THE BUILDINGS OF IRELAND
FOUNDING EDITORS: NIKOLAUS PEVSNER
AND ALISTAIR ROWAN

SOUTH ULSTER
THE COUNTIES OF ARMAGH,
CAVAN AND MONAGHAN

KEVIN V. MULLIGAN

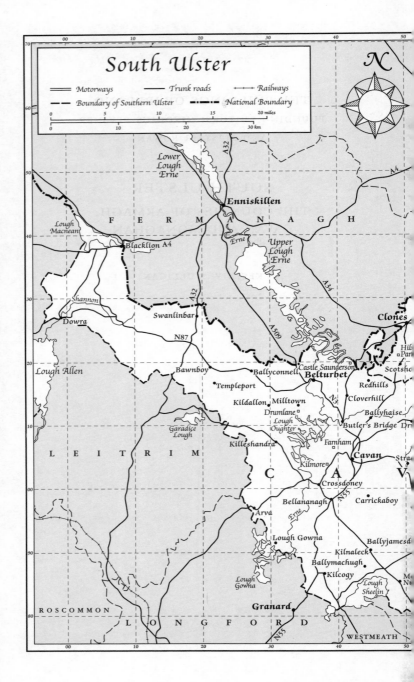

South Ulster

Motorways　　　Trunk roads　　　Railways
Boundary of Southern Ulster　　　National Boundary

0　　5　　10　　15　　20 miles
0　　　10　　　20　　　30 km

N

Lower
Lough
Erne

A32

Enniskillen

F　E　R　M　A　N　A　G　H

A4

Lough
Macnean

Blacklion A4

Erne

Upper
Lough
Erne

Shannon

A32

Swanlinbar

N87

A34

A509

Clones

Dowra

Lough Allen

Bawnboy

Templeport

Ballyconnell

Castle Saunderson

Belturbet

Hil
Par

Scotsho

Kildallon　Milltown

Drumlane

Redhills

Cloverhill

Ballyhaise

Garadice
Lough

Killeshandra

Lough
Oughter

Butler's Bridge　Dr

L　E　I　T　R　I　M

Farnham

Kilmore

Cavan

Stra

V

C

A

Crossdoney

Bellananagh

Arva

Erne

N55

Carrickaboy

Lough Gowna

Ballyjamesd

Kilnaleck

Ballymachugh

Kilcogy

Lough
Gowna

Lough
Sheelin

M
N

ROSCOMMON

Granard

N55

WESTMEATH

L　O　N　G　F　O　R　D

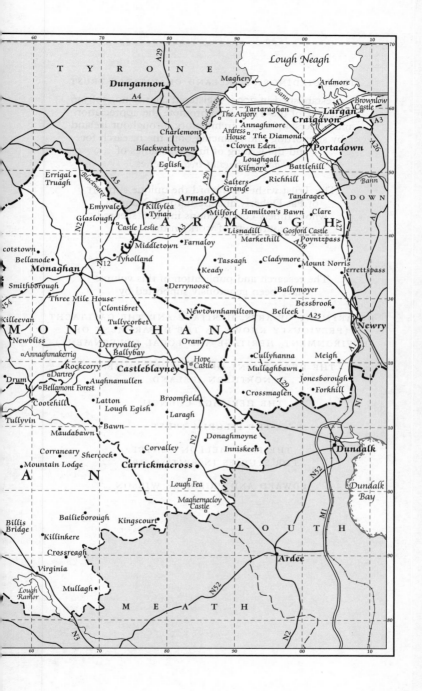

THE BUILDINGS OF IRELAND CHARITABLE TRUST
was established in 2005, registered charity no. 398546
The role of the Trust is to promote the appreciation
and understanding of architecture throughout Ireland
by supporting and financing both the research for
and the writing of future volumes of
The Buildings of Ireland series

The Trust wishes to record the unique support
of Pat Doherty and Bernard McNamara
whose timely contributions in 2008 secured
the continuity of work on the series

The research and publication of this volume
have been generously supported by

DEPARTMENT OF ARTS, HERITAGE AND THE GAELTACHT
(PREVIOUSLY KNOWN AS THE DEPARTMENT OF
ENVIRONMENT, HERITAGE AND LOCAL GOVERNMENT)

THE DEPARTMENT OF THE ENVIRONMENT,
NORTHERN IRELAND

THE HERITAGE COUNCIL

THE PILGRIM TRUST

THE PAUL MELLON CENTRE
FOR STUDIES IN BRITISH ART

EDWARD AND PRIMROSE WILSON

South Ulster

THE COUNTIES OF ARMAGH, CAVAN AND MONAGHAN

BY

KEVIN V. MULLIGAN

THE BUILDINGS OF IRELAND

YALE UNIVERSITY PRESS
NEW HAVEN AND LONDON

YALE UNIVERSITY PRESS
NEW HAVEN AND LONDON
302 Temple Street, New Haven CT 06511
47 Bedford Square, London WC1B 3DP
www.pevsner.co.uk
www.yalebooks.co.uk
www.yalebooks.com

Published by Yale University Press 2013
2 4 6 8 10 9 7 5 3 1

ISBN 978 0 300 18601 7

FOR JIM REYNOLDS
AND IN MEMORY OF
JIM MCALEESE

CONTENTS

LIST OF TEXT FIGURES AND MAPS

Every effort has been made to contact or trace all copyright holders. The publishers will be glad to make good any errors or omissions brought to our attention in future editions.

MAPS

PHOTOGRAPHIC ACKNOWLEDGEMENTS

The photographs were almost all taken by the author, Kevin Mulligan. We are grateful to the Heritage Council and the Paul Mellon Centre for British Art for support in providing the photographs. We are also grateful for permission to reproduce the remaining photographs from the sources as shown below.

Esler Crawford: 47

© National Trust Images / Andreas von Einsiedel: 48

MAP REFERENCES

The numbers printed in italic type in the margin against the place names in the gazetteer of the book indicate the position of the place in question on the index map (pp. ii–iii), which is divided into sections by the 10-kilometre reference lines of the National Grid. The reference given here omits the two initial letters which in a full grid reference refer to the 100-kilometre squares into which the county is divided. The first two numbers indicate the *western* boundary, and the last two the *southern* boundary, of the 10-kilometre square in which the place in question is situated. For example, Ballymachugh (reference 4080) will be found in the 10-kilometre square bounded by grid lines 40 (on the *west*) and 50, and 80 (on the *south*) and 90; Mullaghbawn (reference 9010) in the square bounded by the grid lines 90 (on the *west*) and 00, and 10 (on the *south*) and 20.

The map contains all those places, whether towns, villages or isolated buildings, which are the subject of separate entries in the text.

FOREWORD AND ACKNOWLEDGEMENTS

The South Ulster volume is the fourth in the *Buildings of Ireland* series. The geographical coverage of the counties Cavan, Monaghan and Armagh sits snugly between the first and second volumes, *North West Ulster* (1979) and *North Leinster* (1993). Its aims remain true to the original series begun in 1951 by Nikolaus Pevsner with *The Buildings of England*, sharing his intention that architecture should be better understood and enjoyed by all. The format continues the Pevsner model. An overview of architectural development in the region and a chapter on building materials introduce the gazetteer, which provides the substance of the book. This is arranged alphabetically with entries devoted to towns and villages, including dispersed buildings; some important examples of the latter are treated separately. Locations are indicated on the regional map on pp. ii–iii, with the relevant grid reference noted in the margin at the beginning of each entry. The arrangement of buildings within the principal towns follows a hierarchy, with cathedrals, churches and religious buildings placed first, followed by public buildings and so on, and concluding with sites in the neighbourhood. It has been necessary to exclude a small area of south-east Armagh which forms part of Newry and its hinterland; it made more sense to retain this for a future volume dealing with County Down.

What has been covered is, one hopes, as comprehensive as it could be for the scope of such a work, for the time that it has taken to complete, and as the task of just one person. The thought often occurred that if this work had been carried out sixty years earlier, at the time Pevsner began the series, it would have comprised a very different volume; quite naturally different in many ways of course, but fundamentally in the richer pickings of buildings to see. Consequently there are instances where the tone of this volume must become a little melancholy, where a building, particularly in the Introduction, must be spoken of in the past tense; too frequently is this true of the buildings one would most like to have seen – confirming that invidious relationship between the best of buildings and woe that was spoken of by Maurice Craig.

However, work on this volume commenced at the tail-end of an extraordinary era of economic growth, on a scale not witnessed since the C19. Looking back over that period now, and the pace of new building that occurred, it might seem that one had been watching a strange time-lapse sequence. Fieldwork commenced in May 2005 with Cavan town, and then switched to County Monaghan, followed by County Armagh, and finally back to

County Cavan, where visiting was completed in 2011. Research and writing-up of entries was generally undertaken immediately. Although Cavan town was the first place to be visited, writing its entry was delayed, and so its completion necessitated a return visit some years later. It would have been deeply satisfying to record more instances where 'progress' had been good for architectural heritage; it is regrettable that this has not been so. Cavan, in both town and county, seems to have suffered more than its share of ill-considered building because attitudes to good planning have evidently been in poor supply; but right across the region there are instances where the architectural potential of this extraordinary age of prosperity has been squandered on dull buildings and insensitive repairs. This should not detract from what has been achieved, however, and in towns like Cootehill in Cavan, Carrickmacross and Clones in Monaghan, Loughgall in Armagh and Armagh city itself, a better balance appears to have been found between the causes of development and preservation; it is to be hoped that this volume will contribute to improving that balance.

Every effort has been made to ensure that this volume contains all the best buildings in South Ulster as well as many that are ordinary, offering thereby a satisfying diversity and recognizing that architectural appeal need not depend solely on architectural display. The structures which contribute most to our sense of place are frequently everyday buildings, those that enhance the quality of their environment with quiet ease. Indeed, such little-known but authentic structures are often among the most engaging buildings in South Ulster. It has not been possible to see or to treat every good vernacular building, whether farmhouse, mill, school or shop, and the absence of any particular structure from the gazetteer is therefore in no way intended to detract from its merits. Similarly the inclusion of a building does not in any way imply an entitlement to access, and it is important to stress that the privacy of owners must be respected.

The research for this volume was initiated by Alistair Rowan, compiled over several years, mostly with support from students or former students at University College Dublin, and set down in a series of twin lock files that provided the essential starting point for writing up the individual buildings. C19 secondary sources, ranging from familiar topographical works to the various and voluminous *Builder* magazines, provided the core material, augmented by a disparate collection of C18 and C19 primary sources, with some C20 sources also. The material contained in these files has since been absorbed by the online *Dictionary of Irish Architects*, compiled by Ann Martha Rowan at the Irish Architectural Archive. In this format architectural subjects are being continuously brought up-to-date, which in the absence of any research assistants for this volume has made the task of locating historical information much less difficult. I have also benefited immensely from information, material and observations supplied by friends or colleagues in the fields of art and architectural history; those to whom I am especially indebted include Anne Casement, Willie Cumming, the late Desmond FitzGerald (the Knight of Glin), Liam Fitzpatrick, Tony Hand, William Laffan, Rolf Loeber, Patricia McCarthy, Philip McEvansoneya, Edward McParland, Michael O'Neill, Finola Reid, Ann Martha Rowan, Philip Smith, Ronan Teevan and James Stevens Curl; David Lawrence helped to remedy the deficiences in my knowledge of stained glass and took the trouble to read through many of the entries, offering helpful corrections for which I am very grateful; Terence Reeves-Smyth has been extremely kind with his time and expertise, and readily made available enormously helpful copies of historic material.

Without exception, great courtesies have been shown by those employed in public institutions – librarians, archivists and assistants, some unknown to me by name, but who also deserve to be remembered and acknowledged; amongst them are the staff of the county libraries of Cavan and Monaghan, the Public Record Office of Northern Ireland, and the libraries of Trinity College Dublin and the National Library of Ireland, where Tom Desmond has been especially helpful. The Irish Architectural Archive is the principal resource for architectural history, and the value of its collections is greatly augmented by its fine staff, led by David Griffin. Within South Ulster, Armagh Public Library is a rather special, atmospheric place, and Carol Conlin, Thirza Mulder and Lorraine Frazer are worthy custodians who have each been immensely helpful to me; in the same context I am also deeply grateful to the former Dean of Armagh, Patrick Rooke.

Many individuals, including members of various organizations and groups, were willing to provide valuable assistance and showed remarkable enthusiasm for the work and its aims; among those acknowledged with sincere gratitude are Rosemarie and Henry Armstrong, Frances Bailey and Demelza Parker-Williams of the National Trust for Northern Ireland, Ivan Bolton, June Brown, Noel Carney and Andrew McCaul of Dartrey Heritage Group, Shirley Clerkin of Monaghan County Council, Bishop Joseph Duffy, Christopher Fitz-Simon, Sean Gartlan of the Carrickmacross Resource Centre, George Knight, Samantha Leslie, David McCready, Laurence McDermott and Grace Moloney of the Clogher Historical Society, John Madden, George and the late Nixon Montgomery, Jack and Sir Richard Hanbury-Tenison, Nigel Rofé and Oliver Brady of Bawnboy Development Association, and Leigh Vage of Armagh Cathedral.

Although much of the preparation of this volume has by its nature been largely a solitary activity, the people encountered along the way have enriched the experience. Gratitude is therefore due to the owners who granted access, many of whom are named above for having gone further in providing information or allowing me to copy historic material in their keeping. In this age of distrust – of the electric gate – reluctance to accommodate and suspicion of motive were rarely encountered, and indeed the overall interest and enthusiasm with which enquiries have been greeted has been heartening; I would especially like to acknowledge the Rev. William Gillespie, Richard Farrelly, Andy Gray, the Rev. Robert Kingston, James Kingan, John Howell, Ivor Lendrum of Clones, Valery Mahony, Mr and Mrs David Montgomery, Sean Moran, Hazel Pickins, the sisters of the St Louis Convents in Monaghan and Carrickmacross, especially Sr Rita in Carrickmacross, the late John Shirley, Sam Wilkins, and Primrose Wilson. Unfortunately two less encouraging experiences stand out: the overly timorous, perhaps God-fearing, churchwarden in Armagh who could not be persuaded to open his church, and the guardian of an important country house in Monaghan who believed a brief glance at its exterior was more than sufficient for serious architectural scrutiny. Much more entertaining was an encounter with another caretaker, who promised access to his church in return for his being driven to the nearest town in order to procure a bottle of whiskey; having obliged, I returned to find the building unlocked, as always.

Special thanks are due to Alistair Rowan, founding editor of the Irish series, who sagely inducted me into the *Buildings of Ireland* and with admirable patience steered the process from the very start right through to completion; always willing to share his expertise and to offer encouragement, he has shown many kindnesses as well as undertaking to read drafts of the text and to devise the tours. I would also like to acknowledge the members of the board of the Buildings of Ireland Charitable Trust, especially its chairman John Hayden and treasurer Stewart Roche, while Colum O'Riordain as secretary has been of great assistence, always responding to queries with characteristic efficiency and good humour.

In the final stages it was enormously enjoyable to work with Emily Lane, a consummate copy editor who kept my spirits up as my cyber-companion for many months, and who in her close reading of the text displayed an extraordinary and deeply reassuring thoroughness. At Yale University Press, Simon Bradley has been a patient editor who has shown exemplary care with the text, and I am very grateful to him and to Catherine Bankhurst and Phoebe Lowndes for making the arduous task of putting the book to bed a consistently smooth process. Martin Brown drew the maps, and Judith Wardman compiled the index. A special word of thanks also to Sally Salvesen who has always taken a close interest in the series and offered much-appreciated encouragement.

I am privileged to be part of a large and supportive family, and to have in my mother and late father exceptional parents; but in particular I wish to thank my brothers Brendan and William who accompanied me on some of the visits; William also kindly tolerated being imposed upon to draw some of the text figures, while Leo entrusted me with valuable photographic equipment – these are the advantages of sibling fidelity.

Finally, I thank most especially my wife Claire for her love and constancy, and my boys, Hugo, Will and Míde, for all their fun, but most of all for always reminding me of what really matters.

INTRODUCTION

The South Ulster landscape is predominantly a shapely one, of a diversified scenery that gives an abiding picturesque quality to its everyday buildings. Some fifteen thousand years ago a great ice sheet, having macerated rock from the mountains of Ulster, moved southward and dissolved, depositing mounds of boulder clay and dense poor-draining gleys that formed an undulating assembly of small hills in a great tract reaching between Donegal Bay and Strangford Lough. From the highest vantages one might well seem to be gazing over the frozen swell of a great verdant sea, as the three counties at the core of this region – Armagh, Monaghan and Cavan – offer a changing landscape of near horizons that was well adapted to small farming societies. Together, these characteristics contribute a certain lyrical quality to the scenery.

This unfolding landscape makes South Ulster Ireland's greatest lakeland, sometimes appearing post-Diluvial in extent, from the great expanse of Lough Neagh (151 sq. miles / some 400 sq. km) that floods the N boundary of Armagh to the Lower Erne system that divides Cavan, seeping into the district between the towns of Killeshandra and Cavan to become a tortuous watery filigree.

Occasionally the small hills give way to eminences: the ridge of the Fews Mountains spreads benignly down the centre of the south Armagh landscape, in contrast to Slieve Gullion, which strikes a more numinous presence in the SE corner of the county. In Monaghan only Mullyash achieves a contour greater than 1,000 ft (just over 300 m). In south Cavan Slieve Glah, Loughanlea, Carrickaboy and Bruse Hill are all prominent, but become less significant against the expansive upland wildernesses of Slieve Rushen, Benbrack, and the Cuilcagh Mountains, which share their summit with Fermanagh and help to transform the narrow W extension of the county into a rugged, exposed land. All these uplands are thinly inhabited, with few buildings, almost all of which are in the vernacular tradition.

If this South Ulster region appears to hold a greater distinction for its landscape than for its buildings, there still exists within it much that is interesting, satisfying and good. So often it is the simple buildings of the countryside – the tidy farmhouse in a cluster of barns or the tree-girt parish church – that fix the landscape in our minds, paradoxically blending in while standing out against this untidy, sometimes sodden land textured by small fields and high hedges, narrow roads and lanes. Frequently the pattern is enlivened by the more orderly ensemble of country-house demesnes, dense tree-belted landscapes that from the CI8 had fully exploited the natural characteristics of the environment.

The impression of these counties is not remotely bucolic, however, and the old reality of an undulating inland terrain of lakes and marshes that gave such difficulty of access is still partially true; this is emphasized even more by the contrast with the prosperous plains of North Leinster. Throughout its history, the landscape characteristics of South Ulster presented a barrier, a physical and political frontier, the interior only accessible by fording the Erne system or negotiating difficult passages through the densely thicketed hills. As a result it remained fiercely independent, and largely cut off from outside influence.

The challenging characteristics of the region did not inhibit early settlement, and the first human presence can be traced to Mesolithic hunters and gatherers of *c.* 7000 B.C. whose flints have been found on the shores of Lough Neagh. Three millennia later, farming activity of a Neolithic society had begun to open up the forest to accommodate animals and cultivation. These people left what are the earliest standing structures in South Ulster, in the form of court tombs and dolmens or portal tombs. While these are not strictly within the ambit of this book, examples worthy of attention have been highlighted when they are easily accessible within a district.

COURT TOMBS are the earliest form, with a pincered stone forecourt that seems to have been designed as much for ritual purposes as for burial. The best examples are in Armagh, at Ballymacdermot and Clontygora (both near Meigh), each with a deep forecourt expressed like an open jaw of misshapen dentures. They are now misleadingly stripped of their covering cairns of loose stone, but it is only in their denuded state that we can fully appreciate the structural ingenuity of our primitive forebears. With DOLMENS that achievement is especially evident, as at Ballykeel (Mullaghbawn), also in Armagh. Formed of several great orthostats supporting a massive capstone, these basic structures give an impression readily absorbed in local tradition, revealed by the 'Giant's Grave' names on old Ordnance Survey maps.

The monumental nature of the Neolithic tombs is the key to their survival. Little that was impressive or lasting was built by the succeeding population, as increased warfare brought instability. Even as the Norsemen made their first bloody assaults in the late C8, pouring in from the NE, they never penetrated significantly beyond the coast, and left no enduring influence other than to bestow on the province its name, *Ulaidh Staor* – 'land of the Ulaidh' – anglicized as Ulster.

In the pre-Christian Iron Age the region now associated with south Armagh and Monaghan had provided the natural boundary to the kingdom of the Ulaidh, a dynastic family group or clan that ruled a wide confederation of petty kingdoms, and whose capital was based at Emain Macha, known today as Navan Fort (*see* Armagh). This series of great hilltop earthworks w of Armagh city is the major prehistoric monument in Ulster, its significance rivalled only by the seat of the high kings at Tara. Around this time – *c.* 200 B.C. – the natural defences had been greatly enhanced by an intermittent series of extensive EARTHWORKS, threaded through the drumlins of the entire region between Down and Sligo. These linear earthworks – essentially parallel ditches and palisaded banks – constituted a formidable defensive barrier, comparable to the Hadrianic wall constructed across the north of England two centuries later.

Traditionally the principal access to Ulster has always been controlled in this region where the drumlins gradually yield to the more challenging outline of Slieve Gullion. Passage through the lowlands of Louth was directed to the bottleneck of the Moyry Pass, 'the gap of the north', tellingly celebrated in the early *Táin Bó Cúailgne* or 'Cattle-raid of Cooley', which places Cú Chulainn or Cuchulain here, heroically maintaining the right of single battle at fords to withstand the onslaught of the armies of Queen Medb of Connacht, who waged war against Conchubair, King of Ulster.

When the texts of this extraordinary tale were first being written down at the beginning of the C8, the Ulaidh had already lost their capital at Emain Macha to the rising Uí Néill dynasty. By then a new spiritual emphasis had been created just 5 km to the E at the monastery founded by St Patrick in Armagh, which evolved from the C5 to become the pre-eminent Christian site in Ireland and seat of the archbishop; its primacy was recognized by the High King Brian Boroimhe (or Boru) in 1005, and it endured as the most developed medieval settlement in South Ulster.

The region gradually developed into a medieval marchland, pitting an intractable, thinly populated Gaelic world against the more densely developed and ostensibly civilized manorial society of Leinster that developed after the C12 Anglo-Norman invasion. By breaking through the treacherous Moyry Pass in 1177, John de Courcy was able to establish a Norman foothold in eastern Ulster, but his was to be the only enduring one in the region, secured principally because of its access to the sea. Otherwise an Anglo-Norman presence is scarcely found.

For the remainder of the medieval period the 'Great Irishry', led principally by the O'Neills, were to remain secure beyond the drumlins, untouchable in a land of war, living quite literally beyond the Pale, the fortified area of English rule centred on Dublin. Throughout this period the inhabitants of South Ulster seem to have been largely indifferent to architecture; even the buildings of religious foundations rarely rose above the ordinary, and today the medieval legacy barely extends beyond a few rubble remains. Buildings never fare well in political struggles, and many of the key episodes in Irish history occurred in these wild borderlands. Such was the situation in 1586 that Sir Henry Bagenal, reporting to Court for his father who was Marshal of the Army in Ireland, observed that 'buildings in this country are none, save certain olde defaced monasteries'.

The Gaelic lords' domestic security was typically supplied by simple hilltop ring forts or by crannogs, small artificial islands that are still to be seen on the edge of innumerable lakes. Their greatest weapon was the ambush, perfected in this ideal landscape: so it was that during the Nine Years War (1594–1603) Hugh O'Neill, Earl of Tyrone, gained victories over the English at Clontibret in 1595 and more decisively at the Yellow Ford in 1598. It was only when O'Neill abandoned the Moyry Pass in 1600, allowing Lord Mountjoy and his forces to break through, that the fate of Ulster was ultimately decided. And it was only in defeat and through the pursuit of the Plantation of Ulster, for which preparations began in 1609 as a lasting political settlement, that a solid building tradition in Ulster can be considered to have begun.

The area of the three South Ulster counties amounts to 4,479 sq. km (1,729 sq. miles, 447,900 hectares); Cavan is the largest, half as big again as its two neighbours, with Monaghan only marginally larger than Armagh. The topography favoured small units, so both townlands and farm holdings are smaller than the Irish average. In the mid C19 farms in each of the three counties averaged 8–10 acres, and small sheltered farmsteads in a patchwork of hilly fields, 'tilled and tame', reached by meandering lanes, are still very much predominant in South Ulster, a sometimes hungry landscape that was perfectly captured in the poetry of Patrick Kavanagh, born on a small farm in Inniskeen, Co. Monaghan.

The 1841 census figures, compiled on the eve of the Great Famine, give a population of 675,993 for the three counties – 243,158 for Cavan, followed by Armagh with 232,393 and Monaghan with 200,442. In the same period official figures of the land fit for cultivation show almost the reverse – 83 per cent for Monaghan, 78 per cent for Cavan and only 52 per cent for Armagh (because of Lough Neagh, Armagh is over 5 per cent water). The most productive lands were concentrated in lower-lying areas, essentially the central lakelands of the Erne in Cavan, the Blackwater Valley region of north Monaghan which extends into Armagh to coalesce with the more expansive Lough Neagh basin, and the fertile and famed orchard country, drained by the Bann and its canalized tributary, the Newry River, which defines most of Armagh's E boundary. Deep glacial tills rewarded modest agricultural enterprise, but by the C18 the labour-intensive processes of the developing linen industry helped to counteract the limited capacity for food production. Many South Ulster families relied heavily on this cottage industry, given a reasonably secure living by their close involvement in the diverse aspects of the business – growing flax, spinning, weaving, finishing the cloth and bringing it to market.

Gradually as the C17 Plantation settlement of English and Scottish tenants in Ulster paid off, the countryside was given a firm economic structure, so that by 1800 Ulster had developed some fifty market centres where the population was in excess of five hundred. Because so much of the linen industry was based in the country, most towns remained relatively small even when reasonably prosperous. Armagh had become one of the largest linen markets in Ulster in the late c18, with a population of almost 2,000, but its architectural character, still today very much Late Georgian, is the result largely of the permanent residency of the primate of Ireland from 1770. Today most towns in South Ulster are no more than medium-sized market towns, though the best concentration of buildings will be found there, the streets having evolved around a market place where a market house and courthouse, the principal commercial buildings, and perhaps a parish church, tend to dominate still.

Historically, and largely because of the success of its linen industries, Armagh has always been the most prosperous county, and as a result it holds all the major towns in the region. While demographic decline was universally severe in the c19, the population of Armagh never fell below half what it had been in 1841. There was a greater haemorrhage from the more isolated, less productive districts: by 1961 the populations of Cavan and Monaghan were only about a quarter what they had been in 1841. When not forced to emigrate, the poor and destitute, chiefly the landless, were drawn into the larger towns, and of these the increasingly industrialized centres of Armagh were better equipped to provide employment. As the c19 progressed, the economic centre of gravity shifted more and more towards East Ulster and its developing capital in Belfast; in South Ulster, Armagh was gradually superseded by Lurgan and Portadown, which along with the newly formed utopia of Bessbrook looked to Belfast, becoming industrial behemoths, rising equally in prosperity and architectural interest.

In 2001 the combined figures for the three counties stood at just under 280,000, with more than half accounted for by Armagh. Its disproportionate share must largely be attributable to the substantial shift in population caused by the promotion of the new city of Craigavon in the 1960s, the most ambitious architectural enterprise undertaken in Ulster since the Plantation, and just as controversial.

EARLY CHRISTIAN ARCHITECTURE
AND MONUMENTS

Despite the significance of the region for the establishment of Christianity in Ireland, what remains of the EARLY CHURCH falls far short of expectations. A handful of sites in each of the counties can be identified with the traditions of the Celtic Church founded by St Patrick in the c5. The dearth of buildings is generally thought to indicate that the earliest churches were constructed of perishable material, even of mud and timber, but predominantly of timber. The shrine tomb at Clones copies a form of gable-ended oratory similarly invoked in the small

Romanesque church at Kilmalkedar in Kerry, where splayed
finials seem to emulate a kind of timber saddleback roof. Timber
was eventually replaced by stone before the C10, and the *Annals
of Ulster* confirm the existence of a stone church in Armagh as
early as 789. But new structures were conditioned by the experience of the builders, who imitated earlier forms within the limitations of their materials. This is shown in the small single-chambered
western church of Killevy (Meigh), the only example of the early
period in South Ulster to survive, albeit as a roofless ruin, where
the massive cyclopean w doorway is an example of the most
primitive kind of lintelled construction. Throughout Ulster most
older church sites consist of a miscellany of fragmentary ruins of
rectangular single cells of a similar size, with little more than a
standing gable and no distinguishing architectural detail, which
are almost impossible to date accurately. Most are likely to represent medieval or later parish churches; too easily their sparing
character is mistaken for evidence of greater antiquity.

Where architectural details do survive, they are out of context,
and when connected with early church sites they reveal little
about architectural character and more about the willingness of
Christianity to absorb some of the complexities of the pagan
culture it sought to supplant. Only a forgotten iconography can
explain some of the exhibitionist SCULPTURES associated with
church sites, such as the crude sheila-na-gig from the vanished
church of Lavey (Strathdone) or the gross heads – half-human and
half-deity – found at Trinity Island, Castleterra and Clannaphilip,
all in Cavan. More fragments of uncertain origin in the old (now
Church of Ireland) Cathedral in Armagh are equally bewildering,
and surely pagan in their meaning; among several impious-looking
heads are the so-called Tandragee Idol, posed as if for a fight, and
a more grotesque figure with the ears of an ass. At Kilnasaggart
in south Armagh an inscribed phallic standing stone is set in an
enclosure associated with early Christian burials, adjoining one
of the great roads of ancient Ireland between Tara and Emain
Macha, evoking the encounter between the competing traditions
of paganism and Christianity in the Early Middle Ages.

Ancient church sites tend to be on a height within a circular
enclosure, reflecting the dominant settlement pattern of the raths
that developed in Iron Age society. Armagh may have good
reason to claim primacy as the pre-eminent Patrician foundation:
its first church is traditionally dated to 457, and thought to have
been situated below the great oval rath, two centuries older, that
can still be traced in the circular street pattern. The prominence
of the Church of Ireland Cathedral today tells of the eventual
capture of the hilltop; but to understand the early buildings on
the site there is nothing more than suggestive archaeology and a
catalogue of the events that brought repeated destruction. The
Annals of the Four Masters record the most devastating, in 1020,
when the great stone church, round tower, and two other stone
churches were destroyed. Clones is a C6 foundation associated
with St Tigernach; it has the most complete early monastic
ensemble of church, round tower and high cross, but the ruined

Armagh, St Patrick's Cathedral (C of I), Tandragee Idol.
Drawing by K. Mulligan, 2012

church is considered to be no earlier than the C12. Drumlane 19
was possibly founded by St Columba; here the details of the
church are late medieval, though earthworks to the s seem to
reveal the extent of the original complex. At Inniskeen a C19
parish church occupies the site associated with the ancient
monastery.

The ROUND TOWER is undoubtedly the most iconic building
of the Irish monastic tradition, and examples are found at Clones,
Drumlane and Inniskeen. Others are known to have existed at
Killevy and Mullynagolman. Clones, the earliest, is usually dated 17
no later than the C10; also the most complete, it remains a signal
presence in the landscape, lacking only its conical roof. These

buildings are referred to in the various annals as *cloictheach* or
'bell house', but it is sometimes suggested that they also served
as watchtowers and as places of refuge in times of attack: at
Drumlane the usual location of the entrance well above ground
level is followed, but with a window directly above that seems to
have been specifically provided for defence. The fact that round
towers were generally erected in the most intense period of Viking
disturbance, between the C9 and C11, might well support the
theory of a protective function; but on the other hand the tower
in the landscape was more likely to attract unwanted attention,
and its shape would have made it a natural flue rather than a
refuge. Whatever the primary purpose of these towers, the masons
had developed a very remarkable structure, thick-walled and
carefully proportioned, with a gentle taper that is skilfully true in
each case.

As monuments HIGH CROSSES are better represented in South
Ulster than any other element of the Irish monastery, though they

Armagh, Market Cross.
Engraving after Jonathan Bell, 1812

can now be found only in Armagh and Monaghan, and none is complete. The ten or so surviving examples have affinities with crosses found further N at Arboe in Tyrone and along the nearby Blackwater Valley, so they may be considered to form something of a distinct group. These sandstone crosses are all of the classic nimbus type set on a pyramid base. Only at Clones and on the fragmentary and worn remains of a cross now in the Church of Ireland Cathedral in Armagh does the carving attain the richness seen at sites such as Clonmacnoise, Kells or Monasterboice. Precise dating remains problematic. None can be considered earlier than the C10, or later than the C11, with perhaps the earliest represented by the largest and most important group at Tynan. There were at least six crosses in the monastery precincts of Armagh in the C12, some perhaps serving to define the sanctuary boundary. Viewing the fragments in the Cathedral today, battered and eroded, one cannot escape the sense that these are poor reminders of the riches of the capital of the Early Christian Church in Ireland.

15

14, 16

MEDIEVAL ARCHITECTURE

It is difficult to offer a historical account of the medieval architecture of South Ulster in the absence of anything like the range of buildings in the neighbouring counties. A quick and efficient process of colonization, and reform based on a gradual exposure to Continental European experience, helped greatly to redefine the structure of Irish society and to bring organization to the Church in the C12; but the impact was initially of a limited nature, most of all as a consequence of the failure of the armies of the Norman King Henry II of England to penetrate the region. Even after the remainder of the country was firmly subdued as a new Irish lordship, with the centre of English power affirmed in Leinster, the Anglo-Norman conquest brought little more to these three Ulster counties than a handful of hastily erected earthwork castles that proved to be both short-lived and strategically useless.

Without an overthrow of the existing clan structure, the region was almost completely isolated from the economic patronage and manorial society established elsewhere by the great Norman barons and their knights. As a consequence the spread of new architectural influences was slow, and constrained by a reluctance to adopt superior techniques. Armagh was the most developed medieval centre, so it is not surprising that there is a tradition that a CASTLE was erected here by the Lord Deputy in 1236, but nothing is known of the building. The situation becomes a familiar story throughout the region. A few motte-and-bailey castles on the periphery such as those at Inniskeen and Maanan (Donaghmoyne), and even fewer further N, at Clones and Belturbet, served only to support short-lived incursions. The strong castle

3   of Clough Oughter (Killeshandra) stands as a reminder of a brief
     concession obtained from the O'Reilly chief and a fleeting push
     NW by Walter de Lacy in the C13. This is a singularly impressive
     stone tower, unique both for its circular form and for its situation
     on an island in Lough Oughter, but, like the mottes, it too even-
     tually fell into Irish hands. The history of the castle in South
     Ulster only truly begins in the Tudor period.

     It was in ECCLESIASTICAL BUILDINGS that new develop-
     ments in architecture took form. At first the process was slow,
     fostered by reform in the early C12, initially at Armagh and even-
     tually throughout the country, leading to an intensive period of
     building that continued long after the Norman invasion. The
     results, however, are barely visible today. With the extraordinary
20   survival of the great decorated doorway at Kilmore in Cavan and
     a collection of stone fragments in a few tattered ruins in each of
     the counties it is just about possible to follow the critical transi-
     tion from Romanesque to Gothic that brought Irish architecture
     into line with European medieval traditions from the C12 onwards.

     The opening up of an Insular Celtic Church to Continental
     influences occurred along pilgrimage routes to Rome, bringing
     a wider awareness of European forms. In Ireland, the control of
     church offices by the laity had become an increasingly central
     issue, as Continental emphasis on canonical life began to take
     hold and the norms of the Roman Church were introduced.
     From the late C10 the Church in Armagh had epitomized the old
     order, its abbacy controlled by the Clann Sínaich, who for two
     centuries appointed unordained and married men as successors
     to Patrick. Reform synods at Cashel (1101) and Rathbreasail
     (1111) sought to replace this with ordination and celibacy, and
     to reorganize the entire administration, establishing a parish
     system of governance, initially in twenty-four dioceses divided
     between Armagh and Cashel. At Armagh the reforms were initi-
     ated when the unmarried Cellach was appointed abbot in 1105
     and consecrated as bishop the following year.

     Continental influence was first reflected in CHURCH PLANS,
     by the extension of the typically short nave to provide a chancel.
     In South Ulster a subtle legacy can be found in the longer undif-
     ferentiated naves of a few surviving structures, best exemplified
21   in the ruins of the C13 churches at Trinity Island and Annagh
19   and the later example at Drumlane, where the chancel is likely
     to have been separated solely by a timber screen.

     Cellach's efforts at reform invested the Church with a new
     vigour that was partially manifest in an extensive programme of
     rebuilding and new consecrations which, in his own province, is
     indicated by the re-roofing of the 'great stone church' of Armagh;
     the foundation in 1126 of a large priory of Augustinian canons
     dedicated to SS Peter and Paul was particularly significant
     because it introduced the novelties of the cenobitic tradition – the
     aisled cruciform plan, a cloistered 'great court', refectory, dor-
     mitories, storehouses, and cellars.

     After Cellach's death, his successor Malachy finally curbed the
     attempts of the hereditary laymen to reassert control over

Armagh, and ultimately became the most important advocate of reform in the C12. The Cistercian order that he introduced in 1142 never came to South Ulster; here it was Malachy's involvement in the spread of the rule of the AUGUSTINIAN CANONS, with their more flexible observance and pastoral outreach, that has most relevance. Two nunneries were recorded in Armagh town by 1144, and at least forty houses existed throughout the N by the time of Malachy's death in 1148. The nunneries at Armagh and Killevy essentially involved the reorganization of existing establishments, as did Drumlane, settled in the same period by canons from Kells and rebuilt a century later.

There is no clearer illustration of the great advance of architectural ideas in the early medieval period than the contrast between the practical unadorned simplicity of the primitive W doorway of the early church of Killevy and the richly elaborated Romanesque doorway reused at Kilmore Cathedral in Cavan in the C19, where the Hiberno-Romanesque style appears fully developed. Uncertainty surrounds its origins, but its appearance is almost certainly due to the geopolitical circumstances of the O'Reilly kingdom of East Breifne, which developed a more permeable frontier on the edge of the Norman world.

Malachy's unfinished reforms were achieved at the Synod of Kells in 1152; additional provinces of Dublin and Tuam were created, but Armagh reasserted the primacy granted to it by Brian Boru. New religious orders brought new styles of building that were quickly adapted to local ideas and topography. Before the first half of the C14 there were thirty-three Franciscan

Armagh, St Patrick's Cathedral.
Engraving, 1739

FRIARIES in Ireland, most of them in existing settlements, including Armagh and Cavan (Monaghan followed in 1462). Maelpatrick O'Scannail, Archbishop 1261–70, brought the Friars Minor to Armagh in 1263, and three years later rebuilt the Cathedral. O'Scannail's cathedral, with the Franciscan friary, introduced the cruciform plan. But of the six medieval churches still existing in one way or another in Armagh in 1618, only the ruined nave of the friary gives visual evidence of an ancient ecclesiastical tradition. The medieval cathedral was extensively repaired over the centuries and is now encased in C19 masonry. Conforming to the Franciscan rule of poverty, the simple architecture of the Friary is only likely to have impressed in terms of scale; it is still claimed as the longest friary church in Ireland.

With its position beyond the Pale, South Ulster was deprived of opportunities for architectural patronage in the late medieval period. In Armagh, for instance, the archdiocese was divided between the 'two nations': the archbishop, no longer natively chosen, was resident *inter Anglicos*, among the English, his residence and jurisdiction confined within the ambit of the Pale, while his seat lay *inter Hibernicos*, among the Irish, deep inside the Gaelic territories, administered through the dean. The difficult Ulster geography combined with low populations was reflected in larger parishes supporting relatively few churches, contrasting with a greater concentration of pious laity further S.

Our knowledge of the development of MEDIEVAL ARCHITECTURE in South Ulster must rely on few examples. A tall cusped lancet in the E gable of Annagh Old Church (Butler's Bridge) is a rare survivor from the C13. Perhaps attesting to the growing permeability of the frontier, and perhaps to its links with Kells, a cusped ogee window, albeit incomplete, is found in the nave N wall at Drumlane. The most complete example of the kind, in a simpler form, is in the W gable of the old parish church of Loughgall. The stem of the font of the Church of Ireland cathedral in Armagh, copied from the medieval font for Cottingham's C19 restoration, offers a single intimation of a well-developed late medieval sculptural tradition in South Ulster. In Monaghan there is even less evidence: the best of the late medieval period is now represented by a small lancet in the gable at Killeevan and just a few interesting fragments, including sculpted heads, from the ruined church site at Mullanacross (Errigal Truach). The church at Drumlane was repaired in 1436 and it was probably then that it received new tracery in its E window, the most elaborate of its kind now surviving in the region.

POST-MEDIEVAL FORTIFICATION

When Henry VIII was proclaimed King of Ireland by the Irish Parliament in 1541, absolute sovereignty was still dependent on the reach of the Crown being extended permanently into Ulster.

The following year, under the Tudor policy of surrender and regrant, Conn Mór, the O'Neill chief, accepted the subinfeudation of his estates, whereby in return for surrendering his lands to the Crown he was awarded a charter for the lands he formerly owned and was created Earl of Tyrone. But in an age when loyalties were easily betrayed, the conquest of Ulster remained elusive, and Elizabeth's continuation of her father's expansionist policies was disrupted by the disputed succession of the O'Neills.

It was during the campaign against Shane O'Neill in 1557 that the full force of the Tudor expansion was first experienced in South Ulster, unleashed by the unremitting Thomas Radclyffe, Earl of Sussex, who on entering the precincts of Armagh spared only its cathedral, which was retained as a stronghold, and fortified with 'impregnable ramparts'. Fortification provided the key to successful conquest and introduced the most striking architectural innovation in the region. Sussex's continuing campaign was endorsed by Elizabeth's determination to push the frontier beyond Armagh, into the heartland of O'Neill power. The policy was greatly advanced in 1574 when Walter Devereux, Earl of Essex, erected a rectangular fort to control the Blackwater ford, the gateway to Tyrone. Later, after the resurgent Gaelic lords were led into open rebellion by Hugh O'Neill, 2nd Earl of Tyrone, in 1595, their successes in South Ulster seemed poised to reverse the entire conquest. However their advantage was soon lost by error and delay, and ultimately victory for the Crown was claimed by Charles Blount, Lord Mountjoy, a brilliant strategist, who had arrived as Lord Deputy in 1600. O'Neill's submission at Mellifont in 1603 finally brought Gaelic independence to an end.

Mountjoy's campaign against the Earl of Tyrone during the Nine Years War introduced a more developed, effective military infrastructure. With O'Neill the most powerful figure in Ulster, possessing home advantage and command of a well-armed force estimated at 6,000, it was the very least that was required. Advances in the use of artillery had spread throughout Europe, and Mountjoy's FORTS reflected this, invariably formed as elaborate polygonal ramparts with angled bastions, built hastily first of earth with timber palisades and usually later given greater definition and permanence in stone. The shapes could be varied, though always based on precise geometry, even where topography or existing features might have enforced a more irregular outline. The most effective artillery forts have a star form, and this was adopted for the outer enceinte at Monaghan and later p. 459 at Charlemont when its defences were elaborated by Sir Phelim O'Neill after its capture in 1641. This form and the even more popular square enceinte with corner bastions that was employed throughout Ulster, including the first rebuilding at Charlemont p. 260 c. 1611, are among the citadel designs promoted in Buonaiuto Lorini's third book on the art of fortification, first published in Venice in the late C16. Assisting Lord Mountjoy in Ulster was *Sir Josias Bodley*, first stationed here in 1598 and continuing until 1601, by which time most of the new forts had been erected. In 1602 Bodley was Governor of Armagh, and although he was

made Director-General of the Fortifications in Ireland in 1613,
it is unclear how closely he may have been involved with the
designs in South Ulster. The more likely originator was his principal assistant, the Dutch engineer *Levan De Rose*, who has been
connected to the crucially important fortifications at Moyry in
1601. He probably also planned Mount Norris. Of the forts
themselves, only ghostly outlines in the landscape now attest to
the existence of Mount Norris, and even less exists at Blackwa-
p. 260   tertown and Monaghan. In the first rebuilding of Charlemont its
inner enceinte was given the more regular square trace that was
also used at this time around the Plantation castles of Edward
Blayney in Monaghan, and again during the Williamite wars of
the late C17 when two separate earthwork defences of this kind
were erected at Belturbet by Colonel Wolseley.

The visitor in search of the quintessential symbol of medieval
power in Ireland, the TOWER HOUSE, will find only disappointment. It seems to have begun to be relevant in South Ulster only
in the C16 and remained relatively rare. Proof of its existence now
rests primarily on just two substantial buildings. The stout late
C16 castle of the O'Reillys at Tonymore near Kilmore may well
reflect the response of local Irish chieftains to the increasingly
30   militarized politics of the late medieval period. The austere tower
built to claim the Moyry Pass is the most complete example of
the type in South Ulster (*see* Jonesborough): in June 1601 Lord
Mountjoy directed Levan De Rose hastily to produce an effective
plan to secure the 'Gap of the North' inexplicably abandoned by
Hugh O'Neill. The result is a simple square three-storey keep
with rounded corners set within a bawn.

PLANTATION AND RESTORATION
ARCHITECTURE

Only after the Plantation of Ulster, conceived by James I in 1609,
had been commenced in 1610 were widespread and concerted
building campaigns undertaken in the region. The results alas
proved short-lived, and the insurrection led by Sir Phelim
p. 260   O'Neill, begun when he seized Charlemont Fort in October 1641,
brought renewed trauma, ensuring that the new communities
would be all but effaced. Such vestiges as survive leave the
impression that most buildings of the C16 and C17 had barely
advanced from medieval traditions. As so little remains, it seems
sensible to consider the architecture of South Ulster apart from
fortification largely in terms of epoch-shaping events – the Plantation and the Restoration.

The self-imposed exile of the earls of Tyrone and Tyrconnell
in 1607, four years after their submission at Mellifont, offered
James I the opportunity to bring an orderly resolution to Ulster,
using Plantation as a process of colonization both to settle the
province and to advance the Reformation. By September 1610

the estates of the Gaelic lords had been systematically confiscated and redistributed, principally to 'undertakers' and military servitors who were required to build on their new lands as a demonstration of lasting commitment to the project and its defence, and to plant their estates with loyal English and Scottish tenants as a mainstay of future stability.

TOWNS, a novelty in this underdeveloped region of wilderness, forest and bog, were central to the Crown strategy, providing havens for the new settlers and the infrastructure to acculturate the native Irish to the English ideals of improvement. Most of the building initiatives of the Plantation proved to be ephemeral, and today little more than the names and occasionally the layout of the new settlements survives. They were eagerly begun by the undertakers, whose progress was periodically reviewed by commissioners; the inspections conducted by Lord Carew (1611), Sir Josias Bodley (1613), and Captain Nicholas Pynnar (1618–19), along with the official and private work of the cartographer Thomas Raven, provide detailed surveys that enable us to visualize the architectural character of the Plantation town and its buildings in South Ulster.

Of the twenty-three new towns proposed under the articles for the Plantation, four were in Armagh and three in Cavan; these were inevitably associated with some existing settlement, selected largely for strategic reasons. Armagh was an obvious choice. Mount Norris and Charlemont were chosen as established military bases, but the development of both stagnated in the C18, and they now endure only as villages, having been eclipsed by newer landlord towns nearby. Tandragee was probably chosen as the former centre of the O'Hanlon territory. In Cavan, the county town already had a well-developed market place, while Belturbet retained its strategic relevance, established first in the C13. In contrast, Virginia – named after Queen Elizabeth – was entirely new, designated precisely because it was conveniently midway between Cavan and Kells. Indeed, when the programme for the Ulster Plantation was initiated in June 1610 it was to Cavan that Sir Arthur Chichester travelled in order to 'begin that Great work'.

Although siting and layout were carefully considered, there was apparently no strict master plan like those initiated at Newry in Co. Down and by the London Companies further N in Derry and Coleraine. In a contemporary scheme for Monaghan, which lay outside the formal provisions of the Plantation and was privately settled, great ramparted defence works are shown within which an orderly street plan seems to have been conceived, if not actually built. The enormous rectilinear enclosure formed around Castle Raw implies a similarly ambitious urban scheme, but this was forsaken when Sir Anthony Cope chose to develop a less orderly plan at Loughgall, close to a second bawn he had built at Drumilly.

Ultimately, the overall shape of towns in South Ulster was determined by place: the topography of the existing settlements of Armagh and Belturbet was unlikely to yield to a new formal

plan. The principal features are one great street – never perfectly
straight – and provision for a churchyard and market place, often
at opposing ends, as at Carrickmacross and Portadown. Between
these foci the shape of the town was largely defined by the long
narrow curtilages laid out on either side of the street, rather as
medieval burgage plots had been. The colonial accent was set by
the distinctly English half-timbered 'cage houses', which being
so combustible were foredoomed by the unsettled conditions of
the C17.

Belturbet, granted its charter and incorporated in 1613, possessed thirty-four houses of this kind within ten years. John
Taylor, granted the manor of Aghieduff in Cavan, introduced a
colony of English and Scottish settlers at Ballyhaise. Eighteen
families were thriving there ten years later. Perhaps this was the
same John Taylor who in 1622 proposed to plant the Earl of
Essex's land in Monaghan with hardy Scotsmen. The town of
Killeshandra, granted to Sir Alexander Hamilton and developed
by his grandson, Sir Francis, was planted with moderate success,
thirty-four 'English-like' houses being built here before 1641. In
contrast, although Portadown had developed a market by 1631,
it then possessed only fourteen houses for English settlers around
the market place. Nearby, the Brownlows, who had been granted
two manors comprising some 2,500 acres, brought six carpenters,
one mason and six workmen to effect their obligations, which
they did efficiently by 1619, laying out Lurgan as a well-paved
town of forty-two houses inhabited by English families. This
predominance of carpenters over masons seems further evidence
of the prevailing building technology. All these towns were
destroyed after the 1641 rebellion. Lurgan was the first to be
attacked, torched by Sir Conn Magennis. Brownlow's own castle
and bawn survived however, the castle being, like most planters'
houses, a well-built three-storey block of 'stone and brick layed
with lime'.

The BAWN, a fortified enclosure which undertakers were com-
pelled to build, not only secured the family and its livestock but
also underpinned the defence of the Plantation. Typically this was
a near-square enceinte with circular or angled projections on two
or more of the angles. There were imposing bawns at Lurgan
and Monaghan; Sir Edward Blayney's bawn at Castle Blayney
had walls 18 ft (5.5 m) high and a complex plan. A bawn tower
still stands at Farnham, dressed up in Georgian garb as a garden
building, but preserving a vaulted interior. The Earl of Essex's
bawn at Drummond Otra (Carrickmacross) is shown in Thomas
Raven's 1634 view. Hamilton's bawn survives only in the village
name. Rubble walls at Bawnboy may well be part of the original
bawn. There is more at Gosford, in the generous moulded
archway and twin lodges that were retained as an entrance to the
later demesne.

When it comes to DOMESTIC ARCHITECTURE, assessing
planters' houses in South Ulster is hampered by abject losses,
though not all were maliciously destroyed. The origin of Elm
Park (Killylea) as an early C17 house of the Maxwell family in

Castle Blayney.
Engraving by S. Hooper, 1791

Armagh is recorded on several stone plaques preserved on what now appears a mixture of Georgian and Victorian buildings. The influence of Scotland, prominent in Plantation architecture in the N and W, seems not to have been as prevalent in South Ulster. Belturbet Castle, built by Sir Stephen Butler in 1611 and shown in a painting of 1770, offered the silhouette of a commanding block with round, conically roofed bartizans like those on the Watergate at Enniskillen, only a few kilometres distant. In 1624 Sir Edward Blayney was one of those who experienced difficulties in attracting Scots to settle on his estate, but late C18 views of Castle Blayney suggest a typical Plantation castle, a tall gabled structure with mullioned windows and corner bartizans corbelled outwards in the Scottish manner.

Raven's view of Drummond Otra depicts the kind of tall gabled Jacobean mansion that was well represented in Ulster. Charlemont, because it survived until 1920 and was photographed, is the best understood example of this decidedly English form. Nicholas Pynnar's view of 1624 shows Toby Caulfeild's recently completed 'stone house' as a tall keep at the heart of the artillery fort, but in reality it seems to have had stockier proportions to its square plan. There are ruined remains of C17 castles at Derrywarragh, Redhills and Castle Raw, where the plan p. 423 adopted the more unusual form of a Greek cross. At Clones a doorway in a portion of the bawn was revealed by excavations in 2000. More substantial walls survive of the Old Palace at Kilmore in Cavan.

The relatively complete survival of Maghernacloy in Monaghan and Richhill in Armagh goes a great distance to atone for

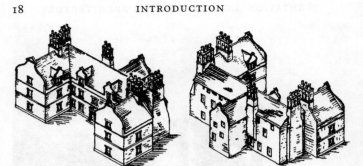

Richhill Castle.
Isometric drawings by E. M. Jope, 1960

31 the dearth of buildings of the C17 in South Ulster. Maghernacloy Castle, built shortly after 1618, is like an Irish tower house but lower; its oblong plan has a projecting tower at one corner and, unusually, an almost central stair-tower. The clearest transition from castle to house seems first to appear in the unfortified building at Richhill Castle. Begun probably about 1664, it is the closest evocation of a genuine C17 house, with dormered attics, Dutch gables, and big decorated chimneys. The basic U-plan is elaborated by a projecting stair as at Maghernacloy, but more integrated; inside, the heavy oak staircase is the real thing.

The beginnings of renewal were experienced immediately after the Restoration in 1660, coinciding with a period of sustained economic growth until curtailed by the war of 1689–91. By 1685 the Lord Lieutenant, Lord Clarendon, could observe the marked changes being brought to the landscape of the country, with 'many buildings raised for beauty, as well as use, orderly and regular plantations of trees and fences and enclosures throughout
p. 338 the Kingdom'. Castle Leslie was remodelled after 1665 and given a remarkable semicircular gable in the centre of the façade. Sadly
47 it does not survive. Ardress House preserves at its core, behind its elegant Late Georgian façade, the modest plan of an undefended brick farmhouse of the last decades of the C17. The chimneystacks projecting from the end gables of Farren Connell (Mount Nugent) betray its origins as a similar late C17 house with a single-pile plan.

The diminutive pedimented tower of the gatehouse of Charlemont Fort is the purest CLASSICAL BUILDING of the Restoration era. The old gatehouse was improved in 1673 by the Surveyor General, *Sir William Robinson*, but the present building may in fact be the work of Robinson's successor, *Thomas Burgh*. The two men shared responsibility for the erection of BARRACKS in Ireland from 1697, and a plaque bearing the date 1699 under the initials 'WR' and the less well-carved 'TB' can still be seen on the remains of the barracks at Belturbet. Robinson and Burgh are the very first architectural personalities to emerge in South Ulster.

The Reformation brought a period of stasis where ECCLESI-ASTICAL BUILDINGS were concerned, and even though the Plantation settlement clearly provided an impetus for new churches, little of any importance has survived, and the most noted work now belongs to the time of slow recovery following the Restoration. Burned by Shane O'Neill in 1566, the medieval cathedral of Armagh was still only partly roofed in a devastated city when peace was, for the time being, restored in 1603. The extensive repair commenced by Archbishop Hampton in 1613 was completely undone by the violence of 1642, and it was only after the Restoration that Primate Margetson was able to commence a programme of rebuilding. His cathedral was a relatively plain cruciform church, distinctive for the candle-snuffer roofs over the buttressed and battlemented aisles. The Old Cathedral of Kilmore in Cavan, greatly altered, is no more than a plain three-bay hall and perhaps was always so; it remains antique enough in its appearance, and the wooden columns supporting the gallery have the proportions and the want of finesse to be genuine C17 work.

The Reformation had a clear impact on church planning, restricting use to corporate worship, with a preference for plain halls in which the chancel was downplayed. The modest single-cell church at Ballymoyer, begun in the first half of the C17, is a perfect example of this kind, though otherwise relatively undistinguished. The cruciform plan of the parish church built at Belturbet in the early C17 is perhaps explained by the form of a predecessor. More importantly, it is the only building of its age still in use in the region. The character of its original appearance lingers in its triple lancets and plain roughcast walls.

Magheross Old Church in Carrickmacross was rebuilt in 1682. It is difficult to say whether it incorporated anything of its predecessor, destroyed in 1641, apart from the evident reuse of masonry in the E wall. There is little to suggest anything of its former architectural character; its importance perhaps lies in that it is an early example of the ubiquitous hall-and-tower type that was to be dominant in the two succeeding centuries.

The T-plan Killeshandra Old Church is arguably the finest Restoration building in Ulster, a handsome evocation of the improving architectural eloquence of the age. That it is such a solitary example fills one with regret, not just for what may once have existed, but also for what might have been if more peaceful circumstances had prevailed. Its creation resulted from the slow resurrection of Killeshandra in precisely the same period as Magheross, and while that lacked the discernment of a single patron (with just a small committee headed by Bishop Boyle of Clogher), the medieval church of Killeshandra was remodelled and enlarged in 1688 solely by Sir Francis Hamilton, who emblazoned his achievement on the entrance gable.

23, 75

p. 96

22

29

26

EARLY GEORGIAN ARCHITECTURE

The 'Glorious Revolution' of 1688 that put the Protestant William of Orange on the throne of his Catholic father-in-law James II was determined on Irish soil by William's victory over James at the Battle of the Boyne in July 1690. A decisive settlement, however, was achieved more completely with the redistribution of lands not protected under the articles of the Treaty of Limerick, which had ended the war in Ireland. The Catholic share of ownership throughout Ireland, already diminished after the rising of 1641 by the Cromwellian settlement of 1652 and that of 1662 following the Restoration, was reduced further by the Williamite confiscations. From then on power was consolidated in the hands of a Protestant minority, who would preside over a century of peace and prosperity. With an idealized sense of *noblesse oblige* landlords gradually reordered the environment of their adopted country so that the C18 became an age of 'IMPROVEMENT', when experimentation and innovation brought advancements in agriculture, trade and industry. The promotion of the linen industry in particular brought such prosperity to Ulster that it steadily moved from being the poorest province in Ireland to become the most prosperous by the end of the C18.

In the opening decades of the C18 Colonel Brockhill Newburgh of Ballyhaise was very much the kind of improver to be emulated. His father having married into earlier planter stock, Newburgh epitomized a new class of innovator, men who became members of parliament, served on the Linen Board, and promoted improvement by example on their own estates, cultivating them in every sense and, in Newburgh's case, building an exemplary house and a model village where the inventive market house was deemed not unworthy of Vitruvius or Palladio. His 'indefatigable industry' was lauded in a eulogy published twenty years after his death: Samuel 'Premium' Madden, co-founder of the Dublin Society which advanced the causes of agricultural and economic improvement, praised Newburgh specially because he had built his house and offices comprehensively in brick as a precaution against both fire and damp. Rarely since Lord Deputy Strafford's unfinished great house at Jigginstown in Co. Kildare of 1637 had brick been used on such a scale.

The earliest building endeavours down to the time of Queen Anne and into the era of George I inevitably involved the rehabilitation and remodelling of existing structures. The problems faced by patrons are typified by the experience of Lord Weymouth, proprietor of half the town of Carrickmacross, who in 1698 instructed his agent to find 'some good architect from Dublin' who would undertake the conversion of the former residence of the Bishop of Clogher in the town into a grammar school. His intention presumably was to procure the expertise of someone like Sir William Robinson or Thomas Burgh. That his agent settled on the talents of the local mason-architect *John Curle* implies either that architectural talent was scarce in Dublin or that most were too busy for work in the provinces. There is no doubt about the level of competence Weymouth expected of his architect: he was concerned at the prospect of employing a provincial like Curle, writing: 'I could have wisht you had given me some account of him, as to what buildings he has made, where he lives and wether he undertakes to build by the great.'

Richhill and Castle Leslie (Glaslough) were both brought up to date by changes to the fenestration and the provision of new classical doorcases. Sash windows replaced the old-fashioned mullions at Charlemont, while Maghernacloy lost all defensive concerns when the plan was re-oriented. The Old Palace at Kilmore was twice enlarged; the front wall and its plan can still be traced, but nothing more substantial is known of the architecture. This make-do-and-mend approach combined with poor survival rates presents its own difficulties when attempting to ascertain or confirm any dating, and is a problem for an analysis of trends. p. 338 31

More can be said about the DESIGNED LANDSCAPE that enveloped these Early Georgian houses. Formal influences of French, Dutch and Italian garden design became prevalent in the C17, conceived as a complex setting for houses and expressed through a series of rigid geometries with radiating avenues, *allées*, parterres and terraces. These formal tastes endured well into the C18 and were extensively displayed in South Ulster: good evidence exists for ambitious designed landscapes in a number of demesnes, particularly in Cavan. This is perhaps in part due to the fact that conditions were more settled there than in the adjoining counties, though survival in Monaghan and Armagh has been more markedly affected by the later fashion for naturalized landscapes. Most are now represented by isolated features and ghostly vestiges, but one of the most ambitious landscapes can still be traced in the farmland surrounding Belville, an old demesne near Bellananagh that was developed by Thomas Fleming *c.* 1713 with a prodigious display of water features. Generally ambition was uninhibited by the landscape: at Castle Hamilton a formal *allée* of elms was aligned with the W front to terminate in a vista of Killeshandra. The atmosphere of the old landscape created by Bishop Goodwin lingers, and many of its original features still persist at Kilmore. At Ballyhaise a series of terraces with water features stepped down between the house and the river. 37

Even where the country-house landscapes could be ordered in truly extravagant ways, the buildings themselves tended to remain subordinate. Early Georgian commentators typically offered no greater insights than that the buildings shared attributes of 'convenience' or were 'well modelled' and 'delicate'.

Most COUNTRY HOUSES erected in the C18 lacked both the scale and the sophistication to reflect ideas and tastes emanating from London. Few architects can be firmly associated with the buildings of South Ulster before the second half of the C18, and so it becomes a matter of great significance that in his short illustrious career *Sir Edward Lovett Pearce* should be the first figure to be well represented in the region. Pearce's importance as an architect of striking originality emerges in designs for three buildings with which his name can be indisputably connected, and in a handful of houses that at the very least offer an acknowledgment of his wholly sophisticated manner. Like his probable associate Sir John Vanbrugh, his father's cousin, Pearce was an innovator in classicism. His independent taste and eclectic approach reveal him as a disciple of Palladio; he had first-hand knowledge of the great architect's buildings, and rivalled the leading exponents of the Palladian taste in Britain under Lord Burlington.

The spirit of Palladian architecture espoused by Pearce was given its fullest expression at Bellamont Forest, a cubic block in red brick, built *c.* 1728 for Thomas Coote. Here the villa ideal is brought fully developed into the South Ulster landscape. It is impossible to overstate the importance of the building as the embodiment of the ideas of Palladio, whose *Quattro libri dell'architettura* had been Pearce's companion in the Veneto in 1724. Its portico introduced the monumental temple front to Irish domestic architecture (though it was not until the end of the century that a portico in this form and on such a scale would appear again on an Irish house), and as a sophisticated, practical rural retreat at the heart of a landed estate Bellamont may be said to have provided the model for countless minor Irish houses down to the middle of the C19. In its design intended to be seen from every side, Bellamont is as fully developed and perhaps even more confidently independent than Mereworth in Kent, the first emulation of the Palladian villa in these islands, designed by Colen Campbell and built just as Pearce began preparing his plans. Given its great importance, it is disappointing that Bellamont had no direct influence on the buildings of South Ulster. It was of greater consequence for the development of Irish architecture beyond this region, and chiefly for Pearce's erstwhile assistant Richard Castle. The most direct influence from it is the top-lit bedroom lobby, which recurs in two houses by Castle, Russborough and Bellinter.

If Bellamont is the purest expression of the compact Palladian villa in Ireland, then it is not surprising that Pearce should also have been the first to promote the elaborated Palladian model that set a central block between wings, with his completion of Castletown in Kildare after 1722. He was also probably designer of the extraordinarily ambitious house at Summerhill in Meath of *c.* 1730, where the particular arrangement of centre block with elaborated quadrant wings terminating in pavilions has some affinities with the original layout of Ballyhaise, known only from a sketch of 1746. That innovative house has traditionally been attributed to *Richard Castle*, but even if its evolution was complicated by several phases, its overall appearance – the architectonic massing, especially the arrangement of lower square towers – speaks out more clearly of the inventiveness of *Pearce* and of ideas transmitted through Vanbrugh than of Castle's more ponderous style. The use of similar square towers is evident in the surviving example at Lismore Castle (Crossdoney), though the

Ballyhaise, conjectural elevation.
Drawing by L. Mulligan, 2012

abandonment of this important house at the end of the C19 and the eventual demolition of its central block deprives us of the opportunity fully to consider another example of this kind of expanded, essentially Palladian, plan.

Even if the structures themselves may never have materialized, *Pearce*'s surviving designs for two buildings in Loughgall, an agent's house and a market house, warrant attention for the consistency they offer with the restrained Palladian aesthetic of Lismore. The scheme for the agent's house (labelled 'Office House'), prepared for Robert Cope, impresses only for its complicated H-plan, as the elevation remains close to the plainest of Vanbrugh's astylar inventions, with its ground-floor arcade, small porthole windows and emboldened imposts. The main front of the market house has a conventional arcaded ground floor, but the end gable has a large Diocletian window over a tripartite opening set under a pediment in a manner close to contemporary designs by Lord Burlington ultimately derived from Palladio's ideas for the Villa Valmarana at Vigardolo.

Bellamont was designed by Pearce for his uncle, Thomas Coote, and it is often through close family connections that attributions to his work are intimated. While its present appearance and condition in no way suggest Pearce, the 'cottage' in Cabra demesne near Kingscourt was a small sophisticated villa p. 404 which he may have designed for his cousin, Mervyn Pratt. It included a broad pedimented frontispiece and big Diocletian window that again invite comparison with the Villa Valmarana.

Also in Monaghan was Gola near Scotstown, another house in p. 531 which it was possible to detect affinities with Pearce's brand of understated classicism. Burnt *c.* 1923 and demolished save for one wing, this was a five-bay block given sophistication by single-storey wings with Venetian windows; the same motif was more prominently displayed in a most remarkable lantern-topped attic tower that straddled the roof, a structure that only finds comparison in Ireland at Woodlands in Co. Dublin, a house usually accepted to be by Pearce. Adding poignancy, the disembodied tower was rebuilt on a church at Urbleshanny (Scotstown), incorporating other fragments from the house.

It is against the usual order that *Richard Castle* should be less firmly identified with the buildings of South Ulster than the short-lived Pearce. Castle had come to Ireland in 1728 from Central Europe, where he had studied fortifications and canals, and in 1730 Pearce gave him responsibility for completing the Newry Canal. Pearce died in 1733, and Castle became the principal exponent of the Palladian style and the leading country-house architect before 1750. However, he features in South Ulster only for a possible involvement with Ballyhaise. The row of lunettes on the stable block at Cabra is closely similar to his designs for the stables of Leinster House in Dublin of the 1740s; indirectly too his shadow passes over the vaulted stables at Hilton and Dartrey, for both of which evidence places construction after his death in 1751.

Contemporary sources make it clear that most MINOR EARLY GEORGIAN HOUSES were neither strikingly original nor architecturally distinguished, with the status of proprietors only barely expressed. Any number of two-storey gable-ended houses with uncomplicated tripartite plans, no more than one room deep, were conceived and built by artisans and lived in by a broad spectrum of proprietors and tenants ranging from the minor gentry and their agents to linen families, millers and clergymen. None of the examples survives without alteration, but there are sufficient details amongst them to confirm the prevailing characteristics of the type. Two early houses worth mentioning are Portnelligan, built for Richard Cross c. 1735 and well preserved, and Upper Thornhill, still reasonably intact but decaying. Both are gable-ended blocks one room deep, hardly more sophisticated than a vernacular farmhouse, but they are longer than usual, and both interiors retain Early Georgian joinery.

Gradually as the century progressed a preference emerged for symmetry in both elevation and plan, reflected in the frequency with which five-bay houses occur throughout the country. Without even entering a typical structure such as Jonesboro House, clues to the arrangement of the plan are to be read from the disposition of the windows, where the wider spacing on either side of the central bay indicates the tripartite plan and the generous hall. Round the back a tall round-headed window in the centre signals the stairs on axis with the hall, as at Lisdoogan (Bellanode). The earliest houses tend to have steeper roofs, often with small attic windows high in the end gables flanking the stacks, but in most cases what distinguishes them most is their doorcases. At Dundrum near Tassagh the main architectural interest is provided by its tripartite round-headed fanlit doorcase, with side-lights of a sub-Palladian or Venetian type, similar to the example at Gola and relatively widespread. Doorcase designs throughout the Georgian period were freely copied from pattern books, as demonstrated for instance by the lugged surround with pulvinated frieze at Donaghmoyne, and the refined pedimented Doric doorcases of Richhill and Jonesboro House.

Larger examples of the five-bay house begin to appear after 1750, simply conceived by scaling up the proportions of the typical block and raising it on a basement. By adding a second range of rooms behind, a double-pile plan was achieved. Monalty at Carrickmacross, built c. 1770, expands the five-bay block to its acceptable limits with three storeys. In many instances the rect-angular plan is elaborated in the shape of a T by a central return to accommodate the stairs, an arrangement that survives at Mount Irwin.

Occasionally a design will rise to a point of stateliness – at Ballinahone (Armagh) with a pediment or with modest wings as at Jonesboro House. Dungillick (Emyvale) is the best preserved of all the Early Georgian houses and is a variant of every rule. Houses with hipped roofs are less common, certainly before 1750. Ballyconnell Castle of the 1750s is among the largest now known, made more sophisticated by resting its roof on a stone eaves course with an ornate profile. Only in exceptional cases does an awareness of the classical grammar of Palladianism become evident, and even then only tentatively. The application of Pal-ladian motifs to give a bolder emphasis to the central bay was generally rare in South Ulster. Its early use at Gola has been noted; Bingfield (Crossdoney) is the most substantial house where it occurs, while at Ashgrove (Milltown) it raises a solidly compact farmhouse out of the ordinary, as the familiar tripartite doorcase is echoed in a Venetian window above and repeated again as a blind motif to the sides.

The transition from an old-fashioned preference for a shallow, economical arrangement of rooms to a more developed double-pile emerged in the C18 as a development of interests in Palladian planning. Bellamont introduced the most developed double-pile plan in South Ulster, but the impact, with a few exceptions, is barely perceptible before the middle of the century. There are, however, important instances where the plan displays some inno-vation. Ballyhaise introduced the bowed or *bombé* projection to Irish domestic architecture, in a form that is closest to French Baroque architecture of the C17. In Britain William Talman had experimented with the idea of bowed projections and an axial oval saloon before the end of the C17. At Ballyhaise the bow is given full expression as a semi-oval form, anticipating an interest in geometric planning that would gain widespread currency only during the Neoclassical period. The only comparable cases where a circular bow is continued into the plan in this way are at another Pearcean brick house, Arch Hall in Co. Meath, and later at Wardtown in Co. Donegal (1740).

p. 182

p. 169

EARLY GEORGIAN INTERIORS have survived only fitfully in South Ulster, and continue to be under threat through derelic-tion and insensitive alteration. The old house at Castle Hamilton, lost long ago, was said to have had a hall that was the 'largest of its kind in the Kingdom', ornamented with pilasters and niches; similar in scale to Pearce's House of Lords Chamber in Dublin, the claim was perhaps justified. Decoration in Bellamont and Ballyhaise is architectural, best in the saloon at Bellamont, where the flat ceiling is boldly garlanded and bordered with the square rose-filled coffers that Pearce favoured, based on Palladio's treat-ment of Corinthian halls, a motif that was to appear again in the work of Richard Castle at Powerscourt and Russborough. At

38, 39

Ballyhaise the best early interiors survive in just two rooms, the Peacock Room and the Saloon, both with 'curiously finished' stucco in their vaults, the latter's walls plastered, with raised and fielded panels.

Though the survival of the Early Georgian interiors of minor houses is especially poor, largely because of continuous alteration, these are sufficiently well understood for one to state that they were typically characterized by chunky cornices and doors with lugged or shouldered surrounds and raised and fielded panels, a combination that was widespread in Ireland and endured for a decade or so beyond the mid-century. Good instances are found at Lisaniske (Carrickmacross) of *c.* 1740. The best of the joinery was usually produced for the staircase; the finest, perhaps surprisingly, is not in the country but in Monaghan town, where Aviemore has a handsome richly carved
55   dog-leg staircase. Fellows Hall (Killylea), rebuilt after a fire of 1752, was also given a handsome dog-leg staircase with characteristically thick newels and sweeping handrails.

In considering CHURCHES of the Georgian period in South Ulster it is the buildings of the former Established Church that are of greatest significance. Few new buildings were undertaken before 1770. In Monaghan, however, a church was built on the Diamond in 1725; it is now known only from the Rev. Daniel Beaufort's tantalizing reference to it as a building of 'Casselian stile' and from others who intriguingly referred to its 'ugly narrow tower' shaped as 'an irregular pentagon'. It was replaced entirely
57   in the early C19. Some of the fabric of St John's Church at Dartrey demesne belongs to the brick church built by Richard Dawson in 1729, but its original character has been subsumed by successive Gothic remodellings. In Cavan, the plain tower of the C17 parish church was given simplified Gibbs surrounds to its belfry in about 1750.

Much better is the survival of early C18 FUNERARY MONUMENTS, which tended to be retained or transferred as churches
33   were rebuilt. Among the earliest is the Hamilton monument at Killeshandra of *c.* 1713, a massive Corinthian aedicule attributed to *David Sheehan*. The handsome Ionic aedicule for Josiah Campbell, †1722, in the church at Aughnamullen, with a graceful swan-neck pediment and carved military trophies, is signed by *J. Lamont*, a sculptor otherwise unknown. A much grander
34   display of this kind is found in the unsigned monument in Templeport erected to John Blachford, †1727. The best collection of Georgian funerary sculpture is naturally to be found in the
65   Church of Ireland Cathedral in Armagh. The monument to Dean Peter Drelincourt, †1722, includes the fine recumbent figure of the Dean by *John Michael Rysbrack*. By far the most important
64   is the statue of Sir Thomas Molyneux of 1752, entirely Baroque in feeling, the only Irish memorial by *Louis François Roubiliac* – originally intended not as a funerary monument but for a garden building at Castle Dillon. The church at Belturbet has several unsigned sculptural monuments of the Georgian period that are also worthy of notice.

LATER c18 ARCHITECTURE

After Pearce and Castle, there were limited opportunities apart from public works, and consequently there are few ARCHITECTS working in the region after 1750 who can be named with any certainty or whose involvement was of great importance or duration. Of those who do appear, most, like Castle, had forged their early careers outside Ireland. *Christopher Myers* had arrived from Lancashire in the 1750s to become the most prominent architect in Ulster, but in the S of the province he was represented only with his design of 1761 for the bridge over the Bann at Portadown, since replaced. William Brownlow of Lurgan claimed that the Sardinian architect *Davis Ducart* (Daviso de Arcort) was 'dropped into this kingdom from the clouds, no one knows how, or what brought him to it'. We still do not know, but once established he was brought northwards by his involvement in 1767 with the Tyrone Navigation, and it was presumably through Archbishop Richard Robinson's shared interest in that project that Ducart came to produce the design for the Archbishop's   44 Palace in Armagh. *George Ensor* appears to have served as its builder (he was paid over £10,000 in 1775), and since there is little of Ducart in the finished palace it seems likely that Ensor took on overall responsibility as designer.

George Ensor's career demonstrates the gradual development of a native profession in the C18, partly encouraged by a strong dynastic tendency within the trades. His family had not long been in Ireland, his father having come from England to work as carpenter on Pearce's Parliament House in 1729, and both George and his half-brother John adopted architecture after successfully combining the role of contractor and designer: John Ensor succeeded to Richard Castle's practice, having been employed as his clerk and measurer from 1740, while George Ensor joined the office of the Surveyor General in 1744. His association with the county of Armagh can be traced to 1760, when he married Sarah Clarke of Ardress, a property to which he succeeded in 1778.   47, 48 While his buildings show a tendency towards Palladianism, he was alive to the delicacies of Neoclassicism in the fashionable improvements that he made to Ardress in the 1780s. As George Ensor's name is also associated with several buildings in Armagh town, including the Infirmary and a prominent terrace on Lower English Street, it is likely that evidence for more will emerge.

As before, most buildings were the work of anonymous LOCAL BUILDERS, whose designs were governed by their own traditions, modified to a greater or lesser extent by an awareness of developing fashions and the demands of their patrons. The identities of some of the masons and carpenters working in the region are known, even if the full extent of their works in not. *Whitmore Davis* was perhaps a typical practitioner, described as an 'architect and bricklayer' and resident in Newbliss in the early 1760s. In 1774 two local builders, *Henry Byrne* and *John Green*, sent their drawing of a brick house built by them in Carrickmacross the previous year to George Shirley, in answer to his intention to make his portion of the town 'as much improved as Lord Weymouth's'. Their competent if old-fashioned building still dominates the Main Street. However, even though Green offered a decent proposal for a new market house in the town, Shirley showed his reluctance to give over full control of an important public building to a local, submitting to his agent in 1779 a design for a more sophisticated building by the Warwick architect *Thomas Johnson*. The appearance of the market house, now demolished, is not recorded.

The lack of clarity surrounding George Ensor's role on the Archbishop's Palace in Armagh exemplifies the difficulties that exist in apportioning responsibility for building design. Richard Louch, William Johnston and John Harvey were all active in Armagh in the second half of the century, but in each of the buildings with which their names are connected it remains unclear whether they acted solely as contractors or may also have had some responsibility for the design. Like Ensor, *Richard Louch* combined his trade as carpenter and builder with design. He settled in Armagh, where, benefiting from the largesse of Archbishop Robinson, he, with *John Harvey*, completed the Infirmary in 1776. He may also have been involved in the building of the Archbishop's Palace, as in 1775 he made a measured drawing of its doorcase to send to Dublin. *William Johnston* was the father of the well-known architects Richard and Francis Johnston, but little is known of the man himself, or of his career; he is recorded in 1775 as the builder of Knappagh House, which he may well have designed; and he appears, like John Harvey, conducting measurements at Drumsill House near Armagh (demolished) in 1789.

There was occasionally a role for the AMATEUR ARCHITECT: the *Rev. Daniel Beaufort*, rector of Navan and Collon, who freely offered his opinion on architecture and gave proposals to neighbours and friends, suggested some alterations to Edenderry House (Eglish), while *Samuel Hayes*, a more pretentious architectural aficionado, central to the development of Neoclassical taste in the capital, designed the Monaghan Market House in 1792.

Dawson's Grove at Dartrey in Monaghan – rebuilt, then demolished, but known from a measured survey of 1843 – offers a sense of the transition in tastes occurring after 1760, blending as it did the canon of Palladio with elements of a lighter, purer form of CLASSICISM that was just then gaining hold through an increased awareness of Greek and Roman detail. It was built before 1768 for Thomas Dawson, who as a Grand Tour dilettante in 1751 had fallen in with Lord Charlemont and his circle on the Continent. On their return to Ireland, Charlemont led Neoclassical taste in Dublin, confining his patronage there rather than on his patrimonial estates in Armagh, while Dawson seems to have been no less discerning in his choices when he began to enhance the family seat in Monaghan. Myers and Ducart were the only architects in South Ulster who might have been capable of such an undertaking; but except perhaps for Myers' works at

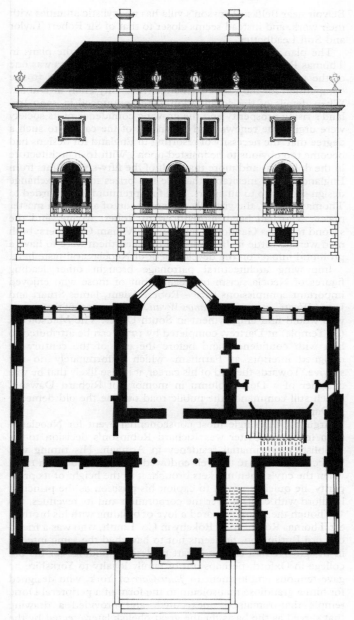

Dartrey, Dawson's Grove, elevation and plan.
By K. Mulligan, 2012

Belvoir near Belfast, Dawson's villa has no stylistic affinities with their work, and instead seems closer to that of Sir Robert Taylor and Stiff Leadbetter.

The plan of Dawson's Grove is close to one of the plans in Thomas Rawlins's *Familiar Architecture* (1768). Rawlins was one of the many English architects who submitted designs to the competition for the Royal Exchange (now City Hall) in Dublin. When details of the competition were announced in 1769 Ireland's rising prosperity and the growing confidence of its society were urging the renewal and expansion of the capital to such a degree that 'the necessity of resorting to England for designs had become too obvious to be insisted upon'. With Irish architecture in the doldrums and more than half of the fifty-six entrants from England, it was inevitable that the top prizes for the Exchange design should go to outsiders. The first premium was awarded to Thomas Cooley, the virtually unknown son of a London master mason who had been apprenticed to Robert Mylne, and the second to James Gandon, a pupil of Sir William Chambers; both men were to settle in Ireland, and between them were to have a profound impact on the development of Neoclassical taste here.

Improving architectural patronage brought other leading figures of Neoclassicism to Ireland, but of those who enjoyed important commissions here – Robert Adam, James Stuart and James Wyatt – it was only *James Wyatt*, the youngest of the group, 51 who would find employment in South Ulster. The Mausoleum (or Temple) at Dartrey, completed by 1774, can be attributed to him with confidence, and before the end of the century he designed interiors at Farnham, which unfortunately do not survive. Towards the end of his career, it is also likely that he was 50 designer of a Doric column in memory of Richard Dawson, which still commands the public road outside the old demesne at Dartrey.

Arguably the single most consequential event for Neoclassicism in South Ulster was Richard Robinson's decision to re-establish the primatial residency in Armagh. His timing was perfect: appointed to the well-endowed but neglected see in 1765, when the city's linen markets brought it to the height of its prosperity, he quickly moved to exploit his position as the principal landlord with control over the corporation and its revenues.

Though the Primate shared a love of building with his brother, Sir Thomas Robinson of Rokeby in Co. Louth, who was a friend of Lord Burlington, he seems not to have had the same interest in design. He had chosen Wyatt to design buildings for his old college in Oxford; perhaps out of family loyalty to Yorkshire he gave tenuous employment to *John Carr* of York, who designed for him a grandiose mausoleum in the form of a peripteral Doric temple that remained unexecuted, and provided a drawing 49 that served as the basis for the great obelisk later erected by the Archbishop. In his first year Robinson instituted repairs to the Cathedral and began setting out a demesne.

44 The ARCHBISHOP'S PALACE was the largest house of the later Georgian period, initiated in 1766 and only completed in

1775. For the first house in the three counties to be built entirely of ashlar one might have expected a more ambitious design, but the exterior is backward-looking, the original doorcase and the Palladian alternating pediments on the garden front seeming to look back rather than forward to the refinements of the Neoclassical style that would later distinguish Primate Robinson's long tenure in Armagh. In many ways its design stands for the static condition of Irish architecture before 1770. Robinson's initial choice of *Davis Ducart* and *George Ensor* was not particularly auspicious. Even by the time he came to choose *Thomas Cooley* as his architect in 1770, Robinson seems not to have been attached to any particular stylistic manifesto.

Having snapped up such exciting new talent so soon after the Exchange competition, the Primate is frequently accused of gradually stifling the great promise of originality that Cooley had shown in Dublin. However it was always unlikely that commissions outside Dublin would offer the opportunity for brilliance displayed in the Exchange, and it is likely that Cooley's work in the capital was limited by the demands of his official position as Inspector of Public Buildings from 1774 until his death ten years later.

Typically Cooley's buildings stand up to critical scrutiny; composed in either classical or Gothic styles, they are characterized

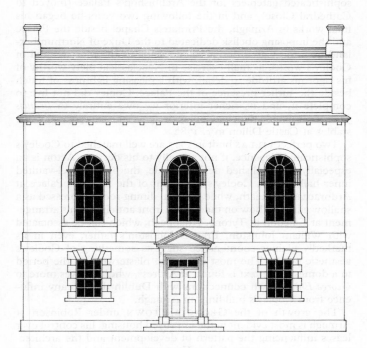

Armagh Public Libary, elevation.
Drawing by K. Mulligan, 2012

by an uncompromising refinement of detail. However, a noticeable unevenness is present across the range of PUBLIC WORKS he undertook in Armagh, his characteristic brilliance sometimes subordinated to more practical considerations. Even so, Cooley's contribution to making Armagh one of the most appealing Georgian towns in Ulster is assured. His earliest recorded work there

p. 31 is the Library, opened in 1771 and later greatly extended, but with its handsome three-bay façade still legible at the centre of the N elevation. In 1776–8 Cooley completed the houses on Vicars' Hill, distinguished from their neighbours by the display of more attenuated proportions. The Barracks of *c.* 1773 and the Gaol of 1780 both demanded a degree of austerity not accom-

p. 123 modating of aesthetic finesse. The Royal School of 1774 is the most novel of these institutional buildings, with its display of a castellated Gothic style, even if its plan is functional and its details are ordinary.

The impression one gains is that Robinson's demands on Cooley were more practical than aesthetic, and doubtless his intentions were greatly restrained by considerations of cost. It is only with the later buildings, completing as Robinson prepared to take his final departure from Ireland and perhaps motivated by personal aggrandizement, that Cooley appears to have been given greater latitude for his creativity. In 1780 he designed sophisticated gatepiers for the Archbishop's Palace (moved to Cathedral Close), and in the following two years he began his

44, 46 final works in Armagh, the Primate's Chapel beside the Palace
49 and the imposing obelisk dedicated to the Duke of Northumberland, revising Carr's design. The Chapel is the most refined of Cooley's works, a small exercise in Neoclassical piety worthy of his rigorous attitude to detail, with a pleasing lightness of touch beside the surlier presence of the Palace. Cooley did not live to

46 complete it, and its richer interior we owe entirely to *Francis Johnston*. Outside the city Cooley designed the exceptionally fine stables at Castle Dillon in *c.* 1782.

Two perfect VILLAS built in 1775 are well matched to Cooley's
45 sophisticated elegance, if not actually to his designs. Acton is an especially accomplished design; inside, the plain barrel-vaulted inner hall invokes Cooley's treatment of the Bishop's Palace at Ardbraccan in Meath, while the oval dining room expressed as a shallow elliptical bow on the garden front anticipates his arrangement at Caledon in Tyrone. Knappagh, which can be associated with William Johnston, Francis Johnston's father, even in its markedly plainer countenance suggests something of Cooley's aesthetic purity. The most important plasterwork of the period

48 in a domestic context is found at Ardress, where it owes more to *George Ensor*'s own connections with Dublin than to any influence from Cooley's buildings in Armagh.

The growth of the GEORGIAN TOWN under Robinson at Armagh is most evident in the improved housing, his control over leases influencing the pattern of development and the architectural character, so that Arthur Young could justifiably claim that Robinson had made it a 'well-built city of stone and slate'. This aspect of urban improvement was not confined to Armagh, and in many of the towns in South Ulster the influence of improving landlords can be seen, with the introduction of at least one gentrified street or precinct on which uniform, well-proportioned town houses occur, with generous sash windows and handsome fanlit doorcases; the Main Street of Markethill, Farnham Street 7 in Cavan, and Lake View, a terrace of five houses in Monaghan, are just some of the examples to be found.

Samuel Hayes's Market House in Monaghan of 1792, with its 69 understated rustication and Adamesque panels with drapery festoons and paterae above each bay, remains the most noteworthy Neoclassical design outside Armagh. Castle Blayney (now altered and in a sad condition) of 1799 was designed by *Robert Woodgate*, a pupil of Sir John Soane. His indebtedness to Soane was dem- p. 237 onstrated outside in his use of low pediments, large tripartite windows set in recessed arches, and a shallow bow, and inside by the central top-lit stair hall.

Nature had ideally prepared the landscape of South Ulster, pooled with natural serpentine waters, for the creation of ornamental DEMESNES. A good many owe their formation to the Georgian era, and of these the most expansive was Farnham, which remained uniquely unspoiled to the end of the C20. However, the best now remain in Monaghan, where Hilton Park has the finest landscape in the tradition of Lancelot 'Capability' Brown. Dawson's Grove, whose especially watery landscape is shared across the county border with Bellamont Forest, was the most acclaimed in its time for containing all the elements of the ideal landscape in Ireland, and celebrated in the late C18 paintings of Thomas Roberts, William Ashford and Gabriele Ricciardelli. The most important Irish designer in the Brownian tradition was *John Sutherland*, whose earliest work is at Derrymore, laid 52

Farnham.
Chromolithograph by A. F. Lydon, 1860s

out from 1777 around a charming *cottage orné* of which he may
have been the architect. Sutherland continued to design into the
first two decades of the C19, but taste soon developed for the
Picturesque.

When we turn to CHURCHES, of the rebuilding in 1763 of St
Salvator at Glaslough only the emphatic moulded eaves course
of the nave now remains. At Ballyconnell, however, the prevailing
classical taste is well represented. Tomregan Parish Church, built
in 1757, is very much a building of 'Casselian' quality and style,
and even if it were not the only well-preserved example of its date
in South Ulster, it would command a place as one of the finest
churches of the period, notable for its unusual bows and fine
ashlar, and for the bold plaster detail in its surviving interior.

In 1772, as Treasurer to the Board of First Fruits, Primate
Robinson introduced legislation which provided for 'erecting of
new chapels of ease in parishes of large extent' in his own diocese
of Armagh, as well as encouraging clergy to build houses for
themselves on glebe lands. Perhaps it was in response to this
legislation that one of the earliest commissions afforded to
Thomas Cooley was for a set of twelve 'standard' church designs.
Now preserved in Armagh Public Library, these range from
modest three-bay single-cell designs to a more substantial hall-
and-tower type, including one with a spire. Of the designs, eight
were in an understated Georgian Gothic manner, with pointed
windows and the plainest Y-tracery. The remainder were small
single-cell classical buildings with pedimented frontispieces and
a variety of elaborate classical bellcotes. It was the hall-and-tower
designs with Gothic detailing that were favoured in the churches
erected during Robinson's building campaigns. Two still in use
closely follow Cooley's designs. One is St John's at Lisnadill of
1772, with a tower almost exactly like that in Cooley's 'Design
No. 9'. St Aidan's at Salters Grange, built a year later, is more
elaborate. Cooley's designs were also followed at Keady,
Camlough and Newtownhamilton, while at Carrickmacross the
apse has the flavour of Cooley's designs. Essentially the same
hall-and-tower type continued to be favoured into the C19, in a
more concerted and widespread church-building campaign that
commenced after the first parliamentary grant in 1778 towards
the work of the Board of First Fruits.

Among Church of Ireland FUNERARY MONUMENTS, later
Neoclassical taste is represented by *John Bacon the Younger*, with
the monument to Richard Robinson, Lord Rokeby, of 1802 (with
a bust by *Joseph Nollekens*), in Armagh Cathedral. *John Bacon the
Elder* executed the classical relief to the Rev. John Jones, of 1794,
for the church of Mullaghbrack. The most elaborate monument
of the Neoclassical period occurs in a different context, with the
moving sculptural group by *Joseph Wilton* installed in 1774 in the
Dawson Mausoleum at Dartrey.

The discriminatory measures instituted against Catholics
soon after the defeat of James II in 1690 were extended in the
early years of the C18 to include restrictions on the clergy. Even
with limited enforcement of the penal laws and widespread

continuation of religious activity, C18 CATHOLIC CHURCHES have a largely fugitive presence in the building record. Sources are full of references to 'mass-houses', thinly disguised vernacular structures of mud or stone, invariably thatched, which disappeared as it gradually became possible to erect buildings of greater pretension. The establishment in 1760 of the Catholic Committee marked the beginning of a relaxation of religious discrimination, which received official recognition in the series of Catholic Relief Acts from 1778 that culminated in full emancipation fifty years later. Only a handful of the churches built in this era survive in the region, all, regrettably, now disused and abandoned. Two chapels in Monaghan, Lathlorcan of the 1780s and Drumcatton built in 1796, are no more than modest two-bay halls in roughcast with simple pointed windows, now much altered. In Cavan, the chapel at Kildoagh, built as a long thatched hall in 1796, best exemplifies the endurance of the simple 'mass-house', barely distinct from a barn. The only overt references to function are the large pointed sashes with a busy display of Gothick Y-tracery. Inside, it has the most common arrangement, with the altar set against the long s wall and gendered galleries filling the two ends of the 'nave'.

The older rural buildings of the PRESBYTERIAN CHURCH have on the whole fared just as poorly as their Roman Catholic counterparts. They share the same modest character and a preference for plain halls and T-plans. At Croaghan near Killeshandra the small church established in 1670 was rebuilt in 1742 as a simple gable-fronted hall. Cahans near Tullycorbet is a large four-bay hall of 1779, later enlarged and now abandoned, but important for its intact furnishings. Outside Ballybay, Derryvalley, an exemplary building still in use, is a substantial plain Georgian hall of 1786 with half-hipped gables and big Gothick sashes. Tassagh, built in 1777, and Tyrone's Ditches at Jerrettspass, perhaps not much later, follow a T-plan and are plainer still.

60

ARCHITECTURE AFTER 1800

In 1799 the Speaker, Isaac Corry, and the Chief Secretary, Lord Castlereagh, are said to have convened at Derrymore near Bessbrook and there, in the large drawing room with its generous bay window, drafted the terms for the Act of Union. In January 1800, as the Parliament voted away its own existence, agreeing the transfer of political power to London, national pride was severely deflated, but its convictions remained alive.

52

Catholic support for the Union was largely based on the belief that the removal of impediments to high office and parliamentary representation would follow. Once the Catholic electorate had been mobilized politically, showing its strength in Cavan and Monaghan by electing pro-Emancipation candidates in the general election of 1826, the goal was at last achieved in 1829. Growing confidence and changing attitudes are evident in Catholic church building, which began to increase significantly after 1810 as aspiration turned to expectation. Funding for the Established Church of Ireland increased substantially in 1816; its building programme greatly accelerated in the succeeding twenty years, as older parish churches were repaired or rebuilt and new churches established in newly devised parishes, even where congregations went down or barely existed, resulting in the ubiquitous hall-and-tower churches erected across the land. In economic terms, sustained growth from 1760 laid the foundation for prosperity in the early C19, and with Irish agricultural exports growing dramatically during the Napoleonic Wars, the early decades of the new century were marked by a widespread increase in building activity; towns expanded and their market centres were renewed as a response to improved trade. In addition, the Government spent freely to uphold the stability of the Union, expanding its infrastructure with new courthouses and gaols. In the countryside larger country houses began to appear, displaying a greater enthusiasm for different architectural styles.

From the turn of the century buildings were increasingly being entrusted to IRISH ARCHITECTS, whose education had been boosted by the establishment of the Dublin Society's School of Architectural Drawing in 1764. With Gandon retired by 1808, Francis Johnston and Richard Morrison, both Irish-born, stood at the head of a maturing architectural profession in the capital. Both were to have a central role in the progress of the profession – Morrison for his part was knighted in 1841 – and both were to influence the development of more eclectic styles. Both were widely employed on important public and private commissions. Their direct involvement in South Ulster is more limited, and *Richard Morrison*'s only recorded commission is at Rossmore Park. However they influenced pupils and assistants, with *William Farrell, William Murray, John Bowden* and *John B. Keane* all employed in the region before 1830. Several English and Scottish contemporaries were to gain important opportunities here; but, recognizing the improved standing of Irish architecture, Thomas Hopper, whose early career had been distinguished by Gosford Castle, could write to Morrison from England in 1839: 'It has always appeared to me as a libel upon the Gentry of Ireland that they should import from this Country talent inferior to their own native genius'; he even claimed to have refused further opportunities to be employed here in deference to the Irish profession.

Over the ten years that Archbishop Robinson was employed in regenerating the town of Armagh, his discovery of a remarkable protégé in *Francis Johnston* proved to be of great importance to Irish architecture. In 1778, the eighteen-year-old Johnston was sent by Robinson to Dublin to train in Cooley's office. By the time of Cooley's untimely death in 1784, Johnston possessed the maturity to assume the role of architect to the Primate, displaying great panache at once with his completion of the interior of the Palace Chapel. After Robinson left Ireland in 1786, however,

there were fewer opportunities to build in Armagh, and consequently there is much less there to show the range of Johnston's
powers. The Observatory of 1789, the last of his works for the
Primate, has a miniature Doric porch exquisitely detailed in a
way that set the tone for his masterpiece at Townley Hall in Co.
Louth. That concern for precise detail is shown in a more idiosyncratic way on the doorcase of Dobbin House of 1812, almost
certainly also his design. Unfortunately Johnston never enjoyed
a fresh commission in South Ulster equal to his talents, and he
designed no new houses here. Cloverhill involved a substantial
remodelling of a mid-Georgian house, begun in 1799; at Loughgilly he merely added wings to the glebe house in 1806, for the
brother-in-law of his patron at Townley Hall. The additions to
Farnham of 1802 were his most important private commission
in the region; still this was not an ambitious or innovative project,
though the surviving columns of its Doric portico are as pure an
expression of the Greek Revival as is to be found anywhere in
the country.

Johnston was appointed architect to the Board of Works in
1805, and in this capacity he returned to Armagh in 1808 to
design the Courthouse. The remainder of his buildings in South   p. 121
Ulster are works of quiet sophistication, revealing a temperament
leaning towards understatement and a preference for clean linear
expression with shallow surface recession; often it is only the use
of segmental- or round-headed arches that keeps the buildings
from severity. These are the qualities that are present in his additions of 1806 to Drumsill House (bombed, then demolished) and
in other buildings attributed to him such as the houses for the
model Palace Farm built on the Primate's demesne, and the
Farnham School in Cavan, while the Cavan Royal School of 1819
and St Luke's Hospital in Armagh of 1820 bring these characteristics to an institutional idiom. In church design, however, St   79
Mark's in Armagh of 1811 was no more adventurous than
Cooley's own paper-thin Gothic style.

Johnston retired in 1826 and died three years later. *William
Murray*, his cousin, who had joined the office in 1807, inherited
the practice. He had been appointed assistant architect to the
Board of Works in 1822, and succeeded Johnston as its architect
in 1827. He immediately began to make an impression on
Armagh, largely through the patronage of Lord Charlemont. But
he was not an original designer, and the results often lack assurance. His most impressive commission is a commanding terrace
of five houses in Charlemont Place designed in 1827. Murray's   72
most important commission in the county, the rebuilding of
Castle Dillon in 1844, resulted in an austere, monotonous block.
The Savings Bank off the Mall in Armagh of 1838 is a more
thoughtful Neoclassical design, nicely proportioned, with well-
judged detail, the best of his work.

Johnston's restrained mode is dominant in the numerous
CLASSICAL COUNTRY HOUSES built in the first half of the C19.
The prevalent type is a well-proportioned two-storey villa with
basement and a pleasing three-bay frontage. The plainest kind,

such as Tullyvin House, is rendered or roughcast, without quoins
or other minor architectural elaboration. In all instances the
fenestration is distinguished principally by smaller proportions
on the upper floors, but at Glynch House (Newbliss) the ground-
floor windows are set in shallow relieving arches in the manner
favoured by Johnston, creating what has almost come to be
accepted as a building type. Hipped roofs with eaves borne on
slender timber brackets seem to have been preferred above all
else. Generally houses after 1800 give an impression of greater
solidity, sometimes achieved by nothing more than a clever
arrangement of an L-plan, where two adjoining fronts are presented to form an impression of greater depth and substance;
this is done for instance in Armagh at Crow Hill, by the mysterious *Brownlees*, and at Glenaul Park (Eglish), probably also his.
53 The L-plan might occur in a single-storey format as well, as it
does at Loughooney. There were also solid rectangular blocks
with broad five-bay fronts relieved only by a rectangular tripartite
window set above the entrance, a manner that prevailed to a
greater extent beyond the three counties.

In most of these houses a simple porch with boxy proportions,
usually given no greater embellishment than a cornice and blocking course, contributes to the impression of bulkiness. In the
more consciously architectural designs, porches, and less frequently porticoes, display classical elements, often with a taste
for Greek detail; the best were *Johnston*'s at Cloverhill and Newbliss House, both lost. At Glynch the pedimented porch with its
pared-down Doric columns has a fine simplicity suggestive of
Richard Morrison. It was in the architecture of his former assistant
John B. Keane that Morrison's architectural mannerisms were
most faithfully emulated, but Keane's two substantial houses in
South Ulster, Stradone House and Ballybay Castle, have both
been demolished. At Belturbet the house built for George Knipe
has long disappeared; the Knipe Mausoleum, however, bears the
Morrison–Keane imprint in a proud Greek Revival design.

The finest building within this group of more architecturally
pretentious houses was Cornacassa in Co. Monaghan, a smart
cubic block inspired by Johnston's Townley Hall, demolished in
1934. In 1835 *James Jones* of Dundalk drew up ambitious plans
for Hilton Park, which would have transformed the house into
the grandest classical mansion of the region; a memory of his
project survives in the extraordinary stoa-like ride for horses.
Today, the largest surviving classical house of this period is The
Argory in Co. Armagh, designed by *Arthur & John Williamson*,
Johnston's Dublin-based cousins, who were principally involved
with speculative development in the capital. Arthur Williamson
also designed the Bann Bridge at Portadown.

After Johnston, *William Farrell* was the most widely employed
architect in the region in the first half of the c19. Much of his
work was undertaken after 1823 in his capacity as architect to the
Board of First Fruits. Farrell had served as a clerk at the Board
of Works under Johnston until 1810, and his work from this time
has a clarity of form and moderation of detail that is close in

feeling to Johnston's more reserved style. The most marked difference between them is that Farrell's buildings develop a greater stolidness, occasionally betraying a weakness for overscaled detail. This is seen clearly in the heavy entablatures at Rathkenny (Tullyvin), where the corners of the building stand proud in a manner that characterizes much of the architect's mature work. At Kilmore in Cavan a few years later he scaled up the same design for the See House, where the details work better on a larger block. Kilmore afforded Farrell the opportunity to employ a form of large tripartite window that he particularly favoured, its divisions formed as pilaster-like mullions with heavy console brackets. The same device was widely used on doorcases at this time, often to support a broad segmental fanlight. Farrell's penchant for bold strip quoins and tripartite windows puts him forward as the architect for the wings at Ballyhaise, added before 1837.

54

37

A feature common to many Late Georgian houses, though not frequent in South Ulster, is the shallow bowed projection. Typically bows occur singly, at the centre of the façade as at Thornhill (Smithborough); more unusually, *Farrell* placed the bow in an offset manner on the garden front of the See House at Kilmore. The most articulate use of bows in the region came in the form of symmetrical projections at either end of the façade, known at Woodville House of *c.* 1757, Coolderry of *c.* 1770 (demolished), Ballymoyer House of *c.* 1770, and on the N front of Elm Park (Killylea) of 1803, where narrow bows are extended to the full height, right on the ends of the broad three-storey façade; twin bows are known to have been used on the garden front of Newbliss House (demolished) and at Drumsill (also demolished), built *c.* 1786 by a master mason, *William Lappan*.

The Newry architect *Thomas Duff*, who shared Farrell's interest in big tripartite windows, first gained employment in South Ulster in a supervisory capacity, overseeing the building of The Argory in 1820 where he later seems to have designed the neat porticoed gate lodges and made proposals for a Greek Revival chapel on the estate. He was also employed as clerk of works at Gosford Castle for almost a decade before his death in 1848, and for Lord Gosford he designed the Courthouse at Markethill of 1842. Something of its bulky character is also evident at St Macartan's Seminary in Monaghan, an imposing astylar composition designed by Duff in 1840.

p. 344

102

Looking at his other works, one gains the impression that Duff, unlike the architects examined so far, was more comfortable when working in a Gothic mode. His earliest example in this manner in South Ulster is St Patrick's Grammar School in Armagh of 1836–8, where he favoured a Tudor style, but little of that is prominent now. It was perhaps this job, if not his command of the style already evident in Newry and Dundalk, that led to the most important commission of his career, the new Roman Catholic Cathedral of Armagh. His archaeological interest in Gothic was demonstrated in an ambitious Perpendicular design inspired partly by King's College Chapel in Cambridge with the

p. 40

Armagh, St Patrick's Cathedral (R.C.).
Engraving, 1880

addition of transepts, twin w towers and a massive crossing tower
to accord with the significance of the building, begun in 1840.

In LANDSCAPE AND GARDEN DESIGN, John Sutherland's
place was eventually taken by the Scottish designer *Alexander
McLeish*, a pupil of J. C. Loudon, who had established himself in
Ireland by 1814. His style of gardening blended formal elements
like parterres with informal shrubberies, adopting something of
Loudon's emphasis on individual, exotic plants. McLeish considered himself as much an architect as a gardener, and was
widely employed as such. Between 1821 and 1824 when working
for the Marquess of Headfort at Kells he was also involved in
laying out the Headfort sporting estate in Virginia, creating a new
avenue; he seems to have been responsible also for remodelling
Virginia Lodge in an understated Tudor style, as well as designing
the gate lodges in a cottage style. Several of the buildings in the
village may also be his. In 1822 he appears to have had some
connection with Castle Hamilton, perhaps even being involved
in the design of the house, which shared his brand of chaste classicism, the kind he also employed on a gate lodge for Knappagh
in 1827.

Tastes in landscape design absorbed the romantic ideals of the
Picturesque Movement. These sought to promote the contrast
and unpredictability present in nature as opposed to the stagey
blend of formal clumps and rolling lawns that characterized the
Brownian format. The informal plantations that rise over the
watery landscape around Castle Blayney (now Hope Castle, at
Castleblayney) are the enduring legacy of its designer, *William
Sawrey Gilpin*, leading exponent of the Picturesque, author of
Practical Hints upon Landscape Gardening (1832), and a nephew
of the Rev. William Gilpin, the pioneering figure of the movement. A garden terrace was often employed with the intention of
'softening off art into nature in the same way that an artist softens
off hardness of outline in his picture'. Just such a terrace garden
was employed at this time at Lough Fea, overlooking its evocative
landscape where the romance of the picturesque is captured in

Monaghan, Rossmore Park.
Chromolithograph by A. F. Lydon, 1860s

natural rock outcrops and caves heightened by an association with the mythical Irish giant 'Finn McCool' whose rocky 'chair' lies buried in the woods.

Among NON-CLASSICAL COUNTRY HOUSES, buildings of the Picturesque Movement are now few in South Ulster. The rustic cottage of the Maxwells at Killykeen survives; Carn Cottage, a decorative Regency house near Kildallon, is being reclaimed by nature to a degree worthy in itself of the Picturesque. Instances of the castle style are not plentiful either. A lone turret in a field is all that now remains of Clare Castle, the earliest known example of the type in South Ulster. The taste for Gothicizing older houses begins with Cabra Castle (Kingscourt), the result of several phases of remodelling and enlargement begun modestly in about 1808; by 1837 it was a larger and more rambling composition with a convincing picturesque silhouette. *George Papworth* transformed Killevy Castle (Meigh) in 1836 into a toy castle. The remodelling of Castle Saunderson by *George* 94 *Sudden c.* 1835 is indicative of the developing interest in more accurate forms of historicism, in this instance cribbed from Edward Blore's work at Crom in Fermanagh. At Rossmore Park *Richard Morrison*, during a short-lived partnership with his son *William Vitruvius Morrison*, introduced a blend of Elizabethan and Jacobean styles that reflected the younger Morrison's observations of English Gothic and Tudor domestic architecture made at first hand at the tail-end of a European tour in 1821.

William Vitruvius Morrison's application of his unique experience to the architecture of the practice coincides with the moment when scholarly attitudes to architectural detail began to affect Irish buildings. *Thomas Rickman*, whose only significant Irish building is not far from Rossmore, at Lough Fea, is among the most important figures of the Gothic Revival in the generation before Pugin, largely because he was the first person successfully to devise a systematic classification for the styles of Gothic architecture, published in 1817 as *An Attempt to Discriminate the Styles of English Architecture from the Conquest to the Reformation*. Lough Fea was designed in partnership with *Henry Hutchinson* and begun in 1825. Unfortunately Rickman's plans do not survive, and despite the importance of the house its layout and interior have not yet been made accessible for study; for the present it is only possible to assess it in a remote way. Lough Fea is one of the most interesting buildings of its kind, the façades of the core building displaying an austere blend of Jacobean and Elizabethan ideas. Rickman retired before the house was complete, and building of the wings with the chapel and Baronial Hall was undertaken from 1838 by *William Walker* with *George Sudden*. Walker, whose earlier career can be traced to Warwickshire, is only now emerging as an important figure in Ulster: based in Monaghan in the 1840s, he designed the classical Market House at Ballybay, remodelled or rebuilt Drumreaske in Tudor style, and produced designs in a similar manner (unexecuted) for Bangor Castle in Co. Down and a house on Lough Erne.

p. 411

After Lough Fea, houses in Tudor Revival style are few in South Ulster and like Rossmore Park have fared poorly. Castle Shane of 1836, burnt in 1920, was a massive, staid expression of an Elizabethan idiom; an altogether more modest building in the Tudor style is Lanesborough Lodge, now in ruins but still showing a typical array of steep skew gables, label mouldings and mullioned windows. Kilnacrott of *c.* 1839, with its extraordinary *porte cochère*, though reduced in size is well-preserved, with a Regency feeling that is surprising for its date.

p. 487

Thomas Rickman is just one of the established figures of the Regency period to produce designs for Ireland after 1800. John Nash, Thomas Hopper and William Henry Playfair made a lasting impact with designs for large Gothic and classical country houses. Of these *John Nash* had the most extensive practice in Ireland, and particularly in Ulster, where he was first employed at Killymoon in Co. Tyrone in 1801, and later in the same county at Caledon, where he worked over a long period on alterations for the 2nd Earl of Caledon. It was perhaps while working there that he made proposals for Tynan Abbey, a modest scheme for a Tudor Revival house. The building and Nash's drawings for it were destroyed when the house was set on fire in 1981, but photographic records of both confirm that although Nash's plans were not followed, the more fanciful result can still be associated with his work in so far as it adopted elements of his castle style. The loggia across the garden front is a feature that he used on both Gothic and Italianate houses. It is this feature, still to be seen among the ivied ruins of Wood Park (Killylea), that causes Nash to be connected with the alterations of *c.* 1830 to that small Georgian house. Stylistic analogy and its close proximity to Caledon and Tynan also suggest that Nash designed the Gothic

p. 567

Drumbanagher.
Wood engraving, 1846

gate screen at Castle Leslie, noteworthy for its distinctive ogee pinnacles, and the rather grand battlemented frontispiece applied to the lodge.

Thomas Hopper was like Nash a successful and prolific architect who had been favoured by the Prince Regent, later George IV, but he never enjoyed the same degree of employment in Ireland. Gosford Castle in Armagh, begun in 1819, was one of the most *p. 344* important commissions of his career and the very first Norman Revival castle of its kind in these islands. But by 1834, although Gosford was still far from complete, Hopper was finished with the country, exclaiming to his patron, 'I have always felt a sorrow that I ever went to Ireland.' A Neo-Norman scheme perhaps inspired by Gosford was proposed for the Church of Ireland Cathedral in Armagh by *William Farrell*, when as Diocesan Architect he was consulted about its repair and possible rebuilding; his design however never left the page.

William Henry Playfair was essentially a classicist. In 1829 he had designed a large Italianate house for Maxwell Close, Drumbanagher. Maxwell Close was the brother-in-law of Charles Brownlow; as a student in Edinburgh Brownlow had shared lodgings with the young Playfair at the home of his uncle, Professor John Playfair, and he may well have effected the introduction. Buoyed by the success of Drumbanagher, Playfair first proposed a grand 'Roman Villa' design for Lurgan Castle, but 93 then accepted a complete change in style. He called the resulting house his 'Elizabethan Child' and proudly considered it to be 'more like an old manor house than any modern attempt I have yet seen'.

In CHURCH BUILDING, the annual Government bounty paid to the Board of First Fruits grew from £5,000 yearly in 1785–1807 to £10,000 in 1808 and 1809 and £60,000 in 1810–16, before being reduced to £30,000 in 1817–21. Parliamentary funds were granted without restrictions, and in 1808 an Act of Parliament increased the Board's fiscal autonomy. By the 1830s it is estimated that more than £1,000,000 had been advanced towards buildings for the Church of Ireland, including glebe houses. For churches, the Board chose to concentrate the funds – in the form of loans or grants – on a major programme of building and repair. In 1832 there were 30 per cent more churches in Ireland than there had been in 1787. By 1814 *John Bowden* had been appointed sole architect to the Board. A pupil of the Dublin Society Schools, apprenticed to Richard Morrison, Bowden is first detected in the region in Monaghan in 1814, when he succeeded *John Behan* to produce plans for the County Gaol (demolished). In 1819 he supervised the building of *Francis Johnston*'s Royal School at Cavan, but his proposals for courthouses at Cavan and Monaghan were frustrated by his death in 1822. It is as architect to the Board of First Fruits, credited with the design of most of the hall-and-tower churches built from 1814 until his death, that he made the greatest impact on the region. Rarely do his plans survive. Drumlane, designed in 1819, is an exception, and from that it is possible to attribute to him other churches, such as Mullagh of 1819 and Drumsallan of 1821, all picturesque buildings that owe a great deal to the format of Cooley's late c18 models. Invariably they are modest roughcast halls of three bays with pointed windows, originally sashed in timber, like those surviving at Mullagh; almost all were built without chancels, and were fronted by a neat three-stage tower, usually articulated with moulded strings, with battlements on the taller belfry stage and spiky corner pinnacles on the larger buildings. Inside, the tower accommodates a small vestibule, often circular, with stairs to the gallery. Even in larger churches the tower is rarely flanked by twin vestries, as it was in many late c18 examples. Bowden also carried out extensive alterations to older churches, usually recasting them in a similar mould, as at Kildallon in 1815 where he added the tower, as perhaps he also did at Mullaghbrack, and more certainly with the enlargement of Tandragee in 1818. In some instances, usually in larger parishes and through local influence, other designers were employed: both Bowden and *Richard Elsam* were associated with Urney Parish Church in Cavan town, built in 1816, while the Cavan-born *Arthur McClean*, who made his later career in Canada, appears to have worked at Virginia; in such instances the results are much richer, with livelier silhouettes.

William Farrell's preference for classical styles meant that, like Cooley and Bowden before him, he was interested in the Gothic primarily for church commissions. After Bowden's death, when responsibility for each of the provinces was divided between four architects, Farrell took over responsibility for the diocese of Armagh, a position he continued to hold under the Ecclesiastical Commissioners who replaced the Board of First Fruits in 1833, remaining in the post until 1843, when he was succeeded by *Joseph Welland*. Newbliss, a cruciform church bristling with needle-like pinnacles, and Mullaghglass, an unusually bulky single cell with an elaborate Regency Gothic front, are *Farrell*'s most original designs. Monaghan of 1836 is his largest new church, with plaster rib-vaults. By far the most distinctive of Farrell's church designs are the single-cell rural churches built across the province after 1830, with examples in South Ulster too numerous to list. The plan, a small gable-fronted hall with thin lancets and an ornate bellcote, was repeated with minor variations. At its simplest the building was finished in roughcast with little ornament, like Clontibret of 1840. If greater elaboration was called for, it was usually given by means of a battlemented porch and a flurry of pinnacles like those at Errigal Truagh of 1834. Inside, the roofs were often carried on distinctive cast-iron trusses, novel at the time, left exposed, as at Derrylane. Farrell used much the same design in 1838 at Killeshandra, where he enlarged the proportions to suit an urban setting, while at Ballyjamesduff, of 1834, he simply enhanced the standard plan by fronting it with a square tower.

The major ecclesiastical project of the time was the restoration of the medieval cathedral of Armagh, begun in 1834 by *Lewis Nockalls Cottingham*, who also restored the English cathedrals of Hereford, Rochester and St Albans. When he took it on the building was structurally unsound and marred in its appearance by an accumulation of poor repairs; and given that restoration as a science was still in its infancy, the result looks like a product of the 1830s more than one of the Middle Ages. It was criticized at the time, but was largely forgotten in the acrimonious debates concerning church restorations later in the century.

23, 75, 76

p. 101

The improved agricultural conditions of the country in the early C19 are reflected in the widespread construction of new MARKET HOUSES. One of the earliest examples of the astylar three-bay block that was to be the dominant pattern in the first two decades of the C19, and by far the most architecturally accomplished, with open arches on the ground floor, Venetian windows and a pedimented frontispiece, was Belturbet (*c.* 1730, demolished). A neat small example was built in Rockcorry in 1805, possibly by *Benjamin Hallam*, with a single recessed arch on each façade, their imposts linked by a continuous platband. The linking motif recurs at Bailieborough of 1818, with three bold round-headed arches on the ground floor. Ballyconnell of *c.* 1830 and Ballybay of 1848 by *William Walker* bring the form up to the mid-century. A different, especially attractive, arrangement where the three central bays are recessed on a broad five-bay front with a classical plaque between *œil-de-bœuf* windows on the first floor can be seen at Ballyjamesduff of 1813 by *Arthur McClean*, repeated at Bellananagh in 1821. The Market House at Arva, of *c.* 1833, had an even more elaborate layout, its central pedimented block originally placed between short three-bay loggias terminating in smaller pedimented wings. *William Deane Butler* produced a rich, stately building in the Clones Market House of 1844, which overwhelms the Diamond with its tall proportions and abundant decoration.

68

The COURTHOUSES built after 1800, at least in the larger towns, were usually more overt in their classicism, often with a preference for Greek that was well suited to the expression of

p. 121

civic authority. Each county town in South Ulster received a new building. The first was *Johnston*'s Armagh of 1809, a handsome Neoclassical building, but constructed, to Johnston's dismay, with columns too slender for the portico. At Cavan *William Farrell*'s responsibility for the design of 1824 is demonstrated by his usual concern for strengthening the corners and a fondness for the kind of decorative play to be achieved through gentle surface recession, particularly when dealing with broad expanses of solid wall. Monaghan of 1827 with its engaged Doric portico is a rare display in a classical idiom by *Joseph Welland*, who trained under Bowden and was chiefly a church architect. Outside the county towns, *William Deane Butler* is usually named as the architect of the Courthouse at Cootehill and, because it is similar, of Ballyconnell. Both stand out for their clearly delineated façades and the use of bold mutules to support the eaves, a characteristic of Butler's work. His pupil *William Caldbeck* has become associated with one particular courthouse design used throughout the country, a neat exercise in classical simplicity, of which most were in fact built before he established an independent practice in 1844. The standard scheme places a large two-storey ashlar-faced hall with a pronounced eaves cornice between short recessed wings containing matching entrances. The wide currency of the format has naturally led to confusion over its originator; *Butler* is known to have been involved with some, and several others are attributed to county surveyors. The earliest recorded example is the building at Carrickmacross of 1837, which is usually said to be by the Monaghan County Surveyor, *Edward Forrest*; essentially the same design occurs again in 1840 at Clones, where Forrest was consulted.

VICTORIAN ARCHITECTURE

Emancipation brought about a steady increase in CATHOLIC CHURCH BUILDING, but the earliest structures continued to follow in the vernacular tradition. The T-plan remained a prevalent type, particularly in Cavan. On the whole, the Gothic enrichments found in most Roman Catholic parish churches are eclectic, understated, and, before about 1860, remote from the convictions of Pugin and the controversies of the Gothic Revival. Even when St Laurence at Belleek (1849), a rare building of the Famine years, was embellished with angle buttresses, pinnacles and a bellcote, it still remained very much the conventional T-plan church. The bellcote on the gable was to become increasingly prevalent, often as older thatched roofs were replaced by slate and given steeper pitches with kneelered gables; together these offer the only outward sign of growing discrimination. And as re-roofing became the most common Late Victorian improvement, new trussed roofs were invariably exposed internally in a manner that clearly owes something to contemporary concerns with structural honesty.

Most popular to the end of the century were plain lancet halls of three to five bays, plainly rendered, with stone dressings used sparingly if at all – a cost-efficient solution when Catholic church-building was funded voluntarily by congregations from exiguous resources. Examples include the small St Peter, Collegelands (Charlemont, before 1845) and the very large Glennan (1837). St Mary, Staghall (Belturbet), begun in 1846 on the eve of the Great Famine, is the most ambitious of its type, with a brash pinnacled frontage. Successive failures of the potato crop between 1846 and 1849 brought mass starvation and emigration; building activity resumed gradually in the 1850s, and old patterns and old-fashioned tastes continued to endure: St Bartholomew at Knockatemple, rebuilt in 1858, was adorned with battlemented Tudoresque doorcases.

Often a developing awareness of Gothic detail is signalled by an ashlar bellcote, though it is sometimes set at the back, as if in apology. The most consciously pretentious Catholic churches to develop in the C19 are those with towers. The first examples are barely distinguishable from their Protestant counterparts except for the inflated proportions of the hall and the presence of a cross floating over the tower battlements. St Mary at Ture of 1843 has perhaps the best proportions, though the architectural details are weak. The parish churches of St Kilian, Mullagh and St Patrick, Keady, both of 1857, are confident structures finished entirely in stone. The contemporary T-plan church of St Mary at Clontibret, an assured design with E.E. detail and an assertive w tower, still relied on the traditional combination of roughcast walls and dressed stonework. Numerous churches acquired towers later. The plain lancet hall of St Mary, Latnamard (Newbliss), was transformed by the ornamental tower and spire added in 1867. It is also common to find a tower centred against one of the side walls, like the one added by *William Walker* to the Holy Family, Ballyosion (Errigal Truagh) in 1844.

Rarely are architects named for any of these buildings, and the parish priest is credited with the more ambitious designs, being often named as builder by a plaque on the building – for example the *Rev. John Conaty* at Mullagh. Exceptions are *Richard Hynes* of Newry, who designed the churches at Mullaghbawn and Bessbrook, and the Belfast architect and pupil of Thomas Jackson *Jeremiah R. McAuley* – later ordained as a priest – who designed the hall-and-tower church at Tandragee of 1852. *James Hughes*, an architect and contractor based in Charlemont, is known to have rebuilt the church at Castleblayney in 1851, but his building was subsumed in 1869 by the work of the Dundalk builder-turned-architect *John Murray*. Murray may well have remained faithful to the essence of Hughes's style, since it is fundamentally rural in feeling.

It seems strange that *John Murray* should have been so restrained at Castleblayney, his position as a serious architect of the Gothic Revival having by then been impressively asserted. He had already begun St Patrick, Drumintee (Forkhill), a big aisled and towered church with primitive Gothic detail. Murray's respect for the memory of Pugin was more perfectly

Monaghan, St Macartan's Cathedral (R.C.).
Engraving, 1868

demonstrated in an executed scheme for a new w front for St Peter at Lurgan, modelled on St Giles, Cheadle, widely held up as the most complete embodiment of Pugin's vision for the Christian church.

The Irish architect who best understood Pugin's vision, *James Joseph McCarthy*, had by 1866 already made a significant impact in South Ulster, having taken the biggest prizes with the new cathedrals of Armagh and Monaghan, and the equally impressive

St Joseph at Carrickmacross. McCarthy, a former pupil of William Farrell, was a Dublin architect; he had espoused the Gothic Revival early, current with the growth of the Ecclesiologi-cal movement and the writings of Pugin in the 1840s, and his career developed just as the Catholic Church embarked on its most ambitious and prolific building phase. In his writings and through his membership of the Irish Ecclesiological Society, which he helped to found, he promoted the revival of the Early English and Decorated or 'Middle Pointed', and effectively became an arbiter of what constituted correct Gothic. He prac-tised what he preached, endorsing the tenets of Pugin's ideology with his archaeological approach to Gothic detail, his concern for structural honesty, and the application of a functional ration-ale to the layout of churches. McCarthy's mature buildings display a preference for the 'Middle Pointed', ostensibly inspired by French Gothic architecture of the C13. In his cathedrals the style could be usefully applied to create striking, expensive-look-ing buildings seen in their time as magnificent acts of piety and a demonstration of national confidence, and viewed today gener-ally as triumphalist symbols of a resurgent Church. At Armagh Roman Catholic Cathedral, where McCarthy began his South 80, 81 Ulster career in 1853, the twin spires acknowledge Pugin's cathe-dral of St Chad, Birmingham (which Pugin had introduced to Irish audiences in the *Dublin Review* in 1841), though in his overall approach to detail McCarthy's dreams were of Chartres, superimposed on the incomplete carcass of *Duff*'s building. He dispensed with the crossing tower and translated the architec-tural detail from English into French, most noticeably in the tracery and the soaring W spires. St Joseph at Carrickmacross, begun in 1861, shows how McCarthy could transmit the same triumphalism on a more constrained site. The tautness in the treatment of the surfaces and the crisp geometry of the tracery are enduring hallmarks of his work, as is the clear differentiation of the elements of the plan, with an offset tower and spire (com-pleted in 1898 by *G. C. Ashlin*). He was committed to using local materials. At Armagh and Carrickmacross the pale limestone resulted in clean-limbed buildings with highly refined details, but at Monaghan Cathedral, also begun in 1861, a more diversely coloured stone was available and the architecture could become more melodramatic. The result is more decidedly High Victorian *p. 463* in feeling, enhanced by a wilfully asymmetrical plan. The spire was completed after McCarthy's death by William Hague, who would also take over the completion of the interiors at Armagh.

William Hague, after McCarthy the most important native figure of the Gothic Revival, reached his maturity with a taste for High Victorian indulgence. He was born in Cavan in 1836, and his prolific career is well represented in the region. He was the son of a successful building contractor, *William Hague Sen.*, whose known work is dominated by buildings for the Established Church, including two sophisticated Gothic Revival designs of the 1850s at Quivvy (Belturbet) and Cloverhill, and the biggest plum, awarded in 1857, for the construction of St Feidhlimidh's 78

Cathedral at Kilmore. The younger Hague began his architectural career in the London office of Sir Charles Barry, spending four years there in the 1850s, just in time to experience Barry's work on the Houses of Parliament but too late to encounter Pugin personally. By then Barry had already begun his affair with the Italian palazzo style, and where churches were concerned considered that 'deep chancels, high roodscreens and pillared aisles' were wholly anachronistic. This does not seem to have discouraged Hague, who had returned to Cavan by 1859 to spend the next forty years, most of it in Dublin, predominantly as a church architect. St Patrick at Ballybay, begun in 1859 when he was twenty-three, was his first significant commission, and shows him as a keen upholder of Pugin's formative tastes. After Ballybay the exquisite church at Butler's Bridge shows Hague fully developing an interest in the rich potential of materials, using structural polychromy, sculptural enrichment, repoussé capitals and darkened timber to striking effect. This concern for elaboration characterizes much of his work in Cavan, with the High Victorian excess of rusticated stonework, carved capitals and stops, and a clear preference for shafts of polished marble; their employment with corbels to frame a doorway or chancel arch becomes something of a leitmotif. The greatest freedoms were taken with smaller churches, which invariably begin as steep gable-fronted halls with bellcotes, but are so diversely expressed that no two buildings are alike. Corravacan (1866) is a solid-looking single cell with ponderous Gothic detail; Milltown (1868), gaunt, with awkward angles, is altogether more idiosyncratic, miniaturizing the expression of a larger aisled nave to the point of ugliness. If any criticism may be levelled against Hague's work, it is that his larger churches fail to captivate in the same way; given equal prominence whether in town or country, they tend to share the same kind of brooding presence, with unforgiving exteriors of dark limestone and in most cases with an incomplete tower. Killeshandra (1862) is decidedly sombre, its stonework tending to coarseness; Kingscourt (1869) is by far the most assured of the larger churches, more pronounced and varied in its detail, all richly finished. Hague's later churches, such as St Joseph at Monaghan, begun the year before his death in 1899, adopt a taste for highly textured surfaces using uniform blocks of rusticated stone; this reflects the influence of *T. F. McNamara*, a former pupil who became managing assistant of the firm, and who continued the practice into the C20 in partnership with Hague's widow.

Joseph Welland is the dominant figure associated with CHURCH OF IRELAND CHURCHES after 1843. As a protégé of John Bowden, he was appointed architect to the Board of First Fruits in 1823, with responsibility for the Tuam province, a role he continued to fulfil under the equally well-endowed Irish Ecclesiastical Commissioners. In 1843 he took control of Armagh, having been appointed sole architect to the newly reorganized Commission, and worked exclusively for that body until his death in 1860. Most of Welland's works involved additions to older hall-and-tower churches, usually a vestry and porch and, occasionally, a chancel, executed in stonework to a high standard but with minimal Gothic detail. New windows often had stone tracery, while new roofs invariably had their heavy timber trusses exposed internally. Drummully (Scotshouse) and Swanlinbar, both built in 1844, are among his earliest new churches in the region, solid rectangular halls in a matter-of-fact Gothic style. Within a decade, however, Welland had begun to apply Ecclesiological principles, not least in his planning, typically with a lower chancel and a gabled porch and lean-to vestry diagonally opposed on the nave, that resulted in a reliable and adaptable economic formula used until the end of his career. Variations on the theme of a small gable-fronted hall with a bellcote, built entirely in stone (rubble or hewn with smooth dressings), steeply roofed and usually with twin lancets in the nave and graded lights at the E end, all with quarry glazing, appear at Annaghmore (1856) and elsewhere. Welland could equally apply these principles to larger churches with aisles and towers, where the massing was usually made more picturesque by the addition of a broach spire, as with his big aisled Drumcree Parish Church (Portadown) of 1854.

After his death in 1860 Joseph Welland was succeeded by his son *William J. Welland* and by *William Gillespie*, who had been his assistants. Appointed joint architects to the Ecclesiastical Commissioners before the end of the year, they worked as *Welland & Gillespie* until the office was abolished in 1870 following Gladstone's Irish Church Act, which disestablished the Church, stripping it of its privileges so that it became a voluntary body. Much of their work involved the provision of new robing rooms, refenestration and repewing, but additions to existing churches became increasingly more extensive, to include chancels (e.g. Dartrey, 1870), aisles (e.g. Poyntzpass, 1861) and transepts (e.g. Cootehill, 1861). Lurgan, rebuilt in 1861, is the first and largest of their buildings in the region, a conservative blackstone church with E.E. detail and a soaring helm spire. Gradually their work begins to reveal a more individual, even playful, accent, with features such as sharp roofs, and lancets with a more primitive, sharper outline. The design of Bessbrook (1866) could never have come from the senior Welland office a decade earlier: its use of structural polychromy is striking and everything is exaggerated, to spiky and unorthodox effect.

Assisting Welland & Gillespie in their works in South Ulster, though the full extent of their involvement remains unclear, were the Armagh-based architects *Alexander Hardy*, appointed District Inspector to the Commissioners in 1854, and *William Turney Fullerton*, employed in a similar capacity. Fullerton built a rather accomplished blackstone church with a spire at Battlehill in 1856, which suggests he may have been closely involved at Lurgan. In 1862 *James Franklin Fuller* was appointed architect to the North-West Division based at Killeshandra, but appears not to have carried out any substantial ecclesiastical works in the region. *James E. Rogers*, a pupil of Benjamin Woodward who designed some memorable churches for the Meath diocese in the late

1860s, was employed at Redhills House in the same period and
seems the most likely designer for the rugged polygonal chancel
at Killoughter, Redhills. Several other architects with no direct
affiliation to the Commissioners brought greater variety. The
London architect brothers *Raphael Brandon* and *Joshua A.
Brandon*, authors of some important practical books on English
77   ecclesiastical architecture, added an aisle to Aughnamullen, their
only work in Ireland, which shows a flair for elaborate traceried
windows. *James Rawson Carroll*, who had worked for a time in
the Brandons' office, designed St Andrew, Drumaloor (Butler's
Bridge), in 1869, a neat lancet hall with a polygonal chancel. In
1854 *Roderick Gray*, whose career began with road-building
in Connaught and who was to become County Surveyor for
Fermanagh in 1834, designed a bulky, austere Gothic hall with
a quirky offset tower at Quivvy (Belturbet) and in 1858 a fancier
106   small Gothic school in Clones. The Newry architect *William
Joseph Barre*, who had trained under Thomas Duff, enjoyed
numerous commissions in Armagh and Monaghan during his
short, prolific career, which ended suddenly with his death in
1867. His originality and diversity are displayed in two smart
84   churches, St James at Rockcorry of 1854, a perfect compact
design that shares Welland's concern with functional planning,
and Kilbodagh of 1859, the year before Barre moved his practice
to Belfast. The remainder of his works were of a minor nature;
he added a chancel to Ballymoyer in 1863, and transepts to
Loughgall a year later.

The London architect *William Slater* was to receive the most
significant commission from the Established Church in South
Ulster, when he was appointed in 1857 to design a new Church
78,   of Ireland cathedral for Kilmore in Co. Cavan. Slater began his
p. 394 architectural career apprenticed to R. C. Carpenter, a follower
of Pugin approved of by the Ecclesiologists; he inherited his
practice in 1855. It was undoubtedly these affiliations that earned
him the commission, whose promoters sought to build their new
cathedral to the memory of the C17 Bishop of Kilmore, William
Bedell, a vigorous reforming cleric who had been made popular
by the C19 Evangelical movement in the Church. Although a
most evocative building, Kilmore is not in any sense a pioneering
design, conceived as a closely massed cruciform church with
good Dec tracery but a short crossing tower. In 1863 Slater took
as his partner *Richard Herbert Carpenter*, the son of his former
master, and in 1866 they added a chancel and side chapels to St
79   Mark in Armagh, rich with Dec windows. Also in 1866 they
designed a perfect small church at Ardragh for Evelyn Philip
Shirley of Lough Fea, who seems to have been motivated to build
by his concerns for the future of the Anglican Church in Ireland.
After Slater's death in 1872, R. H. Carpenter formed a partnership with *Benjamin Ingelow*; they reordered the interior of the
23, 76   Church of Ireland Cathedral at Armagh in 1886–90, introducing
greater Ecclesiological integrity.

After Slater, English figures of the Gothic Revival are represented only in minor works, though worthy of some notice. The

leading Gothic Revivalist *William Butterfield*, a central figure of the Ecclesiological Society, designed the ornately covered font at Ballymoyer of 1865; at Salters Grange, Edward Blore's pupil *Philip Charles Hardwick* designed the font and probably also the pulpit and reading desk.

In the years after Disestablishment church-building and improvement works contracted considerably. Two architects whose work in nearby country house design led to sizeable church commissions were *Frederick A. Butler*, who added a chancel and vestry to Killylea in 1874, and *George C. Henderson*, who designed a ponderous gable-fronted church at Aghabog in 1875. The deep polygonal chancel and intersecting vestry at St Salvator at Glaslough, of 1888 are probably the work of *W. H. Lynn*, carried out while he was engaged at Castle Leslie. Though *J. F. Fuller* was widely employed in Leinster by the Representative Church Body, set up to replace the Ecclesiastical Commissioners, his only work in South Ulster was the substantial enlargement of Portadown in 1885, which included a new polygonal chancel. *Thomas Drew* was greatly influenced by Lynn, whose 'artistic feelings . . . seemed to have acted . . . as a charm, and to have completed the development of his powers' during an apprenticeship served with Charles Lanyon. Drew was the pre-eminent church architect of the Late Victorian period, knighted on Queen Victoria's birthday in 1900, whose pleasing additions to Seagoe in 1890 and alterations at Armagh Cathedral in 1902–3 effectively bring the building activities of the Church of Ireland to a close.

Victorian PRESBYTERIAN CHURCHES form a smaller but more diverse array of buildings. Those of the first half of the century were, like their Catholic counterparts, of a generally modest nature, barely showing any progression from the C18. The simple Gothic hall, typically gable-fronted, in roughcast or smooth render, is found in rural and urban situations, often with pleasing variety. Another type, common in the 1830s, is the bulkier three-bay hall under a hipped roof, with the minister's house usually set back on one side, as at Bellasis (Billis Bridge, 1837), or projecting at the rear to form a T-plan. Bellville (Ardmore, *c.* 1862) is a unique rural church in polychromatic brick. Otherwise, the urban churches are best, frequently by established, mostly Belfast-based, architects, gradually more consciously architectural, occasionally classical but more usually fully Gothic. The Presbyterian church at Keady to which *W. J. Barre* made alterations in 1857 is a stiff, nominally classical building; in contrast, the linen centres of Portadown and Lurgan offered a flamboyant stuccoed classicism: Barre's gaily painted Bridge Street Presbyterian Church in Portadown is a full-blown classical exercise with a giant Corinthian portico, designed in 1858, the year before his award-winning entry for Belfast's Ulster Hall. First Lurgan, with its slightly Baroque touches, might be his, were it not for the awkward proportions. Otherwise Gothic Revival prevails. Barre designed Clones in 1858 with earnest Gothic detail. Armagh Road, Portadown (1868), is an assured Gothic church by *Boyd & Batt*, the Belfast partnership founded by John Boyd and William Batt *c.* 1862. The partnership was dissolved in 1871 and afterwards *John Boyd* alone continued to find work in South Ulster. In 1874 he designed Glennan (Glaslough), a fully Gothic church with tower and transepts and his favoured use of five lights set in a segmental pointed arch. The Belfast architect *Robert Young*, a pupil of Charles Lanyon, was much employed as a railway engineer before going into partnership with John Mackenzie in the 1860s. The firm of *Young & Mackenzie* became the designers preferred by Presbyterian congregations, and later architects of countless red brick behemoths for the industrial magnates of Armagh, Belfast and Derry. The most ambitious church in the region by this firm dominates the Mall in Armagh, a full-blown Gothic design of 1878, ambitiously spired. The last major building for the Presbyterians is by *W. J. M. Roome & R. S. Boag* of Belfast, who in 1900 kept vigorous Gothic tastes alive when they recast the Late Georgian Tudor-style hall in Monaghan.

The architectural ambitions of other religious congregations tended to be more understated, with the exception of the METHODIST CHURCHES in the county towns. The smallest is the ashlar-fronted hall in Monaghan of *c.* 1861. The former Wesleyan chapel in Cavan of 1858 is a competent early work by *William Hague*; it had a broach spire, since removed. An idiosyncratic classical style was favoured in Armagh after the 1835 church was remodelled, first *c.* 1860 and later in 1888 by *J. J. Phillips*, to whom the ersatz stilted arches of the façade are due. *John Boyd's* imperious stuccoed church of 1858 in Portadown is, with its sophisticated Corinthian portico, by far the most flamboyant.

QUAKER MEETING HOUSES are few, but two deserve notice: Lurgan of 1880 by *F. W. Lockwood* is a large and richly stuccoed Italianate design; Portadown of 1905 by *Joseph Chandler Marsh* is altogether different, expressed in an Arts and Crafts manner with a combination of classical and Venetian Gothic elements.

The population more than doubled in the century leading up to the Early Victorian period, and living conditions among the poorest became increasingly abject. A sense of social responsibility developed in response, and was largely directed into building projects still present in the housing, schools, hospitals, workhouses – and prisons – that were provided. In 1838, the year of her coronation, Queen Victoria's Government enacted the Irish Poor Law Act, which, based on the model introduced in England four years earlier, brought the WORKHOUSE system to Ireland. Devised as a means to cope with destitute families, this nationwide system was administered initially through 130 unions, each provided with a workhouse, usually built close to the larger market towns. By 1843, 113 workhouses had been completed, the remainder by 1847. Each followed one of the standard plans devised by *George Wilkinson*, who having proved himself with workhouse design in his native England was appointed architect to the Poor Law Commissioners in 1839. With the exception of Bawnboy, those built in South Ulster were all erected by

1842, sharing the same symmetrical layout, with a nominally Tudoresque design especially evident in the gabled administration block at the front containing the receiving rooms on the ground floor and a board room above. The main block behind was a much more formidable edifice, with the separate accommodation for men and women extended as wings on either side of the officers' quarters at the centre; the dining hall and chapel extended as a deep central spine from which the kitchens and laundries with their respective yards projected on either side, while the infirmary and sick wards were accommodated in a narrow range at the very rear of the complex.

When a further thirty workhouses were built between 1849 and 1853 the architecture remained formulaic and basic. The sole example of this campaign in South Ulster, Bawnboy of 1851, has a completely different character, essentially vernacular in feeling, its principal advance being an inversion of the typical layout. With the abolition of the workhouse system in the Republic of Ireland in 1925 and in Northern Ireland in 1946 some disappeared, and only the entrance blocks at Castleblayney and Monaghan remain. Many were adapted as hospitals or care homes, and Armagh and Cavan are still in use as such; Carrickmacross, enlarged in 1850, is the best preserved, still retaining its original complex.

Workhouses stood in stark contrast to the privately endowed welfare provided by ALMSHOUSES. In South Ulster there are three architecturally diverse examples: two by unknown designers in Monaghan, the simple Widows' Almshouses at Rockcorry of 1847 and the more ornate brick and terracotta Blayney Almshouses at Castleblayney of 1879, and the Shiels Almshouses in Armagh city of 1868 by *Lanyon, Lynn & Lanyon*, in a Ruskinian Gothic style. 104

105

The ASYLUMS and HOSPITALS erected in the rest of the Victorian period are fundamentally conservative, governed by the demands of efficiency. *John McCurdy*'s St Davnet's in Monaghan was the largest of its kind in the country when it opened in 1867. At what is now St Luke's Hospital in Armagh *John Boyd* made additions to Johnston and Murray's asylum buildings in the 1860s–70s; but for the Hill Building there in 1895 *J. J. Phillips & Son* abandoned their usual reserve for an overbearing château style.

Stylistic prudence abides in the CONVENTS and SCHOOLS of the various religious orders, collectively an unprepossessing group of later Victorian buildings, though most designed by leading church architects. The first, St Catherine's in Armagh of 1857, is an early work by the Dublin architect *John Bourke*, popular for his taste in dour classicism more evocative of the Late Georgian era. However, with the ambitious building of St Patrick's Diocesan College in Cavan, designed in 1869, *William Hague* introduced the mode of institutional Gothic that would remain popular into the C20, enduring largely in the hands of *John J. McDonnell*. Hague's design in Cavan is carefully balanced between economy and display, with an unrelenting façade slightly relieved by modest Gothic enrichments. Spare but more attractive is the school by *Charles J. McCarthy* attached to the convent of St Louis at Carrickmacross (1888).

State schools were provided by the Board of National Education, whose architect in the 1840s was *Frederick Darley*, a former pupil of Francis Johnston. Darley favoured a straightforward Tudor Gothic for the schools he built throughout the country, exemplified in the District Model National School of 1848 at Bailieborough. After the Board of Works assumed responsibility in 1856, its newly appointed architect *James H. Owen* designed model schools in both classical and Gothic styles. His Monaghan Regional Model School of 1860, in an indifferent Gothic style with steep gables, contrasts oddly with the Minor Model Schools in Lurgan of 1861, an ambitious Italianate design in red brick and sandstone. Equally sumptuous is *Young & Mackenzie's* Watt Endowed School of 1873, also in Lurgan, remarkable for its uplifting Arts and Crafts-inspired manner, barely credible for a firm otherwise dourly inspired at this time.

Other schools were privately financed, and in many instances conceived as part of the wider development of landed estates. At Quivvy (Belturbet) the Earl of Lanesborough built a school house in the same Tudor Revival style as his house. The National Schools at Poyntzpass display a quirkier stylized architecture that is sometimes attributed to *William Henry Playfair*, because of his work nearby for the Close family. In 1860 *W. J. Barre* invested the Erasmus Smith School at Tynan, a small rendered building, with a mildly Italianate character, in contrast to the red brick school and teacher's house of 1861 that he designed for the Cope estate at Loughgall. Different again, the school at Kildallon retained its vernacular character when it was rebuilt in 1861 to the memory of Lady Catherine Saunderson.

The Tudoresque school house at Bessbrook of 1875 looks like typical estate architecture, but it is in fact an expression of the more ambitious social concerns of the Quaker John Grubb Richardson, whose entrepreneurial spirit was so representative of the age. Rapidly developing the town's linen industry through the C19, Richardson successfully combined business development with social and environmental responsibility by directing much of the profits into the creation of a model industrial environment for his employees. Buildings were used to improve their living and working conditions, and to provide a social and spiritual framework. The same Victorian attitudes are present in the provision of HOUSING SCHEMES by most of the larger linen producers in Armagh, from small-scale rural operations like those at Darkley, Glenanne and Laragh to the enormous schemes, mostly of red brick, which greatly expanded such primary industrial centres as Lurgan and Milford in the later Victorian period.

p. 199

The entrepreneurial spirit of the Victorian age was served by the development of transport systems, which opened up incalculable opportunities for an increasingly industrialized society. In the early decades of the century NAVIGATION SYSTEMS seemed to offer the best solution, with the prospect of linking Belfast and Limerick via the Erne and Shannon systems. Following advice from *Thomas Telford*, the Ulster Canal Company began work in 1830, with *William Dargan* as contractor and *William Cubitt* as engineer. From Charlemont the canal went to Middletown and on to the summit at Monaghan, whence it descended to Smithborough and Clones, reaching the Erne at Wattle Bridge in 1841. It was abandoned in the 1920s, leaving vestiges such as the lock house at Smithborough. Work to link the Erne with the Shannon at Leitrim, through the challenging terrain of Belturbet and Ballyconnell, was completed in 1859, but by then any advantage was lost to the miracle of railways.

The early RAILWAYS of South Ulster were driven principally by the thriving linen markets, which increasingly depended on communication with Belfast. The Ulster Railway was begun in 1837 to connect Belfast and Lisburn with the primary linen centres of Armagh. It was laid out through the Lagan Valley by the Antrim engineers *William Bald* and *Thomas Jackson Woodhouse* and constructed under the direction of William Dargan, who would soon rise to become a leading railway entrepreneur. It reached Lurgan in 1841 and Portadown in 1842, but the extension to Armagh that involved bridging the Bann with an elaborate timber structure was not completed until 1848. The Dublin & Drogheda Railway, whose engineer was *Sir John MacNeill*, a former pupil and assistant of Telford, opened its line in 1844; an extension of the line by the Dublin & Belfast Junction Railway reached Dundalk in 1849, with the promise of opening up more of the province. Also in 1849 a branch line linked Dundalk and Castleblayney, and by 1850 the Dublin rail line had been extended N between the mountains towards the Ulster Railway, which itself was extended S from Portadown through Tandragee and Poyntzpass to Goraghwood. Connecting the lines was only made possible by the technical brilliance of MacNeill, who designed an awesome eighteen-arch masonry viaduct to span the Bessbrook River at Craigmore near Bessbrook in 1852. The selection of Portadown as the junction, making it the primary transport hub in the region rather than Armagh, was determined by physical factors. Through the next two decades railway fever continued apace, extending the network to most of the large towns in the region. The physical challenges of the South Ulster topography largely determined the sequence of routes, so that the easiest lines were laid down first, with the majority established by 1870. Both the principal N–S line and its structures remain integral to what is still the most important route in the modern railway network.

Despite the closure of the majority of the subsidiary lines in South Ulster, several RAILWAY STATIONS remain. Regrettably some of the finest have been lost, such as Armagh and Portadown. Those of the original Ulster Railway favoured a bold Italianate idiom on the model of its Belfast terminus with its arcuated stuccoed portico, a design usually attributed to the railway's engineer, *John Godwin*, but made popular by *Charles Lanyon*. The effect of *Sir John MacNeill*'s lost Portadown station with its magnificent polychrome brick survives on a slightly reduced scale in his Monaghan station of *c*. 1862. *George*

Wilkinson, retired by the Poor Law Commissioners in 1855 and later appointed architect to the Board of Control for Lunatic Asylums, was also widely employed by the railway companies. His designs too show a preference for Italianate classicism, but altogether more modestly conceived. His best design is the perfectly formed small station at Crossdoney of 1855. Later stations are always plain, with none of the industrial novelties of the railway age. This is evident in the larger terminus at Cavan of 1862 for the Midland & Great Western Railway, similar to his station at Clara, Co. Offaly. Wilkinson rarely ventured Gothic in his railway work, but it was the preferred style of *William G. Murray*, architect to the Dundalk & Enniskillen Railway. His vigorous twin-gabled Gothic station at Cootehill of 1860 is usually the reason for the attribution to him of the exceptionally refined Gothic stations at Tynan and Glaslough, both of *c.* 1859; however these are now recognized to be by a London architect identified only as *Mr Clayton*. Murray was also capable of greater restraint, adopting a sterner irregular gabled design for Newbliss and Ballybay. In 1876 the different standard-gauge companies were amalgamated into the Great Northern Railway Company: controlling most of the rail transport in the southern portion of the province, this became the second largest and most prosperous of the Late Victorian companies. From then on the buildings were the work of MacNeill's successor, *William H. Mills*, who produced the most familiar of Late Victorian railway stations, to straightforward designs, most of them boldly expressed with horizontal polychrome brickwork, and usually with round- or segmental-headed windows, with marginal-glazed sashes – all occurring on the rural halt at Cloverhill. The usual polychromy is notably relinquished at Belturbet, where Mills employed rock-faced limestone on the station shared with the Cavan & Leitrim Railway. The stations for that line surviving at Templeport and Ballyconnell have all the characteristics of his work.

PUBLIC BUILDINGS continued to absorb a sizeable portion of public expenditure and to receive deserving architectural treatment, generally in freely conceived styles. The Mechanics' Institute in Lurgan of 1857 is one of the few consciously classical public buildings, a richly stuccoed Italianate block with a campanile. It was the winning competition entry by the London architect *William Raffles Brown*, who then settled in Ireland and worked for a time with *John Skipton Mulvany*, whose classical tastes were entirely in sympathy with his own, but enjoyed limited success before his early death in 1866. Surprisingly, *Young & Mackenzie*'s Lurgan Town Hall of 1868, which adjoins the Mechanics' Institute, with its perfunctory astylar manner makes no attempt to upstage its older neighbour. Lurgan's former Courthouse by *Thomas Turner* captures the industrial spirit of the town, a polychromatic building with the air of a railway station, designed in 1872 in partnership with the County Surveyor, *Henry Davison*. *Fitzgibbon Louch*, a descendant of the Armagh architect Richard Louch, spent much of his career in North Ulster but in 1870 he returned to Keady, the Armagh village where he had

108

been married twenty years before, to design the combined Town Hall and Market House, a rich and forceful exercise in Venetian Gothic (bombed in 1970). Much more gratuitously Gothic is the extraordinarily exuberant and uplifting Gospel Hall on the Mall in Armagh, a dizzying gabled, buttressed and many-towered polychrome fancy built as a Masonic Hall in 1884. Its design is usually attributed to *John H. Fullerton*, though the freer, more personal attitude to Gothic may derive from proposals offered by *John McCurdy* thirty years before. The Institute, now the Town Hall, in Bessbrook of 1886–7 by *William J. Watson* of Newry is a richly textured asymmetrical composition in granite which deserves notice as a building with its own personality, but the Town Hall at Portadown of 1890 by *Thomas & Robert Roe* is noteworthy only in so far as its heavy façade of red brick anticipates the eclecticism of Edwardian times.

The architects and patrons of COMMERCIAL BUILDINGS looked to the reassuring orderliness of classicism, and for most of the Victorian age favoured the solid dependability of the Italianate style. One man, *Charles Lanyon*, more than any other took up the theme of the Italian palazzo, pioneered memorably by Charles Barry's Travellers' Club in London of 1830. From 1836, when he was appointed County Surveyor for Antrim, Lanyon was to become the most influential figure in Ulster architecture, elected President of the Royal Institute of Architects in Ireland in 1862 and knighted in 1868. He made the palazzo style popular for the widest range of buildings, from railway stations to country houses. In South Ulster he gave it its fullest expression in the former Belfast Bank (now the Tourist Office) in Armagh of 1851. Nearby, the tall richly stuccoed Northern Bank of 1867 is a work of the expanded firm of *Lanyon, Lynn & Lanyon*. *William Caldbeck*, a pupil of William Deane Butler and architect to the National Bank from 1853 until his death in 1874, employed the palazzo theme in an understated, astylar manner. His bank in Carrickmacross is a generously sited tall five-bay block built entirely of ashlar. On the same street *Thomas Jackson*'s Ulster Bank of 1873 rises to the same stature but without the same stylistic self-assurance. *Sandham Symes*, a pupil of William Farrell, appointed architect to the Bank of Ireland in 1854, developed his own palazzo style, which in his best work is given rich treatment in precise stonework, generally with complex rustication on the ground floor, elaborate aedicules on the *piano nobile*, and a complicated crowning cornice. All these elements are present in the Bank of Ireland at Portadown of 1868. His designs for banks in smaller towns are more economical, usually with stucco above the ground floor. On his retirement in 1879 the practice was taken over by his relation *William Symes* in partnership with *Gerald C. Millar* as *Millar & Symes*, who reverted to a more lavish treatment at Clones in 1892. By far the most creative exponent of the palazzo style was *William G. Murray*, whose most distinguished work was for the Provincial Bank; one of his best buildings is undoubtedly the bank in Cootehill of 1858, a perfect blend of c15 Florentine and Venetian Gothic elements. In

109   Monaghan, the Hibernian Bank of 1874 by *O'Neill & Byrne*
combines Venetian Gothic with a consciously Hiberno-
Romanesque style.

Murray's Cootehill bank is sometimes taken for the work of
William Hague, but Hague's Provincial Bank in Cavan of 1862 is
a much more modest affair, little more than a town house lightly
dressed up in classical garb. Hague's only other commercial work
in the region appears to be the Westenra Arms Hotel in Monaghan, a commission he canvassed for in 1872; it is an Italianate
block of red brick with heavy stone trimmings. The Provincial
Bank in Armagh of 1896 by *Watts & Tulloch* is a tail-end Victorian
design of red brick and sandstone, which in many ways offers a
foretaste of Edwardian bank design.

Civic-spiritedness and personal tragedy are given more diverse
expression in Victorian PUBLIC MONUMENTS. Classicism is
manifest in the simple obelisk at Middletown to David Smith,
Superintendent of the Fever Hospital, an early victim of the
conditions brought about by the Famine of 1847. More imposing
and purer is the silvery obelisk at Monaghan by *W. J. Barre*,
erected in 1857 by Lord Cremorne to commemorate his brother
who had fallen at the Battle of Inkerman. In Lurgan, the Rev.
Thomas Millar, victim of a railway disaster in England in 1858,
108   was commemorated a year later by *John Robinson* with a spired
Gothic design. Its elegance is not shared by *Fitzgibbon Louch*'s
bulky monument of 1871 to William Kirk M.P. in Keady, and is
p. 472   similarly wanting in the otherwise arresting Rossmore Monument in Monaghan, a large domed and spired octagon of 1874
commemorating the young Lord Rossmore. Its design is probably the work of the English architect *E. J. Tarver* (an assistant of
William Burges), whose only recorded Irish work is the idiosyn-
p. 484   cratic Rossmore Mausoleum of 1876. In Cavan the sculptor
Samuel F. Lynn produced a ghostly marble statue of Lord Farnham
in 1871 for the town gardens (now minus its plinth, in front of
the Library). Lynn also supplied the bronze bust for the Leslie
Monument at Glaslough, a handsome Ionic aedicule designed
by his brother, *William H. Lynn*, and erected in 1874. The gardens
of Brownlow Castle are now Lurgan Park, and the fullest expression of Victorian fancy is now found there: the cast-iron Jubilee
Fountain of 1887, moved from the centre of Lurgan.

COUNTRY HOUSE BUILDING in the Victorian period is decidedly less eventful than previously; there were few new great
houses, and much of the work involved only enlargement and
remodelling. Nevertheless the stylistic trends are clearly evident,
and many works stand out for notice. The Scottish architect
William Burn, a pupil of Robert Smirke, became one of most
prolific country house designers in the first half of the C19. At
the height of his success in the early 1840s he was made an hon-
orary member of the Institute of Architects in Ireland and enjoyed
several Irish commissions. The most important of these was the
p. 310   rebuilding of Dawson's Grove at Dartrey for Lord Cremorne,
designed in 1843, where Burn revived the idea of the great Tudor

manor house; demolished a century after its completion, nothing could ever replace it. *Robert Woodgate*'s dignified Neoclassical Castle Blayney was sold in 1853, enlarged and smothered under frivolous stucco in a strange blend of Italianate and Jacobethan decoration; it later became Hope Castle. A much more exhilarating display of Jacobethan taste is found in the fanciful lodges and gate screen at Loughgall, the ironwork of which is dated 1842. These serve a late and dull Tudor Revival house of the 1870s by *Frederick A. Butler*. The small Georgian house at Annaghmakerrig (now the Tyrone Guthrie Centre) was enlarged and reworked in a gentler Jacobethan manner in 1859 by the partnership of *George Henderson & Albert E. Murray*, brother of William G. Murray.

The influence of Deane and Woodward is felt in the extravagant remodelling of Bessmount in 1868, the only truly High Victorian work, with fanciful gabled projections and turrets and an imposing entrance tower, its porch adorned with free naturalistic carvings. The designer is unknown, but the overall effect calls to mind the work of *John McCurdy* and *W. J. Barre*. Barre's only major domestic work in the region was at Tynan Abbey (demolished), where he designed alterations in 1866; he was followed in 1877 by *W. H. Lynn*, and together their work gave the Regency castle a more varied Victorian air. Lynn's true independent strength and versatility are evident in the varied schemes he produced for Castle Leslie, the only major Late Victorian house in the region, which showed him to be equally rigorous within a broad stylistic range – medieval French, Italianate, and more picturesque Scots Baronial – resolved finally in the adoption of a very personal, hard-hitting Tudoresque design. Tandragee Castle, a rather austere and idiosyncratic castle of the 1830s, was ambitiously enlarged *c.* 1850 with a big gabled keep of the kind popularized by Lynn's baronial style.

Hilton Park is the only major Victorian house in a classical style, the result of remodelling in 1872 for the eccentric John Madden, who had rejected the doyen of country house design, Sir Charles Lanyon, in favour of *William Hague*, in whom he saw a 'very clever rising young man'. His faith was rewarded by the transformation of the ponderous C18 house into a work of classical brio. The effect was completed by a monumental *porte cochère*, a fully dressed-up Italianate design, and the interiors were reworked in Victorian taste.

New classical houses were all relatively small, and reflected a preference for an understated Italianate classicism. Dartan Hall (Killylea) of 1856 is a cubic, somewhat austere Italianate villa by *John Boyd*. Derry Lodge at Lurgan is a subtle, single-storey building sometimes attributed to *Thomas Jackson*. Owendoon (Templeport), built *c.* 1850, shows a more sophisticated mind, with its underlying Italianate classicism modestly laced with the kind of Gothic and Byzantine embellishments then being popularized by Ruskin and the architecture of Deane & Woodward.

ARCHITECTURE SINCE 1900

The ARTS AND CRAFTS MOVEMENT is largely represented in
the region with the work of *William Alphonsus Scott*, who in 1905
10 designed houses on the Diamond in Clones in the manner of
C. F. A. Voysey. He kept up his interest in the style with the
Manager's House at Ballyhaise and the Parochial House of
St Michael, Annayalla (Castleblayney) of 1921, the year of his
death. *Young & Mackenzie* showed an early interest in the movement in the late C19, and with The Demesne of 1911, near
Lurgan, produced its most substantial house, a pleasing asymmetrical design of red brick and sandstone.

  Although great civic buildings were in a sense anathema to the
p. 253 spirit of the Arts and Crafts movement, Cavan Town Hall of 1907
is Scott's masterpiece, and the greatest achievement of the style
in Ireland. A singularly original building, it represented a radical
departure from Scott's award-winning Town Hall at Enniskillen
of just a few years earlier, loosely conceived in a Renaissance
style, and demonstrates the movement's concern for honest
expression of materials and high-quality workmanship. Blending
recognizable historicism into the style is the Tudoresque Church
House in Armagh of 1912 by *W. Sampson Jervois* with *R. Caulfield
Orpen*. Also deserving mention is the simple Protestant Recreation Hall in Clones by the local architect *W. R. Potts*, of mass
concrete, a novelty when it was designed in 1922.

  Ferroconcrete construction was most ambitiously explored in
RAILWAY ARCHITECTURE in the first decade of the century with
the Castleblayney, Keady & Armagh Railway, which left two
impressive viaducts designed by *Sir Benjamin Baker* in mass
107 concrete with brick (at Keady) and stone (at Tassagh). These
were followed in 1926 by the extraordinary locomotive sheds at
Clones and Portadown, great ribbed arcs of mass concrete by
Frederick A. Campion, who succeeded William H. Mills as chief
engineer to the Great Northern Railway; only Clones survives,
the shallow concrete vaulting with wide external ribs quite unlike
anything seen before or since.

  As most architects held fast to the principles of traditional
design, the abiding disposition of early C20 architecture is much
less radical. Their enduring preference for classicism is best
exemplified by BANK BUILDINGS, which proliferated throughout
the country in the first three decades of the century, displaying
all the broad eclectic range of Edwardian historicism. The Ulster
Bank at Lurgan, a mildly eccentric design in ashlar of 1911 by
Vincent Craig, is the most stylistically obscure. *G. W. Ferguson* was
a more conservative designer, employing reliable Italianate forms
in his work for the Northern Bank, built expensively with rusticated stone and brick at Lurgan in 1901 and more modestly with
stucco at Bailieborough in 1912. In Cavan, the Hibernian
Bank of 1907 by *Edward J. Toye* and the Ulster Bank of 1911 by
Blackwood & Jury display the red brick and limestone combination favoured in the Late Victorian age. *W. H. Byrne & Son*
preferred Neo-Georgian for the Hibernian Banks of the 1920s,

producing a frivolous Adamesque design in stucco for Kings-court and a more weighty astylar façade for Bailieborough. *Ferguson* was probably responsible for the purely sentimental Neo-Georgian red brick Northern Bank in Ballybay of 1926, a character that was later shared by the big Provincial Bank in Portadown of 1931 by *Blackwood & Jury*.

Simple Neo-Georgian was also the style favoured for much of the routine GOVERNMENT BUILDING projects, exemplified in the pleasing designs for the Royal Irish Constabulary Barracks at Blackwatertown and the Garda stations for Smithborough (1927) and Tullyvin (1931). The many Post Offices erected throughout the country immediately after 1900 also possess a good sense of the requirements of civic architecture. The designs, usually attributable to *Robert Cochrane* and *George William Crowe* of the *Office of Public Works*, often present lively Baroque façades in the widely adopted combination of red brick and dressed stone. Stylistic ease is evident in smaller designs like Belturbet of 1904, in a Dutch Renaissance style, while greater circumspection is shown in larger buildings like Clones dated 1903 and Monaghan of 1907.

The pace of CATHOLIC CHURCH BUILDING continued steadily in the first half of the century, uncurtailed in its ambitions and unperturbed by any contemporary developments in architectural thought. *Scott*, whose practice was dominated by ecclesiastical work and whose approach is normally consistently fresh, is principally represented in Monaghan by minor, mildly distinctive, repairs and additions to rural churches; the most striking of these is the exotic-looking stuccoed tower added to St Lavinius at Killeevan in 1910. St Michael, Annayalla (Castleblayney) of 1919, fundamentally an ordinary Gothic design, is Scott's only new church in the region and in point of originality only displays the rugged muscularity and distinctive massing that characterize much of his later work.

New ideas in architecture generally suggest an Insular attitude, in consequence of the Celtic Revival loosely derived from the architectural features of the early medieval Irish church. The theme was first taken up in the work of *Ashlin & Coleman*, with the Church of the Sacred Heart at Cloghogue of 1911, an aggregate of Lombardic and Hiberno-Romanesque in vigorously textured masonry. The church was dedicated on Easter Day 1916, an auspicious day in Irish history, when revolutionaries seized the General Post Office in Dublin and proclaimed a republic. George C. Ashlin died in December 1921, just four days after the Anglo-Irish Treaty was signed, which established the Irish Free State in twenty-six counties including Cavan and Monaghan. Armagh was by then already one of the six Ulster counties of the Northern Ireland province, established by the 1920 Government of Ireland Act. No great change accompanied the new era of dominion status: in Cavan and Monaghan the post boxes were painted green. Sentimental attachment to Ireland's early Christian heritage continued and found a natural outlet in new church architecture, though this was largely confined to

87

decorative variations on the Romanesque arch. After Ashlin's death the firm of *Ashlin & Coleman* remained committed to the artistic potential of the Hiberno-Romanesque style in Armagh. Their Church of the Immaculate Conception at Tullysaran (Eglish), of 1921, is an evocative and picturesque composition with the iconic Irish round tower rising from the angle of the gable; St Malachy in Armagh, designed in 1935, is a very pure articulation of a basilican church with the simplest Hiberno-Romanesque details. Though these designs were all built in expensive cutstone, the churches share a certain austerity, especially inside, where any sense of power is conveyed by their scale and orderliness rather than by originality or the quality of the decoration.

Originality is unmistakably present in the architecture of *Rudolf Maximilian Butler*, whose independent work from 1908, when his partnership in the Dublin firm of Doolin, Butler & Donnelly came to an end, becomes increasingly idiosyncratic in his attitude to archaeological quotation. Butler, who succeeded Scott as Professor of Architecture at University College Dublin, completed Scott's St Michael, Annayalla in 1923 and, a year later, acknowledged its rugged personality in his own design for the Church of the Immaculate Conception at Scotshouse. Here however his treatment of the detail reveals a more vital and assured individuality, with the creative reinterpretation of Hiberno-Romanesque motifs, referenced most directly in the design of the w gable with *antae*, based on the c12 church of St Cronan at Roscrea, Co. Tipperary. Like Scott, Butler also carried out alterations and additions, and at St Dympna, Tydavnet (Bellanode) in 1923 and Three Mile House in 1924 enriched the existing vernacular character by introducing simple Romanesque features. Later examples of the Romanesque style which should be noticed are St Paul at The Diamond of 1926, a small but highly finished building for the Church of Ireland by *Richard F. Caulfield Orpen*, and the more studied St Patrick at Lissummon of 1933, a miniature Lombardic design built in a satisfying combination of brick and reconstituted stone by *W. H. Byrne & Son*.

p. 187

The Dublin firm of *W. H. Byrne & Son* more than any other dominated Catholic building in the c20. *William Byrne* was a pupil of J. J. McCarthy, and from 1869 was taken into partnership by John O'Neill of Belfast. In 1882, the year before O'Neill's death, he began to work independently, establishing his reputation as a church designer, and in 1902 he formed a partnership with his son Ralph as W. H. Byrne & Son. Works in South Ulster before 1900 are few and of a modest nature, but after William Byrne's death in 1917, when the practice was carried on by his son under the same name, it gradually became one of the most prolific and memorable church builders in the region. Any apparent conservatism in the designs of Ralph Byrne's two 1927 churches, the fully Gothic Revival Cootehill and the twin-towered Lombardic Arva, belies the architect's unrivalled erudition. St Brigid, Glasdrumman (Crossmaglen), a large basilican church, was built in 1926 from the fabric of the mid-c19

p. 307

Ravensdale Park near Dundalk by *Thomas Duff* and *W. H. Lynn*, burned in 1922. Byrne's mastery of composition is demonstrated by the handling of the campanile, as if specially conceived for this site, but in fact a faithful rebuilding of Lynn's tower. The full range of Byrne's architectural interests and his extraordinary command of historic exemplars is demonstrated in the Cathedral of SS Patrick and Felim in Cavan town, of 1939–42. Here ancient Rome, Gibbs and Palladio were all fastidiously studied to produce an unalloyed classical composition. It conveys the true power of the Church at the time, whose ideals had become inseparably entwined with the aspirations of the newly constituted State. Later works typical of the firm are the big stuccoed rectangular halls built throughout the 1940s and 1950s, most attributed after Byrne's death in 1946 to his nephew, *Simon Aloysius Leonard*, who had joined the practice in 1936. The designs, which can be nominally classical or Romanesque, are usually characterized by the contrast between the bulk of the hall with its broad gabled front and the tall, slender tower offset beside it; Aughnaduff (Mullaghbawn) of 1957 is the plainest.

Awareness of MODERNIST ideologies is first manifest in a modest and rather tentative way in the public building projects of the 1930s and 1940s. Most common are schools, hospitals, public halls and public housing schemes, in which functional concerns dominate over expressions of style, and brick remains a favoured material. As a consequence pure Art Deco forms are rare and understated. Though some of the best instances in the country are to be found in new hospital architecture, at the County Hospital in Monaghan of 1937 *John Francis McGahon* with *W. H. Byrne & Son* struggled with the idiom; the result is bland, and but for a tetrastyle portico, characterless. The town's Mental Hospital of 1938–43 by the Belfast architect *C. T. MacLynn* fails to abandon historicism entirely, but with its Art Deco details the overall feeling is unmistakably Modernist. For a more consciously Art Deco style three public halls deserve notice: the Salvation Army Hall in Portadown of 1939 by an unknown designer is the best, with an impressively austere two-dimensional front; for St Mark's Parochial Hall, also in Portadown, *Hobart & Heron* prepared designs as early as 1936, though it was not built until 1954; St Patrick's Parochial Hall in Armagh by *W. H. Byrne & Son* is a late flowering of 1954.

The best school building is represented by the work of *James St John Phillips*, who using red brick with stone trimming designed numerous elementary schools in Armagh. His designs include patent historicism and more abstract Art Deco stylization; the best of each are the Armstrong Primary School in Armagh of 1929 and the Sir Robert Hart Memorial School in Portadown of 1932.

The new architecture of the International Style made a solitary breakthrough in South Ulster at this time, in the Alcohol Factory in Carrickmacross, one of six designed in 1935 for the Irish State by the Dutch architect *J. D. Postma*. Its presence in south Monaghan was to have little impact, as war in Europe brought

economic stagnation, with few opportunities to build. In the
north, however, the work of *T. F. O. Rippingham* deserves notice.
He was architect to the Ministry of Finance from 1922 in the
new Government of Northern Ireland, and Essex Ridge, his
112   weavers' houses of 1944 at Laurelvale (Tandragee), manifest their
Modernist credentials with prefabricated monopitch concrete
111   roofs. The sleek Bairnswear factory (now Armagh Business
Centre) of 1950 with its curved glazed termination redolent of
Erich Mendelsohn is an accomplished work and a rare classic of
the age. From this time the Modernist cause was taken up by
George Philip Bell, a native of Lurgan, who was educated at Liverpool School of Architecture before spending a year in the office
of Sir Alfred Brumwell Thomas and returning to set up private
practice in Lurgan in 1933. From 1939 on he was in partnership
with his brother, *Roger H. Bell*. Lurgan Technical Schools (now
Lurgan College and High School) of 1957–61 have virtual walls
of glass. The Planetarium in Armagh, designed in 1965, was a
novelty of the Space Age and as such an altogether more fitting
outlet for their Modernist tastes, its original good design now
alas spoiled by later additions.

Cavan and Monaghan offer few buildings of distinction from
this era, but Ballybay Community College of 1965 by *Sean
McCann* was, before it was remodelled, a neat podium-mounted
block with all the lightness and elegance of Modernist design at
its best. The more aggressive, bad-mannered tendencies to which
116,   Modernist design succumbed in the 1970s are perfectly displayed
p. 299   in the massive and ruthless Portadown College of 1972–6 by
Shanks, Leighton, Kennedy & Fitzgerald, an impregnable, top-
heavy fortress of reinforced mass concrete. It is saying much
about the achievements of the age that this constitutes the best
building of the failed metropolis of Craigavon, the sprawling city
conceived in 1963 between Portadown and Lurgan to relieve
social pressures on Belfast. Designed more for the convenience
of the automobile and named for Northern Ireland's first Prime
Minister, James Craig, its master plan was drawn up by *Professor
Sir Robert Matthew*.

By the 1970s the Modernist rejection of the past seemed absolute, as buildings fell victim to bombings or changing attitudes,
and the consequent opportunities to build well were squandered.
Design passed from a process of creativity to a strictly utilitarian
function: when *Fitzgibbon Louch*'s exotic Town Hall-cum-Market
House in Keady was bombed in 1970, its lowly replacement
apologized for the extravagance of its predecessor and got on
with business as a small library in miserable brown brick. The
pattern has been repeated elsewhere too often and too poorly,
and the result only serves to offend and depress. Consequently
the buildings that deserve notice following on from the last
decades of the C20 are few, and constitute a rather motley grouping largely devoid of any stylistic identity. Church buildings form
the largest group, though much is searing to the optic nerve; the
113   buildings that merit interest may be listed briefly. St Paul's in
Lurgan of 1963 by *Thomas J. Ryan*, a large oblong church of

concrete and copper, shows remarkable originality while following a conventional plan. At Inniskeen the Church of Mary, 114, 115
Mother of Mercy of 1974 by *Carr, Sweeney & O'Farrell* lays
greatest claim to originality in an exciting whorled plan that is *p. 359*
surprisingly well suited to its drumlin landscape, but is let down,
like so much contemporary building, by ill-judged cheap materials. The basic form of *Patrick Haughey*'s Church of Our Lady at
Maghery of 1977 could easily be confused with a public swimming pool. St Lastra at Donaghmoyne of 1980 by *Patrick Rooney* 117
is a thoughtful and attractive design with a simplicity worthy of
the vernacular tradition.

The 1980s and 1990s pass with little notice other than the
novelty of the grass-roofed Navan Visitor Centre near Armagh of
1993 by *McAdam Design*, its form derived from Neolithic tombs.
For the present, what is of interest in each of the counties may
be represented by three buildings. The Market Place Theatre in 119
Armagh of 2000 by *Glenn Howells* sets a large and assured Modernist building responsibly in a deeply sensitive historic environment, and responds to the difficulties of the sloping site with
remarkable poise. The Johnston Library in Cavan of 2004 by
Shaffrey Associates, on the other hand, asserts itself with blunt
force in a bulky and ambitious composition in red brick, zinc and
concrete. And with the Clones Library of 2006 by *Keith Williams* 121
Architects of London, a spectral Corbusian pastiche, Modernism
becomes old-fashioned, as an interest in historicism seems to
mirror that of a century before.

BUILDING MATERIALS

South Ulster is a region of great geological diversity. The primary
character and orientation of the rock formations found across the
three counties are shared by the Southern Uplands of Scotland,
continuing into Co. Down and extending as a diagonal belt as
far as Co. Longford. The band is divided into two distinct rock
groups. Lower Carboniferous formations constitute the N division, roughly aligned between Cavan and Portadown, and partly
distinguished by the outcrops of older Devonian sandstones at
Slieve Beagh in north Monaghan and Slieve Rushen in Cavan. S
of this line are extensive Lower Palaeozoic formations, principally
Ordovician and Silurian sandstones, limestones and shales, and
it is these materials that are predominant in the buildings of
South Ulster.

The county of CAVAN is largely composed of slate, ranging
from a blueish fine-textured stone around Cootehill to greener
hues close to Cavan; further S towards Virginia it becomes highly
crystalline. Extensive slate quarries were worked around Cootehill in the C19; as an easily wrought material it was highly sought
after for building, laid in thin courses in a way that is still visible
on several buildings in that town. Older sandstones are found

near Cavan, and a quarry at Latt provided an attractive yellow-greyish freestone for the C19 public buildings of the town, where its fine texture is especially well displayed on the Courthouse. The Carboniferous limestone of North Leinster intrudes around Lough Sheelin, and quarries were opened near Virginia whence the stone was distributed for building up to a distance of some 20 km (12 miles). The only other significant limestone deposits in Cavan are at Stradone.

In contrast to Cavan, MONAGHAN is largely composed of limestone and sandstone, mostly of a good quality for building. In the N half of the county the limestone is dark and close-grained; it gives an unappealing gloom to some of the buildings in the county town. Further S it fades to pale pinks and blue-greys, with the best quarries around Carrickmacross. From the C18 it was extracted and burnt to produce lime, the principal constituent in mortars, renders and limewash. For building stone, the most important limestone quarries lay just across the border in Meath, at Barley Hill and at Cortobber, which furnished the cold blue limestone for *J. J. McCarthy*'s hard-edged parish church at Carrickmacross. Elsewhere in that town limestone was often used in conjunction with the local sandstone, especially on buildings for the Bath estate, where the combination is expressed in a crazy but pleasing form of diagonal snecked masonry. In the early C19 the sandstone was raised in large blocks from a quarry at Carrickleck. Its fine-grained qualities made it ideal for building, and it was used to good effect at Lough Fea. Slieve Beagh, which rises in the NW corner of Monaghan, provided a finer, more uniformly coloured freestone from the S slopes at Eshnaglogh. This was especially favoured in the early C19, as seen on St Patrick's Church and Courthouse at the centre of Monaghan. In the C19 much of the freestone used in the region was being brought from Fermanagh, similar biscuit-coloured sandstones from Lisnaskea and Carnmore Hill being favoured right across Monaghan from Clones to Castleblayney.

In Co. ARMAGH, a similarly honey-coloured sandstone from Caledon in Co. Tyrone was supplied to The Argory in the 1820s, where it was blended with trimmings of Armagh limestone. In Armagh itself the qualities of the Georgian town rely as much on the unique local characteristics of its bedrock as on any special attributes of the architecture. The predominant material is a conglomerate of pale grey limestone and pink sandstone that is easily worked, but is today usually associated with poorer quality stonework, left exposed where historic renders have been unwisely stripped off. The stone is found in a broad band surrounding the city and was quarried from Drumarg Down. Lower beds yielded marbles, with reds and greys producing breccias that were frequently used for paving or, when polished, for chimneypieces and other internal architectural elements, as for the shafts in the Roman Catholic Cathedral of Armagh and in the library at Gosford Castle.

Armagh owes its prominence to a limestone outcrop, and the purest seams of the fossil-rich stone were quarried at a site close to Navan Fort. Its quality lies in its uniformity and stability – a consistent pale grey, resistant to weathering, and accepting finishes of the highest standard. These attributes are evident throughout the town, in the deeply undercut profiles of mouldings and cornices, the clean arrises of fillets, pilasters and quoins, and the fresh finishes on surface dressings, ranging from smooth ashlar to chisel work – all still beautifully crisp after a century and a half or more. Nowhere are these qualities better demonstrated than on *William Murray*'s town houses on Charlemont Place and on the profile of the Roman Catholic Cathedral.

Two significant areas of Tertiary extrusion add interesting diversity to the geology of Armagh. Part of the great basalt field identified with Antrim sweeps into the NE of the county around Portadown and extends as far S as Markethill; in both towns, and in Lurgan, it presents as a dark olivine trap, sombre in tone. Commonly called blackstone, its main quarry was at Ballyfodrin near Portadown. Its use spread well into the countryside, where it is prominent in church building, at Drumcree, Tartaraghan and The Diamond. The silvery-grey granite around Slieve Gullion was a result of volcanic collapse, part of a great ring-dyke which emerges magnificently out of the drumlins in the SE corner of Armagh. It contributes a coarse distinctiveness to the buildings of this district, that is enhanced by weathering and receptive to lichens, whereby even the most ambitious structures possess a marked sense of belonging that is appealing. Quarried at Mullaghglass (Jerrettspass), it was preferred over the local basalt at Gosford Castle, and used to striking effect on the Egyptian-style railway arch at Newry and on the Craigmore Viaduct.

Despite such geological diversity, stone is not the prime material displayed in South Ulster buildings. It is often an elusive ingredient, concealed by the traditional finishes of ROUGHCAST and LIMEWASH that once gave an attractive uniformity and familiarity to everyday buildings. In Richard Bartlett's early C17 surveys of the Tudor conquest in Ulster, stone is predominant only in church buildings or in structures for permanent defence. Most buildings, for native and planter alike, appear as simple thatched habitations, built of mud in conjunction with stone, often of local origin, governed by speed and economy.

The picture presented by early C19 sources indicates that little had changed over the centuries. Topographical books endlessly repeat the same description of houses: neat, built of mud, stone or brick, finished in roughcast and whitewash and very often thatched, slate usually becoming dominant only in towns or on the houses of more prosperous farmers. Most common were cottages. With such perishable materials it was vital to build well: at Aghabog in Monaghan in the early C19 cottages built of a combination of clay and straw could be expected to last a 'great length of time' once the materials were mixed well together to form walls 2 ft (60 cm) thick, with an external coat of roughcast. A poorly built house might not last much more than fifteen years. Grander late C17 and early C18 houses were similarly roughcast: an 1838 description of the now lost late C17 house of

Carrickblacker near Lurgan as 'a plain and antiquated looking house, three storeys high, roughcast and white washed' could in essence still apply to houses like Richhill, Ardress and Jonesboro. At Loughgall, the Courthouse of 1746 is not the classical building proposed by Sir Edward Lovett Pearce, but a plain rubble structure, formerly roughcast and whitewashed, as were most of the public buildings in the region.

QUARRIED STONE first became prominent in the form of tooled dressings contrasting with traditional finishes, such as coarse renders. In Armagh as late as 1804 it was still worth remarking that the streets were being 'rebuilt on a regular elevation, and the houses neatly slated', almost all with 'marble window stools [sills], doorcases, and parapets or eve [*sic*] courses'. The use of ashlar was uncommon before the C18. The Archbishop's Palace in Armagh, begun in 1766, was the first house in the three counties to be built entirely of ashlar. *Thomas Cooley* established the tradition with the best of his works here. His use of ashlar to front the stable block at Castle Dillon in 1782 was later complemented by *William Murray*'s house of 1844 in limestone, the joints virtually invisible. By then ashlar was commonplace for larger houses and public buildings.

In the 1830s *Lewis Nockalls Cottingham* overlooked the local soft pinks and pale greys of Armagh when he chose to encase the ancient cathedral in a toffee-brown sandstone quarried from Wilson's Bridge nearby, paired with imported yellow sandstone for the tracery. In the same period, for both of *William Henry Playfair*'s houses in Armagh Old Red Sandstone from Scotland was preferred, shipped in a rough state and worked up on site. For Drumbanagher (Jerrettspass), it was quarried from Garscube near Glasgow where transport by water made carriage relatively easy and economic. For Brownlow House at Lurgan stone of a deeper brown was chosen, from the Stevenson Quarry near Ardrossan, then the best freestone quarry in western Scotland. In 1872, however, when *William Hague* encased Hilton Park in ashlar he chose a buff-coloured sandstone from quarries at Gortnaglush in Tyrone, transported by train to Clones. Perfectly exploited in channelled and vermiculated rustication, this stone had a grittiness unsuitable for finer carving so that Portland stone from Dorset was used instead for the coat of arms on the portico at Hilton Park.

BRICK was extremely rare before the C18. A course of shaped bricks forms a plinth for the ruined castle at Cabra (Kingscourt) in Co. Cavan, and in Armagh the remnants of brick stacks are found on the teetering ruin on Derrywarragh Island (Maghery), neither earlier than the C17. By the end of the century its use was more extensive: the old house at Castle Leslie (Glaslough) had been built of brick until replaced in 1729, and in Armagh later renders conceal the older brick-fronted houses of Ardress and the land steward's house at The Argory. Locally burnt brick later became widely used in vaulting throughout the country, principally for basements, but at Ballyhaise in the early C18 it was given architectural significance as a foil to classical stonework.

Bellamont nearby was also set apart by the use of brick. The practical virtues of the material no doubt appealed to *Sir Edward Lovett Pearce*, and significantly while a Member of Parliament he had attempted to impose standards on the industry. The widespread use of brick in this particular district, especially in the neighbouring demesne of Dawson's Grove (Dartrey), points to an established local tradition. Generally brick was used more sparingly, as proposed in the agent's house at Loughgall which Pearce intended to be 'built of stone with brick arches to the windows'.

51, 57

Substantial local production was well established in the early C19 in a number of places, including Barley Hill near Kingscourt and Derrybrughas in Armagh, where bricks and tiles were being made from the late C17. From the mid C19 mass-produced brick became commonplace, especially in towns. Coalisland brick from Tyrone provided the principal source in South Ulster, but increasingly a wider range was imported from Scotland and England, including black and yellow industrial brick which fed the later C19 interest in polychromy, seen at its most fanciful on the Gospel Hall in Armagh.

Around Kingscourt, GYPSUM (calcium sulphate dihydrate), an essential ingredient in plaster and cement, is still mined today. In the C19 deposits were discovered on the Shirley estate s of Carrickmacross of a very pure gypsum, essentially a greyish alabaster, tending to pink. Polished, it appears as an elaborate Elizabethan-style chimneypiece in the South Room at Lough Fea; later it was used more extensively in the small church at Ardragh, for the reading desk and as a veneer to line the chancel, which has since been removed.

Although for most of the region stone, brick and lime could be easily sourced in the neighbourhood, TIMBER was for the most part harder to procure, and naturally its survival rate is poorer. Many timbers for ordinary houses were traditionally extracted from bogs, where oak and pine and sometimes yew were found preserved and strengthened, and specially prized for cottage roofs and lintels as well as for fencing and gates. Analysis of the timbers in Richhill and Ardress, which retain late C17 butt-purlin roofs of oak, a type derived from English houses that allowed slate to replace thatch as a roof covering, revealed that the oaks were felled in the period of building. In the 1830s, timber from Dawson's Grove demesne, where the trees were noted for their size, was exploited commercially, with pine and oak sold by auction to builders. On the whole, however, timber had to be imported, chiefly brought by water to Blackwatertown, Dundalk, Newry and Portadown. Timber shingles were common in the C18, their light weight especially suited to timber church spires, but they are virtually non-existent today.

The prevalent roofing material before the C19 was THATCH. According to the locality it might be oat or wheat straw, water reed, sedge, heather or flax, usually pinned to the roof with hazel scollops. Now thatch can only be seen on a handful of buildings, most unexpectedly in Craigavon, with a group of vernacular houses on the Bluestone Road (the best of these Bilbrook Cottage), and in Kingscourt on Gartlan's Public House; the most prominent example is Derrymore House (Bessbrook), a late C18 *cottage orné*.

Quarries of siliceous SLATE at Ballynahaigha in Cavan once supplied Cootehill and its district with a coarse roofing material, but Welsh slate eventually overtook all other roofing materials.

IRON, especially wrought iron, is an overlooked yet essential component of historic buildings. Smithies, once a ubiquitous sight at rural crossroads, provided everything from nails, latches and holdfasts to gates and sharpened mason's tools. The most spectacular example of wrought iron was the gate screen of Rich-hill Castle, made in 1745 by the *Thornberry Bros* of Falmouth in Cornwall, lost to South Ulster when it was moved to Hillsborough Castle, Co. Down, in 1936. A fanciful gateway at Loughgall incorporates wrought-iron gates of 1842, signed by *R. Marshall* of Caledon.

Cast iron – a hard brittle alloy of iron and carbon giving enormous strength under compression – was the novel material of the industrial revolution. Its decorative potential was appreciated in the early C19 by *William Farrell*, who favoured a form of pierced iron roof truss in his smaller churches. The Ride at Hilton Park, an impressive open structure, makes use of cast iron both for such trusses and for its Tuscan columns. The foundries of Belfast and Scotland led in the supply of materials, and even the earliest foundry of all, at Coalbrookdale in Shropshire, supplied a Late Victorian fountain to Lurgan. John Corrie established a small forge near Bailieborough in the mid C19 which eventually became one of the largest iron foundries in Ireland, supplying everything from baths and fire grates to manhole covers; it still operates on a reduced scale today.

Corrugated iron – sheet iron given an undulating profile to improve its strength – was developed as an efficient means of roofing larger spans and first patented in London in the early C19. Its convenience and versatility made it highly efficient and cost-effective, and being well suited to prefabrication it began to be used inventively for entire structures, to brilliant effect in a whimsical steepled church at Laragh. In the C20 it became manifest in the ubiquitous and eye-catching domical red hay barn of almost every South Ulster farmstead.

FURTHER READING

Jonathan Bardon's *A History of Ulster* (1993) is an excellent discursive work which should appeal to everyone with an interest in the province. Perspectives on South Ulster as a historical frontier are offered by *The Borderlands: Essays on the History of the Ulster–Leinster Border*, ed. Raymond Gillespie and Harold Sullivan (1989). A useful and well-illustrated guide to the features of the

same territory, especially buildings, is given in Noreen Cunningham and Pat McGinn's *The Gap of the North: The Archaeology and
Folklore of Armagh, Down, Louth and Monaghan* (2001). P. J.
Duffy's *Landscapes of South Ulster, A Parish Atlas of the Diocese of
Clogher* (1993) brings the scope of regional study down to the
minutiae of the townland in an unparalleled work of historical
geography.

General works treating the INDIVIDUAL COUNTIES offer a
useful starting point towards a more detailed understanding of
the history and the society of the region. So far the only volume
for the three counties in the critical series of 'Interdisciplinary
Essays on the History of an Irish County' is A. J. Hughes and
William Nolan (eds), *Armagh History and Society* (1999). For
Cavan there is Raymond Gillespie (ed.), *Cavan: Essays in the
History of an Irish County* (1995). Monaghan is well served by
Peader Livingstone's *The Monaghan Story* (1980), an exceptional
and comprehensive historical monograph which has an impor-
tant bibliography; it is a worthy successor to Evelyn Philip
Shirley's *The History of the County of Monaghan* (1879), a work
distinctly of its time but no less valuable for that. A unique source
for the region, written in the 1830s and never continued to cover
the remainder of the country, is provided by the *Ordnance Survey
Memoirs of Ireland*, ed. Angélique Day and Patrick McWilliams;
Vol. 1 (1990) deals entirely with Armagh, while much of Cavan
and Monaghan are included in Vol. 40 (1998). The standard
contemporary sources for the C19 all remain indispensable: for
each of the South Ulster counties Sir Charles Coote wrote one
of the *Statistical Surveys* for the Royal Dublin Society – *Monaghan* (1801), *Cavan* (1802) and *Armagh* (1804) – detailing the
conditions of local life. For more specific information on towns
and parishes, often with information on buildings, see Samuel
Lewis's *Topographical Dictionary of Ireland* (1837), and *The
Parliamentary Gazetteer of Ireland* (1846).

The EARLY CHRISTIAN and MEDIEVAL PERIODS are well
served by general works. For Armagh, Ann Hamlin's *Historic
Monuments of Northern Ireland* (1983) has been more comprehensively superseded by Ken Neill's *An Archaeological Survey of
County Armagh* (2009), which offers the most thorough treatment of the archaeology of the county down to the medieval
period and includes an exhaustive bibliography. It does however
exclude Armagh city, which is the subject of the *Irish Historic
Towns Atlas*, No. 18 (2007), ed. Catherine McCullough and W. H.
Crawford. For Cavan and Monaghan, Anna L. Brindley's *Archaeological Inventory of County Monaghan* (1986) is a useful if dry
resource which gives terse factual descriptions of recorded monuments, grouped according to classifications. With Patrick
O'Donovan's *Archaeological Inventory of County Cavan* (1995) the
format is more developed, and each section is given a brief introduction. For the county towns, the principal sources are the
unpublished reports of 1989 by John Bradley and Noel Dunne
for the Urban Archaeological Survey (Part xxv, Monaghan; Part
xxvi, Cavan). Though of limited relevance to specific monastic

sites in South Ulster, Harold G. Leask's *Irish Churches and Monastic Buildings* (3 vols, 1955–60) is an important survey which should be read in conjunction with Aubrey Gwynn and R. Neville Hadcock's *Mediaeval Religious Houses: Ireland* (1970). The only collective treatment of church architecture in the region remains the timely and thorough work of Oliver Davies in the 1940s: 'Church Architecture in Ulster', *Ulster Journal of Archaeology* 6 (1943) and 7 (1944). See also T. G. F. Paterson and Oliver Davies, 'Ecclesiastical Remains in County Cavan', *Ulster Journal of Archaeology* 3 (1940), and Oliver Davies, 'The Churches of County Cavan', *Journal of the Royal Society of Antiquaries of Ireland* 78, No. 2 (1948). Round towers as an individual building type are treated in G. L. Barrow, *The Round Towers of Ireland* (1979); Brian Lalor, *The Irish Round Tower: Origins and Architecture Explored* (1999); and Tadhg O'Keefe, *Ireland's Round Towers* (2004). Hilary Richardson and John Scarry's *Introduction to Irish High Crosses* (1990) offers the most accessible treatment; but the chief work in this area is Peter Harbison's *The High Crosses of Ireland: An Iconographical and Photographic Survey* (1992). Surviving castles are few in South Ulster, but the essential works on the subject are Harold Leask, *Irish Castles* (1941); Tom McNeill, *Castles in Ireland* (1997); and David Sweetman, *The Mediaeval Castles of Ireland* (1999). Specifically for Cavan, see Oliver Davies, 'The Castles of Cavan', *Ulster Journal of Archaeology*, Part 1, 10 (1947), and Part 2, 11 (1948), and Con Manning, 'Clough Oughter Castle, Cavan', *Breifne* 8, No. 1 (1989–90).

For the POST-MEDIEVAL PERIOD, the following survey texts remain indispensable: C. E. B. Brett, *Buildings of County Armagh* (1999), a representative selection of buildings, each extensively researched and illustrated, grouped according to type and introduced collectively; Maurice Craig, *The Architecture of Ireland from Earliest Times to 1880* (1989), still the broadest and most readable text; Brian de Breffny and George Mott, *The Churches and Abbeys of Ireland* (1976), the only complete survey; Brian de Breffny and Rosemary ffolliott, *The Houses of Ireland* (1975); J. Graby, *150 Years of Architecture in Ireland: The Royal Institute of the Architects of Ireland, 1839–1989* (1989); Niall McCullough and Valerie Mulvin, *A Lost Tradition: The Nature of Architecture in Ireland* (1987), a useful and well-illustrated examination of typologies; and Edward McParland, *Public Architecture in Ireland 1680–1760* (2001). Caroline Pegum's *Building for Government: The Architecture of State Buildings: OPW: Ireland 1900–2000* (1999) includes an essay by Arthur Gibney recording continuity and change in the Office of Public Works. Specific to the buildings of Ulster are Hugh Dixon's *Ulster Architecture, 1800–1900: An Exhibition of Architectural Drawings* (1972), and *An Introduction to Ulster Architecture* (1975; 2008).

The most important works treating the Plantation are George Hill's *An Historical Account of the Plantation of Ulster* (1872), and more recent studies: Philip Robinson, *The Plantation of Ulster* (2000), and Jonathan Bardon, *The Plantation of Ulster* (2011). With particular relevance for buildings in South Ulster at this time are G. A. Hayes-McCoy's *Ulster and other Irish Maps c. 1600* (1960), a vital visual source, and Margaret Gowan's important study, '17th Century Artillery Forts in Ulster', *Clogher Record* 10, No. 2 (1980).

The evolution of TOWNS is still very well served by Gilbert Camblin's *The Town in Ulster* (1951), but readers are also advised to consider more up-to-date studies: R. J. Hunter, 'Ulster Plantation Towns, 1609–41', *The Town in Ireland: Historical Studies*, No. 13 (1981), and 'Towns in the Ulster Plantation', *Studia Hibernica*, No. 11 (1971). Two further studies are contained in P. Roebuck (ed.), *Plantation to Partition: Essays in Honour of J. L. McCracken* (1981): W. H. Crawford, 'The Evolution of Ulster Towns, 1750–1850', and D. McNeice, 'Industrial Villages of Ulster 1890–1900'. William Nolan and Anngret Simms's *The Irish Town: A Guide to Sources* (1998) is an essential work which contains D. McCabe's excellent select bibliography of publications on Irish towns between 1963 and 1993. Also in this text, Lurgan is treated as a case study by F. X. McCorry, based on a more comprehensive study by the author, *Lurgan: An Irish Provincial Town, 1610–1970* (1993). Another individual treatment of an industrial town is R. H. Blum, *Bessbrook: A Record of Industry in a Northern Ireland Village Community* (1945).

Through the exceptional foresight of the Ulster Architectural Heritage Society (UAHS), the buildings in the principal towns of South Ulster have all been the subject of detailed lists, which treat historic buildings, groups of buildings and areas of architectural importance. These were compiled at a critical time in the 1970s, in advance of statutory protection, and regrettably the published monographs now have an enhanced value for the buildings they discuss which have since been lost. In the Republic, the work was assisted by An Taisce, the National Trust for Ireland, and began with *Monaghan* (1970), followed by *Cavan* (1978); for Co. Armagh, *Lurgan and Portadown* (1968) and *Craigavon* (1971). Armagh city was more comprehensively treated much later: Robert McKinstry, Richard Oram, Roger Weatherup and Primrose Wilson's *Buildings of County Armagh* (1992) contains essays of special interest: 'Architects in Armagh before 1900' by Hugh Dixon and 'The Stones of Armagh' by Philip S. Doughty.

For the treatment of individual BUILDING TYPES, the following should be consulted: Brendan Grimes, *Irish Carnegie Libraries* (1998); Frederick O'Dwyer, *Irish Hospital Architecture, A Pictorial History* (1997); and Peter Galloway, *The Cathedrals of Ireland* (1992). For Ulster, the publications of the UAHS are once again to the fore: C. E. B. Brett, *Court Houses and Market Houses of Ulster* (1973); James Stevens Curl, *Mausolea in Ulster* (1978) and *Classical Churches in Ulster* (1980); Michael Gould, *The Workhouses of Ulster* (1983); Robin Wylie, *Ulster Model Schools* (1997).

J. A. K. Dean's *The Gate Lodges of Ulster* (1994) is the first of a series for the entire country, and is a vital source for COUNTRY HOUSE ARCHITECTURE, a natural companion to Mark Bence-Jones's *Guide to the Country Houses of Ireland* (1988), still the most comprehensive survey. For smaller houses Maurice Craig's

Classic Irish Houses of the Middle Size (1976; 2006) remains a useful study. Examples of the most important Georgian houses appear in *The Georgian Society Records of Eighteenth-Century Domestic Architecture and Decoration*, Vol. V (1913). A more depressing record of houses in Cavan and Monaghan is found in *Vanishing Country Houses of Ireland* (1988), compiled by the Knight of Glin, David J. Griffin and Nicholas K. Robinson. The SOCIAL CONTEXT of country houses and landed estates has become ripe for study, with particular attention being given to the processes of decline, for which the main texts are Terence Dooley, *The Decline of the Big House in Ireland* (2001), and Olwen Purdue, *The Big House in the North of Ireland* (2010).

For the relationships between GARDENS AND DESIGNED LANDSCAPES and buildings, the most valuable studies relevant to this region are E. Malins and the Knight of Glin, *Lost Demesnes: Irish Landscape Gardening, 1660–1845* (1976); E. Malins and Patrick Bowe, *Irish Gardens and Demesnes from 1830* (1980); Patrick Bowe and Keith Lamb, *A History of Gardening in Ireland* (1995); and for the buildings, James Howley, *Follies and Garden Buildings of Ireland* (2004).

Information on Irish ARCHITECTS is found in several biographical dictionaries: Rolf Loeber's *A Biographical Dictionary of Architects in Ireland 1600–1720* (1981) is the essential source for the earliest figures; Brendan O'Donoghue's *The Irish County Surveyors 1834–1944: A Biographical Dictionary* (2007) has many entries relevant to the region. For British architects working in Ireland see Howard Colvin, *A Biographical Dictionary of British Architects, 1600–1840* (4th edn, 2008), which contains all the major figures whose careers extended to Ulster. For engineers see A. W. Skempton, *A Biographical Dictionary of Civil Engineers in Great Britain and Ireland: 1500–1830* (2002). The essential texts for Francis Johnston and Thomas Cooley are Edward McParland's 'Francis Johnston, Architect, 1760–1829', *Irish Georgian Society Bulletin* xii (1969), and *James Gandon: Vitruvius Hibernicus* (1985), with the background to Cooley's career brought up to date by Ruth Thorpe's article 'Thomas Cooley before the Dublin Royal Exchange', *Irish Architectural and Decorative Studies* viii (2005). Anthony Malcomson's monograph, *Primate Robinson, 1709–1794* (2003), is also important. See also Ann Martha Rowan (ed.), *The Architecture of Richard and William Vitruvius Morrison* (1989); and Janet Myles, *L. N. Cottingham 1787–1847: Architect of the Gothic Revival* (1996). The best contexts for Victorian ecclesiastical architects and architecture are provided by Jeanne Sheehy's *J. J. McCarthy and the Gothic Revival in Ireland* (1977) and Frederick O'Dwyer's *The Architecture of Deane and Woodward* (1997).

The standard sources for STAINED GLASS are Nicola Gordon Bowe, *Gazetteer of Irish Stained Glass* (1988) and *The Life and Work of Harry Clarke* (1994). For MONUMENTS AND SCULPTURE, Judith Hill, *Irish Public Sculpture* (1998); Paula Murphy, *Nineteenth Century Irish Sculpture* (2010); and Homan Potterton, *Irish Church Monuments 1570–1880* (1975).

INDUSTRIAL ARCHITECTURE has been treated quite comprehensively in two texts, Ron Cox's *Engineering Ireland* (2006) and Colin Rynne's *Industrial Ireland 1750–1930* (2006). Specifically for Ulster there is W. A. McCutcheon's *The Industrial Archaeology of Northern Ireland* (1980). For CANALS and NAVIGATIONS see Ruth Delaney, *A Celebration of 250 Years of Ireland's Inland Waterways* (1992). Amongst the many publications on RAILWAYS, the most useful treatment of architecture remains Jeanne Sheehy's article, 'Railway Architecture: its Heyday', *Irish Railway Record Society Journal* 12, No. 68 (1975).

For TWENTIETH-CENTURY ARCHITECTURE Sean Rothery's *Ireland and the New Architecture* (1991) is the standard text. Paul Larmour's *The Arts and Crafts Movement in Ireland* (1992) provides a useful context for the early C20. For churches in the second half of the century, see Richard Hurley and Wilfred Cantwell, *Contemporary Irish Church Architecture* (1985) – now somewhat anachronistically titled. For MODERNIST ARCHITECTURE in Ulster, D. Evans, *An Introduction to Modern Ulster Architecture* (1977). Karen Latimer (ed.), *Modern Ulster Architecture* (2006), brings things reasonably up to date; it also contains thematic essays which trace the evolution of Modernist architecture in Ulster by Paul Larmour, David Evans and Charles Rattray, and has a detailed, illustrated analysis of individual projects, some as yet unbuilt, throughout the province.

Several JOURNALS have provided essential material for this volume. For the C19, *The Dublin Builder* and *The Irish Builder* have proved most useful. For articles on buildings and architects, the *Bulletin of the Irish Georgian Society*, which since 1998 has been published as *Irish Architectural and Decorative Studies*, and the *Irish Arts Review* are the most significant, in addition to the *Ulster Journal of Archaeology* and *Journal of the Society of Antiquaries of Ireland*. An ever-expanding outlet for new research is provided by local history societies' publications; of these the following journals have proved the most illuminating: *Breifne*, Journal of Cumann Seanchais Bhreifne; *The Clogher Record*, Journal of the Clogher Historical Society; *Seanchas Ard Mhacha*, Journal of the Armagh Diocesan Historical Society; and the *Journal of the Craigavon Historical Society*.

The fundamental PRINTED BIBLIOGRAPHY for Irish buildings is Edward McParland's 'A Bibliography of Irish Architectural History', *Irish Historical Studies* 26, No. 102 (1988). While the printed format will, hopefully, never be replaced, its potential for disseminating research efficiently has been entirely surpassed by the INTERNET, which provides access to several reliable online resources for Irish architecture. Chief amongst them is the Biographical Dictionary of Irish Architects 1720–1940 (*www.dia.ie*), established by Ann Martha Rowan and maintained by her at the Irish Architectural Archive. It is very much a live resource, capable of being constantly updated. For bibliographic material, Planning and Architecture Design Database Ireland (*www.paddi. net*) covers all aspects of architecture and planning referred to or found in books, articles and theses, and is augmented by a directory of the major architectural collections in Ireland.

Two important INVENTORIES should also be mentioned. The National Inventory of Architectural Heritage, which according to its statutory obligations identifies and records the architectural heritage of Ireland from 1700 to the present day, makes available online the results of its ongoing buildings and gardens surveys (*www.buildingsofireland.ie*); and David Lawrence's inventory of ecclesiastical stained glass for the Church of Ireland can also now be consulted through an online database (*www.gloine.ie*).

For ARCHIVE MATERIAL the Irish Architectural Archive is the principal repository of architectural material in Ireland; its collections can be consulted in its reading room on Merrion Square in Dublin. In Northern Ireland, the Monuments and Buildings Record (MBR) of the Northern Ireland Environment Agency holds extensive information on all aspects of the built environment, including written records, drawings, maps and photographs, which can be consulted at its premises in Hill Street, Belfast.

SOUTH ULSTER

ANNAGHMAKERRIG

TYRONE GUTHRIE CENTRE. 3 km SE of Newbliss. In 1802 a small estate here was purchased by Dr John Moorhead, who presumably built the Late Georgian farmhouse, then known as Leesborough. A straightforward two-storey block of five bays, it was modestly romanced and enlarged into a charming Tudor Revival house after the marriage of Martha Moorhead in 1859 to the soldierly William J. Tyrone Power, son of the C19 actor Tyrone Power. Bequeathed to the Irish State in the late C20 by Sir William's grandson, Sir Tyrone Guthrie, and adapted for use as an artists' retreat by *Fergus Flynn Rogers*.

On a grassy terrace above Leesborough Lough, surrounded by thick shelter belts, the old house is represented by the symmetrical gable-ended main, S, front, its roughcast walls given ample sandstone trimmings added after 1859 by *George Henderson & Albert E. Murray*. They dressed up the front with blocked quoins, a deep parapet, new stacks, kneelers, and an advanced and gabled entrance bay, finished in ashlar on the ground floor between angle buttresses; the windows were enlarged, with blocked surrounds and mullions, and have hoodmoulds on the ground floor. Rooms were added to the N, including a study, resulting in a wider W front which was given twin curvilinear gables and single-storey bay windows. On the E side a new entrance was placed between the main block and a large kitchen wing to the N. The plan completes its zigzag to the NE in a long two-storey office range, of shale with red brick dressings and pretty latticed windows.

The result is much less ambitious than was first considered. An unsigned perspective in the house, possibly by *Henderson & Murray*, proposed an ecclesiastical four-stage stone tower on the NE corner, with Gothic details and a double pyramid roof. A short single-storey link joined this tower to the proposed kitchen wing, a wide gable-fronted block, with three-light cusped lancets, and a half-hipped gable with fussy eaves decoration crowned by an even more ecclesiastical-looking gabled statuary canopy.

Nothing special about the interior. Only the hall is consciously Gothic, the ceiling groin-vaulted with ribs. It leads to a dog-leg stair in dark timber with fretwork balusters. The reception rooms on either side have mid-C19 joinery and standard florid Victorian cornices.

Henderson & Murray also built the FARMYARD, attractive rustic ranges to the N in shale with red brick dressings. Contemporary ESTATE COTTAGES and red brick LODGE, all with distinctive catslide roofs over the porches.

ANNAGHMORE

9050 AH

A rural parish in the orchard country of north Armagh, focused on a small settlement around the parish church.

ANNAGHMORE PARISH CHURCH (C of I). 1856 by *Joseph Welland*. Small, given all the clarity of a Tractarian plan with nave, chancel, transepts and W porch; a lean-to vestry tucked in the angle of chancel and S transept. Squared limestone on a battered plinth with sandstone trim. Steep kneelered gables, a bellcote over the W gable. Nave of three bays with twin lights filled with clear quarry glazing; bigger windows in the gables, with delicate cusped Y-tracery – three lights in the transepts, four in the E gable. Inside, elaborate arch-braced roof with kingposts. Chancel and transept arches in sandstone. – STAINED GLASS. E window, a simple design with small coloured panels by *Alexander Gibbs & Co.* of London, *c.* 1897; chancel N, *c.* 1906, two lancets probably also by *Gibbs & Co.* N transept, Christ the Comforter by *W. J. Douglas & Sons*, *c.* 1934; S transept by *CWS Design*. – MONUMENT. Great War memorial by *McClements*, a quirky Ionic aedicule in grey marble.

CRANAGILL METHODIST CHURCH. 2.25 km SE. An attractive group of rural buildings – church, hall and manse lined up together by the roadside. The CHURCH of 1881 is a small rough-cast hall with stuccoed quoins. Three bays with twin round-headed lancets set between narrow, feeble-looking buttresses. The porch has a pleasing round-headed doorway with spoked fanlight. The trim cast-iron GATES supported on slender ogee-topped piers are by *Musgraves* of Belfast and noteworthy.

The adjoining REV. T. J. ALLEN MEMORIAL HALL of 1958 echoes the simplicity of the church in both scale and materials.

The MANSE is a simple two-storey, three-bay box with a hipped roof and central stacks.

ANNAGHMORE STATIONHOUSE. 1.5 km NE. A plain stuccoed block built for the Portadown, Dungannon & Omagh line of the Great Northern Railway, completed in 1861. A sedate design attributable to *George Wilkinson*: two storeys and four bays with a hipped roof on oversailing eaves. The windows all have Victorian sashes and plate glass, those on the first floor with cambered heads. Off-centre doorway.

CRANNAGAEL HOUSE. 2.5 km SE. Built in 1762 for James Nicholson and enlarged a century later. The original two-

storey house is represented by the gabled ends still showing on
the main block, presumably having had the usual five-bay front
before it was refronted with three bays. The new front, projected forward to create a deeper plan, is rendered, with sandstone quoins, and crowned by a heavy cornice and blocking
course to conceal the junction with the old roof. A small boxy
porch stands before the slightly advanced central bay. Long
service return behind.

CROW HILL. 3 km SE. Eye-catching on an exposed hilltop, a
pleasing Late Georgian house of 1824 by an architect known
only as *Brownlees* (likely to be identified with the *H. Brownlees*
who produced designs for outbuildings for The Argory at this
time), named with his clerk of works, *Christy Nugent*, in an
account book of the Hoope family for whom the house was
built. Replacing an older house on the site, it stands two
storeys over a basement on an L-plan with two adjoining show
fronts, all in roughcast trimmed with dressed stone, with
twelve-pane sashes. Big hipped roof with stone stacks set back
behind the ridge. Broad entrance front of five bays, the central
bay advanced in a narrow projection under a small pediment
pierced with a spoked lunette. The same design is applied to
the three bays of the adjoining front. The entrance, at the head
of a railed flight of steps, is in a wide elliptical arch boldly
expressed with blocked voussoirs; engaged Tuscan columns
frame the door and geometric side-lights; the big leaded fanlight has been lost. The design was evidently successful, as it
was repeated within the year with little or no variation at
Glenaul Park, Eglish.

ARDMORE AH 0060

A parish in north Armagh on the windswept S shores of Lough
Neagh.

ARDMORE CHURCH (C of I). A handsome diminutive hall and
tower for a parish formed in 1765. Rebuilt in 1785, it is
remarkable for its copper spire and striking masonry walls of
snecked rubble. Three-bay nave with twin quarry-glazed
lancets from a C19 refenestration; simple roughcast tower in
three stages with Irish battlements before the octagonal
spire, an 1883 rebuilding of the storm-damaged C18 one.
Charming interior retaining box pews with C18 raised and
fielded panelling; flat plaster ceiling with intersecting ribs.
C19 gallery by *Joseph Welland*. – FONT dated 1875. – STAINED
GLASS. Three-light E window, a late C20 figurative work by
Clokey, Belfast. – MONUMENTS. The Rev. John Evan Lewis
†1874; a Gothic aedicule by *J. Robinson & Son*, Belfast.
– William Leney †1868; a scrolled tablet. – James Forde
†1837; a plain tablet with inverted torches and heraldic
symbols.

ARDMORE RECTORY, DERRYADD. 0.6 km E. A perfect First
Fruits rectory of 1820 in a small wooded demesne on the shore
of Lough Neagh. A two-storey, three-bay block, roughcast,
with tripartite windows, hipped roof and central stacks. The
front is distinguished by its wide, welcoming doorcase: a four-
centred arch recessed in a blocked stucco surround with fanciful geometric fanlight and side-lights.

RAUGHLAN HOUSE. 2 km SE. On a densely wooded headland
in Lough Neagh, W of Kinnegoe Harbour. An impressively
long, two-storey, gable-ended block in an attractive later
Georgian vernacular style. Roughcast, with a mixture of twin
and tripartite Georgian sashes and an elegant off-centre
entrance bow. The doorcase is a quirky timber aedicule with
slender, fluted columns, a partially panelled door, and above
it a flamboyant Baroque tympanum. Said to have originated
in the C17 as a sporting lodge for the Brownlow family, eventually passing by inheritance to the Fforde family; it looks more
C19, with early C20 interventions suggested by exposed rafter
toes, bay windows, and the proprietary cement used for the
tympanum and string-courses on the bow.

The extensive PLEASURE GROUNDS, described in 1837 as of
'luxuriant character' remain impressive, enhanced by considerable later C19 specimens of arboricultural interest.

DERRYMACFALL OLD CHURCH. 3.5 km SW. Derelict. Tiny
cement-rendered C19 hall and porch of just two bays with tall,
round-headed Georgian sashes; decorative bargeboards on the
gabled front.

DERRYMACFALL POST OFFICE (former). 3.5 km SW. At a rural
crossroads. A sizeable mid-C19 gable-ended block of two
storeys and five bays in the rich burgundy-coloured local brick,
all in English-garden-wall bond. To one side a sandstone porch
with stout, vaguely Tuscan, columns over a fanlit door. Big
sashes with plate glass. Behind, an attractive enclosed yard with
buildings of the same red brick.

Opposite, a quaint two-bay HALL in brick with decorative
bargeboards.

BELLVILLE PRESBYTERIAN CHURCH. 1.75 km NW. A pleasing
rural church in polychrome brickwork with pointed windows
set in pairs. Built c. 1862 to a T-plan to combine church and
hall, with the nave in the long eight-bay stem. To one side, the
MANSE is a compact two-storey, gabled-ended stuccoed block.

ST MARY, DERRYTRASNA. 3 km NW. A plain, stuccoed lancet
hall of 1840 with four bays; enlarged in 1907 with transepts; a
forestanding square tower completed in 1926, when side
porches were also added. The tower has three stages with angle
buttresses, fancy blind arcading to the middle stages, and
good crowstepped battlements. Inside, a coved plaster ceiling
patterned with intersecting ribs and large, florid roses – all
surprisingly accomplished Victorian handiwork. Sanctuary
re-ordered in 1987.

BANNFOOT WESLEYAN CHAPEL. 5.75 km NW. 1855. A plain
stuccoed hall of two bays with a small porch wedged between

lancets on the gabled front. Extending from one side, an attractive low vernacular HOUSE in roughcast with five bays.

ARDRESS HOUSE   AH   9050

Elevated in its small demesne skirted by apple trees in the heart   47
of the orchard country of north Armagh, Ardress is, by virtue of
its ownership by the National Trust, the best preserved example
of a gentleman's farmhouse in South Ulster. Outwardly it is a
substantial mid-Georgian house, gracefully composed with a
broad two-storey façade of seven bays in smooth render with
a small Tuscan portico in the centre, later enlarged to nine bays
by the addition of slightly lower, quoined wings with tripartite
windows. Inside, the arrangements are much more haphazard,
reflecting a more complicated if not downright eccentric evolution that eventually thwarted the efforts to maintain the compo-
sure of the exterior.

The core of the present building began as a more modest
gabled-ended brick house of five bays with a basement. It was
probably built for Thomas Clarke, in whose will, dated 1705, the
house at Ardress is first mentioned. The surviving butt-purlin
roof, of a kind similar to those of C17 Ulster houses like Springhill
in Co. Londonderry and Waringstown in Co. Down, confirms the
early date of the building, and the results of dendrochronological
analysis of its oak timbers, obtained in 2009, give a likely felling
date range for the trees in the last decade of the C17. It appears
on John Rocque's 1755 map of Co. Armagh with two small projections to the rear; these were probably later single-storey additions,
given that a U-plan, unless devised with flankers, is unlikely to
have been conceived for an end-gable block of this kind.

In 1760 Sarah Clarke married the Dublin architect *George
Ensor*, a clerk of works in the office of the Surveyor General
whose brother John was assistant to Richard Castle. Employed
on the Archbishop's Palace at Armagh in 1769–75, Ensor had
succeeded to the Ardress property in 1778 and is known to have
been resident by 1783; unsurprisingly he extended the house,
replacing the W projections by building a second gable-ended
block across the rear to form a double-pile plan which accommodated a large drawing room behind the parlour and hall. The
carefully judged portico is probably also to his design. After
Ensor's death in 1803, and before 1811, the house was enlarged
further when the front was extended by two lower wings with
tripartite windows. The parapet, formed at the same time, was
decorated with quirky undulations, waves of dressed stone that
ripple over the copings, punctuated by urns in the centre and
over the wings. Only on the N does the wing form a real building,
accommodating kitchen and bedrooms and given idiosyncratic
tripartite windows on the first floor of a debased Venetian type;
to the S, the 'wing' is merely a wall to give balance to the

composition. One might expect the dining room here; instead it was built to the W, directly behind the drawing room, but bizarrely given no direct communication with the house, originally reached instead by a short conservatory link across the S façade and, informally, by a porch which formerly stood over the back door. Attempts to remedy this poorly conceived arrangement at the time were concentrated on the resulting five-bay S front, which was given greater formality by the addition of quadrant walls, the E one formed against the wall of the original false S wing. The quadrants are handsomely expressed with statuary niches and blind panels and given quoined terminations, but any ingenuity in the design is let down by the awkward prominence of the end gables. The busts in the niches depict the Seasons, with 'Spring' a signed work by *Christopher Hewetson*.

Inside, the original tripartite plan, one room deep, remains evident. The stairs are to one side at the rear; although renewed, they may well originally have been in this position. Today the narrow hall opens on one side into an inner hall through an archway formed in the late C18 to absorb the small room to the N. The parlour lies on the opposite side. Directly reached from here, and the hall, is the late C18 drawing room. This is the best domestic interior in South Ulster, a grandly scaled room with delicate plasterwork enrichments that offer an unexpected display of Neoclassical sophistication – a sample of the Dublin town house transmitted to the provinces by Ensor and almost certainly the design, if not the work, of the stuccodore *Michael Stapleton*. The flat ceiling is a tripartite composition comprising a large circle set between demi-lunes, inspired by George Richardson's *A Book of Ceilings, Composed in the Style of the Antique Grotesque* (1774–6). The large figurative centrepiece depicts Aurora in a two-horse chariot. Oval figurative overdoor panels, and large medallions – Cupid bound to a tree, after Angelica Kauffmann, and Hercules at the Crossroads – on the walls, each garlanded with superfine husk chains and arabesques. Smaller ovals on either side of the chimneypiece depict Ceres and Bacchus. The dining room is similarly proportioned, which might well suggest it was a contemporary creation; its original decoration is unknown, the modest cornice and frieze having been inserted *c.* 1960 as part of restoration works by *Robert McKinstry*. Good C18 dog-leg stairs with carved bracket ends to the treads and slender turned balusters, two to each tread. The half-landing leads into the C19 wing. The small attic stairs rising from the main landing have a balustrade of chinoiserie trelliswork, significantly a form of carpentry used exclusively for secondary stairs in the speculative houses built in Dublin by *Stapleton*.

THE ARGORY
AH

From its commanding situation, looking down on the broad, easy meander of the River Blackwater, The Argory presents the benign façade of a large and unusual Greek Revival house. Built predominantly of Caledon sandstone, now weathered to a dirty beige, it was begun in 1819 for Walter MacGeough, whose family had acquired the lands here in 1740. Its origins are a little unusual too, for despite being a younger son MacGeough had inherited Drumsill House near Armagh (demolished) but was prevented from living there by his father's will, which gave precedence to his spinster sisters. Without waiting for his sisters to marry, die, or oblige him, he decided to establish himself here at Derrycaw, commissioning a new house from *Arthur & John Williamson*, an elusive architectural partnership formed by brothers who were closely related to Francis Johnston and in whose office John Williamson had, for a time, served as a drawing clerk. Importantly, Johnston provides a link between the Williamsons and MacGeough, since he had produced designs for Drumsill in 1805, and as building of The Argory advanced in 1823 he had even stepped in to arbitrate in a dispute with the mason, *Robert Ballantine Sen.* In point of design, however, The Argory is a building largely free of Johnston's exacting classicism, its approach more decidedly personal, even mannered. Since 1979 it has been a property of the National Trust.

As it stands today, the house is a squat, oblong block, two storeys tall, with two opposing fronts of seven bays, plainest to the E, unrelieved but for a boxy porch added in the 1830s, and a tripartite window set above it. The contrasting W façade, which was intended as the entrance front, is of finely channelled ashlar, emboldened on the corners with strip quoins of V-channelled rustication; the three central bays step forward uneasily in two stages, each phase emphasized by the quick staccato of the clean-lined cornice and blocking course. All the elaboration is given to the narrow central bay, with a playful use of Greek Revival detail – simple and unaffected in the treatment of the horned pediment, but of undisputed sophistication in the academic handling of the Doric portico embedded in the wall. Here crisply fluted columns of pale Armagh limestone stand engaged on the corners, supporting a full entablature; then rather than further columns, the entrance is brought forward in a solid block of clean ashlar. Here the tripartite doorcase, of the kind favoured by *Thomas Duff*, who was employed here as executant architect, is formed under a wide, elliptical arch with a deep concave moulding; strange in itself, but as if to emphasize by contrast the overall restraint in the design, a carved lion's head projects as a keystone, with a resplendent acanthus leaf issuing from its mouth. The same quirky mind is at play in the decoration of the tripartite window above, its lugged architrave coming alive with foliate carving, applied solely to the scrolled terminals and the inner surfaces of the lugs. On both floors, the original twelve-pane windows flanking the breakfront were lengthened by one pane later in the C19, increasing the peculiarity of the façade.

Most of the building was completed by 1824. When the architects exhibited their designs at the Royal Hibernian

Academy in 1826 the work in progress referred to seems to have concerned the service wing. Though not a part of the original concept, this must have been an early amendment, given that the main block has no basement storey, only a small wine cellar. Set back on the W front, the wing extends to the N; it was built in at least two phases, with an octagonal library over the kitchen linked to the house by a passage. Enlarged to the E, possibly by *Thomas Turner*, who had made proposals to enlarge the house in 1856, it was destroyed by fire in 1898 and rebuilt on a much reduced scale.

The interior of the house has an abiding atmosphere emanating from the retention of original contents and of old decorative schemes. The architecture itself is rather understated, the plan a straightforward double pile, divided axially by a corridor which extends into the wing to achieve an impressive length. Two entrance halls form the main axis, that to the W flanked by the Drawing Room and Dining Room, that to the E by the Study and back stairs on one side and by the Billiard Room on the opposite side. Rooms are simply treated with moulded cornices, some ceilings later enriched with fussy Louis Quatorze-style centrepieces. Of *Thomas Turner*'s proposals for the house in the 1850s, only his advice to 'put dressings over doors in all principal rooms' was followed. This accounts for the bold Victorian decorations, even upstairs, mainly composed of crisp Greek scrolls, but with further elaboration in the West Hall and Drawing Room, and given fruit-filled scallop shells in the Dining Room. The best chimneypieces, of Carrara marble with Greek Doric columns, have sculpted tablets: in the Drawing Room the Death of Cleopatra and, appropriately, Ceres in the Dining Room.

The spacious East Hall was formed out of the Morning Room in the 1830s when the main entrance was shifted from W to E (internally both halls are equally prominent and still in use). It is noteworthy for its chimneypiece of black Belgian marble and for the large plaster frieze over the inner door depicting a battle with the Amazons, cast in Scotland, copied, it is believed, from the Temple of Athena Nike in Athens. Architecture triumphs only in the West Hall, formed with a bowed end to receive the cantilevered Portland stone stair, described in 1821 as a 'geometrical bracketed staircase', for which *John Dwyer* of Upper Camden Street in Dublin was paid £64. It is fitted with brass balusters, popular at this time, which give an air of unquestionable sophistication, made even more sumptuous by the walls painted to imitate Siena marble. At the foot of the stairs, set into the chequered stone pavement, is the original cast-iron stove, an exquisite Greek pedestal design topped by a copy of the Warwick Vase signed by *E. Thomason*, for which the Williamsons produced a design in 1821 that still hangs in the house.

The staircase rises to an airy landing, extending through the central axis, lit at either end by big tripartite windows, the entire space conceived for the large cabinet barrel organ by

James Bishop. Though commissioned for the house in 1822, it awkwardly cuts into the side of one of the shallow vaults formed at either end of the space. The ceiling enrichments are possibly the work of *Patrick* or *Thomas McAnaspie* – one or other almost certainly the stuccodore recommended by Thomas Duff as the 'principal stucco plasterer in Belfast'. If so, their work here is noticeable only in the odd key pattern to the soffit bands around the landing.

Behind the wing, an extensive group of enclosed YARDS extends to the E, entered formally through an arched GATEWAY in ashlar, topped by an imposing classical urn. This is likely to be the *Williamsons*' work, though *H. Brownlees* is known to have produced a design for the offices in the 1820s, and other, more substantial additions were made in the late C19. The buildings vary from low vernacular ranges in red brick with quarry glazing to more imposing blocks in stone. Of these the finest is the free-standing STABLE BLOCK of 1820, two storeys with five bays, built in limestone ashlar with rusticated quoins and a pedimented frontispiece on two fronts. A substantial domed cupola rises over the roof, one side inset with a clock by *Waugh & Son*.

Adjoining the yards to the N the ramparted FORMAL GARDEN forms part of a scheme laid out by the *Williamsons* in 1821, originally intended to be overlooked by a stable block on a grand scale, designed with herbaceous borders, lawns, paths and two impressive yew arbors. To the N two identical PAVIL-IONS set diagonally on the ends of the curved rampart; rising from sloping bastions of rock-faced masonry, each is a delight-ful square block with rusticated quoins, geometric glazing, and a pyramid roof with polygonal central stack.

The GATE LODGES by the two principal entrances are similar designs of 1835 by *Duff*, who continued to be employed here long after the completion of the house. Small gable-ended blocks of three bays in red brick with frilly bargeboards and gabled porches on granite columns projecting from the centre. Duff's design for a small Ionic temple – perhaps intended as a chapel – appears not have been executed.

On the edge of the demesne, THE ARGORY SCHOOLHOUSE of 1817 is a quaint single-storey block of mottled red brick built in Flemish bond. A long front of five bays: three sashes to the centre with glazing distinguished by small diamond panes in the intersections; matching entrances at each end, the doors flanked by tall narrow side-lights.

Across the road on rising ground is the former LAND STEWARD'S HOUSE. An endearing small house, roughcast over brick, built in 1698 according to the inscription on the plain carved door surround. A gable-ended block of two storeys, with a lower return forming an L-plan. Three-bay front with twelve-pane sashes and a small oval window on the first floor, Neoclassical in form, with webbed glazing bars.

INTRODUCTION

9   Armagh city, the ecclesiastical capital of Ireland, rises on a prom-
     inent outcrop of limestone and sandstone conglomerate in a lush
     undulating landscape between the Callan and Ballynahone rivers.
     Its name is derived from the Irish *Ard Macha*, 'the height of the
     plain', and here St Patrick is said to have founded a church in
     the mid C5. The association with Ireland's patron saint has
     ensured Armagh's pre-eminence amongst ecclesiastical sites in
     Ireland, endorsed by two proud cathedrals, both dedicated to
     Patrick. As with so many Ulster towns, the pattern of violent
     disturbance over centuries means the architectural history of the
     place must be told from a variety of written descriptions and old
     images rather than an interpretation of standing physical remains.
     Leaving aside the ecclesiastical eminence and geographic quali-
     ties that contribute so much to its character and development,
     in architectural terms the appearance today is largely the product
     of the Late Georgian era, resulting in a town easily placed
     amongst the most attractive and well-preserved in Ulster.
         Patrick's association with Armagh seems tentative, but it has
     endured, not least through C7 Irish texts about the saint con-
     tained in the Book of Armagh, which helped promulgate his cult

Armagh, view of the town looking west.
Chromolithograph by W. H. Unger, 1863

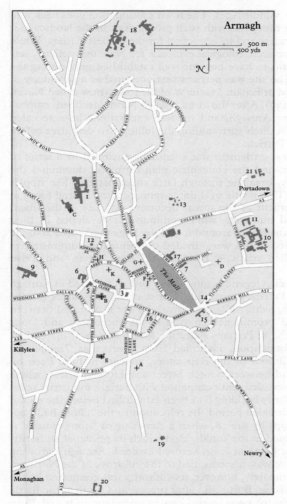

Armagh

500 m
500 yds

Portadown

Killylea

Monaghan

Newry

A	Franciscan Friary	6	County Infirmary (former)
B	St Patrick's Cathedral (C of I)	7	Armagh County Museum
C	St Patrick's Cathedral	8	Royal School
D	St Mark's Church (C of I)	9	St Catherine's College, former
E	St Malachy's Church		Convent of the Sacred Heart
F	First Presbyterian Church	10	Tower Hill Hospital
G	Mall (Scotch) Presbyterian		(former Workhouse)
	Church	11	Shiels Almshouses
H	Methodist church	12	Cornmarket (former)
J	Gospel Hall	13	Observatory
	(former Masonic Hall)	14	Savings Bank (former)
K	Presbyterian church (former)	15	Gaol (former)
		16	Dobbin House
1	St Patrick's Grammar School	17	Charlemont Place
2	Courthouse	18	St Luke's Hospital
3	Market House (former)	19	Archbishop's Palace and
4	Theatre		Chapel
5	Armagh Public Library	20	Palace Farm
		21	Dean's Hill

through the Middle Ages. The town's foundation goes back well beyond that time, and with such prominence in the landscape it is easy to understand its attraction for the earliest settlers. While there is some archaeological evidence for Neolithic activity, settlement seems to have become well established only during the Iron Age. The site was perhaps first occupied as a subsidiary of the royal seat at Emain Macha w of the town (now called Navan Fort: *see* p. 139). After the CI B.C., when Navan declined, emphasis shifted to Armagh, and modern excavations have revealed evidence of a ditch surrounding the hilltop two centuries before the time of Patrick.

The earliest settlement was eventually encircled by a series of oval ditches, and the concentric plan form still dominates the layout today, breaking through later street patterns like ripples on a pond. This gentle oval dome remained the central focus in the development of the town, becoming the site of the major ecclesiastical buildings, while communities developed in their shadow on the slopes around it and the large market place to the E. The settled slopes were divided into thirds as administrative districts called trians – Trian Mór, Trian Masan and Trian Saxan.

The Patrician legend begins with a church founded in Armagh in 445 as Patrick spread his Christian mission amongst the remote Irish, living '*in ultimis terrae*'. Its site is disputed between the elevated prominence enjoyed by its successors and lower ground to the E. Perhaps reflecting local resistance, the earliest Christian foundation, identified from sources as *Teampul na Fearta* or Church of the Repository, appears to have been on lower ground between Scotch Street and Dobbin Street, where excavation revealed that occupation with burials, industrial activity and masonry building had been established before the end of the Early Christian period. Its relocation to the hilltop had happened perhaps by the C8, when a *daimhlaig* or 'stone church' is first mentioned in the annals, after which its primatial authority, for the time being at least, seemed assured. Armagh's growing pre-eminence was, it seems, tied to the influence of the Northern Ui Neill; ultimately, however, its authority was confirmed by the High King, Brian Boru, who after success and death at the Battle of Clontarf in 1014 was carried here in splendour for burial. Even so Armagh's primacy would remain controversial, repeatedly challenged by archbishops of Dublin beyond the Middle Ages, and although its archbishops had been styled Primate of All Ireland since 1365 the matter was only definitively settled in Armagh's favour by Charles I.

Whatever the substance of the foundations here, their early history, as is so often the case with the early Church in Ireland, is told through a pattern of waste and re-edification. In addition to accidental conflagrations, there were the Viking incursions of the C9 and C10. The worst event was in 1020, when the *Annals of the Four Masters* record that the *daimhlaig mór* or 'great stone church', round tower, and two other churches were destroyed, along with their valuable possessions: all was burnt, including the fort, 'without the saving of any house within it, except the library'. Today, nothing even rebuilt after this event survives.

For almost two centuries the head of the church in Armagh had been a layman, until Cellach in the early C12 took holy orders and eventually became the first archbishop. In his time an abbey was founded in 1126 for regular canons of the order of St Augustine; dedicated to SS Peter and Paul, it was until the Dissolution considered to be one of the best of Armagh's buildings. Cellach chose as his successor Malachy, another reformer, who regained the secular properties of the church in 1134. In the second half of the C13 Archbishop Maelpatrick O'Scannail founded the first cathedral on the present site, a building described in 1553 by Lord Chancellor Cusack as 'one of the fairest churches in Ireland'. O'Scannail also built a Franciscan friary outside the town, of which the battered ruin remains. A castle is said to have been built by the Lord Deputy Maurice Fitzgerald in 1236, on a site midway along Castle Street, but nothing is evident there now.

There were intermittent incursions until the end of the C17. Gradually Armagh became a province divided between N and S, Irish and English, restricting the archbishops' jurisdiction outside the English Pale and making Termonfeckin their normal place of residence until the death of James Ussher in 1656. There and later at Drogheda, the archbishops resided safely *inter Anglicos*, among the English, with Armagh administered by the dean, who lived within the town *inter Hibernicos*, among the Irish.

The status of Armagh was reduced by the Dissolution, and diminished even further by the wars against Shane O'Neill. Thomas Radclyffe, Earl of Sussex, destroyed the town in 1557, sparing only the Cathedral, and fortified the site with 'strong raths and impregnable ramparts' as a forward base before the establishment of Charlemont further N. In the same year, the last prior of SS Peter and Paul finally surrendered the Abbey buildings and gardens, then consisting of a large church, some stone chambers, a cellared dormitory, hall, storehouse, and a great court. In 1566 Shane O'Neill burned the town and the Cathedral, leaving it 'foully defaced', seemingly more as a protest against the appropriation for military use of the hallowed ground of the O'Neills – the Archbishop reported that 'he alledgyed such hurtes as were before done to his contrey' – than for any strategic advantage. Before the end of the century, the beginning of the Nine Years War of O'Neill and O'Donnell against the English brought further depredations, reducing the Cathedral to a battered totem over the 'miserable' town. There was little for O'Neill to claim after his defeat of the Queen's army at the Yellow Ford in 1598 and the surrender of the English surrounded in Armagh, and still less to abandon to Lord Mountjoy's advance in 1601. The vivid depiction of Armagh in 1602 by Richard Bartlett, cartographic chronicler for Mountjoy's campaign, shows just a small cluster of cabins standing between the partly roofed Cathedral and the imposing roofless ruins of the Abbey and the church of St Columba to the N of it. Otherwise this desolate 'city of the dead' lay in heaps of rubble, with streets stripped to bare foundations. The desolation was still evident in 1610, when William Camden noted that 'noting remaineth . . . but very few small watled cotages, with the ruinous walles of the monasterie, Priorie, and Primats pallace'.

When the county was shired in 1586 by Sir John Perrot, Armagh's central position had ensured its designation as the county town, but only when English power eventually forced the Irish threat further N, beyond Charlemont Fort, did its future look promising. Thomas Blennerhasset concurred with Camden in 1610, describing it as 'a most base and abject thing' so undefended as to be unable to 'restrain the violence of the wolf' – but he could believe, somewhat presciently, that 'were it a defended corporation it would soon be rich and religious'. Armagh was incorporated in 1613, but was poorly resourced at first. The civil administration was complicated by ownership: Armagh was deemed to belong to the primacy, with the exception of about six acres. The lands associated with the Abbey and *Teampull na Fearta* had been deliberately taken out of ecclesiastical control and ceded to the Crown after the Dissolution, and in 1619 they were granted to Sir Toby Caulfeild and Sir Francis Annesley respectively. Each estate was held independent of the archbishop's control; they were known at the end of the century by the titles bestowed on the grantees' descendants as 'Viscount Charlemont's liberty' and 'the Earl of Anglesea's liberty'. The archbishops as majority owners tenaciously maintained their rights to markets and fairs, asserting their power over the administration and developing the town through agents known as sovereigns. The sovereigns were to keep a steady tiller on urban improvements, and most did that in earnest, though not always without personal advantage. Through much of C17 the Dawson family, descendants of Archbishop Ussher, filled this role, acquiring the seneschalship of the manor of Armagh almost as a hereditary entitlement until Archbishop Lindsay challenged their hegemony in 1714.

Both the archbishop and the owners of liberties encouraged urban development. Armagh was something of an anomaly in the Plantation project, since most of the tenants were native Irish. In 1615 ninety-eight houses were recorded, rising to 123 in three years. As the new town evolved the concentric pattern of the early settlement was preserved, with little deviation, in the street plan: Callan Street and Castle Street to the S follow the form of the inner enclosure, while the outer ditch is clearly defined by Abbey Street to the NW and Navan Street to the SW. Though far short of a wholesale renewal, important measures were initiated by Archbishop Hampton soon after incorporation. His intention to 'replant and re-edify' a town of 'ruinous edifices, creats [huts] and old walls' is demonstrated in a lease to his seneschal, Edward Dodington, which empowered tenants to build English gabled houses of brick or stone with roofs of sawn oak, of which eight had been built by 1622. Some were occupied by members of the Cathedral chapter; of these the best was the rector's, described in 1703 as a two-storey block with attics built of 'extraordinary good brick'. Caulfeild had already effected a settlement on the site of the Abbey of SS Peter and Paul, utilizing part of the ruins to form a 'strong and convenient' house in a bawn with gardens and orchards where he installed a kinsman, and settled fifteen English families in nearby houses.

But violence returned. During the rebellion in 1642 the town, including the cathedral and the recently restored archbishop's residence to the w of it, suffered destruction that seemed as absolute as at any time before. At the end of the C17 the archbishops slowly re-established their authority, though still guiding progress from afar. Early recovery was at first apparent around the broad sloping market place, where a new market house had been erected in 1664, and large houses arose in Scotch Street along the E approach. When the new century opened, there was a sense that architectural fashions were coming up to date: Thomas Ashe, in a survey of the town for Archbishop Narcissus Marsh in 1703, noted oak-framed sash windows on a building in the Market Place (Market Street).

The development of other denominational churches was naturally restricted by the control of the Established Church over most of the town, and eventually it was only facilitated by leases from the holders of liberties. The earliest concentration developed rather fittingly around Abbey Street. The Presbyterian congregation were first, established in 1676 on Dawson land in English Street. They leased adjacent ground on Abbey Street from the 2nd Viscount Charlemont in 1712, and in 1722 built a new church using fabric from the Abbey. The Wesleyans built a church nearby in 1786, while the Catholics leased lands on the Anglesea estate for the original St Malachy's Church, built in Carpenter's Gothic style on what became Chapel Lane.

While the natural dome remained a strong physical character- 9 istic in the evolving street plan, the straight Ogle Street and Thomas Street, created in the 1750s to connect Irish Street and Scotch Street, failed to echo its elegant, generous curves. They did however open up the SE corner of the town to development, advanced in the early C19 by Leonard Dobbin, who had acquired the Anglesea estate. This established a new thriving commercial area which remains so today in these attractive intimate streets.

Archbishop Richard Robinson's decision to establish a primatial residence is the most important event in the architectural history of the town. If Patrick is the towering figure in the early history of Armagh, Robinson, appointed to the see in 1765, tends to be seen as his equivalent in the modern period. His shaping of the careers of Thomas Cooley and Cooley's protégé, Francis Johnston, is arguably Robinson's greater legacy to architectural history.

While his reputation is certainly not undeserved, in most sources it tends to be exaggerated, built largely around Arthur Young's claim that the Archbishop had found Armagh 'a nest of mud cabbins' and endeavoured to create 'a well-built city of stone and slate'. At the time of Robinson's arrival it is estimated that of five hundred or so houses most were still thatched or shingled and only three had slate roofs. Certainly most subsequent visitors were struck by a sense of 'co-ordinated civility': when the Rev. Daniel Beaufort, always a critical observer, visited in 1787 he found it 'improved with many good houses', though not yet handsome. The growth of the Georgian town under Robinson is most evident in the improved housing stock, which trebled between 1770 and 1831 to 1,570 houses. Sir Charles Coote in 1804 found 'the streets being principally rebuilt on a regular elevation, and the houses neatly slated, almost all of them having marble window stools [sills], doorcases, and parapets or eve [eaves] courses'. Not as numerous today as once they were, these orderly terraces, so often pleasing and unpretentious like those on Dobbin Street or along the elegant arc described by Castle Street, typify the unified approach to urban planning that characterizes Georgian towns.

When Young visited in July 1776 he was brought around personally by the Archbishop to view his improvements, which the agriculturalist deemed had 'perfectly changed the face of the neighbourhood'. Robinson was indeed responsible for most of the best buildings, many designed by *Cooley*, as well as improving sanitation by sinking wells, making sewers and paving the streets. On the other hand, his restoration of the Cathedral was at best partial, so that the financial burden of that project passed to his successors. The Rev. John Wesley, who viewed Robinson's buildings in 1787, was naturally a little more disdainful, and considered that in lieu of preparing for heaven Robinson gave too much time to works of temporal utility. The most imposing structure, that kicked off his programme of building in about 1768, was the new Archbishop's Palace, a free-standing block, where he first seems to have employed *Davis Ducart*, but which may actually be by *George Ensor*. Its sobriety certainly anticipates the serious architectural mood of the Late Georgian buildings in the town.

Robinson's single most important act in shaping the expansion of the town was the enclosure in 1773 of the common, a coffinshaped area on low ground to the E where the perimeter had been used as a hippodrome in the C18. This became the long pointed oval called the Mall, lined with buildings on its E and W sides. Once the Courthouse and County Gaol had been completed, addressing each other down the length of the Mall with a parish church as a referee between them, the E side of the old town became a new, polite precinct, with the most important civic and domestic buildings collected here; later in the C19 a workhouse and almshouses joined the existing Royal School in the area of College Hill, and the infantry barracks still crowns the top of Barrack Hill. Robinson eventually abandoned Armagh in 1786; by then ennobled as Baron Rokeby, he retired to England, never to return until his burial ten years later. He never abandoned his dream of making Armagh a university town; but while the ambition continued after his death through a handsome legacy, it was ultimately never redeemed.

As the C18 progressed the market for linen became increasingly vital to the economy of the town, and while milling became prominent in the environs along the River Callan, Armagh never gained the heavy industrialized processes that characterized other prominent linen centres such as Portadown and Lurgan. Henry Inglis observed in 1834 that the town still retained 'evidences not merely of wealth, but of what some would call gentility, for want of a better word'. As a consequence of this distinction the C19 expansion of Armagh was never hurried or especially extensive, even after the arrival of the railway in 1848.

Today the qualities of Georgian Armagh rely as much on materials as on architecture. While some buildings of the Late Georgian period, such as the town houses on Russell Street, are faced in brick, it is predominantly built in grey-to-pale-pink Drumarg conglomerate, attractive for its striking appearance and easily worked (now perhaps too often associated with poorer quality stonework, exposed where historic renders have unwisely been stripped off). The stone is found in a vein surrounding the city, and was quarried at Drumarg Down. The local pale grey Armagh limestone, most extensively quarried at Navan, is in contrast a hard and dense material greatly resistant to weathering, ideally suited as a freestone and superbly employed in most of the public buildings for beautifully crisp ashlar. Nowhere is this better demonstrated than on the hard cliff-like C19 town houses of Charlemont Place. The stone is best seen in suffused autumn sunlight, rarely with greater brilliance than on the gaunt profile of the Roman Catholic Cathedral.

The ancient ecclesiastical traditions of Armagh were spectacularly revived in the C19, beginning with the restoration of the medieval cathedral in 1834, and followed a few years later by the decision of the Catholic Primate to relocate to Armagh and found a new cathedral. Today the historic traditions are maintained by these commanding edifices, enjoying shared prominence by keeping a respectful distance on neighbouring hills.

Armagh was given official city status in 1994. Today its architectural character remains overwhelmingly Georgian, with some unimposing Victorian improvements where the churches alone constitute the chief deviations. Rarely is modern architecture kind to the fabric of a historic town, and in Armagh building plots vacated by bomb blast or economic atrophy have been too hurriedly filled, chiefly with commercial premises that are disruptive, unsophisticated and altogether unworthy of the place.

CATHEDRALS AND ASSOCIATED BUILDINGS

ST PATRICK'S CATHEDRAL (C OF I)

Introduction

In connection with the Viking raids beginning in the C8, the *Annals of Ulster* confirm the existence of a *daimhlaig* or 'stone church' in Armagh as early as 789. Its site is not identified, nor is the location of the 'great stone church' (*daimhlaig mór*) mentioned in association with its burning in 1020, but it is reasonable to assume that it occupied this site. The only impression of its architectural character comes from the description in the *Annals of Ulster* of a nave and chancel, together 140 ft (some 43 m) long. According to the *Annals of the Four Masters* that church was repaired in 1125 after more than a century of partial dereliction; rebuilt in 1145, it was substantially rebuilt again from 1266 by Archbishop O'Scannail to the present plan with aisles and transepts. Repaired by Milo Sweetman a hundred years later, this building appears to have survived the longest, and its ghost endures within the present fabric, most evident in the crypt, which seems to be a largely unaltered medieval construction. In this low vaulted space Archbishop Fleming stored the valuables of the church in 1406 and offered the greater part of it to the citizens of Armagh for the protection of 'lawful and reputable objects'.

It was indeed a secure place, unimpaired by an accidental fire in 1428, even resisting the persistent traumas of the Tudor age. But in 1538, following the Dissolution, St Patrick's crozier, *Bachal Isa*, the 'Staff of Christ', was publicly burnt, and in 1561 Sir William Fitzwilliam adapted the church for victuals, with Lord Sussex reinforcing it in 1563. In the same year the building was briefly restored to Shane O'Neill by the Queen in exchange

Armagh, St Patrick's Cathedral (C of I).
Watercolour by Daniel Grose, *c.* 1830

for loyalty, but it was O'Neill who brought about lasting destruction to the medieval fabric when he burned the Cathedral and
town three years later rather than yield its strategic advantage to
the Crown. Adam Loftus, who had been appointed archbishop
in 1562, despaired of the situation, complaining that he 'could
do no good in his see, as it lieth among the Irish, and produces
but £20 a year for a bare house and eighty acres of ground at
Termonfeighan'; in 1567 he successfully sought translation from
Armagh to Dublin. Efforts were made to repair the building, but
at the end of the century it was still for the most part 'ruined,
broken down and defaced'.

With its spiritual upkeep neglected, the portions of the
Cathedral still roofed in 1595 were occupied by General Sir John
Norris, who raised a parapet to make it defensible and filled it
with a garrison of two hundred men. It remained sufficiently
secure for the defeated Crown forces to retreat to in 1598, carrying with them the body of Sir Henry Bagenal, Marshal of the
Army in Ireland, killed at the Battle of the Yellow Ford, whom
they buried in the s transept before abandoning the site to
O'Neill.

Archbishop Hampton commenced the rehabilitation of the
tattered building in 1613, and diverted church revenues towards
repairs which included raising a new crossing tower and roofing
the aisles, where he inserted 'fayre' windows. But this was only
a temporary reprieve, for the Cathedral was burned again during
the unrest of 1642. It was comprehensively restored between 1663
and 1675 by Archbishop Margetson, and this must largely have
been the structure inherited by Archbishop Beresford before the
early C19 restoration. Jonas Blaymire's engraving of the s eleva-   *p. 11*
tion in 1739 shows a venerable, largely unembellished structure
on a cruciform plan, plainest around the transepts and choir, with
sweeping candle-snuffer roofs over the heavily buttressed and
battlemented aisles. The tower shares its proportions with the
present one, rising above the ridge in a single stage with just one
bay; a corner ogee window is shown in the spandrels below,
a detail of Margetson's C17 tower that is still in evidence on the
tower today.

The most significant C18 alterations were in 1761: they involved
walling off the aisles and effecting a separation of the s transept
from the body of the church, which was newly entered from a
doorway opened beside the transept. The internal arrangements
remained like this until the Cathedral was closed in 1834. When
Richard Robinson was translated to the see in 1765, he reordered
the s aisle for morning service; the Rev. Daniel Beaufort explained
that it was fitted up as a parish church because the choir was
considered too small. Robinson also slated the nave, suggesting
that it had been shingled. Much more drastic was his removal of
the tracery windows, assumed to have been those of 1613: other
than Blaymire's, none of the known views of the building before
the C19 restoration suggests any surviving tracery in the nave,
instead confirming that the openings were filled with 'inelegant
lights', which from appearances were gridded metal frames. In

1782 an ambitious two-stage tower by *Thomas Cooley*, inspired by the tower of Magdalen College, Oxford, began to rise, intended to reach a height of 100 ft (30 m); at 70 ft (21 m) the strain became too much for the arches and piers of the crossing, and Robinson ordered it to be taken back down to its original height. He gave consideration to erecting Cooley's tower over the W end, but abandoned the idea following the architect's death in 1784.

After Lord John George Beresford was translated to the see in 1822 it was probably anxiety about the stability of the old fabric that generated a new sense of urgency. Complete rebuilding was considered, *Thomas Hopper* and the Diocesan Architect *William Farrell* both furnishing designs. Contemporary documents explain the anxieties of the authorities about the 'old decayed building', which they also considered too small. Concluding that the fabric was 'too much decayed and defective in the foundations to admit of repairs or enlargement or any additional weight being put on the foundations', they sought to raise funds to rebuild. Their aims were unsuccessful, ultimately because of concerns over the unsuitability of the existing site, which they were probably unwilling to abandon; discouragement must have followed Farrell's claim that '£3,000 must be buried under ground' just to make the site suitable. In 1831 the Dean, James Jackson, was still suggesting repairs, hoping Farrell might consider relieving the instability by replacing 'the ponderous slating of the roof' with a better material. When in the same year the Dean expressed satisfaction with a plan for restoration prepared by *Lewis Nockalls Cottingham* he revealed the greater extent of his concerns for the structure, believing the proposal for raising the tower just too massive for the old lady to bear. The memory of Cooley's failure was still raw forty years later, when *Francis Johnston* warned that it was 'a dangerous subject' to attempt any considerable works of this kind. The authorities would heed Johnston's warning, leaving Cottingham's evocation of his recently restored tower at Rochester for Armagh a mere pipe dream.

75   Standing aloft in its broad grassy enclosure, the present church is bound to disappoint the antiquarian in expectation of a great medieval cathedral. The works initiated by *Cottingham* in 1834 for Archbishop Beresford involved completely remodelling the architecture, externally encasing the venerable walls of the old shell within a tidier, more coherent mantle. Cottingham restored the cathedrals of Hereford, Rochester and St Albans; Armagh was different, not much larger than a decent English parish church, with an external length of 192 ft (59 m) and width of 128 ft (39 m), and physically in peril. In February and March Cottingham surveyed the fabric, and on 21 May 1834 the Dean laid the foundation stone of the SW pier of the tower. By the time the building re-opened for divine service on 31 January 1840 some £34,000 had been expended, of which only £10,000 came from subscriptions, the balance having been borne by the Archbishop.

The extensive transformation of the fabric illustrates the fact that the older type of 'restoration', even if driven by well-meaning enthusiasm, must stand as a euphemism for destruction. The abiding impression is primarily of a church built entirely anew, and heavily imbued with a sense of an idealized medieval world born of one man's zeal. Chiselled from a toffee-brown sandstone, it stands in contrast to the predominant soft pinks and pale greys of the city. Even if the stone was quarried from Wilson's Bridge not far from the site, there is an unsettling uniformity about it, unexpected for a site of such antiquity, compounded by the fact that in 1840 all the tell-tale undulations of the old graveyard were lost as mounds of earth were carted away in order to lower the ground to the level of the Cathedral floor.

Few commentators congratulated the architect for his work at Armagh. Viewing the Cathedral in 1838, the antiquarian George Petrie, believing that the restorer should have been an 'Irish historical architect and antiquary', accused Cottingham of destroying the antiquity of the building by making it 'a regular English parish church of Tudor architecture, the only style it is probable with which he is acquainted'.

Cottingham's interior ('neat and trim as a lady's drawing room', Thackeray complained in 1842), has been much altered. The High Victorian Gothic Revivalists *R. H. Carpenter & Benjamin Ingelow*, deeply critical of the treatment of the old fabric, in 1886–90 sought to re-establish the ecclesiological integrity by re-ordering and re-fitting the choir and opening it up to the nave, banishing Cottingham's choir screen to the s transept. More extensive alterations of 1902–3 by *Sir Thomas Drew* raised the crossing and reshaped the E end.

Exterior

Seen from the city below, the central authority of the Cathedral is reinforced where the pinnacled E gable with Drew's large traceried window rises powerfully at the apex of the steeply sloping market place. To the visitor entering the railed enclosure from the gateway at Vicars' Hill, on the other hand, the building seems to crouch on the hilltop, an impression given by the low, battlemented crossing tower rising over the ridge in a single stage.

The Cathedral has a straightforward plan: an aisled nave of five bays, with deep two-bay transepts and a deeper three-bay chancel, all routinely buttressed. Its mantle of finely dressed brown sandstone and yellow Penrith sandstone is so neatly homogeneous that only in the upper stages of the tower is there any suggestion that an older structure lies at the core of this building. Emerging in thinly squared courses of Armagh limestone, it contrasts sharply with *Cottingham's* sandstone trimmings below. The tower is essentially Archbishop Margetson's late C17 structure, reworked by *Francis Johnston* after Cooley's ambitious superstructure failed. In restoring the tower to its original (and present) height, Johnston inserted two new bays, restored the battlements, and once again finished it with a stocky timber spire; in 1839 Cottingham had this spire taken down, but otherwise his work on the tower was limited to encasing the spandrels at the base in sandstone, and designing new traceried windows for the belfry.

The chief architectural display is concentrated in the windows. All but the E window are part of the same building programme, with a contrived variety of E.E., Dec and Perp tracery, mullions ranging from slender colonnettes in the transepts to deep chunky profiles in the chancel. Each of the aisle windows is filled with a generous Perp design of three cusped lights with daggers and supermullions to the central light – tracery based on the great window of Westminster Hall, a building central to Cottingham's interest in medieval detail, on which he had published a study in 1822. All were shipped in their entirety from Cottingham's Waterloo Bridge Road premises in London, where *Matthew Frith* supervised the masons.

Otherwise the decoration is limited, and subtly varied, as when the enriched ballflower cornice beneath the eaves parapet of the N transept is exchanged on the S transept for a corbel table in Penrith sandstone, and on the choir the detail is enlarged with a gallery of grotesque heads. Greater architectural consistency is seen in the aisles, where the buttresses are topped with statuary pinnacles; Cottingham intended the aisle walls to have battlemented parapets, simplified from the Irish battlements of the old building. Above is a clerestory of narrow bays with more complicated flowing tracery, introduced by removing the old candlesnuffer roofs that formerly swept over the aisles. These had become decayed by the early C20, and in 1949 *Blackwood & Jury* advised on repairs, though the extent to which their recommendations were followed is unclear.

The transepts have plain lancets and clasping buttresses to the gables, rising into gaunt pinnacles elaborated on the N transept, which houses the chapter room. The N front has a three-light window with heavily cusped tracery above a pointed doorway, deeply recessed, with a single colonnette in the reveals and coats of arms in the spandrels. Plainer elevation to the S, with a lithesome three-light Geometric window under a trefoiled oculus. A sundial of 1706 preserved on the SW buttress, shown in Blaymire's 1739 view, is worthy of attention.

The W front retains the medieval arrangement of three graded lancets, elaborated by Cottingham, under an indented stringcourse, with a deeply moulded pointed doorway below. The aisles flank the gable of the nave with very gently raking parapets between solid clasping buttresses with offsets and tall polygonal pinnacles.

The three bays of the choir are substantially buttressed, as the ground falls away steeply, partly exposing the wall of the crypt. The E front has a low Perp door; the reordered façade above is the work of *Sir Thomas Drew*, who removed the string-course and windows and filled the gable instead with a large Dec window with bristling tracery, an arrangement of five cusped lights in red sandstone, overlaid by heavier mullions rising to hold an inflated trefoil in the apex, all heavily cusped. The buttresses are slender and rise to battlemented pinnacles, given cross-loops, with a toy-like result inconsonant with the seriousness that Cottingham had intended to achieve here.

Interior

None of the evocative gloom or solemnity one might reasonably anticipate: instead, a space that is disappointingly small, and now too brightly painted. Nave and aisles have Tudor-style plaster   23

Armagh, St Patrick's Cathedral (C of I), interior.
Engraving by C. Hullmandell, 1834

ceilings, coved over the nave, ribbed with heavy bosses at the intersections, mostly foliated and some gilded. The plaster decorations too were prefabricated in *Cottingham*'s London workshops. Unfortunately the heightened crossing arch crashes into the ceiling, the result of *Drew*'s early C20 work, making for a sudden change in scale that contributes to the disappointing impression of the nave. The arcade has five chamfered and moulded arches springing from clustered piers, unadorned but for a fillet to the inward-facing shaft, with moulded bell capitals. The general character of the piers was exposed when *Cottingham* removed later thick coats of plaster. A reference in 1837 that piers and arches required a dressing of composition best explains their neat appearance today. Only in the piers integrated in the W wall is there a sense of the older fabric, where the capitals show crude palmate leaves, apparently the 'emblematical sculpture' exposed during restoration.

Cottingham began by strengthening the crossing arches, perhaps as much to receive his projected tower as to stabilize any weakened fabric. He employed ambitious methods, and a 'model of the ingenious contrivance' was displayed at the office of *Mr Smith*, the clerk of the works. Shoring up the structure with timber allowed the crossing piers to be dismantled and rebuilt. A much more intriguing method was required to correct the aisle piers, which leaned substantially outward. The process, based on French experiments and worthy of Viollet-le-Duc, was described in detail by Robert Graham, who witnessed it in 1836 and hailed it as a 'more extraordinary triumph of art': 'By means of iron rods passing thro' the pillars, which were strongly supported and encircled with beams of wood, closed round them with iron bands, the pillars were gradually drawn into their right position by the application of heated charcoal to the iron rods which insensibly drew them into the true perpendicular.' This was apparently attempted only after the lower parts of the piers had been given new foundations and entirely renewed.

23   In 1903 *Drew* raised the flat panelled ceiling in the crossing to improve acoustics and gave it a timber groin-vault. The N and S arches were raised and enriched with applied shafts and stiff-leaf capitals. In the chancel he lined the walls with stone instead of Cottingham's lath and plaster, and removed the plaster tierceron rib-vault, replacing it with a simpler timber-panelled one; in enlarging the E window he removed flanking statuary niches that Cottingham had in 1837 filled with statues of SS Peter and Paul, disdained by Beresford and removed.

76   In the S transept, the REGIMENTAL CHAPEL of 1950 by *George Pace* is an attractive space with altar and reredos of gilded mahogany in a refined, slender classical style. Box pews are arranged on a podium around a central carved stone plinth. Cottingham's choir screen at the S end.

The CRYPT is a low, oblong space beneath the chancel measuring 60 by 24 ft (18.2 by 7.3 m). It is divided into a nave and aisles with five stout polygonal piers on either side, built of rubble and coarsely rendered. Cottingham believed these to be C18 but they support shallow rubble vaults, which in the E end of the aisles reveal evidence of wattle-and-daub construction consistent with a medieval origin. Evidence for pointed openings in the E wall.

Furnishings

Two richly carved C17 oak chairs in the Lady Chapel are the oldest furnishings. The most important of the two is known as the BRAMHALL CHAIR, its surfaces covered with guilloches and scrolled ornament, and on the splat the archiepiscopal mitre and arms of the see with the date 1661. The LECTERN is a heavy oak eagle raised on a traceried tripod base, probably late C18. Another of brass was presented by Lord Clermont in 1879. *Cottingham*'s furnishings suffered when the choir was rearranged in the late C19 by *Carpenter & Ingelow*. The present THRONE of 1890 by *Bowdler & Co.* of Shrewsbury was installed as a memorial to the Ecclesiologist Alexander Beresford Hope †1887, celebrated as a benefactor of the Church of Ireland (his mother was the cousin of Archbishop Beresford, and his older brother owned Castle Blayney). The canopy is richly carved with a heavily cusped ogee arch, which is repeated in the CHOIR STALLS, also by *Bowdler & Co.* Above the stalls, filling the arch to the N transept, is the ORGAN by *Walker* of London, given by Beresford to replace the one by *Snetzler* gifted by Robinson. Originally under the window of the S transept, it was moved and has grown considerably, while still unremarkably cased with pinnacles and gables. The octagonal PULPIT dates from the 1880s, a standard High Victorian type in Caen stone with red and green polished shafts. The REREDOS of Corsham stone, designed by *George H. F. Prynne* and carved by *H. H. Martyn & Sons*, Cheltenham, was installed in 1913; brightly painted and gilded, it is a little too obvious. In the centre a colourful, vibrant panel of *opus sectile* in painted ceramic, the Last Supper, by *Percy Bacon Bros* of London. Behind, in the Lady Chapel, the stone ALTAR, fronted with a blind arcade of crocketed and cusped ogee arches, is by *Cottingham*, as is the REREDOS, a more modest array of canopied niches than those he designed for Magdalen College and St Albans, now filled with chalk-like statues. The stone here is a grey freestone from Farley Down in Hampshire, suited to abundant, clean decoration. The same stone was used for the former CHOIR SCREEN, now closing off a small vestry at the end of the S transept; it has a wide central door under a heavily cusped arch, decorated niches in the side panels, and open crocketed crestwork. The FONT, set on a stepped base under the W arch of the S aisle, is by *Cottingham*, a polygonal, crisply carved work resting on a polygonal stem with angels under Gothic canopies, the motif copied from the circular body of the original medieval font, taken by Cottingham for his museum of medieval art and regrettably now lost; otherwise it shares with all of Cottingham's furnishings 'an English look' complained of by Petrie. – STAINED GLASS. Glazing for Cottingham's restoration was prepared and packed in London by the architect's cousin, the builder *John Orlibar Cottingham*. Since then most of it has been replaced by bright figurative glass, chiefly after 1850 and of uneven quality, the windows in the S aisles repaired after heavy bomb damage in 1957. In the chancel: E window, The Ascension by *Heaton, Butler & Bayne*, *c*. 1903, replacing a *William Warrington* window of 1849; chancel N wall, W window, *c*. 1896, also by *Heaton, Butler & Bayne*; S wall, the Four Evangelists by *Mrs Harriet Dunbar*, niece of Archbishop Beresford; in the S transept, to Archbishop Beresford, 1864 by *Lavers & Barraud*, the design attributable to *John Milner Allen*; W windows in the aisles by *William Warrington & Son*: S side, the Good Samaritan, 1852, and N, Moses, 1854; N aisle, four early C20 windows all attributed to *Shrigley & Hunt* of Lancaster; S aisle, second (1860) and third (*c*. 1858) windows from E by *Clayton & Bell*, both with crude repairs, fifth window by *James Humphries Hogan* of *James Powell & Son*, *c*. 1925.

Monuments and sculpture

p. 8

NORTH AISLE. Damaged and heavily eroded remains of the MARKET CROSS, an early C10 high cross moved inside from the churchyard in 1916, having been vandalized a century before in the Market Place, where it had been erected in 1763. Apparently one of at least six crosses known to have been in the monastery in the C12, though there is a tradition that in 1439 Archbishop Prene removed a large cross from Raphoe to Armagh. It consists of the baseless shaft, now in two pieces on a modern base, with a fragment of the cross, missing the arcs of its pierced nimbus, resting beside it on the floor. The surfaces have carving, with a number of hollow depressions noticeable on the shaft. The subjects as discernible are as follows. W face of the cross: the Crucifixion and Christ in Glory. E face of the shaft, reading up from the bottom: Adam and Eve, Noah's Ark, the Sacrifice of Isaac, and the Arrest of Christ. W face of the shaft: Annunciation to the Shepherds, Adoration of the Magi, Baptism of Christ. N side panels: the Three Children in the Fiery Furnace, decoration, the Raven brings bread to St Paul and St Anthony, and two standing figures. S side panels: David and Jonathan(?), David and Goliath, and David and the Lion.

64

MONUMENTS. Nathaniel Whaley †1737 and Elizabeth Vincent †1736; a plain marble plaque. – Sir Thomas Molyneux †1733 by *Louis François Roubiliac*. The only Irish memorial by this great C18 sculptor, a sensational statue of the physician Molyneux of the Castle Dillon family, in white marble, resting a large open book on a broken column. Full of Baroque verve, it stands on a pedestal carved with an allegorical relief of sickness, also by *Roubiliac*, interpreted as Molyneux depicted in the role of Aesculapius assisted by Hygeia. Shipped to Ireland in 1752 for an unrealized garden building in Castle Dillon demesne, it was installed here in 1840. – Major Andrew

Craig †1877; an arched tablet with winged angels carved in relief. – Captain Alexander Duke Simpson †1874; a cruciform Gothic plaque signed *Gaffin & Co.* – Lieutenant-Colonel Philip E. Kelly †1918 at Dadizeele, by *Kathleen Shaw*; a bronze tablet framed in a pattern of Celtic interlace. – Dean Peter Drelincourt †1722. A large inscribed plinth in grey marble with a gadrooned lid on which the recumbent figure of Drelincourt rests. The plinth is signed by *W. Coleburne*, London. This is probably the *William Colebourne* (fl. 1694–1727) recorded as working with both John van Nost the Elder and the English-born William Kidwell, who settled in Ireland before 1712. The effigy, a highly engaging and expressive sculptural work, is signed by *John Michael Rysbrack.** – Archbishop Marcus Gervais Beresford †1885 by *John Taylor*; a recumbent effigy. – Archbishop William Stuart †1822 signed by *Sir Francis Chantrey*, 1826. The kneeling primate on a plain plinth: in every sense a pious work. – Dean Francis George Le Poer McClintock †1924; a small Gothic plaque under an enriched hood with foliate stops. – Archbishop Robert Bent-Knox †1893; a marble bust by *Joseph Whithead* on a cusped Gothic arch.

SOUTH AISLE. Arranged on the floor of the aisle a collection of mostly primitive early Irish sculpture, some presumably collected from the site. Remarkable are the so-called 'dogs', a primitive cow- and calf-like pair of animals; the distinctively boisterous Iron Age Tandragee Idol, a primitive torso depicted with one hand raised to the opposite shoulder; and in two pieces a figure with the ears of an ass, posed like a sheila-na-gig. Also a cased collection of carved heads, some from late medieval hoodmoulds like those shown over the aisle windows in late C18 views.

MONUMENTS. Robert Turner †1904; a bronze plaque decorated with Celtic interlace, signed by *Kathleen Shaw*, 1909. – The Rev. Thomas Carpendale †1817 by *John Smyth*. Against a pyramid of grey marble an allegory of Death, a mourning female figure holding a downturned torch, standing on the Bible and resting her arm on an open book on a central winged stand with an elaborate funerary urn and more books; on the opposite side a caduceus, orb, scroll, and two more books (Carpendale was master at the Royal School). – Archbishop Richard Robinson, Lord Rokeby †1794. Above a marble plaque, a portrait bust usually attributed to *Joseph Nollekens*; the setting by *John Bacon the Younger*, 1802. – Archbishop Lord John George Beresford †1862; a recumbent effigy by *Baron Pietro Marochetti*, installed in 1864 under the central aisle bay. – Elizabeth Beresford †1870; brass script in a square plaque richly framed with coloured marbles. – Colonel Samuel Kelly †1806, Colonel William Kelly †1817, and Colonel Dawson Kelly †1837. An exceptionally intricate Gothic design, with

65

p. 7

66

---

* Proposals by *Benjamin Brown* in 1839 to add a margin of black marble and pediment of veined white marble seem not to have been carried out.

canted canopies projecting over the centre brimming with miniature filigree and recessed niches to the side with trumpeting
angels set over knights in medieval armour, by *Cottingham*, who
exhibited designs at the R.A. in 1838. – Thomas Osborne Kidd,
†1855 at Sebastopol; a wide plinth supporting a marble plaque
adorned with an imposing heroic relief signed by *Thomas Farrell*.
– Turner Macan, Persian interpreter to the commanders in chief
in India †1836; a simple Greek stela with acroteria, by *Joseph
Theakston*. – Archbishop William Alexander †1911; a half-length
Churchill-like portrait offering a benediction with a raised arm,
in white marble on a plain plinth, by *Kathleen Shaw*, 1914.

NORTH TRANSEPT CHAPTER ROOM. The earliest memorials
are hidden here beyond the public realm. Two colourfully
painted Carolean plaques to members of the Charlemont
family, in exquisitely decorated frames of sandstone with a
blend of fine Renaissance ornament and Elizabethan strapwork, filled with Latin script and surmounted by the Caulfeild
arms. The smaller one to the N, Elizabeth Caulfeild †1694; the
larger one to the S, William, 1st Viscount Charlemont †1671,
also commemorating his father, William, 2nd Baron Caulfeild
†1640, erected by the 2nd Viscount in 1698. – Between these,
James Caulfeild, 4th Viscount and 1st Earl of Charlemont
†1799, and his family; a densely scripted black marble plaque
of 1883 unworthy of this great art patron, simply adorned with
the Caulfeild arms in white marble. – Joshua McGeough
†1756; large allegorical figure of Hope on a square tablet in
the manner of *Thomas Kirk*. – John Martin Carr †1812; a
plaque with inverted torches at the sides and an urn above, by
J. Robinson, Belfast.

CRYPT. Amongst the discarded fabric and broken monuments
stored here, one fragment of Neoclassical design for the
Rev. Henery (*sic*) Jenney †1758 is signed by *Simon Vierpyl*.
Numerous burials between the piers in the W half, including
Archbishops Robinson and Beresford; also long established
as the burying place of the McGeough-Bond and Caulfeild
families, including the celebrated James Caulfeild, 1st Earl of
Charlemont.

Precincts

In the CHURCHYARD, beside the boundary wall opposite the W
entrance, is a fragment of another HIGH CROSS, sometimes called
St Patrick's Chair, found near here in the late C19. It consists of
a base and a small portion of the shaft with some heavily eroded
sculptural decoration.

VICARS' HILL. An enclave of handsome terraced Georgian
houses to the W of the Cathedral. The first four houses at the
N end were built for clergymen's widows and endowed by
Archbishop Boulter in 1724. The individual two-storey, three-
bay design bears an uncanny resemblance to Plate XI of the

Twelve Designs for Country Houses by the Rev. John Payne of 1757, and may have inspired that. Elegant in their simplicity and proportions, with a preponderance of wall over window; architectural focus is on the doorcases, as in Payne's design, with an emphatic Gibbs surround and angular triple keystones in smooth sandstone. The walls are roughcast, with stone sills and a chunky eaves cornice below big slate roofs. Twelve-pane sashes with diminutive six-pane windows above, cleverly designed to open by disappearing into the wall-head. Archbishop Robinson added three more houses, designed by *Thomas Cooley* and built by 1776, to accommodate the Diocesan Registry and the vicars choral, and in 1780 began the last four. The latter include a music hall, remodelled by *W. J. Barre c.* 1858 and distinguished from the rest by its heavy C19 doorcase with engaged Tuscan columns. The ground falls away to the s, and the end house, built last, in 1794, has three storeys over a sunken basement. Façades of three or five bays; while the windows vary in size and position, all are set in plain blocked limestone surrounds like those of the nearby Infirmary. Doorcases here of a simple design, with Tuscan pilasters in dressed limestone, a moulded archivolt, and small keystones around the fanlight, which in some cases survives as a spoked design.

SEE HOUSE. Cathedral Close. Rebuilt in 2010; a plain exercise in Postmodern Tudor by *Stephen Leighton*.

CHURCH HOUSE. Abbey Street. 1912 by *W. Sampson Jervois* with *R. F. Caulfield Orpen*. A large limestone hall in an Arts and Crafts-inspired Tudor style on a sloping site near the crest of the street. Built as a memorial to Archbishop Alexander, whose arms are displayed on the street front. Set on an exposed basement with wide, steep-pitched gables in rock-faced masonry and ashlar quoins. Large mullioned windows in the gables with hooded segmental heads and five cusped lights. Neat octagonal ridge ventilator on the roof. Inside, the hall occupies the main space above offices and meeting rooms, with a cruciform plan under an impressive groined barrel-vault with wide foliated ribs.

ARMAGH PUBLIC LIBRARY. On the crest of Abbey Street, at the intersection with Callan Street and Cathedral Close. Founded by Archbishop Robinson in 1770 to house his collection of C17 and C18 books, a distinguished Neoclassical block in limestone ashlar, designed by *Thomas Cooley* and opened in 1771. Twice extended, first in 1785, when additional living accommodation was built to the w, and more substantially in 1845, as the only prominent work in the very short career of an architect formally identified only as 'Mr Monserrat', who was placed first in a competition for the design; traditionally thought to be John Monsarrat, he is now identified as *Robert Law Monsarrat*. *Cooley*'s building was a modest but suave gable-ended block on a square plan with a two-storey, three-bay front, recognizable in the three central bays on the N front with their refined eaves entablature. The library was

p. 31

accommodated in the tall upper storey, where round-headed
windows are set in recessed arches with prominent archivolts on
short consoles. These have a boldness that is uncharacteristic of
Cooley. Designs, preserved in the building, show the original
entrance in the centre of the low ground floor; in one unsigned
drawing it was proposed as a pedimented doorcase, flanked by
small Georgian sashes with Gibbs surrounds. Such an old-
fashioned approach to the detail suggests that in his execution
of the building Cooley actually modified an existing scheme,
perhaps by *George Ensor*. The drawings signed by Cooley seem
to indicate as much, simplifying the ground floor, as built, and
proposing to dispense with the consoles for finer Neoclassical
touches around the windows, only partly followed.

In the original layout the entrance was shared between the
ground-floor keeper's lodgings and the library, which was
reached by stairs at the back of the axial hallway. The arrangement must have proved inconvenient: a separate staircase was
built in 1820 at the E end, spoiling the appearance of the building, until *Monsarrat* added a single gently recessed bay at each
end of Cooley's block, simultaneously enlarging the library and
creating a three-bay entrance front and staircase to the E. On
the old front, the new work was united under an extended
modillion cornice, all elaborated with a balustraded parapet.
Cooley's frieze and architrave were not continued, and, as on
the E front, blind attic panels were introduced above the first-
floor windows. The three central windows are linked by
moulded archivolts and flat impost blocks which are not shown
in any of the C18 designs; the recessed panels on which the
windows rest instead of sills are shown in one of *Cooley*'s drawings, and so possibly they are also part of revisions by him to
an earlier scheme. The entire ground floor was remodelled with
channelled rustication; the old N entrance was retained but
simplified, and it and the adjoining windows were sunk in
square-headed recesses with a plain architrave. The architecture of the new E front is more complicated than the old N one,
with a narrow central bay advanced under a pediment where
the frieze and architrave, alluding to Cooley's design, are interrupted by a bold Greek inscription, ψυχης ιατρειον (*pseuches
iatreion*) – literally 'psychiatry', taken here to mean 'the healing
place of the soul'. The first-floor windows have pediments on
scrolled brackets, varied with a wider bay in the centre under
an elliptical arch with a segmental pediment inset with a niche
on a balustraded apron. The doorcase has a thin cornice on
consoles.

Inside, a cantilevered staircase with cast-iron balusters flies
across the back wall and leads directly to the library. The
original designs do not suggest an enriched interior; the
arrangement with a gallery running round all sides is the same
in its enlarged form, but the gallery now has decorative cast-
iron balustrades and is reached from a spiral staircase within
the room. The ceiling is compartmented with an enriched
dentil cornice and palmette frieze in the main panels, bordered

with sunken panels in the soffits that are crammed with acanthus roses and Greek Revival interlace.

CATHEDRAL CLOSE CLERGY HOUSES, inside the E entrance to the churchyard. Of 1855 by *John Boyd* (contractors *McCullough & Ross* of Armagh). A pair of semi-detached houses with a long S front, displaying tall brick chimneys and a prominent crowstepped E gable with the date 1854; limestone, in a vague castellated Tudor style. Refurbished in 1991 by *Leighton Johnston Associates*.

101

ST PATRICK'S CATHEDRAL

Introduction

Nowhere is C19 Catholic triumphalism more evident than in this assertive Gothic church of the primatial see. From its prominent exposed site on top of Sandy Hill, the Cathedral with its twin piercing spires looks across to the hilltop city and the crouching Church of Ireland Cathedral at its apex. (The political and symbolic importance of the building in its relationship to the city determined its orientation: the façade faces S, not W. The traditional liturgical directions will be used in the description that follows.) From its earliest conception in the late 1830s this was to be Ireland's Jerusalem. Today it remains a proud edifice, architecturally evocative of Chartres, while in its setting, atop steep slopes now shaped into rippling grassy terraces and seemingly endless steps, it stands with all the iconic power of the Sacré Cœur in Paris.

Until Emancipation, Catholic archbishops were restricted from coming within 3 miles of the city, but when William Crolly was appointed archbishop in 1835 he seized the opportunity to re-establish his deprived church within the ancient see. The site on *Tealach na Licci*, 'Sandy Hill', was obtained on lands outside the control of the Established Church, leased from the Earl of Dartrey; its location here would later be justified by associating it with the site for a new church providentially revealed by the Saint in the legend of St Patrick and the fawn.

Cottingham when working at Armagh in 1837 had been asked to furnish plans, but the commission went instead to *Thomas Duff*, who began by building a seminary on the E portion of the site in 1838. Two years later the foundation stone for the Cathedral was laid, and building commenced to a design shown in contemporary engravings as a rigid essay in the Perpendicular style. Greatly elaborating on his recently completed Cathedral of Newry, Duff added transepts, twin W towers, and a massive

p. 40

crossing tower to accord with the significance of the building.
The sheer scale of the undertaking was such that *The Builder*
wrote of the immense cost involved in the foundations alone,
which necessitated the soil to be excavated to a depth of as much
as 60 ft (18 m).

Progress was repeatedly halted. From 1845 famine diverted
attention and funds away from the building, and when Thomas
Duff died in 1848, followed by a cholera epidemic in 1849 and
the death of Archbishop Crolly the same year, the impetus was
lost. Crolly's successor Paul Cullen showed no appetite for completing the works, and only after his translation to Dublin in 1852
was any enthusiasm restored. By then the building had been
raised to aisle level, described as 34 ft (10 m) of walls for £26,000,
apparently without any tracery. *J. J. McCarthy* had replaced Duff
in 1851, but work only resumed in 1854, when Archbishop Dixon
designated Easter Monday 'Resumption Monday'. Much had
changed in the intervening period, not least in the progress of
the Gothic Revival, which by then had fully absorbed Pugin's
obsessive manifesto. Although Duff's designs were furnished to
the building committee by his widow, it was natural that
McCarthy would wish to depart from them, preferring a more
idealized C13 French Gothic idiom. The existing fabric obliged
him to follow Duff's plan, a straightforward one with aisled nave,
choir, ambulatory and transepts, with towers flanking the w
front. He dispensed with Duff's signal crossing tower, however,
and most of the Perp paraphernalia – the crocketed pinnacles,
battlemented parapets, and corner turrets to the gables. In trans-
lating English into French, McCarthy disguised minor architectural solecisms largely by redesigning the tracery, notably
with unrepetitive flowing tracery in the clerestory; he also gave
the w towers spires, and by raising the pitch of the roof drew
the proportions heavenward. The contractor was *Thomas
Byrne* of Belfast. By 1859 the building was ready for roofing and
glazing.

When Archbishop Dixon died in 1866 work again stopped,
but the spires were eventually built between 1869 and 1873 by
Archbishop Daniel McGettigan, and the dedication took place
on 24 August 1873. Funds were lacking, however, and work on
completing the interior did not resume until a decade later, when
William Hague was employed by Archbishop Logue to design the
furnishings, including the rood screen, for which Hague sourced
materials and sculptors from Italy. After his death in 1899 work
was continued by *Thomas F. McNamara*, and the interior was
finally completed by *Ashlin & Coleman*. They vaulted the aisles
and in 1904 began a comprehensive scheme of decoration,
executed by *George Wooliscroft & Son* of Staffordshire. Much of
Hague's and McNamara's work was destroyed when the sanctuary was reordered in 1982 by *McCormick, Tracey & Mullarkey*;
reordered again with some improvements in 2003 by *Rooney &
McConville* of Belfast. Extensive conservation of the fabric was
completed in 2003 by *Gregory Architects* of Belfast.

Exterior

Built of pale grey Armagh limestone faintly tinged with pink, quarried from Ballybrannon below Navan Fort. The walls are of punch-dressed ashlar with smooth dressings, nicely evident in the plinth, which has a bulging ogee to the upper moulding that is characteristically Tudor and a reminder of the beginnings in *Duff*'s design. The sheer height of the spires, 210 ft (64 m) tall, gives all the architectural emphasis to the liturgical w front. Here, rising from a podium, is an uncomplicated symmetrical arrangement of twin buttressed towers flanking a large Dec gable window before ascending into hard-edged broach spires with diminishing lucarnes. The doorways are Duff's squared-headed Perp design, larger in the centre with a deeply recessed arch, four slender shafts to the reveals and traceried soffit panels, all brought forward by *McCarthy* and flanked by St Patrick and St Malachy in canopied niches of Dungannon sandstone. Over this a statuary arcade with gabled niches which *Hague* filled with Carrara marble statues of the eleven faithful apostles by *Pietro Lazzerini*. Flanking the door, towering statues of *c.* 1904, also by Lazzerini, of the two archbishops primarily responsible for building the Cathedral, each in white marble on a sculpted Gothic plinth; to the r. William Crolly †1849, with a plan of the building, and to the l. Daniel McGettigan †1887, standing beside a model of the tower. In the simplified tower entrances the hoods terminate in carved headstops, showing St Brigid with St Malachy on one side, and Archbishop McGettigan with St Oliver Plunkett on the other. Above the windows here and on the sides *Duff*'s ogee-shaped hoods survive, noticeably with an uncarved finial to the N.

The aisles are buttressed, with five bays between the towers and transepts. The windows are all traceried with three cusped lights under trefoils. The transepts project by two bays and on the gables have flanking turrets, lower on the w side and converted into clasping buttresses as a deliberate distortion of Duff's design. On each front a wheeled window is set high in the gable above a large Dec window; below, on the N side, another Perp doorway with a handsome panelled architrave.

In front of the Cathedral, the impressive terraced approach with broad flights of steps was completed in 1887. It is possibly the work of the landscape gardener *William Sheppard*, who was at this time laying out the adjoining cemetery.

Interior

Spellbinding, with an atmospheric brilliance owing to the stupendous scale of the tall, narrow nave and a superabundance of shimmering mosaic decoration. Eyes are immediately drawn upwards to the hammerbeam roof, a complicated design with gilded angels projected from the hammerbeams and painted enrichments by *Oreste Amici*, one of a host of Roman artists involved in the decoration, showing the lives of Irish saints in medallions amongst arabesques.

The five-bay nave arcade has moulded arches on tightly clustered piers with crisp capitals and bases. *McCarthy* preferred single, massive piers, but these were in place by the time he assumed responsibility, leaving him to redesign the clerestory and introduce a triforium. Here there are paired cusped arches on polished shafts with foliated capitals. The recesses behind are too shallow; darker decoration would enhance the sense of depth, enough perhaps to suggest a passage. In 1901 *James Kiernan* of Dublin built the tierceron rib-vaults in Bath stone over the aisles and ambulatory, where the crimson tasselled *galeros* of deceased cardinals are eerily suspended in the atmospheric gloom as a *memento mori*. The crossing arch towers over the sanctuary; above it, a mosaic of St Patrick baptizing King Aengus at Cashel. The sanctuary ceiling is groined, decorated with images and texts of the four Evangelists.

Twice reordered, the sanctuary has been at the forefront of post-Vatican II architectural vandalism, destroyed with an uncaring insensitivity to its High Victorian architecture. In the initial reordering of 1982 the interior was denuded of its furnishings, leaving just one side chapel fitted out in the s transept. The entire sanctuary enclosure was opened by removing the mesmerizingly rich marble screens, including the rood screen, and on a newly formed podium a weighty collection of misshapen granite boulders was set (now at Derrynoose). Then in 2003 it was entirely redesigned again in an effort to restore the lost integrity, with a brass screen placed in a curve across the E end and a white stone altar forming an attractive focus. The Lady Chapel is no more than a narrow passageway behind the high altar.

Until 1897 when the Synod Hall was completed, the s transept was screened off as a sacristy; it was converted *c.* 1904 to a side chapel; in 2003 it was enclosed by a screen and a tabernacle installed in the surviving reredos, which in a sense revives the spirit of the original high altar, a decision that can be justified by its true E orientation. The baptistery occupies a vaulted space in the base of the NW tower.

Furnishings

In the sanctuary a shimmering curved BRASS SCREEN at the E end, a little too flimsy, but enhanced with brasswork recovered from the lost C19 choir gates. – The HIGH ALTAR is a large block in white Tunisian limestone, its concave panels sculpted with scenes of Christ in a primitivist style by *Gabriel Gilmore*. – The only surviving element of the 1980s scheme is the CRUCIFIX, The Tree of Life, a highly worthy stylized bronze by *Imogen Stuart*. – The CATHEDRA, given central prominence at the rear of the sanctuary, is a heavy oaken work of *c.* 1900 by *Messrs Beakey* of Dublin. – LADY CHAPEL REREDOS, *c.* 1900, in Caen stone with polished shafts of pink marble, nine bays wide with gabled statuary niches. Furnished as a Marian shrine with statuary by *Earley & Powell* and sculptural reliefs including the Annunciation and Nativity by *Michele Tripisciano*. – s transept enclosed by a BRASS SCREEN related to that of the sanctuary; TABERNACLE installed in the surviving reredos by *Ruffononi* and *Aureli*, all in 2003. – In the N transept the sumptuous Gothic PORCH with flanking confessionals is a virtuoso carved work. – STATIONS OF THE CROSS of 1875 by *Herbert & Co.*, Liverpool; high relief in Gothic aedicules on foliated brackets. – Monumental ORGAN of *c.* 1874, by *William Telford*, exquisitely encased by *Beakey*: decorated with colonnettes and traceried panels, it has a central crocketed gable with short links to tall, towering end projections, all adorned with trumpet-wielding angels whose silhouettes against the clear glazing of the W window contribute a spectral beauty. – FONT. By *Ashlin & Coleman*, *c.* 1904. A sculptured marble octagon supported on short polished shafts of Siena marble with a highly carved oak dome. – STAINED GLASS. Brooding figurative glass, mostly late C19 by *Mayer & Co.* of Munich, whose works are saturated with a preponderance of blood reds and deep blues. E window, the Crucifixion, 1879, by *Earley & Powell*, who added three others *c.* 1904. Two windows of the N aisle adjoining the N transept are by *Hardman & Co.*, Birmingham.

88

Associated buildings

GATE LODGE. 1884 by *William Hague*. At the main (S) entrance to the Cathedral grounds. A small, steeply gabled block on an L-plan with a long, low return. A highly textured Gothic design in squared rock-faced limestone with smooth-faced dressings and a little overwrought symbolic decoration. The gables have twin sashes in heavy moulded frames with deeply carved blind tracery in the tympana, set under hoods with carved heads on the stops. A narrow gabled porch in the angle, buttressed on one side with a deeply recessed trefoil over the door; inset is a small relief with the legend of St Patrick and the fawn.

SYNOD HALL. 1894–7 by *William Hague*. Linked to the NE angle of the Cathedral by a short single-storey cloister passage. A large two-storey, gable-ended block in limestone ashlar, five bays wide, with the fourth bay advanced and gabled to effect a cruciform plan. Sparsely decorated but amply fenestrated with Perp tracery, largest in the main gable. The main doorway is reused from *Duff*'s Cathedral, probably intended for the s transept.

ST PATRICK'S PAROCHIAL HALL. Cathedral Road. 1954 by *W. H. Byrne & Son*. A bulky Art Deco-style hall bordering on the colossal, drably cement-rendered. Broad gabled front, three storeys tall with strip quoins, narrow vertical metal casements tightly grouped in threes, and a wide entrance recessed under a flat concrete canopy. The builders were *P. McKenna & Sons*.

ARA COELI. The Catholic Archbishop's Palace, directly behind the Cathedral. As built in 1875 by *J. J. McCarthy* for Archbishop McGettigan, a characteristic Late Victorian clerical residence, a mildly Italianate two-storey stuccoed block with rusticated quoins, dentilled eaves cornice and a hipped roof; two two-storey bay windows. Enlarged in 1928 by *Ashlin & Coleman*. The main front is long and asymmetrical, the windows all sashed with plate glass in segmental-headed stucco frames. The entrance in the centre of the original house is now offset to one side under a shallow projecting porch with flat Corinthian pilasters of granite and the arms of Cardinal MacRory in the keystone.

Behind, set into the hillside, is the CARDINAL TOMAS O'FIAICH MEMORIAL LIBRARY. 1996 by *P. & B. Gregory*. Rectangular in plan, low-slung and shed-like, it has a hipped lead roof 'floating' as projected eaves over a clerestory strip window. Walls clad in blue limestone, with the entrance offset in the eight-bay front between narrow vertical windows in a square-fronted projection. The ridge is glazed to form a spine extending down the end slopes and lighting the offices inside. These are ranged along the spine so as to separate the public rooms to the front from the collections stored behind. Unpretentious and functional.

ST PATRICK'S GRAMMAR SCHOOL. Beside the Cathedral to the NE. 1836–8 by *Thomas Duff*, extended in 1870 and again in 1907 by *Ashlin & Coleman*, with further additions of 1940 by *Thomas McLea*, and 1951 *by James R. E. Boyd Barrett*. Founded by Archbishop Crolly as a seminary when the lease of Sandy Hill was first obtained. It consists of two substantial blocks set at right angles, all drearily cement-rendered. *Duff*'s building to the W is a two-storey, eight-bay block in an unadorned institutional Tudor style, with narrow kneelered gables to the end bays and mullioned windows set in chamfered reveals. This range is linked to the later buildings by an angled four-storey tower with flat-topped polygonal buttresses, where the entrance is set in a projecting Tudor arch. This later block, in which it is difficult to determine the different phases of construction, is larger and plainer than its counterpart, three storeys tall with nine bays; the windows are dormers on the upper floor and unusually arranged on the ground floor as narrow lights paired under small square windows, most probably the work of *James R. E. Boyd Barrett*.

OTHER CHURCHES ETC.

FRANCISCAN FRIARY RUINS. S of the city centre, on low ground just off the avenue to the former Church of Ireland Archbishop's Palace. Fragmentary, somewhat disappointing remains that belie its former substance, with what is still said to be the longest friary church in Ireland. The building was founded by Archbishop O'Scannail in 1263, and the *Annals of the Four Masters* record that it was built under the patronage of MacDonnell Galloglagh ('of the Gallowglasses'), Fermanagh chief of Clan Kelly. The remains are those of a rectangular church consisting of nave and chancel, together 50 m (just under 164 ft) long. Enough survives to allow the visitor standing in the doorway in the w wall to appreciate the impressive length; greater powers of imagination however are required to reconstruct the s aisle or the domestic buildings and cloister on the N side, of which no trace now remains, though bond stones at the w end of the N wall indicate their earlier existence. The w front stands sufficiently intact, with the ragged remains of buttresses on each corner, retaining between them the basic arched form of the entrance, stripped out, with only the moulded base stones remaining of the doorway and the lower portion of the w window above. Two arches of the s arcade survive, stripped of ornament, but with enough evidence from the base details to reconstruct a single shaft applied centrally to the thickness of the piers, and a quadrant moulding to the outer edges. Of the c15 tower added between nave and chancel to complete the standard Franciscan arrangement there is no more than the outline of its foundations. Suppressed in 1542, the Friary had become ruined by 1596 when Hugh O'Neill staged an ambush from within the walls. In 1620 the land was granted to Archbishop Hampton, and it was eventually enclosed within the c18 demesne of Archbishop Robinson.

ST MARK (C of I). Off the E side of the Mall, approached by an impressive avenue of limes. Initially a large Regency Gothic church built in 1811 and consecrated in 1814 as a chapel of ease by Archbishop William Stuart. Known locally as the 'garrison church', it also served as a chapel to the adjacent Royal School. *Francis Johnston* provided the standard hall-and-tower design, and his forestanding three-stage tower survived the rebuilding of the nave with aisles by *William Farrell* in 1830; enlarged again in 1866 by *Slater & Carpenter* with polygonal chancel and side chapels. The tower, of limestone ashlar, has clasping buttresses with blind loops and a tall belfry stage below a decorated parapet and corner pinnacles ornamented with sweeping Chinese-like gables. Behind, vestry and stairs in a battlemented block with angled buttresses and sharply pointed lancets, before the wider, boxy nave. Walls of snecked rubble in Armagh conglomerate with grey limestone dressings. Nave of five bays with buttresses and deep battlemented parapets, all with the same spiky pinnacles as the tower. Squarish mullioned aisle windows, gallery windows with delicate iron Y-tracery, all under emphatic label mouldings. The buttressed chancel, of squared limestone with smooth dressings, projects beyond the gabled two-bay side chapels with set-back buttresses. The windows have Geometric tracery with hoods, elaborated in the gables. A small gabled porch projects from the s chapel, and from the N a low vestry with lancets and a hipped roof. The contractor for the 1860s works was *John Waldron* of Abbeyleix.

Inside, a circular vestibule under the tower and a narrow passage beyond lead to the nave. The nave has a wide, depressed plaster vault with ribs and large gilded bosses, carried on clustered columns passing through the galleries. Similar vaults over the galleries. Moulded limestone chancel arch on short corbelled piers. In the chancel an exposed timber roof with arch-braced trusses; on either side, two-bay arcades on solid round piers with foliate capitals originally opened to the chapels, now rearranged as a vestry and organ gallery.

FURNISHINGS. The tall two-tiered PULPIT, by *J. J. Phillips*, 1896, is a Caen stone octagon with a flying staircase, deeply carved with an open arcaded front and polished marble shafts. – FONT. A crisp octagon with panelled decoration. – STAINED GLASS. The best are two in the E bays of the aisles: 'She had done what she could' (1920) and 'The Virtuous Woman' (1926), by *Ethel Rhind*. The remainder are greatly inferior late C20 figurative works, several by *David Esler, Leadlines Studio*. – MONUMENTS. In the organ gallery, two of a similar design. The Rev. Robert Miller †1840 by *Thomas Kirk*; large obelisk-shaped plaque with a relief carving of an angel in clouds above a portrait medallion. – William Lodge Kidd †1851; plainer, in grey marble decorated with inverted torches and a snake eating its tail. – In the vestry: Robert Riddall †1873; a scrolled tablet. – Charles Smyth Cardwell †1859; a grey marble tablet with inverted torches. In the S aisle: Isabella Hardy †1888; an enriched quatrefoil plaque. – The Rev. Robert Haig †1847; a simple classical tablet. – Arthur Irwin Kelly †1841; a stylized classical tablet on scrolled brackets, by *R. Ballantine & Sons*, Dublin. – Mary Helen Chomley †1884; a brass plaque, by *Maguire & Son*, Dublin. – In the N aisle: John Stanley †1846; a plain shield. – The Rev. William Ball †1821; a white tablet surmounted by a Neoclassical urn. – Meredith Armstrong †1868; a white tablet under a draped sarcophagus. – Robert Gray †1950; a pedimented marble tablet.

On the approach is the CROZIER HALL of 1850, built by Archbishop Beresford. A picturesque Tudor-style hall with steep roofs and label mouldings to the windows; pretty glazing in square geometric patterns. Seven-bay front in smooth render with a two-storey gabled projection at each end, before the end bays, rather like a parochial school with matching doorways in the gables. Later additions at the sides. The GATE LODGE on Victoria Street is a modest Late Victorian gabled L-plan block in squared limestone with carved dressings. Plate glass and a simple Tudor-arched doorway. The only embellishments are chamfered corners to the gable.

ST MALACHY. Irish Street. 1935–8 by *Ashlin & Coleman*, replacing a fine pre-Emancipation chapel on Chapel Lane. A large basilican church in a Hiberno-Romanesque style, built of quarry-faced Navan limestone with smooth-faced dressings. The contractors were *P. McKenna & Sons* of Armagh. A deep plan of nine bays overall, six-bay nave with three round-headed lancets to each bay of the clerestory, low twin-gabled transepts, and a tall apsidal chancel. Tall kneelered gable on the main front; raking aisles detailed with corbel tables in a rather pedestrian way. Shallow staged recession to the gable with three graded lights set over a blind arcade above the entrance. The simplified Romanesque doorway has three orders with chevrons and angle colonnettes. Inside, bright with a clinical coldness. Nave arcade with round arches decorated with chevrons on round piers of grey polished granite with strange oversailing abacuses deeply formed rather like a biscuit tin. The ceiling is a plaster barrel-vault with shallow coffers and flat ribs springing from pilasters between the clerestory windows. Plaster groin-vaults in the aisles. Side chapels with rich mosaic. Renovations in 2005 by *O'Daly, O'Neill & Associates*. – STATIONS OF THE CROSS. Gothic aedicules by *Franz Mayer*. – STAINED GLASS. Richly coloured figurative glass by *Hardman*, London.

FIRST PRESBYTERIAN CHURCH. On the w side of the Mall. 1878 by *Young & Mackenzie*. An assertive and ambitious design sited on the corner with Russell Street, its attenuated spire providing a central emphasis on the w side of the Mall. A highly textured Gothic church in rock-faced limestone, richly ornamented with Dungannon sandstone trim. Raised on a basement above street level, the main front is gabled with a large five-light Dec window and a buttress to one side with heavy crocketed pinnacles. Aisles, and an offset three-stage tower, with a belfry set amongst pinnacles and an octagonal spire with lucarnes. Four entrances, the main doors twinned at the centre with crocketed gables and pinnacled buttresses around deeply recessed arches with shafts in the reveals, fitted with heavy sliding doors, a novelty. Mouldings and tympana with foliate enrichments. Five-bay nave with buttresses and cusped lancets; large twin-light traceried windows above. Gabled porch to the N.

Inside, beyond a short lobby with spiral stairs at either end the nave is an impressive galleried space under a panelled tunnel-vault. The horseshoe-shaped galleries of dark timber are carried on slender octagonal pillars with stylized capitals, which extend through the gallery frontals into an arcade with stilted pointed arches. Re-ordered in 1901 by *H. C. Parkinson*. – STAINED GLASS. In the E gallery by *Heaton, Butler & Bayne*, London; another, similar, opposite is unsigned. – MONUMENTS. The Rev. Jackson Smyth †1890, by *Purdy & Millard*, Belfast. An elaborate Gothic aedicule in Caen stone with polished marble shafts. – Douglas St George Morrison †1917. A plain tablet encircled by a husked garland with a portrait cartouche, also by *Purdy & Millard*.

THE MALL (SCOTCH) PRESBYTERIAN CHURCH. On the w side of the Mall. 1837–40. Built by Third Armagh and known as the Scotch Church. Low-relief classicism in crisp limestone ashlar. A broad front of three bays with a giant order of Ionic pilasters with deep entablature and blocking course, advanced and paired in the centre to support a pediment. On the frieze, the inscription 'The Scotch Church MDCCCXXXVII'.

Channelled rustication around segmental-headed windows on the ground floor; square-headed windows above in lugged surrounds, splayed in Egyptian style. A wide doorcase with scrolled brackets on pilasters supporting a cornice.

METHODIST CHURCH. Abbey Street. A quirky classical church, set back from the street at an angle with a small railed forecourt. Nothing survives of the church built here in 1786 and preached in by John Wesley. Rebuilt in 1835 as a three-bay hall; additions in 1860–2 by *W. J. Barre*. Completely remodelled in 1888 by *J. J. Phillips*, who extended the plan with a new façade; the contractor was *John Collen*. (The extent of the early C19 church is evident where the limestone quoins remain exposed on the N elevation.) A pedimented frontispiece in ashlar projects between convex single-bay quadrants in stucco. The ground floor has shallow channelled rustication; a simple pedimented doorcase in the centre with consoles and a panelled surround is flanked by small leaded windows in stylized aedicules with segmental pediments. A deep frieze between the storeys; shallow projecting plinths on the corners of the frontispiece with Ionic pilasters above – these with bold capitals and partially fluted shafts. Three graded lights on the first floor give it an odd appearance: stilted segmental arches with wide architraves on Ionic pilasters with thickly fluted aprons.

Angled snugly beside the church is the stuccoed front of the large four-bay METHODIST HALL by *W. J. Barre*, built in 1859 as the Wesleyan School. The narrow two-storey front has blocked quoins, a moulded string-course between the storeys, and a pedimented projection with banded rustication around a tall recessed arch. The doorcase has a floating segmental pediment on paired brackets; a wide segmental-headed window with slender mullions above. Paired segmental-headed windows on the street front, originally with shouldered stucco frames, now with metal frames on the first floor.

85 GOSPEL HALL (former MASONIC HALL). The Mall. There is nothing demure about this diminutive Gothic hall of 1884 by *J. H. Fullerton*. A boisterous upstart in polychrome brick, predominantly of red with black-and-yellow dressings, and carved limestone details. Something of a surprise from this usually sedate architect, perhaps going back to plans for the hall presented by *John McCurdy* thirty years earlier. The gabled front is stepped with projecting brickwork, and buttressed with flanking towers, on one side squat and circular with a conical roof, on the other a tall chisel-roofed campanile, both slated and finished with decorative leadwork. The entrance is elaborate, set in a gabled projection with twin pointed doorways framed in pointed arches on short colonnettes with foliate capitals, with a plate-traceried oculus above. The hall of just three bays is buttressed, with a steeply pitched roof where a delightful small flèche sits astride the ridge. Inside, meeting room on the first floor under a timber-panelled cusped vault.

PRESBYTERIAN CHURCH (former). Now part of ST PATRICK'S TRIAN VISITOR CENTRE. On a height off Abbey Street. In

use by First Armagh from 1722 until 1879 and by Second
Armagh from then until 1915. The church of 1722, the date on
a plaque under the E window, replaced a 1676 meeting house
of 'lime and stone' off English Street, described by Thomas
Ashe in 1703 as 'one of the greatest meeting houses in the
north: there are in it three large galleries, a pulpit and seats
below stairs made very regular and uniform and the congregation very numerous'. The new church was also a large one, two
storeys in limestone rubble on a Greek cross plan. The gables
were three bays wide with segmental and square-headed
windows. During the rebuilding Jonathan Swift observed the
use of stone from the old Abbey of SS Peter and Paul and was
wryly amused to see how these 'fanatical Puritans were chisel-
ling popery out of the very stones'. The vernacular character
of this building was lost in the early C19 when the walls were
raised and the N gable was widened to form aisle-like porches
with Tudor-arched doors on the corners, under a sweeping
candle-snuffer roof; the main gables were also given large Perp
windows, though the Georgian openings still appear as ghosts
in the walls. – MONUMENT. On the outside of the W transept,
the Rev. Alexander Fleming †1851, a Grecian marble plaque
in a limestone Tudor-hooded frame.

ST CATHERINE'S COLLEGE (former CONVENT OF THE
SACRED HEART). Convent Road. The Sacred Heart, a teach-
ing order, was brought to Armagh by Archbishop Paul Cullen,
and in 1857 a convent was designed by *John Bourke*. A bulky
three-storey block in squared limestone with ashlar dressings,
now weighted down on either side by hulking late C20 additions. The main front has eleven bays, the three central bays
advanced with quoin pilasters and gabled as an open pediment
filled with a clock face above a statuary niche. Bourke's penchant for round-headed Georgian windows is evident here in
the central bays and across the ground floor. A handsome classical porch with boxy proportions shelters a pilastered doorcase under a broad webbed fanlight. Some interiors rebuilt
after a fire in 1964. Jutting out to the l. are the bond stones
of the former chapel, added in 1885. The original 16-acre site
has now been much built upon. – The TECHNOLOGY AND
DESIGN block is the most commanding of an assemblage of
low, spreading additions of *c.* 2007 by *Patrick Haughey*. It faces
the rear of the old convent with a large square atrium, extensively glazed, with a shallow bow-shaped roof, recessed between
sloping blocks in contrasting colours.

   Behind these, to the S, off Windmill Hill, is ST CATHER-
INE'S PRIMARY SCHOOL of 1937 by *Hugh Lamont*. A large
two-storey block in red brick with sandstone dressings and a
hipped roof. The main front has eleven bays with strip pilasters
and massive casements between, originally with metal frames.
The three central bays are slightly advanced with a two-tiered
classical frontispiece in ashlar with fanlit door, pilasters, entablatures, and a pediment with dentils over the upper central bay.
At each end, discrete five-bay wings project rearward with a
narrow gabled link between.

Across the road St Brigid's High School is an irregular U-plan of 1971 by *McLean & Forte* in red brick with flat over-sailing roofs.

The GATE LODGE at the N entrance is a tall gable-ended Victorian block, two storeys and two bays in polychrome brick with elaborate pointed arches to the gables.

CHURCH HOUSE, Abbey Street. *See* p. 107.

FIRST PRESBYTERIAN CHURCH LECTURE HALL. College Street. 1857 by *W. J. Barre*. A free-standing two-storey block, mildly Italianate, with six bays to the front and a low hipped roof with elaborate scrolled brackets, set in pairs around the eaves. Channelled rustication in stucco on the ground floor with segmental-headed windows and matching fanlit entrances in each of the end bays. The first floor, in chequered Flemish-bond Belfast brick, seems too squat for its tall round-headed windows, which rest on a continuous sill course. The windows here and below have plate glass with horizontal glazing bars. Over the two central bays the eaves are raised into an open segmental pediment, and inserted in the space below is an open bible in limestone surrounded by the text 'Train up a child in the way he should go'.

PROTESTANT HALL (former), Abbey Street. *See* Youth Hostel, p. 133.

PUBLIC BUILDINGS ETC.

COURTHOUSE. 1809 by *Francis Johnston*. Given due authority at the N end of the Mall, but now difficult to appreciate across the busy traffic streams and the formidable tall railings that surround it, though of themselves rather elegant and well designed. A polished Neoclassical block in limestone ashlar with a tetrastyle portico. Single-storey façade of five bays, with three entrances behind the portico and large windows in the side bays. The surface is carefully layered, with smooth panels that project gently around the windows in the side bays, pulled in just enough on the corners to reveal rusticated quoins. Plain frieze above separated by a thin sunken channel, breaking the flat surface of the panels as a shadow line before a sharply profiled cornice and blocking course. The ample round-headed windows each rest on a large panelled block and have moulded archivolts with a prominent keystone; the impost architraves are given a subtle Doric suggestion, with tiny guttae projecting beneath the frieze, a detail repeated across the portico, where the impost is threaded between the pilaster responds. A half-window above the main entrance, and niches in the arches over the side doors.

The order of the portico is Roman Doric, but even to the untrained eye the columns are rather too slender for the weighty pediment. Johnston was employed here in his position as architect to the Board of Works, and though surviving designs show an astylar building (between arched gateways)

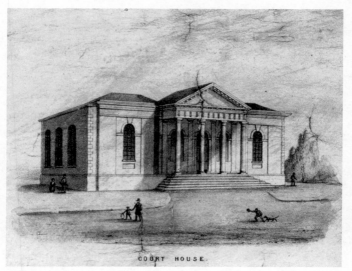

Armagh, Courthouse.
Drawing by J. O'Hagan, 1855

without the portico, he evidently amended this to provide one in the finished design. The problems with its proportions arose because he did not personally oversee the work; when it was built he complained that his design had not been followed: 'the managers (an attorney and others) were prevailed upon by some of the workmen to reduce the diameter of the columns (I suppose for the greater convenience of getting the stone of which they are composed) and have thereby ruined the portico'.

Johnston's plan was a standard tripartite one, with the Crown Court and Record Court flanking a central hall and staircase with a two-storey suite of offices behind. Remodelled internally with a three-storey addition to the rear in 1861–3 by *Henry Davison* with *Thomas Turner* and *Thomas Drew*. Later internal works were begun in 1965 by *Albert Neill*, but the building was extensively damaged by a bomb in 1993, resulting in a more thorough refurbishment *c.* 1994 by *Stephen Leighton*. Significantly for the appearance of the building, the roof was renewed successfully, covering the central well that had given rise to cumbersome independent roofs over the side bays – probably another departure from Johnston's design. The impressive railings enclosing the front were also part of these works.

To the E, the former PROBATE COURT of 1860 is a discreet Victorian L-plan block in red brick with sandstone dressings, set on a rusticated basement. Now a restaurant.

MARKET HOUSE (former), now ARMAGH CITY LIBRARY. Set on a podium at the lower end of the steeply sloping Market

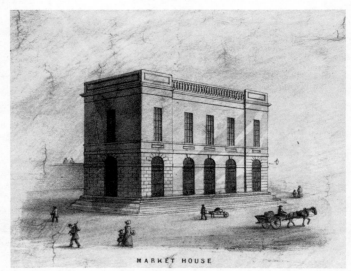

Armagh, Market House.
Drawing by J. O'Hagan, 1855

Place, on the site of the 1742 market house, itself a replacement of a C17 predecessor. A large astylar block, in Armagh limestone ashlar. Built in 1815 by Archbishop Stuart, whose benevolence is recorded in the frieze over the E front; enlarged in depth and given an additional storey in 1912. Initially a two-storey block, just one bay deep, with two opposing five-bay fronts, E and W. The principal front faces E, where the lower two storeys preserve the original design: end bays gently advanced with V-channelled rustication containing a single arch on the ground floor; three segmental arches in the centre with bold console keystones; on the first floor tall Georgian sashes resting on a continuous string; at the top, above the added second storey, the original frieze and balustraded cornice with central open segmental pediment containing a clock face. At the sides, the rustication continues on the ground floor; originally a single central arch below a tall sash window. Seamlessly enlarged in 1912 by *John Caffrey*, to serve as the Municipal Technical School. The contractor was *Robert Cullen* of Portadown. The plan was effectively made square by doubling the depth to the W so that the sides are now also of five bays; the height was raised by an additional storey of reduced proportions, giving it altogether a greater presence in the street. To the W, repeating the arrangement of the original façade, the three central bays step forward, reusing the pediment but with the addition of a pedimented Tuscan doorcase.

ARMAGH PUBLIC LIBRARY, Abbey Street. *See* p. 107.

Armagh, Royal School.
Engraving, 1819

ROYAL SCHOOL. College Hill. One of five schools founded in
Ulster by James I in 1608, reconstituted in 1627. Originally on
Abbey Street, in 1774 it was moved here to a new building for
one hundred boarders designed by *Thomas Cooley*. Archbishop
Robinson contributed most of the funds towards the £5,078
cost, the remainder being given by the Rev. Dr Arthur Grueber.
A rather formidable U-plan block in conglomerate rubble with
sparse Tudor detail. A central two-storey, three-bay block is set
deeply within a courtyard between three-storey, seven-bay
wings which present narrow battlemented fronts with just two
bays to the street; a low battlemented wall with a cloister
behind runs between the wings, screening the courtyard from
the street. The entrance projects slightly in the centre of the
screen wall with a concave Tudor arch under a hoodmould, the
symmetry now spoiled by another simpler entrance on one
side. The central block, originally of a single storey with a
raking battlemented gable, was given an additional storey in
1849 with a cornice and straight battlements matching those
of the wings; it is now joined to the wings by short single-bay
links. All amply fenestrated with Georgian sashes in chamfered
reveals, with labels on the central block. Here, between the
storeys, the arms of George III are flanked by those of archbishops Robinson and Beresford.

GAOL (former). Dominating the s end of the Mall with a long
formidable front of three storeys and fourteen bays, broken by
two pedimented entrance projections with quoins. Sheer institutional classicism. The l. projection was the centrepiece of a
nine-bay block of 1780 by *Thomas Cooley*, much more tamely
expressed than his earlier Newgate Prison in Dublin. This
was later mirrored to the E, perhaps in 1819, when *Francis
Johnston* is supposed to have made alterations and additions to
remedy what was considered to be a bad plan. Built in Armagh

conglomerate with limestone dressings, most expressive in the entrance bays, where channelled rustication with radiating voussoirs and vermiculated blocks surrounds the doorways; these are plain round-headed openings with barred fanlights, set in a recessed arch with side-lights. The ground floor is arcaded, originally blind but for lunettes resting on a continuous impost within shallow recessed arches. The present windows throughout are not those of Cooley's design. The rear of Cooley's block is clearly shown in James Black's important view of Armagh of 1810 as fronting three small yards with a short central return. By 1834 a larger area to the rear had been enclosed and a hospital built in an independent T-plan block. Later, between 1837 and 1850, *William Murray* made proposals to enlarge the complex, introducing the popular radial plan in new blocks. Although his designs were approved, it is unclear how far his proposals were advanced beyond the bulky, three-storey B wing of 1846 which bears his initials and those of the builder, *R. Clarke*; certainly his intention to remodel Cooley's front with battlements was not executed. Plans for a new wing by *John Boyd* were accepted in 1853 and further works by him in 1865 were contracted to *Thomas Ross*. These involved alterations to the boundary walls and to the main front, where Boyd added a deep parapet over the cornice and enlarged all the openings, giving the upper floors segmental heads and blocked surrounds; above the doorways he replaced what had been lunettes in Cooley's design with a tripartite window and introduced triple lancets above; on the r. side these replaced the gallows, which were removed for the conversion of this wing to a residence for the governor. Closed in 1988. At the time of writing proposals were being considered for conversion as a hotel.

ARMSTRONG PRIMARY SCHOOL. *See* p. 129.

OBSERVATORY. College Hill. A simple, understated classical building, rather like a glebe house, begun in 1789 by *Francis Johnston* as the final contribution in Archbishop Robinson's architectural legacy to Armagh and part of his ambition to found a university here. Built as an observatory and astronomer's residence, it is a two-storey, gable-ended block on a half-basement, rising from an open area with a double-pile plan. Walls in thinly coursed blocks of Armagh conglomerate, trimmed with limestone. The entrance front to the N has three bays with chamfered quoins, a thin cavetto eaves cornice and a deep parapet; twelve-pane Georgian sashes on the ground floor, nine-pane above. Sweeping steps lead across the area to a miniature distyle porch with Roman Doric detailing that anticipates Johnston's portico for Townley Hall in Co. Louth. On the garden front a bowed central bay rises to the attic observatory, formed as a copper-domed cylinder. A plaque set between the storeys proclaims the motto: 'The heavens declare the glory of God', the opening of Psalm 19.

Inside, a standard symmetrical plan, sparsely decorated with touches of understated elegance, evident especially in the delicate Doric cornice of the hall. As a deep passage the hall divides the plan, leading to a circular stair-tower at the rear; here spiral stone stairs rising from the basement are coiled round a limestone shaft that finishes in a fluted band before blossoming into a plain vault that supports the telescope in the attic above. Beyond these stairs, a short flight of steps from the first-floor landing, lit by a wonderful glazed half-dome, leads up to the observatory. The equatorial telescope mount of 1795 is a brass-framed trapezoid by *John & Edward Troughton* of London. The dome, its surface still beautifully clad with reeded timber, rotates on brass tracks and is considered the only surviving c18 example of its kind.

A free-standing domed observatory TOWER was built to the E in 1827, possibly also by *Johnston*, and now housing a 15-in. reflector, the first telescope commissioned from *Thomas Grubb*. In 1835 a low four-bay wing, projecting before Johnston's small kitchen wing, linked the tower to the main block; it was designed by *William Murray* to house various measuring instruments. In 1841 one of the bays was raised into a square tower (now an anemometer station) to house the Sisson Zenith sector, designed to measure the zenith distances of stars, part of a collection from the King's Observatory at Kew gifted to Armagh by Queen Victoria.

GATE LODGE in rubble, a charming single-storey block with a hipped slate roof, angled against a gatepier with a large Gothick window with external shutters in the gable.

COUNTY INFIRMARY (former). Abbey Street. Initially an institutional Georgian block of 1767 by *George Ensor*, finished in 1776 by *John Harvey* and *Richard Louch*, and altered in 1849. Two storeys over a basement with a big hipped roof. Astylar classicism in coursed conglomerate rubble with smooth limestone dressings – rusticated quoins, moulded cornice, and windows in blocked surrounds with triple keystones. On the nine-bay front the three central bays break forward under a pediment. Originally there were twin entrances on either side of the breakfront, set in primitive Gibbs surrounds with an arched fanlight. The r. doorway was moved to the centre in the early c20; at the same time, plate glass replaced the Georgian sashes. Further wards, funded by the Lill Bequest, were added in 1843 by *J. J. Johnstone*, resulting in the long irregular N front of squared limestone with projecting pedimented stacks. Further minor additions by *J. H. Fullerton* in 1848. A new surgeon's house, an L-plan block in reconstituted stone, was added to the S in 1934 by *Young & Mackenzie*; this has since been linked to the main block. The buildings were adapted in the 1990s for Queen's University Belfast by *Ian Donaldson*.

DOBBIN HOUSE. No. 36 Scotch Street. Built in 1812 by Leonard Dobbin, Sovereign of the city, who had acquired the Anglesea estate and began to develop it commercially at this time. Usually attributed to *Francis Johnston*, the building served as the Bank of Ireland, of which Dobbin was agent. A tall dignified block on a half-basement, set well back from the street in a railed garden. Well-proportioned front, three storeys and three bays in limestone ashlar with large Georgian sashes between blocked quoins, finished with a thin eaves cornice and blocking course. Elegant railed steps lead up to the central doorcase, which is a delight: a wide segmental arch over four engaged Tuscan columns with a Doric entablature carved in such low relief that it appears mirage-like; all enhanced by leaded side-lights and a webbed fanlight with a projecting lantern case. Lower buildings on either side treated as wings, neatly expressed on the corners at the street line with a Neo-classical urn above the angle of the eaves. Squashed in at the sides, narrow link walls with a webbed oculus over a plain doorway. Converted for sheltered housing in 1980 by *G. P. & R. H. Bell*.

ORANGE HALL (former MALL SCHOOL). On the E side of the Mall. 1818, not unlike a reduced version of Francis Johnston's Royal School in Cavan. Originally a neat composition, two storeys tall with advanced pedimented end blocks linked by a colonnade, built in limestone ashlar with blind segmental arches on the ground floor and tripartite windows above under low raking pediments with plain mutule blocks. Now looming above these, swallowing up the central master's house, is a bulky cement-rendered hall of *c.* 1950, with three large and closely grouped bays under a big hipped roof. Between the end bays a flat-roofed, partially glazed link replaces the colonnade and now accommodates a railed balcony reached from the hall.

LINEN MARKET (former). Dobbin Street. 1820, probably by *Francis Johnston*. A forlorn gateway with a cupola, originally between long narrow ranges built for the Linen Market, now the entrance to an unbecoming surface car park bounded by low walls. A square tower of limestone in two stages with V-channelled rustication on the lower stage, vermiculated on the quoins and radiating voussoirs of the archway. Short clock stage in smooth-faced ashlar below a cornice and blocking course. The louvred cupola, rising on a low hipped roof, is domed in lead with an ironwork finial. A rusticated gateway with ball finials on the S boundary is another stranded remnant.

CORNMARKET (former). Dawson Street. 1827. Built by Arch-bishop Beresford and clearly inspired by the Linen Market; a little too late for *Johnston*, who had retired. Three parallel sheds in the NE corner of the former SHAMBLES, with a long façade extending S along Dawson Street consisting of a square tower and cupola between low rubble ranges with three narrow blind arches with slit openings and pedimented end blocks. The tower, of squared limestone, has a round-headed gateway with large radiating voussoirs set under a segmental relieving arch; nicely moulded cornice with blocking course before the tall timber cupola, more elaborate than at the Linen Market, with panels, clock faces, and rounded gables with oval vents to the dome. Blind three-bay end façade on Cathedral Road, attractively expressed with small recessed arches flanking a shallow pedimented breakfront with a relieving arch and square-headed doorway. Regeneration scheme for the Shambles initiated in 2012.

CHARLEMONT PLACE. 1827–30 by *William Murray*. A terrace   72
of five Late Georgian houses, unusually tall, a fragment of a
great Neoclassical design, like a dislocated portion of a Bath
or Edinburgh streetscape; the drastic collapse in scale to the
semi-detached C20 houses to the S adds to the sense of an
unfinished work. Set back from the street with three storeys
and basement in finely tooled Armagh limestone ashlar with a
blocking course and an enriched modillion cornice to the
eaves. The façades are generously proportioned, with three
bays to each house, the windows crisp unadorned voids in the
wall, tallest on the first floor, where they rest on a continuous
string and have a variety of delicate cast-iron balconies. The
entrances, reached by a short flight of steps, are offset, with
Doric columns set in a concave arch and leaded petal fanlights.
Contrasting with the elegant restraint of the exterior, the interiors have rich Victorian plasterwork, best preserved in Nos. 4
and 5. All restored by *R. McMullan & N. Robinson* after bomb
damage in 1989.

ARMAGH COUNTY MUSEUM (former CHARLEMONT PLACE
SCHOOL). The Mall. The building of 1834 is usually attributed
to *William Murray*. A trim prostyle Ionic temple set in a small
railed garden on a corner, built of limestone rubble with
dressed trim, fronted in smooth pale limestone ashlar with
three narrow round-headed sashes between the columns, set
in shallow arches with moulded imposts and architraves.
Flanked by entrances in low set-back blocks. Short-lived as a
school, it was converted in 1857 by *Edward Gardner* for the
Armagh Natural History and Philosophical Society. The
County Museum since 1931. Extended with large brick additions to the rear in 1957 by *John McGeagh & Alan Dorman*.

TOWER HILL HOSPITAL (former UNION WORKHOUSE).
Tower Hill. 1841 by *George Wilkinson*, alterations 1900 by *Henry
C. Parkinson*. The standard Tudor-style design, in limestone, to
an orderly symmetrical plan. The builder was *Sinclair Carroll*.
The administration block is to the fore in the usual way, a
gabled five-bay front in squared masonry with plate glass and
decorative bargeboards. Windows in chamfered reveals, with
the doorway and subsidiary windows joined in the centre
under a continuous hoodmould. *Parkinson* extended this to the
S, adding a low three-bay block, slightly advanced, with large
mullioned windows. Behind, the principal range is a long
three-storey rubble block with dormered attics between twin-gabled end bays. Refenestrated, with quarry glazing now
remaining only in the dormers.

TOURIST OFFICE (former BELFAST BANK). English Street.
1851 by *Charles Lanyon*. A miniature banking palazzo in sandstone. Three-bay front with shallow recessed arches and a
heavy modillion cornice and balustraded parapet. Fielded rustication to the piers, simplified above with plain channelling
and radiating voussoirs. In the central arch, a rusticated

doorcase with vermiculated blocks and a dentilled pediment which holds up a massive heraldic wolf and seahorse supporting the arms of Belfast. A blank Baroque cartouche forms the keystone above, flanked by keystone heads over the round-headed windows, in plate glass with slender marginal glazing bars. Inside, the former banking hall is a lofty space with plaster panels on the walls and a coved ceiling on an enriched cornice, compartmented around the centre with borders of guilloche and rosette ornament.

The former MANAGER'S HOUSE behind pre-dates Lanyon's work. A handsome Late Georgian town house in rough-cast with rusticated quoins; two storeys on a raised basement with a three-bay parapeted front, Georgian sashes, and a handsome doorcase in a blocked surround with a rectangular leaded fanlight.

SHIELS ALMSHOUSES. Tower Hill. 1868 by *Lanyon, Lynn & Lanyon*. Built with the provisions of the 1864 bequest of Charles Shiels, a Co. Down cotton manufacturer. A modestly scaled group in a rugged institutional Gothic idiom, nominally Ruskinian in its details. Laid out to a U-plan in two-storey ranges of squared rock-faced limestone with sandstone dressings and plate glass. Projecting gabled end bays with half-dormers between; offset on the angled NE corner a three-stage clock tower, more richly treated, with red sandstone banding, engaged colonnettes to the corners, and a steep bell-cast roof. To the E a detached L-plan block with the same detailing.

ARMAGH BUSINESS CENTRE (former BAIRNSWEAR FACTORY). Railway Street. 1950 by *T. F. O. Rippingham*. A two-storey mass-concrete range, long and assertively horizontal, sleek like an ocean liner, with a taller service tower projecting at one end. Clad in pale brown brick, punctuated with small square perforations; reconstituted stone dressings and continuous wide mullioned windows, ceasing before three porthole windows. At the opposite end the entrance is in a modest canopied projection, and on the adjoining narrow end bay the stairs rise in a vertically glazed Mendelsohnian bow.

PLANETARIUM. Below the Observatory on College Hill. 1965–7 by *G. P. & R. H. Bell*. A large zinc-domed drum with a low trapezoid to one side. A classic of the new Space Age, with a big square entrance projection following the curve of the drum and clad with a chequer of large pyramidal tiles. Now destroyed by a hodgepodge of later additions.

MARKET PLACE THEATRE. An unashamedly Modernist building, intruding with spectral brilliance on the established urban scene. The design is by *Glenn Howells*, the winning entry in an international design competition in 1995. Opened in 2000, the building responds well to the challenging terrain with a tiered, modular design set on the N side of the steep W slope of the Market Place. Two main cubic blocks, upper and lower, are set at right angles to each other with a wide glazed link between. The walls are clad with small rectangular panels of white reconstituted stone, flecked with fossil-like inclusions but stacked vertically so that the overall effect is spoiled a little by the unevenness of the joints. The upper block is on a podium with a stepped approach, further exalted by an extended flat concrete canopy supported on slender pilotis which returns across the glazed link. Inside, bright and clinical.

JOINT SECRETARIAT BUILDING. Upper English Street. 2009 by *DA Architects*. This takes the place of the bomb-damaged Town Hall, converted in 1909 from the 1794 Tontine Building by *John Caffrey*. A stagey planar front clad in polished Armagh limestone, disrupting the lines of the streetscape with indecisive fenestration. Ostensibly three storeys tall, with an off-centre square projecting plane where two bays are pierced with regular square-headed windows disposed to one side of a vast squared entrance bay with an angled glazed wall deeply set behind; five layers of strip windows recessed to one side. Angular, attention-seeking stuff.

120

TOUR

The most practical place to begin a walking tour of Armagh is by the Ulsterbus Station, immediately beyond the Courthouse at the N end of the Mall. There are two public car parks here, one behind the Courthouse and the other on the opposite side of the street serving the Bus Station. The tour that follows will take about an hour and a half. It contains optional extensions adding extra streets and buildings worth seeing, and may be curtailed towards the end.

The obvious place to start is in front of *Francis Johnston*'s delicately scaled Courthouse (*see* Public Buildings, p. 120). It faces the WAR MEMORIAL of 1926, by *C. L. Hartwell*, with a female allegorical bronze holding a bay wreath and palm symbolizing Peace with Honour; sombre and dignified. From here there is immediately an optional extension: to the r. (E), a gateway and red brick lodge mark the entry to the grounds and 'Astropark' of the Armagh Observatory. Here, a curving drive passes the ARMSTRONG PRIMARY SCHOOL of 1929 by *James St John Phillips*, a large formal design in red brick with sandstone trim; to one side a grandiose open-fronted brick shed with six stout Roman Doric piers. The drive leads through woodland to the Observatory buildings themselves (*see* p. 124). From here not one roof of the urban sprawl of the city can be seen, though the roar of distant traffic can be heard. On the way up, branch off to enter the visitors' car park for a magnificent view of *McCarthy*'s Catholic Cathedral and its former seminary (St Patrick's Grammar School: *see* pp. 109 and 114), silent and serene on their hill to the w.

To have an initial sense of the historic city, visitors should walk from the Courthouse along the E side of THE MALL. Here at the NE corner is traditionally the first house built on the Mall, SOVEREIGN'S HOUSE, now ROYAL IRISH FUSILIERS

MUSEUM. It was built in 1809 by *John Quinn*, possibly with *Francis Johnston*, for the wily Sovereign Arthur Irwin Kelly, who is said to have appropriated materials from the construction of the Courthouse, leading to the two buildings being popularly named the Cat and Kitten. Two storeys and basement, three bays, in squared limestone; the doorcase was originally in the centre of the façade, but was later moved to the set-back porch on the N. Rebuilt internally. It is followed by the Late Georgian houses of Beresford Row and, most notably, by Charlemont Place (*see* p. 127). After a bathetic interruption of small C20 houses comes the diminutive Ionic portico of the Armagh County Museum (*see* p. 127). A little beyond, after a row of Late Georgian houses in coursed pink conglomerate, a gateway on the l. opens to a tree-lined avenue that leads uphill to St Mark's church (*see* p. 115). There follow the Orange Hall, built in 1818 as the Mall School (*see* p. 126), and the surprise of HARTFORD COTTAGE, a lively single-storey cottage in polychrome brick of 1880, possibly by *J. H Fullerton*. Set back in a garden, the central entrance between contrasting end projections, under a slate roof with exposed rafter toes. Eight later C19 houses, mostly in red brick, restore the street line, ending in a stuccoed pair with dramatic semicircular bay windows rising cylinder-like to the eaves. In the distance a view opens to the former Gaol, enlarged and altered from *Thomas Cooley*'s building of 1780 (*see* p. 123).

To the l. of the Gaol, prominently sited at the convergence of the Mall with Victoria Street and Barrack Hill, is the former SAVINGS BANK, a neat Neoclassical box of two storeys in limestone ashlar with three fronts, by *William Murray*, who exhibited his plans in 1838. Ground floor with channelled rustication; on the corners of the first floor Murray's favoured panelled pilasters rise to a plain frieze below a thin eaves cornice and blocking course, with acroterion blocks at the corners. To the Mall a three-bay façade, the centre gently advanced with a raised name plaque and a handsome Ionic tetrastyle portico with acroterion blocks. It shelters a fanlit doorway with console brackets and side-lights. Bay wreaths over the first-floor windows to Victoria Street.

The SW end of THE MALL is now given over to traffic in all directions. Turning back N, on the W side are three very different churches: the Gospel Hall of 1884, the Gothic Presbyterian church of 1878 and, a little beyond, the Mall or Scotch Presbyterian Church (*see* pp. 118, 117, 117). The trees that surround the green mask much of the terrorist destruction of the 1970s–80s and the uninspiring commercial development that has recently taken place. Halfway up the Mall a path crosses the green to the ROYAL IRISH FUSILIERS MEMORIAL, commemorating the South African war of 1899–1902, a well-modelled statue of a bugler sounding the last post by *Kathleen Shaw*, 1906.

Returning to the W side of the Mall, the road passing the side of the church with the steeple, RUSSELL STREET, leads into the oldest part of the town. On the N side, a recessed row of three-storey Late Georgian town houses in chequered red-and-yellow brickwork with attractive fanlit doorcases; the name, MELBOURNE TERRACE, records the popular Whig Prime Minister, Viscount Melbourne, who led the country at the accession of Victoria in 1837. Beyond them are three larger single-bay houses, an oddity in themselves, of which the last, once a Post Office (1860–82), has a notable shopfront: five clustered columns with foliate capitals support an extraordinary curving fascia with virtuoso carving of enormous crisp acanthus leaves and roses. On the s side of the street, JIM BURTON INSURANCE is the former late C19 Hibernian Bank, a simplified Italianate design in the manner of *Sandham Symes*, with an austerely plain limestone ashlar front of four bays, the central two advanced; segmental-headed windows with plate glass, and matching fanlit entrances in the end bays. Adjoining to the w is CONSTABULARY HOUSE, the former Royal Irish Constabulary barracks of 1883, in a clean Tudor style with mullioned windows including a square oriel on the first floor, gables over the end bays, and tall brick stacks.

At the end is UPPER ENGLISH STREET, following the ancient curving route below the top of the Cathedral hill. To the r. a nice view of the Catholic Cathedral spires and to the l. a continuous street of three-storey houses, small in scale, mid-C18, with some stone doorcases. The BANK OF IRELAND began life in the early C18 as a town house of the Rev. Nathaniel Whaley; it then became a hotel, where Thackeray stayed during his tour of 1843; now after bombing it is little more than a façade, unwisely stripped of render but retaining a provincial Gibbsian doorcase. Beyond it, the ULSTER BANK occupies the four r.-hand bays of a seven-bay pair of Late Georgian houses built by *John Quinn* for William and Thomas McWilliams, framed between rusticated quoins, with Georgian sashes.

To the s, the street rises to enter an irregular open place, backing uphill towards the Protestant Cathedral, and confusingly called MARKET STREET. Beyond the former Market House (now Library; *see* p. 121) is the NORTHERN BANK by *Lanyon, Lynn & Lanyon*, a towering stuccoed Italianate block of 1867 with two richly ornamented four-bay fronts. The ground floor has round-headed windows deeply set under a continuous archivolt with guilloche ornament and large keystones. The first floor is treated as a *piano nobile*, with windows under segmental pediments filled with ornament on scrolled brackets with swags; plainer lugged surrounds above, before a heavy bracketed cornice. Inside, the banking hall has a high compartmented ceiling on slender iron columns with Tower-of-the-Winds-like Composite capitals. The contractor was *James Connor* of Belfast.

From here the tower and gable of the E end of the Cathedral are seen in a perfect stage-set view, with wide steps rising to sets of houses before the trees of the churchyard. Those with energy may extend the walk, continuing round the corner and away from the Bank, to SCOTCH STREET – a straight street created in the 1750s – at the end of which, at No. 36, is Dobbin House, built in 1812 for Leonard Dobbin, Sovereign of the city, who began to develop this area commercially (*see* p. 93). The street now terminates in a dispiriting pool of swirling traffic, but the returning walk is worthwhile for the evolving streetscape, with grand views of the Northern Bank and a pleasing irregularity in the roofs of the smaller houses that line THOMAS STREET – another mid-C18 straight street – in a picturesque way.

Now back to MARKET STREET and up the hill towards the Cathedral by a stairway faced with ceramic reliefs of Armagh markets and fair days. The houses on the s side, Nos. 8–18, were restored (or more properly recreated) in 1992 on the basis of a drawing by Cornelius Varley showing what they looked like probably in 1808. Opposite them on the N, the Market-place Theatre (*see* p. 128). Above that, inside the churchyard, the clergy houses of 1855 and See House of 2010 (*see* p. 107).

6 At the top of the hill, turn l. into CASTLE STREET, a pleasantly curving collection of smaller C18 buildings now fronting the grass and trees that rise around the Cathedral instead of a complementary row of houses, as once was the case. Some walls from the back yards of the demolished houses remain in places to provide on-street parking, a poor recompense for what has been lost. At the end of the street, Nos. 48–58 make a good group of larger C18 houses. Here WHALEY'S BUILD-INGS have two large three-storey bows to the rooms at the back and a low three-arched arcade opening to a passageway and pend. Of IRISH STREET, which runs s downhill from here, only five old houses remain.

At this point on the Cathedral hill, historic Armagh comes to an abrupt end, where a sea of housing – mostly small-scale, mid-C20 buildings – extends to the s and w. Uphill, railings and a now locked gate once connected directly with VICARS' HILL, twelve mid-C18 houses (*see* p. 106) fronting the Cathe-dral. Here the modern visitor must circumnavigate the hill. The dark stone stalk of an early C19 WINDMILL becomes visible in the distance on the w, five storeys with sharply battered sides. Returning round the garden wall of the Vicars' Hill houses, CALLAN STREET reaches a wide junction with a good group of public buildings, the former County Infirmary on the l. (*see* p. 125), *Thomas Cooley* and *Robert Monsarrat*'s fine Armagh Public Library on the r. (*see* p. 107) and Church House (*see* p. 107). On up the hill to the Cathedral GATES, installed by Archbishop Alexander in 1912.

From here the visitor may follow Cathedral Close, past *Thomas Cooley*'s elegant late C18 GATE PIERS, moved here in 1963 from the old Archbishop's Palace to serve the See House (*see* p. 107), and past John Boyd's clergy houses again, from where Market Street leads back into the town.

Passing between Armagh Public Library and Church House, a more rewarding route leads back downhill to an intriguing jumble of houses across the road from the former Infirmary: the house at the top is clearly C18, with a canted two-storey porch and offset door; then comes an assertive, symmetrical house of c. 1890 with a pair of tall and narrow three-storey bay windows, in hot red brick with a modillion eaves cornice; and finally a T-plan C18 house (No. 40) with an excellent early doorcase in stone (closely similar to that of Coolmain House, Tyholland) and a tiny semicircular window in the gable pediment of the projecting arm of the T. This building has extensive offices – derelict at the time of writing – and gates with big stone piers opening into a yard. Fifty years ago there were many more buildings like it surviving in Armagh.

Round the corner, Dawson Street and Abbey Street converge at the former PROTESTANT HALL (now the Youth Hostel). This mid-C19 pilastered, two-storey stuccoed building, with pediments on the two adjacent fronts, is excellent in the streetscape, yet decidedly odd. Of the two streets ABBEY STREET, lined by three- and four-storey Georgian houses, is much the older, curving back and stepping down the hill until the superb surprise of the METHODIST CHURCH, with its bulging stuccoed front (see p. 118) and down the side yet another view of McCarthy's twin spires. Near the bottom of the street on the r. is the former Presbyterian church (see p. 118), now part of ST PATRICK'S TRIAN VISITOR CENTRE, locked behind a galvanized metal fence wholly unworthy of the area.

Where Abbey Street meets UPPER ENGLISH STREET, the corner is marked by the tall and shapely gable of the FIRST TRUST BANK (former Provincial Bank) of 1896 by *Graeme Watts & Tulloch*. Three storeys with a rusticated ground floor in sandstone ashlar and red brick with copious sandstone trimmings above. To the S, the modern POST OFFICE AND SORTING OFFICE, dissolving in its mediocrity all sense of the historic city centre. Beyond it, almost opposite the junction with College Street, the former Belfast Bank of 1851, now the Tourist Office (see p. 127), does a far better job in terms of architectural responsibility within an urban setting. Beyond the College Street junction to the N, on the E side, the SEVEN SISTERS is an imposing terrace of town houses, now bereft of one through demolition, built c. 1768 for Dr John Averell, Dean of Limerick, and attributed to *George Ensor*; conglomerate rubble, each with three bays and a tall sandstone doorcase with a thin cornice on consoles and rectangular fanlight, only one preserving the original light, a fanned Gothic design. Beyond these to the N are the varied stuccoed façades of the CHARLEMONT ARMS HOTEL (originally the irregular seven bays on the l.), which survived the rebuilding of the interior after a bomb in 1972. Opposite is the Secretariat Building of 2009 (see p. 129).

A short extension of the tour might follow the roadway N, turning l. into CATHEDRAL ROAD at the intersection with Dawson Street. The main façade of the former Cornmarket (see p. 126) faces Dawson Street, with a railed enclosure behind, lined by two rows of later C19 red brick terraces, set at right angles to each other and now called EDWARD STREET. The steps to the

Catholic Cathedral are opposite the NW corner of the market.
Visitors should not fail to mark the legend of St Patrick and
the fawn carved on the tympanum of the gate lodge front door
(*see* p. 113).

NEIGHBOURHOOD

ARCHBISHOP'S PALACE (former), now ARMAGH CITY AND
DISTRICT COUNCIL OFFICES. Reached off Friary Road. The
names of *Davis Ducart*, *George Ensor* and *Thomas Cooley* have
all been associated with the design of this building, though
there is conclusive evidence only for Ensor's involvement. A
payment of over £10,000 to him in 1775 suggests, at the very
least, that he was the builder. Archbishop Robinson had first
mooted the idea of moving the primatial residence to Armagh
in 1766 and by February 1769, the year in which the demesne
was enclosed, it was stated in official documents that he 'hath
already erected and covered in the shell of a house for himself
and his successors'. This date firmly places the building before
Cooley's arrival in Ireland, though the sober façades do have
the chaste character of his buildings under Robinson. *Davis
Ducart* is named as the architect in the *Freeman's Journal*
in 1770, and he seems a reasonable possibility, given his
employment at the time on the Tyrone Navigation with
which Robinson was also closely involved. But there is little in
the architecture here to suggest his idiosyncratic hand, apart
perhaps from the bold orchestration of the windows on the
garden front, and the interior seems not to have been completed until 1775, by which time he was certainly no longer
involved, so there seems little choice but to opt for *Ensor* as
the executant architect.

44   Today the impression is of a ponderous free-standing block
in limestone ashlar, grandly proportioned if somewhat too
restrained in character and decoration. Originally built with
two storeys on a rusticated basement, in the early C19 the plain
eaves entablature was raised to provide an additional storey for
Archbishop Beresford. Unwisely, the proportions of the upper
floor were not sufficiently diminished, leaving an awkward if
more monumentally solid-looking building. This work is invariably attributed to *Francis Johnston* and dated to 1825; the
internal decoration looks a decade later, though, making his
successor, *William Murray*, seem more likely. The main front
has nine bays with decidedly reticent decoration limited to
straight entablatures over the windows on the ground floor; its
original two-storey form compared closely to *Cooley*'s main
elevation for the Bishop of Meath's Palace at Ardbraccan,
designed only a few years later, suggesting that if Cooley was
not the designer here, the Armagh design influenced its Leinster subordinate. The original doorcase, replaced by the present
porch, is now known only from a measured drawing made in
1775 by *Richard Louch* to send to Dublin; its arrangement of

Scamozzian capitals, pulvinated frieze and subsidiary arch is redolent of *Pearce*'s treatment of the terminations to the colonnades of the Dublin Parliament House. The porch was added as part of the early C19 works, and from similarities with Castle Dillon can be attributed to *Murray*. It is essentially an octagon, given a distinctly Baroque flourish by twin Ionic columns set at an angle on the outer corners with a complete entablature. The pilaster responds are repeated on the angled inner walls to flank the windows in the sides of the porch. Above the central first-floor window is an oval guilloche filled with the arms of Archbishop Robinson, with drapery swags suspended from the Primate's crozier. The date 1770 carved in low relief above supports the belief that this was a later addition by *Cooley*, corresponding exactly to a drawing for the arms found with his proposals for Ardbraccan. The garden front has seven bays rather than nine, so the windows are more generously spaced, those on the ground floor resting on a continuous sill, with alternating pediments that hint at an old-fashioned Palladianism that gives further assurance to the idea that Cooley is unlikely to have been involved in the building in any substantial way.

The plan is five bays deep, a straightforward double pile with rooms ranged round a square entrance hall with two staircases placed side by side to the front of the building. The Rev. Daniel Beaufort in 1787 visited the Palace when it was complete, and found it 'very ill-designed for the expense' and rather dismissively described the interior with a brief sketch: 'In the house there are six bedrooms, his graces is below – the drawing room too small, the hall neither hall nor parlour.' Most rooms are simply decorated in the weighty classicism of the mid-Georgian period, with nothing surviving that could be suggestive of Cooley's elegant touch; in the entrance hall, an enriched Doric cornice with an ebullient C19 rose to the ceiling. The most impressive space is the main stair hall, with an open-well staircase generously terminated with a large scroll. The plasterwork here is notable, with an unusual arcuated cornice filled with frilly leaves and open ballflower pendants below. The soffit has a guilloche band, and a rocaille Vitruvian scroll frieze runs between the first and second floors. The ceiling of the stair hall is C19, with an enriched modillion cornice and a whorled acanthus rose set in a large circular panel bordered with crisp foliate ornament similar to Murray's decoration at Castle Dillon.

PRIMATE'S CHAPEL. Set at right angles to the main façade   44
of the Palace, this perfect little temple front emerges from a small grove with all the good breeding of a refined Neoclassical monument. The prostyle portico, set on a podium, has a calm austerity with its unfluted Ionic order, crisp entablature, dentil cornice and low pediment; its features in pale, finely droved limestone ashlar contrast with the sober, leaden lumpishness of the Palace. *Thomas Cooley* began the chapel in 1781 for Archbishop Robinson; the interior was completed by *Francis*

Johnston. Four-bay nave and a short, square chancel, the plinth, string-course and entablature continued round all sides. The windows, resting on the string-course, are tall round-headed sashes in shallow recesses, unadorned but for the leaf-draped keystones that emerge quietly from the smooth wall surface.

Inside, Cooley's restrained approach was abandoned for a more sumptuous delicacy, with plaster enrichments by *Johnston*. The lower walls are wainscoted in oak, and above this flat Corinthian pilasters punctuate the walls as Cooley intended; his plain entablature was however revised by Johnston, with an enriched modillion cornice and a lacy Neoclassical frieze with urns and palmettes linked by lyre-shaped arabesques. Similarly the segmental vault of the nave was elaborated with shallow coffers with double borders and flat alternating roses; the lower vault over the chancel has polygonal coffers. Over the entrance, the gallery is a small apsidal space with theatrical drapery and a frontal with elegant Italianate balusters. – FURNISHINGS. The canopied ARCHBISHOP'S THRONE in the centre of the N wall, of timber, has a nicely panelled frontal and fluted Corinthian columns under an open pediment with the archbishop's mitre set on a plinth. – STAINED GLASS. Bright C19 figural panels at the E end; the Good Samaritan in the E window is a late C19 work replacing an C18 window by *Francis Eginton* of Birmingham.

Behind the chapel, the STABLES form a compact Palladian quadrangle in conglomerate rubble with limestone dressings, rebuilt in 1859 by *W. J. Barre* after a fire. A handsome five-bay front addresses the Palace, with a central pedimented breakfront filled with a tall rusticated arch, well-spaced windows in blocked surrounds, quoins and a square, domed cupola on the ridge above.

The ROKEBY OBELISK is a monument of considerable poise set on the wide brow of Knox's Hill in the demesne. Although now stranded in a golf course, it retains its relationship to the Palace, aligned squarely with the S front. Up close the scale is stupendous, a towering pinnacle of limestone ashlar raised on a tall plinth set above two courses of V-channelled masonry. Begun in 1782 by *Thomas Cooley* to a design sketched by *John Carr* of York, and completed after Cooley's death in 1784 by *Francis Johnston*, it was built to commemorate the friendship between Archbishop Robinson, by then ennobled as Baron Rokeby, and the 1st Duke of Northumberland. Cooley and Johnston made the obelisk taller and more slender than in Carr's design and elaborated the plinth with sunken panels, beautifully bordered by acanthus leaves. The E and W sides have a Latin inscription, while the royal arms and those of Northumberland appear respectively on the N and S sides. High on the W face the Robinson arms are displayed under a baron's coronet between bay fronds; the E face displays the more elaborate primatial arms over the insignia of the Order of St Patrick.

The PALACE FARM, inside the W boundary at the S end of the demesne, is a charming model farm, probably by *Francis*

Johnston, built between 1790 and 1804 when Sir Charles Coote remarked that 'his grace's farmyard, implements of husbandry and mode of culture, afford a bright example to the gentry'. A large quadrangle fronted by twin farmhouses linked by a gate screen with tall ashlar piers. Each house is a two-storey, three-bay Late Georgian block with a hipped roof and central stack, the ground-floor windows set in shallow segmental arches with twelve-pane sashes; smaller nine-pane windows above. Now cement-rendered, with plain limestone dressings. The doorway is in the centre under a thin bracketed ledge: a simple trabeated design with blind side-lights and a spoked segmental fanlight. Behind, the two-storey w range has a shallow breakfront with a pigeon loft in the pediment.

PRIMATE'S COTTAGES. Outside the demesne wall, on the Keady Road. A row of single-storey late C19 houses in squared limestone, with a two-storey gabled block with Tudor hood-moulds rising in the centre.

DEAN'S HILL. College Hill. A tall, cement-rendered Georgian block, built in 1772 for Dean Hugh Hamilton with three storeys on a half-basement and gabled ends, altered in 1887 by *J. H. Fullerton*, and extended to one side in 1896 by *H. C. Parkinson*. The front has four bays with Georgian windows and a large central doorcase in an aedicule, squashed between narrow ten-pane sashes. The doorcase, reached across the area by a sweeping flight of steps, is crisply executed in limestone and heroic in scale, with Tuscan pilasters, entablature and pediment and a semicircular spoked fanlight. Inside, a double-pile plan with a large central hallway and the stair to one side. Enriched cornices and lugged doorways in the main rooms.

BALLINAHONE. Off Hamiltonsbawn Road. A substantial Georgian house, described as 'new built' in 1779, but in appearance two decades older, and likely to be older still if the sundial on the gable, dated 1685, belongs here. A broad two-storey block raised over a half-basement, with a pedimented breakfront and big stacks over the end gables. The walls are roughcast, with channelled ashlar on the lower half and upper quoins of the breakfront and on the outer quoins. The triangular arrangement of the windows on either side of the breakfront is odd, one placed centrally over two. The doorway, reached by a broad flight of steps, is a simple round-headed opening with a keystone, flanked by small sashes, now like all the other windows filled with plate glass.

ST LUKE'S HOSPITAL. Loughgall Road. Initially built 1820–5 by *Francis Johnston*, the first of nine district asylums he proposed to the Commissioners for the Erection of Lunatic Asylums as their architect. It follows the standard second-class design, for one hundred inmates, consisting of a two-storey central block advanced between long ranges for male and female inmates, with two further ranges radiating in a large enclosed yard behind. The plan is based on the corridor system, with rows of sleeping cells backed by a corridor. The contractors were *McCartney & Ballintine*, overseen by *William Murray*. Murray added the domed cupola, clad in copper, in 1824, the date displayed on the weathervane. In 1860–2 *John Boyd* added day rooms, a dining hall, kitchen store, laundry and stables, and between 1875 and 1879 he almost doubled the accommodation by extending the front range with large blocks projecting at each end; he also added a large recreation hall in the former kitchen yard to the rear, distinguished by its ornate metal window frames. For this the contractor was *Richard Cherry* of Loughall. *Johnston*'s two-storey, five-bay central block, built of squared limestone with smooth dressings, still dominates with its pedimented end bays. It was remodelled by *Boyd*, who formed a canted entrance bay embellished with a Tuscan order and increased the fenestration on either side with camber-headed windows and plate glass. The central block is flanked by narrow stair-towers (now adapted with entrances), with the long thirteen-bay range recessed behind, remodelled by Boyd when he extended the front with narrow sashes on the ground floor and removed the open veranda shown in Johnston's design. Towering behind the l. range is a bulky Italianate water tower, probably of the same period, in quarry-faced masonry with dressed quoins and three stages topped with machicolated eaves. By 1886 there were 273 inmates; more additions followed in 1891–3.

Eventually a detached hospital for 150 patients was built on an elevated site to the rear in 1895–7. This is the HILL BUILDING, by *J. J. Phillips & Son*. A disquieting Frenchified extravaganza in rock-faced limestone to a symmetrical H-plan, disrupted only by a chisel-roofed tower to one side. The central building is a five-bay, two-storey block with staged recession, mullioned windows, and an emphatic modillion cornice and parapet. Behind this the mansard roof is busily arranged with tall stacks to the fore, pedimented dormers, and an elaborate gabled attic window in the centre, all embellished with iron ridge cresting and fanciful moulded copper ridges. The entrance has a porch with Ionic columns; across the lower, buttressed wings, short glazed verandas with ornate cast-iron supports like those of a railway platform. The wings step forward at the ends, flanked by domed polygonal towers, and reduce to single-storey blocks with hipped roofs and canted fronts. The copper domes of the towers and numerous ridge ventilators enliven the freakish silhouette. New entrance gates of 1900 by *J. C. Boyle* of Armagh, now disused. Further alterations and repairs in 1940 by *McLean & Forte*, and in 1979 by *G. P. & R. H. Bell*.

There are three CHAPELS within the grounds. The earliest and most publicly sited, on the N corner of the boundary with its entrance from the street, is a small classical chapel, built as part of the additions of 1875 by *John Boyd*. A four-bay hall in squared limestone with kneelered gables and porch with moulded copings. The doorcase is a pedimented Baroque design filling the gable. Round-headed windows with raised keystones, elaborated with traceried iron frames. The small Gothic church (C of I) facing the main front is a late C19

design, probably by *J. J. Phillips*. A four-bay buttressed hall and
chancel in red brick with red sandstone dressings, with a steep
slate roof, bellcote gable, and porch to one side. Inside, simple
architecture with tapering trusses to the roof, strengthened
with iron ties. Small windows in Tudor arches with figurative
stained glass by *CWS Design*. St Mary's Chapel beside the
approach to the Hill Building is by *J. J. Phillips*. A six-bay
lancet hall with a polygonal vestry, set chancel-like on the E
gable, and on the W a small gabled porch with a canopied side
entrance. Built in rock-faced limestone with red brick trim.
Inside plain, with a timber-panelled ceiling and exposed
wrought-iron ties.

GREENFIELD MANSE. Newry Road. 1852. A boxy, two-storey
house, three bays wide and two bays deep, in red brick with
ornate stucco dressings, thin eaves cornice, and a hipped roof
with central stacks. The front has a narrow central bay gently
advanced and a shallow porch with square pillars. On either
side, wide segmental-headed window openings with bracketed
hoods and a central mullion separating round-headed sashes;
on the first floor the windows have twelve-pane sashes in
lugged frames resting on a continuous limestone string-course.
At the rear a short stair return. Here, out of sight, a large
limestone plaque records the erection of the building by the
Second Presbyterian congregation for the Rev. William
Henderson in 1852.

LITTLE CASTLE DILLON. 2.3 km NE. A modest two-storey
block of five bays between low three-bay wings with massive
slate roofs. The proportions look Early Georgian, with bulky
stacks projecting from the gabled ends. All in roughcast; the
fenestration now spoiled by leaded casements and gaping rectangular openings on the ground floor.

ANNACLARE. 3 km NE. A small Regency villa, fronting an attractive quadrangle of farm buildings. Single-storey with attic in a
gable-ended roughcast block. A slate roof sweeping to the front
unites two bay windows and a wide depressed arch, forming a
canted porch. Two slender polygonal posts support the arch
and frame a delicate timber doorcase with lithesome reeded
pilasters, a rectangular fanlight, and side-lights filled with lacy
leadwork. Twelve-pane Georgian sashes, narrowed with eight
panes in the sides of the bay windows.

OULART VILLA. 3 km NE. A sizeable Late Victorian house in
chequered Flemish-bond red and yellow brick with rusticated
limestone quoins, understood to have been built for the County
Coroner. Two storeys with attics; four-bay front with a bold
eaves cornice on brackets, formed into an open pediment.
Boxy brick porch with cornice and limestone blocking course.
Tripartite sashes with plate glass.

NAVAN VISITOR CENTRE. 2.7 km SW. 1993 by *McAdam Design*.
A visitors' centre to the adjoining Iron Age site of Emain
Macha or Navan Fort. This enclosed hilltop earthwork above
the plain of Macha had once been the capital of Ulster, the
royal stronghold of the kings of Ulaid, occupying a central

place in Ulster mythology. The Centre is built discreetly into the landscape, with a design caught between the ideas of a Bronze Age henge, an Iron Age stone fort and a Neolithic passage tomb. Essentially two grass-roofed domes, following a plan of two intersecting circles. The funnelled entrance on one side is lined with snecked rubble walls, converging on a low grassy ledge supported by two short stocky pillars with flared capitals. The entrance opens into a central top-lit atrium with twelve tall pillars. Round the back a sunken service yard exposes an ugly two-storey curving façade built in fair-faced blockwork with textured concrete blocks – a tired, out-dated building, the result of poor materials and novelty architecture.

2090   # ARVA   CN

A small market town in east Cavan on the border with Longford, beside the waters of Garty Lough. The surrounding lands were acquired in the early C17 by the Achesons of Markethill, and after the establishment of a bleaching mill by Arthur Bell in 1762 the dependent settlement was modestly developed over the course of the succeeding century by the Achesons, by then ennobled as earls of Gosford, before they sold the estate in the 1870s.

ARVAGH PARISH CHURCH (C of I). 1819. On the edge of the town, in a small graveyard. A small Board of First Fruits hall-and-tower type, probably by *John Bowden*, enlarged later with a modest N transept. Toy-like three-stage battlemented tower, now incongruously unrendered to reveal a mixture of rubble with squared masonry and cutstone dressings. Three-bay roughcast hall with lancets, nicely expressed with fine hood-moulds. A traceried timber window with quarry glazing survives in the transept.

CHURCH OF THE SACRED HEART. 1927 by *W. H. Byrne & Son*, replacing a T-plan church of 1846. An ambitious twin-towered church in an Italo-Romanesque style, set at an angle against the street at the top of the town, but with little advantage, being somewhat too prodigious for its restricted site. Built of squared blue limestone with abundant silver granite for dressings, sparing in detail. The contractors were *Sean Mulligan* and *Charles Doyle* of Mullingar. Aisled nave and deep projecting apse. On the broad and imposing gabled W front, with low lean-to aisles, a rose window is held between slender square campaniles, giving a strong sense of symmetry. The interior is more overtly Hiberno-Romanesque, displaying *Ralph Byrne*'s typically well-informed approach to architectural detail, though his introduction of classical mouldings seems incongruous. Six-bay arcade on plain shafts with polygonal capitals, weak zigzag ornamentation to the arches. Barrel-vault divided by wide transverse ribs springing from plinths on foliated corbels between the clerestory windows.

ARVA LIBRARY AND COURTHOUSE. The former Market House. Given every advantage on the central Market Square, facing down the main side street. An early C19 design in a spare classical style, based on the market house at Collon and built for the 2nd Earl of Gosford, who also considered similar schemes for Markethill. Designs preserved among the Gosford papers, one dated 1833 (possibly by *John Farrell*, who was clerk of works at Gosford and at this time signed a design for the sessions house at Markethill), show a central pedimented block flanked by short three-bay ranges terminating in smaller pedimented blocks. These were presumably destroyed when the building was enlarged *c.* 1912 with closely matched two-storey, three-bay stuccoed blocks by *James Reilly*. The surviving pedimented section is somewhat overwhelmed by these additions, like a breakfront in an otherwise undistinguished stable block. Two storeys in pale sandstone ashlar with a finely tooled finish; on the ground floor is a large round-headed arch with an unusual tapered chamfer; above, three bays on a deep moulded string-course; simple corbel blocks to the pediment and a lunette formed for a Diocletian window. No evidence now of the ogee-domed cupola proposed in the drawings. The C20 additions are rather domestic-looking; one side is differentiated by a small bay window on the ground floor and a central segmental-headed doorway with side-lights.

BANK OF IRELAND. An understated end of terrace house providing a bookend on one side of the Market Square. Two storeys, roughcast, with a deep double-pile plan giving twin gables to the square; four-bay front with corbelled brick eaves, plate glass, and on the ground floor a broad corbelled fascia in stucco above large deep-set windows, all presumably by *Adam G. C. Millar*, who remodelled the building in 1929.

ULSTER BANK. A plain mid-C20 block in red brick of two storeys and four bays, with twelve-pane sashes under a thin eaves cornice and blocking course.

NEIGHBOURHOOD

CORLISBRATTAN METHODIST CHURCH. 4 km N. 1803, restored 1903. A sequestered Gothic hall, small and awkward in its proportions. Plainly rendered with lancets, large and pointed in the gabled ends, narrow with rounded heads and set in pairs on the two-bay sides.

CHURCH OF THE IMMACULATE CONCEPTION, CORRANEA. 4.5 km NE. A rugged Gothic church set against the lumbering outline of Bruse Hill. Built 1925 by *W. H. Byrne* in rock-faced rubble with silver granite dressings. The builder was *Felix O'Hare* of Warrenpoint. Attractively buttressed W gable with a narrow central breakfront filled with tracery, crowned by a tall offset bellcote; seven-bay nave with cusped lancets changing to sexfoils in the last three bays. Straightforward arrangement of nave and chancel with gabled projections on each side for a porch and sacristy, creating a cruciform plan. Inside, an impressive hammerbeam roof and a graduated tripartite arcade at the E end with slender quatrefoil piers and stiff-leaf capitals.

PRESBYTERIAN CHURCH, DRUMKEERAN BLACK. 5.5 km NE. A squat three-bay roughcast hall of *c.* 1839, with smooth quoins, square-headed windows, and a big hipped roof. Entrance offset in the narrow two-bay end elevation. Remodelled in the mid C20. Former MINISTER'S RESIDENCE, a two-storey block, set back on one side.

DERRYLANE PARISH CHURCH (C of I). 5.5 km NE. 1833 by *William Farrell*. The standard three-bay single-cell design, here in the service of the parish of Killeshandra. Rubble with limestone dressings; a broad gabled front with stout buttresses at the corners and an ashlar bellcote, all finished with spiky pinnacles. The windows have simple iron tracery and quarry glass. Inside, the original roof with exposed iron trusses remains. – STAINED GLASS. E window: the Ascension, by *Irish Stained Glass*, 1968. Otherwise the furnishings are later C19.

RECTORY. Beside the church. A two-storey roughcast block built in 1875. Well-proportioned front three bays wide with a segmental-headed doorway, a low hipped roof, and central stacks. Its Victorian age is most apparent in the unusual sash windows arranged with nine panes over a single pane of plate glass.

The former SCHOOLS nearby are contemporary with the church and being similar to Kiffagh (Kilnaleck) were built by the 5th Lord Farnham, based on one of the designs published in *A Statement of the Management of the Farnham Estates* (1830). A large two-storey roughcast block of five bays with entrances in lean-to projections recessed at either end. Rectangular quarry-glazed windows survive on the first floor.

HOLLYBANK HOUSE. 1 km W. A Late Georgian house of two storeys and three bays with a handsome fanlit doorcase and side-lights; known as Laurel Bank in 1837 when it became the home of the miller William Norton. Smooth-rendered with rusticated quoins. Enlarged in the early C20, when a plain three-bay entrance block with bay windows was placed at one end to form an L-plan.

AUGHNAMULLEN   MN

A varied rural landscape with an extensive lake system S of Ballybay. The name *Ath-na-Muillean*, 'the ford of the mills', reflects a long milling tradition in the area that reached its height in the early C19 under the Cunningham family, whose mills were employed in finishing coarse linens. By 1835 the mid-C18 bleaching industry was generally in decline, but eight mills in the Creeve district continued to be powered by the waters of its lakes. Most of these were large buildings, generally three storeys high, with drying lofts in the upper storeys over the beetling mills. The best survivor is at Corrawillin, but it is principally the mill houses, with distinctive wide cutstone doorcases, that remain prominent in the landscape.

When the Rev. Daniel Beaufort was faced with the prospect of the incumbency, he was unimpressed to find 'a miserable shabby church' and the rector's wife scurrying off to 'a meeting of seceders, to hear a journeyman tailor'.

CHRIST CHURCH, AUGHNAMULLEN PARISH CHURCH (C of I). An attractive rural church at a crossroads. Originally of the standard hall-and-tower type; the hall was substantially enlarged on two occasions, and the three-stage rubble tower is now overwhelmed by a disproportionate nave of four bays with a polygonal chancel. The tower is a simple rubble-built affair in three stages marked by sharply bevelled string-courses, topped with plain battlements and short octagonal pinnacles. Small lancets in the W wall, flanking the tower, survive from the original hall. In the mid C19 the Rev. Charles Porter added a N aisle to designs by *Raphael Brandon* and *Joshua A. Brandon*, exhibited at the Royal Hibernian Academy in 1847. Set tight to the N boundary, this interesting structure is unfortunately largely concealed from the visitor. Built in rubble with sandstone dressings, it incorporates a projecting vestry at the E and a quaint dormered window over the W end to light the gallery. The hidden treat is the elaborate and individualistic late medieval tracery, of which the finest examples, with heavy cusping, are at the ends of the aisle (as the church is skewed and the chancel projects beyond the aisle, the visitor needs to go round the back to discover this). In 1863 *Welland & Gillespie* drew up plans for a new church; ultimately the work was limited to alterations, but these were sufficient for the church to be reconsecrated in 1864. The chancel, with conventional cusped lancets, was added, and the entire S wall was rebuilt in a more regular masonry pattern with dressed limestone trim; its striking and individual fenestration, with hard spear-like lancets, pairs widely spaced beneath small trefoils in the nave, a triplet before the chancel, seems to represent a conscious break with the decorative indulgence of the N aisle tracery.

Internally the church is simple: a four-bay N arcade with 77 alternating round and octagonal piers, a plain scissor-truss roof and a nicely timbered gallery, both of the 1860s. – STAINED GLASS. Patterned designs with roundels of the Evangelists, 1864, attributed to *William Henry O'Connor* of London. – MONUMENTS. The primary interest is offered by an early C18 monument on the S wall commemorating Josiah Campbell †1722, by *J. Lamont*, from the old church on the site. A very fine classical aedicule in limestone and white marble. Ionic pilasters support a swan-neck pediment; the pilasters rest on a gadrooned base and are supported on brackets that frame a marble panel carved with military trophies. – Captain Francis Johnston †1862 and his wife †1864; a white marble quatrefoil. – The Rev. Charles Porter and his son, the Rev. William Porter, missionary †1909, by *Lendrum*, Clones. – Richard Allen Minnitt †1877; an elaborate carved Gothic monument in sandstone with a crocketed gable. – Sarah Tardy †1885; Gothic, in sandstone with short polished marble colonnettes, by *Harrison*, Dublin. – Also by the *Harrison* firm, Mary Anne Tardy †1884 and Francis Chamley Montgomery DSO †1901.

ORANGE HALL. 1886. N of the church, a neat little single-storey building of domestic appearance. Rubble with red brick trim. Simple bracketed eaves, rising to form an off-centre gablet bearing a plaque with the date. Behind is the former SCHOOL-HOUSE, a two-storey building of the same character.

MILL MORE (formerly AUGHNAMULLEN HOUSE). Entered off the crossroads. A modest early C19 house, described in 1835 (when it was the residence of Thomas Brunker) as a 'neat house of modern architecture'. Rectangular gable-ended block of two storeys and three bays with a lower two-storey block abutting the W gable set well back and just one bay wide but three bays deep. All roughcast with raised quoins. An exceptionally refined timber doorcase is set in a moulded stone surround with elongated leaded side-lights under an elliptical fanlight decorated with nice ogee-headed petals.

MULLANARY GLEBE. 1 km N. The former rectory for the parish, a long Georgian house with a varied front set handsomely above Mullanary Lake. The datestone over the door proclaims 1770, and the architecture largely agrees. Originally a gable-ended two-storey block of seven bays raised high over a basement, dominated by a wide canted bay in the centre and a broad flight of steps that rise to the blocked cutstone doorcase. Roughcast, with eaves gutters carried on carved corbels based closely on modillions. In the C19 a large two-storey range was added to the E with a projecting two-bay pedimented front, built to accommodate a large dining room, service rooms and additional bedrooms. Inside the main block the original tripartite plan remains, with two modest reception rooms disposed on either side of the octagonal entrance hall and a small but elegant stair directly behind. The rooms are plain, showing C19 alterations, but much of the C18 fielded panel joinery survives.

CUMRY LODGE. 2.5 km NNE. A smart C19 villa bearing comparison with nearby Bowelk. One-and-a-half-storey gable-ended block, roughcast with big sash windows. Wide doorcase framing a webbed fanlight and elegant geometrical patterned side-lights. A central round-headed window above the doorway shelters under an eaves gable. Neat vernacular yard complex adjoining. Occupied as a manse in the late C19.

CORRAWILLIN MILL. 2.5 km NE. Large unpretentious C18 corn mill. A big vernacular block of seven bays with one of the end bays projecting to accommodate the wheel house. Originally of three storeys, but given a fourth in the C19 – the height of the original structure evident on the gables. Tightly constructed rubble walls with brick and limestone trim. Simple three-bay MILL HOUSE to the w with an adjoining row of WORKERS' HOUSES on the roadside. All important reminders of a once extensive local industry.

DRUMFALDRA. 2.5 km NE. A sober early C19 mill house of solid appearance, built by John Cunningham, who had an extensive milling business nearby. Two storeys, roughcast with limestone trim. L-plan with two similar fronts, each with a projecting pedimented central bay. Low hipped roof with wide eaves supported on plain timber brackets set in pairs. The principal front is of three bays; all the windows are of equal height with marginal glazing, distinctively arranged in the side bays as bipartite sashes with a central mullion and heavy stone frames. The familiar wide cutstone doorcase in this instance has a very shallow elliptical fanlight supported on plain bracketed pilasters. The five-bay garden front is much plainer, with plain sashes, larger at first-floor level to light the bedrooms; most of the ground floor contained the service rooms.

BOWELK. 3 km NE. An Early Victorian house built for one of the prosperous milling families. A tidy two-storey, three-bay block of squared rubble with red brick trim, nicely proportioned, with larger windows on the ground floor. Gable-ended with wide bracketed eaves and a central gablet over a plain round-headed sash. Below this is a handsome doorcase with a wide elliptical fanlight and side-lights, each decorated with pretty leadwork. The house fronts a large enclosed yard.

CREMORNE GREEN. 3 km NE. Ruinous. An unusual house with asymmetrical fronts of three bays commanding an exposed hilltop site. The first of the mill houses in the milling district served by the Creeve lake system, though now, sadly, as a burnt-out shell, it must be placed last. Built by the Jackson family in the mid C18 and remodelled in 1785; in 1837 it was the residence of Mr J. Jackson. It stands two storeys over a basement which is completely exposed to the rear, transforming the scale. Roughcast over rubble walls. Wide oversailing eaves indicate later remodelling; the roof space accommodated attic rooms, evident from the line of small windows placed in an orderly fashion below the big gable stacks – the brickwork set into distinctive stone troughs, rather as they are at nearby Carnaveagh. Remains of a small enclosed porch on the entrance front and traces of flush frames to the window openings. It deserves closer study.

CREEVELANDS. 3.5 km NE. Of c. 1810. A handsome Regency villa which was once the focus for a very elaborate milling complex: no fewer than four mills were in evidence here in the early C19. A two-storey, three-bay block of rubble with brick and limestone dressings. Wyatt windows on the ground floor; charmingly naïve carved segmental-headed doorcase, formed of engaged columns with Composite capitals set between plain pilasters with rudely moulded brackets. The house sits in the centre of one of the ranges of a quadrangular yard, so that it appears to have lower wings. In 1835 the residence of Mr S. Cunningham.

CARNAVEAGH. 3.5 km SE. Of *c.* 1790. One of the most characterful of the mill houses in the Creeve district. A tall roughcast Georgian block of ample proportions, with a generous doorcase that gives the S front a cheerful countenance. Three storeys over a raised basement, with three not quite symmetrical bays, increasing to five on the N, garden, front. Big sashes on the ground floor with remarkable twenty-four glazed panels; above these, the windows diminish progressively in size. The tripartite doorcase, with an elliptical webbed fanlight, engaged Composite columns and side-lights, would not look out of place on Dublin's Merrion Square, though the uneasy treatment of the pilaster responds and the varied Neoclassical decoration in the frieze are a touch provincial. Massive red brick stacks, now roughcast, rise over the gables and are distinctively treated to incorporate narrow round-headed attic windows beneath a course of thin projecting stones that forms an unusual stepped band extending across the gable. A variation of this unusual treatment occurs at Cremorne Green. Evidence below the stacks indicates that the E gable was originally entirely windowed, with at least three bays on each level – an extraordinary feature, with no close comparison – closed in the C19; those on the end bays have since been reopened. The plan is compact and economical, with the rooms disposed around a square entrance hall. The stairs are placed to one side at the front and lit by round-headed windows in the W gable. In 1835 the residence of James Cunningham. Restored 2010 by *Jan Hermans.*

BAILIEBOROUGH   CN

A formally planned market town set between hills in the centre of the county, named for William Bailie, a Scottish undertaker of the Plantation who was granted the lands of Toneregie (Tanderagee, not to be confused with Tandragee in Armagh) by James I in 1610. In 1619 ten families of British birth had been settled in the vicinity of an incomplete castle, where in a corner of the bawn Bailie and his family inhabited a single-storey vaulted house, 20 ft (6 m) square. The Castle was completed ten years later, but nothing of it survives; it is understood to have been at Crocknahattin, 2 km NE of the modern town, beside Bailieborough Lough, where later proprietors resided until the early C20. The only suggestion of an early defensive settlement close to the modern town lies immediately S of the Main Street at Tanderagee, where a sizeable MOTTE is located on rising ground, surrounded by a deep fosse.

By the end of the C17 Bailie's property had fallen into the possession of the Stewarts of Lurgan, who retained ownership through most of the C18. Though part of the estate was sold in 1749, it was eventually regained through inheritance, passing to Thomas Charles Steuart Corry of Rockcorry in 1793. The only impression of the Georgian town comes from a brief description in 1789 which indicates that the impressive Main Street had been formed by then, opening into a square central MARKET PLACE like those of Cavan and Kingscourt. This is borne out by some of the tall three-storey HOUSES lining the street. The best of these, still dominating the old market place, is the premises of B. O'REILLY, a venerable Early Georgian house with a beautifully proportioned long symmetrical façade, seven bays wide, with later simple timber shopfronts flanking a central closed archway.

The Bailieborough estate was sold c. 1813 to Colonel William Young, a director of the East India Company, recently returned to Ireland. Young was evidently an improving force, overseeing the establishment of public buildings and developing the market so that by 1842 it had become the largest in the county. William's second son, John, succeeded in 1835 and despite a busy political career that culminated in the governor-generalship of Canada and ennoblement as Baron Lisgar, he continued improvements from afar, bringing the district workhouse and model schools to Bailieborough, the latter at the expense of Cavan. In 1862 it was claimed that the town had risen rapidly in the previous two years, with twenty new houses completed and more in progress. The failure to attract the railway stifled any further substantial growth, and the Youngs' association with the town ended with the death of Lady Lisgar in 1895. Lord Lisgar's house, known as the Castle, in every appearance a large Regency block, had been extended and refronted c. 1875 as a rebarbative Victorian Gothic pile. It was sold in 1900, reconstructed after a fire in 1919 by A. C. Coleman as a novitiate, and finally demolished in 1942; the demesne is now a forest park.

OLD CHURCH RUINS. Off Church Street. The walls of a Late Georgian church, a single cell with just two bays and an apsidal E end. Gabled W front with two widely spaced lancets high up. On the SE corner, where the pointed doorway is located, the wall plane is gently stepped back with a stone cavetto cornice extending from the re-entrant angle. Window openings in the nave are large and pointed with red brick trim. The graveyard is brimful of burials, including the forebears of the American novelist Henry James.

MOYBOLOGUE PARISH CHURCH (C of I). Church Street. In 1830 the vestry condemned the old parish church and resolved to replace it with a new one; begun in 1833 and probably by *William Farrell*, it is sited immediately E of the old one, crowning a small hill at the end of the Main Street. The design is a continuation of the old Board of First Fruits hall-and-tower type, the only distinction given to the upper stage of the tower, where the corners have polygonal buttresses that rise into pinnacles above the battlements. Three-bay nave with angled buttresses at the front and plain lancets with hoodmoulds, and a narrow chancel. Rubble with sandstone dressings. Vestry, s transept and porch at the SE corner by *Welland & Gillespie*, 1865–6.

Inside, the nave is roofed with the exposed iron trusses favoured by Farrell; scissor trusses in the transepts. Narrow, moulded chancel arch with hood. – FURNISHINGS. High Victorian, by *Welland & Gillespie*. – PULPIT. Octagonal with pink marble shafts. – STAINED GLASS. Y-traceried E window filled with patterned glass. Transept: colourful Celtic patterned memorial window to Sir John Young, Baron Lisgar †1876, by *James Watson & Co.* of Youghal, 1906. The remainder C20, unimpressive figurative panels, one signed *Irish Stained Glass*, Dublin. – MONUMENTS. The Rev. Charles Claudius Beresford †1848; a Neoclassical pedimented tablet by *D. McCullough*, Armagh. – William King †1872; a plain pedimented tablet. – Joseph Clarke Argue †1915; an inlaid alabaster plaque. – John Robert Coote †1918; a pedimented tablet with polished shafts, signed *W. Lendrum*, Clones.

ST ANNE. Discreetly sited between the Virginia and Golbolie roads. A sizeable cruciform church of 1838, replacing a modest L-plan building. Forestanding square tower of 1854, in three stages with battlements, pinnacles and a bloated pyramid roof in copper. Chancel, baptistery and sacristy added in 1868; flat-roofed aisles and porches of 1962 by *Simon Aloysius Leonard* of *W. H. Byrne & Son* are rather ungainly additions between the transepts and tower. All roughcast with stone and stucco dressings; expansive roofs renewed with copper *c.* 1962.

Inside, the broad nave has a plaster wagon roof with thin arch-braced trusses. The transepts open through a triple pointed arcade with moulded arches on painted shafts with varied foliate capitals – all 1860s details. At the w end the creation of the C20 aisles is jarring; here the nave walls have been opened up in the most rudimentary way, supported on each side by three short pilotis that form a kind of low and dismal horizontal arcade. – Elaborate sculpted REREDOS of 1895 with statuary, set in niches under crocketed gables. – STAINED GLASS. All C20. – STATIONS OF THE CROSS, 1956, lucid paintings, sombrely coloured, by *George Collie RHA*. – MONUMENTS. Set high round the walls. The Rev. Matthew McQuaid †1861; a plain slate tablet. – The Rev. John O'Connor †1902; a cusped marble panel.

PAROCHIAL HOUSE. 1912 by *J. J. McDonnell*. A two-storey, three-bay roughcast block in a vernacular style with sloping copper roof over a deep moulded cornice.

TRINITY PRESBYTERIAN CHURCH. Virginia Road. Of *c.* 1887. A small five-bay buttressed hall of squared, rock-faced limestone with yellow brick window trim. Gabled front with a lean-to porch with gabled entrance in the centre, three graded lancets above, and a small projecting canopy at the apex crowned by a polygonal copper spirelet.

Immediately behind is the CHURCH HALL of 1911, of squared limestone with red brick dressings and decorative bargeboards.

WESLEYAN CHAPEL (former), now an arts centre. Shercock Road. 1833. A small three-bay lancet hall of cubic proportions with a small gabled porch added later. Cement-rendered with dressed quoins and a big hipped roof. Embellished in the C20 with a moulded brick eaves cornice, ridge cresting, and coloured glazing.

The MANSE to the side is the familiar compact two-storey, three-bay block in roughcast with a steep hipped roof and central stacks.

COURTHOUSE. 1818. Set back at the W end of the Main Street with a deep plan, a stocky, no-nonsense two-storey block with a distinguished porch. Three-bay front, rendered with dressed quoins, stuccoed window reveals, and a low hipped roof with exposed rafter toes to the eaves. The porch added in 1834 is broad with a flat roof, nicely articulated with widely spaced pilasters flanking the doorway, rising to a frieze with corbels supporting a thin, square cornice. Inside, beyond offices and stair hall, is the large courtroom, a double-height space remodelled c. 1910 by *George Beckett*, with a flat coffered ceiling, lit by windows in the upper level.

Incorporated in high walls at the side is the former BRIDEWELL of 1834.

LIBRARY (former MARKET HOUSE). 1818. Replacing an older market house at the centre of the Main Street. A two-storey block with a hipped roof, built of rubble with thick sandstone dressings. Front of three bays with a gently projecting pedimented central bay; a simple plaque in the gable pediment, now weathered, reads 'Colonel Wm. Young MDCCCXVIII'. Emphatic round-headed arches, now glazed, on the ground floor, with imposts linked together by a thick platband.

BECKSCOURT. Kingscourt Road. A solid-looking mid-Georgian house, two storeys with attics expressed in small windows high on the gable-ends. The front has three bays with the central entrance bay deeply advanced and gabled. Lower service wing on one side to the rear, evidently added later: a plaque over the back door is inscribed 'Revd. A.C. 1807'. Interior greatly altered, though corner fireplaces and some raised and fielded joinery remains. In 1837 the seat of the Rev. E. Mahaffy.

TANDERAGEE HOUSE (former FEVER HOSPITAL). Virginia Road. According to contemporary newspaper reports, built in 1847 to the designs of Mr Johnstone of Armagh, presumably *J. J. Johnstone*. A gable-ended two-storey block with central stacks, built of squared blue limestone with liberal dressings, in a formidable Tudor Gothic style. Five-bay main front; the projecting central bay has a steep kneelered gable, an oriel window on the first floor, and a square porch with a hipped roof. Tall mullioned windows with Tudor hoods; two-storey bay window in the E gable. Briefly a convent in the early C20, repaired in 1928 by *Michael Grace*.

DISTRICT MODEL NATIONAL SCHOOL. Cavan Road. Tudor Gothic, in low ranges, to an irregular plan. Originally an infants' school, built for Sir John Young in 1845 to a U-plan in squared limestone with ample dressings and decorative glazing; soon afterwards adapted by *Frederick Darley* to accommodate the District Model National School which opened in 1850; made more irregular by additions in the 1870s and 1882, though all in matching style with kneelered gables and Tudor label mouldings.

MASONIC HALL (Bailieborough Lodge No. 796). Raised on a height in a walled enclosure, closing the E end of the Main Street and facing the parish church at the opposite end. A gay little polychrome building of *c.* 1878 built as a Presbyterian school, possibly by *J. H. Fullerton*. A gable-ended block, four bays wide at the front with a large gabled entrance projecting off-centre. Red brick with dressed stone quoins and bands of yellow and black brick, lively and zebra-like around the windows and doorway. At the entrance a stone string-course, ceramic tiles, and colonnettes framing the doorway. Big three-light gable window to the street. The roof is slated, with a fish-scale pattern across the middle, and has a slender pyramid-roofed spirelet atop the centre of the ridge. Long, low return in roughcast added to the rear in 1926 by *J. Coleman*.

GARDA STATION. Barrack Street. A mid-C19 gabled-ended block with two storeys and five bays, of squared limestone with dressed quoins and Tudor hoods; the entrance projects off-centre under a narrow kneelered gable.

NATIONAL IRISH BANK (former NORTHERN BANK). 1912 by *G. W. Ferguson*. Set behind a railed garden on the Main Street, on the site of the Georgian market house. A refined Italianate block in stucco of two storeys and five bays with nicely confected decoration. Compact, with a hipped roof on a bracketed eaves cornice. Plate-glass windows recessed in richly moulded surrounds, linked on both levels by continuous string-courses decorated with a Greek key.

BANK OF IRELAND (former HIBERNIAN BANK). Main Street. 1924 by *W. H. Byrne & Son*. A long stuccoed block in a revived Georgian style with a limestone porch. Two storeys; banded rustication and plate glass on the ground floor; eight tightly spaced bays above, with twelve-pane sashes resting on a continuous sill; then a full eaves entablature with a thin cornice and deep blocking course. The porch, surmounted by stout stone urns, has an open pediment on pilasters framing a rusticated round-arched doorway. A slender chimneystack towers over the detached N gable.

NEIGHBOURHOOD

GLEBE HOUSE. 1.4 km s. 1811. On the Kells Road, in a small romantic demesne with beech groves. A handsome Late Georgian roughcast block, of two storeys on a basement, with

a hipped bell-cast roof and central brick stacks. The main front
has three bays with Wyatt windows on the ground floor and a
broad, gently advanced central bay with a round-headed, fanlit
doorway, now concealed by a boxy Victorian porch set over the
area and awkwardly squashed between narrow side-lights. On
the garden front, an unusual segmental bow projects on the
basement and ground floor only, with three sashes crammed
closely together. Inside, the staircase is to one side, opening
through a segmental archway. Provincial Regency details, with
plain ceiling cornices and reeded pilasters framing windows
and doors.

Enclosed STABLEYARD nearby with whitewashed rubble
buildings.

CORGLASS PRESBYTERIAN CHURCH. 4 km N. An important
Late Georgian church in a vernacular Gothick style, built by
the Rev. Robert Montgomery in 1795 for a congregation established here in 1714. To the long seven-bay hall a gabled entrance
was added in 1902; here, the space above the big round-headed
doorway is filled with small plaques, pithily recording the
building's architectural history. The smallest is a reference to
the works of 2001 which spoiled the old exterior, replacing the
roughcast and hoodmoulds with flat cement render and dis-
carding elegant Gothick sashes for fake plastic casements.
Happily the inside fared better, and the Georgian box pews
with raised and fielded panelling remain; a raking gallery
extends the length of the hall, carried on iron columns.
– MONUMENTS. The Rev. Patrick and Mrs Jane White †1862;
a white marble tablet topped by a draped urn. – The Rev.
Thomas Robert White, †1906; a tablet with fluted pilasters by
Lendrum, Clones.

RELAGH BEG CHURCH RUINS, SRAHAN. 5 km SSE. In a well-
formed circular enclosure with revetments, directly beside a
motte and bailey, with superb views over open countryside.
The remains of a sizeable late medieval church associated with
St Fintan of Moybologue. Visible today are the substantial
rubble remains of the s transept (20 ft by 16 ft, 6 m by 4.8 m),
a portion of the nave N wall (18.5 m / 60 ft 6 in. high), and
fragmentary sections of the chancel walls. The original plan is
confused by numerous later dry-walled grave enclosures. The
chancel fragments stand as solid walling with a pronounced
batter, and it is evident from the s portion that the transept
was added later. Here the gable preserves the upper dressed
stones of a rectangular window and a Tudor hoodmould with
a plainer opening of similar size directly below. Inside, a
blocked window on the E wall; a fireplace on the first floor
seems to indicate domestic use, by the priest.

The GRAVEYARD has much to reward the curious. In an
enclosure within the nave is a wonderful assembly of small
cross fragments, richly carved with figures and two with
inscriptions and dates of the late C17. Among an engaging collection of early grave markers is a large recumbent slab with a
relief of a cleric in medieval attire, bordered by worn text. The

sleuth will find more inscribed stones in the walls around the entrance.

In the C18 the area around Ballybay supported a successful linen industry. The watercourses feeding the Creeve lakes and Lough Avaghon link a collection of mills (now abandoned and derelict) that helped modernize the bleaching process and ensure a thriving market for flax and high quality linens here. Before that revolution Ballybay comes across as nondescript, part of lands acquired by Patrick Beaghan in the C17. In 1712 Edmund Beaghan sold it and thirty plowlands to his brother-in-law, the Rev. Henry Leslie, whose family were absentee landlords until the early C19, when *J. B. Keane* was employed to design a large house beside the town. In their absence the linen industry was promoted by members of the Jackson family, who had established the markets and built a market house about 1750. Between 1783 and 1824 the value of linen sales doubled. The industry went into decline, however, and although a new market house was built by the Leslies in 1848 ultimately the trade died out. A good mix of C18 and C19 buildings still dominates both sides of the Main Street, which meanders as an elongated S-shape from N to S. Halfway down on the W side where the curve is most pronounced, four three-storey houses are set back, breaking the street line to form what is still rather grandly called 'the Square' – the old market place, site of the Jacksons' market house.

CHRIST CHURCH, BALLYBAY PARISH CHURCH (C of I). At the top of Church Street in a small rectangular graveyard. Overall an unprepossessing structure, standard late C18 four-bay nave with a three-stage rubble tower and ample limestone dressings, plain battlements and short spiky pinnacles. Built soon after the parish of Ballybay was formed in 1796. Transepts possibly later, perhaps part of alterations in 1822. Elegantly elongated cusped timber tracery windows light the nave. Chancel added in 1881 by *J. H. Fullerton*, the contractors *Irwin Bros* of Ballybay. The E window in sandstone is a more elaborate exercise, Dec, with triple cusped lancets arranged beneath two generous quatrefoils. Plain interior, with no trace of the gallery added in 1816. Simple exposed kingpost trusses added with the chancel. Caen stone chancel arch with pink marble shafts, braided capitals and a sinuous hoodmould ending in carved heads. Chancel trusses and pine panelling nicely expressed in an unusual manner to follow the form of a cusped arch. Sandstone sedilia with two cusped arches supported on a red marble column, a pleasant surprise.

FURNISHINGS. ALTAR. Carved oak by *James McKean* of Laragh, late C19. – ORGAN. Donated in 1895 by Andrew

Carnegie and dedicated to Surgeon-Major Thomas Parke. – STAINED GLASS. Chancel: E window, the Good Shepherd by *Jones & Willis*, London, 1930, a copy of their window for Christ Church, Totland Bay, Isle of Wight; S window to Robert A. Mollan †1982: a Benedicite designed by *Meg Lawrence* and made by *David Lawrence*, 2005, a modern work of rare quality. N transept: the Sower by *Clokey*, Belfast, 1951. S transept: the Resurrection, also by *Jones & Willis*, after 1931; a watercolour design dated 1930 is displayed in the church. – MONUMENTS. Charles Albert Leslie †1838, a mourning figure in low relief by *Richard Westmacott*.

Outside the gate, CHURCH HALL (former BALLYBAY NATIONAL SCHOOL). Single-storey T-plan block, roughcast with hoodmoulds and decorative bargeboards. Built in 1838 and enlarged in 1878 by *J. H. Fullerton* under the patronage of R. C. Leslie French.

ST PATRICK. 1859–78 by *William Hague*. Big and conspicuously sited on the Monaghan Road, with a strong and resolute tower and spire. In 1857 proposals for a new church were sought and two years later the building was begun to designs by the young ambitious architect William Hague. He was twenty-three. Unsurprisingly, it is not a prepossessing work. A straightforward design in E.E. with broad expanses of dark blue limestone rubble and buff sandstone dressings – in effect somewhat ponderous, but in quality exceptionally good. The contractor was *George Burnett*. Cruciform plan – nave, aisles, chancel and transepts, though unusually the latter project from the chancel, an arrangement explained inside by the use of the transepts as side chapels. The three-stage tower on the SW corner, built last in the 1870s, is by far the most ornamental feature, with a fine ashlar broach spire with lucarnes. Entrance on the S side of the tower, through a moulded sandstone arch with colonnettes, hoodmould and carved headstops. Clerestory more frugal, with widely spaced small paired lancets, an arrangement repeated with taller windows on the aisles. Even with tall three-light windows in the gables, the result must have been a dimly lit, atmospheric interior. It is now flooded from skylights added along the aisle roofs, not without detriment to the architecture and the atmosphere. A plain scissor-truss roof rising from a high moulded cornice gives an impressive sense of scale, enhanced by the four-bay arcade carried on barely disguised Tuscan columns. Above the spandrels a register of blind oculi with dogtooth surrounds gives slight relief before a dull expanse of wall between deep-set clerestory windows. Richly ornamented chancel arch, carried on short engaged columns of polished marble resting on corbels, a device favoured by Hague. Sanctuary reordered and consequently dull. Side chapels without elaboration; S chapel replaced by a new entrance with an incongruous external timber porch. – STAINED GLASS. Mostly C19 in the colourful manner of *Mayer*; the three-light E window, nicely framed with colonnettes and hoodmoulds, depicts the Crucifixion with SS Patrick and Macartan.

Parochial House. The original, presumably also by *Hague*, was a typical two-storey, three-bay block with hipped roof and high stacks and a Gothic window on the first floor. It was demolished in 1991 and replaced by a rather banal building.

Second Ballybay Presbyterian Church. Hall Street. 1834. A massive six-bay hall built by a Dissenting congregation from Derryvalley, with an odd gabled front in a modest Perp style. The wide two-storey front of three bays has been stripped, apart from its rendered 'pediment'; the elements would read better if the entire front were re-rendered. However, it remains an attractive, assured composition built of neat horizontal rubble, framed by tall slender corner piers of sandstone ashlar. The rear elevation is simpler, with a half-hipped roof instead of a gable; to satisfy the symmetry of the S elevation one of the piers floats above the eaves on the SE corner only. The great bulk of the building is softened by very attractive fenestration: paired lancets with marginal glazing set in sandstone surrounds under emphatic hoodmoulds with nice bulbous stops. Those in the upper register are larger, an arrangement probably explained by the existence of a gallery, removed when the building was remodelled in 1888. The interior, after an entrance lobby and rooms to the rear, is a plain space of considerable volume, brilliantly lit, with a plaster ceiling with Victorian centrepieces and a simple moulded cornice. Raking GALLERY at the W end inserted in the late C19, with an elaborate floral cast-iron balustrade by *W. MacFarlane & Co.*, Glasgow, whose name is stamped on the supporting columns. – FURNISHINGS. All in pitch pine. – ORGAN by *Norman & Beard*, 1913. – MONUMENTS. Identical Gothic tabernacles on the E wall, flanking the organ, 1896, to the Rev. John Harris Morell, builder of the church, and his son, the Rev. James Morell †1914.

Second Ballybay Manse. A large, inelegant two-storey house built for Edward Keelaghan in the early C20. Seven-bay front, pebbledashed with stucco quoins and reveals, dominated by two-storey canted bays flanking a porch with two slender Tuscan columns supporting an ungainly concrete balcony.

Our Lady of the Sacred Heart and St Joseph's Nursing Home. A convent was established here in 1931 in a late C19 house on the Clones Road. The principal building is a plain two-storey, three-bay block with single-storey canted bays. The adjoining HILDEN HOUSE, acquired for a nursing home in 1947, is an early C20 two-storey block with a gabled front and a ground-floor veranda between canted bays. Additions of 1970 by *Martin Feeney*.

Market House. 1848 by *William Walker*. A handsome and dignified two-storey, four-bay pedimented block at the corner of the Main Street and Church Street. An interesting and perfectly balanced classical essay by an architect otherwise known as a designer in the Gothic idiom. The earlier Georgian market house in the middle of the Main Street was found to be in very poor condition in 1835, and subsequently demolished. Nothing is known of its appearance, but when Walker designed a new building for a new site, under the patronage of the Leslie family, he chose an established form with an arcaded ground floor, the arches elegantly articulated in moulded architraves with projecting keystones, resting on solid ashlar piers, carefully defined in the two advanced and pedimented centre bays, and given extra strength by the use of rusticated pilasters on the corners. Continuous platbands form a wide frieze between the storeys. The upper band runs through the sills of the first-floor windows, which have moulded architraves and straight entablatures. In the centre of the upper floor a panel bears the date in Roman numerals. Hipped roof with bracketed eaves, neatly applied to the raking elements of the pediment. Well-constructed in squared limestone with a paler ashlar trim. The contractors were *Clarke & Co.*, Monaghan. A new entrance and steps in a projection to the rear were added in 1943.

RAILWAY STATION (former). Castleblayney Road. 1860 by *William G. Murray* for the Dundalk & Enniskillen Railway, started four years after the line from Castleblayney was opened. An attractive and varied design with an understated Gothic character, dominated by the two-storey gabled stationmaster's apartments with long differentiated single-storey wings on either side. Windows mostly in depressed pointed arches. Built from the local limestone rubble with dressings of Fermanagh sandstone, now rendered on the rear elevation. The contractor was *John Nolan*. The new STATIONMASTER'S HOUSE built at the end of the C19 follows a standard design by *N. A. Mills*: a one-and-a-half-storey gable-ended block in red and yellow brick with a central gabled window on the upper floor.

HALL STREET NATIONAL SCHOOL AND TEMPERANCE HALL. 1878–83. Pound Hill. A simple and pleasing building. Single-storey, roughcast, with big Victorian sash windows. The two-storey, three-bay teacher's house to the rear is a simple gable-ended block of coursed rubble.

BALLYBAY COMMUNITY COLLEGE. Carrickmacross Road. 1965 by *Sean McCann*. An unusually sophisticated provincial school building. A light and elegant rectilinear structure, well integrated with its surroundings. The principal flat-roofed block, with rows of vertical glazing, rests with ease on a solid podium. The purity of the original concept now lost as a result of alterations and extensions of 2005 and 2010 by *McGarry Ni Eanaigh Architects*.

BALLYBAY CASTLE DEMESNE. There is now no trace of the substantial mansion designed in 1830 by *J. B. Keane* for Charles A. Leslie. The house, known as 'the Castle' presumably in reference to an earlier, unrecorded building on the site, stood on the E side of Lough Major. It was burnt in 1921 and demolished. Keane exhibited his design at the Royal Hibernian Academy in 1830. Photographs show a large Neoclassical house, two storeys over a raised basement with a rectangular plan. The principal front was ample, of three bays with a Doric portico set between advanced end bays. The house clearly followed lessons of scale and articulation learned from *Richard Morrison*'s villa designs: the arrangement was close to the design for Mount Henry in Laois. The longer side elevation, of five bays, echoed Morrison's side elevation for Castlegar in Galway, with its central pedimented section advanced with a relieving arch extending through two storeys. Of the interior nothing can be said other than that there are accounts of an entrance hall with marble columns, most likely scagliola, long familiar in Irish country house design.

No substantial features are evident in the DEMESNE other than part of the walled garden, some outbuildings, and remains of some good planting. A small astylar GATE LODGE on the Castleblayney Road, set in a formal railed entrance with gabled ashlar piers, is also by *Keane*.

OTHER BUILDINGS. The buildings lining the MAIN STREET are in general simple, unprepossessing C19 houses with plain stuccoed fronts. Occasionally the remains of some C18 houses are evident under the surface ornament. The POST OFFICE, for instance, occupies a tiny part of a greater eight-bay elevation, with nicely proportioned upper storeys now rendered and divided by a bold stucco string-course. Further s THE TAVERN, rebuilt in 1911 by *J. F. McGahon* in a Neo-Georgian style, stands out on the W side as a substantial red brick block of six bays and three storeys with a strong presence in the streetscape, and good stucco detail. An older red brick building further s on the same side is the LIBRARY, early C19 in appearance and possibly the public library mentioned in the town in 1842. Looking like a town house, it forms an end of terrace building of three storeys with a wide façade of brick laid in Flemish bond with sandstone quoins. Two multi-pane sash windows to each of the upper floors. On the ground floor the original doorway survives to the l., with slender fluted columns and spoked fanlight. To the r., a later arrangement: a straight-headed doorway, flanked by bipartite plate-glass windows. The houses on the E side of the former market place make an important contribution to the urban form, but offer little of architectural interest – even less since they are now fitted with ugly shopfronts. However, given the monotony of many planned streetscapes, the curious arrangement of the fenestration, with paired sashes in the intermediate storey, is an oddity that invites some attention. Much more formal amongst these is the BANK OF IRELAND (former NORTHERN BANK). Built in 1926, probably by *G. W. Ferguson*, it looks more like an English market house than a provincial Irish bank. The banking hall is accommodated in the advanced and pedimented three-bay section with a lightly rusticated stuccoed ground floor and precise stretcher courses of deep red machined brick. The manager's house to the r. appears too tightly inserted into the streetscape. S of this the former BANK OF IRELAND of 1879 by *Sandham Symes* is a modest Italianate design with strong horizontal emphasis and an unhappy combination of materials. The brick ground floor, with segmental-headed openings and bold sandstone keystones, rests on a lower register of black stone and sandstone trim, all in contrast to the plainly rendered upper storeys, of which the third was added in 1900. Further N, TOM MCGINNITY on the W side of the Main Street, an early C19 building, later remodelled as a bank, is remarkable for its tall brick and stucco front concealing a sweeping mono-pitch roof, all employed to give it presence in the streetscape. Lively and idiosyncratic Victorian shopfront, supporting a Doric entablature on roll mouldings. Amongst these brick-fronted houses and the plainly rendered houses that dominate, the former MARRON premises, a substantial five-bay building with central carriage arch, has squared random masonry and red brick trim. The traditional shopfront to the l. of the arch just survives, its simple architecture ignored in the creation of a crude and ill-proportioned counterpart on the r.

Later housing is represented by an attractive terrace of five local authority houses lining the S side of CHURCH STREET. Built by *Francis Keelaghan* in 1911, they offer a nice combination of black stone and red brick trim on the ground floor with a rendered upper storey.

NEIGHBOURHOOD

SPRINGFIELD. 2 km N. Simple but pleasing small late C19 villa of two storeys and three bays with the central bay advanced and gabled. Canted bays on the ground floor with an emphatic moulded cornice. Associated with the family of Sir Edward Carson.

ROCKMULLAN HOUSE. 2.5 km N. A solid house, of two storeys and three bays, squat in its appearance. Fanlit doorway and big sashes with Gothic glazing all replaced in a late C20 remodelling.

DERRYVALLEY (FIRST BALLYBAY) MANSE. 0.8 km E, on the Clones Road, 2 km from Derryvalley, whose C18 Presbyterian church (*see* below) it served. A small but ornamental house of 1895. Two-storey, three-bay block with corbelled eaves, a hipped roof and yellow brick stacks. The central bay is advanced and gabled with decorated bargeboards. Canted bays on the ground floor. Quaint timber porch.

OUR LADY OF KNOCK, BALLINTRA. 3 km SE. A hall church, on the site of an exceptionally fine T-plan barn church built here before 1788, which served as the parish church for Ballybay until the late C19 and was demolished in 1938. Designed by the contractors *William & Jack Cunnane*, it is a handsomely detailed design. A rendered seven-bay hall with raised quoins and gables with kneelers repeated in E and W projections that accommodate the chancel and a gallery respectively. Bright interior with an attractive and novel segmental plaster vault interrupted by flat ribs carried on short risers supported on the side walls. The intervening spaces are filled with a plaster Gothic frieze of cusped lancets. The chancel and gallery display clumsier plaster ornament.

BALLYBAY RECTORY. 1 km w. 1799. A relatively plain gable-ended block of two storeys and three bays over a raised basement, harled. Now with an unpleasant modern roof with boxed eaves, though retaining a pair of attic windows in each gable. Handsome and unusual windows with fanlights on the ground floor; originally fitted with Wyatt windows, replaced in the C19 with less appealing paired sashes and plate glass. Later porch. Modern housing spreading from the town threatens to diminish the attractive rural setting overlooking Rectory Lake.

HILLCREST. 1.5 km w. A familiar Georgian single-pile design. A tall two-storey, five-bay, gable-ended block over a raised basement with a plain doorcase and sash windows, its charm masked by a hard and uncomfortable coat of cement; the only light relief is found in roll mouldings applied to the reveals.

60 FIRST BALLYBAY PRESBYTERIAN MEETING HOUSE, DERRY-VALLEY. 2.3 km NW. A perfect Georgian hall built in 1786. Substantial rectangular block with half-hipped gables, all beautifully articulated with big Gothick sashes – six bays on the main front, reduced to four on the rear elevation, with a smaller pair in the gables. Unrendered rubble walls, but with a form of tuck pointing which effectively makes the surface read as ashlar. Wide cutstone doorcase with a blocked surround on the s gable with interestingly studded double-leaf doors and Gothick fanlight. Plain interior, reordered with replacement furniture in the C19. – MONUMENTS. Major David Nelson V.C. †1918; a brass plaque by *Robinson*, Belfast.

In a corner of the church grounds is DERRYVALLEY OLD SCHOOL, a pleasing composition of 1836. Long five-bay, single-storey block over a raised basement containing two classrooms on the upper level. Roughcast, with a low hipped roof and two brick stacks rising between the bays on the front wall. Central entrance reached by a long flight of railed steps.

To the NE on an adjoining site is the COMMUNITY HALL, built as a meeting house by a seceding congregation in 1800 and imitating the C18 church on a smaller scale: a long six-bay block with half-hipped roof. Cement render and uninspired replacement windows make it very dull.

SE of the church is DERRYVALLEY HOUSE, a modest Georgian gable-ended block of two storeys and three bays. Roof attractively finished with graded slates. Rubble walls, now exposed, revealing alterations to the fenestration in the C19 when windows appear to have been reduced in size. Some C18 window joinery evident inside. In 1837 the residence of T. McCullagh.

CRYSTALBROOK. 3 km NW. Little is known about this big Edwardian house, its suburban character a surprise in this deeply rural area. The tiled roof, Tudor-style gables, entrance veranda and leaded Art Nouveau windows would not look out of place in south Co. Dublin. An L-plan with two adjoining gabled ranges of two storeys, largely roughcast, with cambered window heads of red brick. The principal range is slightly higher, with three bays on the main front under a wide half-timbered gable, a Tudor feature effected in smooth render and bearing the letters CB. The tall central window, with clear crystal-like Art Nouveau glazing, lights the stairs. A bay window projects to one side on the ground floor, its roof continued to form a veranda that wraps around the corner to cover the entrance porch in the angle between the ranges. Single square chimneystack in red brick with attractive vertical detailing.

CREEVAGH PRESBYTERIAN CHURCH. 3 km NNW. Two dates are proclaimed on the gable, 1789 and 1900; the overall appearance of the building agrees with the latter. Trim gabled Gothic hall, smooth-rendered with raised quoins. Small lancets carefully balanced on the principal front, flanking a plain Perp doorway with a larger window over. The same paired lancets light the hall. Small pointed lunette with cusping isolated in the E gable.

BALLYCONNELL CN 2010

A small market town on the River Woodford beneath Slieve Rushen, close by the ancient border between Breifne and Fermanagh. Ballyconnell first emerges in the medieval period as a centre of the territory of the Magaurans, whose chiefs surface in skirmishes with the neighbouring Maguires, O'Rourkes and O'Reillys. In 1609 Cormac Magauran sold the surrounding lands comprising the manor of Calva to Captain Richard Tyrell, who held them briefly before the Plantation in 1609, when 1,500 acres were granted to Walter Talbot and Hugh Culme. It was Talbot who promoted the Plantation settlement here, raising a strong CASTLE at Annagh, on the E side of the river; built of stone and lime, it was three-and-a-half storeys tall with two flankers, described in 1622 as located 'in a very good place and convenient for the strength and defense of that parte of the country which is an abscure [sic] and bordering corner of the countie'. The Talbots forfeited the property in 1641 and by the time of the Restoration it had been granted to Captain Thomas Gwyllym, who renamed the settlement Gwyllymsbrooke. In 1724 the soldiering Colonel Alexander Montgomery of Convoy in Donegal paid £8,000 for the town, which by then had been granted a patent to hold markets. On the Colonel's death in 1729 the estate passed to his nephew, the Rev. George Leslie, who rebuilt the castle in the 1730s on a different site. His son, also George, assumed the name Montgomery, and began shaping the modern town, building a new parish church, and eventually rebuilding his father's house, which had burned in about 1764. George Leslie Montgomery died in 1787 and the estate was placed in chancery. The town continued to develop, gaining several public buildings in the 1830s. In 1856 the estate was sold, and divided principally between the 4th Earl Annesley and George Roe, who acquired the part of the town with the castle.

The town received its second patent in 1767, and weekly markets, a flour mill and nearby bleaching greens were well-established before the end of the c18, as the main street developed parallel to the river, extending NW of the bridge. By 1830 it had grown to 153 houses with a variety of trades, and soon after acquired a market house, but the linen trade was already in decline, and Ballyconnell reverted to being an 'inconsiderable place'. Its advantageous location opened the town to trade when the River Woodford was canalized in the 1850s between the Shannon and the Erne, and in the 1880s the Cavan & Leitrim Railway arrived. Ultimately, however, neither of these links had any great consequence.

58   TOMREGAN PARISH CHURCH (C of I). Singularly attractive, a pleasing study in curves on the edge of a grassy bluff. Built *c.* 1757 under the patronage of George Leslie Montgomery, supposedly on the site of the Magauran stronghold and an older church. Ostensibly a modest hall, but most unexpectedly for its date, it has bows breaking out at the ends and from the centre of the principal, S, front; these are curved only at the sides, with a flat face. The walls are of ashlar, rising from a plinth to a cavetto cornice set under a low hipped roof. The windows – lancets with timber tracery and small panes, set in chamfered frames with thin hoodmoulds – were inserted when the building was enlarged *c.* 1820. This involved seamlessly extending it to the N to form a T-plan and giving it a three-stage buttressed tower set well back behind the main front, architecturally independent, with battlements, pinnacles and a needle spire. As part of these works, the W bow was squared off to accommodate a vestry beside the main entrance, the seams for the work most evident on the N face.

The church is entered through a striking carved doorcase with a lugged architrave and curvilinear pediment. Inside, a stair is accommodated on one side, within the curve. Rare indeed is the survival of most of the Georgian interior, with the kind of bold plaster detail found in *Richard Castle*'s work.

59   The nave is an intimate space with galleries to the W and N and heavy plaster arches framing the chancel and the Montgomery pew in the S bow. A low C19 coved ceiling of timber panelwork disagrees with the thin plaster cornice from which it rises, but the bold architectural emphasis given to the chancel is enough to distract the eye. The arches describe a generous arc springing from short pilasters, with a keystone formed as a Baroque cartouche, set under heavily moulded spandrels. The chancel is more richly treated, with scrolls and raised and fielded panels in the soffits and gilded fronds in the spandrels. The words 'God is Love' are borne in a central panel over the arch, corresponding to the Montgomery crest and motto, 'Honneur Sans Repos', displayed over their pew.

The soffit displays clouds set against a sunburst, framed by a Vitruvian scroll, while on either side of the (later C19 traceried) E window the decalogue is set in lugged egg-and-dart frames, rising at the top into festooned swan-necks to frame a garlanded dove. Repewed, with Victorian furnishings, by *Joseph Welland*. – MONUMENT. Sarah Ainsworth Story †1829. A grey marble tablet with an eared pediment; set within a deep circular recess, an allegorical figure in white marble, resting on an urn, signed 'Temistocle Livornese Scolpiva' – presumably the work of the Leghorn sculptor *Temistocle Guerrazzi*. – STAINED GLASS. Traceried E window: the Good Samaritan, signed *A. L. Moore & Co.*, London, *c.* 1876. S transept: twin light with The Angel and the Women at the Tomb and the Faithful Warrior, also signed *Moore*, *c.* 1914.

89

Inside the porch is the so-called TOMREGAN STONE. Brought here from Tullymongan Hill (Cavan), where it is believed it formed the top of the door, it is a carved triangular stone, usually dated to the C12. The carving depicts a male figure, greatly foreshortened, with arms extending from an elongated bearded head with staring eyes, and clutching indeterminate objects in each hand; below the arms the stone is rebated, with the splayed legs and genitalia represented in low relief.

OLD CHURCH. Doogary Road. Disused but maintained. A trim lancet hall of squared limestone, built in 1843 by the Rev. P. Donegan P.P., replacing a 'thatched building undeserving of any description'. On the front under a kneelered gable the doorway has a steep Tudor arch with hoodmould, flanked by narrow lancets; three graded lights above. The sides have four tall lancets, most with twin sashes. Surrounding the third bay, a large masonry arch appears to represent a provision for future expansion into transepts. In 1956 a new sanctuary and a classical campanile were proposed by *Simon Aloysius Leonard* of *W. H. Byrne & Son*, but these were ultimately abandoned for a new church.

OUR LADY OF LOURDES. 1968 by *W. H. Byrne & Son*. Set on tarmac and lording it over its petite predecessor, a vast concrete church with the scale of an aircraft hangar: a bulky seven-bay hall, with a broad angular gabled front and a tall narrow tower at the rear. Built of pulvinated blocks, with nine tall mullioned strips cast *in situ* as a centrepiece to the gable, inset with alternating panels of concrete and glass mosaic – the only interesting element of the design.

METHODIST CHURCH. Main Street. Of *c.* 1869. A plain, well-finished Gothic hall of just three bays in squared limestone with prominent quoins. Gable-fronted, with a tall round-headed doorway and twin lancets above. Larger pointed windows to the nave, also in wide cutstone frames, sashed, with simple Y-tracery.

COURTHOUSE. 1833. Similar to the Courthouse at Cootehill. In a large railed forecourt off Church Street, a two-storey classical block with broad proportions and a rather heavy appearance; three-bay front of squared masonry with a central pedimented breakfront. Pediment and eaves defined by a thin projecting course of stone on widely spaced blocks. On the lower storey blind windows set in shallow segmental arches flank a sandstone tetrastyle portico with thin square pillars. The upper storey has a large tripartite window in the centre and windows in the side bays set in square-headed recesses resting on a continuous string-course. Interior remodelled in 1919 by *Patrick J. Brady* following a fire.

MARKET HOUSE. A heavy limestone block, set well back on the Main Street. Built *c.* 1830, and in 1842 considered 'rather an elegant edifice'. Sharing a family resemblance with the Courthouse, it is an astylar block of two storeys and five bays. Clean ashlar on the ground floor and squared rubble above, the separation between the two marked by a continuous platband. A steep hipped roof is carried on a simple modillion eaves cornice, rising into an open pediment with a clock over the central bay. The usual emphasis is given to the three central bays with wide segmental arches set in shallow recesses that rise through to the windows of the upper storey. The end bays are narrower, with round-headed recesses, inset with a fanlit door on one side only. Altogether the proportions are rather tall, leaving the small four-pane windows of the upper storey somewhat lost in the preponderance of walling.

OTHER BUILDINGS. On the E side of CHURCH STREET, the LIBRARY is an ill-proportioned but quaint three-bay hall occupying the former Presbyterian church, with a narrow Gothic gabled front overwhelmed by big lancets and a glazed Tudor-arched doorway. The Edwardian MASONIC HALL sits squarely opposite the Courthouse, with a severe gabled front of rusticated limestone ashlar with dressed quoins and three round-headed lancets. Beside the church, behind elaborate Victorian entrance gates, GLENDOON is a modest, smooth-rendered Regency house of two storeys with shallow hipped roofs oversailing on bracketed eaves and a well-proportioned three-bay front with plate glass and an engaged stucco portico; greatly enlarged *c.* 2000 when a new block with bowed ends was built behind in concord with the overall design. Opposite, elevated well above the street, ROSEBANK is a modest, one-and-a-half-storey Victorian villa on a T-plan; three bays to the front in squared limestone with wide windows set in shallow segmental arches, a fanlit timber doorcase, and a gabled window above.

In the centre of the MAIN STREET, the three-storey ULSTER BANK of 1910 by *Blackwood & Jury* stands out prominently, as much for its want of architectural appeal as for its scale. Four bays; plain stuccoed ground floor, sandstone ashlar upper floors with windows set in pairs, awkwardly rising into dormers on the top floor. On the same side, the premises of J. McBARRON preserve the only traditional shopfront in Ballyconnell: a trim symmetrical design with big plate-glass windows, slender pilasters and consoles, and raised lettering painted to imitate lapis lazuli.

On the outskirts of the town to the NW, the former RAILWAY
STATION, c. 1885 for the Cavan & Leitrim Railway. A
long building in the polychromatic brickwork favoured by
W. H. Mills for the Great Northern Railway, with a two-storey
central block of three gables.

BALLYCONNELL CASTLE. Beside the Erne, N of Ballyconnell
Bridge. Derelict for years and now stranded in a housing
development, the 'castle' is no more than the tidied, reroofed
and glazed shell of the mid-Georgian house built to replace
the one erected by the Rev. George Leslie in the years following
his succession to the property in 1729. The site he had chosen,
closer to the town than the Plantation castle, appears to have
been a new one. The Rev. William Henry in his *Description of
Lough Erne* of 1739 wrote of the newly completed house as
being of 'hewn stone without, and elegantly finished stucco
work within', adding curiously that 'the front is diversified with
dark and light coloured stones, resembling a pavement'. That
house was destroyed by fire *c.* 1764, and nothing of it is evident;
the house of his son, George Leslie Montgomery, stands today
as a no-nonsense two-storey block, just two bays deep with a
lower return. The main front has seven bays with nicely balanced fenestration and a small semicircular porch, altogether
neat and solid in its appearance, with smooth-rendered walls
relieved only by a sandstone trim applied to the plinth, sills, a
string-course between the floors, and a good moulded eaves
cornice. The windows are sashes with twelve panes on the
ground floor and six panes above. Described in 1830 as 'not
remarkable for any architectural beauty' largely because of
additions 'giving it a medley appearance'; most of these were
swept away in the C20.

SLIEVE RUSSELL HOUSE. 1.5 km N. Derelict. An attractive
Victorian lodge of two storeys with substantial returns. Main
front of four bays, one end bay slightly advanced and gabled.
Built of close-jointed squared limestone with raised ashlar
quoins. The windows, sashed with plate glass, are trimmed in
red brick later stuccoed over to imitate rustication. The roof
is carried on paired eaves brackets and has diagonal chimneystacks of red brick with limestone trim. Depleted of its
outbuildings and garden, though still retaining a small, well-
planted park, the house looks out over a vast industrial prospect of quarry and warehousing.

BALLYHAISE   CN   *4010*

In 1610 the manor of Aghieduff was granted to John Taylor, an
undertaker for the Plantation of Ulster. He built a strong bawn
of lime and stone above the ford of the River Annalee and introduced a colony of settlers. Within ten years, eighteen English and
Scottish families were living here in relative prosperity. The

manor of what was by then called Ballyhaise was conveyed by Brockhill Taylor to his son-in-law, Captain Thomas Newburgh, following the latter's marriage to Mary Taylor in 1656, and it was their second son, Colonel Brockhill Newburgh, who built the present house, a commanding red brick classical block set proudly above the river crossing. In the twenty years before 1715 he had spent the enormous sum of £4,500 on consolidating his estate, expending a large portion on improvements, so that for a visitor in 1738 it possessed a 'beauty and magnificence' that could compete with any in Ireland. In 1703 Brockhill Newburgh and Thomas Nesbitt were overseers in the rebuilding of the BRIDGE at Ballyhaise, clearly designed as an improvement over the old river ford, but also, as a imposing eight-arched structure squarely aligned with the house, part of a much greater gesture, allowing the house to address the impressive rising landscape that was gradually enriched in a grand manner.

Colonel Newburgh was eulogized as one of the great improving spirits of the new political order established after the Battle of the Boyne: 'with indefatigable industry he inclosed, cultivated and improved'. The same grand idea was behind the formation of the village to the SE, essentially conceived as a small circus, placed to terminate an impressive straight approach from Cavan to the SW. A slightly irregular decagon was formed of two-storey houses, 'all arched' within. The circus opens to the N and E, now intersected by straggling roads that fail the initial grand design; these originally led to a triangular fair green on one side, and on the other to the approach to Newburgh's mansion, with the parish church set importantly between the village and the house. The most striking element of the circus was the 'fantastical' MARKET HOUSE sited in the centre, long vanished. It was a circular building, in the opinion of some 'not unworthy the plan of a Vitruvius or Palladio', and indeed considered to bear no 'distant resemblance to the Pantheon'. The descriptions invite comparison with a contemporary design for a polygonal summerhouse by *Sir Edward Lovett Pearce*, whose assistant *Richard Castle* has long been associated with Ballyhaise. In 1736 the market house collapsed. Rebuilt, and described in 1837 as 'an arched edifice built of brick and of singular appearance' and in 1842 as a curious building on arches, though curiously it does not appear on the contemporary Ordnance Survey map.

The grandeur of the idea is spoiled today by the absence of the Market House, and more completely by the removal of one whole side of the circus and the late C20 mistreatment of the surviving buildings, grossly disfigured by unseemly alterations. The visitor's disappointment is carried through to the unattractive ribbon development and poor building design that has been allowed to line the approach.

CASTLETERRA PARISH CHURCH (C of I). A hall-and-tower type; its origins lie in an older C17 nave, largely rebuilt in 1820, probably by *John Bowden*, to a standard design consisting of a three-bay nave with a forestanding square tower in three stages with battlements and pinnacles. Enlarged *c.* 1860 with S transept, an extra bay to the E and a small vestry to the N. Refenestrated at the same time, with Romanesque windows with two-light tracery. Rubble with dressed sandstone.

Inside, W gallery and a kingpost roof. – STAINED GLASS. E window: Resurrection themes, 1888, possibly by *Joshua Clarke & Sons*. S aisle: the Good Samaritan and the Beloved Physician by *Alexander Gibbs* of Bloomsbury, London. – MONUMENTS. Ralph Harman †1807; above an inscribed tablet with inverted torches, a relief of an angel flying heavenwards among clouds, in white marble against slate, signed [*John*] *Smyth*, 14 Westland Row, Dublin. – William Humphrys †1834; a simple marble plaque with inverted torches and a snake eating its tail; the same composition used again for Anna Maria Humphrys †1837, a signed work by *Thomas Kirk*. – William Humphrys †1872; a scrolled tablet by *Coates*, Dublin. – The Rev. Baptist Barton Crozier †1878; a scrolled tablet by *W. Lendrum*, Clones. – John Winter Humphrys †1884; a scrolled tablet also by *Lendrum*. – Lieutenant William Humphrys †1906 at Pachmari in India; a sandstone aedicule. – Nugent Winter Humphrys †1931; a stone aedicule.

ST MARY THE VIRGIN. After the new cathedral for the diocese of Kilmore was completed in Cavan in 1942, the old building was dismantled and re-erected in Ballyhaise, replacing a more modest pre-Emancipation T-plan church of 1810 closer to the village approach. The present building had evolved in Cavan as a pre-Emancipation chapel of 1823, enlarged with a new chancel, galleries, transepts and S porch in 1853, and raised to cathedral status in 1862. The design was simplified here, the chancel and transepts omitted, so that essentially it has reverted to its earlier character: a seven-bay hall of squared biscuit-coloured sandstone, with the later square battlemented porch rebuilt, minus its steep pinnacles, in the centre of the S wall. The exposed position of the church, set in a vast car park, contributes to its bulky appearance. The three-bay W front is held between angle buttresses, with a bellcote rising over a narrow offset projection in the centre. The fenestration here is plain, with lancets set above narrow square-headed windows, all with chamfered reveals and hoodmoulds; in the nave big lancets, and a larger traceried window in sandstone on each side before the final E bay.

Inside, no attempt was made to revert to the Victorian richness of the old interior, or to recreate the elaborate rib-vaulting; instead, *W. H. Byrne & Son*'s involvement is evident in the high, gently cambered ceiling, simply treated with a wide margin and a moulded cornice. The nave was made even larger and more vacant when the wall separating the sacristy was demolished in 1982. Sanctuary re-ordered 2000 by *Richard Pierce*. Undistinguished.

BALLYHAISE HOUSE, now BALLYHAISE AGRICULTURAL COLLEGE. 0.4 km NNE. A stirring, unexpected Early Georgian red brick house of the Pearce–Castle school, grandiosely set above the public road, facing down to the narrow crossing of the River Annalee. There is an instant feeling that this house was once the centre of a much more extensive, grander idea, its relationship to the surrounding landscape possessing all the complexity of a grand Baroque design. It was built for Colonel Brockhill Newburgh, and in the *Particulars relating to the Life and Character of the Late Brockhill Newburgh Esq.* Jonathan Swift is reported to have declared that Ballyhaise was 'not only the best, but the only house he had seen in Ireland'. The true splendour of the setting and its power to awe in the early c18 survive in a brief account of 1739, written by the Rev. William Henry: 'There is an ascent to it by several terraces from the river, which are adorned with ponds, jets d'eau, fruit and flowers . . . scarce any house in Ireland has so brisk and lively an aspect.' Henry felt he could not do justice in a description of the house, but he points to the wider sophistication of its 'gardens, vistas, avenues, circular walks, roads and plantations rising to the tops of all the hills around'. Eventually these features gave way to the taste for a more natural environment.

It was to architecture especially that the Colonel gave most encouragement, his eulogist in the *Particulars* claiming that 'no gentleman of a private fortune gave juster and more useful specimens than Mr Newburgh'. The design of Ballyhaise was indeed innovative: the *bombé* façade made its first appearance here in Irish domestic architecture, and so too did the corresponding oval interior, prefiguring a volume that would not find popularity until the appearance of James Wyatt and Thomas Cooley in the Neoclassical period. However, it was the structural use of brick that singled Newburgh out as progressive. The house was entirely vaulted, on both levels, ostensibly against the hazards of fire. Perhaps this was also a signal that the new political order was here to stay: to contemporaries it was a house 'made to last for ever'.

The design for Ballyhaise has long been attributed to Richard Castle, though there is no contemporary evidence to support this; there is perhaps little even in the building itself that speaks out in favour of his involvement. There is a graceful quality here, especially in the subtle use of the orders – the 'elegance of fancy' – rare in Castle's work. And all the evidence seems to suggest that the house was completed before Castle had established himself in Ireland. The date usually suggested, 1733, seems improbable, given that Newburgh died an old man in 1741: his reputation as a great improver is unlikely to have been based on such a late achievement. If not Castle, then *Sir Edward Lovett Pearce* naturally comes to mind, and the house sits perfectly within his œuvre. The extensive use of brick rests more comfortably with Pearce than Castle, as at Cashel Palace, Henrietta Street in Dublin, and of course at nearby Bellamont. The use of a stone frontispiece against brick is also characteristic of Pearce and not of Castle; and so too is the distinctly Vanbrughian bridging of the chimneystacks, even if here it is

36

only as simply articulated as it is on Bellamont. The apparent influence of William Talman on Bellamont may also be relevant for Ballyhaise: the experimental use of the bow and the oval saloon, inspired by C17 French traditions, begins in these islands in the late C17 with Talman.

However, our understanding of Newburgh's innovative house is complicated by uncertainty. That the building belongs to several phases, but is essentially a major Early Georgian reworking of an existing core, is most noticeable on the main, E, façade, where distinctions in the brickwork evince changes in height, perhaps for the creation of the crowning entablatures; and the stone frontispiece with a steep pediment curiously independent of the roof certainly has all the appearance of an afterthought. However, all of this was certainly in place by 1746. That the house then also possessed a more complicated layout with wings is now known from a hastily produced sketch made by the Durham architect Thomas Wright while touring Ireland. His drawing confirms Ballyhaise as a building of the Pearcean school, the massing made more complicated by lower subsidiary blocks flanking the centre (where the present C19 pavilions stand), overlapped by low arcaded quadrants terminating in what appear to be octagonal or circular pavilions rather like the little domed belvedere towers that Pearce employed in a similar position at Summerhill.

Ballyhaise was always a house of less substance than its imposing roadside presence suggests. Raised on a half-basement, the Early Georgian house comprises the central two-storey, seven-bay block and its stone frontispiece, with lower, two-storey wings just one bay wide set back gently on either side. These wings would seem awkward were it not now known that they once formed part of the elaborated, well-balanced arrangement depicted by Wright. When the quadrants and end pavilions were swept away they were replaced by robust C19 pavilions. The primary material throughout is Flemish-bond red brick, satisfyingly contrasted with a pale sandstone, crisply worked for all the architectural details, including the entire pedimented frontispiece. Here, superimposed classical orders frame the three central bays, Ionic over Doric, each subtly articulated by clean-limbed pilasters rather weakly projected to support a full entablature. Set on low plinths, the Ionic pilasters have Scamozzian capitals, paired with a pulvinated frieze to support a rather steep crowning pediment – too steep, perhaps, because the order below is a little too crowded by the fenestration. This apparent unease is most obvious in the doorcase, a narrow lugged frame set tightly between the pilasters with a miniature segmental pediment filled by a scallop shell. Across the Georgian façade the windows are all of an equal size, with twelve-pane sashes in simple lugged frames. Below, a thin string-course continues through the upper plinth mouldings of the frontispiece. Above, a continuous deep stone band on which the first-floor windows rest, aligned with the Doric entablature, also unites the centre block and the wings. It is mirrored by the eaves cornice, which only partly conceals the roof. Breaking over the blocking course is a series of slate pyramids that represent an early roofing form; importantly, the pediment remains independent of the central roof, so that when it is viewed from the side it seems to teeter, reinforcing the impression that the frontispiece must have been a later addition.

Regrettably the Georgian wings were swept away after the house was sold to William Humphrys *c.* 1800, to be replaced by large pavilions – containing a drawing room and dining room – at either end, each with a single bay framed by broad sandstone strips, too wide to be pilasters, recalling *William Farrell*'s use of such bold vertical elements at the See House of Kilmore in Cavan. Tripartite windows are framed by slender bracketed pilasters and straight entablatures that also correspond with Farrell's work. The s side elevation has four bays facing out over a terrace created for a long Victorian curvilinear conservatory in the manner of *Richard Turner*, since demolished. The rear, w, front is rather uncomfortably embraced by lower Georgian farm buildings, that part only so far as to reveal the three-storey bow with its commanding plumpness. The façade is disappointing; part is covered with roughcast, raised around the red brick window surrounds so that it must be a later finish, while the bow has smooth render, with the effect that it looks like a different building. As on the e front there are seven bays, though here mainly with round-headed windows, those on the first floor cambered instead. The ground-floor windows retain their chunky Early Georgian glazing bars and crown glass, some with bullions. The entrance in the centre of the bow has an interesting arrangement. The shouldered stone surround has heavy carved brackets that support a thin ledge, projected as a balcony for another doorway directly above, where one might imagine the improving landlord standing to declaim. Now closed, it has a blocked surround and an open pediment on brackets, framing the arched doorway within.

INTERIOR. The plan is relatively straightforward: at the centre, a large entrance hall and an oval saloon beyond; flanking the hall two square rooms with a staircase behind them on either side; the stairs were probably not originally in this position, but perhaps in the subsidiary towers in the wings. The hall is generous, though not now grand, with its complicated brick vault plastered without any ornament. The floor is paved in the traditional Georgian combination of Portland stone and black marble, and the chimneypiece is a plain Gibbsian design with an open pediment on brackets in highly polished Kilkenny marble. The best Georgian interiors survive in just two rooms, the small Peacock Room on the s side of the hall and the oval Saloon. Both justify the reference to 'curiously finished' stucco in the vaults seen here in 1738. In the Peacock Room, above a modillion cornice is a cross-vault with wide parallel ribs, each decorated with mouldings and a central husk margent, con-

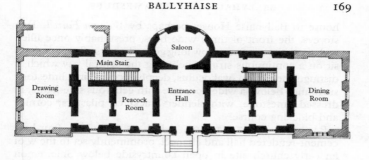

Ballyhaise House.
Plan by K. Mulligan, 2012

verging in the centre on a wonderfully heavy oak-leaf wreath,
the *sine qua non* of the Pearce and Castle decorative repertoire.
The Saloon is a modest space, resembling the small circular
tower rooms of the Pearcean Arch Hall in Co. Meath. Imperfectly symmetrical, it has walls with simple raised and fielded
plaster panels, a thin dentil cornice, and a shallow coffered
dome with an oak-leaf wreath in the centre. The chimneypiece
in the narrow curve of the N wall has a simple architrave in
Kilkenny marble, beautifully embellished with a fish-scale
console keystone, carved exactly like those below the ground-
floor windows at Bellamont. The lugged tablet in an egg-and-
dart frame above, a staple of Early Georgian design, is copied
on the opposite side.

The main staircase to the S, of the early C19, is a timber
cantilevered design, carried upwards with an awkward elongated grace. Crammed in around the walls at ground level are
a series of attractive arched doorcases, blending slender Gothic
pilasters with Neoclassical fans to the overdoors. The secondary stairs to the N are treated as mural stairs and open off a
small rectangular antechamber. The result is an unseemly passageway to the wings, where the largest rooms, the Drawing
Room and Dining Room, were created in the early C19. These
have modest cornices, elaborate joinery, and decidedly old-
fashioned overdoors with enriched floral friezes. The bedrooms
on the first floor are plain, all with coved brick ceilings, plainly
finished as at Bellamont, most with a heavy rectangular border.

Since 1905 Ballyhaise has been an agricultural college, with
the usual institutional accretions, most of which are happily
situated to the w, beyond the yards. The solid-looking two-
storey early C20 MANAGER'S HOUSE is by *W. A. Scott*. The
single-storey GATE LODGE opposite the entrance is a handsome Regency design, probably by *William Farrell*. It has a long
five-bay front with a trellised screen across the three recessed
central bays, twelve-pane sashes in shallow recesses in the end
bays, and a big hipped roof on bracketed eaves.

LISNAGOWAN. 1.5 km NNE. The ruins of an attractive Regency
villa in roughcast with limestone dressings. Built as the dower

house to Ballyhaise House, perhaps by *William Farrell*. Two
storeys, the front of three wide bays, presumably once filled
with tripartite windows, now long gone. The first-floor windows
sit on a continuous string, including the central bay which is
distinguished by an oval oculus, deeply recessed in a limestone
surround. Below, a wide doorcase with generous side-lights, in
dressed limestone, with slender bracketed pilasters, cornice
and blocking course.

ST PATRICK, CASTLETERRA. 1 km SE. 1829. A four-bay,
cement-rendered hall and chancel, prominently set to the W of
an early church site in open countryside below Shantemon
Mountain. In the porches, a medieval grotesque head and two
sandstone stoups that probably come from the old church.

LISDUNVIS GLEBE. 2 km SE. A solid Late Georgian house on
a commanding hilltop site. Two storeys on a basement with a
steep hipped roof. Three bays to the front with a handsome
fanlit doorcase in a blocked surround. A long single-storey
whitewashed vernacular range extends to the E, enclosing one
side of the stableyard; further E and detached is a formal three-
bay, two-storey COACH HOUSE in rubble and red brick.

5090   BALLYJAMESDUFF   CN

A market town established by the C18: in 1744 Isaac Butler found
here an infantry barracks, two inns, and about twelve houses near
'a rivulet with a stone bridge' dividing the town. The present
town retains an unusual triangular plan that leads to a confusing
network of streets, all eventually seeming to converge on the
expansive market place, where the yearly market for black cattle
was understood by Butler to be 'the greatest in ye kingdom'.
The plight of the historic town is all too evident here, as the
buildings are so disfigured by unsympathetic alterations that their
Georgian, Regency and Victorian origins can only be suggested
by the forms and proportions. If Paddy Reilly were indeed to
come back to Ballyjamesduff, as appealed to do in Percy French's
famous ballad of 1912, he might just recognize the tall three-
storey house with its wide eaves rounding the corner of Anne
Street and Dublin Street, or the perfect bracketed shopfront on
Bride's public house on Market Street – that is if he had not
already turned round, confused and saddened by the generic
overdeveloped suburbia sprawling out to greet him.

BALLYJAMESDUFF PARISH CHURCH (C of I). 1834 by *William
Farrell*. Set in woods above the town. Essentially Farrell's standard single-cell design, similar to Larah (Stradone) but here
enlarged with a solid-looking tower. Plain roughcast hall of
three bays with a short chancel and angle buttresses to the W,
part polygonal with pinnacles. The windows are quarry-glazed
lancets with thin Geometric tracery. Tower of three stages with

battlements and pinnacles. Inside, the usual exposed cast-iron
trusses.

ST JOSEPH. 1966 by *Philip Cullivan*. Dominating the E approach
into the town, a showy angular barn in brown brick and painted
concrete with a big gabled front and square offset tower.
Replacing a church 'advanced but not finished' in 1840. Now
rather dated and tired. The centre of the front steps forward,
the entire wall above the entrance meshed with diagonal piercings cast in concrete; similar fenestration to the E. Over the
entrance a thin oversailing ledge extends on one side to intersect with the tower. The tower rises in plain brickwork before
an abrupt ledge and a concrete belfry with a sharply truncated
roof and a big metal cross hung off the corner; a vertical register of hexagonal openings and a grid of square piercings
decorate adjoining faces. Some architectural interest on the
sides, where three copper-clad gables, grouped together in the
centre, sharply break over the moulded eaves course, suggesting something greater that might have been. Inside, nothing of
particular interest; again all brown brick and painted concrete.
The feeling is claustrophic, with a weighty pitched roof to the
nave, intersected by a series of triangular serrations presumably intended to evoke a medieval vault and clerestory but with
windows only in the centre.

METHODIST CHURCH. Set back on Market Street. Derelict. A
small early C19 lancet hall of just two bays. Roughcast with
dressed window frames and hoodmoulds.

MARKET HOUSE. 1813 by *Arthur McClean*. A broad-fronted two-
storey block angled to address the wide market place. Handsomely ordered and well-proportioned front of five bays with
a hipped roof. The three central bays are recessed beneath the
eaves, with wide segmental arches in ashlar on the ground
floor; otherwise the walls are roughcast with stone dressings,
the end projections held between blocked quoins with round-
headed openings on the ground floor and square sashes above.
In the centre, between *œil-de-bœuf* windows, a limestone plaque
brings the glory of the Peninsular Wars to the provinces:
'Erected in MDCCCXIII A year memorable for the Glorious
Achievements of Marquis Wellington'.

COURTHOUSE. Derelict. Built or remodelled in 1927 by *Patrick
J. Brady*. A modest gable-fronted building with a porch, set in
a railed enclosure on the Stradone Road and more like a
Masonic Hall. Roughcast with wide strip quoins and plinth in
smooth render. The courtroom is a three-bay block with big
segmental-headed windows; two-bay projections at one end
and behind, both with handsome chimneys.

CAVAN COUNTY MUSEUM (former POOR CLARES CONVENT).
1881 by *William Hague*. Behind the church, enveloped by beech
trees. A towering block in a familiar institutional Gothic style,
sparsely decorated but abundantly fenestrated with big Victorian sashes and plate glass. Roughcast with dressed quoins and
stucco reveals. Three storeys with a hipped roof and massive
end stacks arched over large windows set high in the gables.

The main front has eleven bays, the entrance in a narrow gabled projection squashed into the centre. A two-storey former classroom block adjoins on one side, and a lower primary school of 1954 extends to the E.

ULSTER BANK (former NATIONAL BANK). Chapel Street. A plain gable-ended block with a stuccoed front of three storeys and four bays, prominent only for its scale. Altered in 1922 by *John V. Brennan*.

GARDA STATION. Granard Street. Quaintly set behind a stone-walled front garden, a pleasing single-storey Neo-Georgian design developed in the 1930s. A low roughcast and rendered block of five bays with sash windows; the three central bays are set between projecting pedimented end bays, nicely articulated with the windows set in a shallow relieving arch under the open pediment.

Beside is the large PAROCHIAL HALL of 1949 by *Patrick Gaffney*.

NEIGHBOURHOOD

CASTLERAHAN. 4.5 km S. A large medieval ringwork castle set on an impressive height with broad panoramas to the S across the numinous cairn-topped spread of the Loughcrew Hills in Meath. In about 1618 Nicholas Pynnar noted in the district of Castlerahan an 'old castle, newly repaired' and a square bawn with 12-ft (5.7-m) high walls and two flankers. There are still traces of a large rectangular structure and the suggestion of two circular towers, all set about by steep banks with a deep fosse between.

5   CASTLERAHAN OLD CHURCH. In a corner of a large enclosure, as an appendage to the banks and ditches of the ringwork castle. The well-preserved ruins of a small rubble church, used until 1834; in 1837 it was described as 'ancient' and in very indifferent repair. Gabled single cell of just two bays with a simple lancet in the E gable; doorcase robbed from the W gable. Inside, both gables show sockets for hefty purlins. Nave windows shortened, but their straight reveals suggest a C17 or C18 date, perhaps as a rebuilding of the medieval church. The GRAVEYARD is large, with good C18 monuments, both primitive and abundant.

ST MARY, CASTLERAHAN. 5 km S. Elevated on a sheltered site. A large cruciform church built *c.* 1834, rubble with smooth limestone dressings, in an unadorned Gothic style with plain lancets. Too plain for its broad bulky proportions. Nominal pediment on the W gable and a square, Tudor-style window above the pointed doorway. Inside, after a succession of C20 alterations, a vast dull and disengaged space. – MONUMENTS. All simple tablets, the best to the founder of the chapel, the Rev. John Reilly †1842, signed *R. Ballantine*, Dublin. – The Rev. Michael Brady †1872, by *Dennany*, Glasnevin. – The Rev. James Brady †1866, by *Farrell & Son*, Glasnevin.

BALLYMACHUGH

A rural parish on the N shore of Lough Sheelin.

BALLYMACHUGH PARISH CHURCH (C of I). A small Late Georgian three-bay hall with a shallow chancel and a squat pinnacled tower, all in roughcast with tooled limestone dressings to the lancets and tower battlements; enlarged *c.* 1837 with a transept. Inside, a bright boxy hall retaining its flat plaster ceiling. – ORGAN by *Telford & Telford*, housed in a handsome architectural case of oak with Corinthian pilasters and a raking pediment. – STAINED GLASS. E window by *Mayer* of Munich, 1904. – MONUMENTS. John Bell †1822, an armorial plaque. – John Tatlow †1824; a sarcophagus-shaped plaque surmounted by a Neoclassical funerary urn. – Another similar, to Anthony Tessington Tatlow †1828. – Dora Maxwell †1861; a Neoclassical tablet with inverted torches and a snake eating its tail, signed *Alexander Ballantine*, Dorset Street, Dublin. – The remainder, William Tatlow †1869, Barry Somerset Maxwell †1897, Lady Florence Farnham †1907, and Charlotte Maxwell †1910, all signed *C. W. Harrison*, Dublin. – On the approach to the church, the Carmichael vault is crowned by a large architectural MONUMENT in granite, a true aedicule with stiff-leaf capitals to the columns presenting a playful incongruity.

SCHOOLS. A Late Georgian roughcast block of a decided domestic character. Two storeys tall and three bays to the main front with a small boxy porch, Georgian sashes and wide bracketed eaves under a hipped roof and central stacks. Shared with the petty sessions in the early C19. Disused at the time of writing.

ST MARY, BALLYNARRY. 1.75 km NW. 1831. A plain T-plan lancet church, enlarged in the late C19 with a chancel and several small additions. Inside, elegantly plain. – STAINED GLASS. Mixed figurative works. E window of *c.* 1912; later windows by *George Walsh* and *Kevin Kelly*.

BALLYMOYER

A rural parish and townland 4.5 km NE of Newtownhamilton, named for the MacMoyer family, hereditary keepers of the C9 Book of Armagh.

BALLYMOYER OLD CHURCH, BALLINTEMPLE. Ruinous. A rare early C17 church, now choked with ivy. A large single cell with rubble walls and just two bays to the nave and two to the E gable; plain round-headed openings; at the W a doorway and a bellcote with twin piercings on the gable. Unusually there is a large chimneybreast inside, rising between the windows on the N wall to a short stack on the eaves. The present ruin

replaced the so-called 'Eight mile church' recorded here in the
c16. Abandoned shortly after it was rebuilt, it was brought into
use again after partial re-roofing by Archbishop Robinson in
1775, and its fabric was deemed to be in good order in 1810,
but it was replaced by the present parish church in 1822. Part
of its 'fine oak' roof still survived in 1842.

ST LUKE, BALLYMOYER PARISH CHURCH (C of I). A deeply
attractive church, large and imposing, with an irregular plan
that belies its origin as a standard hall and tower of 1821. In
the second half of the c19 the building was radically remodelled in two phases that were so successful as to make it appear
one design. The result is a powerful evocation of Late Victorian
ecclesiology. Nave, chancel and vestry with a forestanding buttressed tower, the old structure given a steeply gabled roof,
with a polygonal external stair set to one side and a delightful
small apsidal porch adjoining it in the angle of the nave. These
additions were probably begun by *Welland & Gillespie* after
1860. Walls of squared blue limestone, hammer-dressed, with
a punched granite trim, entirely encasing the older walls save
only on the nave S wall where the random rubble remains
evident. Otherwise the earlier structure only suggests itself in
the forestanding position of the tower; its survival is confirmed
in the exposed internal fabric of the upper stages.

In 1863 *W. J. Barre* was employed by Jane Synnot to add the
two-bay chancel to house a memorial window to commemorate her husband Marcus, who had died in 1855. Barre also
added a vestry to the S, refurnished the sanctuary and nave,
and replaced the old nave roof and ceiling, presumably steep-
ening the pitch; the nave was also entirely refenestrated, with
Geometric sandstone tracery. The builder was *B. McGinnis* of
Newry. The tower was probably remodelled in 1877 when the
porch was added, the date carved on the kneelers flanking the
doorway. The treatment of the upper stage as a gabled belfry
recalls the tower of Newtownhamilton, which suggests that
Welland & Gillespie completed the works in the decade following Barre's death in 1867.

Attractive interior, with an open timber roof of scissor
trusses set in pairs with arched braces decorated on the under-
sides with chevrons. Sandstone chancel arch on twin shafts
with stiff-leaf capitals; delicate timber ROOD SCREEN, its base
inset, somewhat oddly, with classical stone balusters. The
REREDOS is a heavy work in Dungannon sandstone with shafts
of Connemara marble displaying *Barre*'s expressive Gothic
detail. The BAPTISTERY, in the tower, opens off the nave
through a narrow pointed archway. It is a richly decorated
space lined with *Minton* tiles on the dado and floor tiles to a
Pugin design. The highlight is the FONT of 1865 by *William
Butterfield*, installed by the Rev. Garret Wall to the memory of
his young son. Though a relatively plain octagonal design with
paired shafts, there is a good assemblage of coloured marbles
and a truly medievalizing counter-weighted iron dome with gilt
foliate bosses. – STAINED GLASS. Plentiful and good. Chancel:

three windows including three-light E window, *c.* 1864 by *Thomas Earley* of Dublin; in the nave, fine windows by *Hardman & Co.* of Birmingham, one *c.* 1864, the rest *c.* 1877. – MONU-MENTS. Sir Walter Synnot †1821; an elaborate Neoclassical tablet with portrait medallion. – Major-General FitzRoy Hart-Synnot †1910; a simple plaque inset with enamelled arms.

RECTORY. A modest early C19 roughcast house of two storeys and three bays with a hipped roof. The entrance is in a slightly lower central projection, flanked by small lean-to wings, so that it all looks slightly back-to-front.

ST MALACHY. A spruce early C19 hall of five bays with the N wall canted in the centre. Elaborated externally in the late C19 with stucco and a gabled porch to one side that is nicely finished with short angle buttresses and granite dressings. The windows have twin lights in blocked surrounds with moulded splays and very thin hoodmoulds. A slate plaque in the E gable records the dedication and gives 1835 as the date of origin.

LURGANA HOUSE. 1.5 km NE. An attractive Italianate house on an asymmetrical plan, built *c.* 1862 by Parker George Synnot to enlarge an existing Georgian mill house, which partly survives in the plain two-storey wing to the S. The new block has two storeys with wide eaves on chunky modillions and three fronts, all elaborately stuccoed with channelling and vermiculated quoins on the ground floor. Main front of three bays, advanced on one side, with a tall, overlapping porch projected from the re-entrant angle; attractive recessed doorcase with brackets under a squat segmental fanlight. Tripartite windows on the ground floor and paired sashes in elaborate lugged surrounds on the first floor; plate glass now artificially divided with adhesive glazing bars. Large enclosed FARMYARD to the S with low rubble buildings.

BATTLEHILL

ST SAVIOUR, BATTLEHILL (C of I). 1856 by *William T. Fullerton*. An attractive Gothic Revival church, with buttressed nave, chancel and tapered steeple, built as a district curacy to Kilmore. The square tower is offset, embedded in the nave wall with diagonal buttresses and converting to an octagon at belfry stage, where each face is gabled with finials over a louvred lancet. Walls of squared blackstone trimmed with dressed limestone, used also for the belfry and spire. The contractor was *Richard Cherry* of Loughgall. Nave of five bays with twin cusped lancets and clear quarry glazing. In the E gable three graded lights, in the W two lancets with a cinquefoil over. Inside, a hammerbeam roof with kingposts over cement-rendered walls, lined to imitate ashlar. – STAINED GLASS. In the E window the Ascension, by *Clokey*, Belfast; in the W window late C19 patterned glass; in the remainder, colourful naïve work by *Calderwood Stained Glass*. – MONUMENTS. Crane Richard Bush †1858; a small Neoclassical tablet, by *Edwardes & Co.* of Oxford Street, London.

The adjoining RECTORY is a compatible design of 1869 by *Boyd & Batt*, two storeys in coursed blackstone with pale sandstone trim. Front of three bays with a small porch centred between gables graduated in scale to achieve asymmetry, all with bargeboards ornamented to different designs.

Between the church and rectory, the SCHOOLHOUSE is a neat low building, also in blackstone, with yellow brick trim. Central gabled porch flanked by narrow sashes set in pairs.

BALLINTAGGART HOUSE. 1.4 km N. A tall free-standing Late Georgian block, built not long before 1833 and in 1835 the residence of Mr Todd. Two storeys on a basement with attics, a half-hipped roof, and central stacks. Roughcast over rubble, and red brick. Front of three bays with twelve-pane sashes; later C19 porch projecting over the area. The plan is symmetrical, with a central entrance hall incorporating an impressive open-well stair, extended into a short return at ground level and rising all the way from basement to attic, lit in two stages by tall round-headed windows. Decoration limited to restrained plasterwork: a reeded cornice in the drawing room and a vine-leaf band in the dining room.

DERRYHALE HOUSE. 0.6 km NE. A compact, two-storey square house, built *c.* 1850 in red brick with a low hipped roof on oversailing eaves and short central stacks. Three bays to the front and sides, with nine-pane sash windows over twelve-pane. The doorcase has a simple spoked fanlight in a semi-ellipse over Tuscan columns.

ST PATRICK. 1833 and 1907. A rural chapel with a distinctly odd belfry pasted on to the front. The standard cement-rendered hall of four bays arranged on a transverse plan, evident in the two porches projecting from the end bays. Dilapidated by the early C20, when *W. A. Scott* added a short chancel opposite a solid concrete belfry set centrally between the porches. A harsh and unharmonious structure is now made uglier by later slate cladding. Scott was more successful in his refenestration, piercing the walls with paired lancets under oculi and hoodmoulds as an economical kind of plate tracery. The interior is unremarkable, despite a good terrazzo floor of 1942 and Tardis-like confessionals.

LOUGH BAWN. 1.2 km NE. An attractive Regency villa set in an older demesne, between two linked lakes, Black Lough and the larger Lough Bawn. For centuries the estate formed part of the MacMahons' principal territory, but by the C17 it had come into the hands of Captain William Barton of Carrickmacross.

His relative, Bryan Norbury, is named as resident in 1697, about the time when the estate passed to Henry Tenison as part of a marriage settlement. By the end of the C18 it was in the possession of William Barton Tenison, who seems to have been only an occasional resident. His son and namesake built the present house *c.* 1815, after a fire destroyed its predecessor. In a rare turnaround, the estate, having passed out of the hands of the Tenisons in 1921, was bought back again five years later.

The new house is a stocky Neoclassical block of great appeal, very much in the manner of *William Farrell*, given modesty and presence in equal measure, and as much as the landscape demanded. Front of three bays, with a salient central bay and Wyatt windows on the ground floor set tightly within recessed segmental arches. Walls roughcast with stucco quoins and a plinth. Windows carefully proportioned, diminishing on the upper storey, before a hipped roof with oversailing eaves on paired brackets. Unusually, the ridge is raised between the large central stacks with two dormers neatly inserted to light the attic. In the C20 the windows were united under a flat roof and the space between them filled by an Adamesque relief. The original plan was a straightforward L-shaped block with some minor adjoining elements. Today lower two-storey ranges project from the rearward corners, added or extended in the C20, but done so sensitively that the changes are imperceptible. Another C20 alteration was the removal of a boxy single-storey porch and its replacement by an engaged Tuscan portico, a clean and competent exercise in smooth concrete that frames a refined timber doorcase, modified in the same period, with an elliptical petal fanlight and big marginal-glazed side-lights.

Inside, two large rooms flank a square hall, originally with adjoining front and back stairs immediately behind it. Both stairs were altered in the C20, when a corridor was formed to connect to the N wing. New stairs were formed between the old and new blocks, reusing the balustrade of an older stair. A large and attractive timber-panelled dining room dominates the N wing. The decoration throughout is refined, though understated – best in the entrance hall, with good joinery, simple cornices and a vine-encircled centrepiece.

The RUINS below the house, near the water's edge on a peninsula in Lough Bawn, gained definition as an 'abbey' on C19 maps. There is nothing romantic or ecclesiastical in their present overgrown appearance, and it is more likely that they represent the original house, understood to have burnt in 1809. What remains is a small rectangular structure, rubble-built and originally lime-plastered, now only, and perhaps always, single-storey with a basement. The long sides have three and two bays respectively with a single bay on the short end wall addressing the lake. The fragmentary remains of additional walls at the other end indicate that this was part of a larger structure, possibly one of the projecting wings of a U-plan C17 house, perhaps retained as a summerhouse after the new house was built.

CORLEA PRESBYTERIAN CHURCH. 2 km NE. A trim rectangular box of *c.* 1840 with an attractive four-bay front and a hipped roof. Pebbledashed with blocked quoins and cut limestone window reveals. The pointed openings have simple Y-tracery frames with elaborately glazed iron casements. The entrance, a plain door, is tucked away on the rear elevation. Repaired in 1939 by *W. R. Potts* of Clones.

CORLEA MANSES. 2 km NE. Two houses are associated with the Presbyterian church. The earliest is a compact Late Georgian block of two storeys and three bays set in trees on high ground behind the church. Rubble with red brick trim and an attractive doorcase with side-lights and an elliptical webbed fanlight. This was replaced by a new house close by the church: a Late Victorian two-storey, three-bay block, cement-rendered with big blocked quoins; camber-headed openings on the first floor and bay windows with sweeping lead roofs on the ground floor, all with plate glass.

BAWNBOY   CN

A small village in NW Cavan which owes its origins to a settlement undertaken by Sir Richard and George Grimes, who were granted the estate under the Plantation in the C17.

BAWNBOY HOUSE. Derelict. A severely plain and solid two-storey block in smooth render, the result of various C19 remodellings of a smaller Georgian house. An ample façade with tall windows and a gabled C20 porch; five bays on the ground floor and four bays above, where the origins of the house may in part explain the unusual spacing of the central windows, closer together and out of alignment with those below. A low hipped roof projects on paired eaves brackets. The Georgian house appears to have been one room deep, with the usual arrangement of drawing room and dining room flanking the hall. When the plan was doubled in the mid C19 these were enlarged and given enriched plasterwork cornices and vigorous leafy pendant roses. Perhaps as a result of the pre-existing house, the enlargement lacks coherence, with a Victorian staircase with iron balusters set to one side at the back of the hall. Several bedrooms retain Georgian six-panel doors.

N of the house there are substantial rubble walls terminating in a D-shaped enclosure, perhaps the remains of a small C17 BAWN established by Sir Richard and George Grimes. Although associated with farm buildings in the C19, a large half-tower projection on the SE angle does suggest itself as a bastion.

ST MOGUE. 1978. A strange unforgiving design in red brick with a broad, low façade, which looks impregnable but for a small brick porch with a glazed front and a thin oversailing concrete canopy. A heavy copper-clad lid appears to hover over a continuous strip clerestory, rather giving the building the appearance of a public swimming pool, a characteristic shared with the Church of Our Lady at Maghery and St Theresa at Sion Mills in Co. Tyrone, both by *Patrick Haughey*, who must also have designed this. – STATIONS OF THE CROSS. In bronze by *R. Gourdon*.

WORKHOUSE (former). 1851–2 by *George Wilkinson*. Designed to accommodate five hundred inmates at a cost of £4,000. Its imposing presence is improved by the sloping site. Not the architect's familiar Tudoresque design of the 1840s, but a more sedate roughcast group of long two-storey ranges, more vernacular in character, with simple square-paned mullioned windows. The buildings are laid out in an inversion of the typical segregated plan fronted by the administrative block: here the gable-fronted dining block is brought forward and made central to the plan, flanked at the front by long accommodation ranges.

CURLOUGH CHURCH. 6 km W. A sizeable hillside T-plan chapel, erected in 1851 by the Rev. P. Smith and built of squared brownstone with dressed quoins and thickly framed lancets. Extended in 1910 and made cruciform by *W. A. Scott*, who added a chancel and a new vestry in quarry-faced masonry, set alongside an existing gabled vestry. Because of the sloping site, the entire E front rises above a series of open segmental vaults, serving no other purpose and displaying too much architectural brio when contrasted with the quiet informality of the original design. The contractor for these works was *Francis Duffy* of Monaghan. The W gable is treated as a blind façade with a stepped projection in the centre which presumably once rose into a bellcote, removed in the late C20 when the roof was renewed and given crude concrete barges. The interior displays little of Scott's originality, with a clumpy late C20 roof of exposed queenposts formed of laminated timbers. Short arcades to the transepts with three pointed arches on polished shafts with bell capitals, unadorned but for a stylized volute emerging to support the angles of the abacus. The chancel arch is supported on free-standing minuscule shafts that rest on corbels. Repairs of 1919 by *Patrick J. Brady*. – STAINED GLASS. Three-light E window: the Crucifixion by *State Glass Co. Ltd*.

BELLAMONT FOREST CN 6010

In Ireland no house better embodies the villa ideal than Bellamont Forest, a cubic red brick house, standing conspicuously on a high grassy dome surrounded by the expansive waters pooled by the River Dromore. It was designed *c.* 1728 by *Sir Edward Lovett Pearce* for Thomas Coote, the younger son of Richard, Baron of Coloony, and a Justice of the King's Bench. Viewed today it is perhaps difficult to appreciate fully its significance for the spread of Palladianism in Ireland. As a sophisticated rural villa just like those of the Venetian nobles on the *terra firma*, Bellamont stood throughout the C18 in the centre of a large landed estate, combining politely assured architectural *gravitas* with all the practical convenience of a country retreat. Even if the scene is more pastoral, the climate more changeable than in the Veneto, Bellamont is Ireland's Villa Rotonda.

Nepotism and self-conscious modernity were probably the instrumental factors in Thomas Coote's decision, relatively late in life but perhaps in concert with his son Charles, to replace the old house of his uncle, situated nearby. Pearce may have been employed solely by virtue of his relationship to the family as a nephew of Coote's first wife, but there was then no-one else in Ireland who could have designed a building like this. Pearce's association with the design was first recognized from a related proposal preserved amongst his drawings, a plan only substantially different from Bellamont in its idea for a portico set *in antis* rather than prostyle as built. It clearly originated as a variant of Palladio's Villa Pisani. Pearce's knowledge of the Palladian villas had come at first hand, from the buildings themselves, having visited the Veneto in 1724 with the *Quattro libri* as his companion.

Few Georgian visitors seem to have quite appreciated the architectural importance of the house or even acknowledged its authorship, their impressions shaped instead by the natural beauties of the demesne. Not even Mrs Delany, one of the earliest visitors (in 1732), who knew Pearce and even in a small way promoted his career, showed any awareness of its significance or the identity of its designer. In 1778 the Rev. Daniel Beaufort was rather disingenuous in his remarks, considering it 'though a modern building' to be 'very inelegant and ill contrived'. Some years later Sir Charles Coote was also critical, his view poisoned perhaps by being the illegitimate son of the louche Earl of Bellamont; inheriting the baronetcy but not the house in 1800, he wrote soon after, in 1802, that it cannot 'be justly called a good family house: nor can it be said to be as extensive a mansion as is suitable to so splendid and spacious a demesne. Its figure being a square is also hostile to the appearance it should command, and opposes any improvement of the addition of wings, which, if of another plan, might yet be added to a happy and pleasing effect.'

The house has a strange prismatic purity, rising freely as it does, four-square, on its water-girded mound, described by Mrs Delany as a 'carpet hill'. Unlike many Georgian houses, Pearce's design was unfettered by the presence on the site of an existing house. Its predecessor, nearby on Hoop Hill, was most likely an inherited O'Reilly stronghold, adapted haphazardly in the Irish way, from which the Cootes were only too willing to break free. That there is something unreal about the villa's emergence from the hilltop is in part due to its materials, which are principally red brick, laid in Flemish bond. The use of brick is of interest here as a central component in the design, and as an element in the structural success of Palladio's villas. It is important here too because Pearce as an M.P. was instrumental in encouraging and regulating the use of bricks for building.

The brickwork is enhanced by a liberal use of sandstone dressings, most prominent and most elaborate on the main, w, façade, not least because of the great portico. Here, the ground floor is raised over a partly rusticated basement, executed in V-channelled ashlar, now ending abruptly where a dry moat was later created round the house. Quoins and attenuated window surrounds with pediments and long fish-scale consoles emphasize the *piano nobile*. Above this a deep string-course marks off the first floor as an attic storey, which is quoinless and – in perfect accord with the Palladian manner – given as much prominence here as for example at the Villa Foscari. Instead of an eaves cornice, the walls rise to form a parapet, coped in stone with a weak cornice so as greatly to conceal the hipped roof. This marks the house out from its Italian predecessors and from contemporaries like Mereworth, and so too does the absence of a crowning dome, sacrificed here for the practical necessity of chimneys. The four brick stacks are tied together two-by-two by arches that deliberately echo the central arch on the sides below, but more directly seem to reflect an idea absorbed by Pearce from his kinsman, Sir John Vanbrugh.

The prostyle Doric portico does not share the richness of its Continental predecessors, and with its scale and solitary prominence gives the impression of an afterthought. Pearce's design had proposed a portico *in antis*, with an open loggia at the expense of the Entrance Hall. Noticeable seams in the masonry of the plinth on either side of the portico may indicate that the change of idea took place during the course of construction; also there are subtle distinctions in the quality of the details framing the windows under the portico, overall less refined when compared closely to those in the end bays. Furthermore, the existence among Pearce's drawings of an unidentified villa design by *William Talman* with a comparable arrangement suggests that Talman may well have superseded Palladio here as a source of inspiration. The application of a temple front to domestic architecture was an idea espoused by Palladio, a great columnar front conferring a kind of moral dignity to the architecture and its patron; Vanbrugh considered that 'no production in architecture is so solemnly magnificent' as a portico. At Bellamont, the carving of the metopes with musical instruments suggests the more pleasurable, cultured aspects of the villa, rather than the military conventions more ordinarily associated with Doric architecture.

The plainer side elevations have four carefully spaced bays. Pearce deftly handled the vacancy on the central axis by placing all the ground-floor windows on a continuous string and linking the two central bays by an arch, to form the classic Venetian window motif derived from Serlio; quixotically, on the s side this arrangement was elaborated with engaged columns. Over these are the windows of a mezzanine, and then the attic. On the rear,

E, elevation, the recession of the central bays displays a kind of articulation not unpractised by Palladio; while one might reasonably think of the Villa Godi, a more convincing source of inspiration might be Vanbrugh's studied orchestration of planar surfaces. Here it is practised only enough to toy with Palladio's cube, and perhaps more importantly it reflects Pearce's concern with reducing the potential weakness of the corners: by elaborating the fenestration as Venetian windows – originally blind – he deals with any unresolved emphasis otherwise required on the shallower end bays. There is also modest embellishment of the central bay on the *piano nobile*, set in a lugged frame, with a bracketed cornice above; Pearce's plan indicates that the whole effect here was intended to be more imposing, with an elaborate perron across the area with the central bay giving access to the Saloon.

The INTERIOR has all the expected compactness of a Palladian villa, now with improved symmetry, a fire some years after the building was completed having resulted in the remodelling of rooms on the N side. Now as originally, Entrance Hall and Saloon dominate the central axis on the *piano nobile*, the scale of the rooms perfectly matched to the dignity of the porticoed entrance. To the E, the Dining Room and Drawing Room flank the Saloon.

Two stone staircases are discreetly placed flanking the Entrance Hall, faithfully following Palladio, so as not to get in the way. The MAIN STAIR, hardly bigger than the servants', is tightly

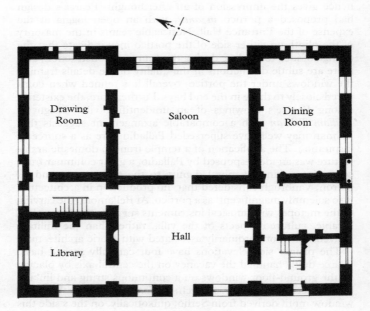

Bellamont Forest.
Plan by K. Mulligan, 2012

compressed in a narrow space with straight iron balusters and none of the theatre that has come to be associated with later country houses; a vaulted ceiling at the top, delicately embellished, is enough to set it apart. Below, the BASEMENT is occupied by the kitchens and servants' quarters, all vaulted, with the main rooms disposed off a spinal corridor and the largest directly corresponding to the Saloon. Above the ground floor on either side is an independent MEZZANINE, an arrangement that corresponds to Palladian practicality, and to the *ammezzato* in the Villas Rotonda and Foscari, where space was maximized by setting smaller rooms alongside 'magnificent'. It is clear that for visitors the grand gestures were controlled through the main approach, limited inside to the *piano nobile*, where with the state rooms the architectural experience was effectively complete.

The stone-paved ENTRANCE HALL is treated simply, with a high coved ceiling above a plain modillion cornice that gives a wholesome integrity to the volume. The Attic austerity of the space is given great stateliness with circular niches above the doors, each with an emphatic egg-and-dart frame of delectable quality encircling a marble bust, C18 originals of classically posed figures which are an integral part of the architectural design. Directly behind is the SALOON, larger and naturally architecturally richer, given its importance as the great room of the early C18. Here the plasterwork is elaborate: above an enriched Corinthian cornice the flat ceiling has an ebulliently garlanded central oval bordered with square rose-filled coffers that owes something to Palladio's treatment of Corinthian halls. For the marriage of the Earl of Bellamont in 1774 the Saloon walls were given shouldered frames, principally to receive his flamboyant portrait (now in the National Gallery of Ireland, Dublin) and the more restrained pendant of his wife (now on loan from a private collection to the Wernher Collection at the Ranger's House, London), both by Reynolds, and the *Death of Dido* after Guercino which still fills the end wall.

The Saloon is now flanked by similar rooms, the Dining Room and Drawing Room. The DINING ROOM to the S, surviving from the original plan, has a high coved ceiling, boldly coffered above a deep entablature with a dentil cornice and an enriched rinceau frieze; the entablature and the engaged screens of fluted Ionic columns at the ends are late C18 introductions, possibly replacements. At the E end, the awkward collision of the round-headed window and the frieze is explained by a later C19 opening of the blind windows in the end bays. Out of the ruins on the NE corner, a Library (now the DRAWING ROOM) was formed by dispensing with the mezzanine rooms immediately overhead. It mirrored the Dining Room opposite, and was given a similar coved ceiling, though its more refined geometric coffering takes it stylistically closer to the Neoclassical period, probably to coincide with the works undertaken after the Earl's marriage. At the same time, or perhaps earlier, the surviving mezzanine rooms on both sides were given new brick jack-arch ceilings, a fireproof method of construction that became common in the early C19.

38

The Early Georgian CHIMNEYPIECES are rather varied in the main rooms; in the Entrance Hall a spare, elegant Doric design in painted stone with free-standing columns and dosserets projected at each end; in the Saloon a simple design with sculpted brackets, in pale breccia with carved white marble trim; in the Drawing Room grey marble with thick mouldings and big scallop shells, supporting shelves on either side; in the Dining Room a C20 variant of that in the Saloon. The present LIBRARY in the NW corner of the ground floor, although its ceiling was altered after the fire, has a simple moulded chimneypiece of Kilkenny marble, one of several in the house with a signature scallop shell – the *sine qua non* of the Irish Early Georgian interior.

The modesty of the main stair does not prepare one for the wonderful columned BEDROOM LOBBY on the first floor at the centre of the plan. The encircling effect of its Tuscan order and oval lantern – an oblique reference perhaps to the centralized plan of Palladio's Villa Rotonda – compensates for the absence of a dome. It was a theme to be revived later at Russborough and Bellinter by Richard Castle, to whom the Palladian torch was passed and in whose hands it was to burn somewhat longer, if a little less brightly. The surrounding BEDROOMS have plain coved ceilings with a raised central border, each a perfect distillation of those in the Drawing Room and Dining Room, of which every Modernist architect embarrassed by ornament might be proud.

Bellamont was inherited in 1800 by Charles Johnston Coote, one of the twelve illegitimate children of the Earl of Bellamont. It was sold by George Coote in 1875.

BELLANANAGH   CN

A sizeable crossroads town. The C18 fabric was destroyed by fire in 1794 but was not of any architectural consequence. A very fine early C19 market house and some good vernacular houses remain; much of the provincial urban charm has been lost, with one side of the central intersection conspicuously rebuilt in jarring red brick.

ST FELIM. 1978 by *Gaffney & Cullivan*. A big triangular cement-rendered hall with discordant roof pitches, unmercifully set above the town. A work of unforgettable ugliness, the uninspired successor to a church of 1869 by William Hague.

The visitor will however be rewarded by the dignified classical MEMORIAL behind the church. It looks 1840, but was erected in 1894 for Philip Smith of Kevit Castle. An exacting Greek Doric column of silver granite on a square plinth with diagonal corner projections topped by domed anthemion blocks. The column suffers the wonderful absurdity of a Celtic cross placed proudly on its abacus.

MISSION HALL. A modest early C20 gable-fronted hall in roughcast with round-headed lancets.

MARKET HOUSE. 1821. Set back on the Main Street, with the same broad-fronted design as *Arthur McClean*'s building in Ballyjamesduff. A two-storey block of five bays in roughcast with limestone dressings. The three central bays are deeply recessed under the hipped roof, with segmental arches in ashlar on the ground floor; the end bays are held between blocked quoins with niches on the ground floor, now opened to a window on one side, with square sashes above. Set between *œil-de-bœuf* windows on the first floor, a classical tablet records the date of erection, under the patronage of James Stewart Fleming of Belville.

BELVILLE. 2 km N. A modest Late Georgian farmhouse in a much older demesne, extensively described in an Early Georgian topographical account for the Physico-Historical Society of Dublin *c*. 1750, when it formed the 'convenient and very delicate' seat of Thomas Fleming. The present house is a two-storey, gable-ended block in cement render with blocked quoins. The three-bay front has Georgian sashes and a central Gibbsian doorcase in sandstone with a triple keystone, probably from the older house, described as 'a square building, well modelled and finished, admitting 3 fronts'. Lower two-storey two-bay C19 wing on one side, in rubble and red brick. C19 yards clustered behind, but unfortunately nothing of the old offices, tantalizingly described as 'one entire range of buildings, with an arched stable supported by pillars & pilasters of stone finely cut, the window and door cases of hewn stone, the whole so neatly done & well contrived that it is looked upon as a pattern'.

The DESIGNED LANDSCAPE had waterworks that included a pool before the house, a cascade, and two ponds or canals of prodigious length, placed at right angles somewhat as at Antrim Castle so as to make a T-shape, the shorter pond extending to 1,554 ft (474 m) with a breadth of 54 ft (16.5 m). It certainly warranted the attention given to it in the account for the Physico-Historical Society, which for its rarity deserves to be quoted here:

> The south view terminates in a fruitery of an acre walled in (formerly a Danish fort) on the top of a hill having great plenty of choice fruit in great perfection. In the western prospect there is a variety of water works, terraces and diagonal walks; a slope 24 perches long, 46 foot deep with falls of water, and dark walks; below the slopes there is a beautiful pleasure house, the upper very elegant, fitted to a bowling green, the lower room in the nature of a mock grotto, here one may take a boat on the end of a canal 74 perches long, 54 foot broad, and may from there sail into a much longer canal, having in view fine meadows, groves . . . on the east side there is a bason near the house, with a long, rising prospect to the top of an high hill and deerpark.

Now from the densely wooded hilltop site of the old fruitery, directly s of the house, many of these elements can still be discerned – the radiating formal avenues flanking the now dry

T-shaped pond and the deerpark. Of the architectural features unfortunately only FLEMING'S FOLLY survives. Now ruinous, this four-square rubble structure crowns a rocky height behind Belville, and is visible from far around. Its scale is deceptive: inside the stumpy mass the cubic volume is suggestive of an imposing grandeur, with slender salient piers giving strength to the corners and just possibly the basis for some engaged classical order. It has the characteristics of a banqueting house, with a fireplace in the N wall, a large window opening to the E, and two deep arched recesses in the massive W wall. These support a mural stair entered beside the doorway in the S wall that once led to some kind of viewing platform, but now delivers the intrepid visitor to the perilous broken wall tops. A recess over the entrance probably contained the device of Thomas Fleming dated 1713 that is now preserved in Ballintemple Church.

ST PATRICK, BALLINTEMPLE (C of I). 2.4 km SE. 1821. A trim hall-and-tower church, outside the town beside the River Erne, replacing the medieval church across the road of which only the graveyard survives. The standard First Fruits design, in roughcast with limestone dressings. Three bays, pointed windows with twin cusped lights and quarry glazing; a pedimented vestry in the centre of the nave N wall. A short chancel was added in 1931. The tower is tall and square, with three stages and simple battlements. A circular vestibule in the tower leads into a plain hall with galleried W end and exposed kingpost trusses. – MONUMENTS. Above the vestry door the flamboyant arms of Thomas Fleming, carved in slate, dated 1713, believed to have been brought here from Fleming's Folly in the demesne of Belville. – Elizabeth Coyne †1852; a plain tablet of white marble framed in limestone with a naïve Neoclassical urn. – Ensign Robert Smith †1868 at Sealkote in India; a white marble table by *J. Craven* of Portsmouth. – The Rev. Stuart Smith †1849; a plain Gothic tablet by *J. Robinson & Son*, Belfast, 1880. Three large battlemented MAUSOLEA, projecting from the graveyard, contribute an architectural frisson among the more conventional gravestones.

Adjoining the graveyard, the former SCHOOLHOUSE is an attractive vernacular building. A gabled-ended, roughcast block of two storeys and two bays, built 1925 by the Rev. R. J. Walker to adjoin a lower three-bay C19 block with nicely paired eight-pane sash windows and an off-centre gabled porch.

BELLANODE

A small crossroads village in the large rural parish of Tydavnet, no more than a dispersed group of houses, a parish church and a picturesque three-arched stone bridge crossing the River Blackwater. The parish name recalls the C6 saint Damhnat (also identified as Davnet or Dympna), and the earliest ecclesiastical site is the old graveyard some distance NNE near the church of St Dympna, Tydavnet, with notable richly carved C18 headstones.

TYDAVNET PARISH CHURCH (C of I). 1830 and 1867. A large hall-and-tower church with transepts. Originally 'roughcast and whitewashed', now with unrendered walls of squared limestone and dressed trim. Four-bay nave with quarry glazing and three-stage battlemented tower with pinnacles. The transepts have older Gothick sashes; in the w gable a plain oculus on either side of the tower lights the gallery. In 1865 the Ecclesiastical Commissioners announced that the 'ancient church' was to be restored, and in 1867 it received a new roof, gallery and seating and new plate-traceried E window by *Welland & Gillespie*. The contractor was *Henry Sharpe*. The best part of the interior is their barrel-vaulted timber ceiling with ribs and tie-beams carried on deep projecting brackets. – STAINED GLASS. Brightly coloured figurative glass and a patterned window with scripture of 1886, signed *Cox, Sons, Buckley & Co.*, London. – MONUMENTS. Mostly by *W. Lendrum*, Clones, none especially good.

   MITCHELL MAUSOLEUM. A large rudimentary C19 structure beside the tower: low rectangular box of limestone rubble with two large plaques in recessed arches. The SCHOOLHOUSE is an attractive three-bay roughcast hall with porch, rebuilt in 1903.

ST DYMPNA, TYDAVNET. 3.5 km NNE. Large cruciform church with understated Romanesque Revival details. Built in 1784 to a standard T-plan with galleries and Gothic windows, greatly enlarged in 1923 when *R. M. Butler* formed a new five-bay nave to the w. Butler retained the old church as transepts in the new

Bellanode, St Dymphna, Tydavnet.
Perspective, 1923

arrangement, adding porches and a bellcote over the s transept gable. The new work is distinguished by squared rock-faced masonry for the nave and more finely hewn ashlar for the porches and bellcote, in contrast to the snecked rubble and irregularly squared masonry of the old. The gabled w front is a simple composition, with offset buttresses placed farther from the quoins than is typical or reasonable. Romanesque doorway, inspired by early Irish examples: three unadorned arches with inclined jambs given hard-edged reveals and simple imposts. The keyhole shape is repeated in the three round-headed lancets above it and in the plainer, paired nave windows. Inside, the spaces are plain, simplified in the late C20 when the sanctuary was extended into the nave on a raised platform of industrial bricks. Exposed timber roof of kingpost trusses with arched braces springing from corbels. – STAINED GLASS. Three-light E window with SS Dympna and Michael, stylized and richly coloured in the manner of *Harry Clarke*.

An earlier CHURCH SITE is represented by a small enclosed graveyard nearby to the s, possibly the early Christian site associated with St Damhnat. Today it is distinguished for its C18 headstones, a memorable display of folk art that is rich in symbolism: the many upright stones are carved in high relief to display various heraldic and biblical themes, along with the more familiar *memento mori* of coffins, hourglasses, and skulls and crossbones.

RACONNEL. 2.5 km E. Derelict. A medium-size Late Georgian house. Symmetrical roughcast block of two storeys over a basement with a hipped roof on wide eaves brackets. The seven-bay front has big Georgian sashes, the central three expressed as a shallow bow, and an underscaled limestone doorcase with Tuscan pillars supporting an arched fanlight. Interior remodelled in the C20, though retaining late C18 and mid-C19 plaster cornices and joinery. Good outbuildings of rubble and red brick. The residence of Colonel R. Lucas in 1837.

DRUMREASKE. 1.5 km SE. Derelict. A plain Tudor Gothic house on high ground overlooking a small wooded lake. Built *c*. 1840 for Alexander Mitchell, agent to the Shirley estate, probably by *William Walker*, who was involved here while working at Lough Fea. Long and low two-storey front of six bays, symmetrical but for the off-centre position of the entrance porch and a canted bay window. Walls roughcast with wide rectangular mullioned windows in dressed stone frames with stucco hoodmoulds. End bays advanced and gabled with ornate bargeboards, pendants and finials and a rectangular bay window on the ground floor; between these gables smaller gables, embellished like their larger counterparts, disrupt the eaves over the first-floor windows.

To the rear, one- and two-storey FARM BUILDINGS in adjoining ranges enclose an attractive yard. The single-storey range has six brick carriage arches; rising over one of these, a Tudor gable with a square plaque of *Minton* tiles displaying a now damaged 1840s date and the arms and initials of Alexander Mitchell.

On the opposite side of the road the large GATE LODGE is more picturesque. A one- and two-storey roughcast block with tall diagonal brick stacks and three diminishing gables with carved bargeboards; the central gable bears a heraldic shield with the three upright fishes of F. W. de Vismes Kane, who acquired the estate later in the C19.

LISDOOGAN. 1.5 km SE. Originally a small gabled Georgian block of two storeys and five bays, twice enlarged. In the mid C19 a narrow two-storey range was placed across the rear, with a large round-headed window in the centre of the first floor lighting the stairs. Then *c.* 1900 a large stuccoed block with a boxy porch was placed across the front of the old house, large enough to exist independently of it. Two-storey, with raised quoins, hipped roof and fussy bracketed eaves, it has camber-headed windows with moulded architraves, distinctively arranged in pairs on the ground floor and above the porch. Two-storey bay windows on the side elevations. Decent and solid FARM BUILDINGS to one side are contemporary with the older house. In 1882 the residence of James Mitchell.

KILMORE PARISH CHURCH, KILNAHALTAR (C of I). 2.5 km SE. A trim hall and tower in an ancient enclosure. A monastery was founded here in the C6 by St Aedhan – Aedhan Mac Aonghusa, a follower of St Mochta. Its name, *Cill Mór Aedhain*, 'the great church of Aidan', reflects its importance in the Middle Ages, as does the townland name of Kilnahaltar (*Cill na h-altora*, 'church of the altar'). The monastery was attacked and destroyed by the local Uí Chremthainn clan in the C8, and revived only to be attacked again in 1206 by Hugh de Lacy, Earl of Ulster. The present site holds a great deal of archaeological promise, evident in the varied undulating ground behind the church, with some curious indeterminate protrusions that seem unlikely to be associated with graves. There is strong visual evidence of an artificial escarpment some 12 ft (4 m) in height, with an external ditch 9 ft (3 m) in width. There are also two bullaun stones, boulders with artificial cup-like depressions that are a feature of monastic sites, generally associated with the grinding or pounding of herbs and roots, much like an apothecary's mortar. In the post-medieval period the site endured as a place of worship while its religious significance diminished.

The old church, perhaps itself a later rebuilding, was described as ruinous in 1622, and was completely rebuilt in 1788 to a regular plan, 60 ft by 30 ft (18 m by 9 m), originally with a small vestry on the N side. Roughcast, apart from the tower, which is built of uncoursed rubble with dressed stone string-courses defining its three stages; the upper stages have louvred openings, enlarged on the belfry stage where the parapet has short battlements and corner pinnacles.

Inside, the nave is neat and nicely proportioned, with a very small breakfronted gallery carried on slender iron columns, reached by a compact timber stair in the tower with attractive Gothic detailing. The Ecclesiastical Commissioners granted funds for repairs in the 1830s – perhaps the works *Joseph*

Welland is known to have proposed, which included a new roof, seating and a pulpit desk. The roof is exposed with plain scissor trusses, alternating with kingpost trusses; the latter are nicely treated with curved braces and have unusually well-detailed lower braces springing from moulded corbels in the nave wall. Welland also replaced all the windows with Y-traceried windows with quarry glazing that enhance the simple elegance of the architecture. Chancel added in 1862, with a new vestry projecting on the s side. – STAINED GLASS. Three-light E window: the Good Shepherd, deeply coloured glass in a fresh painterly style by *M. Healy*, 1911. Nave S: vivid figurative glass in the late C19 tradition, by *Campbell Bros* of Belfast, installed *c.* 1901. – MONUMENTS. Two fine marble plaques in the nave, both Neoclassical in style. The finer, to Myrtilla Schomberg †1839, with a draped urn, is unsigned. – The plainer monument to her husband, the Rev. George Schomberg †1847, is by *L. Hughes* of Dublin.

Outside, a large uninscribed TOMB is a fine architectural piece in its own right. It has an ashlar front framed by solid piers with moulded recessed panels and domed capstones; between them a lopsided curved gable fronts an impressive barrel-vaulted crypt formed of large rough-hewn blocks.

To the W, below the tower, the well-preserved ruins of the PARISH SCHOOL, with a datestone over the door recording its erection in 1828. A substantial two-storey block with rubble walls and red brick trim, built with funds raised by subscription and a grant from the National Board for Education.

The GLEBE HOUSE is a handsome Georgian building on the adjacent wooded site, contemporary with the church, built with a donation of £100 from the Board of First Fruits in 1792. A large two-storey-over-basement block with an attic storey revealed on the gable ends. Three bays to the main front, the entrance in the centre, in a compact little porch with recessed Tuscan columns. The garden front on the opposite side, where the basement is fully exposed, presents a more imposing façade of five bays.

BRANDRUM. 3 km SE. Derelict. Tall Late Georgian house of two storeys over a raised basement with a five-bay front and a three-bay bowed projection to the side. Handsome doorcase with side-lights and a wide elliptical webbed fanlight. Inside, an elegant circular stair hall with cantilevered timber staircase and domed ceiling, illuminated from above, Pantheon-like, by a round roof-light. Associated with the Cole family, who had been granted an estate here in the C17.

BELLEEK   AH

A small village, once a Tudor garrison, now bordered to the E by the impressive walls of Lord Gosford's large C18 deerpark.

ST LAURENCE O'TOOLE. 1849. On a height at the end of a
straight avenue off the Main Street. The builder was *Arthur
Bennett* of Ballyheel. A modest stuccoed church on a T-plan
with lancets. The entrance gable has angle buttresses with
awkward pinnacles and a bellcote. Inside, gallery in the stem,
and altar on the long E wall; flat panelled ceiling of pitch pine
with a carved Gothic pendant in the centre. Simple coloured
C20 glass by *James Watson* of Belfast.

ST LUKE, CARRICKGALLOGY (C of I). 2 km N. 1827. An attractive rural hall and tower with chancel projection. Cement-
rendered with granite trim. Three-stage battlemented tower
with pinnacles and three-bay nave, unusually with small
hooded lancets; larger three-light E window; all the windows
with metal frames and plain glazing. Interior a model of elegant
simplicity, without the heavy hands of the Ecclesiastical Commissioners. Nothing more than a shoebox furnished with box
pews, yielding to form a polygon in the aisle for a now vanished
stove.

CARRICKANANNY CHURCH. 2 km NNE. A dull late C19 hall
with large pointed windows and simple Y-tracery. In the gable,
a canopied statue of the Virgin over the doorway.

BELTURBET   CN   3010

A sizeable hilltop market town filling an embrace of the River
Erne, long settled because of its position on a vital fording point
S of the river's course into Lough Erne. Its origins are found on
the rocky outcrop forming Turbet Island beside the present river
crossing. On this elongated islet a steep shouldered motte rises
over a large double-fossed bailey erected in 1210 by King John's
Justiciar, John de Grey, as one of seven strongholds along the
Erne Valley extending Norman control into the NW. Intended to
isolate the Irish of Ulster from Connacht, by 1213 it was abandoned after the incursions of Aedh O'Neill, but ultimately it
continued to be used to patrol the river crossing on the boundary
between the medieval kingdoms of East Breifne and Fermanagh.
The remains of a stone tower on the summit of the motte, probably of the C16, suggest an enduring significance.

The modern town came later, in 1600, when its strategic
importance for provisioning Enniskillen during the Nine Years
War was recognized with the erection of a bridge and the establishment of a garrison, which developed along the E riverfront
through the C18. In 1611 Sir Stephen Butler, a grantee of the
Plantation, built three houses, a forge and a 'fair house after the
English manner' which crowned the hilltop to overlook the river
crossing. In 1730 this was described as a 'lofty, square house,
divided into several large rooms and apartments', and it was still
standing in 1770 when the painter Thomas Roberts represented
it as a commanding block with three circular angle towers.

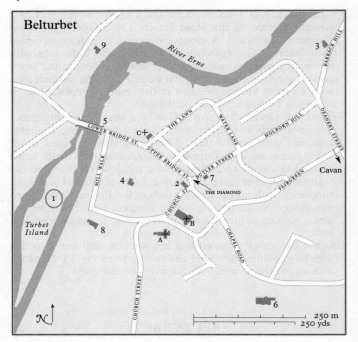

A	St Mary (C of I)
B	Church of the Immaculate Conception
C	Methodist church (former)
1	Motte and bailey
2	Town Hall

3	Barracks site (former)
4	Glebe House (former)
5	Kilconny Bridge
6	Railway station (former)
7	Post Office (former)
8	Erne Vale (former Distillery)
9	Riversdale House

Belturbet was granted a charter and incorporated in 1613; by 1622 there were '34 howses builded'. On Palm Sunday in 1642 the town was torched. Today the parish church is the most prominent survivor of the C17, a large cruciform church with a C19 steeple, now joined by its C20 Roman Catholic counterpart. Two square bastioned forts offering temporary defence in the Williamite campaigns, erected in 1689 by Colonel Wolseley, may still be traced, most visible beside the parish church, where triangular spurs are clearly defined along the Sern escarpment to the site. The patronage of the Butlers as earls of Lanesborough exerted a benign influence on development, and gradually as the Georgian town expanded on both sides of the river, in response to the growing significance of water carriage to its trade, Belturbet quickly became the most prosperous town in Cavan. Development was, and still is, largely concentrated on the E side. A cluster of streets evolved around the site of the Butler castle, now long vanished, its prominence overtaken on the Diamond by a handsome market house, existing here by 1730, since replaced by a more sedate C20 building. Like most Ulster towns, trade in cattle and linen was vital to the local economy; in the angle formed by Bridge Street and Main Street, the narrow streets, including Weaver's Row, are a reminder that the town provided the principal flax market for the region, its importance declining in the late C18 even though the markets endured. Industrial growth continued in the C19 with the establishment of a distillery and mills beside the river; operated by Messrs Dickson, Dunlop & Co., the distillery was capable of producing 100,000 gallons annually.

However the role of Belturbet as a military station continued to define the character of the town as it developed. Despite its prominence, or perhaps because of it, when John Wesley passed through in 1760 he found the town filled with 'Sabbath-breakers, drunkards and common swearers in abundance', there being in it neither 'papist nor presbyterian'. The Lawn, once part of the hanging castle gardens reaching down to the river, is a smart terrace of houses where the officers once resided. The extensive riparian barracks survived into the C20, but now in the C21 their place is taken by a public park; of their former existence only the Georgian gatehouse remains, along with some ruins and foundations overlooking the river.

St Mary (C of I). A sizeable steepled church crowning the hilltop but not always prominent within the townscape. Built close to the castle in the early C17, it is the only parish church of its age in the region still in use. Cruciform in plan, it was recast in 1814 when a new tower and adornments to the N transept were added. The original C17 character remains apparent in the spare roughcast walls with their distinctive quarry-glazed windows: three graded lancets with rounded heads under a stepped cavetto hoodmould. In contrast the E window is pointed, with Y-tracery and a hood, perhaps from an older church; its location behind the altar seems to reinforce the notion that a Gothic or pointed style was considered more emblematic of salvation. Heavier transomed windows in the transepts are later, probably inserted in the 1820s, when the N gable was crenellated between diagonal buttresses with tall pinnacles and given a round-headed doorway with slender engaged shafts. This enrichment, not repeated on the other gables, seems as if intended to suppress the dominance of the tower, rebuilt on the site of its Georgian predecessor with a short link to the nave. The embattled tower is built of squared limestone and ashlar with diagonal buttresses on the three stages, topped by spiky pinnacles and an octagonal spire; scale and effect are somewhat overwhelming against the relative vernacular modesty of the old church. A broad gabled vestry of 1861 by *Welland & Gillespie* now clutters the NE angle.

Inside, shallow sexpartite vaults in plaster with ribs and foliated bosses are works of 1828. Handsome w gallery with concave sides, on clustered shafts with raised and fielded panels on the frontal, where the Farnham arms are displayed in the centre; similar galleries also in the transepts. – FURNISH-INGS. Exceptional Georgian scroll-top ORGAN CASE of mahogany with a carved eagle bracket supporting the central pipes. – Octagonal FONT in Perp style, 1863 by *McCullagh* of Armagh; sculpted from dark red marble with bold mouldings. – Octagonal Gothic PULPIT, richly carved in dark oak, and REREDOS, both part of improvements of 1886 by *R. Langrishe*. – STAINED GLASS. E window: 'I am the Good Shepherd', *c.* 1912, attributed to *Mayer & Co.* – MONUMENTS. The best in the chancel S wall: Francis Whyte (date illegible); grey limestone and white marble, a mid-Georgian pedimented tablet with side scrolls, surmounting obelisk, and an armorial apron with flamboyant quarterings set between scrolled brackets, flanked on either side by a draped oval plaque surmounted by a lamp. – To the E, Sarah Whyte †1752; to the W, Francis Whyte †1778. Similar designs: both fine white marble ovals set in drapery with an Aladdin's lamp above. – Henry Richardson †1766; a plain bowl-shaped limestone plaque. – Beneath the W gallery: Bedell Howard Stanford †1776; a white marble oval bordered by reed fronds. – Others: John Gumley †1840, by *Manderson*, Dublin. – The Rev. Andrew W. McCreight †1868; a pedimented grey marble tablet, signed *John Robinson*, York Street, Belfast. – Francis Jermyn †1915, by *Lendrum*, Clones.

In the graveyard, the KNIPE MAUSOLEUM is a large early C19 Greek Revival block of the *Richard Morrison–J. B. Keane* school. Ashlar-fronted sarcophagus with panelled antae, a low horned pediment, and an Egyptian door. The MAUDSLEY MAUSOLEUM is a plain ashlar box in limestone with an eaves cornice. To the S, the remains of two diamond-shaped corner redoubts form a steep escarpment at the edge of the site, relics of its fortification during the Williamite wars.

CHURCH OF THE IMMACULATE CONCEPTION. Succeeding a C19 Gothic chapel located downhill, this bulky stuccoed hall of 1954 by *Simon Aloysius Leonard* of *W. H. Byrne & Son* crowns the hilltop site at the expense of its more ancient neighbour. Its similarity to Drung is explained by the fact that the motivating priest, James Brady, was responsible for both parishes. Here an understated Romanesque style is used, expressed in the arcaded front with its shallow roof pitch and corbel table. The latter is continued along the five-bay side walls, punctuated by four big round-headed windows and three graded lancets at the E end, separated by buttresses. A free-standing polygonal tower on a square base is poised rocket-like beside the church. Disappointing, over-scaled interior with a high ceiling gently cambered and divided into panels; apse more of a niche, in a roped and chevroned frame. Reordered in 2002 by *Noel Smith* and *Richard Pierce*; still rather bland.

BELTURBET CONVENT NATIONAL SCHOOL. Upper Bridge Street. 1909 by *W. H. Byrne & Son*. A more substantial convent completed by the same architects just twenty years earlier was demolished to make way for this two-storey L-plan block in smooth render with segmental-headed windows. Institutional architecture at its plainest.

METHODIST CHURCH (former). The Lawn. 1903, succeeding a church established here by 1837. A steep gabled hall in squared rock-faced limestone with three closely grouped lancets and an offset gabled porch. Now a residence.

TOWN HALL. The Diamond. 1927 by *Patrick J. Brady*. The handsome old cupola-topped market house with its series of Venetian windows dominated this site from the mid C18. Brady repaired it in 1915, and then replaced it with this less venerable gable-ended block of two storeys with a broad seven-bay front, partly roughcast, with quoins and simple channelling on the ground floor. The design is modestly classical, with bracketed eaves cornice and string-course, both simplified as a straight ledge, the three central bays slightly recessed and given a weak, steeply pitched pediment; casement windows, in rounded arches on the ground floor.

BARRACKS SITE. Barrack Hill. The sizeable cavalry barracks developed here in the C18 were largely demolished in 1985 to become a public park beside the river, but what survives is of some interest. An arcade of three arches from the old riding school stands out as a curiosity at one end of the defensive platform over the riverfront. Nearby, set into the low wall that bounds the edge of the platform, is a carved plaque bearing the date 1699 under the initials 'WR' with a more crudely carved 'TB' placed below; the monograms may be of some significance if taken as referring to the Surveyor General, *Sir William Robinson*, and his successor, *Thomas Burgh*, who at this time were responsible for the erection of barracks in Ireland, enabled by an Act of Parliament in 1697. The complex was greatly enlarged over time: extensive stabling was built during the surveyor-generalship of Arthur Jones Nevill between 1744 and 1752, so that by 1837 the barracks accommodated 101 horses and 156 non-commissioned officers. In 1753 Nevill's successor, Captain Thomas Eyre, employed the Derry architect *Michael Priestley* with *John Priestley*, probably a relation, to carry out substantial works. These may well have included the mid-Georgian HOUSE which survives as a gatehouse on the E boundary; locally identified as the commanding officer's residence, it is a handsomely solid two-storey L-plan block with a big hipped roof covered in chunky slates. The main front to the street has three bays, now much altered but retaining small lunettes in the end bays of the upper floor with thick limestone surrounds and triple keystones, repeated in a blind rectangular window on the ground floor; this kind of rustication is one of the hallmarks of Michael Priestley's work.

GLEBE HOUSE (former). Mill Walk. An imposing Late Georgian block set below the town and above the river. The property was acquired by the church in 1810 and the house built by 1837. Two storeys over a basement, with a lower stable block forming a wing to the side; all in roughcast with limestone dressings. The main front has three bays with a modillioned eaves cornice, hipped roof and big central chimneystacks. The narrower entrance bay with an elaborate pedimented doorcase is slightly recessed between the end bays, which have limestone quoining and big tripartite windows with straight entablatures on the ground floor. Joined by a short link is the two-storey stable wing, just one bay wide, with an open pediment on corbels and a tall recessed arch on the ground floor that recalls *Francis Johnston*, though the heavy-handedness of the house seems more characteristic of his nephew, *William Murray*.

KILCONNY BRIDGE. An impressive three-arched stone bridge spanning the wide Erne with broad elliptical arches and angular cutwaters. Built of squared limestone with rusticated voussoirs and ashlar parapets, it was designed in 1836 by the first Cavan County Surveyor, *Alexander James Armstrong*, and financed with £1,700 from the Board of Works. The contractor was *James F. Johnstone*.

RAILWAY STATION (former), now a community and visitor centre. Chapel Road. 1885 by *W. H. Mills*, for the Great Northern Railway. A straightforward company design, in rock-faced limestone rather than the usual polychromatic brick. A long single-storey range with a two-storey stationmaster's house abutting one end. Segmental- and round-headed windows with marginal glazing bars. The entrance has five bays gently breaking forward under a gable with a timber canopy. Between 1887 and 1959 the station was shared with the Cavan & Leitrim narrow-gauge railway.

KILCONNY HOUSE. w, across the bridge. A two-storey late C19 block in rough-hewn limestone with black and yellow brick dressings and a hipped slate roof. Front of three bays, the end bay stepping forward with a two-storey canted bay; single-storey porch in the angle to the side. Windows mostly set in pairs with cambered heads and plate glass.

OTHER BUILDINGS. On the E side of THE DIAMOND, the POST OFFICE of 1904 by *Robert Cochrane* and *G. W. Crowe*, a crouching gable-fronted building in a flamboyant Dutch Renaissance style with a lower shaped gabled to the side, built in the usual combination of red brick and limestone dressings. The doorcase is a fanciful Baroque design with rusticated bottle-shaped columns and a scrolled pediment, set beside a big transomed window. The builder was *John McNally* of Cookstown. On a neighbouring low stone wall a bronze SCULPTURE, 'Geraldine and Patrick' by *Mel French*, 2007, depicting two life-size figures seated on a stack of large folios, recalls the tragic killing of two teenagers by a bomb in 1972. Behind the Town Hall, the MASONIC HALL is a vernacular two-storey building in roughcast with plate-glass windows; four bays, with a gabled breakfront and a plaque over the door bearing the date 1901. On BUTLER STREET the ULSTER BANK is a stuccoed Victorian house of two storeys and three bays with rusticated quoins, large tripartite sashes and a bracketed eaves cornice; the lower flat-roofed cash office to the side was formerly worthy of attention, with channelled rustication and emphatic eaves cornice – all now obliterated. Across the road behind impressive railings is the former MANSE, built for the now demolished Presbyterian church of 1857 by *William Hague*. The house, probably also by *Hague*, is a straightforward two-storey, three-bay block in rubble with sandstone quoins, red brick dressings and a steep hipped roof with central stacks. The ORANGE HALL on Deanery Street has a two-storey gabled front of 1874 in squared limestone with dressed quoins and yellow brick window dressings.

On the E bank by the river walk is ERNE VALE, the two-storey Late Georgian residence associated with Dickson, Dunlop & Co.'s distillery founded in 1825. Actually two houses in a gable-ended block of eight bays, roughcast with rusticated quoins, Georgian sashes and a leaded fanlight; alterations include timber bay windows on the ground floor and a battery of red brick Victorian chimneys on the ridge. Enlarged *c.* 1846. Most of the distillery buildings, originally grouped to the rear, had disappeared by the early C20.

NEIGHBOURHOOD

RIVERSDALE HOUSE. N of the bridge. A tall and compact Late Georgian house of two storeys with attics, pleasantly sited on a riparian site facing the town. Gable-ended block of three bays with twelve-pane sashes and a broad open porch with corner pilasters and an arched entrance. The gable chimneys are unusually formed as three independent square stacks, each rising to an eight-pointed limestone coping block.

ERNE HILL GATE LODGE. Cavan Road. A surprise in the ribbon development on the outskirts of the town. A prim Regency lodge in the manner of *Richard Morrison*, sometimes attributed to his former assistant, *J. B. Keane*. The design consists of a stuccoed symmetrical block under a low hipped roof with oversailing eaves and a crowning chimneystack, held between narrow side projections with arched trellis screens of elaborate ironwork. The central block has thick pilaster strips incised in a Soanean manner, with the wall deeply recessed between them; in the centre a single bay window projects with a bracketed sill and tripartite window with arched frames and marginal glazing bars. The gates and house of George M. Knipe across the road, which this lodge formerly addressed, have been replaced by a golf course, housing, shops and car parking.

ST MARY, STAGHALL. 1 km SW. A big lancet hall prominent in the open countryside, built in 1846 on a site donated by Lord Lanesborough and enlarged with a chancel in 1863, possibly by *William Hague*. Five-bay buttressed nave with bellcotes at both ends; a showy entrance gable, three bays wide, with a large lancet under an ogee hood in the centre and statuary niches above, all held between clasping buttresses with soaring pinnacles. The battlemented porch with domed pinnacles has a less spiky profile, bearing contrasting domed Tudor pinnacles instead. Re-roofed with concrete eaves *c.* 1983.

Inside, a flat plaster ceiling with large sunken panels, installed in 1964, encloses the originally exposed queenposts while leaving the lower truss members visible as a series of ornate brackets. The arcaded W gallery is a virtuoso display with twin statuary niches, decorated in Gothic filigree to an extraordinary extent. The mouldings of the pointed chancel arch spring from a fussy selection of short shafts and angel consoles in the manner favoured by Hague. In contrast to the plainness of the nave, the chancel walls are enriched with a great deal of applied ornament, including a sort of blind triforium arcade. E window of three cusped lights framed by tall slender shafts with foliated capitals. – MONUMENT. The Rev. Phill Donegan, founder of the church †1853. A marble tablet flanked by torches with a horned pediment, signed *Farrell & Son*, Glasnevin.

ST PATRICK, DRUMALEE. 3.5 km E. A satisfying small Gothic Revival church, designed in 1868 by *William Hague* for the Rev. J. Dunne. Buttressed nave of just three bays with paired lancets behind a steep gabled front with clasping buttresses, nicely ordered fenestration and a soaring belfry. Built of squared limestone with bands of dressed sandstone and polychrome brick arches to the windows. Inside, an airy space made serene by painting out the dark timbers of the exposed roof trusses. Wide chancel arch, its inner arch springing from short marble shafts on profiled brackets. The arch perfectly frames the busy crocketed spirelets of a High Victorian marble reredos by *James Pearse* – not a unique provincial survivor but an import, gifted in 2000 from the side chapel of J. J. McCarthy's Mary of the Angels, Church Street, Dublin.

LANESBOROUGH LODGE (formerly Quivvy Lodge). 5 km NE. The ruins of a modest early C19 Tudor-style house set on the tip of an elevated promontory in the Lough Erne system, surrounded by the loughs of Quivvy and Derrykerrib. The seat of the absentee earls of Lanesborough, who had established the castle of Belturbet in the early C17. A long and narrow two-storey block with kneelered end gables, three bays with wide mullioned windows, and a canted entrance bay advanced in the centre. Enlarged in 1846 for Henry Cavendish Butler with offices enclosing a kitchen and stableyards to the rear.

Along the avenue, the former SCHOOLHOUSE is a long mid-C19 block in squared limestone with gabled projections; also in ruins. Framed between tall yews at the entrance, the large Gothic GATE LODGE dated 1859, built for the 5th Earl of Lanesborough whose arms are prominently displayed on the front. An asymmetrical design in squared limestone with quarry glazing. Single-storey front with an offset open porch and two-storey gabled ends with decorative bargeboards. Discreetly enlarged *c.* 2000.

CHURCH, QUIVVY (C of I, former), now a residence and recording studio. 5 km NE. 1854 by *Roderick Gray* of Enniskillen. A

large gable-fronted church with an unusual offset tower, built
on the edge of the demesne of Lanesborough Lodge under the
patronage of the Countess of Lanesborough, who laid the
foundation stone. In squared limestone with sandstone dressings. The contractor was *William Hague Sen.* A buttressed hall
of four bays with richly glazed iron lancets. The steep entrance
gable is severely plain and solid-looking, with clasping buttresses and a gabled porch, pierced only by a tiny quatrefoil
below the apex. The square tower is tall and stocky, unusually
buttressed at the base with a continuous offset along one side;
the solid shape is rather nicely expressed above, with chamfers
on the corners. The overall sense of solidity is once again
enhanced by small quatrefoils piercing the upper walls, before
a pronounced cornice which surrounds the over-generous
pyramidal base for a short octagonal belfry and its squat spire.
Closed in 1986.

BESSBROOK AH

0020

An industrial utopia developed in the late C19 around an established linen mill on the River Camlough. Today orderly terraces
of houses are dominant, leaving little sense of its pre-industrial
origins. On high ground above the town, at Magheranely, earthworks survive from the early C17 defences of Sir Toby Caulfeild,
whose descendants, the earls of Charlemont, owned the town
until the late C19. A linen mill with bleaching green was founded
here by the Pollock family in 1760, which passed to Joseph Nicholson in 1802. According to official records the spinning mill was
the largest in Ireland. It fell into decline when the scutching mill
was destroyed by fire in 1839, but was rescued in 1845 by John

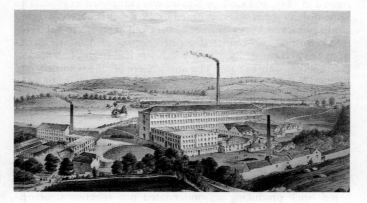

Bessbrook Flax Mills.
Chromolithograph by M. Ward, *c.* 1855–60

Grubb Richardson, who approached its development with a mes-
sianic zeal based on Quaker principles. The remove from Newry,
where his works had been, suited Richardson's 'rooted aversion
to be responsible for a factory in a large town'; here he had the
'desirable condition in my sight of enabling us to control our
people and to do them good in every sense'. The commercially
and morally inspired philanthropy of the industrial revolution
that established Sir Titus Salt's contemporary Saltaire and the
later Port Sunlight was here enhanced by Richardson's particular
controlling attitude to his workers' welfare, expressed in the
promotion of work, education and leisure for all in an atmosphere
of total abstinence. Corrupting influences were banned; no
public house or pawnbrokers were allowed, and consequently
there was no need for a police force. His son James Nicholson
Richardson summed up its ethos in an early C20 parody:

> From far-famed model Bessbrook,
> Where Bacchus is unknown,
> Where lack of public-houses
> Hath starved him of his throne
> (Police, pawn-shop nor publican
> Come nigh this realm of ease,
> The anxious call it in their wrath
> 'The City of Three P's'.)

Clearly this was conducive to the success of the Bessbrook Spinning Company; the town grew steadily through the late C19, as
did the mill, an industrial behemoth of granite that continues to
loom disproportionately over the small streetscapes. Its success
was unrivalled in Europe, supporting a workforce of 2,000. The
population peaked in the 1880s when some 3,000 lived in 700
houses built of rubble granite and red brick with individual
gardens or communal allotments. These were developed from the
mid C19 in two large squares linked by the existing Fountain
Street with parallel streets between; Charlemont Square was
started in 1855, and College Square was completed in 1890. The
same orderly spirit was continued in the neat rendered Arts and
Crafts houses of Abbey Terrace of 1913 and in the more standardized red brick and rendered council houses of Mount Charles
from 1939 onwards. By then the industry had begun to stagnate,
eventually closing in 1967. The atmosphere of lulled industry and
Richardsonian idealism was completely shattered when the mills
became Europe's largest helicopter base at the end of the C20.
Today it is once again a peaceable place. The churches are all
uphill, at the W end of the town.

CHRIST CHURCH (C of I). 1866–8 by *Welland & Gillespie*. The
contractor was *Matthew Doolin*. Roguish. A large and deeply
attractive Gothic church, exceptionally well finished, with
walls of random close-jointed Mourne granite and bands of
red brick producing an understated but effective structural
polychromy. Cruciform, with a large, steeply roofed nave, transepts with twin gables, and shallow polygonal apse; to the W a

slender offset tower with a spire entirely of yellow and red brick. Fenestration quite varied: mostly quarry-glazed lancets set under pointed arches of alternating red and yellow bricks with limestone keystones, but plate tracery in the nave and transepts; large, elaborate plate-traceried window of red sandstone in the w gable, above four small cusped lancets. The interior is attractive. The steep roof accommodates a high waggon vault marked by regular transverse ribs and intersected by a pair of arches opening into each transept, divided by an arcade resting on a stone column, with bizarre brick arches. Robustly detailed gallery at the w end.

SS PETER AND PAUL. 1873–5 by *Richard Hynes* of Newry. A simple cruciform church, plainly rendered, with lancets. Gaunt w gable dominated by an eccentric triple lancet window set in a shallow projection with expressive blocked quoins narrowing to support a gabled bellcote in ashlar. Interior galleried, with handsome Gothic joinery, exposed kingpost roof, and colourful sanctuary mosaics. – MONUMENT. The Rev. Michael McKevitt, P.P. †1874.

BESSBROOK PRESBYTERIAN CHURCH. Church Street. A trim Gothic church built in 1856 and enlarged in 1865. Five-bay buttressed hall with walls of random granite and plain lancets. Extended with a simple three-bay block to the w resulting in a T-plan. In 1876 this portion was raised to accommodate galleries, with small lancets set in gablets along the eaves.

To the N, the MANSE is a simple three-bay block of 1858, since enlarged. Roughcast with stuccoed quoins and entablatures to the ground-floor windows. The central bay is advanced and gabled and the first-floor windows extend upward in gablets above the eaves.

METHODIST CHAPEL. Church Street. 1873. A short, angular roughcast hall and porch with meagre red brick trim. Three bays, with triangular-headed windows.

FRIENDS MEETING HOUSE. 1864. A large and unusual building, in the woods of Derrymore demesne. 'Rustic' best describes the architecture of this great lumbering mass of squared granite with heavy eaves cornice, rusticated quoins, red brick window trim and replacement timber cross-mullioned windows. Essentially a T-plan building, mostly expressed in two storeys and dominated by a four-bay hall to the E. The main entrance is in a two-storey, three-bay block with an independent hipped roof that fills the NW angle. In the opposite angle a small single-bay projection from the first floor balances precariously on a single granite column to form an open porch. Between these elements the s gable exudes a provincial Georgian quality in the continuation of the moulded eaves cornice across the steeply pitched gable to form a pediment complete with brick oculus.

NATIONAL SCHOOL (former). College Square. A standard piece of estate architecture with hoodmoulds and pretty openwork bargeboards, built in 1875 to replace the original schoolhouse of 1853. A symmetrical single-storey design of five bays, the three central bays recessed under an open veranda on cast-iron columns between gabled end bays. The original latticed casements replaced by sashes with plate glass and marginal glazing bars.

CONVENT AND PAROCHIAL SCHOOL. Off Church Street, enjoying sensational views of the Mournes. 1902 by *John J. McDonnell*. Familiar institutional Gothic, built to accommodate eighteen sisters, a chapel and schools. A two-storey composition on a high basement, consisting of a long central range of seven bays between advanced and gabled end bays. Cement-rendered walls with stuccoed window surrounds, elaborated in the gables with decorative tympana above the first-floor windows. The entrance is a wide segmental-headed opening with glazed Gothic panels. Inside, the standard plan with spine corridor and central stairs in a gabled projection to the rear.

TOWN HALL (former INSTITUTE). College Square. 1886–7 by *William J. Watson* of Newry. A large two-storey block, nominally Gothic, with nicely textured walls varied between coursed granite and finely worked dressings. Asymmetrical front with four narrow bays and an off-centre porch between contrasting end projections; to the N wide and bulky with a hipped roof and rows of narrow mullioned windows, to the S gabled and more consciously Gothic, with a three-light window on the first floor under a pointed arch with a traceried tympanum. All the windows have plate glass and are set in chamfered reveals, the sashes in the N projection shaped to follow distinctive profiled heads formed by the mullions. The town clock is set high in the gable under an arching hoodmould; in the adjoining roofs three neat cusped lucarnes light the attics. Interior furnished with dark pitch pine; the main hall occupies a parallel gabled range behind and has an open timber roof.

BESSBROOK MILL. At the heart of the town, extending along the Derrymore Road. Disused. An enormous complex of C19 industrial buildings, really impressive only in terms of scale. The main block, built in long blocks of granite ashlar, has five storeys and a relentless battery of windows on each level. Surrounded by expansive low sheds with north-light roofs.

BESSBROOK RENT OFFICE. Church Street. 1866. A quirky little asymmetrical building of three bays, rising into a sharp gable to the W. Granite rubble walls with polychromatic brick trim, Georgian sashes with brick hoods, and roof patterned with fish-scale slating. Small brick diamonds in the gables, a motif found in the late C19 lodges of Derrymore House. Delightful polychromatic gate piers to the W with adjoining merloned pedestrian arch.

Behind, a row of taller rendered HOUSES, variously altered.

MOUNT CAULFEILD. Chapel Road. A long gable-ended C18 house, gaily remodelled with Tudor features in the later C19. Built, as the name implies, by the Caulfeild family who were then proprietors of the town, and acquired by John Grubb Richardson in 1845. The C18 T-plan house remains distinct in the long rectangular form of the entrance front and is evoked not least by the presence of two Georgian sashes with flush frames high in the N gable. The remodelling, probably by *Thomas Jackson & Sons*, was completed after 1867 when the house was given by Richardson to his son as a wedding present. This involved altering the symmetrical two-storey front by the addition to the S of a gabled projection with bay windows, repeated on the garden front, and the placing of a curvilinear gable to the N over the two end bays. A heavy moulded eaves cornice, gabled attic dormers and tall narrow brick stacks were also added. The windows were widened in blocked stucco surrounds and filled with plate glass; the upper and lower halves of the sashes, in chunky frames, are unevenly proportioned, the central divisions more like mullions than glazing bars – a distinctive window repeated in several Richardson houses of this period (the Wood House and Moyallan in Co. Down), regardless of the style. Enlivening the overall character is the distinctive diaper-patterned roof slating and attractive Jacobean strapwork in stucco on the N gable. The open timber porch with its fanciful pagoda roof has vanished, replaced by an ugly glazed concrete box.

THE WOOD HOUSE. Derrymore Road. A large gabled Victorian house of *c.* 1870, possibly by *Thomas Jackson*. Built for John Grubb Richardson as his main residence, near the town, inside the demesne of Derrymore House. Two storeys and rather plain, relieved only by varied gable projections. Roughcast with a continuous sill course between the storeys, simple timber bargeboards and irregularly proportioned plate-glass windows, some with stout central mullions of the kind employed at Mount Caulfeild.

DERRYMORE HOUSE. SE off the Derrymore Road. A large thatched *cottage orné*, successfully distilling Palladian, Gothic and vernacular ideas. Built *c.* 1777 for Isaac Corry, Chancellor of the Irish Exchequer, and described in 1803 by Sir Charles Coote as 'without exception the most elegant summer lodge I have ever seen'. It may well be the work of the landscape designer *John Sutherland*, who Coote says was employed by Corry to lay out the demesne. Modest in scale, a single storey over a basement, on a U-plan formed by three discrete blocks; two long, low ranges joined in the Palladian manner by short curved vestibules to a larger central block. This results in a deep entrance court where the sense of the vernacular is strongest. The walls have an uneven lime render with Georgian sashes under the roofs, thatched now with water reed and not dressed in the vernacular manner. The principal front is to the S, where the central block has a big mullioned bay window to the drawing room flanked by quatrefoils set under hoodmoulds in shallow square recesses. The scale of the bay window is exceptional for a house of this kind, with an extraordinary eighty-two panes. Further mullioned windows in the side elevation and wings are an amusing irony in the house of the man responsible for the Irish window tax – or would be, except that these very designs benefited from the concession that any

52

window, regardless of size, could be considered as one for taxation purposes if its dividing members were less than 12 in. (30.5 cm) wide.

Shortly before his death in 1813, Corry sold the property to Sir William Young, who added a large boxy entrance front with an elaborate fanlit doorcase across the end of the court, flanked by lower flat-roofed wings extending across part of the canted ends of the adjoining ranges. This was removed after the property had been acquired by the National Trust; its former existence explains the odd transverse hipped roofs and doorways facing across the entrance court.

Inside, the main space is the drawing room, known as the Treaty Room from the tradition that Corry and Lord Castlereagh drafted the terms of the Act of Union here. It is a generous room, taking up most of the central block, though plainly treated with a high coved ceiling. The only notable architectural features are two circular niches on the rear, fireplace, wall to answer the quatrefoil windows flanking the bay window.

The fine DEMESNE, considered by Coote to have been laid out according to 'the correct and elegant taste', is one of *Sutherland*'s earliest known works, in the naturalistic style, planted with as many as 140,000 trees.

CRAIGMORE VIADUCT. 2.5 km E. 1852 by *Sir John MacNeill*. A stupendous run of eighteen arches built for the Dublin & Belfast Junction Railway, spanning the Bessbrook River valley. Built in local rock-faced granite with slender, tapering piers, it extends over a distance of 1,400 ft (417 m) and cost £50,000.

EGYPTIAN ARCH. 3 km SE. 1851. A poetic monument to C19 engineering brilliance that powerfully evokes the entrance pylons to the New Kingdom temples of Karnak and Philae. A striking alternative to the stock railway arch, and apparently a modification of a design by the Dublin & Belfast Junction Company engineer, *Alexander Schaw*, perhaps made by *John Skipton Mulvany*, whose iconic Midland & Great Western Railway terminus at Broadstone in Dublin had just been completed. The contractors were the *Moore Bros*. Gently projecting from routine embankment walls, it is formed as a single arch of rock-faced granite between two sloping abutments faced in crisp ashlar that once supported a great oversailing cavetto cornice. The arch itself is round-headed, skilfully converted to a lintelled arch by the extension of the rusticated masonry into shallow spandrels at the corners which end abruptly in sharp arrises defining its angular form between the two textures of the stonework. Even with the reduction of its cornice by half, surely the most elegant railway arch in Ireland.

CAMLOUGH OLD CHURCH (C of I). 2 km S. Ruined hall and tower, built in 1772 to one of *Thomas Cooley*'s 'standard' designs for Archbishop Robinson. Three-bay hall with a forestanding battlemented tower in three diminishing stages. Nave walls of snecked masonry with granite Y-traceried windows. Redundant when the new church was completed at Bessbrook in 1868.

ST MALACHY CARRICKRUPPEN, CAMLOUGH. 2 km SW. A low
T-plan chapel, apparently of 1816. Roughcast with stuccoed
quoins and plain Y-tracery. Unusually with external stairs to
the galleries, rising in straight flights from the angle of nave
and transepts up to small square porches. Remodelled interior,
plain, with timber-panelled ceiling and exposed trusses. –
STAINED GLASS. A vibrant figurative E window of the 1940s
by *Earley & Co.* – MONUMENT. The Rev. Michael Montague
†1873; a crocketed limestone gable with polished marble shafts.

BILLIS BRIDGE   CN   5090

Rural crossroads between Cavan and Virginia.

ST BARTHOLOMEW (C of I). 1 km NE. 1843 by *Joseph Welland.*
A large hall and tower set in a grove of beech trees, built of
limestone rubble with sparse dressings. Nave of four bays with
lancets; tower forestanding in three stages. Additions to the
tower by Welland are recorded in 1855 but all looks uniform,
with rather pronounced strings, modest battlements and spiky
pinnacles. Unusually, there are windows on two levels on the
W gable, flanking the tower. Seamless enlargements of 1860 by
Welland & Gillespie involved an extra bay to the nave, and a
chancel with a new robing room intersecting on the SE corner;
the old robing room was replaced by a shallow N transept. The
contractor was *William Hague Sen.* A dark timbered interior
with exposed scissor trusses. – FURNISHINGS. Compact alabaster READING DESK signed *Harrison*, Dublin; octagonal
PULPIT with polished shafts; ORGAN in a charming Regency
Gothic casing. – STAINED GLASS. Three-light E window: 'I am
the Resurrection', 1906, attributed to *Jones & Willis.* – MONU-
MENT. William Pratt †1917; a scrolled plaque signed *B. Taylor*,
Dublin.

ST MARY, CLANNAPHILIP. 3 km NE. 1974. A downright ugly
building unworthy of its purpose. More an engineered object
than architecture. A broad gabled block overwhelmed by a
gambrel roof and strange overhanging slate aprons. The main
front is a special oddity, wilfully muddled: cement-rendered
walls with vertical strip windows flanking a crazy-paved central
panel of silver granite. Entrances on either side set under
ridiculous floating hipped canopies, clad in slate. On one side
a tall steel bell-tower with a palisaded belfry looks like some
kind of medieval gallows. Interior unimaginably poor. The only
object of interest is a primitively inscribed plaque from a
church at Termon nearby, dated 1811, displayed in the porch.
    Surprisingly, this was an established ecclesiastical site, asso-
ciated with an ancient chapel of the O'Reillys. Now a late
medieval grotesque head embedded in the back of a makeshift
statuary niche partly of reused ashlar is all that visibly

survives on the site of the earliest church and its successors. Tradition identifies the heavily wrinkled head as a portrayal of the Cailleach Gearagain, the witch eradicated by Patrick's zeal.

BELLASIS PRESBYTERIAN CHURCH. 2 km SE. A bulky three-bay hall like Glasleck (Shercock), with a hipped roof and a lower two-bay MINISTER'S HOUSE set back on one side. Smooth-rendered walls with strip quoins. Its erection in 1837 by the Rev. John King is recorded on stone plaques recessed between the windows.

0030   BLACKLION   CN

A small street village situated in the extreme NW of the county, between the McNean Loughs on the border with Fermanagh. Only the Late Georgian vernacular MARKET HOUSE stands out for notice on the corner of the Main Street, a handsome two-storey, three-bay end-of-terrace building in dressed stone with a broad segmental archway in each of its two fronts.

METHODIST CHURCH. 0.5 km W. A tall, four-bay lancet hall with a small gabled porch, in smooth render, for which the foundation stone was laid on 20 April 1849.

TERMON OLD CHURCH. 2 km W, by Lough McNean Upper. The ruins of a substantial rectangular church of late medieval date comprising undifferentiated nave and chancel, measuring approximately 69 ft by 20 ft (21 m by 6 m). Built in coursed field rubble with tiny unelaborated rectangular windows piercing the nave, equally small loop windows in the chancel, and a carved three-light, round-headed E window. Sockets internally at the W end evince a timber loft.

KILLINAGH PARISH CHURCH (C of I). 2 km SW. Of c. 1850 by Joseph Welland. A charming small church, in a simplified Tractarian Gothic, built of squared rubble with smooth dressings. Steeply roofed nave of four bays and lower chancel, both with lesene buttresses on the outer corners and quarry-glazed lancets. Small gabled side porch, and lean-to bell-chamber on the W front serving the bellcote on the gable above. – STAINED GLASS. In the centre of the nave, on either side: the Good Shepherd and the Resurrection, both signed Jones & Willis, London & Liverpool, c. 1910.

KILLINAGH GLEBE. 2 km SW. A handsome Regency house of cubic proportions on an L-plan, two storeys on a basement. Front of three bays with a fanlit doorcase set in a shallow recess; large twelve-pane sashes on the ground floor, nine-pane above.

ST PATRICK, KILLINAGH PARISH CHURCH. 2.5 km SW. 1846, enlarged and remodelled in 1934 by James Donnelly under the patronage of Sir Patrick McGovern. On a triangular island between two roads, a small lancet hall of four bays with a two-bay chancel in roughcast with stucco trimmings. Kneelered gable, with a bellcote and porch. Inside, an open timber roof with queenpost trusses. – STAINED GLASS. E window: vividly coloured early C20 figurative design in the manner of the *Earley Studio*, Dublin. – MONUMENTS. The Rev. Hugh de Lacy †1875, by *Farrell & Sons*, Dublin. – The Rev. John Smith †1893, by *J. Delany*, Monaghan.

UPPER THORNHILL. 4.5 km SW. Secluded in an attractive, treed landscape, an Early Georgian gable-ended farmhouse with a long, low two-storey front of six bays with a squat gabled porch added later. Smooth cement render has now given the front a dour appearance, not helped by crude window replacements. The true vernacular charm of the building is preserved in the roughcast rear façade, where some original sash frames survive, and on the windowed gable which retains ovolo timber mouldings on the slate overhangs. Inside, just one room deep, the rooms reached from a corridor running across the front; entirely vernacular in feeling, with whitewashed walls, a large arched central hearth, flagged floors, and some raised and fielded joinery.

BLACKWATERTOWN

AH 8050

A street village where today only the presence of the River Blackwater suggests its former strategic importance as a frontier post in the wars against the Tyrone O'Neills. A town evolved from the defences commenced here by Walter Devereux, Earl of Essex, in 1574. The Earl of Tyrone's risings always began with an attack on the Blackwater Fort, and he successfully destroyed it and the river crossing in 1595; rebuilt by the Lord Deputy, Thomas Burgh, as 'an eyesore in the heart of O'Neill country', it fell again, to be eventually reclaimed in 1601 by Sir Arthur Chichester, commander of the Crown troops in Ulster; it was rebuilt for the last time in July the same year by Lord Mountjoy, following a triangular plan with bastions on the apexes. Nothing of this strong and compact structure remains now. In more peaceful times the river was opened up to navigation and the settlement prospered for a while, from its quayside transporting corn and potatoes by Lough Neagh to Belfast. In 1788 the Rev. Daniel Beaufort found it a 'good, brick-built village'. Trade was further enhanced when the Ulster Canal opened in 1842; the former importance of this activity is evident at the N end of the Main Street in two facing warehouses, that on the E side a three-storey block with striking snecked masonry. Otherwise just one C18 house stands out, with a long two-storey front and an attractive Tuscan doorcase with open pediment.

PRESBYTERIAN CHURCH. 1898. Simple lancet hall, roughcast, with wide stuccoed quoins and four pointed bays. Gable-fronted with a pointed doorway flanked by lancets and the date on a plaque above it.

NATIONAL SCHOOL (former). 1867. Marking an intersection at the top of the village, a plain roughcast building in two abutting blocks forming an L-plan. Large camber-headed windows.

ROYAL IRISH CONSTABULARY BARRACKS (former). An early C20 two-storey block. Neo-Georgian: nicely proportioned five-bay front with the three central bays on the ground floor set in recessed arches; steep hipped roof with a short single stack in the centre and tall eaves stacks on the end walls.

BUSINESS CENTRE. 2007 by *Daly, O'Neill & Associates*. A curving two-storey range with projecting gabled end bays. The main front has a modest elegance reminiscent of a C19 stable block, with cement-rendered walls, tall windows on the first floor set in pairs, and wide segmental arches on the ground floor – unfortunately let down by cheap metal frames.

BROOMFIELD

MN

7 km SE of Castleblayney

ST PATRICK. 1898 by *G. L. O'Connor*; interior 1941 by *Thomas J. Cullen*. An ambitious solid church that sits heavily on its rural site. The foundation stone was laid by the Bishop of Clogher and the Archbishop of Melbourne; the builder was *James Wynne* of Dundalk. Straitened E.E. Gothic in style, with a

Broomfield, St Patrick.
Drawing, 1901

cruciform plan and a tall four-stage belfry tower at the sw corner. Architecturally quite passionless but for the highly expressive masonry, a hard pale limestone sourced locally, pitch-faced and worked in closely gauged courses, giving the exterior the appearance of a hard amphibian skin. The gabled w front is especially plain, with a severe pointed doorway set in a double-chamfered reveal flanked by small lancets, and a triple-light window and hoodmould above. Tall lancets, between buttresses, light the four-bay nave. The tower muscles in on the w front, strengthened by clasping buttresses with offsets rising all the way to the upper stage; between them each stage is defined by moulded string-courses – at the lower level related to the w front and on the upper stage taken round the buttresses to give the belfry greater emphasis; the top is finished with a straight balustrade pierced with quatrefoils, and four gable-fronted pinnacles with crockets. Internally the details are plainer, the present interior reconstructed after the building had been seriously damaged by fire in 1940. A two-bay arcade with high pointed arches supported on square piers clad in polished Aberdeen granite opens to the transepts. The present ceiling forms a pointed vault with simple transverse ribs. Reordered in 1985. The original high altar in Caen stone and marble, destroyed in the fire, was by *E. Sharp*. – ARTWORK. Batiks in the transepts by *Bernadette Madden*, 1986. – STAINED GLASS. E window: the Crucifixion, by *Abbey Stained Glass Studios*, Dublin, 1997. – Adjoining the small sacristy on the N transept is a hexagonal TOILET BLOCK added in 1985.

The PRESBYTERY is also by *O'Connor*, 1910. A large two-storey cubic block of five bays with flat triangular-headed windows. Hipped roof with chimneystacks carried on the outside walls.

AN EAGLAIS. 1841. Former Presbyterian church, now a roadside diner. A short four-bay hall with a broad gabled front, cement-rendered, with tall pointed windows and a diminutive Tudor-arched doorway. The interior retains exposed kingpost trusses, some monuments, and the pulpit niche embellished with Gothic plasterwork.

MOUNT CARMEL GLEBE, sometimes called BROOMFIELD. A low two-storey block of *c.* 1800. Understated five-bay front, roughcast, with a shallow hipped roof over wide eaves on paired brackets. Timber doorcase with slender Tuscan columns and spoked elliptical fanlight. Glazing bars removed in the late C19, resulting in oddly proportioned sashes with plate glass on the first floor. Circular window tucked in under the eaves in each end wall. A former rectory, it is described in 1835 as a small house and the residence of Mr Henry Kenny. Across the main road, the PARISH CHURCH of 1841 which it served has been demolished. The foundations, outlined by a pavement, indicate a rectangular structure lined with buttresses, angled at the corners, suggesting one of the typical gabled halls of *William Farrell*. Nicely detailed Gothic gates and cemetery survive.

BROWNLOW HOUSE *see* LURGAN

4010   BUTLER'S BRIDGE   CN

A small village on the River Erne, 6 km N of Cavan.

83   ST AIDAN. 1861 by *William Hague*. Fronting the street, beside
     the five-arched bridge that gives the village its name. This small
     Gothic church is an early work, clearly intended to impress
     with sophisticated and carefully considered indulgences, by a
     self-conscious young architect whose family came from this
     locality. The pride must extend also to the contractor, who was
     William Hague Sen. A polychromatic design just when that was
     becoming fashionable, yet still novel enough to be excused by
     the Dublin *Builder* as an economic solution to a decorative
     imperative in a design that 'couldn't afford ornament so gained
     as much effect as possible by contrast of materials'. Built in
     squared buff sandstone with pale grey limestone dressings
     employed in bands and as quoins, with red-and-yellow brick
     voussoirs to the windows. The contrast is kept up in two-toned
     slating to the roofs. The plan is relatively straightforward, with
     a narrow aisled nave and a deep apsidal chancel with side
     chapels, separated from the lean-to aisles by gables to indicate
     transepts. On the W front the aisles are set back with curved
     triangular tracery and lower gabled porches below linked by
     short side passages to the entrance gable. The angle of the tall
     gable is misshapen on one side to support an open columnar
     belfry, carried up as a steep polygonal spirelet.
          The interior is as refined as it is unusual, with an arcade of
     just three bays with pointed arches on lithesome cast-iron
     columns enriched with repoussé capitals, each with different
     exotic foliage. This structural delicacy creates the impression
     of a broad nave, with a continuous panelled timber ceiling well
     lit by tall lancets in the aisles, set in groups of two and three.
     The transepts are expressed only in the widening of the arcade
     and their transverse panelled roofs. Ribbed plaster ceiling in
     the apse, separated from the nave by a trefoiled arch on
     enriched corbels. – STAINED GLASS. Three lights in the chancel
     and three graded lancets in the organ loft, all with bright figu-
     rative glass by *Thomas Earley*, *c.* 1870.
     URNEY OLD CHURCH. 2 km NW. A ruined late medieval church
     in a secluded waterside site. Rubble walls of a rectangular nave
     with a substantial W wall, separating an annexe, containing a
     decent pointed doorway and stairs in the thickness of the wall;
     once divided into two barrel-vaulted chambers with an upper
     floor served by the stairs, this was probably the priest's accom-
     modation. A narrow slit window with a deep splayed reveal is
     evident in the E gable through the dense ivy.
          Nearby on the picturesque River Erne is an imposing Victor-
     ian BRIDGE, a two-arch structure in rock-faced ashlar with a
     narrow carriageway.

DERRYHEEN PARISH CHURCH (C of I). 2 km SW. A low-lying rural church overlooking the floodplain of the River Derryheen, built to *William Farrell*'s most ubiquitous chapel of ease design, for a parish formed in 1834. Three-bay rubble hall with lancets and a short gabled chancel. W gable with a pinnacled bellcote, square corner buttresses with spiky octagonal pinnacles, and a similarly buttressed battlemented porch in the centre.

ANNAGH OLD CHURCH. 2.5 km NW. In a circular roadside enclosure overlooking Annagh Lough, the remains of a medieval rectangular single-cell church ruined since the early C17. Today among the overgrown rubble walls the two gables stand complete, and in the battered side walls an entrance and windows are suggested on the S side. The principal feature is in the E gable, a tall C13 cusped lancet, narrow, with a deeply splayed reveal dressed internally with sandstone quoins, carved with a slender shaft to the angles which rises to a bell capital on the impost; the pointed arch is elaborately formed of short voussoirs deeply cut with roll mouldings. Externally, the opening is simply framed by a roll moulding under a beaded dripstone.

ST ANDREW, DRUMALOOR (C of I). 3.5 km NW. 1869 by *James Rawson Carroll*. The contractor was *Robert Smith*. A simple lancet hall of four bays, rectangular in plan, with a gabled W front, S porch, and polygonal chancel continuous with the body of the church; all with steep slate roofs. Built of rock-faced limestone with smooth dressings. Bellcote, oculus and cusped lancets in the W gable; paired lancets in the chancel.

CARRICKABOY   CN   4090

Rural crossroads 7 km S of Cavan town.

CARRICKABOY OLD CHURCH. The foundations of a small rectangular church, in a walled cemetery, overgrown and impenetrable at the time of writing. The entrance, however, is rewarding: twin polygonal piers of limestone, dated 1860 and signed by *Thomas Stafford* in large script below the vanished caps; handsome wrought-iron gates with arrow spikes and a stile to the side with a flight of projecting limestone slabs.

ST MATTHEW, DRUMAVADDY. 0.5 km W. 1865, rebuilt 1957 by *Patrick Gaffney*. A dull cruciform building in roughcast with stucco trim. Bulky proportions, with round-headed lancets. Inside, flat plaster ceiling with a wide, pronounced border. At the E end, the wall plane is interrupted to accommodate a recessed sanctuary, the simple architectural play enhanced by side-lighting recessed behind the walls.

DENN PARISH CHURCH (C of I). 1.5 km NE. Early C19 hall-and-tower type, built of rubble with limestone dressings. A compact three-bay hall, unusually with a hipped roof, giving it a sense of independence from the tower. The windows are pointed with hoods, now rather badly fitted with plastic casements; wider E window where the timber Y-tracery survives. Also on the E end, above the eaves, two squat polygonal turrets in dressed limestone are chimney-like projections that appear decorative rather than functional. The battlemented tower has three stages with ball-topped pinnacles. A plaque over the door records the date 1815, the vicar, the Rev. Joseph Drum, and the churchwardens, Thomas Heaslip and Patrick Fagan. Small vestry added in 1868.

DECORATED STONE. Beside the NW corner, a rectangular stone pillar of unknown origin or date, now much weathered and easily mistaken for a headstone. Surfaces are heavily punch-dressed, with chamfered corners above a decorated band; images on each face seem predominantly of an equine nature, including a pair of rampant winged horses on one side.

Across the road, the former SCHOOL is a small, single-storey rubble block with a hipped roof. Three bays to the front; though narrowed, the quarry-glazed windows are still unusually large.

ST MATTHEW, CROSSKEYS. 5 km SE. 1839, replacing a T-plan building described as 'old and dilapidated' in 1837. A bulky, three-bay gabled hall, smooth-rendered with limestone dressings. Sides expressed in two stages with blocked quoins at entrance level and strip quoins above. Round-headed windows set high on a continuous string-course to define the stages, with ashlar lesenes between. Enlarged c. 2008 with a broad cumbersome porch set across the W gable incorporating an ungainly, offset square tower. Inside, a plain rectangular hall. – STAINED GLASS. Richly saturated figurative glass by *Earley & Co.*, Dublin. – MONUMENT. The Rev. Patrick Gilroy †1871, by *Harrison*, Dublin.

CARRICKMACROSS   MN

INTRODUCTION

Carrickmacross is an attractive market town set in the varied countryside of south Monaghan; a group of small lakes and closely wooded landscapes dominate the hinterland to the S, while more open vistas characterize the agricultural landscape to the N. It remains a town of two halves, reflecting its division in

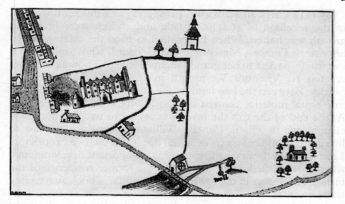

Carrickmacross, map of the town.
Drawing, 1736

the C17 along the centre line of its main street between two prominent absentee landlords. The E side formerly belonged to the Thynne family, viscounts Weymouth and later marquesses of Bath, and the W to the Shirleys, descendants of the 1st Lord Ferrers, in whose possession it nominally remains. They developed a modern town in a spirit of co-operative competition over the course of the Georgian period, resulting in a legacy of good buildings.

The town stands on a low ridge. The ascent is steep from the S until reaching the S–N Main Street where it levels out to form a wide thoroughfare, dipping briefly before rising again to the N where it is forced to divert E around Gallows Hill, an eminence that supports the hollow masonry cylinder of an C18 windmill. Wide three-storey houses of 'respectable appearance' dominate both sides of the long street, with the vistas closed by the spiritual and temporal foci of the town – the Church of Ireland parish church to the S and the Courthouse to the N. This main artery is intersected here and there by a few straggling side streets; those to the W slope down into the valley of the small River Proules. In its boggy flood plain to the S the Irish settlement of Magheross had developed, where according to tradition there had been a church since the C7. Later it provided power for a mill.

Walter Devereux, 1st Earl of Essex, was granted the barony of Farney by Queen Elizabeth in 1576 but did not live long enough to build a permanent base here, and it was the 3rd Earl who, between 1628 and 1633, erected the castle at Drummond Otra, on an elevated site to the S above Magheross. The castle illustrated by Thomas Raven in 1634 was a robust three-storey block with gabled projections and high diagonal stacks set in an elaborate bawn, with battlemented walls, circular bastions and a central pedimented gateway. It was laid waste after 1641, used as a quarry in the C18, and rebuilt as the residence of the agent to the Bath estate, then as the St Louis Convent.

By 1612 Carrickmacross was prospering as a market town, but in the rebellion of 1641 the castle and church were fired and growth was halted. When Essex died in 1646 the estate went to his sisters: Frances, Marchioness of Hertford, whose inheritance eventually passed to her granddaughter, wife of Thomas Thynne, created 1st Viscount Weymouth in 1682, and Lady Dorothy Shirley. Between the two families the estate was gradually divided into equal moieties centred on Castle Street, now Main Street. At the end of the C17 the town was leased to two London merchants, one of whom, Captain William Barton, was the last to live in the castle before its eventual decay. Of the two proprietors Lord Weymouth was the first to initiate important developments, when in 1698 he sought to convert the former residence of the bishop of Clogher in the town into a grammar school, succeeding to do so in 1711.

By the late C18 the town could be described as 'a good market town and improved of late into great figure and trade'. The Shirley side eventually followed Weymouth's initiative, and in 1774 *Henry Byrne* and *John Green* wrote to their landlord George Shirley, in response to his stated desire to have the w side 'as much improved as Lord Weymouth's', enclosing a plan and elevation of a brick house erected by them in the town a year earlier. At this time the development of the Main Street remained focused on the s half, around a market house, apparently an old structure built with material quarried from the ruined castle. As it occupied the centre of the street it was shared by the two estates in their promotion of the town. In 1779 Shirley sent to his agent a design for a new market house by the Warwick architect *Thomas Johnson* (drawn by his son, *John Lees Johnson*), a neat single-storey classical building with Tuscan pilasters framing three arched bays. *John Green* had provided a simpler design, but Shirley was reluctant to give over full control of an important public building to local ideas. It is unclear which of these designs was followed; in 1782 Shirley was given to believe that 'the building is clumsy, by not following my plan'. It was demolished by the early C20 without being recorded. In 1789 – the year the 3rd Viscount Weymouth became Marquess of Bath – a new parish church was given a central prominence, away from the shabby ancient district of Magheross to the s, and so the modern town began to take shape. A new Catholic chapel erected at this time was well removed on the E side, served initially by a narrow lane off the Main Street; this soon provided the impetus for the creation of New Street, opening opposite the old market house, which became a busy commercial side street.

The w side did not always develop apace with the E, and in 1815 it was noted that several houses were 'decayed and not inhabited'. Even with gradual improvements, and the employment in the 1830s and 1840s as clerk of works for the Shirleys of the architect *George Sudden*, to whom several buildings may be attributed, the general impression of the town in 1835 was not very favourable: the houses, though large, 'were badly built and, if examined, are shells only . . . for the accommodation of hordes of country people who . . . frequent them for the purpose of drinking'. The imagery is supported by the town's two principal industries – a brewery located on the W side of the Main Street stretching down to the Proules, and a large distillery further downstream to the SE to which the brewery provided malt, built in 1823 and by 1836 producing 200,000 gallons of spirits annually. Although this complex was quarried for building material in the late C19, substantial ruins may still be seen.

The town did not acquire any architecture of marked formality until well into the C19, the instances of good-quality building noticeably increasing with the economic upturn that followed the Great Famine. The Courthouse of 1837 was the first, its long low elevation set appropriately (and not coincidentally) against the backdrop of Gallows Hill, further reflecting the growth of the town to the N. It was followed by *William Caldbeck*'s National Bank, begun in 1855, forming a rather grand palazzo composition on the E side. The Catholic population was willing to express a new confidence: in 1860 they decided to replace their C18 chapel and called upon the best purveyor of triumphalist Gothic, *J. J. McCarthy*, to achieve this. The Established Church was content to tinker with its building, making only minor alterations.

1861 was to be an important year. The town's landlords continued to develop their interest, and as absentees entrusted their estates to competent, if at times controversial, agents. The most influential of these was William Steuart Trench (author of *Realities of Irish Life*, 1868), agent to the Shirley estate until 1845, and from 1851 until his death in 1872 to the Bath estate. He provided the main impetus for the extensive building activity undertaken in the town for the Bath estate; he built a residence for himself on the site of the castle, and in 1861 created a new market place at the N end of the town, which promoted further growth there. Also dispersed around the E portion are several instances of good-quality estate housing built in the Tudor style typical of such architecture in the second half of the C19. These buildings, which usefully display the Bath coronet and dates of erection, are characterized by distinctive diagonal patterning and the expressive treatment of the masonry.

CHURCHES ETC.

MAGHEROSS OLD CHURCH (C of I). The oldest surviving ecclesiastical remains in Carrickmacross, where a church is said to have existed from at least the C7. Ruined in 1641, rebuilt in 1682, abandoned after 1789, and now ruined, it remains the focus of the original settlement by the Proules, near the ancient well, Tober Inver. Today the irregular churchyard, elevated above the street, is entered by majestic late C17 GATEPIERS with ball finials; especially fine bettered only by those at Killeshandra. At the back of the site sits a long and low hall with a forestanding square tower over the W gable distinguished by its conical spire, a squat twisted finger defining the 29 approaches from the S and SW. The nave is of two bays with wide windows that survive best on the S wall, where shallow arches are evident; basic E window with a pointed arch, repaired in modern times. Walls of uncoursed rubble with traces of a base batter to the E gable. Evidence for rebuilding internally, with reused masonry found at a low level on the E wall and alterations to the splay of the SE nave window. Tower of two stages, a tall lower stage with a camber-headed window to the W and a shorter belfry stage with windows on each face, distinctive for their cambered heads shaped from a single stone, linked by a string-course; further distinction in the broad and flat bands of masonry, uneven but well finished, that clasp the corners. Together these features seem to confirm an early C17 date. The tower is crowned by a battlemented parapet and rubble spire. Inside the tower is a sandstone doorcase, neatly carved with a Tudor arch, perhaps part of the late C17 rebuilding; it bears a graffito date of 1727. Above the door, a carved plaque records the waste and rebuilding of the church in the C17 and names the patrons, with their crests at each corner: Dr Roger Boyle, Lord Bishop of Clogher; William Barrett, Esq.; Robert Hill, Esq.; and Andrew Montgomery, clerk vicar of the parish. The old bell from the tower was removed to St Patrick, Ardragh (Corvalley), in the C19.

INVER LODGE, beside the churchyard to the N. A long two-storey rendered house of C19 appearance, present before 1836. Five bays with a pedimented projection flanked by lean-to projections on the ground floor and gabled windows on the first floor.

ST FINBARR, Magheross Parish Church (C of I). A plain hall on an elevated site with its tower and spire facing N down the Main Street. In 1777 the parishioners had petitioned Lord Weymouth for a new church, claiming that the 'ancient decayed building' at Magheross was 'hastening to dilapidation and ruin'. Concern with the old church's location 'in the midst of a popish country' motivated them to remove to the safety of the town centre. Their petition was supported by Bishop Boyle of Clogher, but progress was to be slow. The earliest practical contribution appears to have been a subscription of £113 from Lord Weymouth in 1786. Perhaps the delay was down to the hunt for a suitable site. Work commenced in 1788 with the demolition of houses on Bridge Street and Carver's Lane (Bath Street); the church was completed by *Henry Byrne* in 1792 for the sum of £600. The building is a plain three-bay hall with a W tower – all harled and unprepossessing, except for the small apse that offers a certain unexpected elegance, perhaps inspired by one of *Cooley*'s classical designs. The third stage of the tower, with its pilaster strips, distinctive arcaded battlements and short corner pinnacles, was probably added later to house the clock and support the octagonal needle spire, all intended to enhance the eminence of the structure within the streetscape (and succeeding). In 1868 *Slater & Carpenter* proposed enlarging the church with the addition of a narrow S aisle, of five bays with an ambitious arcade, and a polygonal chancel; neither was executed.

Interior disappointingly plain. The apse is as though formed with an ice-cream scoop, a large niche without a distinguishing arch, lit by a mid-C19 tripartite window – in effect a debased Venetian window – filled with densely patterned C19 coloured glass. The gallery was extended along the S side in 1845 by *Joseph Welland* but has since been removed. *Welland* carried out further alterations in 1853–4 that included the vestry to the SW and presumably also the elaborate queenpost-truss roof. – STAINED GLASS. In the nave S, two windows showing parables by *James Powell & Sons*, 1860; nave N: 'Miraculous feeding', signed *Harry Clarke Studios*, 1937. – MONUMENTS. Alexander Mitchell †1843; a simple classical tablet on consoles. – James Evatt †1846; a handsome Gothic aedicule in white marble. Agents to the Shirley and Bath estates respectively.

ST JOSEPH. 1861–6 by *J. J. McCarthy*. A major monument of the Irish Gothic Revival, displaying all the attributes that define McCarthy as Ireland's most dedicated disciple of Pugin. It was commenced at the height of his career, a month after his cathedral at Monaghan was begun. Although on the E edge of the town, with its tall grey spire it outperforms its more prominently placed Church of Ireland counterpart. The decision to replace the old T-plan chapel of 1783 was taken by a meeting of parishioners in 1860. The lead was provided by the Marquess of Bath, who also gave the additional site area, the use of stone from his quarry, and a subscription of £300. The foundation stone was laid the following year; the clerk of works was *George Burnett*.

The plan is a standard one, tightly arranged: nave with aisles, transepts, and chancel with N and S chapels; a porch on the N side and an adjoining sacristy and chapel to the NE, all clearly delineated and hierarchically ordered in the Puginian manner. The asymmetrical W front is dominated by a tall S tower with broach spire, incomplete at the time of McCarthy's death in 1882, depriving the building of its symbolic power until their completion by *G. C. Ashlin* in 1898. At the angle of the N aisle and transept a neat polygonal projection in smooth ashlar accommodates spiral stairs to serve the gallery, a feature later repeated on the S side of the tower. The sense that the arrangement is overly compact is explained by the fact that the site available for building on was restricted by the existence of the bishop's house and the C18 church, retained until 1866, thereby forcing the new church into a more confined situation close to the E boundary.

The style is French-inspired Dec Gothic in pale limestone, crisp and sharp-edged. McCarthy's belief that style should be determined by local materials resulted here in a slightly cold structure that is vigorously expressed. Each element is carefully and precisely modelled: clasping buttresses with offsets strengthen the corners, or, positioned singly, define the bays. The tower with its clasping buttresses, offsets, lancets, hoodmoulds and lucarnes increases the Frenchified air; the closeness of the detail to McCarthy's spires for Armagh and Maynooth indicates that Ashlin followed the original architect's design closely, perhaps only adding ribs to the arrises of the spire to enhance its elegant profile.

The windows are notable exercises in geometry, especially those high in the transepts. In aisle and clerestory, paired lancets with cusped heads supporting foils that subtly alternate to reward the inquisitive. The w doorway is gabled, with a deeply moulded recess supported on colonnettes; the extraordinary bulbous capitals were never fully carved but left punch-dressed so they look like Bronze Age vessels, and the label stops are plain blocks.

The interior possesses all the ascetic quality that was, by this time, characteristic of McCarthy's churches. Plainness and simplicity are immediately evident in the lofty nave with its clerestory and in the functional scissor-truss roof carried on plain corbels. The juxtaposition of painted plaster and soft-coloured ashlar stonework offers greater definition to the spaces. The saturated richness of the stained glass creates an atmosphere that is at times gloomy but never dull, especially in the aisles, where a preponderance of blue distinguishes the studio of *Harry Clarke*. Nave and aisles are separated by a pointed arcade of eight bays; the piers are squat sandstone cylinders with octagonal scalloped capitals possessing a medieval quality worthy of *Pugin*, and almost identical to Pugin's piers for Killarney Cathedral. Everywhere, however austere, the detail is accomplished. The principal windows have highly decorated bar tracery: the seven-light E window is essentially McCarthy's earlier w window for Armagh, shortened a little; it is repeated with five lights on the w front, where the organ parts to provide a full view.

After the architect's death the interior was completed by his son, *C. J. McCarthy*, who was mainly responsible for the FUR-NISHINGS, including the altars, reredos and organ gallery. The sanctuary has now been emptied of all but the REREDOS by *P. J. O'Neill & Co.* – STATIONS OF THE CROSS in oils by *Richard King*. – STAINED GLASS. E window: St Joseph and prophets by *Earley & Powell*. Chancel N and s windows: SS Brigid, Patrick, Macartan and Columcille (Columba) by *J. Clarke*. s transept: Madonna in Majesty, by *Mayer & Co.*, c. 1893. s aisle: Crucifixion and Entombment, with almost neon illumination; this and the remainder come from the studios of *Harry Clarke*, c. 1928; St Cearra in the s aisle is the only work bearing his distinctive monogram.

The former Bishop's Residence to the NW, an attractive four-bay house of early C19 appearance with a hipped roof and central stack, was replaced in 1980 by a CURATE'S RESIDENCE, less appealing and rudimentary in its character. The former National Schools of 1834 have also gone. The former High School, now the SCOUTS HALL, was built in 1909 for the

Patrician Brothers. Plain institutional Gothic by *Robert Coulson* and *Joseph Latton*; L-plan with gabled street front, roughcast walls with moulded brick trim. To the E the CATHOLIC HALL of 1905, a gaily painted stucco façade fronting a long plain hall, is a good-humoured exercise in jazzy Baroque classicism.

PRESBYTERIAN CHURCH. Bath Street. A simple four-bay Gothic hall of late C19 appearance set within a small railed enclosure. Squared limestone walls, ashlar trim, and plain lancets with raised cement surrounds. Entrance in a single-storey T-plan projection to the E.

Adjoining to the E stands the JACKSON MEMORIAL HALL of 1927, a big two-storey block with hipped roof, dull but for the interesting vermiculated quoins and platband rendered in stucco.

ST LOUIS CONVENT AND SCHOOL. Beside St Finbarr's Church. Certainly not the most elegant building in Carrickmacross, but probably the most imposing, with the forbidding qualities of its predecessor, the castle. A great rendered mass behind C19 battlemented parapet walls, its gaunt edifice hangs over the S approach to the town with a large crenellated tower rising at the centre of a long three-storey range with polygonal ends.

In 1888 the castle and its grounds, by then the house of the agent to the Bath estate and known as Essex Castle, were acquired by the Rev. Dean Birmingham and given over to the Sisters of St Louis from Monaghan, who established the convent here. A view of Essex Castle in 1888 shows a battlemented tower flanked by long single-storey ranges with a two-storey annexe to the SE. Additions by *Hague & McNamara* in 1903 must have involved the extension of these ranges to three storeys, including an additional storey to the tower and a single-storey battlemented porch. The ground floor retains two large rooms, plainly decorated, on the N side of the tower with a corridor to the rear; the stairs adjoin the tower to the S and rise through the building, lit on each level by paired windows. A chapel occupies most of the ground floor to the S.

By November 1888 stones were being drawn from the disused distillery to the S for the erection of a new BOARDING SCHOOL; the foundation stone was laid the following spring, attended by the architect, *C. J. McCarthy*, and by November it was complete, ready to accommodate fifty boarders. A long and attractive two-storey range in squared ashlar with red brick trim, lit by big four-over-four-pane sash windows on the ground floor with smaller corresponding sashes above arranged in pairs tightly placed beneath corbelled eaves; a two-bay gabled projection with belfry accommodates the stairs on the E elevation. TEACH JOSEPH to the S is a massive brick-fronted block of three storeys, erected in 1962 to provide a large examination hall. The CHAPEL by *J. J. McDonnell*, 1909–12, is a severe Gothic hall in rock-faced ashlar, erected over vaults expressed as an arcade to the W, used as a refectory. Six-bay nave with paired lancets between buttresses; chancel projection to the S with Dec window; sacristy to the SW. Interior stripped *c.* 2000.

Hidden in a corner of the convent complex are the former
BATH ESTATE OFFICES. An interesting collection of mid-C19
outbuildings to the N and E. One elaborate range faces the back
of the former Boarding School with an arcade of five carriage
arches at ground level. Arranged on two levels; mural stairs to
the W add to the collegiate atmosphere and rise through the
building to another, higher yard where the building has a long
single-storey S elevation. The latter can be identified as the
former master workshop, altered in 1866 to create a fireproof citadel.
A neat rendered porch with chamfered corners of ashlar
encloses the two central bays and evidently formed part of the
alterations, though the original date, 1859, and the Bath
coronet are displayed over the door. Steel-shuttered loops on
either side of the doorway and on the corners render the building secure and defensible, along with a wonderful oriel in the
E gable resting on fat corbels, its shutters having loops also –
reminders of less peaceful times during the turbulent steward-
ship of the agent William Steuart Trench. In a letter to the
Under Secretary, Sir Thomas Larcom, at Dublin Castle in
1866 Trench wrote that eight masons were 'hard at work at the
loopholes, porches, and small fortifications'; he explains his
alterations to create a fireproof citadel so that 'a few resolute
men well armed, could hold it for a long time, at least for 2 to
3 days', and adds, 'Of course my proceedings have attracted
much comment and observation in Farney, and it is magnified
according to the usual practice of that credulous people. I am
reported to have several cannon in the place, 1,000 stand of
arms, and to be building fortifications to stand a year's siege!'

PUBLIC BUILDINGS ETC.

COURTHOUSE. 1837, apparently by *Edward Forrest*, County Surveyor, and not William Caldbeck, to whom it has often been
attributed. A solid exercise in classical simplicity, placed to
great effect with its sober façade closing the vista at the N end
of the Main Street. It follows an astylar type most familiar in
the C19, used again with minor variations at Clones. A five-
bay, two-storey rectangular block flanked by short wings, dominated at the upper level by five tall sashes in austere surrounds
with plain entablatures, all resting on a continuous string-
course. The end bays are very gently advanced, with
segmental-headed windows on the ground floor. Between
them, small rectangular panels alluding to cells within, the
central one with attractive glazing. A hipped roof rises from
the bracketed eaves cornice. The entrances are accommodated
in the wings; the wide doorways decorated with carved consoles supporting a heavy cornice seem a little uncouth. The
quality of the stonework complements the simplicity of the
building: the squared pink limestone gives texture to the wall
surface, while crisp ashlar provides refinement to the architectural detail.

UNION WORKHOUSE (former). Shercock Road. 1842 and 1850. Distinguished by the russet colour of the stonework and the (restored) quarry-glazed mullion windows. *George Wilkinson*'s enlargement in 1850 of his standard plan results in a more picturesque composition: the typical five-bay administration block with its advanced end gables is displaced to one side in a fourteen-bay range to the front. This terminates to the E in the gabled three-storey kitchen block, with a solitary Tudor gable on the adjoining roof contributing to the picturesque effect. The range behind is symmetrical, with gabled terminal blocks and square stair-towers that break the roof-line.

The FEVER HOSPITAL, opposite, is a tall free-standing block of 1841 by *George Sudden*, who was then employed by the Shirley estate. Five bays by one, of two storeys, with gabled ends mirrored in the gabled central projection. Good-quality squared limestone walls with red brick trim. The windows are placed directly beneath the string-course on the ground floor and under the eaves above. The building appears to take its stylistic cue from the administration block opposite, notably in the arrangement of the tripartite doorcase with a four-centred arch and flanking windows below a hoodmould.

The NATIONAL SCHOOLS of 1889 face onto Bath Street, an austere block of two storeys and six bays with lower wings and a return. The colour and variation of the squared and snecked ashlar walls create a dizzying effect. The arrangement seems to have drawn its inspiration from the mid-C19 SHIRLEY SCHOOLS, opposite the convent to the W. This is a more appealing free-standing gable-ended block in an amiable Tudor style, possibly by *George Sudden*, hanging off the edge of the street with a two-storey E front falling to a gaunt three storeys on the W side. Gabled projections at either end give access from the street to the upper floors. Squared grey limestone with ashlar trim contrasting with brown limestone on the sides. Simple two-light mullioned windows beneath hoodmoulds, triangular-headed on the upper level, breaking through the eaves with Tudor gablets.

OTHER BUILDINGS

MAIN STREET has a number of solid C18 buildings, including some interesting three-storey houses on the W side. One of these, at the S end, though heavily altered, has a curious miniature pediment and a carved limestone cornice indicating that the buildings here possessed some quality. Further N, on the corner with Parnell Street, one red brick building stands out, the broad five-bay façade of the house built in 1773 by *Henry Byrne* and *John Green* with a pedimented doorcase and Gothic glazed fanlight. For the most part, however, the buildings are plainly rendered; occasionally an attractive fanlight or interesting doorcase survives, less so the original windows. Other more formal buildings are evenly distributed on both sides of the

street. The GARDA STATION is a formidable structure dominating the E side, erected in 1868 as constabulary barracks by
the Bath estate. A tall three-storey block of four bays, with a
small off-centre porch bridging the railed area that helps to light
the basement cells. The hard limestone ashlar front contributes
to its grim appearance; this is largely derived from the boldness
of the detail, whether through the hard edges and projection of
the eaves corbels or the severity of the rock-faced reveals. Substantial end stacks of red brick and limestone trim take the
building well above its neighbours and affirm its assertive stance.

71   Further N is the MARKET YARD built in 1861 as part of a
new Market Square, formed at the top of the Main Street to
replace the C18 Market House in the middle of the street.
Single-storey ranges form a U-shaped courtyard, open to the
street on the W side. Dark grey limestone walls, squared and
snecked, with a paler limestone ashlar employed as an expressive trim. Main block of seven bays, with carriage arch and
clock in a central gabled projection. Bracketed eaves, slate
roofs, and a cupola with leaded ogee cap. Lower parallel ranges
of ten bays sheltering under an overhanging roof supported on
steel ties and a colonnade of slender cast-iron columns. Across
the street, the TOLL HOUSE, now with the overbearing backdrop of a vacuous 1990s shopping centre. Solid diminutive
Tudor, provided in 1861 as a booth for the collection of market
tolls. Coursed, squared masonry walls in the local freestone
with ashlar trim. Gabled to E and W with kneelers and fleur-
de-lis finials; Shirley crest inset above a nicely dressed window
with hoodmould on the E front facing the Market Square.
Tudor doorway to the S. Also at the top of the Main Street,
the SHIRLEY ARMS HOTEL is an oddly proportioned but
attractive early C19 block facing the wide area before the
Courthouse and closing the approach from Monaghan. Two
storeys over a half-basement with a five-bay front centred on
a neat Tuscan porch supporting the Shirley arms in the blocking course. Built of slender ashlar blocks of limestone, with
simple shallow projections for the string-course, reveals and
cornice. A generous preponderance of wall to window on the
ground floor; first-floor windows tightly inserted between the
thin string-course and plain eaves cornice. Behind the blocking
course with its strange central and terminal blocks is a big
hipped roof with wide slates; disappointing squat chimneystacks on the outer walls. Enlarged behind in 2008 by
Aughey O'Flaherty Architects; a thumping great cubic block,
conceived without any feeling for the old building. Interior
greatly altered at the same time.

All the town banks are on the Main Street. On the W side,
the BANK OF IRELAND (former NATIONAL BANK) is the most
impressive, an Italianate palazzo completed in 1856 by *William
Caldbeck* and similar to his designs for Kells and Mullingar,
though of much higher quality. A tall free-standing block set
back from the street behind a railed area and flanked by curtain
walls with integral carriage arches. Three-storey, five-bay front

with projecting end bays handsomely articulated with segmental-headed recesses; all in smooth limestone ashlar, rusticated on the ground floor, and crowned by a plain cornice and blocking course. Doorcases with elaborate surrounds and carved consoles flank the three round-headed windows with attractive Georgian glazing lighting the banking hall. Tall sashes with six-over-six glazing define the *piano nobile*, contrasting with six-over-three panels for the windows above. More modest is the ALLIED IRISH BANK on the same side, early C20, with a subdued astylar front in pale limestone ashlar carved into crisp blocks with dense striations. Two storeys and five bays with subtle recession on the ground floor formed with plain pilasters; windows in plain frames, round-arched entrance to the banking hall on the N. Big sashes in the upper storey with plate glass and marginal glazing; the central bay is given a lugged surround in low relief with scrolled ends and a projecting keystone. Iron balconies to the end bays. (Equally prominent as a landmark is the otherwise modest façade of the funeral directors just S of the bank, an aspirant palazzo expertly painted in shades of grey to imitate faceted ashlar.) Opposite, the more sombre ULSTER BANK of 1873 by *Thomas Jackson* is set back slightly, with short perpendicular side walls that make it appear crammed into its site. Three storeys and four bays in squared dark grey limestone with dressed trim. The ground floor has an asymmetrically placed wide archway with a chunky moulded surround and projecting keystone, carved with the Hand of Ulster, that extends up the string-course, and three narrow round-headed windows resting on a moulded sill forming a unified group lighting the banking hall.

Facing up Bridewell Lane, the former BRIDEWELL is a plain block of 1831, appropriately severe in its expression, with roughcast walls and ashlar trim; narrow plan with six bays and two storeys over a raised basement; ground-floor windows altered. In SHIRLEY HOUSE LANE nearby, a terrace of good solid mid-C19 houses on the N side, is notable for massive ashlar chimneystacks. Opposite, McEneaney's, the traditional Irish shopfront in its unadulterated form, with slender pilasters supporting a big fascia and crowning cornice; double-sheeted door and big shop window still protected by a bicycle rest. Off this street to the S, along a small laneway and opposite the site of Shirley House, principally the residence of the Shirley agent (demolished in the C20), are the former STABLES. Two parallel two-storey ranges of late C18 appearance. The gables have recessed arches linked by a screen wall with good rusticated ashlar piers and timber gates, a very attractive composition. Further W is IVY HOUSE, a very smart little late C18 house tucked away in a small enclosed yard beside the River Proules. Two storeys and three bays, with central gabled projection. Roughcast walls, Georgian windows, and a flat-headed doorcase with a beautiful webbed fanlight.

BATH STREET, which winds to the E in front of St Finbarr's, has some good C19 and C20 housing, and isolated features of distinction – the Presbyterian church and Jackson Memorial Hall. Between Bath Street and O'Neill Street the WEYMOUTH COTTAGES, built in 1870 by the Bath estate, form a row of pretty houses with dormered attics facing onto walled garden allotments. Long symmetrical composition emphasized by the central gabled house with a canted porch. Of interest here is the curious patterning of the masonry, combining the squared pale local limestone with diagonal snecking in a purple sandstone, a variant of a pattern found on other Bath properties on O'Neill Street. Rock-faced ashlar surrounds to doors and windows, like those of the Garda Station, provide additional expression. Pretty carved bargeboards to the end gables; also inset here is the Bath coronet, signalling the buildings of the estate as the work of a common designer.

RAILWAY YARD (former). Between the roads to Donaghmoyne and Drumconrath. The rusticated masonry of the former WATER TOWER and ENGINE SHED, both converted to residential use, are the principal reminders that Carrickmacross was once served by a branch line of the Great Northern Railway.

40   DERRYOLAM GLEBE. Shercock Road. A handsome brick-fronted house built in 1776 by John Garnett, Bishop of Clogher to replace an older house. Presumably the initials 'JC' inscribed with the date on a stone below the eaves in the middle of the front are his. Two-storey, five-bay gable-ended block, sitting high over a half-basement with central gabled stair return at the rear. A pattern-book limestone doorcase, Roman Doric with an open pediment and spoked timber fanlight, gracefully reached over the basement area by a railed flight of stone steps. Sash windows all of equal size. The bricks are laid in Flemish bond with wide mortar joints; above the first-floor windows a noticeable seam in the brickwork indicates that the upper fifteen courses were added later to accommodate an attic storey, lit from the gables; this helps to explain the uneasy proportions of the façade. Typical tripartite plan, two rooms deep with a central staircase projected to the rear to form a shallow T-plan. NW of the house lies a pretty symmetrical two-storey range housing COACH HOUSES AND OFFICES, built, according to an inscription on the façade, by the Rev. Robinson (Dr Thomas Romney Robinson) in 1857. Together these buildings are rare survivors close to the town that continue to enjoy a partially rural aspect.

LISANISKE. Dundalk Road. A place associated with the centre of local MacMahon power in the C17, now the site of a much altered and extended mid-C18 house overlooking a small lake of the same name. A long two-storey block of eight bays with an off-centre canted bay added after 1836. The C18 house, barely discernible in the E portion of the present building, was a typical three-bay, gable-ended block. It was one room deep, with a symmetrical tripartite plan and central dog-leg stairs with balusters grouped in threes that survive in the present – original – entrance hall. The doors leading to the adjoining

rooms have six raised and fielded panels and lugged architraves, which together with the stairs confirm the mid-c18 date.
In 1835 the residence of Adam Gibson. After 1902 the building
was extensively altered when for a time it became a residence
and school of the Patrician Brothers.

NEIGHBOURHOOD

ALCOHOL FACTORY (former). 2 km SE. A bold abstract architectural form, like an assemblage of toy blocks, that announced
the International Style to Co. Monaghan. Built in 1935–8 as
part of an economic enterprise by the new Irish State, which
in 1934 employed *J. D. Postma* to design six alcohol factories
in the N half of the country. The vertical and horizontal contrasts strongly expressed in the cubic massing and strip
windows show influence from the De Stijl movement of Postma's native Holland. A unique steel-frame construction, clad
with riveted steel panels, now concealed behind modern
panels, demonstrating how the cold, hard lines and functional-
ity of Modern Movement architecture is generally best suited
to light industrial buildings.

MONALTY HOUSE. 3 km SE. A striking monolithic block built
c. 1770 for the Bath estate. Three storeys over a half-basement,
gable-ended, with roughcast rendered walls. Attractive central
limestone doorcase with engaged Tuscan columns supporting
a stylized Doric frieze with triglyphs and rosettes, repeated in
the architrave around the delicate webbed fanlight. The original door has an extraordinary number of raised and fielded
panels – twenty in all – and is flanked by small leaded side-
lights. The principal façade is studiously proportioned, evident
in the rhythm of its five bays and the glazing pattern; the
ground-floor windows were given plate glass in the C19, resulting in an unusual nine-over-four arrangement. Internally, a
standard symmetrical plan with well-lit interiors, very restrained
in decoration, arranged around the central stairs to the rear
which were originally emphasized in a shallow outshot. The
staircase, with a generous landing, forms a very elegant composition, with simple balusters and a mahogany handrail terminating in a beautifully formed tight elliptical spiral. In 1835
the residence of Thomas McIlvoy Gartlan. The house was
extended in 1910 by *William Samuel Barber*. He added a three-
storey bathroom return, reached from the half-landings which
he extended, and also a small single-storey wing to the NW.

The rear of the house faces attractive late C18 STABLE
RANGES of rubble with ashlar trim; two-storey T-plan, presenting two adjoining varied façades to the W with interesting
round-headed windows and curious pill-shaped vent loops.
The ground falls steeply to the E to reveal a vaulted understorey. An overscaled road now passes within metres of the
front door, leaving the former GATE LODGE, a simple hipped-
roof structure, stranded on a roundabout.

BALLYMACKNEY HOUSE (KILLANNY). 4 km SE. An engaging and compact Regency villa with all the character of a glebe house, but built for a social equal: it was erected *c.* 1830 to accommodate the land agent to the Bath estate. A free-standing two-storey block on a basement exposed only at the sides, with a high hipped roof on wide bracketed eaves, and central chimneystacks. Main (E) front, three bays by two with Wyatt windows, smaller on the upper storey. Striking segmental doorway with a rusticated stucco band framing a sinuous moulded ashlar surround; inset, a very refined timber doorcase with busy geometric-patterned fanlight and side-lights. The refinement continues into the spacious entrance hall, big and airy with a delicate ceiling centrepiece of leaves and spreading curlicues in low relief. Three doorways in the back wall are framed by high timber arches screening a very elegant staircase retained within the plan and lit by a tall Georgian sash window with Gothick glazing on the rear elevation. Large reception rooms on either side of the hall, with smaller rooms behind, and a secondary stair adjoining the main stair to the N.

PARISH CHURCH, KILLANNY (C of I, former). 4.5 km SE. Ruinous. A little mid-C19 parish church by *Joseph Welland* beside the River Longfield. Three-bay hall with paired lancets, diagonally opposed porch and vestry, and bellcote over the W end. Squared masonry with punch-dressed trim.

ST PATRICK, CARRICKASHEDOGE (THE ROCK CHAPEL). 5 km S. 1855. The perfect country chapel, a small roughcast T-plan built on a rocky outcrop. Gabled W front with paired entrances beneath Gothic arches, topped by an ashlar bellcote with a bell by *Sheridan* of Dublin. Short chancel. The windows, all with blocked ashlar surrounds, are the real architectural interest here: those in the transept gables have a pretty lace-like quality; good Dec W window, in timber; one of the most pleasing aspects must be the use of crown-glass bullions to glaze the apexes of the remaining quarry-glazed lancets. After this the squat E window is somewhat disappointing, as the cusped circles appear to crush the heads of the five lancets; its disparity is explained as a later insertion. Internally the building remains largely undisturbed, apart from the usual sanctuary remodelling. Pitch-pine roof with exposed trusses on corbels that are possibly a later insertion. Wide timber galleries on three sides with scumbling to resemble light oak.

SS PETER AND PAUL, DROOMGOOSAT. 5 km SW. A simple five-bay hall of 1823. Smooth-rendered walls with small C20 gabled porches to the end bay, set beneath the windows which have been shortened to accommodate them. Delicate Y-traceried windows (evident in old photographs and partially surviving on the N elevation) now lost to much plainer replacements. The internal arrangement reflects the enduring popularity of C18 arrangements for hall churches, where the altar is placed transversely along the N wall, flanked by tall pointed windows. Galleries added at the ends in 1844. Late C19 panelled timber roof with exposed kingpost trusses. – STAINED GLASS. St

Michael by *Mayer & Co.* – CHURCHYARD. Decorative cast-iron bell-frame by *M. Byrne*, Dublin.

ST MOLUA, MAGHERACLOONE PARISH CHURCH (C of I). 6 km SW. A charming rural graveyard with many fine C18 monuments shelters this neat hall and tower erected in 1824. This was the site of a much older church; found 'in good repair' in 1622, its traces can no longer be discerned. Two-bay nave with elegant sashes and Y-tracery. Roughcast walls and limestone trim, used to good effect in the three-stage tower for quoins, string-courses, hoodmoulds and spiky octagonal pinnacles. Enlarged in 1891 by *J. H. Fullerton*, who added the chancel and vestry of squared rock-faced ashlar. – Carved REREDOS by the rector, the *Rev. C. M. Stack, c.* 1918.

MAGHERACLOONE GLEBE HOUSE. 6 km SW. 1824. Quietly hidden in a miniature demesne opposite the church is the very elegant gable-ended house erected for the Rev. Patrick Mathias Cumming to coincide with his rebuilding of the church. Three bays and two storeys over a half-basement. Roughcast with big windows, most attractively arranged with paired sashes, and a simple trabeated doorcase with a wide spoked fanlight and geometric-patterned side-lights. Good wholesome architecture that takes its place comfortably between formal and vernacular building traditions.

CASTLE LESLIE *see* GLASLOUGH

CASTLE SAUNDERSON   CN   *4010*

Today Castle Saunderson is a dark forbidding shell on grass-grown terraces at the centre of a picturesque water-girded demesne. Even in ruin, this large Elizabethan evocation in limestone is impressive; the pitch-black vacancy of the fenestration captivates, while the combination of crisp ashlar, refined detail, smooth render and a competing array of textured rock-faced towers conveys a Hogwartian air of mystery and menace. Robert Sanderson, the son of a Scottish planter settled in Tyrone in 1613, began the first castle here after he was awarded lands in Cavan in 1654. The tumults of the late C17 saw it destroyed by James II's forces in 1689, despite Sanderson's apparent Jacobite sympathies. There is no evidence that it was immediately rebuilt, and it is unlikely to have been substantially revived in any way before the end of the C18. The new house is usually credited to Francis Saunderson, around the time of his marriage in 1779. By then family ambition had been expressed in unsuccessful efforts to claim the extinct Castleton peerage of the Saundersons of Saxby, for which the spelling of the family name was changed. This Late Georgian house continues to make itself felt in the symmetry of the long two-storey entrance front facing E and in the proportions of its windows, dressed up with Tudor hoods and chamfered reveals but retaining their original sashes before the building fell

94

into ruin. The tripartite plan was retained, the generous reception rooms on either side of the central hall being suited to the baronial demands of the new architecture, which otherwise completely subsumed the old house. This dramatic remodelling was undertaken by *George Sudden* and was well under way in December 1835, when Nathaniel Clements wrote to Lady Leitrim that he 'stopped an hour or two' to breakfast with Alexander Saunderson of Castle Saunderson, who was 'altering and castellating' the house. The transformation of a restrained Georgian house into a new and ambitious architectural form was just then about the most fashionable and novel building exercise. The result owes a good deal to Edward Blore's contemporary works at Crom in Co. Fermanagh, not far away, which in fact Sudden was to rebuild after a fire in 1841. The relationship between the two buildings is further strengthened by the fact that the families had been connected since 1825, when Alexander Saunderson's brother married the sister of Blore's patron, Colonel John Crichton, later 3rd Earl of Erne.

The closest resemblance between the buildings is in the massive three-storey entrance tower, Burghley-inspired though in a purer castellated form, which sits gauntly in the centre of the old E front; its rock-faced octagonal turrets and big mullioned-and-transomed windows contrast with the flanking rendered walls and vertical Georgian windows. Battlements above the old sandstone eaves cornice and narrow square rock-faced towers on the corners with false machicolations complete an effective transformation here, as at Crom giving the house just one symmetrical façade. The sides were unhindered by the old house. That to the S has projections at the ends, varied in height and texture but sharing Tudor gables and sufficiently advanced to allow a four-bay battlemented loggia – shorter but finer than that at Tynan – to extend between them at ground level. A two-storey service wing extends at right angles and continues as a long single-storey orangery, a little reminiscent of Nash's Camelia House at Shane's Castle in Antrim, with buttressed walls and wide Tudor arches before a square terminal tower. The N front is more vigorously textured, a tight huddle of projecting bays with an octagonal entrance tower placed off-centre. From here lower ranges disappear to the W, enclosing one side of the STABLE-YARD, attractive roughcast ranges forming a large enclosure behind the castle. Abandoned and stripped out in 1920, the house lay derelict until the interiors were completely rebuilt in the 1980s; alas damaged by fire a decade later, it has returned to its former state.

Even unkempt, the DEMESNE LANDSCAPE has a deeply enchanting quality, gently falling away from the castle to the lakes formed by the meandering embrace of the River Finn. Great oaks frame the extensive vistas in the park and attest to a long history.

CASTLE SAUNDERSON CHURCH (C of I). Along the avenue in a sombre grove of yew trees, a small melancholic Perp hall with an eye-catching spire. In existence in 1837, and possibly the rebuilding or remodelling of an older structure, the design almost certainly by *George Sudden*. A three-bay hall with pinnacled gables, built of rock-faced masonry like much of the Castle. Tall Tudor-headed lancets between buttresses, with angle buttresses on the gables. The tower rises from a square with angle buttresses, then turns octagonal for the belfry with an elaborate corbel table, and ends with a stocky ashlar spire. At the w end, the entrance to the crypt projects to support a form of box tomb; the approach is flanked by large, well-worn C17 grave slabs, one of them carved with a heraldic panel. The interior is a cubic hall with a flat ribbed ceiling; over the w door, a flamboyant sandstone carving of the Saunderson arms, probably C17; the remainder of the walls lined with rather plain C19 and C20 tablets.

CASTLEBLAYNEY MN <i>8010</i>

A small market town set on a ridge amongst the hills surrounding the spreading waters of Lough Muckno. Castleblayney remains a frontier town, its foundation set out in 1612 in a patent to Sir Edward Blayney, a prominent soldier in the Nine Years War. As Seneschal of Monaghan Blayney was granted substantial lands here to secure the supply communication between Newry and Monaghan by establishing a midway halt for royal troops. He was also committed to raising a large castle 'at his own charge', and *p. 17* a tall gabled structure with Scottish corner turrets within an elaborate bawn was built at Onomy beside the town. Like most of the castles of this generation it was short-lived. Blayney, created Baron Blayney in 1621, died in 1629, and his son Henry failed to hold the castle against a devastating attack by Hugh Patrick Mac Dubh MacMahon at the outbreak of the rebellion in 1641. Henry was killed at the Battle of Benburb in 1646 and afterwards the estate was sold to a London merchant, Thomas Vincent. Later, in what seems like a deft manoeuvre, Lord Blayney's grandson married Vincent's daughter and thus restored the estate to the Blayney family.

The rights to hold a weekly market and yearly fair, granted in 1613, no doubt ensured the initial development of a town here, but it faltered with the turmoil of the mid-century. Recovery was slow, so slow that only five hearths were taxed in 1663. No significant improvement was witnessed in the following century, and two decades before its close there was little to impress the Rev. Daniel Beaufort in this 'ugly straggling small town'. By the end of the century, however, all had changed, and a new era commenced under another famous Blayney soldier, Major-General Andrew-Thomas, 11th Lord Blayney, later a hero of the Napoleonic wars, to whom the shape of the modern town is due. Promotion of the linen trade, laying out the market place and erecting a market house ensured economic growth. He created an extensive demesne around the shore of Lough Muckno and in 1799 built a compact Neoclassical mansion near the battered remains of the former Plantation castle. In 1796 Lord Blayney had married Lady Mabella Alexander, daughter of the 1st Earl of Caledon, and when between 1810 and 1814 he was a prisoner of war in France he relied on his wife's father and brother to manage his Monaghan estates. To his brother-in-law he wrote in 1813:

> The freedom of my sentiments on religion are fully recorded in the separate buildings for divine worship ably executed near the town of Castleblayney, where I have contributed both in money and furnishing ground, to the Roman Catholic, the Presbyterian, and the Established Church, so as for each to have a place suited to impress them with good moral principles in their separate avocations . . . My affectionate regard for the county of Monaghan and for Ireland in general is noticed . . . by forming a suitable establishment, planting and improving the face of the county, and introducing a better mode of agriculture in hopes the example would be followed.

In 1853 the estate was sold to Henry Thomas Hope, who remodelled the house, and it became Hope Castle.

Most C19 visitors made much of the quality of the housing and the absence of any thatched buildings within the town. This was largely due to favourable leases – low-rate and long-term – allowing the inhabitants to build solid and enduring stone houses that remain as legacies in the town's character today. The plan combines elements of a traditional market town with a regularly planned estate town. The large Market House and the triangular Market Place form the focus for the principal street, a wide thoroughfare, predominantly commercial, lined with three-storey buildings. On the E side of the Market Place the buildings are more genteel, mostly two-storey houses that defer to the formal entrance to Hope Castle. In contrast to many other large towns, the churches lie on the periphery and fail to dominate the skyline. The Catholic church lacks a spire, and its Protestant counterpart has been largely appropriated for the castle demesne as a picturesque incident in the lakeland scenery.

ST MAELDOID, MUCKNO PARISH CHURCH (C of I). 1858–60 by *Joseph Welland*. Set against the landscape of Lough Muckno, this is a sombre but compact and Ecclesiologically sound church dominated by an offset tower on the NW corner with a stocky broach spire, a late work by an experienced church architect, probably designed in conjunction with his son, *William*. The contractor was *T. H. Carroll*. This was the third church here. The first was built in 1622. It was replaced in 1810 by a new building, to which a tower and spire were added in 1818, and that church was completely rebuilt in 1858. Grey rubble with a trim of Scottish sandstone. The plan is cruciform, though irregular, with the N transept projecting further to accommodate, between it and the tower, a two-bay aisle with a gabled porch projecting at the W end. All the architectural emphasis is thus on the N elevation, which faces the approach. The tower is bold and expressive, in two stages with emphatic angle buttresses, adjoining the more demure W gable which is pierced by generously separated lancets under a multifoiled opening. At the E end a polygonal apse with offset buttresses between the bays lies partially obscured by the small vestry projecting from the N transept. In nave and aisle paired lancets set below foils and quarry-glazed; in the transepts, more elaborate tracery in Dec style that echoes the E window of the adjacent Catholic church, as if to confirm the neighbourly coexistence of the buildings.

The interior is simple and spacious, with a modest three-bay N arcade and tall sandstone arches revealing the transepts on either side of a simpler chancel arch. The roof is of particular interest for its alternating series of simple scissor trusses and more elaborate kingposts with arched supports. At the W end the richly decorated timber organ loft supports a very fine mid-C19 ORGAN by *Conacher* of Huddersfield. The area below the loft was very sensitively closed in the late C20 to provide administrative accommodation. – STAINED GLASS. Transepts: *c.* 1880, attributed to *O'Connor & Taylor*; nave S wall: by *Joshua Clarke & Sons*, Dublin, 1923. – MONUMENTS. Nave S wall: Charlotte Angerstein †1863, daughter of Lord Blayney, by *T. Gaffin* of Regent Street, London. – Mathew (*sic*) Singleton †1865, by *Coates*. – Andrew Foulis McMath †1875, by *Coates*. – BELL of 1673, presumably from the old church, by *Henry Cilbury*.

Inside the entrance gates, N of the present church, the foundations of the OLD PARISH CHURCH remain. It was a simple rectangle with a porch at the W end of the S wall. The footings of massive angle buttresses remain on the E side. It now encloses a simple masonry MAUSOLEUM for the Blayney family.

ST MARY, MUCKNO PARISH CHURCH. Though colourful and prominently sited, this church stands out as something of an anomaly. As if in deference to its Church of Ireland counterpart behind, the opportunity for post-Emancipation triumphalism so commonly seized elsewhere was eschewed and the early C19 building was simply allowed to grow organically with the needs of the congregation. Though now reasonably large, its size is tempered by the consistent symmetry and simple orderly expression of the architectural detail. This is a cheerful uncomplicated building, completely rural in feeling: smooth-rendered walls with Gothic stone trim, now all painted in a lively coordinated scheme. The present building developed out of a church built in 1805 by the Rev. Edmund Maguire. In 1803 Major-General Lord Blayney had granted the site on a long lease apparently with the proviso that a church, with a slated roof of foreign timber, be built within five years. The building was not completed until 1814; in its original form it seems to have followed the C18 tradition of the transverse plan with the altar on the long wall. Extensive rebuilding by *James Hughes* in 1851–6 produced the present cruciform plan, the old church becoming the transepts. Hughes's work was substantial enough for the church to be rededicated in 1861. Even in the hands of an ambitious architect such as *John Murray*, who made some improvements quite soon afterwards, in 1869, the building remained quiet. Essentially Murray must have provided the Gothic trim – angle buttresses in smooth ashlar blocks with crocketed pinnacles, moulded gable copings, and subtle string-courses and hoodmoulds – which as executed is pious provincial stuff. In 1929 *J. F. McGahon* extended the nave by three bays and carried out other alterations and repairs. He remained faithful to Murray's work, moving the w gable and flanking it with identical side porches, expressed as miniature transepts. The gables repeat the angle buttresses but here project emphatically, if absurdly, below the offsets.

The interior is high and airy, with a long five-bay nave and a big raking gallery lit by a triple lancet window at the w end. Timber-panelled ceiling borne on thin scissor trusses; in the w half, the newer timbers of McGahon's extension can be clearly distinguished. Deep chancel with decoratively painted walls and E window of three-light ogee lancets; simple vaulted ceiling of moulded plaster panels decorated with quatrefoils. The chancel arch is flanked by side altars sheltered under shallow recesses, treated in effect as blind windows with rich Dec marble tracery. The same quality is emphasized in the unusually sophisticated (and, more remarkably, surviving) sanctuary rails.

The CANON'S HOUSE is an attractive one-and-half-storey cottage of three bays with the central bay advanced and gabled. Perhaps by *J. J. McDonnell*, who enlarged the Parochial House in 1911.

FIRST PRESBYTERIAN CHURCH. Keady Road. A simple three-bay hall. A plaque over the door records the date 1787 and the Rev. John Davys as the builder. The gabled front has been embellished and is now more expressively ecclesiastical than is usual, possibly part of the additions of 1930 carried out by *J. F. McGahon*. The combination of roughcast and smooth render gives texture and variety to a well-balanced composition, with a central doorway flanked by tall lancets and surmounted by a three-light window with good carved tracery and quarry glazing, united under a continuous hoodmould. Three-bay E elevation with half-hipped roof.

MANSE. Keady Road. 1871 by *John Murray*. Lord Templeton and Mrs Hope paid for the building, which was to be in the Gothic style. The contractor was *W. Belshaw* of Armagh. Murray showed ample dexterity in responding to the demands of a different faith, and the result is suitably understated. A neat Z-plan arrangement with a familiar asymmetrical two-storey front of five bays. The two end bays to one side are advanced and gabled with plainly ornamented bargeboards. A single-storey porch with a pointed doorway is tucked into the angle. The building is roughcast; the window openings have depressed pointed arches, now fitted with unpleasant frames. A single-storey canted bay projects on the four-bay side elevation. Adjoining to the s is the PARISH HALL of 1891, built as a lecture hall by *John Harvey*; the contractor was *T. White* of Castleblayney. A decent, if somewhat cheerless, cement-rendered hall of five bays with a projecting porch, lifted a little by raised quoins and ornate bargeboards.

CONVENT OF MERCY, LAUREL HILL. New Street. 1910. Impressive institutional Gothic by *J. J. McDonnell*. The contractors were *Patrick Ritchie & Co.* of Belfast. A U-plan complex dominated by a big, near-symmetrical N front of roughcast, dressed with smooth and moulded render details, all uniformly applied so that different stages in the building are not evident in its present appearance. A long central two-storey range, irregularly fenestrated, is placed between projecting gabled end bays. The entrance, an elegant pointed opening with an ornately traceried fanlight, occupies an advanced and gabled central section; above the doorway is an elaborate, tightly squeezed composition with a canopied niche filled with a statue of St Patrick, flanked by lancets resting on blind traceried panels. The central bay projects on the rear (S) elevation as well, where a buttressed limestone bellcote rests on the gable above a big Perp window that lights the stairs. The gabled E block forms part of the original composition, and projects as two bays on the principal front. It has recessed trefoils and quatrefoils under hoodmoulds arranged over the first-floor windows. The design is varied to three bays on the corresponding W block, built later to house the CHAPEL. This is a very simple affair inside, originally a small hall of just three bays, extended to the W in 1949 by a further four bays under a parabolic vault, with a polygonal apse lined with marble. – STAINED GLASS. Lancet windows in the apse feature Irish saints and include the image of Christ by *Harry Clarke*.

An enlarged SCHOOL COMPLEX to the rear includes a nice vernacular corrugated-iron-clad hall and the Convent National Schools of 1912, also by *McDonnell*. Understated institutional Gothic expressed on a long single-storey range with big mullioned windows set high in the walls between buttresses with offsets. A gable with kneelers on the N end is balanced by a mid-C20 flat-roofed extension, projecting not unsatisfactorily from the SE corner. Two handsomely detailed copper ridge vents break the long roof-line.

COURTHOUSE. An assured building prominently sited on the Market Square. Big, with cubic proportions, in the kind of stuccoed classicism regularly employed by *William Farrell*, though difficult to read to any advantage because of its sloping triangular site. A market house had been erected on this spot in the late C18 to encourage the linen trade; a mid-C19 sketch by George Victor Du Noyer shows a building typical of its kind, not unlike the later market house in Ballybay: a two-storey block with four bays, arcaded on the ground floor, the central bays advanced and pedimented with a crowning bell-turret. In 1856 the decision was made to combine a new courthouse and market house in one structure. There is no reason to believe that the present building incorporates any fabric of its predecessor. The principal (w) front faces down West Street, presenting a skewed view of a compact three-bay, two-storey block dominated by a polygonal cupola with a copper ogee dome. The articulation is eloquent: the central bay advances slightly with a continuous platband, decorated with guilloche, between the storeys, and the ground-floor windows are set in relieving arches on either side of the central round-headed door. The raised stucco quoins are more emphatic, extending to a bold eaves cornice and blocking course. Over the central bay, the cornice arches to receive a clock face. The arrangement of the ground floor as a blind arcade is continued on the two-bay end blocks of the long eight-bay s elevation; the four central bays, deeply recessed, open up to form a single-storey loggia – all presented with a modest formality as civic-minded architecture. Less elegant is the N elevation, where the ground falls away sharply to reveal a severe, towering edifice on a hard rock-faced and arcuated basement storey, almost Piranesian in effect. The three central bays project deeply; chamfered corners here, with niches in the ground-level rustication, fail to soften the harsh appearance.

WORKHOUSE (former). Shercock Road. 1842 by *George Wilkinson*. The surviving front range of one of Wilkinson's standard plans, arranged, as at Carrickmacross, with the front administration building disposed off-centre. Walls of squared bluestone with sandstone trim. Extensively remodelled, with nasty c20 tiled roof.

OTHER BUILDINGS. WEST STREET forms the main E–W artery leading directly into the Market Square. Here three-storey buildings predominate. On the N side, the ALLIED IRISH BANK (former PROVINCIAL BANK) is a simple three-bay town house of three storeys with a stuccoed front, presumably applied in 1880 when *Samuel P. Close* added a new cash office in a single-storey annexe. Here three arched windows under a simple entablature carry a balustraded parapet. On the same side, the POST OFFICE of 1908 by *J. F. McGahon* has a more austere, four-bay façade with string-courses forming prominent bands between the storeys. On the s side of West Street, the much more formal red brick and sandstone façade of *Sandham Symes*'s BANK OF IRELAND of 1874. A routine Italianate composition with a bracketed doorcase and wide segmental-headed window in the ashlar-fronted ground floor, which is framed by plain pilasters that rise to a pair of stylized brackets supporting square blocks and in effect form a giant shopfront in stone. The upper floors are of a fine machined red brick with sandstone trim. Adjoining to the E is a narrow three-bay house, PINE & POTTERY, with each floor independently expressed in varied Victorian stucco enrichments under a crowning pediment. Leading into the MARKET SQUARE, a

more restrained tone is set by simpler rendered two-storey
fronts as the sides of the square converge on the entrance to
Hope Castle to the E. Though many have been greatly altered,
the formal tone is retained in the symmetrical fronts, elaborate
timber porches, and sloping canopies with scrolled iron brackets over some of the doorways.

The most ornate and unified composition of the estate town
lies on the S side of CHURCH STREET, where a row of seven
very picturesque late CI9 ESTATE HOUSES sit between two
pairs of former gatehouses. Nicely varied one-and-a-half-
storey dwellings in squared blackstone with red brick trim; they
have ornate dormers and sloping canopies over the doorways,
either set under the eaves and shared between two houses or
continued from the roof slope as catslides. Unlike their identical plainly roughcast and gable-fronted counterparts of the
early CI9 to the N, the GATEHOUSES adjoining the houses at
the S end are more formal Victorian stone buildings, with big
rusticated gatepiers closely set between them. Here the N
house, dated 1877, is more elaborate, built in squared limestone with a trim of sandstone ashlar. The street front has an
unusual central gabled projection of two bays that narrows to
form a pier between the ground-floor windows. The entrance
is on the side elevation, inside the gateway, under a deep
arched recess. Above this is a plaque carved with the mono-
grammed initials of Anne Adele Hope (†1884), who was presumably also responsible for the corresponding block to the S,
the SEXTON'S HOUSE, altogether a less picturesque three-bay
building with big expressive segmental-headed windows.

There are few buildings worthy of attention on YORK
STREET, which forms the S approach to the town. Dominating
the W side are the BLAYNEY ALMSHOUSES – a handsome
parting gift of the 12th and last Lord Blayney, who died in
1874. A striking formal terrace in red brick with terracotta
ornament, built in 1879 for 'single elderly persons of good
character from Castleblayney'; the expressive brickwork forms
pilasters and string-courses that boldly define the bays and
divide the two storeys, achieving a kind of latent classicism.
Big bell-cast tiled roof with massive stacks on the front slope.
Originally built to provide twenty units, back-to-back, it was
refurbished and converted to ten residences by *Teague & Sally*
in 2004. The gabled CARETAKER'S LODGE forms a pleasing
introduction to the buildings on the edge of the walled formal
gardens. Further N along the street under a big wrought-iron
arch boldly proclaiming the name, an avenue rises uphill to
CONABURY HOUSE, a plain three-bay, two-storey block with
a high hipped roof over bracketed eaves and tall red brick
stacks. Lower wings extend on either side. Although a house
can be confirmed here in 1840, the present building largely
owes its appearance to *J. F. McGahon*, who carried out alterations in 1917 for John F. Smyth. A RAILWAY STATION was
established off New Street in 1849 for the North Western
Railway. The site has been largely developed for housing, but

the late C19 STATION HOUSE survives as a plain cubic block, irregularly fenestrated, with wide eaves on paired brackets.

CASTLE BLAYNEY

Later HOPE CASTLE. The visitor in search of Sir Edward Blayney's castle, built after 1612, will be disappointed. An official report witnessed it under construction, within a large bawn with 18-ft (5.5-m) high walls of lime and stone 'well flanked w'th bulworkes'. Though at that stage the walls of the castle were just 6 ft (1.8 m) high, it was deemed 'a fayre and spacious house of stone work . . . the walls of a great thickness w'th vaults'. The bawn had alternately a circular and a square flanker opposed on each of the corners, those flanking the gatehouse three storeys tall and large enough to accommodate 'two or three rooms or lodgings a piece with chimneys'. Blayney's castle was taken in 1641 by the rebellious MacMahons, leaving a ruin whose appearance is known from late C18 views by Grose, Fisher and Beranger. Three storeys over a basement, with two principal gables, wide mullioned windows on each level and high corner bartizans, it appears a typical Plantation castle. In fact a C16 plan shows it to have adopted an H-plan, more common to English mansions. The sophisticated layout of the rooms outlined in the plan coincides in several ways with Gervase Markham's idea of a 'plain man's country house' published in *The English Husbandman* (1613). Markham, like Blayney, had been a captain under the Earl of Essex's command in Ireland.

p. 17

The precise whereabouts of the castle and its complex are not known, though in the early C19 it is described as close to the Georgian house. Identifying the site is confused by another substantial fortified structure to the E in Concra Wood, shown on maps as a sort of eight-pointed star rather like Augher Castle in Tyrone, warranting Sir Charles Coote's description of it in 1801 as 'curious and whimsical'; it seems more likely that it was conceived as an ornamental garden building. Nothing of either of these ruins may now be seen above ground.

When the Rev. Daniel Beaufort visited in 1787 he thought that though the demesne was beautiful it was demeaned by a 'wretched habitation'. How this related to the old castle is unknown, but evidently its condition justified replacement. In 1784 the estate had been inherited by the 11th Lord Blayney, then an adolescent. In 1799 he commissioned the design for a new house from *Robert Woodgate*. Woodgate, articled to Sir John Soane in 1788, had come to Ireland in 1791 to supervise works for Soane at Baronscourt in Tyrone, where he earned the praise of the agent as 'a lad of much address, seldom embarrassed, and full of resources'. Three years later he decided to pursue an independent career. Blayney may have looked to *Thomas Cooley*'s house for his father-in-law at Caledon, also in Tyrone, as a source of influence for the new house. So proud was Woodgate of his design for Castle Blayney that he wrote to

Soane in 1799 enclosing a small-scale set of drawings of 'the first House I ever Built' as a student's modest tribute to his master, carrying with it a desire that future fortune might allow a more fitting token of his 'attachment and fidelity'. By 1805 Woodgate was dead and his future potential was lost. Soane, who kept Woodgate's letter in his London house, will have seen enough in Blayney Castle to appreciate it as a progeny of his own designs for Tendring Hall in Suffolk.

The visitor in search of Woodgate's building will also be disappointed. The house was remodelled and almost doubled in size in the mid C19, and now sits gauchely on a tarmac platform, overdressed like a wedding cake, internally incomplete, and rather soulless. Woodgate's interiors survived until its conversion into a hotel in the 1980s; were they still in existence, some of the inventive genius of Soane could have been savoured in the design of his respected pupil. Sadly there is little to be proud of here now, even less as a result of a malicious fire in 2010.

The four outside walls of Woodgate's building survive, as do the sketches which he sent to Soane, so that with a little peeling off of C19 embellishments the original cubic block can be revived in the mind's eye. The entrance front was originally on the E side; it was of five bays, the end bays projecting with tripartite windows under recessed arches on the ground floor, rather like those at Soane's Shotesham. The entrance occupied a similar arch in the centre, with a big fanlight flanked by big sashes; otherwise the plainness was relieved by two small Neoclassical panels decorated with swags in the spaces above the windows. Less conventional were the shallow pediments over the cornice on the salient elements, pierced by impossibly small lunettes much like raised eyebrows against the parapet. This oddity is explained by an unusually shallow roof pitch, slated so as to allow the lower course to project slightly over

Castle Blayney.
Elevation by K. Mulligan, 2012

the blocking course, meaning that the pediments would throw off rainwater along the cornice which served as the gutter; Woodgate explained that 'by introducing the pediments the gutters are all of one length of lead [so] that no solder or laps are necessary'. Roof-lights were provided on the inner slopes. On the five-bay s front the three central bays project under a wider pediment, just enough to allow the downpipes to be discreetly placed in the re-entrant angles – with the virtue, expressed by Woodgate, that 'they rather add beauty to the building than deface it looking [instead] like a bead'. A shallow bow punctuates the N elevation, a feature then almost universal in Irish country house planning. The kitchen was in a separate wing to the w, set back behind the line of the N front, and originally formed part of a U-plan court.

The axis in Woodgate's plan was E–W, focused on the square entrance hall. There was a conscious, though imperfect, symmetry on the longer N–S axis, particularly on the first floor. The staircase was placed in the centre, to allow the surrounding rooms to address three dramatic prospects. A third of the ground floor was given over to the drawing room, which extended across the entire length of the s elevation, inspired perhaps by Soane's gallery at Baronscourt. On the N side, the bowed dining room was flanked by small drawing rooms. The architectural spaces, and especially the use of shallow oval domes on pendentives, gave the interiors an excitement that was so characteristic of Soane, and they also reflected his taste for clearly defining the surfaces by geometric borders – Vitruvian scrolls, narrow guilloches and Greek-key patterns – heavily modelled to create shadowy reaches in the details. Not a trace of any of these features remains. Besides the unusual scale of the drawing room, the principal excitement was offered by the top-lit stair hall. A complex and restricted geometric space, this was the most Soanean aspect of the plan: designed around an apsidal staircase, with a dome carried on pendentives and deep barrel-vaulted side bays, it is a variation of the theme of the drawing room at Wimpole Hall in Cambridgeshire on which Woodgate may have worked with Soane. In Woodgate's plan the stairs appear impossibly small, which may explain their enlargement as a dog-leg later in the C19. The small room in the NW corner, described by Lord Blayney as 'the Glory Hole', was presumably similar to the ladies' drawing room on the NE side. Like the stair hall, this was a well-developed architectural space with a shallow oval dome on pendentives and recessed niches in the walls repeating the external motif framing the tripartite windows on the E front.

In the early C19, probably coinciding with the succession of the 12th Lord in 1834, a single-storey bowed projection was added on the E front, perhaps with some internal reorganization of the plan. The roof was also replaced, and the attic storey raised, with windows in the parapet.

In 1853 the 12th Lord Blayney sold the estate to Henry Thomas Hope, the immensely wealthy son of Thomas Hope of

The Deepdene in Surrey (and owner of the Hope Diamond). Forsaking the sophisticated Neoclassicism of his father, he renamed the house Hope Castle having enlarged and remodelled it in a frivolous kind of Italianate classicism. This is most apparent in the cresting along the roof-line – fanciful scrollwork above the parapets with urns and ball finials that is neither Elizabethan nor Jacobean. All the details were tricked out in stucco, including vermiculated quoins and moulded window architraves with straight entablatures and bracketed sills. The segmental pediment on the s elevation, replacing Woodgate's shallow raking pediment, retains a flamboyant cartouche branded with the initials of Mr and Mrs Hope.

Hope also created a showy symmetrical entrance front by extending the N elevation to the w, advancing the external wall of the kitchen range in line with the main block, and there duplicating the existing bowed front. What was now the central bay was marked by tripartite openings on two levels, expressively treated with vermiculated rustication. The entrance remained in the main block, but was moved to the N by a square porch added to the original bow; Woodgate's fanlit doorway was reused under an exceptionally fragile-looking cast-iron canopy. A larger open-well staircase accommodated behind the new central bay with access from Woodgate's secondary staircase was the only substantial alteration affecting the plan of the original house. The remainder of the service ranges on the w side was removed and replaced by a single-storey four-bay block on the s that provided a new dining room opening directly off the drawing room. This low element contrasting with the main block gave the building an unfinished appearance, and indeed it was unfinished at Hope's death in 1862. Other substantial works to complete the sw corner in a uniform manner may have been curtailed by his widow, who inherited the property and in 1868 was said to be 'amiably carrying out the designs of her late husband'. Their daughter Henrietta Adela had married Lord Lincoln, soon to be 6th Duke of Newcastle, and on Mrs Hope's death the property passed to that family. Between 1900 and 1904 Queen Victoria's son, the Duke of Connaught, resided here when Commander of Forces in Ireland. Sold in 1928, it was occupied from 1943 to 1974 by Franciscan nuns, then later acquired by Monaghan County Council. They leased it in the 1980s to a hotel; most of the c19 additions were demolished, and Woodgate's interiors were gutted. Finally, it was badly damaged by arson in 2010.

The STABLES to the w, now also gutted by fire, comprise a U-plan block with a pedimented central range; of two storeys in squared limestone with sandstone and red brick trim; remodelled in 1865 with a grandiose pedimented gateway linked to the side ranges by railings. The ironwork, by *Shekleton* of Dundalk, includes the tether rings fixed on either side of the doorways.

The creation of the extensive lakeside DEMESNE is largely considered a late c18 development, evident in 1772 when lands

around the castle began to be taken back soon after the original
grant of leases. The designed landscape here relies greatly on
nature, improved in 1832 by *William Sawrey Gilpin*, who had
been employed by Lord Blayney's nephew at Caledon in 1829.
Gilpin planted the islands to give greater variety; adopting the
same approach to composition that he employed as a successful landscape painter, he viewed the landscape in three distinct
parts – distance, middle distance and foreground – with formal
emphasis given to the foreground as the means to frame the
entire composition. No trace now of the picturesque island
cottage visited by John Ynyr Burges of Parkanaur in 1825,
known as 'Belfast', to which Blayney retreated in desperation
to escape boring company. The entire demesne has deteriorated in public ownership since the 1980s.

The TEMPLE, set on Concra Hill with dramatic views over
the lake and the distant house, is an elegant and sophisticated
Neoclassical building, now abandoned as a sorry ruin in scrub
in the unnatural environment of a golf course. The front has
fluted Ionic columns *in antis*; behind, the doorway is flanked
by niches with blind panels above, an arrangement loosely
echoed on the side elevations, where a central round-headed
window set in a relieving arch is flanked by smaller windows
below blind panels and framed by pilasters. The effect recalls
Soane's stables at the Royal Hospital Chelsea, so *Woodgate* may
have been involved in its design. Mid-C19 drawings, made
before alterations, show the columns unfluted and a plainer
cornice without dentils, while the parapet above is treated as
an open balustrade. The plan identifies the principal space as
a square tea room, with a stair to the rear giving access to a
flat roof. A pitched roof was added *c.* 1860.

TOWN LODGES. Of *c.* 1870. Derelict. Two stately Italianate
houses of two storeys and three bays addressing each other at
the end of the approach from Market Square. Rusticated
ground floor in crisp limestone, red brick upper storey with
limestone trim, crowned by an eaves cornice and heavy blocking course. Three round-headed windows grouped closely
together on the ground floor, each with richly scrolled iron
grilles under the heads. The N lodge is doubled in size to the
N with an entrance facing the park; it may have served as a
dower house. The buildings are linked by a large formal railed
entrance with rusticated ashlar piers and ornate ironwork; the
end piers, large and square in plan, double as pedestrian gates
and entrance porches to the lodges.

TEMPLE LODGE (formerly South Lodge). 3 km SE. 1880.
A large and highly picturesque lodge with an Arts and Crafts
flavour. Squared limestone in thin courses with ashlar trim and
tiled roofs. Irregularly planned, with varied elevations.
Windows deeply set in chamfered reveals, occasionally paired
with mullions, and some with dormers on the first floor;
coloured glazing in the upper panels, patterned like St Brigid's
crosses on the ground floor. Narrow main block with a gabled

entrance projection to the N; on the E the roof sweeps down to the front wall. The E gable has its lower corners dramatically cut away under massive rippling corbels so that it reads as a diamond shape; windows under corbels and a projecting gabled stack in ashlar between two further windows complete this curious elevation. Two short ranges, contrasting hipped and gabled roofs, are set at right angles on the S elevation. A large C20 addition, in sympathy but barely successful, extends to the SE.

NEIGHBOURHOOD

FRANKFORD PRESBYTERIAN CHURCH. 2 km NE. A congregation was established here in 1750, though the present church looks early C19. A trim four-bay hall, roughcast with half-hipped roof. Nice understated architecture, handsomely fenestrated with timber Gothic windows, all marginal-glazed with coloured glass; round-headed doorway in the W gable diagonally placed beneath the gallery window; simple Geometrical oculus in the E gable.

ALL SAINTS, DOOHAMLET. Of c. 1860. 6 km W. A smart and assured gabled chapel completed at the same time as St Mary, Clontibret, and likely to share the same unknown designer. A six-bay lancet hall with chancel. Rendered, with well-spaced stepped buttresses in limestone with sandstone trim. Robust gabled front with angle buttresses, filled with three graded lancets, all well-finished in soft sandstone surrounds. Directly below, with the same simple sophistication, the pointed door sits in a wide chamfered recess with plainly incised lines. The ashlar bellcote was added in 1882. Good internal timber porch to the W. Disappointing interior. Timber-panelled ceiling with braced scissor trusses.

ST MICHAEL, ANNAYALLA. 6 km NW. A massive rugged structure designed in 1919 by *W. A. Scott*, built to replace an C18 mass-house that survives as a ruin to the N. Scott exhibited his designs for the church at the Royal Hibernian Academy in 1921, the year of his death, leaving supervision of the building to *R. M. Butler*, who completed it in 1923. The architect's expressive use of stone – rock-faced limestone, in contrasting shades of pale and deep grey – and the hard, heavyweight forms all combine to give this building its macho appearance. The W front is characteristically muscular, its essentially simple gabled form greatly obscured by Scott's typical massing of the central bay around a heavily buttressed bellcote rising above a gabled porch. Heavy square piers break through the eaves, anchoring the primary W gable; they are repeated on the transept gables but abandoned on the chancel. The quality of stoneworking in this building can be seen not least in the big roofs that are covered with small chunky slates. The plan is cruciform: a five-bay nave, transepts, and a deep chancel.

Confessionals at the W end of the nave are set within enlarged bays handsomely expressed externally with a subsidiary gable. The windows are simple lancets with blocked surrounds.

Inside, the space is big but dull, except for the wide chancel arch that rests on stocky limestone columns with smaller arches opening to the side chapels. This tripartite arrangement is repeated across the transepts. Scissor-truss roof. – The ALTAR incorporates good Celtic Romanesque columns. – STAINED GLASS. In the E window the Crucifixion; in the side chapels, the Virgin and Christ.

The PAROCHIAL HOUSE to the S is also by *Scott*. A thrifty two-storey block of three bays with a central gabled section in stone. Here the pitch is steep, evident also on the end gables, where the rear roof slope sweeps noticeably lower on one side and is bell-cast. The first-floor windows are pushed close to the eaves, marking Scott's debt to C. F. A. Voysey, but they have lost the leaded metal windows that make this architecture so distinctive.

CAVAN

INTRODUCTION

Cavan, set amid the benign contours of the South Ulster drumlin belt, is a large market town originating in an established Gaelic settlement in the centre of the highly developed O'Reilly lordship of East Breifne. Two castles, one inside the town and another to the SE on Gallows Hill, once signalled its ancient beginnings; no traces of either may be found today, just an unusually high concentration of earthen ring forts in the hinterland. A Franciscan friary dedicated to the Blessed Virgin, founded here in 1300 under the patronage of Giolla Iosa Ruadh O'Reilly, suffered the typical sequence of burnings, and only the ruined tower of the old parish church that replaced it on Abbey Street hints at any older associations.

Although the friary and town were burnt in 1468, there is evidence for a market here in 1480; thanks to the town's proximity to the Pale and the absence of tolls, its fortunes endured throughout the medieval period because of trade. The *Annals of the Four Masters* record a devastating fire in 1575 that burned 'the great monastery and the town of Cavan from the great castle

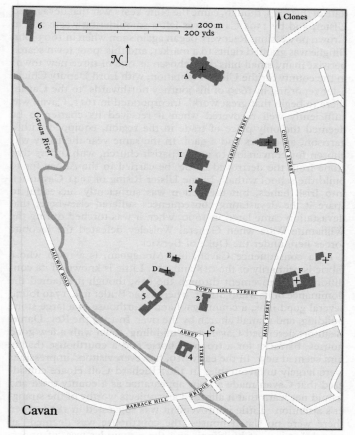

↑ Clones

200 m
200 yds

𝒩

Cavan River

RAILWAY ROAD

FARNHAM STREET

CHURCH STREET

A

I

3

B

E
D

TOWN HALL STREET

5

2

MAIN STREET

ABBEY STREET

C

F
F

4

BRIDGE STREET

BARRACK HILL

Cavan

A	Cathedral of SS Patrick & Felim	I	Courthouse
B	Urney Parish Church (C of I)	2	Town Hall
C	Church ruins	3	Johnston Central Library
D	Scots Presbyterian Church	4	Farnham Schools
E	Wesleyan chapel (former)	5	Gaol (former)
F	Poor Clares Convent and	6	Railway station (former)
	St Joseph's Chapel (former)		

downwards to the river'. A quick recovery is suggested by the fact that all these features are present on a rare map of 1591. From this it appears that the town had grown substantially to become a large urban centre stretching along a N–S axis lying hard against the E uplands of Tullymongan Hill. The Main Street, fully lined with houses, opened out in the middle to a square market place with a market cross; out of this to the W, Bridge Street (now Plunkett Street) led to a crossing of the River Cavan, which flows parallel to the S end of Main Street. Soon after the

date of this map, though, came the Nine Years War that devastated
Ulster, and by 1595 Cavan was left a smouldering waste and in
Crown possession. Recovery began again soon when in 1603 John
Binglie was granted rights to a market, and this 'poor town seated
betwixt many small hills' was chosen as one of three new towns
in the county for the Ulster Plantation, with Lord Deputy Chichester reporting in 1609 of his journey northwards 'to the Cavan,
there to begin that great work'. Incorporated in 1611, Cavan was
sufficiently well recovered when it received its charter to be
deemed the only place of trade in the region, equipped with a
garrison, an assizes and a gaol. In the same year the friary was
chosen for conversion to a new parish church, with orders that
stone from the destroyed castle 'be carried to the Abbey for to
build the school withal'. In the Ulster Rising of 1641 Cavan fell
into Irish hands, but the action was sufficiently successful to
spare it the devastating consequences suffered elsewhere; that
devastation came later, in 1690, when it was torched during the
Williamite Wars when General Wolseley defeated the Jacobite
forces here under the Duke of Berwick.

As a consequence Cavan, like Monaghan, is a town whose
fabric is primarily of the C18 and C19. Little is known of its condition or improvement through the C18, though it retained the
dominance of its Main Street, where Isaac Butler in c. 1740 found
several good inns, a county gaol and courthouse in a large stone
building, and a small church by the river. In 1787 the Rev. Daniel
Beaufort described Cavan as a 'middling' town with a few good
houses, barracks for a troop of horse and a courthouse that to
him seemed new. In the early C19, however, visitors' impressions
were largely unfavourable. In 1807 Richard Colt Hoare considered that Cavan made a poor appearance as a county town and
'could not learn that it afforded any objects worthy of the stranger's attention'. Little improvement was suggested in 1824, when
there were no slated houses, the courthouse was deemed 'an
unsightly piece of building', and the remainder was 'of unpretending character thickly daubed and patched as well as considerably prolonged with rows of mere cabins'. But by then the
influence of the Maxwell family, Lords Farnham, who were the
town's principal owners, must already have been evident. They
began to direct a steady pattern of growth through the century
with the creation of Farnham Street as a wide thoroughfare to
the w, parallel to the Main Street, that reinforced the linear
emphasis of the urban layout. It must have been planned by 1816,
when the new parish church was erected at the N end, its impetus
perhaps begun when the Gaol was erected at the S end in 1810.
Formally conceived as a mall with a linear park along its E side,
Farnham Street began to fill up as the best buildings were established along the w side, beginning with the new Courthouse
completed in the 1820s. Eventually the spaces between were filled
in with Protestant churches, while tall terraces provided an
orderly gentility on both sides over its considerable length (in one
of these houses on the E side the entertainer and artist Percy
French was a resident in the late C19). Such formal developments

became standard in C19 towns; here they were achieved without shifting the focus away from the narrower, flowing axis of the Main Street that remains the commercial heart of the town. All the churches are still spread out along Farnham Street, culminating at the N end in the two major churches, where the steepled tower of the Church of Ireland held its advantage over the Regency Gothic barn of the Catholic church opposite until that was replaced by the overwhelming C20 Cathedral and its babelesque spire.

Additions to the town in the late C20 and early C21 have been at the expense of the traditional weave of the older fabric, and some of the best buildings have now gone: the Gaol, elevated at the S end of Farnham Street and designed by *Richard Elsam* in 1810 with a formidable gateway, was demolished in the 1930s; the Georgian Market House with its boldly rusticated windows stood on the Main Street until replaced in 1972 by a pitiful Post Office; also on the Main Street was the County Infirmary, an imposing block with gabled end projections and a broad pedimented doorcase, designed by *William & Francis Farrell* in 1849. The replacement building here (Dunnes Stores) has the inflated blandness demanded by modern retail centres, and elsewhere new architecture continues to be raised amongst traditional forms with all the subtlety of a throbbing thumb. This is especially evident in the hulking apartments that chill the surviving terraces on Mill Street; on the E side of Farnham Street, the Johnston Library replaces *J. F. Fuller*'s Farnham Hall with all the forced insensitivity of stark Modernism, its heavy cubic form in bright red brick, glass, zinc and unpainted concrete set among public buildings that were more quietly developed here in the C19. Only in the tiered and contoured apartments designed in 2003 by *Fitzgerald Kavanagh & Partners* against the steep slope of Cock Hill at Aughnaskerry, to the E of Church Street, have new buildings so far attained a level of success deserving of critical notice.

118

CATHEDRAL OF SS PATRICK AND FELIM, AND PRECINCT

With the most majestic and the last of the great cathedrals by *Ralph Byrne* of *W. H. Byrne & Son*, of 1939–42, classicism in Ireland seemed to come to a spectacular final flowering in this provincial town. Set on a grassy rise off Farnham Street, its proud steeple and classical portico compensate for a less than imposing site on the edge of the town. This is an exceptionally monumental design. A century after Emancipation, it cannot be taken for a display of triumphalism: instead, it proclaims ecclesiastical dignity, establishing an architectural alliance with the majesty of Rome and St Peter's See at a time in Ireland when the bonds between the Church and the newly independent State were being woven tightly together. Still very much a building for architectural purists, it was controversial in its time as a threat to Modernism and it has been too easily dismissed with labels like 'sham

Renaissance', or viewed with suspicion as part of the European classical tradition tainted by the agendas of the Fascist states.

The visitor who leaves aside the squabbles between arch-conservatism and Modernist cant will find a building purely of its time that is deserving of greater respect for its blend of C20 inventiveness and classical veneration; and only by time has it been denied its worthiness within the Neoclassical tradition. As a contemporary of Lutyens, whose colleague *Alexander Meldrum* assisted on this building, Byrne had a thorough understanding of the classical vocabulary, which once properly understood and applied can always appear new; certainly the design of Cavan leaves an abiding impression that the building could not belong to any other time.

The predecessor was a modest pre-Emancipation chapel, enlarged, and in 1862, two decades after the Bishop of Kilmore had made Cavan the administrative centre of the diocese, designated cathedral of Kilmore. The decision to replace it was made as early as 1919, when Bishop Patrick Finegan complained that the old church was unbecoming. *W. A. Scott, T. F. McNamara* and *R. M. Butler* all eagerly offered their services to the Bishop and in 1922 the disused Gaol site at the s end of the street was acquired for the new building. However lack of funds postponed the project until 1937, and by then it had been decided to abandon the Gaol site in favour of one beside the old church. In November the building committee approached *Ralph Byrne* for preliminary designs in varying styles with a capacity of two thousand people. In September 1938 the building contract was awarded to *John Sisk & Sons,* and work began in October. The classical orders provided a forceful symbolism for an authoritarian church, but the choice of design appears to have been driven more by economic considerations at first: Bishop Lyons had rejected Gothic on grounds of expense, and he approved the steeple in the chosen design because it would compensate for the lowly position of the site. Curiously, the church authorities believed that the Gothic and classical styles had been successfully blended in the design: at the foundation stone ceremony in 1939 Dr P. A. Beecher, Professor of Sacred Eloquence at Maynooth, explained: 'The spirit of the classical style is to stretch its lines along the ground; that of the Gothic to seek the sky.' The Cathedral was dedicated on 27 September 1942 and consecrated five years later. The final cost was £209,235. (The old church was afterwards rebuilt at Ballyhaise.)

Cavan is Byrne's best work, his erudition evident in a composition more architecturally coherent than his slightly earlier cathedrals at Mullingar (1932) and Athlone (1935). It shares with them the form of a great long nave with aisles and transepts and a low copper dome over the crossing that deserved more emphasis. However, here he closely studied his James Gibbs, and formulated a design that successfully elaborates on the theme of St Martin-in-the-Fields in London. Perhaps the most influential of Anglican churches, Gibbs's design had been used in Irish church architecture a century and a half before by Francis Johnston, who invoked its steeple for his Dublin church of St George, Hardwick Place. As Byrne's office had surveyed Johnston's building he must have known it well, but he returned to the original to evolve a suitably Romish w front for Cavan. Although it cost a good deal less than its midland counterparts, with its scale and grandeur it looks a great deal more expensive, and is given enhanced stateliness by its masonry, which continues a long Irish tradition of combining Wicklow granite with Portland stone.

Exterior

Set on a wide podium with steps at the top of a ramped approach, the front is showy and formidable, branded in *Byrne*'s own way with shallow rustication at ground level below the impost mould-ing. Pre-eminence is awarded to the giant Corinthian tetrastyle portico. Reducing the portico from Gibbs's hexastyle arrange-ment results in a more imposing two-storey block and allows greater elaboration in the side bays, where pilasters are layered and step forward before the corners, the projection extended through the entablature in an arrangement that suggests Michel-angelo more than Gibbs. The unifying entablature crowns the front with its heavy modillion cornice, blocking course and closed parapet. The sculpture in the pediment, where the risen Christ is shown with outstretched arms between the kneeling figures of St Patrick and St Felim, is by *George Smith*. The steeple completes the formal power of the front, attenuating and mildly varying the St Martin's design, while raising it from the roof inside the w wall as Gibbs had so innovatively done two centuries before. In 1941 when the copper cross was put in place the spire attained a height of 220 ft (67 m). The small, pimple-like copper domes over the side bays, while a little unresolved, reduce the isolation of the steeple and invest the front with an added *gravitas*. They are Byrne contributions, and join favourite motifs throughout the design, such as swags indiscriminately repeated. His tendency to toy with convention is apparent in the fenestration: the upper windows are severe piercings set over thin rectangular panels in shallow unadorned recesses that are pushed up to the level of the frieze, thereby forcing the architraves to return into the jambs; Byrne here displays an individualism that has all the playfulness of Giulio Romano in the way the voussoirs are set to drop slightly towards the keystone. In the entrances, classic Gibbsian designs are followed but adapted with all the elastic potential of the vocabulary; over the side doors the triple keystones are greatly enlarged, thus deepening the frieze before a thin cornice with a sculpted panel in a lunette above. The main door, flanked by niches under the portico, is a simpler design, wide and squat with a semicircular fanlight.

The side elevation eschews the giant order, perhaps as too much of a good thing; here the entablature is simplified, return-ing to full power only in the pedimented projections of the tran-septs. The bowed, half-domed projections on the transept ends

and flanking the w front are the most handsomely articulated
elements of the design, once again evoking Gibbs, this time
taking ideas from his unexecuted design for a round church in
London. A subsidiary Doric order of pilasters is employed here
and on the aisles, where it produces an unsatisfactory contrast
with the plain, fully fenestrated clerestory; the bulkiness of the
aisles is exaggerated by limiting the windows to alternate bays
where they are set in a concave recess, framed by the pilasters
that support a continuous deep entablature. The effect is compounded by the awkward return of the aisles along the transepts,
upsetting the overall rhythm.

On the sides as on the main front enrichment is limited mostly
to swags and festoons; up close these seem lumpish and uncouth,
but their stylization is typical of the time. Only in the lower frieze
does the decoration appear misplaced, the husk-draped roundels
tied to the pilasters repeating a motif favoured by James Gandon
that here seems to demand a more refined Neoclassical frame.

Interior

110   A deep nave 106 ft (32 m) long and 41 ft (12.5 m) wide, with a
trabeated arcade like that of the Early Christian basilica of
S. Maria Maggiore in Rome, progressing E with all the spare
rhythmic elegance of Brunelleschi's S. Lorenzo in Florence. The
ceiling is flat, with a massive enriched cornice with long mutule
blocks and a coved border filled with swags and bows; the surface
is divided into three square panels filled with shallow domes,
probably suggested by the aisle ceilings of St Martin's, here
encircled by rich floral bands; the aisle ceilings repeat the domes
in a simpler way. The square-headed clerestory windows are
pleasing inventions, a blend of High Renaissance classicism and
Georgian Baroque set in lugged surrounds with a broken entablature and a cartouche at the base.

Economy and Byrne's appreciation for materials combined to
leave surfaces with untreated finishes, giving an unexpected
avant-garde look to the design. What must have seemed strange
upon completion has mellowed over time, the smooth gypsum
employed for pilasters, window soffits, capitals and stucco work
now a dull pink that contrasts with the pale green cement-rendered wall surfaces, enhanced in the upper areas with stippling
to give heightened texture. The columns of polished grey Pavon-
azzetto marble, furnished by *Dinelli Figli* of Pietrasanta and fitted
by *Earley & Co.* of Dublin, give a sense of Antique gravity. They
are returned at the E end to support arches in the classic Venetian
form favoured by Palladio and Serlio, a composition that screens
the crossing and is repeated before the shallow apsed E end with
its thin register of twelve arched lights set high in the wall above
the altar. The crossing, a top-lit dome raised on pendentives, is
flanked by the barrel-vaults of the transepts, which are richly
coffered in a way inspired by the Basilica of Maxentius in Rome.
Forming a narrow axis with apses at both ends, the transepts

forcefully recall Palladio's treatment of the transepts in the church of the Redentore in Venice; the careful, subtle revelation here nicely demonstrates Byrne's competence in fusing classical ideas.

In the sanctuary apse above the altar, the MURAL of the Resurrection is by *George Collie*, who also painted the STATIONS OF THE CROSS. – The other FURNISHINGS were largely shared between *Hearne & Co.* of Waterford and *T. & C. Martin* of Dublin. – PULPIT by *Maguire & Short*, carved by *A. J. Breen*. – Terrazzo floors by *Oppenheimer*. – STAINED GLASS. The earliest, in the N transept, is signed by *James Clarke* of Frederick Street, Dublin, and dated 1919. The heads of the Twelve Apostles in the apse are by *Earley & Co.* Most of the remainder are by *Harry Clarke*, dated before 1934, brought here in 1993 from the Sacred Heart Convent in Leeson Street, Dublin. Dazzling, jewel-like figurative work in deep blues with unmistakable almond-shaped eyes.

PRESBYTERY. 1962 by *W. H. Byrne & Son*. Set along the N boundary on the site of the Temperance Hall. A plain two-storey block in granite ashlar with a long six-bay front, irregularly spaced windows (originally sashed), and a flat roof. An arched doorway in Portland stone is set to one side. The contractor was *P. Elliott & Co.*

OTHER CHURCHES ETC.

URNEY PARISH CHURCH (C of I). 1816 and *c.* 1854. Usually attributed to *John Bowden*, though *Richard Elsam* was paid for plans in 1815 and the design noticeably bristles with ornament, unlike Bowden's usually conservative approach. A large church with a W tower and spire, on a triangular site at the intersection of Farnham Street and Church Street. The main front shows a lively architectonic, modular composition of porch, tower, vestry, nave and transepts stepping forward with diminishing widths. Begun as a hall-and-tower type, with a boxy four-bay nave in limestone rubble, greatly enlivened by crowstepped battlements and angle buttresses with crocketed pinnacles. Windows in three-centred arches under hoods, with timber mullions and iron casements. The tower is linked to the nave by a half-bay projection. All the lively Gothic enrichments are carried through here and on to the diminutive porch projecting from the W face of the tower; here the side entrances have boldly framed Tudor arches with panelled doors deliciously patterned with Gothic motifs. Enlarged by *Joseph Welland c.* 1854 with plain transepts and chancel, where the Perp windows are wider with stone tracery. The contractor was *William Hague Sen.*

The interior is an impressive galleried space with exceptionally flat quadripartite vaulting, defined with ribs and bosses springing from plaster corbels borne aloft by winged cherubs with heads like porcelain dolls. Elaborate timber galleries carried on lithesome clustered shafts, with panelled frontals filled with large Tudor roses; the shafts are unnervingly eschewed across the W end, where the corners are elegantly bowed outwards. – FURNISHINGS. PULPIT and PRAYER desk by *R. Langrishe*, 1887, in Caen stone with Irish marbles, carved by *Charles W. Harrison*. – STAINED GLASS. Varied figurative glass, some heavily patterned and most of it weakly coloured. E window: by *Ward & Nixon*, c. 1850; S transept: by *Clayton & Bell*, c. 1858; N transept: 1876, attributed to *Ward & Hughes*; nave: by *Mayer & Co.*, 1900; the remainder by *Clokey*, Belfast, 1937. – MONUMENTS. A small selection, the best in the chancel: John Maxwell, 2nd Earl of Farnham †1823; an imposing composition of 1826 by *Sir Francis Chantrey* in white marble, classical in feeling, against an anomalous Gothic backdrop of limestone, with a reclining Lord Farnham taking farewell of a kneeling figure. – Nathaniel Sneyd †1833, 'whose valuable life was terminated by a maniac in the streets of the metropolis'; a plain white tablet topped by a bust, probably by *Thomas Kirk*. – In the gallery: the Rev. Joseph Story †1838 by *Thomas Kirk*; a large obelisk-shaped plaque in white marble with a favourite relief carving of an angel in clouds set above a funerary scene. – Commodore Alexander Saunderson Barrow, †1860 at St Malo; a Neoclassical tablet surmounted by an urn, flag and anchor.

'THE FRIARY'. In an overgrown graveyard on Abbey Street. The site is associated with the Franciscan Friary of St Mary, founded in 1300, and the ruins are known as the Friary, though what remains is the surviving tower of the C17 Church of Ireland parish church, which closed in 1815. Of the Friary, the *Annals of the Four Masters* record the burial in 1330 of its founder, Giolla Iosa Ruadh O'Reilly; it suffered greatly in the C15 during clashes between the O'Reillys and the forces of the Pale, and by the late C16 its decline had followed the O'Reillys and its property was confiscated. In 1594 Captain Dowdall had it reinforced as a garrison, but the buildings appear to have been destroyed again in 1608, perhaps as the town was renewed for the Plantation, when a new parish church and school were established here. After the rebellion of 1641 the friars briefly returned to the site and re-established buildings, described in 1646 as a 'marvelous structure in the Ulster fashion, the church, cells, refectory and all other apartments being of wood and roofed with sods'. They were finally expelled in 1650 and a parish church rebuilt. The tower is a plain structure in limestone rubble with three diminishing stages. Round-headed windows in the upper belfry stage and doorway on the W face, all with simplified Gibbs surrounds, correspond to recorded works of c. 1750. Good C18 corniced gatepiers. Remarkable now chiefly as the supposed burial place of the mid-C17 Catholic heroes Eoghan Ruadh O'Neill, Myles 'the Slasher' O'Reilly, and Archbishop Hugh O'Reilly.

SCOTS PRESBYTERIAN CHURCH. Farnham Street. 1836. A diminutive Tudor-style hall and battlemented porch with

gables matching those of the main front, both fulsomely
adorned with spiky finials on the corners and apexes. Built in
squared limestone with sandstone dressings. The hall has three
bays with large timber Y-traceried windows in blocked surrounds. Better hooded twinlight in the porch, with stone mullions and timber frames. Enlarged to the rear with a lower
four-bay block in rubble with brick dressings and square-
headed windows.

The MANSE stands forward, nearer the street front. A two-
storey Victorian house of three bays with twin gables, formerly
adorned with decorative bargeboards and finials. Squared
limestone with red brick trim. Crudely altered in the late C20,
with ugly brick-and-glass infill between the gables and the loss
of the balcony over the entrance, the bargeboards, and the
paired Victorian sashes.

WESLEYAN CHAPEL (former). Farnham Street. 1858 by *William
Hague*, and so far his earliest known commission. A modest
and competent design with none of the vigour of his later work.
A single-cell lancet hall of four bays with a plain gabled front
to the street with angle buttresses, three-light Dec window, and
an offset entrance tower, now truncated, the octagonal broach
spire having been removed when the church closed. Walls of
squared limestone with sandstone dressings. Converted to
office use in the late C20 but retaining inside an exposed purlin
roof with arched trusses, decorated in the spandrels with
Gothic motifs.

The MANSE stands forward on one side. An equally tidy
design, probably also by *Hague*, two storeys in squared limestone with yellow brick trimmings, a hipped roof and tall
central stacks. Front of three bays with Victorian sashes set in
pairs on either side of the entrance, which projects from the
centre under a hipped roof.

POOR CLARES CONVENT AND ST JOSEPH'S INDUSTRIAL
SCHOOL FOR GIRLS (former). Now largely occupied by
CAVAN COLLEGE OF FURTHER EDUCATION. 1862–4 by *John
Ryan*, and later. Integrated with the terrace on the W side of
Main Street in an unusual arrangement for an Irish religious
institution, even more so for a closed order: an L-plan block
with a three-storey, six-bay street façade of rubble with red
brick trim and Georgian sashes and a Gothic tower gently
projecting at the S end, all that now proclaims the building's
former purpose; rising above the eaves, its odd-looking pyramidal upper stage is explained by the removal of the belfry and
spire in the C20. A Gothic aedicule with polished shafts and a
crocketed gabled is tucked away high on the tower's S elevation.
The original six bays were extended by a further three to the
N, the work distinguished by improved stonework. Behind the
tower, extending W, the return to the rear is more obviously
institutional, nominally Gothic, with walls of squared masonry
trimmed in yellow brick and triangular-headed windows with
plate glass. The complex was enlarged in the C20 at various
times with plain rendered blocks ranged loosely around an
irregular yard, including an INDUSTRIAL SCHOOL of 1910 by

W. A. Scott, dormitories of 1931 by *Patrick J. Brady*, and a rebuilding of the dormitory wing in 1943 by *W. H. Byrne & Son* following a tragic fire which claimed the lives of thirty-five female orphans and an elderly cook.

At the very rear, between car parks, ST CLARE'S CHAPEL was built as ST JOSEPH'S CHAPEL for the convent in 1881. A long gable-ended block in a sparse Gothic style, with walls of squared rock-faced masonry in buff-coloured sandstone, trimmed with yellow brick. The main front (N) has a gabled porch offset to the E between tall lancets, and is divided from the two-storey W end by a buttress; here triangular Gothic windows with concave sides are set over paired lancets. Plainer ten-bay S front where the four central windows are grouped in an ascending pattern under a gabled oculus with a discreet doorway to one side.

PUBLIC BUILDINGS ETC.

COURTHOUSE. Farnham Street. 1824 by *William Farrell*, with later alterations. (*John Bowden* had proposed a design, but died in 1822.) Farrell's design survives and was used again at Carrick-on-Shannon. The contractors were *Williams & Cockburn* of Dublin. A broad distinguished front in honey-coloured sandstone ashlar, five bays wide with solid pilasters holding the corners; the three central bays are slightly advanced and pedimented with a tetrastyle Tuscan portico. The windows above are recessed in a tripartite arrangement with a Wyatt window between standard sashes, which gives an overall Schinkelesque appearance. The side bays are blind, with round-headed arches in shallow recesses on the ground floor and rectangular recesses above. The sides are built of rubble, four bays deep with the typical massive round-headed sashes employed in most courthouses at this time. Alterations and additions in 1866. Doubled in size to the rear *c.* 1985, cheaply built in exposed concrete blockwork with an absurdly proud hipped slate roof. Internal alterations in 1928 by *Patrick J. Brady* and again in 1987 by *Charles D. Ellison & Sons*.

TOWN HALL. Town Hall Street. 1907–10 by *W. A. Scott*. Contractor *William O'Callaghan & Sons*. A masterpiece in the Arts and Crafts manner, massive and solid, with a striking, rugged originality. Seen from Farnham Street the tall commanding silhouette has all the authority of a medieval keep, explaining perhaps the contemporary view of it as Neo-Norman. However there is nothing here to align with any of the revivalist tendencies of the time: instead, Scott relies solely on massing and the careful interplay between fenestration and recession to achieve bold architectural effects. Walls of brown sandstone rubble from a local quarry at Latt. The building is essentially arranged as two interlocking gable-ended blocks with a long, low, buttressed projection to the rear, under a big slate roof broken by large triangular dormers. The main front of seven bays is

Cavan Town Hall.
Drawing, 1910

formed symmetrically, with three broad bays, the central one ascending as a taller, narrower block that is placed as it were cross-wise in the centre and raised above the main ridge to form the imposing entrance gable. An enhanced vertical emphasis results from the way in which each of the corners, including those of the central block, is articulated, by means of paired strip buttresses with shallow projections that continue above the eaves where they are brought together under a deep coping so as to read as square towers. The perspective view published in *The Irish Builder* in 1910 shows that the architect had intended to finish these towers more simply, tying them together across the front with brick arches flying above the intervening eaves, and to plaster the recessed wall surfaces of the main bays, evoking some sense of Voysey's white-walled simplicity and giving bolder definition to the towers. The vertical lights set in the recessed planes between the 'pilasters' have a defensive quality, and the contrast with the main windows could not be more striking. These are enormous rectangular openings with mullions and flush casements in the manner of Voysey; all are square-headed except for the largest, with a segmental head, recessed in a brick arch above the entrance and opening on to an iron balcony. Below, the doorway is low and unadorned, funnelled in the thickness of the wall. Inside, a tight staircase with sweet fretwork balusters leads to the council chamber in the roof space, an unimposing room now tastelessly refurnished like a cheap hotel. Inside the return, a large public hall with a steeply pitched roof of exposed arch-braced trusses.

MASONIC HALL. Farnham Street. 1885. An odd-looking Gothic hall with varied fenestration. Two storeys in squared limestone with dressed quoins and patterned slating to the roofs. The front has a large gabled bay with big mullioned windows, rectangular below and Tudor-arched on the first floor; to the r., slightly set back, the narrow entrance bay; above the shouldered door a triangular window with concave sides, and a plaque with Masonic symbols giving the date.

JOHNSTON CENTRAL LIBRARY. Farnham Street. 2004 by *Shaffrey Associates*. An outlandish successor to *J. F. Fuller*'s benign Farnham Hall of 1876 which formerly occupied the site, and a disruptive neighbour amidst the old-fashioned gentility of the street. Strangely unwelcoming for its purpose too; a bullish and preposterously overscaled block, where smooth red brick, glass and zinc cladding coalesce into an ungainly angular composition, its main, burdensome overhang to the street front hubristically borne on puny concrete cantilevers. Much more successful inside, the main library bright and airy with an open plan.

FARNHAM MONUMENT. Farnham Street, in front of the Library. 1870 by *S.F. Lynn*, who exhibited a model of the design at the Royal Hibernian Academy in 1872. Erected by the tenantry in memory of Henry, Baron Farnham, who was killed in the Abergele railway disaster in 1868; it was unveiled in December 1871 in the centre of the town gardens, and moved across the road after the gardens closed. Minus its plinth, still a dignified design, executed in brilliant white marble, with Lord Farnham portrayed in full regalia in a thoughtful pose.

GARDA STATION, Farnham Street. *See* p. 258.

PROVINCIAL BANK (former). Farnham Street. Designed in 1862 by *William Hague*, the year he moved his practice from Cavan to Dublin. A tall, detached stuccoed block in a simple astylar classicism with subtle mannerisms. Three storeys over a basement with a three-bay front, the entrance in a single-bay projection to one side. Rusticated ground floor with tall windows in shouldered surrounds and a stuccoed Ionic entablature above, the bold cornice serving as a continuous sill course to the first-floor windows; lugged architraves, thin keystones and pulvinated brackets add quirkiness to the first-floor window surrounds. The upper floors are smooth-rendered with rusticated quoins below a crisply defined eaves cornice with a pulvinated frieze.

BANK OF IRELAND (former HIBERNIAN BANK). Main Street. 1907 by *Edward J. Toye*. An imposing Italianate design in red brick and limestone. Three storeys and five bays with big Victorian sashes. The ground floor is ashlared, extending into arched single-storey wings, with a simple Tuscan order framing the entrances in the end bays. The first-floor windows are plain, resting on the entablature and intruding into the moulded string-course above; the upper storey is more elaborate, with round-headed windows in lugged frames with keystones projected into a bold modillion eaves cornice. Deep parapets with open balustrades, boldly interrupted in the centre by a gabled attic dormer.

FARNHAM SCHOOL. Of *c.* 1800. On a spacious site at the S end of Farnham Street. Vernacular classicism with all the quiet sophistication of *Francis Johnston*. A compact design which might well have been proposed as a model farm, rather like the Archbishop's Palace Farm at Armagh. The master's house is a central two-storey block, with a moulded eaves cornice, hipped roof and central stacks. Roughcast, with a three-bay entrance front, nicely proportioned. Nine-pane sashes on the first floor; handsome recessed doorcase, set in a segmental arch with scrolled brackets, Grecian cornice and a squat webbed timber fanlight; the ground-floor windows are also set in shallow segmental arches, with the sills extended out to the reveals of the arches. The motif is repeated in the single-storey classroom wings, with paired sashes and parapets.

ROYAL SCHOOL. Reached from the s end of College Street. 1819 by *Francis Johnston*, and later. As one of the Ulster Royal Schools founded in 1611 during the Plantation, no provision was made for a permanent schoolhouse. First housed amid the ruins of St Mary's Friary, the school had a largely neglected and peripatetic existence in the c18, moving between rented buildings in the town and for a time to Cootehill before the present building was completed. The grandfather of Richard Brinsley Sheridan, Dr Thomas Sheridan, whom Swift described as 'the most learned person I know in this Kingdom', was master in 1735. Despite standing amongst a mélange of non-descript structures added from 1991 onwards and gruesomely disfigured by external concrete stairs, Johnston's building is still fundamentally an attractive three-storey block in the spare Neoclassical style he usually reserved for institutional buildings. The work was overseen by *John Bowden*, with *John McMahon* as contractor.

Now drably cement-rendered and dismally refenestrated, the main front to the E consists of a generously spaced three-bay block held between single-bay wings, gently advanced with pediments, and on the ground floor Johnston's favoured device of a tripartite window set in a relieving arch. The wings extend deeply to the W, with a short central stair projection set between them here to form the building's E-shaped plan. A thick plat-band extends around the entire building, forming a continuous sill to the first-floor windows, and drawing attention to the fact that the fenestration at this level is blind on three sides of the building, concealing the reality that most of the internal accommodation extends to just two storeys. The purpose of this unusual feature was to harmonize with the s wing, where the MASTER'S HOUSE really has three storeys. It presents an altogether plainer five-bay façade to the s, and here is the entrance proper, with generous spacing on each side of the central bay containing the doorcase. This is a singular design set in a recessed segmental arch, elegant in its plainness, with tall narrow side-lights extending well above the doorway; now obscured by a crude aluminium porch. Inside, the master's house has a standard tripartite plan around a central hall, a small groin-vaulted square space opening directly into the apsidal-ended stair hall with an impressive flying timber stair.

The classrooms are served by a separate stair in the central return.

BROOKVALE. Railway Road. Beside the River Cavan, a handsome small house in an understated Regency cottage style. A smooth-rendered block to a T-plan, with Georgian sashes and tall diagonal stacks. Just two bays to the main front, projected as a gable on one side with a canted bay on the ground floor supporting a pretty trellised canopy to the window above. Associated in the later C19 with *William Hague Sen.*, whose builder's yard was located on Market Street.

RAILWAY STATION (former), now the offices of the *Anglo-Celt* newspaper. Of *c*. 1862 by *George Wilkinson*. The railway came to Cavan in 1856 as a branch of the Midland & Great Western, and the station was built for the Dundalk & Enniskillen Railway when a new line from Clones opened in 1862. The contractor was *William Hague Sen*. In Wilkinson's spare Italianate idiom: a plain two-storey block in squared limestone with dressed quoins and a hipped roof. The four-bay front is asymmetrical, the end bay gently advanced on one side. Altered and greatly enlarged to the side to link with the former engine house.

TOUR

The best place to begin a tour of Cavan is at the Cathedral (*see* p. 245). A car may be parked here, or if not in the road below in front of the Cathedral. Looking down from the tall portico, a modest row of two-storey slated and rubble-built houses can be seen to the l., fronting the triangular and wooded grounds of Urney Parish Church. The side of the Courthouse appears on the r. (For church and Courthouse *see* pp. 249 and 252.) The visitor should descend the wide paved slope, patterned by grey and white composition-stone slabs and divided by stone steps, to the road, here called Farnham Street.

Rounding the railed and bull-nosed corner opposite, walk s down CHURCH STREET, a classic C19 Irish town scene, with a block of seven houses, Nos. 51–63, facing the gates and E end of the church. Where the church grounds end so does most of the historic streetscape. Opposite, Church View opens to the l. and continues uphill, turning sharply as a dog-leg around the base of Cock Hill. Here one gains a view of the impressively tiered APARTMENT COMPLEX of 2003 by *Fitzgerald Kavanagh & Partners*, which exploits the difficult contours with remarkable success. Back on Church Street, only a three-bay house and a terrace of houses, late C19, with shiny brick fronts and big chimneys, survive before recent commercial buildings take over. DUNNES STORES of 1994, on the r., replacing the County Infirmary of 1849, is a vast low Postmodernist white cement block with thin pediments and square windows in the upper storey. It faces a long block of fake Victorian shops on the l., brick-built and too tall for the style adopted.

After Dunnes Stores, Thomas Ashe Street leads off on the r., while the line of Church Street continues s. Here its name changes to MAIN STREET. This thoroughfare offers a satisfying if modest accumulation of C19 houses, of painted render or of rubble stone, with brick surrounds to the upper windows. At the entry to the Main Street, on the l., a pend opens to St Clare's Chapel and Convent Court, apartments where the convent block is now manacled by iron galleries and a bulky enclosed stair. Back in the street, the stone front wall of what was St Joseph's Industrial School of the Poor Clares Convent (see p. 251) has been opened to make shopfronts on the ground floor. A reduced Gothic turret survives at the S end. Now comes an older house, roughcast, six bays by two storeys with a central pend and, soon after, the FARNHAM ARMS HOTEL, a tall five-bay four-storey block, not improved by the partial exposure of rubble on its façade. Opposite the hotel, a bank building with a more ordered façade. Back on the l. side, the ULSTER BANK of 1911 by *Blackwood & Jury*. Five bays and three storeys in limestone and red brick. Prominence is given to the ashlar narrow central bay supporting the bank's arms in the middle of the balustraded parapet. Sash windows, irregularly proportioned, are set together in pairs with Tudor hoods and thin moulded sills displaying the architects' usual tendency towards classical irreverence, continued in the engaged emaciated Doric columns on the ground floor and the boldly hooded doorway set to one side.

The bank faces the MARKET SQUARE, with the harsh Modernist POST OFFICE of 1972 by *John O'Brien* of the *Office of Public Works*; two storeys, flat-roofed, unworthy of the site and its function. *Imogen Stuart*'s archaeologically inspired THREE HANDS FOUNTAIN of 1989 is here. On a circular stepped podium, a dolmen-like composition formed by three massive travertine blocks, sculpted as hands, to symbolize peace and reconciliation. Originally flanked at the base by two pools. Now no longer a fountain; and this evocative modern monument is certainly not helped by the utilitarian glass-and-steel shed erected over it.

The MAIN STREET from this point is quite unspoilt, with several three-storey gabled blocks of different height built as rows. Immediately on the r. is the impressive Bank of Ireland (*see* p. 254). After Bridge Street, on the r. is a large ten-bay block of three houses, perhaps *c.* 1850, with a wide central pend. BRIDGE STREET runs downhill to the r.; its name is misleading, since Cavan makes nothing of its river, whose water is forced into a narrow channel and is constantly hidden behind buildings. The bridge is anonymous. A little beyond the bridge, before the bottom of the street, turn l. into River Street, a narrow passageway bordering the river, to find LIFEFORCE MILL. This vernacular complex of two- and three-storey corn mill buildings was redeveloped and enlarged in a five-year programme which began in 1990. Then the main buildings, of coursed limestone rubble with cutstone dressings dating from the early C19, were dismantled in Drogheda and transported to Cavan as the centrepiece of the scheme. The mill preserves a working *MacAdam* water turbine of 1846. From here, downstream at the end of RIVER STREET, half of a mid-C19 two-storey house is constructed on a tunnel half over the water. Back to Bridge Street. ABBEY STREET takes a curving line to the N with the three-stage ruined tower known as the Friary (*see* p. 250) rising solitary in a graveyard of rough grass and large sycamore trees. Here the road curves to join FARNHAM STREET, the principal thoroughfare of the modern town. Turn l. past the delicately scaled Farnham School (*see* p. 254) to the Fleadh Cheoil roundabout with 'Fiddle Head' by *Joey Burns* at its centre, a wood and metal SCULPTURE of the stock of a violin.

Now turn N. All the major public buildings of the town line FARNHAM STREET, with the Cathedral at its N end. Halfway up, where Town Hall Street opens to the r., the handsome side of *W. A. Scott*'s Town Hall (*see* p. 252) is visible. Continuing N, on the l. the former Wesleyan chapel and manse of 1858 (*see* p. 251). Just beyond is the Masonic Hall (*see* above), then a cluster of handsome Late Georgian houses built on an ambitious scale. Thomas Ashe Street then comes in on the r. Just beyond on the l., the Johnston Central Library of 2004 (*see* p. 254). Rather lost between its bulky overhang and a large tree, and deprived of its plinth, the marble statue of Lord Farnham (*see* p. 254). *William Farrell*'s Courthouse of 1824 (*see* p. 252) follows. Opposite, set back behind trees, the large Postmodernist GARDA STATION, built as three attached pavilions with a pyramidal slate-roofed skylight to the central block, dates from 1991, designed by the *Office of Public Works*. Further on on the l., set in isolation, the former Provincial Bank (*see* p. 254).

NEIGHBOURHOOD

CAVAN GENERAL HOSPITAL, LISDARN. 1.25 km NW. 1977–88 by *Robinson, Keefe & Devane*. A spreading flat-roofed design, raised in tiers behind the low, obtusely angled single-storey front. Largely symmetrical in plan with a series of internal courts. Gloomy, in discouraging brown brick, with windows set in recessed vertical panels, all capped with bulky concrete overhangs. Laundry, stores and mortuary form a compact group to the S, dominated by the tall stacks adjoining the large lean-to boiler house.

Ranged along the SE flank is ST JOSEPH'S HOSPITAL, the former Sanatorium of 1938 by *Winters & Tyndall*, a long two-storey block in red brick with lower ancillary ranges, all reasonably handsome and well built.

WORKHOUSE (former). 1.5 km N. A well-preserved example of *George Wilkinson*'s standard design, built in 1841 to accommodate 1,200 inmates. Set prominently to the fore, the administration block has the familiar gabled Tudoresque facade of two storeys and five bays, here executed in good-quality squared local limestone. The limestone is exchanged for sandstone for the finer window trimmings, which results in a pronounced pattern to the chamfered reveals. Decent pierced timber bargeboards survive here, and also on the twin gables that terminate the ends of the more extensive three-storey accommodation range, which, as usual, is set well back behind.

To the SW, the former FEVER HOSPITAL of 1847 is a freestanding three-storey H-plan block, built of limestone rubble, imposing but altogether more rudimentary in its details. Five bays to the front with the end bays deeply projected as nononsense kneelered gables. Adapted in the early C20 as Cavan County Hospital and later as St Felim's Geriatric Hospital. Largely disused at the time of writing.

ST PATRICK'S DIOCESAN COLLEGE. 1.5 km NNW. 1869 by *William Hague*. A forbidding Gothic design with an overwhelming symmetrical front of three storeys with at least twenty-three bays, plate-glass windows, steep slate roofs and a battery of brick stacks. Unrelenting institutional austerity is moderated by the varied rhythm of the windows between the big three-bay gabled wings and the square battlemented stairtowers with pyramid roofs set in the angles between them. The narrow entrance gable in the centre is consequently weak, though considerably emboldened by a large recessed arch and Gothic decorations. Built in squared sandstone with ample dressings to the projections and red brick window trim. The contractor was *William Hague Sen.* The main stair projects in a central square return with flanking lean-to and a big fourlight window. The CHAPEL extends from the E wing, a polished little apsidal building with aisles with cusped lancets. Additions and alterations in 1907 by *J. J. McDonnell*; harmonizing W wing of 1939 by *W. H. Byrne & Son*. FARM BUILDINGS of 1941 by *Patrick Gaffney*.

GLENLARA HOUSE. 1.5 km SW. Set proudly overlooking Lough Swellan, a small gable-ended Victorian house in roughcast with Georgian sashes and decorative bargeboards. Two storeys, with a three-bay front where the central bay is advanced and gabled and the ground-floor windows are flanked by unusual thin vertical recesses. Bay windows with plate glass in the gables.

MOYNE HALL. 3 km S. This was the site of a Plantation castle, its existence now evident only in the moulded corbel base of a corner turret, boldly projected from an outbuilding of the present C19 house. A richly stuccoed Victorian villa, Moyne Hall was designed in 1862 by *William Hague* for James Fay, whose arms are borne in a pediment over the entrance front. The contractor was *George Buchanan*. A two-storey block with a deep plan on one side. Three bays to the front with rusticated quoins and tripartite windows, all elaborated with aedicules. The pedimented entrance bay advances from the centre with Tuscan columns supporting a balustraded balcony to the twin round-headed windows on the first floor. Plain, irregular façade of five bays to the N; narrower to the S, with a canted bay rising up to the heavy bracketed and open balustraded parapet which surrounds the entire roof. The roof is now flat, remade in mass concrete when all the floors, even the staircase, were similarly composed after a fire, presumably in the early C20.

ST BRIGID, KILLYGARRY. 3.25 km E. 1867 by *William Hague*. The contractor was *William Hague Sen*. A substantial aisled church in a modest Gothic Revival style, with five bays, lancets, and steeply pitched gables. Squared limestone, with polychrome brick trim to the windows and bands of yellow brick in the clerestory. The buttressed w front, flanked by gabled porches projecting from the aisles, has an elaborate polychrome bellcote framing a statuary niche and an enormous platetracery window oddly designed with four cinquefoils. Inside, lofty with an empty feeling. The pointed arcade has squat cylindrical piers of polished limestone with stiff-leaf capitals in Caen stone, now painted. Timber-sheeted wagon roof with unbraced arched trusses resting on corbels. Sanctuary reorganized in 1925, with new ALTARS of red-and-white marble, the gift of P. J. Lawler of Pennsylvania. – STAINED GLASS. SS Brigid and Phelim, 1909.

8050   CHARLEMONT   AH

The most important bridgehead on the Blackwater, established by Charles, Lord Mountjoy, during the Nine Years War against

Charlemont Fort, detail of map.
Drawn by N. Pynnar, 1624

Hugh O'Neill, Earl of Tyrone. In 1602 he built a wooden bridge over the river and on the hill above it a fort in view of O'Neill's castle at Dungannon, which he named Charlemont in his own honour. He passed it to the charge of Captain Toby Caulfeild, whose descendants were intermittent governors. Caulfeild had come to Ireland in 1599 with Essex in command of a troop of horse, and was knighted by King James after the fall of Hugh O'Neill; from here he administered the O'Neill lands in Tyrone after the Flight of the Earls in 1607 and quietly accrued land interests in the region; in 1623 he firmly tied his descendants' roots to the fort when he was made a baron and became Lord Charlemont.

Richard Bartlett's survey made after 1602 shows that the original fortifications extended on both sides of the river – the main fort on the hilltop as a square earthwork, indented with flankers at the corners, and a second elongated work sloping down to the river, answered by a ravelin on the N bank to protect the new bridge. Such was the hasty and impermanent nature of these works that by 1608 they were found to be 'much decayed'. They were rebuilt to a new plan by Caulfeild, the fort adopting a more regular square form with salient corner bastions shaped like those of Enniskillen and Hillsborough. In 1611 the result was described as 'a good fort, fairly ditched, with a strong pallisade and bulwarks. Within the fort are good houses built after the English fashion, and to keep the King's stores of victuals and provisions. Sir Toby Caulfeild, constable there, had 60*l* sterling from the King towards this building. A very fair garden without the rampier, etc.'

When Nicholas Pynnar drew the fort in 1624 the defences had contracted to a hilltop huddle within Caulfeild's artillery fort. For the stone house Caulfeild completed for himself in 1623 Pynnar suggests a grandiose keep at the heart of the fort, with compact tall proportions, similar to contemporary English high towers such as Wootton Lodge, Staffs. (*c.* 1603) or Westwood House, Worcs. (as built *c.* 1612). In reality, from surviving records of the building Charlemont was more diminutive, stout, square in plan, rising through three storeys. The walls were roughcast with the storeys defined by strings, the chimneys tall polygonal brick fingers clustered above the corners like turrets. Its outward expression was rather like Rathfarnham, s of Dublin, but the battlemented bays on the corners of each front with cross-mullioned windows were closer to English traditions; much of the architectural character was destroyed when the windows were replaced by big Georgian sashes. A striking element of the building shown by Pynnar is an elaborate and oversized glazed lantern on the roof, which may well have lit stairs at the core of the plan; a later topographical view before the end of the C17 shows a steep gabled roof, which either discounts this arrangement or indicates alterations. We know nothing of the realities of the interior.

Sir Phelim O'Neill chose Charlemont to commence the rising of 1641, surprising the fort on 22 October. Enhancing the existing defences by adding an outer star-shaped enceinte with ravelins, he held it for the rest of the decade until he surrendered it to Cromwellian forces under Sir Charles Coote. In 1661 William Caulfeild, later 1st Viscount, was made Constable and Governor of the Fort for life, but he sold his interests to the Crown three years later. A garrison was maintained here until 1858. In 1859 Charlemont Fort was bought back by the 2nd Earl of Charlemont, who levelled the fortifications to give the buildings a more picturesque, ornamental setting. In July 1920 the fort was burnt by the Irish Republican Army during the Anglo-Irish War and afterwards demolished. It had been photographed, so its appearance is known.

In 1788 the Rev. Daniel Beaufort described Charlemont as a 'poor village, very well looking – very broad having two rows of good trees along the road'. In contrast to its former strategic importance, Charlemont today consists of a disappointing group of buildings with just one recognizably C18 terrace, adjoined by the quaint Eagle Bar. It had in reality been declining since the early C18, when the Caulfeilds crossed the river to Tyrone, built a new house overlooking the fort there and laid out the attractive town of Moy.

GATEHOUSE. In 1665 the gatehouse to the fort was newly roofed with shingles and a new drawbridge made. Two drawbridges in the thick stone walls inside the ramparts are mentioned in 1691; Beaufort in 1788 simply described the fort as a square with four bastions defended by a drawbridge. This, the sole surviving building, is a forgotten classical gem, its pedimented central tower a shadowy curiosity at the end of a rising beech avenue. Two phases are evident, with the central tower finished in Dungannon ashlar independent of the older flanking lean-to side blocks built of rubble with evidence of small brick niches, long since filled, on the inner face; the only obvious defensive element is the gun loops piercing the wall tops. The building is usually attributed to the Surveyor General, *Sir William Robinson*, who repaired the fort for its governor, Lord Conway (writing to him in 1673 'we are now cutting a graft before the ravelin and preparing for a new drawbridge and entrance'), but it seems more probable that the insertion of the central block is a later work, perhaps by *Thomas Burgh*. He was employed here between 1701 and 1719, twice before and twice after Robinson's death in 1712, on the earlier date spending £120 building drawbridges and gates.

The entrance is a plain arch, now filled with a timber door but formerly protected by a drawbridge; in the space below the cornice are the flamboyant Caulfeild arms, presumably reused from a predecessor, and on either side is a gun loop with deep splays. The pediment is filled with a copper clock face and the roof was once topped with a short louvred cupola. Later evidence from official reports of 1760 noted that 'the watchtower over gateway is new roofed and slated'. The elevation is repeated on the opposite side with a sash window in place of the arms. Inside, the workings of the drawbridge remain evident.

CHARLEMONT COTTAGE. A low Late Georgian house built to accommodate the storekeeper when the adjoining fort became an ordnance depot. The plan is a deep double pile formed of two blocks back-to-back, longer to the rear where wings extend to form a U-plan; on the E side raised over a half-basement. The single-storey front is built of limestone ashlar with five bays, the central entrance bay advanced with a squat open pediment, generously filled with a fanlit doorway. The sides and rear are roughcast over rubble.

CHARLEMONT CHURCH (C of I). Derelict. Built in 1831 to one of *William Farrell*'s single-cell designs. A cement-rendered, three-bay lancet hall with clear quarry glazing, the chancel and a forestanding porch all amply trimmed with cutstone. The porch is battlemented with stout polygonal angle buttresses rising to spiky pinnacles, and the same minaret-like form is used to frame the bellcote. The Geometric E window in pale sandstone is later, probably of 1862, when *Welland & Gillespie* added a narrow lean-to to the chancel in rusticated masonry lit by a triple lancet window. Inside, new seating and a heavy wooden gallery were added; Farrell's pierced iron trusses were retained under a new timber-panelled ceiling.

CHARLEMONT RECTORY. 1 km E. A substantial house in red brick, built *c.* 1900. Two storeys with a broad front of three bays and steep pointed gables with crossed timber barge-boards. Narrow paired sashes on the ground floor under flat concrete hoods and tall pointed windows on the first floor, all with plate glass. The glazed semicircular porch is late C20.

ST PETER, COLLEGELANDS. 1 km SW. The name comes from the fact that Trinity College Dublin owned six of the surrounding townlands. A small lancet hall with a short chancel and a C20 porch which bears a plaque (reset here) with the date 1845 and the name of the pastor, the Rev. John Keating. Four bays with walls of roughcast and dressed stone quoins; stuccoed hoods only to the four lancets of the entrance front. The carved stone crosses on the gables are noteworthy. Inside, a plain shoebox; unexpected is the wide chancel arch, framed by a stuccoed hoodmould stopped with big human heads and the soffit decorated with cusped Gothic panels. – STAINED GLASS. In the porch a vesica of St Peter by *James Watson*, Belfast, 1981.

COLLEGE HALL. 1 km SW. A low two-storey block of five bays with single-storey wings slightly set back at either end. It looks Georgian, but a lease of 1857 shows that the property was acquired by the architect *Peter Hughes*, who was covenanted to build 'one good and substantial house' within ten years. Hughes is little known but was probably his own architect, choosing a plain symmetrical design in the Georgian tradition of the improved farmhouse that was promoted in the drawing schools. The modesty of the design is countered only by the symmetrical formality of the façade. The main block has a low hipped roof with red brick end stacks. Walls cement-rendered, with a sandstone plinth and blocked quoins that are repeated in the wings. A platband coincides with the eaves cornice of the wings and forms a continuous sill course to the first-floor windows; above these the wall finishes in a plain frieze and simple moulded eaves course in brick, both now cement-rendered. The windows of the central block have sashes with twelve panes on the ground floor and nine on the first floor, arranged as six panes over three; the wings have twelve-pane sashes. The doorway is unadorned and reaches no higher than the windows. Low outbuildings of rubble and brick enclose a small yard to the rear.

DARTRY LODGE. 2.5 km S. An attractive small early C19 house of two storeys, three bays wide with a small boxy porch in the centre. Cement-rendered, with plate-glass windows. The former entrance at the front of the porch has a stone doorcase with brackets supporting a straight entablature; it now frames a square window. The double-pile plan is expressed externally in the twin gable-ended blocks placed back-to-back.

CLADYMORE AH

5 km SW of Markethill

ST MICHAEL. Decent old-fashioned T-plan church, built in 1834 by the Rev. Michael Dillon P.P. The three-bay façade was refronted in the late C20 with a harsh, machine-finished ashlar frontispiece in the centre between tall round-headed windows. The new work exudes an awkwardness worthy of C19 provincial chapel design, with angle buttresses that are given odd little skittle-like pinnacles, and a crazy stepped gable pierced to house the bell. Ugly timber Y-traceried windows with obscure glazing. Inside, a bright galleried space. The top-lit sanctuary was reformed in the late C20 as a raised platform and reordered with the usual lumpish pieces of polished limestone. – STAINED GLASS and canvas ALTARPIECE in the unmistakable, unfinished style of *Patrick Pye*.

CLADYMORE PRESBYTERIAN CHURCH, CLADY MILLTOWN. 2 km NE. 1835. A plain rendered block of four bays with tall camber-headed windows and porches in the end gables. – THE MANSE to one side looks mid-C19, a neat two-storey block with three bays, hipped roof, and a round-headed fanlit doorway.

KILCLUNEY PARISH CHURCH (C of I). 3 km NE. A small late C18 roughcast hall; reroofed and re-gabled in 1836 and greatly extended in 1864, when a S aisle and porch were added by *Welland & Gillespie*. This results in two discrete parallel halls, both with quarry-glazed cusped lancets that were inserted as part of these works. The aisle is narrower, with steep gables and walls of squared limestone rubble with cutstone dressings. Inside, the nave opens to the S through a three-bay arcade of pointed arches on square piers. The ceilings have exposed trusses – kingposts to the nave and lighter scissor trusses to the aisle. – STAINED GLASS. Three-light E window of 1896 by

William Francis Dixon of *Mayer & Co., Munich*. It is flanked by scripture panels in hybrid arched Gothic frames carved with Romanesque chevrons, and must be the work of the skilful C19 rector, the *Rev. Henry Hutchings*. – MONUMENT. The Rev. L. H. Robinson †1866; a plain crested tablet signed *Jn. Robinson,* York St., Belfast.

THE ABBEY. Adjoining the church, the unprepossessing parish hall conceals an extraordinary C19 interior, moved here in 1995 from the former rectory. A delightful confusion of Romanesque and Flamboyant Gothic detail, designed and built in 1886 as a private chapel by the artistic High Church rector *Henry Hutchings*. Undoubtedly inspired by nearby Gosford Castle, it is a long, low, timbered hall lit by Romanesque triforium windows with chevrons, slender shafts and scalloped capitals. The roof has hammerbeam trusses with arched braces, frothy pierced work in the spandrels, and between them timber panelling framing colourful diocesan arms. The carving is abundant and diminutively scaled, the best of it in the miniature rood screen with crocketed gables and lance-like pinnacles set incongruously before a large Romanesque window.

CLARE AH 0040

A picturesque milling settlement with a handful of small churches at a crossing of the River Cusher, 4 km SW of Tandragee.

CLARE PARISH CHURCH (C of I). 1840 by *William Farrell & Son*. An endearing rural scene: a small Gothic church set picturesquely behind twin lodges in a churchyard lined with tall beech trees. One of William Farrell's single-cell designs, a three-bay hall fronted by a kneelered gable with a heavy bellcote and very slender blind lancets flanking the door, set in a tall recessed arch. Pebbledashed, with granite dressings. The windows have twin cusped lights and clear quarry glazing.

The LODGES, serving as schoolhouse and sexton's lodgings, are single-storey with lofts under hipped roofs, built of rubble with granite and brick dressings. Five bays to the front with twin quarry-glazed casements with hoods, unusually projected in plain brick. Presumably also by the *Farrells*.

CLARE PRESBYTERIAN CHURCH. 1828, remodelled in the late C19. A sizeable four-bay roughcast hall with stuccoed quoins. Tall round-headed windows in moulded frames. Broad gabled front of two bays with windows recessed in big moulded arches, dwarfing the doorway between; above these a plain frieze extends across the gable, ending with scrolled brackets at the eaves.

Beside it, the ORANGE HALL of 1893 is a plain, roughcast Gothic hall of three bays.

HARRYBROOK. A long two-storey stuccoed block with a hipped roof on prominent brackets. Originally a smaller Late Georgian house, enlarged in 1890 for the Harden family by *J. J. Phillips*, resulting in the imperfectly symmetrical front and Late Victorian stucco embellishments. Five bays with tripartite windows with plate glass and elaborate pedimented entablatures on the ground floor. The central bay has a gable over the Harden crest and motto, formed in stucco above the first-floor window; below, a handsome distyle portico over the Ionic fanlit doorway. The early C19 LODGE opposite the entrance is a neat three-bay block with bipartite windows and a hipped roof.

CLARE CASTLE. 1 km NE. A solitary rusticated turret in thin alternating bands of red brick and pebbles rising into crenellations, in a barren field. Too small to accommodate a room, this decorative angle turret remains a difficult and intriguing clue to the C18 house, an early instance of the castle style built on the Irish estate of the Fane family, earls of Westmorland. For much of the C18 Clare Castle was occupied by the Dawson family – in 1776 by Thomas Dawson M.P., described as 'a man of no property'. It was ruined by 1840. Extensive and much altered yards remain. Part of the demesne follows an attractive wooded nature walk alongside the River Cusher.

ST PATRICK, BALLYARGAN. 3 km E. 1807, rebuilt early C20. An honest small crossroads church with impressive open views to the distant expanse of the Mournes. Rendered three-bay hall with pointed windows and heavy offset buttresses. Simple unadorned doorway with splayed sides and segmental head, flanked by lancets with an oculus above; over the door, a tiny niche and a tiny statue of the patron. Set high on the adjoining nave wall, the slate SUNDIAL is a *memento mori* of 1826, made by *Thomas McCreash* for the Rev. Arthur McGurk with the legend:

> Years following years steal something every day
> At last they steal us from ourselves away
> This plainly shows to foolish man
> That his short life is but a span

Plain interior, with a tidy organ loft in a sparing early C20 idiom, set on a platform over a small entrance hall, fronted by an iron balustrade of simple Gothic arches with stairs to the side. No trace of the altarpiece of St Peter recorded here in 1838.

INTRODUCTION

Clones is an attractive market town, set among the drumlins that rise out of the watermeadows of the River Finn and its tributaries. Its steep streets are laid out along the declivities of one of the more prominent of these gentle rises. The topography is reflected in its name, from the Irish *Cluain Eois*, 'the meadow of the

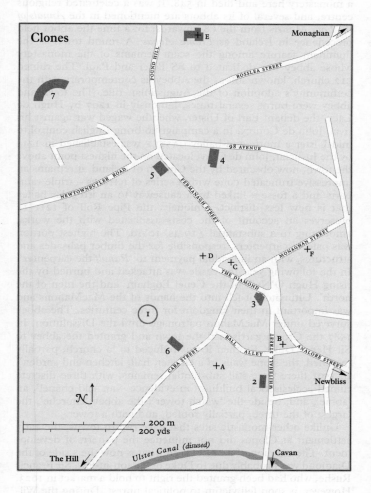

A Round Tower
B The Abbey
C High Cross
D St Tighernach (C of I)
E Church of the Sacred Heart
F Presbyterian church

I Motte and bailey
2 Courthouse
3 Market House (former)
4 County Library
5 Butter Market
6 Masonic Hall
7 G.N.R. Locomotive Shed (former)

height'. Its history and development have been shaped by its peripheral location on the w edge of the county; in the Middle Ages it lay on the edge of the MacMahon kingdom of Oriel, and in the C20 it remains very much a border town of the Republic.

The town owes its origin to the most important religious foundation in Monaghan, associated with Tigernach, who established a monastery here and died in 548. It was a celebrated religious centre, and several of its abbots are mentioned in the *Annals of the Four Masters* from the C8 onwards; for a time the abbot held precedence in Ireland as *Primus Abbas*. A round tower is the dominant feature among the scant remains of the monastery whose abbey was dedicated to SS Peter and Paul. The ruined C12 church, known still as the Abbey, is contemporary with the community's adoption of the Augustinian rule. The town and abbey were burnt several times, famously in 1207 by Hugh de Lacy, the defiant Earl of Ulster, when he waged war against his rival, John de Courcy. In a campaign to bring English control to mid-Ulster a motte-and-bailey CASTLE was established in 1211 by the Justiciar, John de Gray; located on the highest point above the town, now obscured by the Church of Ireland, it remains an impressive truncated cone with a series of terraces – triple ramparts and a fosse – linked by a causeway to an irregular bailey that is now less distinct. Uniquely, the Pipe Roll of 1211–12 preserves an account of the costs associated with the works, amounting to a substantial £19 4s. 10½d. The highest portion was paid to carpenters, responsible for the timber palisades and structures, with an individual payment to '*Ranulf* the carpenter'. In the following year the castle was attacked and burned by the rising Hugh O'Neill of the Cenél Eöghain 'and the men of the north'. Ultimately it fell into the hands of the MacMahons and was important in their kingdom for three centuries. The abbey survived under MacMahon patronage until the Dissolution. In 1587 the Crown garrisoned the town and granted the abbey to Sir Henry Duke. By then it was reduced to 'a church, partially thatched, the stone walls of a cloister, hall, kitchen and garden'. In 1591 there were still substantial remains, with three discrete ruined ecclesiastical buildings in evidence – an 'old chapel', an 'abbie', and, beside the 'watch tower', the abbey 'churche', the largest of the three, partially roofed, and with a tower.

Unlike other monastic sites that gave rise to towns, the early settlement at Clones did not influence the pattern of development. The erection of a CASTLE on what is now the s side of the Diamond was probably due to Duke or his son-in-law, Sir Francis Rushe, who had been granted the right to hold a market in 1623. However, it soon fell victim to political unrest. During the Williamite wars, when the cabins of the town had been 'much destroyed by the townspeople for firing', it was found that the castle was 'full of dung' and in want of 'a great deal of slating, and one of the joists above the dining room floor . . . come from the wall'. It was partly rehabilitated and inhabited by Ensign Lee; the castle was depicted in a view of the town made in 1741, and

Clones, view of the town.
Drawing, 1741

shown partly inhabited, seeming to front a later gable-ended
block that faced into a regular bawn-like enclosure lined on two
sides by lower ranges. Excavations in 2000 at the rear of the
Credit Union building exposed a doorway in a fragment of
boundary wall and probably part of the bawn.

Clones gained a family of constant improvers after Duke's
great-granddaughter, Anne Loftus, married Richard Barrett-
Lennard of Belhus in Essex, son of Lord Dacre. A quarrel
between Richard Barrett-Lennard and his son Dacre forced the
son to spend time in Clones, where he married and became M.P.
for Monaghan. After his father's death in 1696 Dacre Barrett
inherited both Belhus and Clones. In 1755 the family name was
formalized as Barrett-Lennard when they claimed the Dacre title
again. Though the family remained absentees – one agent wrote
admonishingly in 1807 that no proprietor had been in Ireland
since 1744 – they kept a close eye on their estate through a series
of earnest and conscientious agents, who guided them towards
improvements.

By the c18 there was a thriving linen industry, and the modern
town developed around an irregular sloping plateau formed by
two intersecting triangles, known as the Diamond, to which all
the approaches rise steeply. A market house was built in 1745.
According to a contemporary account a number of substantial
new houses had already been built or were planned in the vicinity; the cabins between them and the market house were sched-
uled to 'be tossed when the lease expires, and good two storey
houses built instead of them on a range with the market
house, . . . [to] make that side of the street perfectly uniform'.
Beyond the centre Clones was still in 1801 a town of mostly
thatched houses, but improvements were constantly encouraged.
Sir Thomas Barrett-Lennard's agent Nicholas Ellis in 1840
claimed that 'If I not make Clones a good town it shall not be
my fault.' He succeeded, and the 1840s were to be an important

decade. The town received a workhouse in 1842, and the Ulster Canal arrived as an arc s of the town linking Lough Neagh and Lough Erne. It was never a serious commercial success; the creation of the Dundalk & Enniskillen Railway in 1858 was more influential, and in 1863 the Ulster Railway extended its line from Portadown and Clones became a railway town. The lasting legacy is an exceptionally good housing stock, as rows of good-quality brick and stuccoed houses were built in the closing decades of the C19, such as Fermanagh Terrace and Railway View Terrace on the Newtownbutler Road. Early C20 partition deprived Clones of much of its hinterland, and with that a valuable established economic base. By the end of the C20 the preservation of its architecture was the primary beneficiary of this retarded economic development.

CHURCHES ETC.

17　ROUND TOWER. This solitary tower stands on the boundary of a small oval graveyard enclosure – half in, half out, similar to its counterpart at Kells. The base plinth is visible outside the walls and the tower gently tapers above it to a height of 75 ft (23 m), solidly constructed of snecked rubble with large local boulder stones. The internal diameter at the base is 9 ft (2.7 m). The walls have an internal taper as well, their thickness reducing from 3½ ft (1 m) at the base to 2 ft (0.6 m) at the upper stage, which has disintegrated and is missing its cap. On the E face the stonework is noticeably differentiated, particularly around the entrance, appearing as if hammer-dressed; this is in fact the result of fire damage, giving credence to the annalists' accounts of attack. The entrance is an unembellished trabeated opening, set rather low, less than 7 ft (2 m) from the original ground level. Four similar openings existed at the upper level, only two now intact. Smaller windows set at N, S and E are found in the intervening levels; they could have been intended as look-outs, but equally may have served simply to broadcast the peal. The primitive character of these openings and the absence of any sort of arch indicates an early date for construction, probably C10. Internal excavations in 1856 revealed the remains of several individuals.

　　In the graveyard a short distance to the E is an intriguing
17　SHRINE TOMB, its shape evoking the form of the early oratories of the Celtic Church. Claimed as the tomb of St Tigernach, it is similar to the mortuary or skull houses found in the NW at Cooley in Donegal and Bovevagh in Derry, though it is smaller and differentiated as a sculpted monolith, standing as a single gabled block of hard red sandstone with low sides, just under 6 ft (1.8 m) long and 3 ft (0.9 m) high, heavily weathered and now split by a natural fissure. The gabled ends have lugs at the apexes recalling the splayed finials associated with the saddleback roofs implied by early timber churches and invoked in stone at Kilmalkedar in Kerry. Perhaps erected to

replace a timber predecessor; eroded details in relief along the 'eaves' line suggest the metal clasps or hinges of a wooden casket. The E gable has a recessed panel supporting a relief carving unconvincingly interpreted as a mitred figure. Later, defaced C18 inscriptions on the slopes probably relate to its traditional role as the contested sacred burial place of rival families and associated with unusual burial rites.

THE ABBEY. A curious single-cell church ruin tucked away 18
between Whitehall and Analore streets on a triangular island with graves. Difficult to pin down, though generally accepted as C12, it is a simple quadrangle, greatly disintegrated to the E, with the surviving W gable presented as a truly remarkable two-dimensional ziggurat. The walls are rubble with an impressive outer skin of square ashlar blocks, surviving only partially on the side elevations where there is a noticeable batter. The stone blocks, stacked Lego-like, form a crowstepped gable as a result of lost coping. The doorway has a wide segmental head that extends beyond the jambs, unadorned but well finished in a neat arc of voussoirs tightly locked into the square blocks around it; formed rather like an C18 fanlight, this suggests a later repair to a robbed Romanesque doorway; the worn impost blocks, both carved, one with a clearly discernible canine head, are certainly suggestive of a former elaborate arrangement. A small Romanesque loop with a simple rebated reveal is all that survives of the fenestration; externally formed of just four carved blocks with deep internal splays, it seems C11 or early C12. Externally on the N wall is a small relief carving of a high cross.

HIGH CROSS. A tall decorated cross enclosed by railings on the 15
upper Diamond. It consists of two sandstone pieces on a stepped, undecorated base – the head with a recessed and pierced nimbus, and a collared shaft. Together base and cross extend to 15 ft (4.5 m). The difference in scale between the two carved portions makes for an awkward junction, so that unless there is a portion missing they may come from separate crosses of similar date. The upper portion of the nimbus, damaged in the C19 and repaired, had much decoration, but now because of weathering is worn almost to abstraction. Tentatively dated to the C10 and firmly placed amongst the Ulster group that includes Arboe and Donaghmore in Tyrone, the cross shares with them a similar iconographic programme. The shaft is divided on each face into three panels. The S face is the most legible, reading from the bottom up: Adam and Eve, the Sacrifice of Isaac, Daniel in the Lions' Den; the collar bears illegible decoration with a beaded border; on the lower section of the cross is what appears to be the Entry into Jerusalem; in the cross is another rendering of Daniel in the Lions' Den; in the arms are the Arrest and Pilate washing his hands. The E side continues the New Testament themes, reading from the bottom: the Adoration of the Magi, the Marriage of Cana, the Miracle of the Loaves and Fishes; on the cross, scenes of the Crucifixion. The sides are ornamented with panels of

geometric interlace and raised bosses; figures are depicted on the arms of the cross, one on the W side identified as an angel.

St TIGHERNACH (C of I). Also known as St Tigernach and St Tiarnach. A plain hall-and-tower church with a polygonal spire, this is the best-sited building in the town. Standing on a raised polygonal base to face down the Diamond, it is approached by an impressive flight of steps, which rises pyramid-like to a gateway set high in the buttressed wall. In the gateway wall a stone displays the date 1696, a reference perhaps to the rehabilitation of the old C17 church that occupied this site after it had been vandalized in 1689, when Protestants were forced to flee the town on the accession of James II. It was recorded as a conventional building with nave, transepts and a large battlemented W tower with a low pyramid roof. Although found to be in good repair in 1777, it was entirely replaced in 1823 by *William Farrell*. Given such a prominent site, he seems to have been unwilling to over-dramatize, but he did respond scenically by reversing the arrangement of its predecessor: the tower is positioned at the E end, with a tripartite battlemented projection at the W end that mimics his typical chancel arrangement, comprising a vestibule, flanked by diminutive porches. The tower is a simpler version of his later design for Monaghan, built of ashlar in three stages with simple battlements and stepped angle buttresses, with gentle offsets, and topped by short pinnacles. By contrast the nave is a spartan masonry box of squared limestone. The porches are highly finished in ashlar with angle buttresses and tall battlemented parapets. Farrell's reverse arrangement was completed by *Joseph Welland* in 1858, when the base of the tower was opened to the body of the church as a chancel and given a large traceried memorial window. Welland also added new transepts that bulk out the view, and a small gabled vestry, partially absorbed into the base of the tower and mirrored by another on the opposite side. *Alexander Hardy* was clerk of works. These additions were also built in squared limestone with ashlar trim; *Farrell*'s rich-patterned quarry glazing was reused in the transepts, making them indistinguishable from his work.

The interior is spacious, with a shallow rib-vault and continuous raking galleries around three sides, resting on slender iron columns and reached by a delightful cantilevered spiral stair between the W porches. A wide chamfered chancel arch frames a neat recess filled with a three-light E window with reticulated tracery. – STAINED GLASS. E window: The Ascension, a fine work in pale colours by *Miss Courtney* of *An Túr Gloine*, 1910. – MONUMENTS. A number of good C19 ones in the chancel. Martha Armstrong †1807; a plaque framed by inverted torches with a kneeling figure above, carved in the manner of *Westmacott*. – Sergeant James Graham †1845, hero of Waterloo; a brass plaque. – Cassandra Hand †1868; a tablet with a draped urn.

Tucked into a corner of the Diamond beside the church gates stands the former RECTORY, a simple gable-ended block of two storeys and three bays with plate-glass windows and a handsome Doric doorcase with fluted columns and a segmental sunburst fanlight.

CHURCH OF THE SACRED HEART. A large church with tower and spire on a windswept hill removed from the town's cluster of streets. A late building by *William Hague* – the foundation stone was laid in 1891 – it lacks ambition, appearing uncharacteristically restrained in a by now old-fashioned Puginian E.E. Gothic. The contractor was *P. Nolan*. The plan is the usual cruciform arrangement of nave, aisles, transepts and chancel, with an overpowering square tower set to one side, all clearly expressed externally. There is a pleasing simplicity about the architecture; the surface texture is rich, squared hammer-dressed limestone providing a perfect contrast for the crisp ashlar trim and the sparse Gothic detail. The church was dedicated in 1895; tower and spire were started two years later. Unusually, the three lower stages of the tower are undifferentiated, resulting in expanses of rugged masonry below the belfry level, relieved by a pointed window on the w and s faces. The corners are held by weak offset angle buttresses that terminate in gabled aedicules with blind tracery. The effect is to isolate the belfry stage as an elaborate flourish. It is carried up in ashlar on polygonal corner buttresses with crocketed turrets and crowned by an unaspiring broach spire with lucarnes diminishing too rapidly.

Inside, the church stands out as a rare survivor, perhaps always too spartan to have been interfered with. The nave is lofty and bright with an uncomplicated exposed roof of braced scissor trusses. The arcade has polished columns of Aberdeen granite with high plinths and plain moulded capitals, awkwardly integrated with the pointed arches. Basic lancets light the aisles; paired cusped lancets in the clerestory; large three-light windows in the gables. – FURNISHINGS. The sanctuary keeps its altar rails, rich marble reredos, and altar with a fine relief of the Last Supper. – STAINED GLASS. The E window has bright pictorial glass by *Mayer & Co.*, Munich, 1895. – MONUMENTS. In the N transept, two identical plaques with chalice and crucifix to the Rev. Francis McGennis †1847 and the Rev. James Smith †1868, both by *J. Chapman* of Dublin.

PRESBYTERIAN CHURCH. Monaghan Street. 1858, attributed to *W. J. Barre*. A solid small church with emphatic Gothic detail. Four-bay buttressed nave in squared, hammer-dressed limestone with sandstone trim, and compact Dec windows. The gabled front has bold corner buttresses with pinnacles rising between them, an elaborate belfry-like projection, and a big four-light Dec window with heavy, sharp-edged tracery, deeply recessed like a pastry cutter. Parallel to the church a small gabled porch is slightly set back on one side.

Behind the porch, the SCHOOLHOUSE is a neat block of three bays, added later, with a short link on one side and a lower single-bay addition on the other. The big windows have simple linear tracery.

MANSE. Newbliss Road. Neat late C19 two-storey block with a hipped roof in squared limestone with red brick trim and blocked ashlar quoins. The front has three bays with plate-glass windows and a small rendered porch.

PUBLIC BUILDINGS ETC.

COURTHOUSE. Whitehall Street. In 1840 Nicholas Ellis, the agent to the Barrett-Lennard estate, fought hard with the Grand Jury to locate the sessions house in Clones rather than Newbliss. Having inspected the Courthouse in Cootehill three years before, Ellis forwarded a design to the Commissioners, perhaps to compete with the one which was requested of *Edward Forrest*, the County Surveyor, in the same year. In the end, the building followed the standard plan used extensively throughout the country, which is usually ascribed to *William Caldbeck*, almost identical to the Courthouse at Carrick-macross, which makes it likely that *Forrest*'s version of the design was accepted. Although the builder was the Commissioner of Public Works, the agent persuaded Sir Thomas Barrett-Lennard to invest in cutstone for the front in order to make it 'a building for your grandson's grandson'.

A sombre grey building, with the standard arrangement of a large two-storey block in ashlar of five bays with bracketed eaves cornice, blocking course and hipped roof, flanked by short recessed wings. The stone is sandstone, quarried locally at Carnmore and chosen because it was worked cheaply. The end bays project, with banded rustication at ground level framing a recessed segmental-headed window; between, small rectangular blind panels recessed in the plain surface. Above, the tall windows lighting the court chamber, their elegant sashes defined by slender glazing bars, have straight entablatures and rest on a continuous sill. Entrances and stairs accommodated in the wings, which are partially rusticated with wide pedimented doorcases.

68 MARKET HOUSE (former). 1844 by *William Deane Butler*. An assured classical building with a stately bearing that misses its potential by being semi-detached and placed on an awkward corner of the Diamond. In 1801 there was an 'indifferent market house' on this site, built for Lord Dacre in 1745 by *Stephen Price*; the surviving building accounts indicate that this had a three-bay arcade and campanile, the common type in Ireland. In the 1840s, encouraged by the success of winning the new Courthouse for the town, Ellis, the agent, suggested rebuilding it. He was vindicated, writing to Sir Thomas Barrett-Lennard that 'in beauty it exceeded the plans . . . [it] is the admiration of everyone, so beautiful, so elegant! Wyatt's approbation of the plan is justified by the opinion of all.'

Butler's building is a tall and imposing T-plan block, all in crisp ashlar. The architecture is astylar, with an expressive articulation that is strident and at times eccentric. The

principal front is dominated by a pedimented section of three
bays, deeply projecting beyond the single side bays; much the
same arrangement appears, simplified and without a pediment,
on the side elevation. At the front the pediment is richly embellished, the entablature formed with a modillion cornice which
at eaves level alternates with deep moulded brackets set
between pulvinated panels and a narrow frieze with raised
paterae – details that disappear on the sides. The ground floor
is arcaded, with straightforward moulded arches, graded voussoirs and cumbersome scrolled keystones; the tympana are
screened with scrolled ironwork, each bearing the initials TL
for Thomas Lennard beneath his crest of an Irish wolfhound.
The arches are recessed between lesenes with banded rustication, interrupted by a broad platband and first-floor sill course
that constitutes a pedestal for their resumption as flat strips on
the tall upper storey. The windows of the *piano nobile* rest on
a fluted frieze, forming a blind balustraded apron. The central
bay is emphasized with a tall round-headed window set within
a double arch; on either side the windows are more eccentric,
with lugged segmental heads and straight entablatures. Above
the windows, blind panels give the impression of three storeys,
except in the central bay where a banner displays the date of
erection and supports a shield carved with a scallop shell, the
Hand of Ulster, and a broken bough, all laid over a tasselled
cord and the date 1191. In the pediment, under a baron's
coronet, are the arms of Lord Dacre in Portland stone, taken
from the old Market House and bearing the Barrett-Lennard
motto, 'Pour bien desirer'. The arcade was closed in when the
building became the County Library Headquarters in 1928.
Inside, impressive cast-iron columns with Aeolic capitals; fine
doorcases with lugged architraves. Closed in 2008, its future
is uncertain, with a conservation plan in preparation at the
time of writing.

COUNTY LIBRARY. '98 Avenue. 2006 by *Keith Williams Architects*
of London. Old-fashioned Modernism with standard Corbusian shoebox forms, stacked to three storeys with strip windows,
occasionally with solid placed over void; at its most daring
when the upper floor oversails the pavement. Its backland site
ensures that ambitions for a stagey contrast with the established town character remain unfulfilled. Novel terrazzo facing
makes it fresh-faced.

BUTTER MARKET. Fermanagh Street. 1873. Long U-plan range,
single-storey, in hammer-dressed limestone with a projecting
gabled archway. The Gothic detail is sparse, limited to bargeboards and deep chamfered openings, moulded brick reveals
and quarry glazing. Detached wings flanking the gate screen
present neat gables to the street with a blind pointed arcade,
shields with the monogram of Sir Thomas Barrett-Lennard,
2nd Bt, and ornate bargeboards.

PROTESTANT RECREATION HALL. Cara Street. A charming
and simple Arts and Crafts hall. Designed in 1922 by *W. R.
Potts*, but not commenced for another four years. Constructed

in mass concrete, on a podium with plain buttressed sides. The gabled front has a toy-like quality about it with a geometric innocence in the symmetry of the three bays – big rectilinear windows flanking a squat round-headed door with a gridded fanlight – and the mock half-timbered gable. The best part of the design is the balcony; resting on short pilotis at the corners, it is reached by an impressive straight flight of steps and extends across the bays to support a flat-roofed portico with square Tuscan pillars.

MASONIC HALL. Cara Street. Large early C20 stuccoed hall with a windowless gabled front arranged in two stages. The lower level has strip quoins and a very basic engaged Tuscan portico with square piers over a round-headed doorcase. The upper stage rests on an emphatic ledge-like cornice and has blocked quoins and a false half-timbered Tudor-style gable. Small paired sashes on the side elevation.

ST JOSEPH'S TEMPERANCE HALL. Pound Hill. 1911 by *J. J. McDonnell*. A large T-plan hall, with a single-storey, five-bay range across the front. This is gable-ended with pebbledashed walls and stucco detail. The central bay gently advances as a kneelered gable with a round-headed doorway which has a gridded fanlight and attenuated voussoirs and keystone. Interesting blind Venetian window in each of the two end gables. The builder was *Isaac Copeland* of Belfast.

CASSANDRA HAND CENTRE. Ball Alley. 1858. Picturesque Gothic building, Lilliputian in scale. Built as female schools by Cassandra Hand, the rector's wife, who introduced a successful lacemaking industry to the town. Designed by *Roderick Gray*, County Surveyor for Fermanagh. An L-plan block with a projecting gable at one end, elaborated by an adjoining entrance tower set into the angle and flush with the gable. The walls are in squared limestone with ample dressed sandstone trim, and the windows have quarry glazing. In the gable three tightly grouped lancets are set under a high relieving arch. The tower is an attractive composition, two storeys with a pyramidal roof; on the upper level three ogee lancets with louvres are set in a recessed panel under an unusual frieze of dice-like squares. Internally simple, with exposed scissor trusses and very smart Gothic dado panelling.

FORTVIEW SCHOOL. Newtownbutler Road. 1902 by *Thomas Elliott*. Diminutive Gothic school no doubt inspired by the Cassandra Hand schools, though altogether more forbidding. Essentially cruciform, with walls of rock-faced limestone and punched stone dressings. A square tower adds interest to the front, though it barely softens the grim appearance, tucked into the angle with a steep, sprocketed pyramid roof that contrasts with a smaller gabled porch on the opposite side. On the principal gable two lancets sit under a quatrefoil. The arrangement is elaborated on the sides with four graded lights.

RAILWAY YARD (former). Off Newtownbutler Road. Clones was an important junction on the Great Northern Railway, and in 1860 a station house by *William G. Murray* was built. No trace of it survives, and the site is now dominated by the giant arc of the LOCOMOTIVE SHED. This is an early C20 form of some significance by *F. A. Campion*, chief engineer to the railway company. Built in 1926, it has a curved gabled front with a grid of concrete panels, at the end of a 130-degree arc of shallow concrete vaulting with wide external ribs giving it an appearance like a monstrous earthworm. Further E is a well-preserved ENGINE SHED, *c.* 1860, a long single-storey, five-bay range in coursed limestone rubble with dressed quoins and tall round-headed windows with iron frames.

OTHER BUILDINGS

By far the best buildings may be found on THE DIAMOND, 10 predominately three-storey, and full of presence. Uppermost, adjoining the church wall to the NE, is a terrace of three Arts and Crafts houses by *W. A. Scott*, built in 1905, replacing an impressive group of tall C18 thatched houses. They form an asymmetrical composition with a steeply pitched roof, half-hipped on one side and broken by steep attic gables. The houses are subtly varied, with flush casements, and linked together by a continuous slated canopy over boxy ground-floor bay windows. Two further houses by *Scott* on the lower E side of the Diamond and a terrace on Pound Hill are more conventional; all have the same buttressed brick doorways with segmental heads. On the S side the POST OFFICE, bearing the date of 1903 though drawings for it are dated 1917, is by *G. W. Crowe*, and shows his favoured combination of red brick and stone dressings. It has a two-storey, four-bay façade with a low curvilinear parapet and an expressive, asymmetrical ground floor with rusticated pilasters. On the same side, the former MUNSTER AND LEINSTER BANK, now BARRY, HICKEY & HENDERSON, by *Beckett & Harrington*, 1922, dominates the corner with Cara Street. It is a cubic five-bay block, mildly Italianate, with decorative eaves brackets all made somewhat cumbersome by large plate-glass windows, elaborate stuccoed surrounds and stepped quoins on the upper floors; as a result it sits heavily over the ground floor, which is finished in limestone ashlar with classical detail in an Art Deco style. *Millar & Symes*'s BANK OF IRELAND of 1892 makes a conscious effort to blend with the former Market House which it adjoins. An existing bank was essentially rebuilt to accommodate a larger cash office; the older building had a relatively plain three-storey stuccoed front of five bays with big Georgian windows which the architects dressed up in crisp ashlar with string-courses, raised strip quoins and elaborated eaves with decorative recessed panels, obtained by reducing the windows on the upper storey. The aim was to give emphasis to the first floor as a *piano nobile*, where the windows have segmental pediments on consoles. The end bay is slightly recessed, with a carriage arch, and the four-bay banking hall is arranged symmetrically with segmental-headed openings. Directly opposite, on the N side, the ULSTER BANK is a monumentally plain three-storey, three-bay smooth-rendered block with a basement that turns the corner and descends into lower ranges down Monaghan Street. Once fully Italianate with elaborate stuccoed window surrounds, the exterior was remodelled in the mid C20. The rusticated basement, stylish classical doorcase, and solid eaves cornice, all in sandstone, are survivors of alterations and additions of 1905 by *Lepper & Fennell*. On the E side, the former NORTHERN BANK is an attractive Italianate block that outscales its rivals and successfully squares up to the former Market House. It has a broad stuccoed front of three storeys over a raised basement with a rich cornice, stepped quoins, and tall sashes set in simple moulded frames with horizontal glazing. A bulky classical porch dominates the ground floor and is nicely articulated with recessed arches, moulded architraves, keystone and imposts. The Bank's origin in an older house, confirmed by the rear elevation, accounts for the irregularity of the façade, which appears to be cut short on one side. The adjoining CREDIT UNION, wayward modern classicism deprived of any emphasis, vies for attention with a disruptive roof-line and a showy front of machined Portland stone, unsuccessfully combined with red granite on the ground floor. It makes one yearn for the C18 building it replaced in 2000.

At the lower (N) end of Fermanagh Street, on a corner site, stands the CREIGHTON HOTEL, a substantial three-storey late C19 Italianate block, with a low hipped roof on bracketed eaves. Strong architectural emphasis is given to the fenestration on the two broad stuccoed fronts, joined by a single canted bay on the corner. The windows are all boldly defined, arcaded on the upper floors, with prominent keystones and plate glass.

NEIGHBOURHOOD

CLONBOY and THE HILL. Two identical Late Victorian houses, set in paddocks on adjoining properties along the Belturbet Road, built by Henry Pringle and William Parke respectively, who were related by marriage. A taller variation on Sunnymeade on the other side of the town and probably by the same designer. Each is a substantial, well-finished block of two storeys in squared hammer-dressed limestone and finely tooled trim, with steep hipped roofs, fish-scale slating and large masonry stacks. The front is nicely varied: on one side a two-storey canted bay with a turret roof and on the other two bays set under a wide gable with ornamental bargeboards; between, a pointed doorway under a timber canopied porch. The canted bay is repeated on the side elevations.

SUNNYMEADE. Newbliss Road. A large asymmetrical house built before the turn of the C20 in a faint château style. The walls are highly textured in squared limestone with tooled

string-courses and window dressings. Two principal storeys
and attic. The front has a large three-storey gable at one end
with paired sashes and cross-braced bargeboards; at the opposite end, a canted bay with a sprocketed turret that breaks the
eaves and is repeated on the side elevation; in the centre a large
balustraded portico deeply projecting on square piers. A
similar design was employed at Clonboy and The Hill (*see*
above), presumably by the same hand.

CARRIVETRAGH WINDMILL. 3 km N. A well-preserved tapered
drum of three storeys. Rubble-built with ashlar coping. Interesting twin doorways on the ground floor; small square
windows and a big loft doorway on the first floor. In 1834 it
was described as falling into ruin, having failed first as a spade
mill and afterwards as a corn mill.

BISHOP'S COURT. 1.5 km NE. Late Georgian glebe house. A
plain cubic block, three storeys over a basement, with a sombre
three-bay front, made more so by unforgiving cement render.
Small Late Victorian porch. The basement has been exposed
on the garden front; the result is a rather sheer façade, with
gaping Wyatt windows at ground-floor level accentuating its
gauntness. A lower service range projects into a small yard at
the side.

STONEBRIDGE PRESBYTERIAN CHURCH. 5 km NE. A trim
roughcast hall and porch with a long, low projection behind.
Built for a congregation established here in 1700, though the
present building looks late C19. Nominally Gothic, with just
two widely spaced bays and simple timber tracery.

SCARVY HOUSE. 3 km SSE. A cubic mid-C19 villa. On a modest
scale, not unlike a glebe house, with two storeys over a basement and a three-bay front. The render has been stripped to
reveal tightly coursed rubble walls; against this, plain pilasters
mark the corners and the windows are emphasized by raised
reveals. The front has an assured Tuscan portico hung with
wreaths, reminiscent of the work of the Morrisons or J. B.
Keane, covering a doorcase with a segmental fanlight patterned with circles and long narrow side-lights. The shallow
hipped roof is oddly presented on the front elevation with a
single stack seen in profile, hiding a second stack behind that
reads properly on the three-bay garden front. The arrangement
is explained by the unconventional plan, found in some of
William Farrell's houses (cf. Rathkenny and Kilmore), with
two principal rooms back-to-back and the stairs at the side.
  Very handsome limewashed YARD BUILDINGS, formally
arranged. The principal range has five bays with a central
round-headed opening set in a big recessed archway under a
shallow floating pediment with a small lunette. The archway
leads through to an enclosed court with single-storey stable
ranges on either side. Attractive LODGE of three bays with a
quaint pedimented portico on cast-iron columns.

CLONCURRIN HOUSE. 1.5 km S. A Late Georgian two-storey,
L-plan block with three-bay front. Single-storey porch and
Doric doorcase with eccentric base detail. Given cement

enrichments in the early C20, including window hoods, vermiculated quoins and bracketed eaves. Canted bay to the side.
Inside, elaborate architraves with pulvinated panels and corner
rosettes, similar to Cloncallick. Boxy two-storey gate lodge
with big quoins.

FERNEY HILL. 2.5 km S. Built in 1890 for a Mr M. Maguire, a
town merchant. A substantial stuccoed house of two storeys
and five bays, with a line of barrel-roofed attic dormers giving
it a Frenchified air. The front is quite plain, with low-relief
quoins and plate-glass windows and a handsome tetrastyle
Tuscan portico. Hipped roof with paired eaves brackets; tall
red brick chimneystacks with banding and quoins in yellow
brick. The low ground-floor windows give the house a squat
appearance, which can be explained by original (unsigned)
drawings surviving in the house that show a proposal for a
three-storey block all in banded rustication with the first floor
treated as a *piano nobile*.

CLONCALLICK HOUSE. 3 km SW. A handsome early C19 gentleman's farmhouse with a three-bay front of two storeys and a
half-hipped roof with attics. Simple pleasing proportions and
all nicely roughcast. The windows retain their Georgian sashes,
arranged with six-over-six lights on the ground floor and three
over six on the first floor; the central opening on the first floor
is treated as a Wyatt window. Cute Greek Doric doorcase with
a finely worked frieze. Inside, distinctive architraves with pulvinated panels and corner rosettes like those at Cloncurrin.

ETNA LODGE. 3.5 km NW. An unusual-looking Late Georgian
house. A two-storey, three-bay block in roughcast with a projecting hipped roof, extended slightly on one side to give a
canted bow to one end – probably a later addition. A large
gabled projection to the central entrance bay, generously
glazed on the upper storey to create a well-lit conservatory,
looks early C20.

AGHAFIN HOUSE. 5 km NW. A smart Late Georgian villa, built
in 1836 for a branch of the Madden family of Rosslea and
Hilton Park. Two storeys over a basement, all roughcast, with
a low hipped roof projected slightly on bracketed eaves. The
three-bay front is closely similar to Glynch, a little smaller in
its proportions but with the same setting of the ground-floor
windows in relieving arches with segmental heads, and with a
tripartite window to the centre of the first floor. The porch here
is less sophisticated, projected with a low pediment with
narrow leaded side-lights flanking the door. The plan is
extended rearward by a lower service range with bay windows,
which forms one side of an attractive L-plan yard sunken
behind the house. Inside, straightforward tripartite plan with
stairs on one side of the entrance hall. Simple cornices throughout. In the dining room, a quirky and heavy Doric chimneypiece in black marble; in the drawing room a finer Tuscan
work in white marble with a blindfolded Cupid carved in low
relief on the central tablet.

Charming little GATE LODGE facing the entrance, single-storey to the road with three bays, ostensibly symmetrical but pleasantly wayward with an off-centre chimney and doorway. Small quarry-glazed casements and an elaborately panelled door.

DRUMARD HOUSE. 2.5 km NNW. Attractive, two-storey Late Georgian house in roughcast, with the typical symmetrical front of three bays with an elegant fanlit doorcase.

DRUMARD CHURCH RUINS. 2.5 km NNW. In a field opposite Drumard House. The much reduced and featureless remains of a small single-cell structure (29½ ft by 15 ft, 9 m by 4.6 m), set inside a small oval embanked and tree-lined enclosure. Traditionally the site of the monastery of St Eachaidh.

CLONTIBRET   MN   7020
11 km NW of Castleblayney

Two distinct religious congregations are here, separated along the main road by more than a kilometre. Each has its church and schools with a cluster of modest but interesting buildings nearby. Distances are measured from the C of I church.

ST COLMAN (C of I). A small single-cell church of four bays with an attractive gabled front, set alongside the ruins of the old church. In the medieval period this was Teallachgealla-chain, later Gallagh. The need for a new church was confirmed by Samuel Lewis, who in 1837 found the old church in a very dilapidated state. The foundation stone was laid in 1840 and the new church opened in 1842, but by the following July the roof was found to be dangerous. It reopened in December with the addition of a gallery. The design is by *William Farrell*, and similar to Clare Parish Church. Roughcast, perfectly contrasting with the crisply carved limestone used in the diagonal buttresses and the unusually elongated lancets with hood-moulds. The contrast provides a good deal of the aesthetic appeal of the W front, where three lancets – blind but for the central bay – are arranged around a single-storey ashlar porch with an elegantly detailed miniature gable with kneelers, filled with a shallow recessed arch. Above the W gable a cutstone bellcote with blind pointed niches and a single pinnacle with gables.

Interior beautifully intact, even down to the small stove niches. Well-finished exposed trusses with chamfered members resting on corbels projecting from the cornice; ornate kingposts with curved braces gathered in an octagonal moulded pendant. Neat railed sanctuary with a four-light Perp E window in a recessed frame filled with highly decorative coloured glass. – MONUMENTS. Henry Swanzy †1843; a white marble sarcophagus. – Eliza Jones †1861; a classical tablet with crest and motto. – Henry Swanzy †1742; gravestone embedded in the porch wall.

In the graveyard are the ruins of the OLD CHURCH. Walls of the nave survive to the s, perhaps no earlier than the C17. Evidence for a high-pitched roof is still traceable on the rugged tower over the former w gable, a coarse rubble structure of four stages given a shingled spire in the 1760s which has long since vanished. It survived the razing of the church, apparently because one of the Swanzy family offered the clergyman £1 to retain it! Primitive arched doorway in the N tower wall with crude banded stonework and a big triangular keystone. Beside it, the Swanzy MAUSOLEUM is a plain ashlar box.

Close by, the NATIONAL SCHOOL of 1862 is a simple L-plan block of two storeys, cement-rendered with a three-bay front and a plain Gothic doorway. Between the church and the school, the SEXTON'S HOUSE is a delightful single-storey vernacular cottage of three bays with central windbreak. Lower two-bay addition of equal length to the s. All roughcast.

ST MARY. 1.5 km NW. 1857–62. Large, orderly, and unusually well-considered design, with close affinities to All Saints Doohamlet; the architect is not known. Dedicated in 1859, the tower completed by 1862. Cruciform, handsomely articulated in E.E. with a solid three-stage w tower of limestone rubble with sandstone trim rising squarely through a short gabled narthex. Short chancel also faced in rubble with dressed trim, nave and transepts roughcast with sandstone trim. Each corner of the building is marked by square clasping buttresses topped by octagonal pinnacles with crocketed cones which are abandoned on the E gable. The main door is a recessed pointed sandstone arch in a blocked surround with wide chamfered reveal and hoodmould; the detail is repeated above in a small statue niche. Lancets throughout, arranged as three lights on the transepts and E front. Interior by *F. S. Barff & Co.* of Dublin, and some alterations and additions by *W. A. Scott* in 1911; their contributions have largely been lost in reordering. The space is big and airy; the best feature is the timber-panelled roof with elaborate trusses combining features of the kingpost and queenpost system. The trusses are abandoned over the crossing, where a large irregularly shaped panel is filled with carved radial cusped tracery, perfectly scaled for its height, and appearing almost to float above the altar.

MOYS NATIONAL SCHOOL. 1875. Beside St Mary, a decent schoolhouse to a standard plan. Two classrooms in a six-bay block with hipped roof; entrances in the gabled projections at either end. Blue limestone with pale ashlar quoins and red brick window surrounds.

RECTORY. 0.5 km SE. An impressive T-plan house built in 1742, remodelled in the mid C19, and now much altered. A gable-ended block, three storeys over a basement, originally with five bays on each level; later given a light Gothic mantle when the upper storey was altered to three bays with a hierarchy of Tudor gables, each with a blank shield. Gables mimicked in the c20 single-storey porch which spans the basement area and is flanked by bay windows. The original building can best be seen in the massing, evident on the rear elevation, where the basement lies exposed, revealing the true bulk of the Georgian house.

PRESBYTERIAN CHURCH, LEGNACRIEVE. 2 km NW. 1916 by *Young & Mackenzie*. Plain, rather pedestrian four-bay hall, similar to Braddocks, with the entrance in a large two-storey gabled projection. Roughcast with Roman cement quoin strips and tall round-headed openings in the hall.

PRESBYTERIAN CHURCH, BRADDOCKS. 3 km SW. 1802. Big rectangular hall with gabled projections at either end. Roughcast, with quoins and round-headed openings.

ST MICHAEL, ARDAGHY. 4.5 km NW. The old church here, too 'dangerous for the people to assemble under its decayed and falling roof', was rebuilt in 1877 by *William Hague*. A small rendered Gothic hall with ashlar bellcote; four pointed windows with simple Y-formed mullions. Internally the space has an ascetic coldness, but for Hague's massive kingpost trusses. Completely reordered in 1987 by *Richard Hurley*: the altar was transferred to the W end, and the former entrance porch utilized as an atmospheric sanctuary for the tabernacle. Three-light window to the E, glazed in 1968, with attractively coloured stained glass in the manner of *Richard King*.

CLOVEN EDEN
AH   8050
2.5 km NW of Loughgall

CLOVEN EDEN PRESBYTERIAN CHURCH. A bulky Gothic hall elevated in open countryside. Built in 1791 under the Rev. Moses Hogg to replace an early c18 building of mud and thatch. Rendered, with stuccoed quoins. Five bays with new Y-tracery to the windows that unusually alternate in scale. Refurbished in 2004, when a large porch was added by *Cliff Gordon*. The poet W. R. Rodgers ministered here 1935–46 and lies in the adjoining graveyard.

EDEN VILLA. 1 km E. A modest early c19 house acquired in 1884 as a manse for Cloven Eden Church. Two storeys and three bays with a pretty elliptical-headed doorway with leaded fanlight and side-lights. The walls are roughcast, with unusual fenestration consisting of narrow sashes divided by mullions, those of the lower floor stretching to the ground. The roof is half-hipped with meagre central stacks, all rebuilt in the c20 without the former deep eaves projection to the gables.

EDEN HALL. 1 km E. A plain vernacular farmhouse. Two-storey, gable-ended block in roughcast with three bays and Georgian twelve-pane sashes. A small gabled porch conceals the original entrance and its rectangular geometric fanlight.

SUMMER ISLAND. 1.5 km NW. A large Late Georgian house built before 1833 in an older demesne of venerable oaks. Two storeys on a half-basement with a broad front of five bays with big Georgian sashes. Steps to the entrance where the wide fanlit doorcase has Tuscan columns set *in antis*, a plain entablature, and a wonderful leaded Regency fanlight. Inside, a tripartite, double-pile plan: a central entrance hall flanked by the main rooms and leading through to a spinal corridor and dog-leg stairs beyond. The interiors all have the same early C19 appearance, with restrained plaster cornices. In the drawing room a fine white marble chimneypiece with classical reliefs; the brass insert is signed *Mason*, Clarendon Street.

The main entrance is framed by a delightful pair of Georgian Gothick LODGES, single-storey, roughcast over red brick, with symmetrical three-bay fronts and arched windows with Y-tracery. The front walls are gently bowed, the same shallow curve nicely echoed in the concavity of the back walls.

CLOVERHILL   CN

A crossroads village on the main route between Cavan and Enniskillen, developed in the C19 by the Sandersons beside their C18 demesne of the same name.

ST JOHN (C of I). 1856. A small picturesque church on the village crossroads. A neat Gothic design with a quiet, appealing irregularity more accomplished than the standardized work of *Joseph Welland* and the Ecclesiastical Commissioners, highly finished in squared hammer-dressed limestone with crisp dressings. The designer remains unknown; the contractor was *William Hague Sen.* The plan comprises a rectangular buttressed nave with irregular fenestration, a lower chancel with angle buttresses, and a lean-to vestry to the side. The design is distinguished by a salient entrance tower and spire, set diagonally against the W gable. Some of the windows are cusped lancets with thick hoodmoulds, others have simple tracery with thinner hoods and carved heads to the stops. The tower is square in plan with angle buttresses, changing to an octagon for the ashlar upper stage. The steep spire is decorated with lucarnes and finishes in a weathervane set over an armorial *estoile* of Sanderson. The patron of the church, Mary Anne Sanderson, paid the unnamed architect £62 to design and superintend the building as a memorial to her father, James Sanderson of Cloverhill. Inside, an open kingpost roof with exposed rafters and purlins. Plain chamfered chancel arch. – STAINED GLASS. Three-light E window, bright decorative glass in the manner of *Mayer & Co.* of Munich, 1935.

Across the road, the former TEACHER'S HOUSE is a good example of Victorian estate architecture: a two-storey L-plan block of rubble and red brick, with wide eaves and an off-centre gable.

CLOVERHILL HOUSE. 1758 and 1799–1802. The ruin of a sizeable Late Georgian house by *Francis Johnston*, fronting its mid-Georgian predecessor. The demesne, first established after the lands were granted to Robert Sanderson in 1654, passed on the death of another Robert in 1723 to his nephew, James Sanderson. He, with his wife, Maria Newburgh of Ballyhaise, built a relatively modest two-storey Georgian house, then known as Drumcassidy, distinguished only by a rusticated, fanlit doorway on the S front, now hidden inside a porch within the later kitchen yard. The date 1758 is boldly carved on its keystone. There is little else to confirm the C18 origins of the surviving range, recast as a kitchen wing in 1799 when another James Sanderson employed *Johnston* to enlarge the house greatly to the E. Careful study of signs in the masonry of the N front, now exposed by decay, suggests that Johnston absorbed a greater part of the existing house. The seams visible here suggest that it was a typical gable-ended block with a deep return. The foundation stone of the new house was laid in June 1799; Johnston was paid £22 for his plans, and the work was overseen by *John McEssor*. Johnston's design was for a relatively sedate classical villa, with none of the brio he was then displaying in his designs for Townley Hall in Co. Louth. Cloverhill is the familiar Late Georgian block with a two-storey, three-bay front to the E and a bowed projection to the S, built of rubble and roughcast with a low hipped roof on a wide limestone eaves cornice. The central bays are gently advanced, originally with a lean pedimented Ionic portico, while the ground-floor windows are framed in Johnston's favoured shallow segmental arches. The three-storey N front is more disconcerting, with windows on the top floor breaking through the eaves with pediments – perhaps a later addition, as blocked window openings below would appear to suggest; however, a similar idea is seen in Johnston's treatment of Loughgilly House (Mount Norris).

Varied yards remain, well built in rubble, set amongst the vestiges of a once impressive landscape, including several gate lodges. The main entrance is distinguished by an unadorned TRIUMPHAL ARCH of ashlar between low piers and pedestrian gates. The LODGE, preceding it at an unusual distance, is a large three-bay block with an oversailing hipped roof, three bays to the front with label mouldings and a gabled porch in the centre; spoiled now by the loss of its mullioned quarry-glazed windows and the creation of large windows on the first floor to replace blind panels in the original design. Along the main avenue, brought inside the demesne by the realignment of the public road, is the two-storey RED LODGE, a gingerbread red brick house with timbered oriel dormers and an open porch; enlarged *c.* 1860 from a modest porter's lodge that was probably by *Johnston*, of which the canted front with arched windows is evident on the ground floor. The NORTH

LODGE is a small refined block in squared limestone of *c.* 1840, usually attributed to *Edward Blore*, though *George Sudden* may equally be a contender. Asymmetrical single-storey front with a gabled porch, quarry glazing and bracketed eaves; delicate, flowing bargeboards on the gable-end, with the Sanderson crest and a battlemented bay window below.

PROSPECT HALL. Derelict. A large early C19 roughcast block on a hilltop SE of the village. Two storeys high with a three-bay front, square porch in the centre, and a big hipped roof. Despite its domestic appearance it was a parochial hall.

RAILWAY STATION (former). 1 km E. A small rural station on the Ballyhaise–Belturbet branch of the Great Northern Railway, opened in 1885. The familiar polychromatic GNR design, probably by *W. H. Mills*, with a long front, advanced and gabled at one end, with a wide glazed screen in the centre. Predominantly of red brick with yellow-and-black brick trim.

COOTEHILL   CN

A sizeable market town in north Cavan, situated between the Annaghlee and Dromore rivers. Its development along the old route between Dublin and Clones is traceable today on the serpentine axis of Church Street and Bridge Street. By the time of Sir William Petty's Down Survey of 1654, a castle and houses were already evident here in the townland of Magheranure. The remains of the small parish church established in 1639 are still to be found, elevated above Church Street on the site of an older church.

Cootehill owes its name and its later development to the Coote family, whose founder in Ireland, Sir Charles Coote, acquired

Cootehill, showing All Saints' church (C of I), l., and former R.C. chapel.
Drawing by William Groves, *c.* 1835

lands here in 1605, confiscated from Mulmore O'Reilly for his
part in the Nine Years War, and settled them under the terms of
the Plantation. The name is said to commemorate the marriage
between the 1st Baronet's younger son, Thomas Coote, and
Frances Hill. Colonel Thomas Coote was confirmed in some
17,000 acres in the barony of Tullygarvey after the Restoration,
in 1662, and before 1671 he built a house on Hoop Hill. That
was replaced by his nephew, also Thomas, son of Lord Colooney,
with the Early Georgian house, Bellamont Forest. This later   36
Thomas in 1725 obtained a grant for a weekly market and annual
fair which allowed Cootehill to prosper around its growing linen
industry. Mrs Delany in 1732 found the town like 'a pretty
English Village, well situated and all the land around it cultivated'. With a great many weavers and bleachers centred here
and no fewer than ten bleachyards in the neighbourhood, a visitor
in 1740 could observe that because the 'new town was so tenderly
nursed and cherished in its infancy . . . many of its inhabitants
soon grew rich and brought it to the perfection in which it now
stands'. Because of Coote's particular promotion of the linen
industry, Cootehill was the most prosperous market town in
Cavan or Monaghan throughout the C18. The creation of Market
Street, a wide main street to the NE, and an equally wide approach
from the SE (Station Road), allowed the thriving Late Georgian
town to expand; its scale and formality also reflected well on the
sophisticated ambitions of its promoter, Charles Coote, pomp-
ously immortalized in pink in a famous portrait by Reynolds after
he was created Earl of Bellamont in 1767.

The concentration of growth was controlled by Lord Bellamont, who by his will sought to prohibit further development
along the old axis of Bridge Street and Church Street. In the
early decades of the C19, a market house-cum-town hall (demolished; it stood opposite the Courthouse, on the site presently
occupied by the White Horse Hotel) and a courthouse were
established around the new parish church, scenically placed at
the NE end of Market Street. This remains the main commercial
street, lined for the most part with substantial three-storey buildings, some of red brick but mostly smooth-rendered; of these,
the Bellamont Arms is the best example, with a five-bay front
and carefully proportioned Georgian sashes, each adorned with
a Tudor-style hoodmould.

ALL SAINTS (C of I). The spiky silhouette of the needle spire
and the tall pinnacles of the buttressed tower, held between
battlemented lean-to projections, give this picturesque hall-
and-tower Gothic church of 1819 a deserved prominence. Built
of thin shale rubble with sandstone dressings. Three-bay nave
and gabled chancel with timber windows, Perp in style, with
hoodmoulds and quarry glazing. S transept with sandstone
tracery added in 1861 by *Welland & Gillespie*, with a vestry to
the E, adjoining the chancel. Inside the W door, an octagonal
lobby is flanked by the stair and former vestry. The unspoiled
nave has a satisfying plainness, retaining its flat plaster ceiling
and moulded cornice; at the W end, a raking gallery on slender

clustered shafts with a panelled Gothic frontal. Transept now closed off as a separate space. – FONT. 1901 by *Sir Thomas Manly Deane*. Octagonal, of Caen stone, with four polished shafts and inlaid marble panels. – MONUMENTS. In the chancel: Charles Coote †1842; a plain marble sarcophagus surmounted by an urn, signed *M. & P. Harris*, Great Brunswick Street, Dublin. – In the nave: Brampton Philip Gurdon †1804; an elaborate marble tablet surmounted by a chalice. – Richard Welsh †1845; a simple marble tablet. – The Rev. Philip Brabazon †1845; a Neoclassical tablet with a dove set in the sarcophagus pediment.

ST MICHAEL. A substantial Gothic Revival church, prominently sited on Station Road and replacing a large bellcoted chapel of 1826 located in backlands off Market Street. Begun in 1927, it was designed by *Ralph Byrne* of *W. H. Byrne & Son*. Robust and entirely hard-wearing in its appearance, with highly textured walls of squared limestone and copious smooth dressings. The contractor was *James Wynne* of Dundalk. The plan is straightforward: a tall gabled nave with twin-gabled transepts, buttressed lean-to aisles, a polygonal chancel with side chapels, and a baptistery to the W terminating the S aisle. A battlemented tower, offset on the W gable, rises forcefully over the N aisle with heavy angle buttresses. The interior is tall and well-proportioned, though the nave is rather busy in effect; six-bay arcade with chamfered arches on round shafts of polished granite and spare E.E. capitals, and a heavy hammerbeam roof with iron ties supported on half-colonnettes that rise through the spandrels below. The rib-vaulted chancel is more satisfying, opening through a tall arch supported on clustered shafts with foliated capitals. Twin lancets in the aisles, quatrefoils in the clerestory, twin cusped lights in the chancel, and a large five-light traceried window in the W gable. Sanctuary alterations of 1969 by *W. H. Byrne & Son*; reordered again in 1992, but happily all the Gothic furnishings, altar, reredos and pulpit, remain. – STAINED GLASS. E windows by *F. Mayer* of Munich and London. – MONUMENT. The Rev. Francis Brady †1882 and his successors; a Gothic plaque with polished shafts and crocketed gable signed *Cullen*, Cavan.

PRESBYTERIAN CHURCH. 1877. On Bridge Street, set well back in a small cemetery. A low Gothic hall, possibly to a design by *John Boyd*, in squared limestone with sandstone trim and a wide gabled front with kneelers and buttresses. Replacing a church of 1728 where John Wesley preached in 1778, its date is boldly inscribed on a small gabled porch offset on the main front. Six-bay nave with paired lancets and five graded lights in the gable. Interior plain, with a timber-panelled ceiling and exposed queenposts.

MASONIC HALL (former WESLEYAN CHURCH). Bridge Street. 1868 by *Benjamin Hallam*. A small three-bay lancet hall with an attractive gabled front in squared limestone with rusticated quoins and red brick trim.

Familiar two-storey Victorian MANSE behind.

COURTHOUSE. Market Street. A solid-looking, modestly classical block. Built *c.* 1831 and usually attributed to *William Deane Butler*. Rubble with sandstone dressings. The two-storey main front has three bays with a pedimented frontispiece, a low hipped roof and a corbelled eaves course. The broad central entrance bay is gently advanced, its larger proportions effecting a slightly uncouth appearance. Here on the first floor a large tripartite window framed by consoles and a cornice undermines the prominence of the entrance below; deserving of greater scale, the doorcase is an attractive classical design with a moulded architrave, set between bold consoles that support a raking pediment. On either side, the windows in the end bays are recessed: on the ground floor with square-headed openings (blind on the l. side) set in ashlar under segmental arches with moulded imposts, plainer above with square recesses close to the eaves.

LIBRARY. Bridge Street. 2001 by *Gaffney & Cullivan*. A ponderous pyramid-roofed block with all the usual gracelessness of local authority architecture. On the corner the cement-rendered walls are set back, angled inwards to form a glazed entrance behind giant pilotis. A clock suspended from the ceiling corresponds to the clichéd civic-minded gestures of the 1990s.

ALLIED IRISH BANK (former PROVINCIAL BANK). 1858 by *William G. Murray*. Prominently sited at the top of Market Street, facing the principal approach from the SE. A large Italianate block of two storeys and five bays with an emphatic corbelled eaves cornice and a hipped slate roof. Built of contrasting limestone and biscuit-coloured sandstone, and modestly detailed with a blend of classical and Gothic elements. This is most apparent in the distinctive treatment of the ground-floor windows, which are prominently set in an arcade formed with expanding voussoirs in the C15 Florentine manner; the association is continued in the fenestration, which is here layered: tripartite Victorian sashes overlaid by a central mullion with a Venetian Gothic flavour, consisting of a slender barley-sugar shaft with a foliated capital supporting twin chevroned arches as lower elements of a distinctive rounded tracery. The first floor is given tall windows with plate glass under straight entablatures.

Detached on one side is the stuccoed two-storey MANAGER'S RESIDENCE; also by *Murray*, it is a gable-ended block with a nicely ordered front of five bays with vermiculated quoins, channelled rustication, square bay windows, and a decorated porch projecting from the centre.

Two other banks on Market Street are designed in understated classical styles. The ULSTER BANK, detached and set back from the street, is a gable-ended late C19 stuccoed block with two storeys and four bays. The ground floor is simply rusticated with round-headed windows; bold architraves and quoins to the first-floor windows before a prominent eaves cornice. The BANK OF IRELAND is larger and simpler, adapted

from a three-storey Late Georgian terraced house, when a late
C19 Tuscan shopfront with engaged columns was added to the
ground floor.

RAILWAY STATION (former). 1860 by *William G. Murray* for the
Dundalk & Enniskillen Railway. The contractor was *John
Nolan*. On the edge of the town, off the Shercock Road, abandoned and derelict at the time of writing. A severe Gothic
design, in squared rock-faced limestone with smooth dressings
and twin cusped lights. A compact two-storey block with
steep slate roofs, central brick stacks and gables with kneelers
over the end bays. On the main front, a sweeping slate roof is
set between the gables, descending to a veranda elaborately
supported on timber struts over cast-iron columns with
Gothicized Tower-of-the-Winds capitals; here the passenger
entrance is a pointed doorway set to one side in a heavily
moulded sandstone surround; the porters' entrance is at the
opposite end, set in the side of the gable with an offset
buttress.

NEIGHBOURHOOD

RECTORY, KILLYCRAMPH. 0.5 km E. 1820. A compact block,
two storeys over a basement, in rubble with limestone quoins,
red brick window dressings and a hipped slate roof. Four bays
deep with carefully proportioned fenestration, given taller
twelve-pane sashes on the ground floor. Narrow front of just
two bays with the entrance set to one side, recessed in a large
lean-to porch, now crudely extended to project beyond the
front. The doorcase has a moulded limestone architrave with
a floating cornice above.

CABRAGH HOUSE. 1 km SE. Set atop a prominent drumlin, a
Late Georgian block, two storeys tall, with a steep hipped roof
and central stacks. Perfectly proportioned three-bay front in
roughcast with blocked quoins and twelve-pane sashes. Two
rooms deep, with a three-bay side elevation, and a central
entrance and stair hall combined. Substantial two-storey yard
buildings forming an L-plan behind, of rubble with red brick
dressings.

VERNACULAR HOUSE, LISNASARAN. 1 km SE, just off the
L6082. A rare vernacular farm complex centred on a long
two-storey gable-ended house, extended by a low tin-roofed
shed to one side. The house is built of rubble and whitewashed
with a slate roof. Pleasing front with three widely spaced bays,
each with small Georgian sashes, and an off-centre gabled
windbreak. Inside, some mid-Georgian raised and fielded
joinery survives. The house is set in a small garden, with a
substantial roughcast BARN of two storeys and five bays enclosing the farmyard to the side.

COHAW COURT TOMB. 4 km SE. By the roadside, in rough rocky
ground, remains of a dual court tomb, the best preserved of a
group of Neolithic tombs in the area. Formerly covered by a

cairn; what is clearly discernible now is a long narrow passage divided into five cells, each defined by jambs and sill stones, opening at either end to a pincer-shaped court.

ASHFIELD LODGES. 2.5 km SW. The house of the Clements family has gone, but two lodges survive. The older lodge, on the Redhills Road, is a small, rather heavy Victorian design of *c.* 1882 by *Thomas Drew*, built in squared limestone with rock-faced quoins of red sandstone and further trimmings in red brick. Steeply gabled front, where the tiled roof sweeps down on one side as a catslide to enclose a porch. Here the entrance is formed by a chamfered arch which springs on the corner from a stout sandstone column. A canted bay window to the side displays the flamboyant, exquisitely carved escutcheon of Clements. The same arms appear in limestone on the larger River Lodge, situated off the Ballyhaise Road. Built in an Arts and Crafts manner, either a later work by *Drew* or perhaps by *William M. Mitchell & Sons*, who carried out alterations to the main house in 1931. A two-storey L-plan block of squared limestone, part hung with red clay tiles on the first floor, with vertical half-timbering on the end gables. The main gable projects on brackets over a large mullioned bay window.

Much of the scenic character of the DEMESNE landscape remains, enhanced by the broad water of the River Cootehill. This is crossed near the site of the old house by a low BRIDGE of 1858 with three segmental stone arches with rounded cutwaters and a trellised ironwork parapet; the keystone of the central arch bears the date on the downriver face, and upriver the Clements coat of arms. The nucleus of the old demesne is now represented by a number of quaint Victorian houses of stone and red brick, including the former SCHOOL and teachers' residences, grouped around the picturesque church.

ASHFIELD PARISH CHURCH (C of I). 3 km W, at the edge of the Ashfield demesne, with the former school. Built in 1797 for a perpetual curacy. A three-bay nave with a tall forestanding tower in four stages crowned with diagonal buttresses, battlements, and a polygonal spire. All in rubble with meagre dressings and rusticated quoins to the nave. The church was enlarged with transepts and reroofed in 1861–2 by *Welland & Gillespie*, who also replaced an apsidal chancel with a gabled one, added a lean-to vestry, and introduced E.E. fenestration. The later work is well-integrated, of rubble with smooth sandstone dressings.

Inside, an impressive arch-braced roof with exposed rafters and purlins replaces the Late Georgian ceilings. Three-light E window, Y-tracery in the transepts, and paired lancets to the nave. – STAINED GLASS. Chancel and S transept: bright pictorial glass by *Clayton & Bell*; N transept: rich brooding colours of 1905 in the manner of *Mayer & Co.* – MONUMENTS. The best are in the S transept, including Henry John Clements †1843, a white marble plaque adorned with a draped portrait medallion, by *Thomas Kirk*. – Two gabled stone plaques with polished shafts, to Mary Isabella Clements †1890 and Selina Clements †1892.

CORRANEARY

A rural crossroads between Shercock and Bailieborough, surrounded by small lakes pooled amidst the drumlins. There is no trace now of the castle called Hansborough built here by John Hamilton, who was granted the estate in 1613 – only a small scatter of churches and vernacular buildings.

CORRANEARY PRESBYTERIAN CHURCH. Beside the crossroads, a small Victorian gable-ended hall of four bays. Plainly rendered, with lancets.

ST PATRICK, MAUDABAWN. 4.25 km N. An ambitious Gothic church on a pleasant riparian site, built in 1915 by *J. McGennis*, replacing a building of 1825. An aisled nave with a busy W gable bearing a tall bellcote. On either side, the aisles terminate in heavily buttressed porches; at the E they end in smaller gabled side chapels. Pebbledashed walls with copious pre-cast dressings of concrete, novel for the time and used to good effect with quoins, kneelers, prominent eaves corbels and paired lancets under shared hoodmoulds. Inside, bright and impressive with a timber wagon roof. The nave of five bays opens into the aisles through a pointed arcade on round limestone piers. – PAINTING. 'The Entombment', in a competent Baroque style, donated in 1992 by the Mercy Sisters, Dromore.

KNOCKNALOSSET. 1.75 km NE. An endearing two-storey farmhouse in roughcast with a hipped roof. Something of a split personality. The N front, set in a narrow yard facing a long lofted barn, is simple, with four bays and a small gabled porch on the ground floor; three bays above. Here the windows are all sill-less, mostly with miniature Georgian sashes. A contrast with the more formal S front, which was refenestrated in the Late Georgian period: also of three bays, but with enlarged openings, with tripartite sash windows on sandstone sills. Entrance in an off-centre gabled windbreak. The authentic limewashed interior is a very rare survivor, with low-ceilinged rooms and good C19 panelled doors and shutters. Interesting plan, with five rooms on the ground floor around a long hall with narrow stairs placed across the kitchen at the centre; here a generous arch over the hearth and, piercing the stair wall, the obligatory squint as a window on passing life. Georgian maps show the existence of a house here before 1775, when the lands formed part of the Greville estates.

KNOCKBRIDE OLD CHURCH. 1.25 km SE. On a hillock beside Corraneary Lake, an ivied ruin, possibly pre-Reformation, abandoned in 1825. A single cell built of rubble with simple rectangular openings. A twin-light late medieval window was evident over the W door in 1948.

KNOCKBRIDE EAST PARISH CHURCH (C of I). 1.25 km SE.
1825 and 1870. A large rural church close to the old church
site. The standard First Fruits hall-and-tower design, varied
with a short chancel and a big S aisle. Rubble with sandstone
dressings, hooded Y-tracery and quarry glazing. The tower has
three stages with ashlar lesene strips to the upper stages before
pinnacles and stepped battlements. Greatly enlarged in 1870
by *Welland & Gillespie*, with a twin-gabled N transept with
simple plate tracery and an adjoining lean-to vestry to the E.
Inside, plain open timber ceilings. Box pews in the nave and a
raking gallery with a panelled frontal supported on two impossibly slender iron shafts, modelled as attenuated lotus leaves
and ending with a scrolled flourish. – MONUMENTS. Rebecca
Hinds †1836; a large pedimented tablet bearing a Neoclassical
urn. – Isabella †1855 and Neason Adams †1859; a marble
sarcophagus, by *Manderson* of Dublin. – The Rev. Henry Hugh
O'Neill †1872; a plain tablet. – Charles Stuart Adams †1876;
a marble scroll.

To the E, behind the graveyard wall, a modest farmstead with
a delightful VERNACULAR HOUSE. A long, low block, two
storeys tall and with a formal five-bay front facing the church.
Small windows with plate glass, set to a pleasing rhythm and
embellished in the early C20 with primitive Gibbsian surrounds of stucco fancifully decorated with shellwork. Round
the back a more irregular, purer vernacular front with a small
off-centre gabled porch and quarry glazing. In the wall above
the porch, an exposed fieldstone is elegantly inscribed between
a small Maltese cross and a horizontal frond with 'AD 1833
– Jas McBree'.

ST BRIGID. 2 km SE. 1826. A bulky lancet hall of three bays.
Roughcast with blocked quoins and wide unadorned window
surrounds in dressed stone. Belfry tower offset on the W gable
added in 1962, and looking it: tall, thin and angular with an
open belfry and a low pyramid roof. Inside, an open kingpost
roof. Reordered and repewed 1975. Dull.

DERNAKESH (C of I). 3.5 km NW. 1834. Built as a chapel of ease
to *William Farrell*'s standard single-cell design, closely comparable with Munterconnaught (Virginia). A perfectly preserved
small rendered hall with stone dressings of three bays, gable-
fronted with a pinnacled bellcote and a battlemented porch;
all with square corner buttresses, rising into octagons to
support pinnacles. Short chancel with a tiny lean-to vestry on
one side. Windows quarry-glazed with lithesome tracery.
Interior austerely plain, retaining box pews, cast-iron roof
trusses, and a central potbelly stove.

CORVALLEY MN 7000

A rural crossroads 8.5 km NW of Carrickmacross on the road to
Shercock. Two Protestant congregations were encouraged here

by the Shirley family, who provided lands and endowed the church livings.

CORVALLEY EPISCOPALIAN CHURCH AND SCHOOL. 1839. A pleasing little group sited on a bend in the road. The CHURCH, possibly by *George Sudden*, is a straightforward three-bay Tudor hall, with single-storey porches on each gable, front and rear. Smooth rendered walls with moulded eaves cornice. Big square-headed windows with ashlar surrounds and deep hoods carried on heart-shaped stops – all rather uncouth, especially since the poor replacement of the original sashes. Pyramidal gable finials like those on Lough Fea. The SCHOOLHOUSE is a pleasing contemporary companion with rubble walls and ashlar trim. U-shaped plan formed by projecting Tudor gables representing the classrooms on either side of the central residential range. Good ashlar chimneystacks.

ST PATRICK, ARDRAGH (C of I). 1866–8 by *William Slater*. A perfect small structure, solid and well built. Conceived by Evelyn Philip Shirley of Lough Fea, who was the anonymous author of several tracts concerned with the crisis facing the Anglican Church in Ireland, and intended as a mortuary chapel. In a style that the patron described as 'early Irish', it is picturesquely sited on an eminence in a grove of beech trees. Shirley laid the foundation stone in November 1865 and work began the following May; two years later, in March, the roof of the apse was finished, the chimney was almost built, most of the cutstone for the bellcote prepared, and setting the gable cross only depended on the weather. St Patrick's was consecrated on 13 October 1868. It is an exquisitely crafted building, displaying a use of local materials that would have cheered Pugin greatly. The form is simple. A short four-bay gabled hall with a bellcote over the W front and a delightful polygonal apse to the E with an ashlar roof, beautifully formed like a miniature baptistery. The nave with four drop-arched lancets is framed by offset buttresses, in line with the gables, and buttresses continue around the apse between the bays. The stonework throughout is of exceptional quality, with small squared blocks of rock-faced limestone, quarried locally at Carrickalim, contrasted with the pink hues of sandstone from Lough Fea demesne. The latter was carved into sloping ashlar blocks to roof the apse and the small lean-to porch on the W front, and decoratively to provide the corbels of the eaves course. A curiosity is the treatment of the W gable, with a pronounced round-headed arch reflecting an optimistic provision by the patron for the future enlargement of the nave if required – in effect to become a chancel arch. Within this is a round window with plate tracery of the plainest possible kind: four circles punched through to form the shape of a cross with smaller circles in between. A tall chimneystack projects above the eaves in the NW corner of the nave, an elegant stone cylinder with moulded bands.

The interior is simple, given a monastic air by the arch-braced roof of the nave, carried on small moulded corbels, with pargeting between the rafters – an uncomplicated and expressive structure contrasting with the solid pink blocks of sandstone roofing the apse. The windows and doors set in plain rendered walls are forcefully articulated with alternate blocks of pink and buff-coloured sandstone. Alabaster from a quarry on the Shirley estate was extensively used. In March 1868 blue and red alabaster was being cut to line the apse – since sacrificed for dry-lining. The chancel arch has polished alabaster shafts supported on capitals of Lough Fea stone.

FURNISHINGS. *Slater*'s designs for the furniture survive. The sculptural works were executed by *Sibthorpe* of Dublin. These include a READING DESK, a solid rectangular block of blue alabaster with roll-moulded corner chamfers set on a moulded Caen stone base. Top also of Caen stone. Two face panels of shamrock diaper-work are divided by an engaged alabaster shaft with stiff-leaf capital. – Octagonal FONT of Caen stone with alabaster inlay and shafts of polished Connemara marble. – The chancel floor is covered with *Minton* TILES displaying impressive Shirley quarterings. – The BELL comes from the old church of Magheross (Carrickmacross), presented by the Rev. Dr T. R. Robinson. – STAINED GLASS. All by *Clayton & Bell*. s and N sides patterned with roses, acorns and shamrocks. In the three E windows the True Vine, the Good Shepherd and the Light of the World. The w window depicts the life of St Patrick: his call, his consecration, his preaching to the Irish chiefs, and foundation of the church of Armagh.

MANSE. 0.5 km w of the church, also built on ground granted by the Shirley family. 1872 by *A. T. Jackson* of Belfast. A plain two-storey gable-ended house of three bays with a narrow sharply gabled breakfront in the centre; bay windows in the side elevations. A neat stable and coach house to the rear. Attractive cast-iron entrance gates.

ST JOHN THE EVANGELIST, CORCREAGH. 1.5 km SW. 1861. A ghostly Gothic chapel hemmed in by a small late C19 schoolhouse on one side and a two-storey house on the other. Trim and handsome four-bay hall lit by narrow lancets with simple hoodmoulds. Roughcast, painted brilliant white. Gabled w front neatly defined with clasping buttresses; buttresses repeated in the raised surround framing a pair of Dec windows above a nicely articulated flat-roofed porch with diagonal buttresses. Porch lit by a pair of sweet Perp windows with Art Nouveau-style glazing. Plain interior with a small chancel. Extensively reordered in the late C20, when the ceiling was lowered. Fine timber w gallery where simple Gothic detail remains. – STAINED GLASS. E window depicting St John the Evangelist and the Christians by *Richard King*, 1954.

ST MICHAEL, CORDUFF. 2 km NE. Of *c.* 1900. A severe church in rock-faced limestone with a long and narrow five-bay nave, wide aisles, and a single transept to the s. Uncomfortable in appearance because of its awkward situation in a corner of the cemetery. The tightness of the nave is at first apparent in the steep slate roof, but fully revealed in the hard-to-reach w front.

Here the tall bellcote rises from the upper third of the gable, giving it a gangling appearance that is accentuated by its arrangement in three stages with a wide pointed doorway, long paired lancets, and a round multifoiled window above these. The contrast between the rock-faced limestone and the ashlar sandstone trim expresses these details attractively, but unfortunately was not continued on the side elevations. Interior largely uninspiring. Five-bay arcade with deep moulded arches carried on cylindrical piers with polygonal capitals. Timber organ gallery to the w. Plain but interesting polygonal wagon roof. – STAINED GLASS. Three-light E window by *Ward & Partner*, Belfast, 1918; s transept window by *Harry Clarke Studios*, 1936; s aisle, Baptism of Christ by *Richard King*, 1954.

The PAROCHIAL HOUSE to the w is contemporary. A stout three-bay, two-storey house with nicely considered detail evident in the moulded stone sills and the attractive trefoil-headed doorway. Roughcast with a hipped roof on corbelled eaves.

0050   CRAIGAVON   AH

A failed metropolis, resulting from 1960s policies in social engineering. Craigavon is today a notional place without any clear definition; in physical terms it is no more than an administrative reality, with a borough council that administers a geographically extensive area reaching from the edge of the w drumlin belt to the lowlands by the s waters of Lough Neagh and E across the Bann to Co. Down.

Named after James Craig, Northern Ireland's first Prime Minister, Craigavon was a politically motivated social initiative to relieve Belfast, devised in 1963 by *Professor Sir Robert Matthew*, former Chief Architect of London County Council, on a grand scale with a master plan for a new, modern environment based on integrated planning concepts. By 1966 over 6,000 acres, or 26 sq. km, were designated around Portadown and Lurgan for the new linear city that would absorb the older towns. In the language of the period, a chain of sectors was designated within the 10-mile (16-km) corridor for housing, industry, recreation and education, all based around a tangled road network with outer motorways cut through the boggy terrain to the N, opening up an otherwise remote and isolated hinterland to the wider region. Much of the picturesque pastoral landscapes to the NE of Portadown was swallowed up by a confusion of dead-end housing estates and unappealing industrial estates; despite provision for public transport, the only community foci were provided in widely dispersed services and amenities so lacking in human scale or intimacy as to generate car-dependent populations.

The immediacy of its impact was captured at the time by the historian D. R. M. Weatherup:

The character of country and town has been steadily altered by man's increasing mastery of his environment and the machinery of modern engineering have [*sic*] enabled the natural limitations of the area to be largely set aside. No one returning to Craigavon after ten years' absence will find it any more recognizable than an eighteenth-century traveller would have done after an absence of fifty years – such is progress.

However, the science of social engineering failed to tame human nature, and so in a sense this grand scheme was doomed. Progress was slowed once the project was offered to the public, and ultimately the numbers failed to materialize: ambitiously forecast at 120,000 by 1981, in 2001 the population of Craigavon urban area stood at less than half that. In a place where every convenience was surrendered to the supremacy of the automobile, it could never become an attractive human environment. In any case its future was sealed by worsening economic circumstances and the political instability of the 1970s. The sense of failure is particularly evident today in abandoned housing estates in the central area of Brownlow.

Once the impetus of the original grand vision was lost, and lacking any cohesion from the start, what is left looks like almost any other speculatively driven suburban sprawl between two established urban centres. The cohesiveness of the old towns remains strong, but the impact of continued scattergun planning is all too evident in their environs.

SEAGOE OLD CHURCH. Seagoe Road. In a large, well-stocked cemetery. The fragmentary rubble walls of a rectangular church destroyed in 1641, rebuilt by Valentine Blacker in 1662; in 1687 the vestry resolved that '20 oakes be fallen in lands at kilvergan for shingles . . . the old ones being much decayed through long continuance'. Small additions were made in the early C18, but eventually the building was abandoned in 1816.

ST GOBHAN, SEAGOE PARISH CHURCH (C of I). Seagoe Road. 1814 and 1890. The name of the architect lies in a glass bottle under the foundations, but we may guess *John Bowden* for this standard First Fruits hall and tower, set squarely with extravagant Gothic entrance piers. Built for the Rev. Stewart Blacker and his curate, Richard Olpherts, whose initials are found on a plaque reset on the tower. In coursed blackstone rubble with pale sandstone trim. The tower has three stages with battlements and pinnacles; above the entrance, a heraldic plaque with crossed keys and a bible under a bishop's mitre and oak fronds. Enlarged in 1890 by *Sir Thomas Drew*, who added the s aisle, a new porch to the N, and a new chancel. Drew's work is more vigorous, with rock-faced blackstone masonry, red Dumfries sandstone dressings, offset buttresses, and Perp tracery. The nave was also reroofed and refenestrated with red sandstone tracery. The builders were the *Collen Bros*. Half the costs were borne by Baroness von Stieglitz, who laid the foundation stone of the chancel, dedicated to the memory of her brother, Stewart Blacker, D.L., of Carrickblacker.

Inside, the impressive hammerbeam roof is a surprise, the beam ends handsomely carved with angels. Acknowledging that the design was more elaborate than that of other churches in the diocese, *Drew* produced a far-fetched explanation: because of 'the difficulties of proportions' in the nave, 'a treatment in the manner of 15th-century architecture' was best suited to 'lower pitched roofs and wider spans'. If, cynically, he was chasing a fat fee through expense he at least advocated using pitch pine, because 'left untouched after the carpenter's tools, without varnishing' it would assume 'an appearance as that of old oak'. Rich three-bay S arcade in Bath stone with compound piers and elided stiff-leaf capitals. Similar detail on the chancel arch. – Timber REREDOS profusely carved with Perp designs. – STAINED GLASS. Mostly dark Late Victorian pictorial glass with some smaller, mediocre C20 examples; in the five-light E window the Ascension is an impressive work, *c.* 1881. – MONUMENTS. Numerous, the earliest transferred from the old church: the Rev. Richard Buckley †1796, a handsome oval plaque with swags and garlands, and the Rev. George Blacker †1810, a decorated Tudor arch in white marble. – The best of the rest: Amelia Saurin †1838; a draped urn over a plain tablet. – Eliza Blacker †1846; a hooded square quatrefoil. – Lieutenant-Colonel William Blacker †1855; a plain white heraldic tablet, signed *Jn. Robinson*, Belfast. – The Rev. James Saurin †1879; a brass plaque in a hooded frame of Connemara marble, signed *J. Robinson & Son*, Belfast.

Across the road, the former SEAGOE PAROCHIAL SCHOOLS of 1859. A well-built Victorian schoolhouse in blackstone rubble with sandstone and red brick trim. A nice asymmetrical design to a T-plan; a steep gabled projection on one side with a gaunt bellcote, flanked by differentiated porches. All now rather imposed upon by a nasty pedestrian road bridge, which obscures a plaque on the gable recording the erection of the schools by public subscription under the rector, James Saurin.

ST PATRICK. Derrymacash Road. Built in 1829 as a four-bay lancet hall in snecked blackstone rubble with pale sandstone and red brick trim; given a rather staid rubble tower *c.* 1970 with large Tudor-arched openings, tied to the gable by a narrow glazed link. Inside, altered 1923–6 by *James Patrick Neary*, whose works appear to have included shortening the nave by bringing the sanctuary forward to create a sacristy behind, an undertaking that involved the transfer of the elaborate *opus sectile* decoration of 1913–15 that lines the sanctuary from floor to ceiling. – Imposing HIGH ALTAR by *Antonio Caniparoli*, *c.* 1935, Carrara marble with a tall spired Gothic tabernacle. – STAINED GLASS. An uneven mixture of C19, C20 and C21 works.

BAPTIST CHURCH. Killycomain Road. A conventional but tressed hall, built *c.* 1950 in red brick with lancets and three graded lights in the main gable. Twin entrances in a long flat-roofed block across the front.

PORTADOWN COLLEGE. Killycomain Road. 1972–6 by *Shanks,
Leighton, Kennedy & Fitzgerald*. There is little aesthetic appeal
here, but much to impress in the monumentality of the design.
Spread over a sloping site, a massive block in a Brutalist style
looms above a lower horizontal range in tiers. These essentially
comprise the two key blocks in a larger institutional complex.
Modelled with all the hard-edged sculptural qualities of reinforced mass concrete, exploited in protruding angular volumes
prominently textured from the timber shuttering with bands
of alternating patterns. The TECHNICAL COLLEGE element
towers over a basement podium with massive, over-emphasized
corner pylons on the main front. The portal is a broad recess
with a balconied floor above, over which the glazed upper
floors step back in tiers of unequal height, giving an impression
of movement that has a mechanical quality. Throughout there
is tension in the relationship between the impregnable controlling masses of the structure and the expansive glazed surfaces,
as where the deeply undercut angles cast dark shadows over
the receding square bays of the lower storeys. The sides are less
weighty and less bold: here the bulk of the upper walls is cantilevered over an impressive orderly loggia, with slender square
piers rising through two storeys, each tied to the main structure
by a short concrete link in the middle. The theme comes from
the firm's earlier design of 1968 for Victoria College, Belfast.

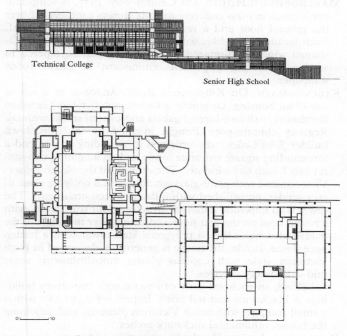

Craigavon, Portadown Technical College.
Elevation and plan

On the longer side elevations, canted brick bays project between the piers at ground level.

Extending away from the front is the lower range now associated with CRAIGAVON SENIOR HIGH SCHOOL. Rather like a stadium building, more balanced and more humane than its towering neighbour, it has a symmetrical front, extensively glazed, with four receding tiers, the middle tiers facing pavements under a deeper oversailing upper tier. The overall effect is not so macho now: the *béton brut* surfaces of the main block have been tamed by a pastel paint scheme, breaking up the cohesion of the group, and as ridiculous as a wrestler attired for the ballet.

CRAIGAVON AREA HOSPITAL. Lisanisky Lane, off Lurgan Road. 1973. Undistinguished architecture on a colossal scale, in varied rectangular blocks of up to five storeys with long horizontal fronts in bands of red brick and strip glazing, broken vertically by tall metal-clad towers.

COURTHOUSE. Off Central Way. An uninviting low rectangular late C20 block of dark brown brick. Two large square towers, marginally varied in height, rise tentatively from the centre like the pavilions of a Buddhist temple, both with pyramidal roofs glazed at the apex; smaller subsidiary projections on the entrance front. The unappealing architecture of entrenchment.

MARLBOROUGH HOUSE. Off Central Way. 1977. A sculptural cubic block in mass concrete with six storeys cantilevered over the ground floor and a recessed service storey on the roof. Each façade is grid-like, with eighteen bays consisting of pill-shaped windows displaced in protruding panels, tapered in section, achieving a pattern reminiscent of garish 1960s wallpaper.

KILLYCOMAIN. Off Killycomain Road. An oasis in a sea of suburban housing. Originally a two-storey, five-bay Georgian farmhouse with half-hipped gables and central stacks with tall Regency chimneypots. Bought in 1880 by the Portadown builder *John Collen*, who enlarged it by adding at one end a forestanding square entrance tower and an adjoining two-storey block with bay windows. The exterior of the old house was Victorianized with plate-glass windows and a unifying cloak of grey render, embellished with inflated stucco ornaments. The tower is an imposing Italianate structure, four storeys tall, with a round oriel on the first floor and, rising over the angle of the balustraded belvedere, a polygonal stair-tower with a leaden ogee dome. Inside, the house is generously decorated in High Victorian style with copious plaster embellishment; some mid-C18 joinery survives.

Behind, an enclosed early C19 YARD with two-storey buildings in blackstone and red brick. Impressive GARDENS within a small compass with much Victorian planting, and, adjoining the house, ornamental rockwork arches.

BEAUMONT. Lurgan Road. An attractive early C20 Arts and Crafts-inspired suburban villa, with walls of smooth plaster trimmed with red brick and half-timbered gables. Irregular plan with deep projections, bay windows, and steep dormered roofs with tall red brick stacks.

NEIGHBOURHOOD

METHODIST CHURCH. Bluestone Road. A bulky, late C19 hall with a two-storey gabled entrance projection. Cement-rendered with three bays to the nave and round-headed windows with ordinary stained glass, the result of alterations in 1910.

MANSE. Bluestone Road. An attractive Late Victorian block, of two storeys and three bays, with gabled ends, and a lower roughcast range to one side which looks earlier. The main front has pebbledashed walls with stuccoed quoins and architraves, and overhanging eaves, exposed rafter toes and carved barge-boards. The windows are camber-headed, with plate glass; the doorcase has a webbed fanlight under a bracketed cornice.

BILBROOK COTTAGE. Bluestone Road. A comfortable vernacular house, long and low, with a roof of reed thatch. Seven bays with Victorian sashes, enlarged at one end in the mid C19 by a lofted annexe of rubble and red brick with a slate roof.

ST JOHN, MOYRAVERTY PARISH CHURCH. Bluestone Road. Pleasing single-cell church of 1869, fronted by a low school-house of 1894 which looks earlier. Three bays with walls of coursed blackstone and red brick trim rebated around the windows, which have segmental heads and sashes with marginal glazing. Small porch of 2006. Inside, plain with exposed kingposts, stained glass, sanctuary mosaics, and a decent Gothic reredos.

BALLINACORR METHODIST CHURCH. Carbet Road, off Charlestown Road. 1845. Small three-bay hall, now with fluted stucco pilasters on the corners and pebbledashed gable and porch, the result of mid-C20 alterations.

ST MATTHIAS, KNOCKNAMUCKLEY (C of I). Bleary Road. 1852 by *Joseph Welland*, with additions of 1859 by *William T. Fullerton*. A modest lancet hall of four bays with bellcote, porch and vestry in coursed rubble with sandstone dressings. Chancel of 1911 by *W. J. Fennell* with three-light E window and but-tressed N projection. – PULPIT by *Young & Mackenzie*, 1872.

Across the road the PAROCHIAL HALL of 1897 is a lively Gothic building of five bays with a central gabled projection; walls of boulder-faced blackstone trimmed with yellow brick. Distinctive iron windows with multiple panes and decorative intersections to the glazing bars.

FAIRVIEW HOUSE. Tannaghmore Gardens, off Ballynamony Road. A long two-storey Late Georgian farmhouse, originally of five bays and subsequently enlarged by two bays. Roughcast with gabled ends, blocked quoins and twelve-pane sashes, slightly taller on the ground floor. The doorway sits in a heavy raised surround with a webbed fanlight. In the small yard to the side, the former coach house of rubble and red brick now houses a small MUSEUM. An extensive public garden was developed in the grounds beside two large artificial lakes formed in 1969.

CROSSDONEY   CN

A straggling street village established outside the walls of Lismore demesne.

LISMORE CASTLE. Perhaps the most lamentable architectural loss in South Ulster. The demolition of the imposing three-storey central block, designed with a spare Palladian eloquence evocative of Sir John Vanbrugh, leaves a tragic void between the imperfect symmetry of the surviving wings.

Lismore was built by Thomas Nesbitt of Brenter Donegal, who came to Cavan on his marriage in 1713 to Jane Cosby, daughter of Arnold Cosby, whose family, a scion of the Cosbys of Stradbally, had settled here in the C16. The date probably lies somewhere between 1722, when Arnold Cosby died, and 1737. In that year Nesbitt sold some of his estates to his brother Albert, a wealthy London-based merchant, who perhaps significantly for Lismore possessed a marriage connection to the Duke of Newcastle that may have pulled the Nesbitts into the sphere of one of Vanbrugh's principal patrons.

After the death of Alexander Nesbitt in 1886 Lismore went into decline, and was well on its way to ruin before the end of the C19. The central block was eventually demolished in 1952. Had it survived, it would have been undisputedly the best Georgian house in the region. The arrangement of the seven-bay block flanked by a lower, square, overlapping tower owed a great deal to Vanbrugh's orderly receding plans; similar

Crossdoney, Lismore Castle, elevation.
Drawing by K. Mulligan, 2012

towers projected as wings to hold the central block are found in his designs for The Vine at Sevenoaks in Kent and his earliest design for Claremont, Surrey. The spare elevations, from the restraint of the classical outline of the pedimented breakfront to the concentration of Venetian windows in the centre, and the fondness for round-headed windows with bold impost blocks and keystones, all evoke Vanbrugh, and the connection of ideas is sufficient to draw in his Irish kinsman *Edward Lovett Pearce* as the probable designer. Nesbitt and Pearce were elected to the Irish Parliament at the same time; and the prominent use of red brick trim in the surviving wings echoes Pearce's instruction for the agent's house at Loughgall to be 'built of stone with brick arches to the windows'.

Along with the wings, only one of the towers still stands today, somewhat forlornly, beside the yawning space where the house stood; across the space is the severed quadrant wall which linked the N wing to the missing tower. The surviving tower has two storeys, the ground floor set on a plinth, so that it is treated, like the house, as an exposed basement, in effect a Palladian rustic with a *piano nobile* above. The walls are built of rubble with sandstone dressings. Its present unhappy appearance is not helped by the low hipped slate roof added above the parapet and the narrow entrance block appended to the side.

The outlying L-shaped WINGS form the main substance of the remains, originally barns and now recast as separate dwellings. Built of rubble with red brick dressings, each has six bays with arched windows on the ground floor and corresponding oculi above. Curvilinear gables are now observed only in the opposing end gables, a signal of Dutch influence that is similarly found, if just before the Georgian period, in the wings of the houses of Shannongrove in Limerick and Springhill in Londonderry.

The DEMESNE is still an impressive landscape; a rustic single-arched BRIDGE survives in the park, while the rising ground behind the house is encircled by several stately circular plantations, some evidently originating as earthen ring forts, the largest of these undoubtedly representing the *Líos Mór* or 'great fort' remembered in the name.

LISMORE LODGE. Derelict. Beside the village, surrounded by magnificent lime trees on the edge of Lismore demesne. A sizeable Late Georgian house, made higgledy-piggledy by a series of large Victorian additions. The core is a roughcast two-storey, gable-ended block on a double-pile plan with a central return; the plan is elaborated by a bow-ended morning room that projects beside the S gable. The main front originally had five bays; an extra bay with a hipped roof was added to the N. The wide timber doorcase with a fanlit segmental arch is now obscured by a bulky two-storey gabled projection with plate-glass windows and a porch, both Late Victorian in appearance, with decorative bargeboards. The same overbearing proportions characterize a service wing that disrupts the roof-line to the N, built of rubble and red brick with big plate-glass windows and a square three-storey tower under a low pyramid roof, projecting from the junction between old and new. Inside, the main house retains the standard tripartite plan with rooms disposed back-to-back on either side of the central entrance hall, with a generous open-well staircase set at the back. Good early C19 marble chimneypieces: in the drawing room, black marble with Tuscan columns and a fluted frieze; in the dining room, white marble with a pulvinated band carved with a bayleaf garland. Heavy Victorian cornices.

BINGFIELD. 1 km NNE. The familiar middle-sized Georgian house, tall and boxy on a half-basement with a shallow hipped roof over a pronounced limestone eaves cornice. Three-storey front, three bays wide, with characteristic bold fenestration of diminishing proportions, all in plain limestone frames with keystones against ruled render. The centre is given the classic mid-Georgian emphasis using Palladian motifs, here with a Venetian window over a wide pedimented doorcase, rather like Ledwithstown in Co. Longford, with Tuscan pilasters framing the door and narrow side-lights. Two-storey, two-bay wing on one side. Original interior details destroyed in the late C20. In the 1760s Bingfield was the residence of Joseph Story, Archdeacon of Kilmore.

RAILWAY STATION (former). 1 km SSE. Derelict. A small Italianate station of 1855 by *George Wilkinson* for the Midland & Great Western Railway. Surprisingly ambitious for its rural situation. A gable-ended two-storey block in rubble with dressed quoins; wide eaves to the gables and a moulded eaves cornice in Roman cement to the two opposing fronts. The platform front has three bays with a wide segmental-headed doorway in the centre protected by a heavy open timber porch; the windows in the side bays are segmental-headed, set in carved limestone frames with tall two-over-four sashes and plate glass. Nearby along the road is the GOODS SHED, a substantial gable-ended block in squared limestone with stone and brick dressings. The roof projects out to form a canopy along the front to the road; hidden from view on the rear façade are seven brick oculi set high in the wall.

ST MICHAEL, POTAHEE. 3.75 km S. Set in the lee of a steep hillside. A trim T-plan chapel in roughcast with modest stuccoed ornament. Originating as a plain thatched barn church in existence in 1820, the building was enlarged with a three-bay nave in 1837 and subsequently remodelled with a W stepped gable and a steeply gabled bellcote. The windows are lancets with hoodmoulds and square stops. Inside unprepossessing, but an attractive gallery survives in the S transept, its frontal ornamented with spiralled wrought iron above square timber panelling, and there is a good C19 oval limestone FONT.

CLOGGY. 3.5 km SW. A handsome Late Georgian mill house by the River Erne. A two-storey, three-bay block with a hipped roof and central stacks, in limestone rubble, originally roughcast, with Georgian sashes and a round-arched fanlit doorway.

Attractive yard behind, enclosed on one side by a two-storey ten-bay rubble range.

DRUMCOGHILL CHURCH HALL. 3.75 km SW. Lost in a sheltering spinney, deep in the countryside. A former C19 schoolhouse, a small single-storey block of roughcast with rusticated quoins and a hipped slate roof. Two fronts, each of five bays, the main front with three pointed arches set between plain doorways at either end. The whole design is brought wonderfully alive by the iron window frames, unusually rich, with elaborate cusped tracery and swirling mouchettes above quarry-glazed casements.

CROSSMAGLEN AH 9010

A small market town formed round a vast rectangular fair green. Existing as a crossroads in the early C17, the town was developed by the Ball family of Urcher House after Thomas Ball established a market here in the late C17. The old town was much ravaged by the Troubles, leaving few noteworthy buildings today.

ST MICHAEL. 1834, with later alterations. A large cement-rendered T-plan church with lancets and a thin offset tower. The tower turns polygonal from a square base, and was given a strange frilly crown and spire in the late C20. The gables have angle buttresses with pinnacles; the w gable is elaborated with three Dec windows under hoodmoulds, the larger one over the door within a large recessed panel. Inside, steep raking galleries with rich Gothic frontals on clustered pillars; the early C19 high-backed benches are fortunate survivors. The roof of open arch-braced trusses looks late C19. The sanctuary is decorated with mosaics framing five graduated lancets with STAINED GLASS, a bright attractive composition by *Mayer & Co.*, Munich.

FREEDOM MONUMENT. 1980 by *Yann Renard-Goulet*. The central event in Cardinal O'Fiaich Square: a large heroic bronze on a granite plinth with an elemental figure rising from the body of a phoenix.

GLENLOUGH HOUSE. Off the Creggan Road, an Edwardian villa set high above the town. A bulky two-storey roughcast block on a deep plinth. The doorcase is a handsome Tuscan aedicule set between two full-height canted bays, crisply expressed with Tuscan pilasters and cornices in stucco.

URCHER HOUSE. Creggan Road. A modest Late Georgian house, gable-ended, with two storeys and three bays and a central fanlit door. Enlarged with wings and picture windows on the ground floor in the C20.

CREGGAN PARISH CHURCH (C of I). 2.5 km NE. A perfect quaint hall-and-tower church on the edge of a precipice above the din of the River Creggan. A small three-bay nave with a short gabled chancel built in 1758, possibly incorporating an older church, to which a three-stage tower was added in 1799. Small lean-to projections flank the nave gable to give the impression of aisles when seen from the E. Uncoursed limestone rubble, with quarry-glazed Romanesque tracery in granite designed by *Joseph Welland* in the mid C19. The tower has three stages, with Irish crowstepped battlements enhancing the overall medievalism of the architecture. Internally, a neat space with a shallow coved ceiling defined by mouldings, with a ribbed star in the centre. Completely refurnished by *Welland*. – STAINED GLASS. Three-light E window with Faith, Hope and Charity, a memorial to Sir Thomas Jackson †1915 signed by *Douglas, Sons & Co.*, Belfast. – MONUMENTS. The best are two elaborate classical compositions supporting figural relief sculptures. The plainest, Richard Donaldson M.D. †1876, is unsigned. – The other, Mary Corr †1880, is by *Pearse & Sharp*, Dublin.

The graveyard is noteworthy as the burial place of a number of C18 Gaelic poets. In the centre, the CHARNEL HOUSE of the Eastwood family is a curious rubble building of indeterminate date, though not an early stone church or *daimhlaig* as is sometimes claimed: it is a small gabled single cell with low-pitched stone roof and half-round buttresses on the side walls. Internally, barrel-vaulted with recesses coinciding with the buttresses.

The former SEXTON'S HOUSE with Gothic windows and the facing former SCHOOLHOUSE provide neat lodges at the entrance. Contiguous with the churchyard is the beautifully planted DEMESNE of the former glebe house (demolished), which in 1837 was 'ornamented with evergreens, rustic seats and walks cut out of solid rocks'. Now a public park.

ST BRIGID, GLASDRUMMAN. 5 km E. 1926 by *Ralph Byrne* of *W. H. Byrne & Son*. A large and unexpectedly sophisticated classical church deep in the countryside. Built of Mourne granite to a basilican plan with nave, aisles, and a tall Italianate campanile flanking the entrance. The explanation for this successful and well-finished building lies in its reincarnation of Lord Clermont's Ravensdale Park near Dundalk, a large house of 1840 by *Thomas Duff* with additions by *W. H. Lynn* which was burned in 1922. In 1926 the Rev. Peter Sheerin P.P., perhaps attracted by the evocative tower Lynn had designed as an addition to the house in 1859, bought the ruins for his new church. It is easy to see the learned mind of *Ralph Byrne* in this clever conversion from domestic design to an evocation of an Early Christian basilica, expressed in an eclectic classical vocabulary. The design minimized reworking of the hard materials. The bold Tuscan modillions are reused, lending a strong primitive character to the pedimented frontispiece. The austere elevations of the house give the nave its marked austerity, though here the ashlar walls are relieved by large shallow recessed areas that define the bays; in each recession the clerestory is expressed as the plainest form of Venetian window, the

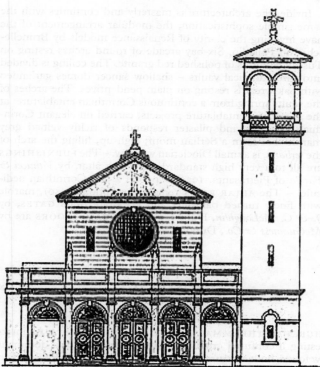

Crossmaglen, Glasdrumman, St Brigid, elevation.
Drawing by W. H. Byrne & Son

members widely spaced and only elaborated around the central arched opening with a raised blocked surround; similarly the aisles are severely expressed, with gentle recession, a few narrow windows, and a high parapet to conceal the flat roof. The tower flanks the entrance just as it did at Ravensdale, rebuilt exactly as Lynn designed it, all 78 ft (24 m) in five stages; the only difference here is the stone cross over the pyramid-roofed open belfry replacing the former weathervane. The arcaded entrance front has five bays with webbed fan-lights, blind in the aisle bays, the central three arranged as doors under a portico. The portico projects slightly, with four free-standing Ionic columns and a heavy entablature below a deep parapet incorporating plinths over each of the columns to support statues of the Irish saints – Oliver Plunkett, Brigid, Columcille (Columba) and Patrick. Above this, a narrow wall pierced by a large circular window flanked by narrow lights, and in the pediment a bright MOSAIC, 'The Lord is my Shepherd', by *Oppenheimer* of Manchester.

Inside, the architecture is masterly and continues with the same simple sophistication, the modular arrangement of the nave invoking the clarity of Renaissance models by Brunelleschi and Palladio. Six-bay arcade of round arches resting on Tuscan columns of polished red granite. The ceiling is divided into three domical vaults – shallow saucer domes garlanded with oak wreaths resting on plain pendentives. The arches of the vaults spring from a continuous Corinthian entablature; at the E end, the entablature projects, carried on elegant Corinthian columns and pilaster responds of richly veined grey marble that form a Serlian motif; high up, filling the arch of the *serliana*, is a small Diocletian window. – The FURNISHINGS are all to a very high standard. The high altar, by *Vanucci & Favila* of Pietrasanta, 1929, supports a fine Corinthian aedicule. – The ALTAR RAILS remain (exceptionally so), marble with finely turned balusters and elaborate brass GATES, by *J. & C. McLoughlin*, Dublin. – The MOSAIC FLOORS are by *McGuinness & Co.*, Dundalk.

6080   CROSSREAGH   CN
                      4 km NE of Virginia

CHURCH OF THE IMMACULATE CONCEPTION. 1874. An interesting if confused cruciform Gothic church with a dominant W tower, built at a rural crossroads by the Rev. J. O'Reilly. Plain five-bay nave and transepts of rubble limestone with ashlar quoins. Lancets with stained glass, very up-to-date in spirit, with polychromatic trim combining red and yellow bricks with limestone ashlar. The effort is lost in the old-fashioned three-stage tower with battlemented parapet and pinnacles, not unlike the example at nearby St Kilian, Mullagh. Inside, a hammerbeam roof nicely decorated and panelled with fail-safe tie-beams. Short three-bay arcade to the transepts with rendered octagonal piers supporting moulded arches. Nasty modern bell-frame to the N, with bell of 1879 by *J. Murphy*, Dublin.

A simple but attractive two-storey, three-bay stuccoed PRESBYTERY with gabled walls stands to the SE in the church grounds. Opposite the churchyard entrance is a wonderful wrought-iron COTTAGE GATE teeming with spirals, certainly worth a look.

QUILCA HOUSE. 1 km SW. An old and wasted demesne where magnificent trees, an ornamental motte, and a picturesque lake are vestiges of the C18 landscape that inspired the author of *Gulliver's Travels*. A modest two-storey farmhouse of *c.* 1940 occupies the site of the C18 residence of the scholar Thomas Sheridan, grandfather of the playwright Richard Brinsley Sheridan and friend of Jonathan Swift. It seemed unlikely that a shambolic house 'in no very good repair' could have survived satirization by Swift in 1725 as 'a rotten cabin' where 'the Goddess Want in Triumph reigns', but it survived through the C18 and received elaborate parlour paintings by the artist and set designer *John Lewis*, paintings that evoked Swift and Sheridan in the company of Milton and Shakespeare. A solitary stone chimneystack – one of Swift's 'chimnies with scorn rejecting smoak' – stoutly rising above the rear return of the farmhouse, and the adjoining range of rubble outbuildings, are a small fragment of the old house where the irascible Dean spent the summer of 1725 and conjured up the utopian world of Lemuel Gulliver.

CULLYHANNA   AH   9020

St PATRICK. Designed in 1890 by *William Hague*. The foundation stone was laid by Archbishop Logue in May 1891 and the building dedicated in 1903. A large cruciform church; nave, transepts and chancel with a large gabled sacristy in the NE angle. A square tower flanks the gabled front, rising in three stages to a low pyramid roof on corbels; the belfry is greatly attenuated, with two tall lancets on each face. The walls are of rock-faced limestone ashlar with dressed trim; the contractor was *J. Wynne* of Dundalk. The W gable is expressed as two storeys with two plain lancets flanking the gabled entrance and two wide pointed windows with slender bar tracery above; a canopied statue niche is set between. The interior was completed after Hague's death by *T. F. McNamara*. A five-bay nave opens into the transepts through twin arches on a polished column of red granite. Impressive open timber roof with arch-braced trusses, unusually well finished with turned kingposts and braces between the central arches. – STAINED GLASS. E window: the Transfiguration, by *Mayer & Co.*, Munich. S transept: SS Columcille (Columba), Patrick and Brigid, by *Clokey*, Belfast.

The PAROCHIAL HOUSE, also by *Hague*, is a greatly altered two-storey, five-bay block with a hipped roof.

FREEDUFF PRESBYTERIAN CHURCH. 1 km S. A plain cement-rendered church, built in the early C18 to a T-plan; remodelled in the late C19, when a small porch was added to the N. Large pointed windows and an oculus in the S gable with ordinary stained glass by *Clokey*, Belfast.

HARRYMOUNT. 2.5 km NW. Derelict. A neat Late Georgian villa. A long single-storey, five-bay block, roughcast, with a wide elliptical doorcase and a low hipped roof, fronting a small enclosed yard. Behind the house an ornamental mound planted with trees with a DOVECOTE on its summit completes this perfect example of the gentleman's model farm.

St OLIVER PLUNKETT, DORSEY. 2.5 km E. 1956. A simple five-bay hall, cement-rendered with stucco quoins, prominent kneelers, and plain round-headed windows.

DARTREY

DAWSON'S GROVE, later DARTREY CASTLE. The red brick
house built in the years before 1768 for Thomas Dawson, later
ennobled as Baron Dartrey and Viscount Cremorne, was radically altered in the mid C19 and demolished in 1946, but its
original character merits attention here. While its brand of
astylar Palladianism was becoming outmoded, its elevations
offered something more completely assured, each element
carefully measured in a way that points towards the knowing
refinements that gradually developed with Neoclassicism. It
stood within sight of Bellamont in the neighbouring demesne,
sharing something of its solid brick countenance, and indeed
the compact plan of the house and its use of a canted bay
display a sophistication and thoroughness not witnessed in the
region since Bellamont.

Christopher Myers and Davis Ducart were the only architects in South Ulster who might have been capable of such an
undertaking; but except perhaps for Myers's works at Belvoir
near Belfast, Dawson's villa has no stylistic affinities with their
work, and instead seems closer to that of Sir Robert Taylor or
Stiff Leadbetter. In so far as family connections have any
relevance for architectural patronage, *Leadbetter* had been
employed in 1760 by Dawson's mother-in-law, the Countess
of Pomfret, and by his brother-in-law, Thomas Penn.

The two-storey, five-bay entrance front was decidedly
restrained, with an urn-topped parapet screening attic dormers;
the only relief was an attractive pedimented frontispiece, where
the entrance and its flanking bays were expressed as an arcade,

Dartrey Castle.
Chromolithograph by A. F. Lydon, 1860s

and the only enrichment was a florid heraldic display in the tympanum. The garden front displayed a bolder, more thoughtful composition, with stone trimmings enriching the brickwork. Here the basement was exposed, giving greater presence to a narrow canted bay rising from a rusticated plinth at the centre, where the windows of the *piano nobile* were united as a simple Venetian window, in contrast to the fuller expression of the form in the end bays. There was nothing new in the use of Venetian windows in this way, as their appearance at Bellamont proves, but the manner in which they were set into a recessed arch here, and in the example on the s elevation lighting the stairs, is of importance: this gave greater articulation to the surface planes and an impression of lightness, in a way that only began to gain widespread currency in the Neoclassical period under Adam and Wyatt. How such advances might have been carried through to the decoration is unknown. The Rev. Daniel Beaufort's assessment of the building in 1777 as 'neat and well contrived but rather heavy both in its external appearance and inside decorations' suggests that it had yet to break from the weighty boldness of older traditions.

p. 29

The plan is also of interest, not least for its closeness to one of the plans in Thomas Rawlins's *Familiar Architecture* (1768). It was a variant of the classic double-pile plan, with the usual axial alignment of entrance hall and saloon and the traditional columnar screen across the back of the hall, but made more distinctive by the disposition of the stairs, set together at right angles on one side of the entrance hall. This is the earliest example of the villa plan that was to remain most popular at the height of the Neoclassical period, even if the saloon was merely bowed at one end (canted externally) and not a complete oval as it is in Rawlins's plan.

p. 29

In 1843 the 1st Earl of Dartrey employed *William Burn* to rebuild the house, renamed Dartrey Castle. Burn encased and greatly extended the old house, giving it all the panoply of the Elizabethan Revival style – gables, mullioned bay windows, domed towers, and tall chimneys – with the repetitive hard-edged detail that characterizes his work. A century later it was sold and torn down; its vaulted basements are now exposed like an open wound on the grassy lakeside terraces. (Elizabethan Revival balustrades, but a modest fragment of Burn's creation, now ornament the garden of Kilnacloy in Monaghan town.)

The extensive DEMESNE, between Rockcorry and Cootehill, shares a dramatic undulating lake-filled landscape with Bellamont Forest. Formed in the early C18 by Richard Dawson, it was recorded by the painters Thomas Roberts, William Ashford and Gabriele Ricciardelli and described by a visitor in 1773 as 'a place which unites in it so many striking beauties. For wood, water and simple unaffected decorations, it far exceeds anything . . . imagination could have formed.' The demesne was greatly enlarged by the Earl of Dartrey, who acquired the adjoining demesne of Fairfield. Ravaged as it is now, many good buildings remain in the landscape, mostly in the estate livery of local red brick, usually attractively combined with a pale limestone. There are a number of GATE LODGES, the best in a picturesque mid-C19 Tudor Gothic with mullioned windows and ornate bargeboards, possibly by *Burn*, who proposed more elaborate Elizabethan entrances. Beside the main avenue two impressive STABLEYARDS are sited closely together; similarly laid out in two-storey ranges with canted wings, all in red brick handsomely contrasted with stone dressings. The older range, associated with the 1760s house and possibly even earlier, has varied pattern-book doorcases and brick vaults on Doric columns like those employed in stables by Richard Castle. The vaults tragically destroyed 2012. The GARDEN HOUSE is an attractive L-plan block of two storeys and three bays with square Georgian sashes, hipped roof, and tall diagonal chimneystacks; perhaps one of the 'neat and ornamental' red brick farmhouses mentioned in 1801.

DAWSON MAUSOLEUM (or Temple). Smothered by a conifer plantation on Black Island, deep within the demesne. A large and refined Neoclassical temple to aristocratic devotion and grief. Originally commanding great scenic advantage, elevated to face the old house squarely across the lake. Erected by Thomas Dawson for his first wife, Lady Anne Fermor, daughter of the 1st Earl of Pomfret, who died in 1769, and completed by 1774. The design is convincingly attributed to *James Wyatt*, based on a surviving elevation close in detail to the executed building which evokes the Pantheon in Rome: a handsome single-storey cube with a top-lit lead dome. As the only light source, this was designed to heighten the emotional drama of the building's *pièce de résistance*, likely to be most potent at dusk or by moonlight: Lord Dartrey's personal anguish rises to a crescendo in a moving sculptural group by *Joseph Wilton* installed in the apsidal recess in 1774.

51   The building is a tall windowless block in local red brick on a limestone plinth. The W front has a rather flat engaged tetrastyle portico in finely tooled limestone with a round-headed doorway at the centre, flanked by blind windows on two levels, an oculus above a rectangle. The pilasters rise to unusual fluted capitals with stylized acanthus leaves supporting a simple entablature with a finely scaled dentil cornice which is continued round the building under a blocking course and high brick parapet. The broad brick expanses of the secondary elevations are relieved by square-headed blind windows, expressed as three bays on the sides and five on the bowed rear elevation. The brickwork (rendered over in the C19 and since exposed again) is all very finely finished, with penny-struck pointing. The dome, recorded by the Rev. Daniel Beaufort in 1778, was replaced in the mid C19 by an ugly hipped roof on oversailing eaves that provided some kind of top lighting. Having become roofless in the late C20, in 2010 the building was given a new zinc and fibreglass dome by Dartrey Heritage Association as part of an ambitious restoration overseen by *John Redmill*.

Inside, *Wilton*'s sculpture, in white and grey marble, is an elaborate virtuoso composition raised above an altar. The figures are grouped round a large funerary urn: from a cloud an angel gestures sympathetically to the approaching life-size figure of Thomas Dawson, whose drapery is clutched by the frightened form of his stricken son. The theme of angelic intercession was current at the time. Wilton employed the same idea in the monument to Lord and Lady Mountrath in Westminster Abbey; and the angel is closely comparable to one in Robert Adam's monument to the Duchess of Montagu at Warkton in Northamptonshire, carved by van Gelder in 1771. Within a year of Lady Dawson's death, her husband was raised to the peerage as the 1st Lord Dartrey, remarried, and set about overcoming his grief (and guilt perhaps) in this elaborate memorial. Undergoing continuing restoration at the time of writing.

ST JOHN THE EVANGELIST, EMATRIS PARISH CHURCH (C of I). At Kilcrow, on a wooded slope near the edge of the demesne, a remarkable church of Late Georgian appearance; some of the fabric dates from 1729, when Richard Dawson built a church here for 'the convenience and accommodation of his family'. It is an attractive structure with a low roof, nave, transepts with lean-to vestry and porch to the E, deep apsidal chancel, and a large Gothic belfry. The body of the church is in red brick, exceptional at the time and reflecting the availability and importance of this material on the Dawson estate. The fabric of the old structure lies in the two-bay nave; since enlarged with buttresses and refenestrated, it bears scars in its brickwork and retains a battered plinth, roughcast, with a distinctive rounded upper moulding. The unusual wide eaves brackets – primitive modillion blocks – may also be features of the older building copied in the later additions. In 1771 Lord Dartrey added the N transept to accommodate a gallery pew, having vacated his for the erection of a pulpit; the S transept and vestry were added later, raised over a low vault that bears the date 1815. The battlemented tower was rebuilt in 1840 without its spire, at which time the nave appears to have been extended to meet it; a stout structure in two tall stages with wide clasping buttresses changing to polygonal buttresses on the tall belfry stage and rising to pinnacles. The chancel of 1870 is a considerate addition in red brick by *Welland & Gillespie*, raised over the sloping ground on a deep masonry base and battered with sloping buttresses and seven cusped lights. The contractor was *James Maguire*. Around the same time the nave windows, formerly Gothick sashes like those of the transepts, were replaced with simple Y-mullions. Architecturally the interior is very plain, with a coved plaster ceiling compartmentalized with timber ribs in the nave and flat ceilings with reeded cornices in the transepts. An elaborate carved Gothic dado lines the chancel. – STAINED GLASS. Pictorial window by *Clayton & Bell*, 1887. – MONUMENT. Charles Dawson †1845, signed *R. Ballantine*, 11 Dorset Street, Dublin.

57

50 DAWSON COLUMN. On high ground by the roadside outside the
    demesne walls. A handsome Doric column 60 ft (18 m) high,
    in finely worked sandstone, commemorating Richard Dawson,
    five times M.P. for Monaghan, who died in 1807. Erected by
    his electorate. The design is attributed to *James Wyatt* and is
    comparable to his column to Sir Edward Coke at Stoke Poges
    in Buckinghamshire. The capital is Greek Doric; of the column
    only the neck is fluted, in relief; the rest is a smooth Roman
    Doric column and base. Surmounted by a Neoclassical funer-
    ary urn with swags and lion heads. Medallions on two faces
    draped with a bayleaf garland bear the Dawson crest and
    motto, *Toujours Propice* – its sentiment aptly sounded in the
    survival of the monument.

61 HOLY TRINITY, CARSAN. 0.5 km NNE. An attractive Gothic
    hall built by the Rev. Francis Gormly in 1841. Four bays,
    cement-rendered with blocked stucco quoins and tall lancets
    with thin hoods and flowing Y-tracery. Inside, a grand reredos
    with fluted Ionic columns.

    KILCROW RECTORY. 0.5 km E. A gaunt Late Victorian house in
    red brick. Two storeys over a basement with a hipped roof on
    paired eaves brackets, and end chimneystacks. The front has
    three bays, the central bay boldly advanced and gabled with a
    simple fanlit door and side-lights. The windows have segmental
    heads and plate glass.

    TOWER LODGE. 1.5 km SW. A fussy red brick house with an
    irregular plan outside the demesne walls. All angles and projec-
    tions, with a gabled entrance hemmed in between a large
    rectangular bay window and an octagonal corner tower with a
    low pyramid roof. Windows with marginal glazing bars and
    Tudor hoods.

    TANNAGH. 1.5 km SW. A Late Georgian house built for a cadet
    branch of the Dawson family. An L-plan block with a long
    two-storey front of five bays, originally of three, with the
    doorway set in a deep alcove in the central bay. Smooth-
    rendered walls with vermiculated quoins; the windows have
    moulded architraves and big Georgian sashes. Canted bay on
    the longer side elevation, extended by ten bays in the C20. Now
    in institutional use.

    The CHAPEL of 1962 is a large cruciform building of brick
    and concrete with steep copper roofs and tall vertical glazing
    in the gables. The designer is unknown.

43 FREAME MOUNT. 2.5 km SW. 1772. A pleasant Late Georgian
    red brick villa erected by Charles Mayne, agent to the Dawson
    estates. Named in honour of Philadelphia Freame, grand-
    daughter of William Penn, the founder of Pennsylvania, and
    second wife of Thomas Dawson, 1st Lord Dartrey. Two storeys
    over a raised basement with a hipped roof and a single bay
    lean-to wing to the side. Three-bay front, the central bay
    advanced with a handsome if old-fashioned tripartite Palladian
    doorcase reached by a broad railed flight of steps. The door is
    a little underscaled, which results in the Gothick fanlight being

extended below the imposts in an unusual arrangement. Above the door and flanking it, elegant tripartite windows that are possibly later insertions.

Inside, the standard tripartite plan, essentially one room deep, with a central stair hall extending into the irregular assemblage of service rooms behind. Old-fashioned joinery, with lugged architraves and raised and fielded panels. The plasterwork is simple and refined: in the dining room a Neoclassical cornice with a low-relief rinceau frieze with urns; in the drawing room a quirky combination of modillion cornice and Doric frieze.

DERRYNOOSE AH 7030
5 km SW of Keady

ST MOCHUA. Large gable-fronted single-cell church with a stepped bellcote. Five bays with plain Y-tracery. Built in 1834; remodelled by the Rev. P. Kelly P. P. in 1854, when it was refenestrated with elaborate stucco frames, now bizarrely set against rubble walls, unwisely stripped of render. Refurbished by *Daly, O'Neill & Associates* in 2003. Inside, a cold unfeeling space with exposed queenpost trusses. As part of the refurbishment works, the sanctuary, designed by *Rooney & McConville* of Belfast, has been opened up and fitted with the globular granite FURNITURE of 1982 discarded from Armagh Roman Catholic Cathedral, here stranded on a polished marble platform. – TABERNACLE. A finely worked late C20 piece in punched silver. – STAINED GLASS. Good early C20 figurative work in the manner of *Clokey*, Belfast.

ST MOCHUA RUINED CHURCH. 1 km NW. Remains of a long, narrow single-cell church. Low section of the N wall and tall narrow portion of the S wall, with a distinct base batter. Opposite, MALACHY'S WELL, a devotional pool of murky water under a rustic arched stone canopy.

LISLEA. 2.5 km N. A small late C19 stuccoed house with a steep hipped roof. Two storeys, three-bay front with a large cubic porch, chamfered window reveals, plate glass and marginal glazing bars.

THE DIAMOND AH 9050

A rural crossroads 4 km NE of Loughgall.

ST PAUL, THE GRANGE (C of I). 1 km SE. 1926 by *R. F. C. Orpen*. A modest, vaguely Romanesque church, highly finished in squared blackstone with pale sandstone trim. Built by a bequest from Richard F. Cope of Loughgall. The contractors were *H. Laverty & Sons*. Five-bay nave with vestry and porch projecting from the end bays. The porch has an expressive offset gable finishing in a broad bellcote. Round-headed lancets with hoods. Inside, a spartan simplicity, with a timber wagon roof over the narrow nave. Romanesque chancel arch with low relief chevron carving. – STAINED GLASS. In the E window of three graded lights, the Adoration of the Magi, 1926, signed *Ward & Partners*, who also executed the simple Art Nouveau glazing in the remaining windows.

On an adjoining site stood the OLD CHURCH, of which all that survives is the free-standing pyramid-roofed brick belfry in a small enclosed yard. In front of that, a SCHOOL recessed between two gable-ended blocks, the schoolmaster's residence and the larger church hall. Attractive mid-C19 H-plan block typical of Early Victorian estate architecture: stuccoed walls with hooded, cross-mullioned windows, quarry glazing, cusped bargeboards and polygonal stacks. The entrance to the school, in the centre, has an attractive pedimented porch on slender square stone pillars.

Beyond these is the RECTORY, a typically gaunt Late Victorian house, set in a gloomy woodland clearing. The kind of strong architectural design of which *J. H. Fullerton* was sometimes capable. Built of squared limestone and yellow brick trim with sashes set in pairs, all with plate glass and horizontal glazing bars. The front is asymmetrical with a projecting pointed gable, the roof on one side sweeping down in a catslide over the entrance to form an open timber porch. The steep roofs project on long 'bookshelf' brackets; unusual tapering stone stacks formed with tall prismatic caps on decorated twin piers. Longer, symmetrical side elevation with a central gable raised over twin lancets.

DAN WINTER'S COTTAGE. 1 km W. A former rural spirit grocers, named after its late C18 owner. The classic Irish *teach fada*, or 'long house': a low, gable-ended thatched cottage of eleven bays, three of which have doorways, all irregularly disposed, with two set in curved windbreaks under the projecting thatch. The walls are rendered, with small twelve-pane Georgian sashes. The scene of affrays in 1795 between the sectarian Defenders and Peep o' Day Boys that culminated, ultimately, in the founding of the Orange Order.

DIAMOND HALL. 1 km N. 1952. A large, unexpected Orange hall, much like the early C20 cinema of a provincial town, but set in open countryside. A buttressed hall, four bays deep, fronted by a tall, uncouth two-storey block. All in red brick with chamfered concrete heads to large rectangular casements. The entrance block has three bays, the central bay projecting under a flat gable. Two tall concrete pillars over the entrance support a railed balcony.

DONAGHMOYNE

3 km NE of Carrickmacross

Historically an important local centre, now a small village focused
on a quiet crossroads. The name *Domhnach Maighean*, 'church
of the little plain', links the place with an early church associated
with St Patrick's mission. The Normans penetrated the ancient
territory of *Airghialla* to establish a motte and bailey here under
the Pipards, replaced in 1244 by Maanan Castle.

ST LASTRA. The old mid-C19 parish church at the centre is a
plain low-lying four-bay Gothic hall, roughcast, remodelled in
1908 by *J. V. Brennan*, who added a sacristy and porch. The
NEW CHURCH of 1980 by *Patrick Rooney* of Boyle, a little to
the S, is a novel round structure, appealing to the eye and well   117
suited to its site. Wide conical roof with a central glazed roof-
light resting on low walls with big leaded windows on the N
side. Interior unfussy but attractive.

DONAGHMOYNE PARISH CHURCH (C of I). 1 km S. Disused.
A Gothic hall and tower, built in 1827, near the site of the
ancient church said to have been founded by Victor, one of St
Patrick's bishops. The *Annals of Ulster* record a Viking raid in
832 when the shrine of Adamnan (Abbot of Iona and biogra-
pher of St Columba) was taken. The church and lands of
Donaghmoyne were later granted to the Hospital of John the
Baptist at Ardee. Nothing of this period is visible above ground.
The old church, ruinous in 1622, was rebuilt in 1641 at a time
when elsewhere most were being destroyed. The present structure lies to the N. Squared limestone walls and crisply carved
ashlar trim. Three-bay nave with shallow chancel and angle
buttresses. A three-stage battlemented tower with pinnacles.
Later vestry to the S. No trace of the font and marble altar
understood to have come from the old church.

    CHURCHYARD. A large limestone Celtic cross to the S marks
the grave of William Steuart Trench †1872, land agent to the
Shirley estate and then to the Bath estate. – Unlocated: the
resting place of the Gaelic poet Cathal Bui Mac Ghiolla
Ghunna †1760.

MAANAN CASTLE. 1 km SW. A striking complex of earthworks   *p. 318*
surrounds a weary masonry stump unworthy of its setting.
A large motte and bailey to the E, surrounded by fosse and
ramparts, was established here by Gilbert Pipard at the end of
the C12 to protect a timber fortification. According to the
Annals of Ulster the stone castle was built in 1244. A stone
causeway to connect the inner bailey to the motte was created
at this time, and perhaps also the second bailey. Yielded to the
Crown in 1302, it passed to the MacMahons and was abandoned by the C15. Now stranded among the fairways of a golf
course.

DONAGHMOYNE HOUSE. 1 km SW. Surrounded by the golf
course. Originally a modest two-storey, gable-ended house of
three bays described as 'modern built' in 1835 and occupied

Maanan Castle.
Engraving, 1845

by William Bashford. Roughcast with tripartite windows in the
end bays, the house was made irregular and somewhat ungainly
in 1894 when *R. P. T. Logan* extended it for the then owner,
John Marshall Bolton. Logan added a projecting gabled block
to the w end in a fashionable Tudor idiom. Here, under the
apex of the gable, are several red brick courses supporting
Tudor-style half-timbering. The arrangement is repeated in the
centre of the façade, where an attic gable is carried on corbels
above the first-floor window. At the same time a boxy single-
storey porch was added, crowned by a big dentil cornice and
pulvinated frieze borrowed from the entablature of the limestone doorcase. The doorcase with its lugged surround looks
mid-C18 and must have come from the front of the original
house. The interior is simply planned, with a small room on
each side of the entrance hall and stairs set in a deep return.
The large room to the w was built as a library with a canted
bay on the side elevation.

GATE LODGE also by *Logan*. One and a half storeys with
three bays and unusual hoodmoulds.

CAPRAGH. 2 km S. On this site beside a stream feeding Capragh
Lough there is the tradition of a monastery affiliated with Mellifont. No visible trace of such buildings now: only a neat two-
arched bridge adjoining the gates and ruined lodge of Capragh
House. The brick core of the C19 house also survives, within
the beautiful parkland of its small demesne. The basement, a
tall two-storey wing of later C19 appearance, and a sunken yard
and stable range to the N are more substantial remains.

LONGFIELD OTRA. 2 km SSE. Derelict. A curious house that deserves closer study, in an old demesne with fine trees. A small but well-built gable-ended block, roughcast, with two storeys over a basement and the entrance in a lower annexe to the rear. Distinctly odd front elevation with just two bays irregularly placed: a single tripartite window on the ground floor to the W and a three-over-six sash above to the E. Nice well-proportioned rooms with decent joinery. Surrounded by a varied collection of good C18 and C19 farm buildings.

DOWRA   CN   9020

A small village developed on the River Shannon, here in its youthful stages, which defines Cavan's border with Leitrim.

COURTHOUSE. In the heart of the village, set well back from the street. A two-storey U-plan block of the 1930s, roughcast with channelled strip quoins, a modillion eaves cornice in timber, and steep hipped roofs. Square-headed mullioned windows in the wings, tall round-headed windows in the central block, set between matching entrances. The doorways have spoked fanlights framed under stuccoed classical hoods on consoles with keystones.

CHURCH OF THE IMMACULATE CONCEPTION, DOOBALLY. 1924 by *Thomas F. McNamara*. A prominent rural church, hard against the hillside, with wide views over the distant valleys below the Cuilcagh Mountains. A large buttressed hall of seven bays with a polygonal chancel and offset vestry, built in squared limestone. A pedestrian W gable holding a porch with kneelers between lancets and three similar graded lights above. Inside, a dark timber roof with braced hammerbeam trusses. – STAINED GLASS. In the three-light E window densely coloured glass in the manner of *Mayer* of Munich.

CORRARD HOUSE. Rebuilding of an older, more modest house in 1925 by *James Donnelly* as a tall gable-ended building of Late Georgian appearance. A roughcast, two-storey block with attics, expressed by windows in the gables. Three-bay front with twelve-pane sashes and well-spaced brackets to the eaves. Stuccoed strip quoins and moulded strings.

DRUM   MN   5010
6 km S of Newbliss

Grandiosely described as a town in Victorian times, now a quiet village. One of the earliest Presbyterian churches in the region was established here at the end of the C17. Now of that only a

small graveyard survives, lying discreetly on one side of the straggling street.

DRUM PARISH CHURCH (C of I). A handsome and well-finished Board of First Fruits hall and tower in a dark local
limestone with greywacke trim. Built in 1828 as a chapel of
ease for Currin (Scotshouse), as a small two-bay hall with
decorative Y-traceried windows and a forestanding tower in
three diminishing stages with pinnacles. Enlarged and altered
by *William J. Welland*, who in 1860 added an aisle to the S; this
stands as a distinct gabled block, with a steeper roof pitch than
the old nave. Quarry-glazed windows with plate tracery, mostly
arranged as paired lancets in finely dressed surrounds, elaborated to three at the E, where they are set under three small
circular openings.
    Internally the old galleried nave was considerably altered
when the S wall was opened up as an arcade with two pointed
arches meeting on a short cylindrical sandstone pier. The old
roof was replaced with heavy hammerbeam trusses; unusually
for a building of this kind, the hammerbeams are elaborately
carved. An old tradition records that during the so-called
Second Reformation of the early C19 people were witnessed
being carried out of the church in a faint, having seen 'visions
and revelations from the Lord'. Restored in 1902.
DRUM PRESBYTERIAN CHURCH. The survivor of the two
churches formerly in the town. Early C19 pebbledashed hall
with brown sandstone trim and half-hipped roof. Big round-
headed windows with Gothick glazing. Two quarry-glazed
lancets on the E gable, where the original entrance is still represented by its stone surround; it was closed in the late C19
when a porch was formed on the opposite gable, the new
entrance reusing the old fanlit timber door.
JOHN ANDERSON. A precious vernacular survivor at the centre
of the village. Early C19 roughcast range combining accommodation, shop and stores behind a long single-storey, irregularly fenestrated front. Two storeys to the rear with stables and
coach houses on the ground floor. The upper floor retains
quarry-glazed casements. Possibly the lodging house mentioned here in 1835.
POST OFFICE. Pleasing one-and-a-half-storey C19 building with
dormers, that looks like a row of labourers' cottages thrown
together.
MINORE HOUSE. A small Late Georgian house of two storeys
and three bays with nicely proportioned sashes. Rubble and
red brick with peach-coloured lime render. L-plan with lower
two-storey wing to the side and a short stair return in the angle
to the rear, lit by a round-headed window with a sash of most
remarkable length that extends through two storeys. In 1835
the seat of Captain Cottingham, who displayed 'much taste
upon a small scale' in the 'highly useful and ornamental
planting'.

ST JOSEPH, CORRINSHIGO. 3 km W. Diminutive gabled hall
and porch, newly built on an old site in 1964 in the tradition
of vernacular simplicity. Four bays with short and wide pointed
windows, leaded, with coloured glass. Pebbledashed. The interior penitential in its plainness.

DRUMLANE   CN   *3010*

Accessible only by a narrow twisting lane, this isolated monastic
complex lies at the N end of Derrybrick Lough, one of the many
peripheral lakes that spill out from Lough Oughter. A diminutive
round tower and low-lying medieval church ruins are the remains   19
of a monastery founded here on the *droim leathain* or 'broad
ridge' in the C6. Its founder is usually given as St Maedhog,
Bishop of Fern; one account, however, says that the future
parents of the Saint, despairing of their childless state, had given
alms to the holy men of Drumlane: thus the monastery would
have been in existence earlier, and credit for the foundation
passes to Columcille – St Columba, Abbot of Iona. The round
tower is the only obvious indicator of this early Christian foundation, although further ruins, now little more than a series of
earthworks to the S, indicate a more extensive complex. Said
to lie on the boundary between the two ancient territories of
Breifne, the site is reputed to be the burial place of its princes.
The *Annals of the Four Masters* record numerous clashes involving

Drumlane Abbey.
Engraving by J. Newton, 1794

the O'Reillys and O'Rourkes at Drumlane, and whether princely
or otherwise, many O'Reillys are recorded on the C18 gravestones
surrounding the church. By the mid C12 Augustinian canons
regular from Kells had established a priory here, dedicated to
St Mary; a century later the *Annals* record the burning of
Drumlane, and it is possible that the medieval church was built
after this fire. After the Dissolution the lands were granted to the
Dillons. The church evidently continued in use as a parish church
into the C18; in 1792 Daniel Grose drew it with its roof intact.

The ROUND TOWER at the NW corner of the church is late
C11 or early C12. Reduced in height, it is now 38 ft (11.6 m) tall.
There is a pronounced division in the stonework more than
halfway up, where neatly laid blocks of lake stone, partly in ashlar,
give way to random rubble – an arrangement that undoubtedly
gave the tower its initial and enduring strength. The doorway,
almost *c.* 10 ft (3 m) above ground, faces S towards the church;
the usual keyhole opening formed by inclined jambs is nicely
expressed here with a raised surround made of large carved
blocks that remarkably extend through the full thickness of the
wall. Similar, smaller, opening above. On the N face, heavily
weathered and now hard to discern, are carvings generally taken
to be a hen and a cock.

The CHURCH RUIN is a long rectangular structure, 107 ft by
24 ft (32.7 m by 7.46 m), possibly the canons' mid-C12 building,
with battered limestone rubble walls and gabled E and W ends.
It owes its distinctive appearance to the multiple sloping buttresses that project centipede-like from the side walls. Now
damaged and a little ragged, these odd triangular anchors when
seen from the gable-end almost give the impression of a basilican
plan. An appeal for alms in 1436 to repair the parish church and
the church of the priory suggests that the E window, the tomb
niches, and the cusped ogee window in the N wall may all be of
that time. More extensive work was carried out in the C17, when
much of the W end was rebuilt, with the repositioning of the W
doorway and the addition of further buttresses. A very pronounced batter makes these alarmist additional supports difficult
to explain, unless they were related to a former roof structure,
but Grose's view suggests nothing unusual there. The W door is
late C13 or early C14: a low round-headed arch in limestone,
carved to a complex moulding with inner dogtooth decoration
and a bishop's head for its keystone; it is set beneath a relieving
arch of rough voussoirs which suggests that it was inserted later,
perhaps when the W end of the church was rebuilt.

The slender pointed E window with splayed reveals retains
fragments of elaborate tracery displaying a combination of Dec
and Perp styles, so that it must be C15. The replacement of the
sill makes a reconstruction difficult. It is easy to establish that
there were three double-cusped lights, supporting smaller openings that incorporated the short supermullions surviving at
the top of the arch. These clearly express the Perp character of
the window, though how they fitted together is hard to understand. The internal surround forms an elegant composition

incorporating lithe pilaster shafts, delicately worked with a single face rib and banded by an intermediate collar. These support slightly varied moulded capitals. The crisp detail appears consistent with the C14, so the tracery may be a later insertion. The external hoodmould is punctuated with carved heads, all C15 in appearance: a bishop in the apex and kings as terminal stops. The s wall has four windows: a square opening lighting the chancel and three regularly spaced pointed windows defining the nave. The two central windows retain elements of simple intersecting tracery with external hoodmoulds. The w opening, ruder in form with an arch of squared limestone voussoirs, is C18. Two windows in the N elevation are also later: that to the w, an untidy opening, contrasts with the pair of small cusped ogee lancets to the E, added in the C15 and now lacking the dividing mullion. Two late doorways inserted in the nave are built of reused masonry; that to the s gave access to a vestry. A reused head with stylized features projects above the arch outside.

Internally the church is now one long uninterrupted space; a short masonry foundation extending from the N wall may indicate the location of a screen that separated chancel and nave. – MONUMENTS. The cavities of two plundered tombs survive on the s wall, relics perhaps of forgotten Breifne princes. The w niche, once elaborate, offers traces of a crocketed gable; only a broken finial remains. A section of raised architrave and the bell-cast base of a colonnette are all that survives of the w jamb. No details remain of the E tomb. Two carved heads have strayed from their original location and been given protection here: one covered with pinholes and heavily eroded, C15; the other, better preserved, though more primitive, probably C13. – Solitary pieces of unrelated stone jigsaws litter the chancel; found and gathered together, they include cusped stone lights, pilaster bases, mullions and capitals, and offer a sense of the elaboration of the former buildings on the site. – Secured against the N wall is a medieval grave slab, its surface carved with interlace, reputedly for one of the O'Farrellys, coarbs of St Maedhog.

EGLISH   AH   *8050*

A rural parish NW of Armagh.

EGLISH OLD CHURCH AND CROSSES. An early Christian site on an isolated hilltop with fragments of two high crosses, possibly C10, and a ruined church, usually dated to 1720 and in use until 1821. The church was a small single cell, the surviving w gable now a raw rubble outline; a plain, largely restored doorway suggests a rudimentary building; the remainder lies evident only in raised grassy banks.

The NORTH CROSS survives in two parts – head and base – united with a new shaft in 1989. Similar to the crosses at

Eglish, High Cross.
Engraving, 1884

Tynan, though much smaller, it is simply bordered on each face with linear mouldings. The solid head, partly restored, has an unpierced nimbus with circular cusps projecting from the arcs into sunken panels; on the N face a single raised central boss with interlace; on the S face a cluster of nine smaller bosses within a circle. The SOUTH CROSS survives as an incomplete weathered head similar to its neighbour, though the centre of each face is decorated with a cup-shaped recess; the upper section reveals that it originally carried a finial.

BENBURB VALLEY HERITAGE CENTRE, MILLTOWN. 1.5 km N. A signal smokestack stretches high over this industrial complex, its slender red brick profile a picturesque incident against the steep wooded valley of the Blackwater. A large flax mill had developed here by the C19 between the Ulster Canal and the Blackwater, near the town of Benburb, Co Tyrone. The principal MILL building is late C19, a large three-storey block with seven bays in squared rough-hewn limestone and red brick dressings; the windows have segmental heads and plate glass. It towers over a low expanse of C20 north-light roofs largely hidden from view behind; at right angles to the front, the DYE HOUSE of 1938 is a low-slung building in red brick, screening older rubble buildings on the mill race. The LOCK-KEEPER'S COTTAGE is a delightful small building in squared limestone, single-storey with a hipped roof. The ends are polygonal, each face with twin sashes under flat angular hoods.

MAYDOWN HOUSE. 2 km NE. Derelict. Beside the Blackwater, just S of Benburb, an attractive roughcast house of c. 1760. A two-storey gable-ended block with attics, with a short return to one side resulting in an L-plan. The front has five bays, imperfectly spaced, with Georgian twelve-pane sashes. The entrance is in a small porch added in the early C19, with a handsome fanlit doorway and side-lights. Inside, the standard tripartite plan with central stairs. Good late C18 joinery: the doors have six recessed panels, arranged with big square panels in the centre between long, thin panels top and bottom. A stone plaque in an adjoining wall is inscribed 'M/W:M 1762' on a raised and fielded panel.

EDENDERRY HOUSE. 1.2 km SE. Built in 1778 as a glebe house, with an elegant tall cliff-like front of three storeys with five bays. The rubble walls are now stripped of roughcast, greatly harming the simple architectural sophistication of the original intention. The doorcase is a familiar Georgian design with engaged Tuscan columns, open pediment, and an ornate webbed lead fanlight; unusually the frieze of the dosserets has primitive-looking ewers carved in low relief. Occupied in 1808 by the Rev. James Tisdall, for whom the Rev. Daniel Beaufort proposed some alterations.

CHURCH OF THE IMMACULATE CONCEPTION, TULLYSARAN. 1.5 km SE. 1921 by *Ashlin & Coleman*. A hard-edged Hiberno-Romanesque essay in biscuit-coloured sandstone. Long nave and chancel with transepts and an offset round tower at the SW corner, crowned with a cone on an open columnar belfry. A small apsidal baptistery projects from the W end of the nave N wall and the transepts have low confessional outshots. The walls are of squared masonry, finely punched, with frugal two-dimensional embellishment. The W gable is emphatically fringed with a corbel table; a statue of the Virgin is set in a gabled niche between windows – here, as elsewhere, plain round arches under hoods – with a modest rose window over. The main door is recessed, the arches emboldened with chevrons; above it in raised lettering is the dedication *Maria sine labe concepta pro nobis* and the date, 1922. Inside, a high roof with exposed scissor trusses; the transepts open through twin arches on a slender compound pier where the shafts have abstract block capitals with unusual arched undercutting. –

STAINED GLASS. Three-light E window with vivid, jewel-like figurative glass, C20.

GLENAUL PARK (formerly Mullyloughan). 2 km SE. 1825. A handsome Georgian house, elevated with broad views to the E across the valley of the Ballymartrim and north Armagh. In every respect its outward appearance is shared with Crow Hill (Annaghmore), built a year earlier, so perhaps this house shares its mysterious architect, *Brownlees*. Built for Joseph Johnston of Knappagh, who laid the foundation stone on 25 March 1825. The house is a two-storey-over-basement block on an L-plan. The main (E) front has five bays with twelve-pane sash windows, roughcast walls with dressed stone quoins, and a low hipped roof with stone stacks set back behind the ridge. The central bay projects under a small pediment, pierced with a little spoked lunette; the same design is attractively applied to the three-bay S front. The entrance is wide, approached by an elegant railed flight of steps similar to those at Dobbin House in Armagh; it has four engaged Tuscan columns with geometric side-lights set between the columns and an exceptionally squat elliptical fanlight framed by long, radiating blocked voussoirs.

HOLY TRINITY, DRUMSALLAN (C of I). 2 km SSE. 1821. On an exposed hilltop, a picturesque church to a familiar Board of First Fruits design by *John Bowden*. Well built in regular squared blocks of limestone with cutstone dressings. The nave has three bays, the windows with twin pointed cusped lights and quarry glazing under hoodmoulds; the same design is used in narrower windows to flank the tower on the W gable, recalling an arrangement common to *Thomas Cooley*'s late C18 churches. The tower has three stages, expressed in thin moulded strings with wide corner lesenes and a tall belfry finishing in stepped battlements and tall pinnacles that give it a spiky appearance. Inside, a circular vestibule, twin vestries, and a boxy nave with a gallery at the W end; the ceiling is panelled, with exposed kingpost trusses. – MONUMENTS. James Johnston †1823; a tall Neoclassical tablet with a standing angel in relief, by *Thomas Kirk*.

KNAPPAGH. 3 km S. This compact square Georgian house with its perfect doll's-house front, built in 1775 for James Johnston, is sometimes associated with the family home of Francis Johnston. Although Francis Johnston was only fifteen when Knappagh was built there is documentary evidence for a possible connection, with payments in the building accounts made to *William Johnston*, which almost certainly refer to the architect's father. Though the family may be more reliably connected with Kilmore House in Co. Armagh, in spirit at least the architecture of Knappagh relates to the pleasing and refined aesthetic sensibilities of Johnston the architect. The sophisticated austerity of the main façade can be found in some of his early works; the garden front in particular has a plainness that is quite absolute, inviting some comparison with his Townley Hall, and in particular with the side elevations of Rokeby, both houses in Co. Louth. Significantly perhaps, Rokeby is considered to be Johnston's first house, completed by him after Thomas Cooley's death in 1784.

Knappagh is a smart cubic block that could as easily have been produced by Cooley. The main front is two storeys tall, set on a semi-basement, with three bays giving a preponderance of wall over window, in contrast to the battery of six closely spaced bays at the back. The central bay breaks forward with a pediment, inset with a small spoked lunette, and the façade is finished by a crisp entablature and blocking course to conceal an attic storey that is only revealed on the side elevations. The entrance, reached across the area by a short flight of steps, is an elegant, round-arched doorway exactly like those by *William Murray* for Charlemont Place in Armagh, with engaged Tuscan columns, fluted frieze and webbed fanlight. The walls are cement-rendered, and the render stands proud of the exposed window dressings, a strange feature found also at Elm Park in Killylea. The windows have large twelve-pane sashes, those of the ground floor resting on a continuous string-course.

There is an impressive array of C18 and C19 FARM BUILD-INGS, mostly two-storey with hipped roofs, walls of squared limestone, some roughcast, and many distinguished by round-headed windows and red brick trim. The artist John Luke (1906–75) escaped from wartime Belfast to live here in the Steward's House.

The former MAIN ENTRANCE was designed by *Alexander McLeish* in 1827 with a now demolished temple-fronted lodge; the gates are flanked by twin trabeated pedestrian entrances formed of massive limestone blocks and joined to convex outer sweeps. GATE LODGE with an asymmetrical single-storey front of four bays and a hipped roof sweeping out on pillars to form a veranda over three bays, before a projecting gabled end bay with a small bay window. It appears to be C19, inconsistent with the brief, unfinished history inscribed on the decorative bargeboards: 'Built in the C18 and renovated in the C20 by . . .'.

DERRYDORRAGH HOUSE. 2 km SW. A handsome Late Georgian house of two storeys and three bays, in roughcast with dressed quoins, steep hipped roof and stone stacks. Central doorcase in a blocked surround with webbed fanlight. A plaque set in the side elevation reads 'William Wilson 1836'.

KNAPPAGH PRESBYTERIAN CHURCH. 3 km SW. A large four-bay hall, roughcast with stucco quoins and round-headed windows in blocked surrounds. The entrance front is gabled with high kneelers. A plaque over the door gives the date 1839.

EMYVALE   MN   6040

A small mill village in north Monaghan beside the River Black-water. In 1788 the Rev. Daniel Beaufort described it as 'a good street village with many houses building'. There was a market

house then, and later a short-lived Methodist church where now
only a small cemetery survives. The street is lined with modest
houses. Just one stands out for notice – a neat DISPENSARY on
the E side designed by *W. A. Scott* in 1905.

DUNGILLICK. 1 km NE. Built *c.* 1720 by the Ancketill family.
Classical vernacular at its most basic and most pleasing. A
two-storey L-plan block which appears to be the result of
enlargement, where the original gable-ended house was integrated into a later C18 hipped block formed at the E end. The
more irregular three-bay S elevation, the original entrance
front, has a simple blocked limestone doorcase, now a window;
on the first floor two early sashes with exposed frames. The
main front is roughly symmetrical, with four bays on the first
floor and just two larger sashes on the ground floor. These sit
close to the ground, most likely the result of enlargement; a
small boxy porch between them perhaps part of the same
alterations.

DUNDONAGH. 2.5 km SE. A pleasing Late Georgian gentleman's
cottage. Long single-storey, gable-ended block with five bays
and an understated fanlit door. Roughcast walls, slated roof
and brick chimneys. A great deal of the attractiveness stems
from the fenestration, with twelve-pane sashes set in flush
frames. Neat farm buildings to one side behind.

ANCKETILL'S GROVE (formerly called Trough Lodge). 2 km S.
A strange Late Georgian house with wings and a large Italianate tower. Apparently built by Matthew Ancketill in 1781 as
a successor to a C17 house, itself successor to a McKenna
stronghold near the site. Its layout is similar to that of the
model farms promoted at this time in the Dublin drawing
schools: a small gable-ended farmhouse of two storeys and five
bays with a projecting pedimented central bay, linked by single-storey fenestrated quadrants to pedimented wings of two
bays with Gothick sashes. The ground floor and wings are
rendered, giving way to regular blocks of pale ashlar on the
upper floor. The central bay is partly obscured by a disproportionate early C19 square entrance block with a hipped roof and
Tuscan doorcase, set excessively to the fore with a short link
to the old entrance. The same inconsiderate sense of aesthetics
and scale is manifest in further alterations carried out in the
mid C19, when a bulky square tower was added to the rear.
The weathervane carries the initials of Matthew John Ancketill
and the date 1852, the year following his succession to the
property. It is an ungainly structure in squared limestone with
dressed trim, rising behind the return in four diminishing
stages to a low pyramid roof that oversails on large eaves
corbels that give it a Lombardic air. From the main approach
the tower rises above the ridge as if from the attic, evidently
calculated to present an arrangement reminiscent of Gola
(Scotstown), though here its proportions unwisely exceed
those of the house. Also at this time, presumably in an (ill-
advised) attempt to complement the tower, the Georgian

Gothick windows of the house and quadrants were given rounded heads, flat hoods and plate glass; they have been replaced even more unsuccessfully since.

To one side, the mid-C19 BARN is a long single-storey range in squared stone with an attractive two-storey gabled centre; this is given interest and elaboration by twin arched openings, nicely meeting on a single column and grouped with an oculus under a large recessed brick arch.

At the end of the straight avenue, the C19 GATE LODGE is a modest single-storey block in squared masonry. Three bays with a projecting gabled porch bearing the Ancketill monogram. To the NW the former LODGE at Creevelea is larger and earlier; built *c.* 1800, it is a single-storey T-plan block with a five-bay front, the central three projecting slightly.

ST PATRICK, CORRACRIN. 2 km S. A small T-plan gable-fronted lancet hall, built in 1811; in 1835 described as roughcast and slated. Of that only the gables survived late C19 remodelling, when the church was reoriented: the altar was moved from a shallow projection in the long E wall to the S end and a new entrance provided in the N gable under a projecting belfry. The E wall was rebuilt in small ashlar blocks and given paired lancets. A W aisle was added in the late C20, with a large monopitch roof; the copper-clad link between it and the nave is so deeply recessed that the aisle has the strange appearance of being detached. Inside, an open kingpost roof. – STAINED GLASS. Richly coloured glass of the early C20 in the manner of *Earley & Co.*

CHURCH OF THE SACRED HEART, CARRICKROE. 4.75 km NW. Small T-plan chapel of 1832 with simple Y-tracery, cement-rendered, to which a new chancel, porches and bellcote, all in squared limestone, were added in 1886. Inside, timber-panelled ceiling, mansard-shaped, with lithesome arched braces, also of 1886. – STAINED GLASS. E window: three graded lights with brightly coloured glass of the 1880s.

ST PATRICK, CLARA. 8 km NW. A trim cruciform chapel, the most northerly in Monaghan. Built in 1787, rebuilt in 1936 by *T. J. Cullen.* Cement-rendered with cutstone trim. Gabled W front with a small porch, three graded lights and a bellcote. Three-bay nave and transepts, with a flat-roofed sacristy extending across the entire E elevation. Inside, an exposed timber roof with functional, unadorned scissor trusses. – STAINED GLASS. The Crucifixion, a vividly coloured work by *Earley,* Dublin, 1938.

ERRIGAL TRUAGH   MN   6040

A rural parish in north Monaghan extending into south Tyrone.

MULLANACROSS OLD CHURCH. The surviving gables of a large late medieval parish church, already in ruins by the early C17.

A straightforward rectangle with uncoursed rubble walls of medieval thickness. A large square-headed opening in the misshapen E gable wall is now filled with a low round-headed doorway; neatly formed of squared voussoirs and chamfered to the outer reveal, it was inserted c. 1687 to give access to the burial ground of the Ancketill family. Fragments of a carved stone window frame survive in the W gable. The surrounding CEMETERY has many good C17 and C18 carved gravestones; two sculpted heads and a sheila-na-gig from the site are now in the Ulster Museum.

ST MUADHAN, ERRIGAL TRUAGH PARISH CHURCH (C of I). A neat little Gothic church built to a standard design by *William Farrell* in 1834. Three-bay hall of coursed rubble with ample cutstone trim. W entrance gable with porch, corner buttresses and bellcote, all with pinnacles – an elaboration of the standard form. The windows are nice, Dec in style with quarry glazing. Short chancel projection with graded lancets and lean-to vestry to one side. Inside, exposed cast-iron trusses. – STAINED GLASS. Bright pictorial window by *Abbott & Co.*, Lancaster, 1902.

Highly ornate GATEWAY with buttressed diagonal piers.

THE HOLY FAMILY, BALLYOSION. 2.3 km SE. Charming pre-Emancipation chapel built by the *Rev. C. McDermott* in 1820. Four-bay cement-rendered hall with thick Y-tracery, emphatic offset buttresses – angled at the corners – and a distinctive belfry tower set against the S wall. The tower, designed by *William Walker* in 1844, is nicely scaled, built with squared masonry in three diminishing stages; the belfry has large pointed openings with gables on each face bearing aloft ball-and-spike pinnacles. Inside, a good timber-panelled ceiling is all that survived late C20 refurbishment.

FORT SINGLETON. 3 km S. Handsome Neoclassical house. Large stuccoed front, two storeys and five bays, with big sash windows, rusticated quoins, delicate eaves cornice and blocking course. The central bay projects, with a tripartite window over a wide fanlit doorcase, now partially concealed by a later flat-roofed porch with an eccentric Tuscan frontispiece on square columns. The standard tripartite plan, doubled in the C19 when a new range was built across the back. An incongruous square tower projects from the wall between these ranges, extending above the eaves to a third storey with crenellations.

FARNALOY
5 km NW of Keady

ST JOHN, DERRYNOOSE PARISH CHURCH (C of I). A bulky hall with a stout forestanding tower. Although a church was established here under an act for building parish churches in the reign of Queen Anne, only the datestone in the tower, 1712, survives. Rebuilt in 1816, the nave has two bays with simple Y-tracery filled with iron frames in a mesmerizing knotwork pattern. Three-light E window with stone mullions. The tower rises in three diminishing stages to battlements and spiky pinnacles. Inside, an open timber roof with kingpost trusses. Good pews with finial-topped ends. – STAINED GLASS. 'Suffer Little Children', set in weakly coloured panels; by *Ward & Hughes*, London, 1892.

ST JOSEPH. 1998 by *Daly, O'Neill & Associates*. An uneventful assemblage of diminishing angular blocks forming nave, transepts and a deep porch. Roughcast, with gables of squared hammered limestone. Expansive glazed timber grids contrast with short rows of tiny square apertures close to the eaves level. Inside, a carpeted warehouse with laminated timber roof and a bowed sanctuary wall of glass bricks.

MADDEN RECTORY. 0.5 km SW. Derelict. A substantial block of two storeys over a raised basement, built *c.* 1825 for the Rev. James Jones, possibly by *William Farrell*. Imposing three-bay front, nicely proportioned with diminishing windows and a shallow gabled projection. Handsome carved doorcase with scrolled brackets and side-lights under a wide segmental fanlight. Windows with marginal glazing. Two-bay side elevation with relieving arches on the ground floor. Good STABLE BUILDINGS to the N, the main range pedimented with a clock face.

ST MARY, AGHAVILLY (C of I). 3.5 km NE. A tall three-bay hall typical of *Joseph Welland*'s mid-C19 work, with quarry-glazed lancets, bellcote, and a large gabled porch. The W and S walls were rendered in the early C20 with an unusual textured finish, perhaps in imitation of the punched limestone window dressings. Three-light E window with Y-tracery. Later vestry to the S.

DRUMHILLERY PRESBYTERIAN CHURCH. 3.5 km SE. 1752 and 1868. Big four-bay hall in rubble and brick with limestone trim. Gable-fronted with three large round-headed windows assembled round a small door. Built or remodelled in 1868 by the Rev. James Macauley. Though the architecture all looks C19, the brickwork of a closed lunette on the rear gable holds a small stone plaque inscribed 1752. The interior is airy, with a flat plaster ceiling in three panels with large roses. – MONUMENT. The Rev. James Macauley †1874; a white marble plaque with inverted torches.

The MANSE opposite is a neat gable-ended roughcast block of two storeys with three bays and a recessed Tuscan doorcase.

FARNHAM   CN   *3000*

Today the historic house of Farnham is overwhelmed by a vast city-scale hotel – a paradigm of the uncontrolled exploitation of historic demesnes that characterized the economic boom of the early C21. Even on one of the largest demesnes in South Ulster, this is an unnerving case of development overkill. The origins of the demesne can be traced to a stone house in a bawn of sods with four flankers that was erected here by Sir Richard Waldron, who was granted 1,000 acres in 1610 under the Plantation. The Waldron tenure was short: Sir Richard died in 1617, and by 1640 the property with its unfinished castle had been sold to the Waldron carpenter Richard Castledyne. Before the end of the century the manor was in the possession of Robert Maxwell, Bishop of Kilmore, who was succeeded by his son, John. John

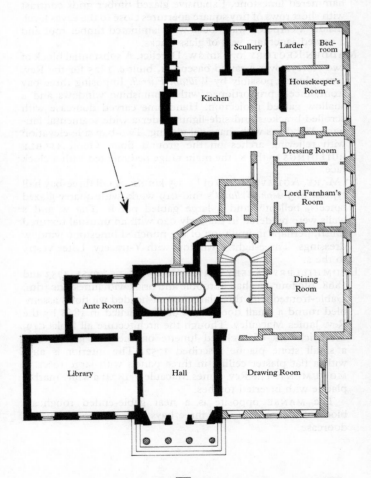

C18 House, retained in 1802, dem. 1961 ■   1802 additions by Francis Johnston ▨

Farnham.
Plan by K. Mulligan, 2012

1.　Landscape near Castleblayney (MN) (p. 1)

2	4
3	5

6	9
7	10
8	

11. Meigh (AH), Ballymacdermot, court tomb, Neolithic (p. 447)
12. Mullaghbawn (AH), Ballykeel Dolmen, Neolithic (p. 493)

| 11 | 13 14 |
| 12 | 15 16 |

13. Jonesborough (AH), Kilnasaggart Stone, C8 (p. 363)
14. Tynan (AH), village cross, C10 or C11 (p. 565)
15. Clones (MN), High Cross, C10 (p. 271)
16. Tynan (AH), Well Cross, C10 (p. 569)

17 | 18
   | 19

36 | 38
37 | 39

47. Ardress House (AH), late C17, remodelled by George Ensor after 1778,
    and later (p. 83)
48. Ardress House (AH), drawing room, plasterwork attributed to Michael
    Stapleton, late C18 (p. 84)
49. Armagh (AH), Rokeby Obelisk, begun 1782 (p. 136)
50. Dartrey (MN), Dawson Column, after 1807, attributed to James Wyatt
    (p. 314)
51. Dartrey (MN), Dawson Mausoleum, c. 1769–74, attributed to James
    Wyatt (p. 312)

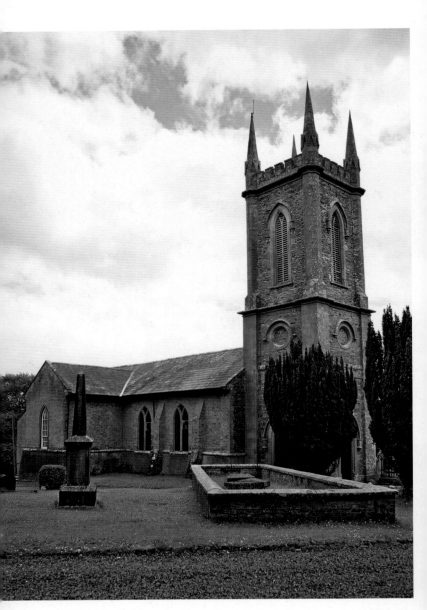

57. Dartrey (MN), Ematris Parish Church (C of I), 1729, tower added
    1840 (p. 313)
58. Ballyconnell (CN), Tomregan Parish Church (C of I), c. 1757, enlarged
    c. 1820 (p. 160)
59. Ballyconnell (CN), Tomregan Parish Church, interior of chancel
    (p. 160)

60	62
61	63

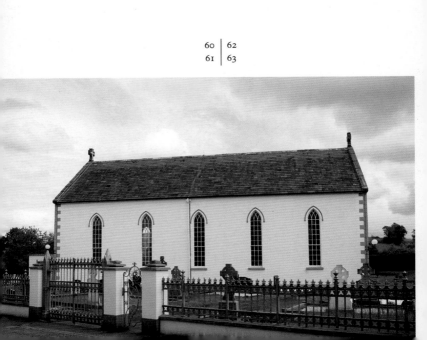

<table>
<tr><td rowspan="2">64</td><td>65</td></tr>
<tr><td>66 67</td></tr>
</table>

64 | 65
66 67

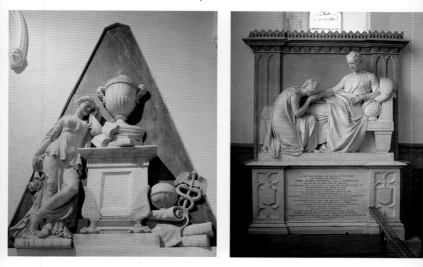

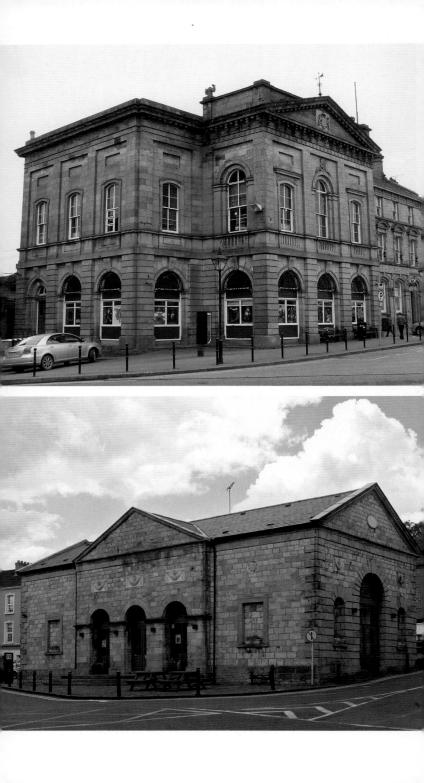

77. Aughnamullen (MN), Christ Church (C of I), by R. & J.A. Brandon, 1847, alterations of 1863 by Welland & Gillespie (p. 143)
78. Kilmore (CN), St Feidhlimidh's Cathedral, by William Slater, 1858–60 (p. 392)
79. Armagh (AH), St Mark (C of I), by Francis Johnston, 1811, enlarged by William Farrell, 1830, and Slater & Carpenter, 1866 (p. 115)

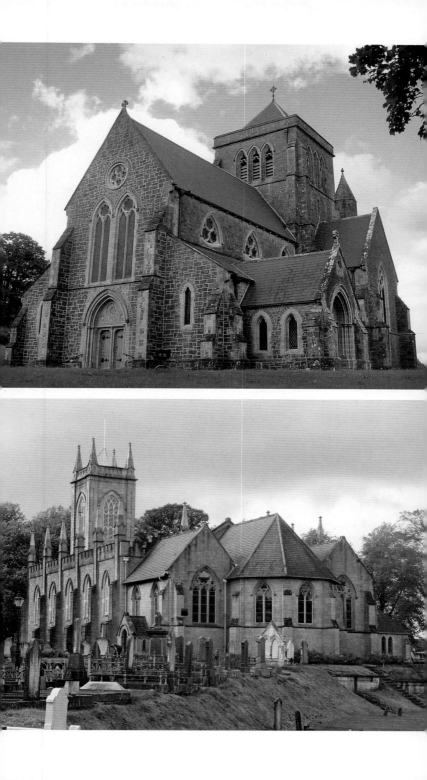

80. Armagh (AH), St Patrick's Cathedral (R.C.), begun 1840, interior of the nave (p. 112)
81. Armagh (AH), St Patrick's Cathedral (R.C.), choir vaulting, by J.J. McCarthy, *c.* 1854–9 (p. 111)

82. Portadown (AH), Methodist church, by John Boyd, 1858 (p. 505)
83. Butler's Bridge (CN), St Aidan, by William Hague, 1861 (p. 210)
84. Rockcorry (AH), St James (C of I), by W.J. Barre, 1854–61 (p. 522)

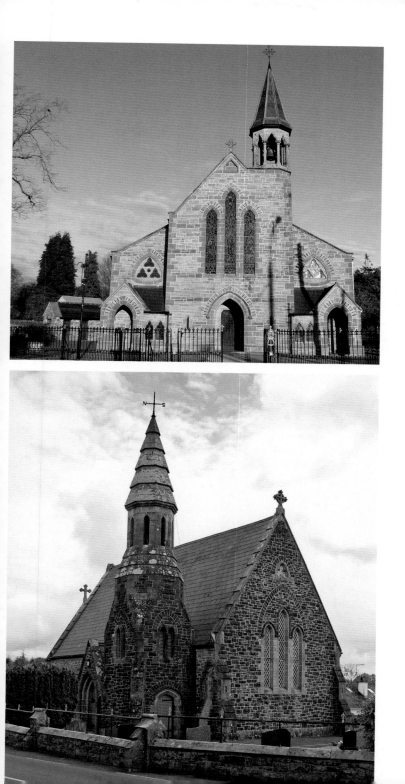

85. Armagh (AH), Gospel Hall
(former Masonic Hall), by
J.H. Fullerton, 1884 (p. 118)
86. Laragh (MN), St Peter
(C of I), 1868 or 1890
(p. 408)
87. Meigh (AH), Cloghogue,
Church of the Sacred Heart,
by Ashlin & Coleman,
1911–16 (p. 448)

93. Lurgan (AH), Brownlow House, by William Henry Playfair, 1833 (p. 436)
94. Castle Saunderson (CN), by George Sudden, *c.* 1835 (p. 227)

97	99
98	100

101. Armagh (AH), Clergy Houses, by John Boyd, 1855 (p. 109)
102. Monaghan (MN), St Macartan's Seminary, by Thomas Duff, 1840–8;
additions by J.J. McDonnell, 1908 (p. 481)
103. Bessbrook (AH), Town Hall (former Institute), by William J. Watson,
1886–7 (p. 202)

107. Tassagh (AH), Tassagh Viaduct, by Sir Benjamin Baker, 1903–11
(p. 550)
108. Lurgan (AH), former Courthouse, by Thomas Turner and Henry
Davison, 1872, with the Millar Memorial, by John Robinson, 1859
(p. 431)
109. Monaghan (MN), Bank of Ireland (former Hibernian Bank), by O'Neill
& Byrne, 1874 (p. 474)

110. Cavan (CN), Cathedral of SS Patrick and Felim (R.C.), by Ralph Byrne, 1939–42 (p. 248)
111. Armagh (AH), Bairnswear Factory (now Armagh Business Centre), by T.F.O. Rippingham, 1950 (p. 128)
112. Tandragee (AH), weavers' houses, Laurelvale, by T.F.O. Rippingham, 1944 (p. 547)

110 | 111
110 | 112

116. Craigavon (AH), Portadown College, by Shanks, Leighton, Kennedy &
Fitzgerald, 1972–6 (p. 299)
117. Donaghmoyne (MN), St Lastra, by Patrick Rooney, 1980 (p. 317)

116 | 118
117 | 119

118. Cavan (CN), Cock Hill apartments, by Fitzgerald Kavanagh &
    Partners, 2003 (p. 256)
119. Armagh (AH), Market Place Theatre, by Glenn Howells, 1995–2000
    (p. 128)

120. Armagh (AH), Joint Secretariat Building, by DA Architects, 2009
(p. 129)
121. Clones (MN), County Library, by Keith Williams Architects, 2006
(p. 275)

Maxwell built a house here, completed before his death in 1713, which retained some if not all of the older castle in its fabric. In 1779 Barry Maxwell, 3rd Baron Farnham, employed *James Wyatt* to remodel interiors in the house. Wyatt had been employed by Maxwell's brother, Henry, Bishop of Meath, to produce ideas for the Bishop's Palace at Ardbraccan, though ultimately it was completed by others; his involvement at Farnham seems also to have been limited, known principally from surviving ceiling designs and for the creation of a new library. The work was complete in time for Maxwell to be raised to the earldom of Farnham in 1785. He died in 1800.

In 1802 his son John James, the last earl, employed *Francis Johnston* to remodel the house and greatly enlarge it. Johnston in effect doubled the size by adding the present nine-bay block to the S, at right angles to the old house, but stepping forward to the W. To the N he created a new eight-bay front with its entrance set in a shallow two-bay projection with a crisp Greek Doric portico. Further service additions to the E, made for the 7th Baron in 1839, were all swept away when the house was again remodelled, by *Philip Cullivan* in 1961, for the 12th Baron, who had rejected more ambitious proposals by *Claud Phillimore*. Most of the older house was demolished and with it all that may have existed of *Wyatt*'s earlier work. What survives now is *Johnston*'s principal addition to the S, a long astylar block, originally roughcast, three storeys tall and nine bays wide, with the three central bays gently advanced as a pedimented frontispiece bearing the Farnham arms. A plain modillion cornice enhances the pediment and continues across the eaves, before a low hipped roof. The twelve-pane ground-floor windows rest on a limestone plinth; those above on a continuous string, subtly diminished, then reduced to just six panes on the upper floor. The three central windows on the ground floor are taller, with rounded heads set in a recessed arch and linked by a limestone impost in a design that clearly evokes Ardbraccan.

Inside, the plan owes its strangeness to the C20 demolition of the C18 block and the retention of *Johnston*'s additions, which had mostly comprised household, staff and service accommodation. It is difficult to understand the logic of the decision, and the consequence is a poorly laid out sequence of diminishing rooms. The old house was on a tripartite plan comprising a deep entrance hall in the centre with a bow-ended staircase behind, flanked by a library and drawing room. With the library, hall and stairs swept away, a more modest entrance front was formed in the shallow three-bay projection that resulted from the retention of Johnston's drawing room and stair which provided the link to the old house. Here in the new 'front' the sandstone columns were reused in a new concrete portico, now leading directly into the side of Johnston's stair hall. This space is elegantly expressed, with apsidal ends and understated Neoclassical plasterwork that seems more suggestive of *Wyatt* than Johnston, suggesting that he copied the stair in the old house that his replaced. The cantilevered sandstone staircase with scrolled wrought-iron balusters

p. 33

gives an impression of weightlessness in a design that seems effortless. The stair hall is linked by a short corridor to a service stair at the opposite end, with the main rooms laid out as an enfilade across the front, formed in 1961 out of the former dining room, Lord Farnham's study and dressing room, and the house-keeper's rooms. Consequently none of these spaces is especially decorated beyond simple Neoclassical cornices, except for the largest, the former dining room, with a quirky modillion cornice. The blocky white marble chimneypiece here is C19 with Greek Revival ornament; in the room at the opposite end is a delicate Wyattesque design in white-and-grey marble, with Neoclassical tripods over the pilasters and in the centrepiece two griffins flanking a funerary urn.

The house is today no more than a frontispiece, its unused rooms providing little more than status to a bland hotel complex, institution-like, spreading this way and that. Designed by *Gilroy & McMahon*, this array of disparate blocks, mostly of three storeys, is in the usual ugly early C21 blend of materials: cement render, masonry cladding, cedar panelling, glass, powder-coated aluminium, and zinc roofing. The main entrance is at the side of the old house, a glazed butterfly canopy rather like an entrance one might expect at a hospital, here opening into the predictable marble-floored and glass-roofed lobby in which the Doric portico stands to one side as a kind of irrational absurdity – a prisoner of the guiding modernist principles surrounding it.

A surprising survival is the unusual solitary GARDEN HOUSE, situated a little to the E of the house, skewed on the high garden wall so as to give it greater curiosity, its origin probably lying in the earliest foundations here. Shamefully abandoned at the time of writing, it is a tall three-storey block in roughcast with just a single bay in the centre and a hipped roof which extends over lean-to projections, stepped back on either side of the main front. Inside one of these projections a heavy Georgian stair leads into a square groin-vaulted room on the first floor.

When Arthur Young visited in 1776 he wrote, 'Farnham is one of the finest places I have seen in Ireland; the water, wood and hill are all in a great stile, and abound in a variety of capabilities.' Today the over-development of this deeply rural setting extends like an infection, spreading to conference facilities built on the walled gardens, and to a scattering of suburban apartments and houses, many vacant and unfinished at the time of writing, which sit alongside abandoned stables and vernacular barns of an important agricultural complex; through the wider landscape the inescapable golf course contrasts incongruously with the pictur-esque character still perceptible in the rest of the demesne.

FORKHILL   AH

A small village in south Armagh, set in the picturesque valley of the River Forkhill.

Parish Church (C of I, former). An attractive small church,
built in 1767 under the patronage of Richard Jackson of
Forkhill House. The C18 building was a plain gabled hall of
three bays with rubble walls, moulded eaves course and a small
W porch. Remodelled with new twin lancets in 1859, when a
belfry and a short chancel projection, integrated with a lean-to
vestry, were added. The result suggests a homogeneous C19
design. Converted to domestic use *c.* 1990 by *G. Fay.*

St Oliver Plunkett. A strange church with warehouse proportions, *c.* 1997. Roughly square in plan, with a gabled frontispiece deeply projecting on a plain arcade with a Romanesque
corbel table, flanked to the E by small arcaded porches.
Cement-rendered walls with tightly grouped straight buttresses
and narrow round-headed windows; all under a massive low-
lying, slate-covered gambrel roof.

Folly Tower. 1 km NW. A late C18 pepperpot tower picturesquely sited on a rocky outcrop on the lower slopes of Cross-
lieve; a squat cylinder with rubble walls and battlements.

St Patrick, Drumintee. 2 km NE. On an exposed rural
hilltop, a prominent and assured Gothic church on a basilican
plan with a three-stage tower, dramatically offset on the E gable
to command the surrounding countryside. Designed by *John
Murray* and begun in 1866, with walls of squared hammered
limestone with dressed blue limestone trim. The detail is E.E.,
with routine paired lancets lighting the aisles and clerestory
and three graded lights in the gables. The contractor was
Arthur Hammond. Though dedicated in 1869, the building
remained unfinished for some years; in 1883 the interior was
still undecorated, and the tower not yet started. In 1896 *J. J.
McDonnell* furnished designs to complete the upper stage,
including an elaborate broach spire with lucarnes; the plans
were never realized, but McDonnell's hand can be seen in the
rusticated stonework of the clasping buttresses and the completion of the upper stage with battlements and pinnacles.

Inside, a five-bay nave is carried on an arcade of moulded
arches supported on columns of tooled limestone, under a
wagon roof with two-centred arched trusses and pierced brass
grilles along the spine. – Monuments. S aisle: the Rev. Bartholomew Campbell †1847; a neat marble tablet. – N aisle: the
Rev. Michael McParland †1853; an elegant Gothic aedicule
with crocketed gable.

Forkhill House. 2 km SE. The puzzling remnant of a larger
house. A tall three-bay, three-storey, gable-ended block with
Gothick casements on the upper levels that until the 1920s
stood on one side, as the servants' and kitchen wing, of a neat
three-bay, two-storey house. This was early C19 in appearance,
with hipped roof, sash windows and a low porch on primitive
square pillars. After the main house was demolished the surviving wing was converted and given plate-glass windows on the
ground floor; these windows replaced a central door flanked
by niches, so might this roughcast block actually represent the
original C18 house?

To one side an attractive four-centred arch – like another at the entrance to the demesne – leads into an attractive FARM-YARD with two-storey roughcast buildings arranged in a U-plan range. Forkhill was the seat of Richard Jackson until his death in 1787.

GLASLOUGH

Sir Thomas Ridgeway was granted MacMahon lands here in 1608; he formed a defensive bawn around 'a little English house', and eventually replaced that with a castle exaggeratedly described as 'magnificent . . . flanked by circular towers with moat and drawbridge'. Nothing survives, but the distinctive castle built by Ridgeway on his Tyrone estate at Augher suggests its possible sophistication. In 1661 on his translation to Clogher the nonagenarian Bishop John Leslie was given £2,000 as a reward for supporting Charles II; with his gift he bought Glaslough, and here he installed his family in 1665. By the time of his death in 1671 at the age of a hundred Leslie had 'strengthened and extended' Ridgeway's Plantation castle and refounded the nearby parish church.

A small settlement had evolved at Tullyree in the shadow of the castle, and it was gradually extended by the Leslies to form the impressive main street that retains a terrace of good two-storey Georgian houses on its w side. The most imposing building is a large C19 coaching inn with attic dormers and mullioned windows, set with a large forecourt at the junction of the side street.

In the mid C19 portions of the main street, including the old village site, were appropriated when the demesne was extended; the parish church was absorbed within its walls, so that today the picturesque village street terminates abruptly at the pretty Gothic lodges that form the entrance to Castle Leslie. Since 2005 extensive new streetscapes have been developed by the Castle Leslie estate close to the old village site; not entirely disagreeable, if a little too many, two-storey stone and rendered HOUSES designed by *Consarc* in an artisan style to suggest a natural expansion of the village.

ST SALVATOR, DONAGH PARISH CHURCH (C of I). A large and evocative hall-and-tower church lost in a dark circle of trees on the edge of the demesne. The soaring tower, in rubble with round-headed openings, is all that survives of the structure built by Bishop Leslie in 1670. It has an impressive five stages, stacked like building blocks, gently diminishing to an ashlar upper stage with crenellations and pinnacles that was added in the C19. The three lower stages were given stepped angle buttresses; even with these additions it is still not quite worthy of the Rev. Daniel Beaufort's 1787 dismissal as a 'heavy ill looking high spire'. The nave was rebuilt in 1763, a fact proclaimed in stone on the s wall. It is boxy, of four bays with walls of well-wrought squared and snecked limestone, an emphatic moulded eaves cornice, and gently pointed windows in plain surrounds. The deep polygonal chancel and adjoining vestry to the s are highly ornamental additions of 1888 of a quality attributable to *W. H. Lynn*, perhaps following his involvement at Castle Leslie; the chancel is stoutly buttressed between simple lancets; the plate tracery in the vestry and the slender minaret chimney rising over the fish-scale slating are unexpected refinements.

Inside, of the C18 interior only the thick-set tower stairs survive; the nave roof has heavy exposed kingpost trusses of the C19. Beyond a plain plaster arch the chancel provides a striking architectural contrast, a sumptuous small space highly finished in Caen stone with a perfectly scaled rib-vault springing from clustered shafts. The capitals are remarkable, carved to varying degrees of artistic competence and completion as if simultaneously by master, apprentice and amateur; this might well suggest the personal handiwork of the patron, *Sir John Leslie*, who was a keen amateur artist. – STAINED GLASS. N wall: richly patterned glass by *R. D. Edmondson & Son*, Manchester, *c.* 1858; chancel: Faith, Hope and Charity, 1883, attributed to *O'Connor & Taylor*, London. – MONUMENTS. N wall: William Young Johnston †1854 at the Battle of Alma, by *R. Kirk*. A sarcophagus-shaped tablet bearing a portrait cameo; resting on it, books, a palette and a lyre, draped with a regimental flag. – Chancel wall: Sir John Leslie, 1st Bt †1916; a simple plaque by *Purdy & Millard*, Belfast. – s wall: Sophia Smith †1903, signed *F.G.* 1904. – James McCullagh †1910; a carved Gothic design with polished shafts, by *E. Stuart*, Monaghan.

MONUMENT. 1874 by *W. H. Lynn* and *S. F. Lynn*. Prominently positioned in the centre of the village, set in a railed section of the demesne wall with a perfect backdrop of Irish yews. A handsome monument, the successful collaboration of two brothers as a tribute to Colonel Charles Powell Leslie M.P. who died in 1872, paid for by his tenants, who subscribed over £500. Portland stone. Raised above a canted water trough on a stepped plinth with scrolled side brackets is a fine Ionic aedicule with segmental pediment bearing Leslie's cypher; it frames a moulded square panel inset with a circular niche bearing *Samuel Lynn*'s bronze bust of Leslie, the design for which he exhibited at the Royal Academy in 1874. The water spouts out from the fearsome iron griffin of the Leslie crest fixed to the base.

RAILWAY STATION (former). Off New Line. 1859. Derelict. Designed for the Ulster Railway, like nearby Tynan, by a *Mr Clayton*, possibly the Brixton architect who later designed the terminus to the Finn Valley Railway in Donegal in 1862. The designs were shown at the Architectural Exhibition, London, in April 1859; the *Civil Engineer and Architect's Journal*, while finding the Tynan station 'absolutely ugly', accepted the Glaslough design as 'a happier conception' and deemed the bell-turret and some of its timberwork 'well devised'. Smaller than Tynan, it is a similar gabled design in rock-faced sandstone, here with two gables side by side, one larger and advancing with a large and distinctively mullioned window to light the passenger hall, divided as at Tynan with small upper panels in a star shape. A gabled porch projects from the smaller gable.

CASTLE LESLIE. Bishop John Leslie's elaboration of the castle is not recorded, other than the implication that it was built of brick. It was extensively remodelled in 1720, when it was made more sedate, less defensive in bearing, than it must have been originally. To the Bishop's son who carried out the works, it was transformed into 'the handsomest house in the three counties', but in 1787 the Rev. Daniel Beaufort found the house 'very old and ugly'. Photographs and engravings record old Castle Leslie as a solid and venerable house, a three-storey roughcast block with gabled end bays very much in the manner of other late C17 houses like Old Bawn s of Dublin or Myrtle Grove in Co. Cork, and in general appearance rather like Richhill, if altogether more imposing, with less projection given to the end bays. While an irregular ridge and massive gable stack hinted at its origins in Ridgeway's castle, nothing can explain the massive rounded gable ballooning over the three central bays, quite unlike anything found elsewhere in Ireland, and really a sort of debased French Baroque detail. The narrow windows with sashes and the pedimented Doric doorcase were also part of the Early Georgian alterations. In 1842 the house was said to have been lately 'modernised and enlarged'; the

Glaslough, Old Castle Leslie.
Engraving, 1879

works probably included the single-storey block surviving today as the billiard room.

Colonel Charles Powell Leslie, the third of that name in succession, first gave serious considerations to rebuilding, proposing in 1856 to spend £16,000 on a new house. By then *Ninian Niven* and others were employed in improving the park and gardens, and a scheme had been made for a grand castellated entrance, for which *Alfred G. Jones* had furnished designs in 1854. However, Leslie was to remain ambivalent about the house; in 1856 he had written to his younger brother and heir, John, that 'the more I see of this country, the more persuaded I am that it is not at all necessary to have anything but comfort in a house: many rooms is a mistake'.

The earliest overall scheme for the house was a proposal by *Lanyon & Lynn* dated 1859. However Leslie remained indecisive, and in 1866 after the London landscape designer *William Broderick Thomas* had marked the trees to be removed for the new house he hesitated and the trees were spared. In 1872 the rebuilding passed to John Leslie, a man with strong artistic sensibilities, and in that same year *W. H. Lynn*, by then in independent practice, produced a number of ambitious and presumably costly schemes, including a dreamy medieval French château with a stout circular entrance tower that recalls Killyleagh in Co. Down; a moderately restrained low Italianate house; and a rigorously picturesque Scots Baronial castle, similar to his earlier, unexecuted plan for Portavo and the contemporary executed designs for Belfast Castle. This design came closest to the form of the finished building, though it proposed a more massive six-storey entrance tower set diagonally against the main block. That feature was eventually pared down, suggesting Lynn's cynical response to the Leslies' drawn-out equivocation on the decision to rebuild.

Work finally began in 1874, the year in which Lynn exhibited his rejected designs for 'a French Renaissance pile'. The contractor was *James Henry*. The sum initially agreed, £19,043, was ultimately increased by £3,000 because of alterations to the plan. As work commenced Leslie, an Italophile and an aspiring artist, departed for Italy, and in 1875 he was in Florence acquiring trophies for his new house from the Aldobrandini Palace sale. Many of the rooms were furnished from this trip; his greatest prize was the ceramic chimneypiece by *Andrea della Robbia*, bought for £30 and installed in the drawing room. In 1876 Leslie was made a baronet, and by 1877 he was able to immerse himself in furnishing the house.

As it stands today, sheltered in woods beside Glaslough Lake, Castle Leslie is a formidable building, a cheerless Tudor Revival design in dark local limestone and red Dumfries sandstone, its hard angular massing, highly textured stonework and extensive plate glass all planned with an impressive sense of the irregular. The N front is dramatically austere, the main block dominant between lower service wings extending at right angles, the walls sparing in ornament: the effect seems a little

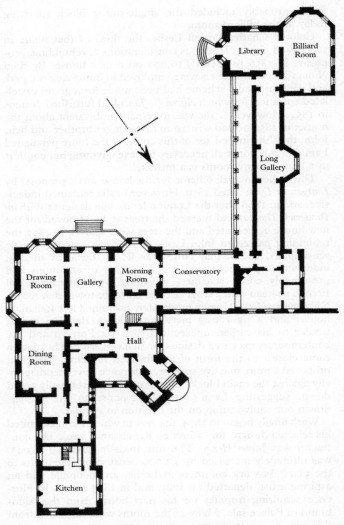

Glaslough, Castle Leslie.
Plan by K. Mulligan, 2012

institutional, if not unwelcoming. The gabled entrance tower
kicks out diagonally, three storeys tall, with a central oriel and
below that a round-headed arch supported on crisp Ionic
pilasters, set to one side. This leads to a porch that burrows
through to the main block; steps rise between a short open
arcade and recesses mirroring that opposite, where the tympana
offer a welcome in the fruit-garlanded words 'Dulce' and

Glaslough, Castle Leslie, stair hall.
Drawing by L. Mulligan, 2012

'Domum' below keystones decorated with the youthful profiles of the Leslie children. The garden fronts to the s and e are less forbidding. The broad e front overlooking garden terraces and the lake is asymmetrical, emphasized by a bay window extended to the attic as a turret and by the recessed kitchen range. Here the exposed basement and attic dormers dramatically increase the sense of scale. The adjoining s front is symmetrical: two-storey bay windows in gabled end bays with three bays in between. The stonework seems less severe here: narrow enriched panels are set over the bay windows, and the contrast between the squared rock-faced limestone and the finely droved Dumfries sandstone enlivens the gaunt, impossibly slender chimneystacks. To the w is a short arcaded conservatory, and at right angles an Italianate loggia, an elegant eleven-bay arcade of Tuscan columns. At the end are the small gabled library and billiard room, in the farthest corner of the formal garden; the arm's-length placing of these rooms was a convention in Victorian planning, but rarely has it been achieved so handsomely.

Inside, a compact, well-considered plan is revealed: none of the rooms is overwhelmingly large, but there is an impressive sense of grandeur. The ENTRANCE HALL is a small and closed square space with a Roman-inspired mosaic floor, dark wainscoting and an elaborate carved chimneypiece with an effusive

100

overmantel. It leads directly to the STAIR HALL, a bright lofty space, the walls crisply decorated with recessed arches, framed by Ionic pilasters that continue into the landing – altogether Palladian in feeling but for the open-well Jacobean-style staircase, a weighty composition with a balustrade of arches with tapered Ionic balusters.

The GALLERY forms the principal axis of the house, the largest space providing circulation. It and the stair hall evoke the hand of Lynn's former partner *Sir Charles Lanyon*, and so were perhaps carried over from the firm's earlier scheme; with its shallow barrel-vault and columnar screen it revisits Lanyon's gallery for Stradbally Hall in Co. Laois designed just a few years before. The room is flanked by large and small drawing rooms. The smallest, the BLUE DRAWING ROOM to the w, is entirely c18 in feeling, with a chimneypiece of richly carved wood surrounding Siena and white marble and a delicate chinoiserie overmantel – the point of departure for effective avian murals of *c.* 2005 by *Nat Clements*. To the E is the larger DRAWING ROOM, with bay windows to S and E and the *Della Robbia* chimneypiece. Behind the loggia a long carefully staged top-lit corridor, with colourful, loosely painted allegories by *Sir John Leslie*, leads to the remote library and billiard room, the latter with a disparate pair of carved wood c18 chimneypieces, best at the N end, the S one heavily restored.

The scene in GLASLOUGH DEMESNE today still tallies with Daniel Beaufort and Arthur Young's c18 praise of the setting with its scenic wood-lined lake. The GARDENS are Victorian. *Ninian Niven* was involved here in 1854, designing a conservatory for the kitchen garden, and in the same year *John Cox* made a proposed layout for that garden. *James Howe* carried out further designs for the gardens and pleasure grounds in 1866. He was succeeded, briefly, by *William Broderick Thomas*. Below the terraces, the BOATHOUSE is a romantic timber structure contemporary with the house and possibly also by *Lynn*. On the NE perimeter of the demesne the FARM-YARD is an attractive rustic building in limestone ashlar with a pedimented frontispiece, presumably the 'excellent enclosed farmyard' seen by Sir Charles Coote in 1801, to which additions were then proposed.

The LODGES form an important collection of buildings, all c19; the earliest are two attributed to *John Nash*, then engaged nearby at Caledon in Tyrone. The remote COTTAGE ORNÉ GATE LODGE (Mullanlary) on the NE corner of the demesne, derelict at the time of writing, is a pretty single-storey gingerbread house with wondrous curvilinear-patterned iron casements, rendered walls, canted end bays, and oversailing hipped roofs supported on iron columns to form a continuous veranda across the front, the eaves greatly enriched by pendant honeysuckle ornaments. The cast-iron entrance gates are stamped *Shekleton, Dundalk*. To the N the GOTHIC LODGE, behind a gaunt tripartite castellated gate screen with distinctive ogee pinnacles, is similar to Nash's design for Longnor Hall in Shropshire; it is a simple rectangle, two-roomed, with a heavy castellated Gothic frontispiece in ashlar framed by octagonal buttresses with a traceried window between. The heavy cast-iron gates with handsome Gothic detailing are also stamped *Shekleton, Dundalk*. The main gate has twin lodges closing the top of the Main Street: a neat symmetrical composition by *Lynn* of *c*. 1872, two storeys with paired crowstepped gables, single-storey side porches, and pretty Gothic glazing. The HUNTING LODGE, built in the 1860s and known then as 'the agency', is a large building in dark rock-faced limestone repeating Lynn's distinctive crowstepped gables. DAWSON'S LODGE to the NW, also by Lynn, is an L-plan block with curvilinear gables and mullioned windows.

ST MARY, GLENNAN. 1 km NW. Built in 1837 by the Rev. Patrick Moynagh. An ignorantly scaled lancet hall, massive in its proportions and modest in its details. Roughcast with rusticated quoins. Four bays, the big three-bay front with windows on two levels and a nasty concrete cross over the gable. Inside, the ceiling is a flat grid, having been lowered in the C20. Plain and effective Ionic reredos.

GLENNAN HOUSE. 1.5 km NW. Solid late C19 house in rock-faced ashlar. Two-storey three-bay block, with central porch, plate-glass windows, hipped roof and yellow brick stacks.

Behind is a small Nonconformist CHURCH. A trim two-bay roughcast hall and porch; pointed windows and a good doorcase with pilasters and entablature.

PRESBYTERIAN CHURCH, GLENNAN. 1.5 km NW. 1874 by *John Boyd*. A neat T-plan Gothic church and tower, highly textured in rock-faced ashlar with smooth sandstone dressings. Three-bay nave with lancets and very short transepts. Five graded lights in the E and W gables. The tower adjoins the W gable, a tall square structure with a steep pyramid roof, nicely finished with fish-scale slating.

MANSE. Attractively sited across a stream beside the church. A small late C19 house of four bays in squared limestone and brick trim with three attic dormers, Georgian sashes, and a canopied entrance with a Tudor-arched doorway.

DONAGH CHURCH AND CROSSES. 1.5 km SW. A small enclosed churchyard, with the low rubble walls of a grave-cluttered medieval church and scattered cross fragments. As the name indicates, this was one of the *domhnachs* or early churches usually associated with St Patrick; its ancient origins are indicated by traces of an outer oval enclosure which can be discerned on older maps. First mentioned in 1306 and ruinous by 1622, the present church is principally of interest to the archaeologist: a small rectangle divided in two by a cross-wall, each part entered by breaches in the N wall. To the N lies a small wheeled CROSS, a short stocky shaft with unpierced nimbus, decorated with chevrons on one side and a weathered depiction of the Crucifixion, of indeterminate date. Socketed base plinths of at least two other CROSSES lie nearby.

GOSFORD CASTLE   AH

1.3 km N of Markethill

Set on a ramparted platform in dense woods, Gosford is a great brawny pile. Large and unforgiving, its castellated form rises mirage-like, a picturesque grouping of square and circular masses with carefully recessed surface layers and an impressive display of Romanesque detailing. Even in pale granite, the architecture appears grave, a brooding grandiloquent expression of an invented past that represents the most assured instance of a revived Norman style in these islands. It was designed in 1819 by *Thomas Hopper* for Archibald Acheson, 2nd Earl of Gosford, paradoxically described in 1815 as 'a good natured and venerable little fellow without political or personal pretensions'. It was however the usual opportunism of the C17 that had brought the Achesons from Scotland on the Plantation tide. In 1610 Henry Acheson was granted the 1,000-acre manor of Coolmalish, though it is unclear whether he built the first castle here, or if it was his brother, Archibald, whose succession to the property in 1628 coincided with the gift of a baronetcy. The castle was renamed Gosford, in reference to the family's origins in East Lothian, and it was as Gosford that Jonathan Swift knew the place when he stayed here on extended sojourns in 1728 and 1729. The Plantation castle, about which nothing is known, had probably been rebuilt by then, and if we can accept the image on an estate map of 1754 its replacement was a seven-bay, three-storey block of Early Georgian character. Its builder was perhaps the 5th Baronet, Arthur Acheson, Swift's introverted and distant host:

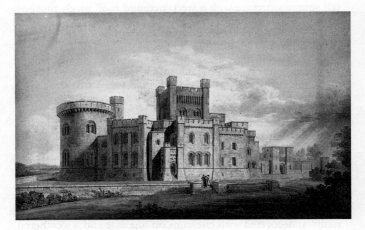

Gosford Castle, principal front.
Watercolour by J. Miller, 1828

Such is the fate of Gosford's knight
Who keeps his wisdom out of sight
Whose uncommunicative heart
Will scarce one precious word impart . . .

That house is understood to have been destroyed by fire in the early C19. By then the family had risen steadily through the peerage, accepting an earldom in 1806 with the 2nd Earl succeeding just a year later. He waited twelve years before embarking on what remains the most ambitious building in South Ulster, a dour baronial fantasy with a massive if not overblown gravity.

Gosford represents the most substantial commission of *Hopper*'s early career, begun by 1820 when he had not yet proved his credentials for so ambitious a work, though he had been favoured by the Prince Regent to work at Carlton House. It was probably Hopper's role as arbitrator in a dispute between Nash and Lord O'Neill at Shane's Castle in Antrim in 1816 that won him the commission here, brought to Lord Gosford's notice perhaps by his agent William Blacker, who had also acted for O'Neill. It is difficult to gauge the role of the earl in the actual choice of design, but there is nothing to suggest that he was the innovator. The Romanesque style was never to become popular, the general view holding that 'the forms of its apertures are inapplicable to our habits'. Hopper's unique feeling for Romanesque forms expressed here, and later in a more ambitious work at Penrhyn Castle in Wales, was undoubtedly conditioned by his birthplace in Rochester. Its numinous C12 castle inspired his decision to focus the picturesque composition of both these castles around a great Norman keep, which he then enriched with studiously transcribed detail from other Norman castles such as Hedingham in Essex, where as it happens he was appointed County Surveyor in 1816.

Eventually, however, Hopper was to express deep regret that he had come to Ireland, so disillusioned had he become with his patron in 1834. Even then the castle was far from complete. Given its size, the building works were naturally protracted, but there were also financial constraints. In 1821 the outbuildings were progressing, with *William Walker* as clerk of works. In 1828 *John Donnelly* had built the principal stairs in Portland stone, 62 tons of the material having been shipped between Weymouth and Newry for the purpose. By April 1833 *James Donnelly* was preparing to organize the plasterers' and joiners' work 'necessary to complete the different apartments'. In January 1834 Hopper wrote expectantly to Lord Gosford, 'I shall be happy to congratulate you on your actual occupation of the castle.' But by then it had taken too long and cost too much, leaving both architect and client weary. Each rather candidly expressed his discontent to the other, Hopper sounding enormous regret after Gosford chose to measure the apparent failures of his building against the success of the recently completed house at Drumbanagher (Jerrettspass): 'I am glad if Major Close admits that he has got so perfect a house and sincerely congratulate Mr. Playfair who is a very clever man although I suspect it has not cost him one hundredth part the thought, and but a small portion of the trouble, which I took to try to make Gosford Castle as convenient and as good as I wished it to be . . . I have always felt a sorrow that I ever went to Ireland. I now consider it a misfortune.' Setting aside the indulgences of artistic temperament, Hopper's misfortune was perhaps to have become embroiled in a dispute between Walker and the contractor, whose side was taken by the patron. Progress was further delayed by Gosford's appointment to the governorship of Lower Canada in 1835. Walker had by then been replaced as clerk of works by *John Farrell*. In 1836 James Graham, the first of the C19 tourists to visit the house, described it as 'entirely modern, indeed not yet completed', with only a few of the rooms inhabited, and orders 'to admit nobody' in Gosford's absence. In 1839 Gosford was recalled and work continued under the superintendence of the Newry architect *Thomas Duff*, who remained until his death in 1848, completing various additions, alterations and improvements valued at £5,400. In 1842 Lord Gosford's agent had cautioned, 'if you can, I think you may continue with strict economy to continue to live here comfortably'. Despite his disillusionment in 1834, Hopper remained involved after the death of the 2nd Earl in 1849 until at least 1854, two years before his own death. Expenditure on the building remained substantial up to 1864, the average annual sum amounting to about £7,000, more than a third of the estate income.

Buildings rarely betray the tortures of their evolution. The castle as it stands today, a collection of brooding, picturesquely grouped masses, all executed in clean ashlar, looks quite unified; but it is in fact the result of two distinct phases. The first and more protracted involved the bulk of the building executed under *Hopper*: in October 1852 the *Armagh Guardian* reported that 'a number of tradesmen are now engaged finishing the remaining wing of this building'. Hopper's work comprises the central keep rising out from the core of the plan over a disparate assemblage of cubic two-storey blocks and a great round tower set to one side. This stout two-storey structure is thrown out from the main block to stand at the end of a wilfully skewed wing in a way that underlines the architect's picturesque approach to the plan. The massing of the core blocks appears both solid and redoubtable, partly achieved by their being set on a tall plinth with quite a pronounced batter. In 1836 James Graham noted that this had first been finished in a composition plaster to mimic ashlar, but soon afterwards it was stripped bare, the limestone rubble wall presumably being thought to have a more convincing medieval appearance. Except for the bold machicolations on the towers, the battlements are rather tame-looking, closed but for the narrowest of loops, extending a horizontal profile across the building which makes the massing seem even more ponderous and the silhouette rather less eventful than one might hope for, or indeed expect, in a building with such picturesque potential. It does however point up Hopper's scrupulous concern for a more authentic Norman profile. On the E side, the original entrance was formed in the angle between the main block and the westerly skewed S wing, projected as a narrow towered gatehouse with a mock portcullis between the two broad projections associated with the Library and Dining Room. This was the main front, and the surfaces here are altogether richer than on the hard-edged N side, which became the new entrance front: a continuous arcaded corbel table runs below battlements; most of the main projections are relieved by shallow clasping buttresses, rising to square turrets, the angles all nicely figured with engaged shafts similar to those at Castle Rising in Norfolk.

The window openings are for the most part disposed in an orderly way, with round-headed forms naturally dominant. Those on the round tower are rather thickly formed and simply treated, with deep recession and bold chamfering increasing the impression of strength; the rest have engaged shafts and moulded

1 Entrance Hall
2 Hall
3 Inner Hall
4 Dining Room
5 Gun Room
6 Morning Room
7 Library
8 Writing Room
9 Drawing Room
10 Housekeeper's Room
11 Kitchen
12 Kitchen Court
13 Family Apartments (upper floors)

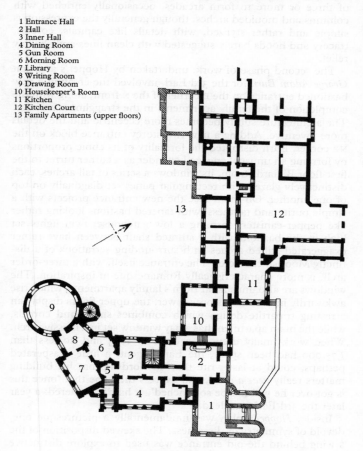

Gosford Castle.
Plan by K. Mulligan, 2012

arches, more richly treated on the main floor with chevroning. The most direct medieval quotation is presented by paired tri-angular-headed windows of the kind found on several Anglo-Saxon church towers such as Deerhurst in Gloucestershire. It seems that most of the enriched window surrounds were renewed as part of the later works: in 1836 Graham had also observed the application of composition over the freestone which had been used for the carved work of 'the sills and ribbits'; although he considered the result a 'wonderfully good imitation of granite', the material seemed to him too obviously contrived and ulti-mately must have proved problematic, to judge by the decay of the only surviving sandstone surround over the original entrance. Across the N front the windows are quite varied, with a marked randomness: square-headed openings fitted with conventional sashes are mixed with round-headed forms, many set in groups of three or more to form arcades, occasionally enriched with columns and moulded arches, though generally the expression is simple and rather stylized, with details like capitals, corbels, tracery and hoods barely suggested with clean lines and shallow relief.

The second phase of work, undertaken by Hopper's assistant *George Adam Burn* for the 3rd Earl, involved the creation a new bastioned entrance on the E corner of the N front, along with the completion of the family apartments in the straggling NW range. The architecture subtly becomes more eccentric and the details more inventive. Adding a new two-storey entrance block on the NE corner, Burn disrupted the formality of its cubic proportions by forming an unusual engaged cylinder as a corner turret to the first-floor Billiard Room, its windows a series of tall arches, each distinctively glazed with rectangular panes set diagonally on top of one another. On the N face the new entrance projects with a simple purity and tautness, with tapered bastions looking rather like pepper-canisters forming a low gatehouse; twin lights set high in the bastions with a stunted shaft between have rather exaggerated stilted arches with surrounding serrations of a dis-tinctly Moorish character. The entrance itself, with a three-order arch, is more characteristically Romanesque in inspiration. The windows are also unusual in Burn's family apartments, which rise awkwardly into a three-storey tower: the upper floors display an arresting tripartite design which combines shafts and corbels, while the main apartment has a bay window set in a massive arch. When work finally drew to a close in 1863 and no less than £75,000 had been spent, the Earl's agent, a little exasperated perhaps, could at last write that 'his lordship has his building matters really *near a close*', and express the hope that 'once this is got over he will not be so pinched'. It hardly mattered: a year later the 3rd Earl was dead.

Inside, *Hopper*'s plan was fundamentally a picturesque one, devoid of symmetry or directness. The skewed disposition of the S wing behind the old entrance was used to explore distinctive shapes in smaller rooms grouped in a way that set up the great circular Tower Room as the climax of the interior. This was the room most worthy of the proportions first intimated by the architecture, finally encountered only after a suspenseful sequence of small irregular rooms. Hopper's original effect remains, even if its power was diminished by the creation of *Burn*'s new approach, distantly located at the opposite end of the plan. Reached through the long side wall, the later ENTRANCE HALL to the NE is an imposing rectangular space, scaled to make an impact with its ceiling supported on great stone corbels decorated in an enriched Byzantine style. There is a convincing sense of medieval informality about it, with at one end a spiral turret-stair to the Billiard Room set in one of the bastions, nicely articulated with an open arcade on diminishing shafts. At the opposite end, Hopper's original plan is reached through a large INNER HALL, ruined at the time of writing but retaining a great canopied chimneypiece, probably by *Burn* – an ugly and absurd composition on short pillars. From here a narrow passage, with plaster vaults and arcaded dados, bisects the plan, cutting directly through one end of the older inner hall to terminate in the triangular vestibule of the old entrance. Flanking this corridor to the E is the DINING ROOM, a large rectangular room with a flat compartmented ceiling supported on corbel heads; around the walls, shallow recessed arches decorated with chevroned architraves and engaged shafts of polished Armagh marble, possibly the work of the Dublin sculptor *John Smyth*, to whom payments are recorded in the accounts. The same material is used for skirtings. The sash windows, otherwise conventional, are noteworthy here, elegantly divided into two tiers of arcuated glazing bars in oak, fully detailed with miniature capitals and bases. Through an archway at the N end is the deeply recessed servery, where John Ynyr Burges in 1862 noted that the 'sideboard or buffet takes a very sightly place amidst a recess of Norman-form columns with massive pendants dropping from its ceiling'.

Behind the entrance hall, the MORNING ROOM is an irregular octagon with a heavy chevroned frieze borne on a corbelled arcade. Beyond is the LIBRARY, a rectangular space like the Dining Room with a similar ceiling, but overall the most exotic and atmospheric interior, full of intended 'gloomth'. Bookcases are recessed under chevroned plaster arches, the side architraves elaborately carved in oak with rope and billet mouldings edging a flowered band. The spandrels are executed in florid fretwork, an extraordinary filigree in timber inspired by Byzantine designs. The narrow chimneypiece is elaborately treated with an integral overmantel mirror with an overlapping arcade, all framed between shafts that terminate in bestial heads derived from the supporters of the Gosford arms. In contrast to the intricacies of the decoration here, the TOWER ROOM verges on the monstrous, its sides relieved by recessed arches, above which is a deep plaster frieze articulated as a blind arcade. The ceiling above overwhelms by its plainness: the flat surface is given a centrifugal design formed of simple ribs, with the main ribs extending through the cove to intersect the frieze, resting there on short shafts that emerge from tapered bases in the spandrels between the wall arches. The chimneypiece has a double order of shafts in Armagh marble with a chequered insert in the same material paired with black marble.

Around 1922 *Henry Seaver* is said to have 'waved his Prospero's wand' over the castle, but it was largely disused and neglected throughout much of the C20. From 2006 it and the adjoining COURTYARD to the NE, a large quadrangular citadel of single-storey ranges and battlemented towers, were carved up to create a number of independent residences to designs by the *Boyd Partnership*.

The DEMESNE, most of it now a forest park, is densely wooded, but remains picturesque despite James Graham's dismissal of it as 'tame, chiefly from the want of water'. Underexplored vestiges survive of the old landscape, notable chiefly for its associations with Swift. Through his friendship with Lady Acheson he made an extended visit to Gosford in 1728 'to sponge for good cheer' following the death of 'Stella' (Esther Johnson), spending his time 'walking and reading and making twenty little amusing improvements'. The place proved a creative retreat, immortalized, if barely described, in verse; for a time Swift entertained the idea of building a summerhouse on the edge of the demesne, as a monument for his posterity to Drapier, the pseudonym he used for pamphleteering against the corrupt exploitation of the Irish currency, so 'That when a Nation long enslav'd, Forgets by whom it once was sav'd . . . This Hill may keep the Name of DRAPIER.' The name endures, but the scheme was ultimately thwarted by Swift's disenchantment with Sir Arthur, whose house and grounds he found to be wasted on such an 'anti-social recluse'.

In the garden, Swift worked independently of his hosts, directing the gardeners to make improvements; the nature of these is not known, and the evidence long overlaid. The principal feature of the older gardens remains the twin FISH PONDS, formerly overlooked by the old house. Moat-like, they flank twin GATE LODGES: small rubble-built blocks with shaped rear gables now temporarily lost in the clasp of vegetation, these are set on either side of the main carriage drive, united by a semicircular archway of undoubted grandeur, with bolection moulding that points to a C17 date. James Graham thought that the entrance was ancient, remarking that it was the intention for it to be retained without gates, so that the new approach could pass through, new entrances having been formed to the E and further S when the demesne was enlarged. At the S end, off the Tandragee Road, the LODGE is a compact and orderly *cottage orné*, a rustic cube decoratively clad in branches with a pyramid roof carried on poles to form a surrounding veranda; its sibling on the E side of the demesne at Drumalack has disappeared.

HAMILTON'S BAWN   AH

A small crossroads village near where John Hamilton in 1619 erected a fortified residence in a square bawn with flankers. It was attacked and destroyed in 1641, and possession later passed to the Achesons of Markethill. Hamilton's Bawn was well known to Jonathan Swift, who mentions a large old house here in 1728 which he immortalized in poetry, staging a mock debate in rhyme between Sir Arthur and Lady Acheson as to whether the building should be turned into a barracks or a malthouse; Sir Arthur seems to have triumphed, and a garrison was in evidence here until the early C19. Today a few well-dispersed vernacular buildings can be found amidst large late C20 housing developments,

GILDEA'S PUBLIC HOUSE. Standing at the crossroads. A long Early Georgian house, two storeys, gabled, with eight bays on the first floor – the rhythm interrupted in the centre – and five irregular bays on the ground floor; all with square openings and now with plate glass. To one side a naïve Gibbsian doorcase, rather attenuated, with blocked surround, triple keystone, straight entablature and a geometric patternbook fanlight. In the gable, above the understated shopfront, a florid if primitive relief of the Hamilton arms provides the only visible association between the founders and the modern village.

DRUMINNIS PRESBYTERIAN CHURCH. 2 km W. Small rural church. A trim stuccoed hall, four bays with gables, blocked quoins and plain round-headed windows.

KILDARTON PARISH CHURCH (C of I). 3 km W. Of c. 1840 by *William Farrell*, to a design shared with his church at Clare. A small single-cell with three bays, lancets and traceried E window of three cusped lights. The original entrance was set in a tall blind arch in the gable, now obscured by a small buttressed porch in squared masonry added by *J. H. Fullerton* in 1885. On the gable, the tall bellcote looks precarious. Atmospheric interior, nicely preserved, with lots of stained glass. The roof has exposed cast-iron trusses. The gallery is a nice work in carpenter's Gothic supported on elegant clustered colonnettes with quatrefoils on the frontal. – STAINED GLASS. Bright figurative glass, mostly C20, attractively coloured and best in the nave. N wall: 'The Light of the World' after Holman Hunt by *W. J. Douglas & Sons*, Belfast, c. 1925; S wall: the Sermon on the Mount by *Clokey & Co.*, Belfast, 1946.

Beside the church the PARISH HALL of 1900 is an attractive vernacular building; a three-bay, roughcast hall with end porches and segmental-headed windows with horizontal glazing bars and plate glass.

AHOREY PRESBYTERIAN CHURCH. 3.5 km NE. Plain C19 lancet hall of four bays, repaired in 1932 by *Henry C. Dorman* and enlarged in 1958. Effective-looking tower with angle buttresses and battlements added in 1973. – STAINED GLASS. 1977 by *Clokey*, Belfast; 1988 by *James Watson*, Belfast.

MARLACCO HOUSE. 3.5 km E. Beside Marlacco Lake, a pleasing, two-storey Late Georgian house in roughcast to an L-plan, built by Robert Boyd after he acquired the lands in 1813. The proportions are stocky, with low hipped roofs and stout redbrick stacks. Three bays to the front with twelve-pane sashes and a round-headed, fanlit doorcase, given fluted columns in the C20. Thoughtful Neoclassical addition of 2008 by *Alistair Coey*, neatly set back on one side. Attractive group of vernacular outbuildings behind in rubble and red brick making an informal courtyard.

4020   HILTON PARK   MN

A large demesne with rolling wooded hills and sheltered lakes on the edge of Scotshouse village. The old townland name of *Kilshanlis*, 'the wood of the old fort', suggests a long history of settlement now represented in a stately Late Victorian structure that conceals a more ancient house at its core. Hilton is the grandest house in Monaghan, a long and plain C18 roughcast block of two storeys and eleven bays, remodelled with an ashlar front for John Madden by *William Hague* between 1872 and 1877.

99 Hague's only substantial addition involved extending the front by a single bay to the N; the real impact was cleverly achieved by excavating the basement, thus enlarging the entire front so as to place the *piano nobile* above a properly expressed rustic – the exposed basement forming a short plinth – entered by a new, palatial *porte cochère* across the three central bays.

Hilton stands in territory once the stronghold of the MacMahons of Roosky, who sold it in 1624 to Sir William Temple, Provost of Trinity College Dublin. Passing to Sir Robert Forth, the estate was greatly expanded in the following decades by his descendants. A survey made by John McKinlie for James Forth in 1713 indicates that a large house had been built in Kilshanlis in the preceding decades – shown simply as a large seven-bay, two-storey, gable-ended block with stout red brick stacks. In 1734 the estate was acquired by the public-spirited Rev. Dr Samuel Madden of Manor Waterhouse in Fermanagh. Madden, whose incentives for the promotion of industry and arts made him famous and earned him the sobriquet 'Premium Madden', bought it for his younger son, John Madden; however by 1786 the Fermanagh estate was let in perpetuity and Hilton became the family's principal seat.

The 1835 Ordnance Survey Memoirs' description of the house as 'grand and imposing in the distance but plain on close examination' is confirmed in old photographs; it was a two-storey, five-bay roughcast block with bold quoins, and slightly recessed three-bay wings also of two storeys added in the late C18, all on a raised basement with a broad flight of stone steps at the front. The doorcase took the form of a Venetian window of the common Early Georgian kind; the side windows were filled in during agrarian unrest in the 1860s. Little but the four walls and the doorcase of the original house can have survived a devastating fire in 1804, and today it is the lingering presence in the plan of a single-pile arrangement with chimneystacks on the rear wall that most seems to hark back to it. The fire occurred in the tenure of the profligate Colonel Samuel Madden, so that restoration in the early C19 was slow, initially with parts simply thatched over to protect the walls. After Samuel Madden's death in 1814 the ruin was greatly rehabilitated by his son, Colonel John Madden. In the 1830s he added a new dining room to the s, and after his marriage in 1835 a nursery wing to the n and a servants' passage across the rear of the old single-pile plan as a link between these blocks. His architect was *James Jones* of Dundalk. Designs by Jones for a Neoclassical remodelling of the entrance front in ashlar, expressed principally in a grandiose Ionic portico, were not executed.

Colonel John Madden died in 1844 when his eldest son, also John, was just eight years old. Years later, his income boosted by £1,000 per annum after the death of his mother in 1870, this intriguing Madden revived the idea of remodelling the house. By then he had grown into a eccentric individual – an outsider and a loner, isolated politically as a Home Rule M.P. and described by his neighbour, Lady Dartrey, as a 'semi-madman'; by the end of the century he was forced to step down as a Justice of the Peace and Deputy Lieutenant. In this context the choice of *William Hague*, an architect favoured by Catholics, seems at first an anti-Establishment gesture. However, in September 1871 *Sir Charles Lanyon* had been consulted at Hilton about plans, with Madden returning the visit to Lanyon in Belfast a month later; yet by early December Hague was paying a second visit to Hilton, concluding plans for works that were eventually to begin the following March. No doubt Madden's view of Hague as a 'very clever rising young man' influenced his preference: his radical plans were more suited to an impressionable and ambitious young architect than to a more staid figure like Lanyon; and having trained as an engineer in London and Paris, it suited Madden to be involved directly with the works.

Madden and Hague's success was to achieve maximum effect with minimum intervention. Madden claimed it was his own idea to expose the basement, removing 8 ft (2.5 m) of earth to create the rustic. Clearing the earth was a massive task which extended well out to the front of the house and on the s side in the formation of the sunken terraces, which in parts required the removal of 14 ft (4.5 m) of earth. The idea had been no doubt inspired by the old house, where the entrance was sufficiently well raised above the ground, reached by a broad flight of steps, as to suggest a *piano nobile*; the old entrance became the central first-floor window. Madden appears to have relished the challenge, acting as his own overseer for the entire works and taking particular pride in the extensive underpinning; begun in August 1872, this involved cutting into the 'hard blue clay' below the old rubble foundations and constructing in 'heavy dressed limestone' virtually another storey below ground. So deep was the underpinning that Madden claimed to have been able to pass under the walls in his hat without stooping! The work, which took three years, progressed in 3-ft (90-cm) sections; most of the front wall of the central block had to be entirely rebuilt.

Hague's remodelling barely betrays the presence of the old house, which still constitutes the principal mass of the block.

What one sees now is a three-storey design with walls of toffee-coloured Dungannon sandstone, supplied by Samuel Howard from quarries at Gortnaglush and transported by train to Clones. The ground floor is emphasized by channelled ashlar on a plinth of heavily vermiculated stonework, extending to the quoins, and the windows are deeply sunken, piercing the masonry through crisp recessed frames. Above this, the windows on the *piano nobile* preserve the long Late Georgian proportions, accentuated by plate glass – installed in 1865 – and embellished on the recessed side bays with pediments that float rather eccentrically above sunk panels rather than entablatures (straight entablatures alone had originally been proposed). The upper floor retains its Georgian sashes. The old cornice and parapet were dismantled and replaced by a crisp cornice and deep parapet decorated by a volley of blind discs across the entire front.

The *porte cochère* is the *pièce de résistance* of the building, reviving in spirit the scheme for refronting the house that had been abandoned in the 1830s. Hague devised a broad and complicated Italianate design, carefully gauged to extend to two storeys, with elegant Scamozzian Ionic columns and pilaster responds, paired in the centre with a pediment, and altogether displaying a lightness of touch effected by its attenuation on high plinths; the balustrade here is based on those of Bramante's Tempietto; in contrast, the cornice carries a balustrade that is more thick-set and at once Victorian, with squat plinths and urns. Howard's bill for the *porte cochère* was £480, the capitals £65 extra, carved in Dublin by *Fitzpatrick & Molloy* of Glasnevin. The arms in the pediment are of Portland stone, as recommended by Hague (the Dungannon stone considered too full of grit); the carving was by *Robert Montgomery*, unfairly deemed by Madden to be 'badly done', though he paid him the £10 10s. to 'avoid litigation with a beggar'.

Round the corner the terraced s front is plain, with four bays; at the w end it is incomplete, the abrupt and jagged termination of the ashlar exposing the old rusticated quoins, left in anticipation of doubling the length of the front. In 1875 Hague had proposed a wing here to accommodate a new dining room and billiard room, centred at this point on a large and ugly bay window rising into the attics to accommodate female servant quarters, with an Italianate tower raised over the servants' stairs at the w end. (In 1877 Madden paid £25 to Hague for these designs, which he wrote were to 'stand over until I am ready to proceed'.)

Internally, Hague was unable to suppress his instincts for brooding Gothic spaces, using plaster vaulting and fitting decorative enrichments in the new ENTRANCE HALL to satisfy this tendency. It was formed in the old basement between a pantry and the housekeeper's room, which became respectively the study and smoking room, the floors of which, having been excavated during the underpinning, now match the new ground level outside. Brightly floored with encaustic tiles supplied by *H. Sibthorpe & Sons*, it is a low space with a shallow barrel-

vaulted ceiling panelled with ribs; Hague's suggestion for an
elaborate painted heraldic ceiling with gilding was not executed.
A short flight of steps to the old basement level leads formally to
the central event of Hague's design, an atmospheric STAIR
HALL, intended by the architect as a 'fine ante lobby' to the
reception rooms. It is lit by two large round-headed windows
filled with brightly patterned heraldic stained glass by *Mayer &*
Co. of London, installed by *Walter Wells* in 1878; in this Madden
heeded the architect's plea to avoid 'the cheap and trashy stuff'.
Much of the light-filled effect intended for this space was lost
when the walls of the lower portion were panelled with oak in
1935. The open-well staircase in dark stained oak with its solid
balustrade pierced with trefoils and quatrefoils was made by *John*
Armstrong, who came here from Parkanaur.

On the *piano nobile* Hague's work was limited to the central
core of the house, leaving the rooms on the N and S ends – the
dining room, C19 stairs and nursery rooms – unaltered. The
DINING ROOM in the SW corner is Gothic, a survivor from
Jones's early C19 additions and still one of the best rooms in the
house. Regency in feeling, it has shallow vaulting springing from
foliate corbels in the corners with flat ribs inset with a cable
moulding. The new principal DRAWING ROOM was formed out
of the billiard room and entrance hall at the centre of the old
house; it could be thrown together with the old drawing room
when a heavy timber archway, since closed, was opened between
them. Each is a large space with a flat panelled ceiling, the
borders deeply enriched with square Tudor bosses, presumably
some of the plaster enrichments supplied by *E. Cross & Sons* of
Lancaster. The parquetry borders are by *C. H. Davies* of London
and the heavy oak cornices over the windows are by *R. Strahan*
& Co. The richly carved Victorian chimneypiece in the new
drawing room is a catalogue piece in statuary marble which was
bought from *Brookes Thomas*, Dublin, for £74. The chimneypiece
in the old drawing room was brought from Italy by Colonel John
Madden at the beginning of the C19; a much finer piece, with
fluted pink marble columns and a fulsome bacchanalian frieze,
signed by a long-forgotten Italian, *Piggiani*. On the N side of the
new drawing room the BOUDOIR was simply given a new ceiling,
a bold geometric design formed with heavy foliate bands, while
the adjoining BEDROOMS retain more refined late C18 cornices.
In some of these rooms extraordinary cast-iron shutters feign
their wooden counterparts; made by the estate carpenter, *Andrew*
Breakey, they are a legacy of agrarian tensions in the 1860s. Most
of the redecoration of the interiors was by *James Gibson & Son*
of Dublin.

The entire family remained in occupation during the works,
Mrs Madden and her young children testing the perils of the
scaffold in the stair hall as they passed from their bedrooms to
the dining room, the only room deemed fit to inhabit. By August
1877 when works were all but complete and some £9,117 had
been spent, Madden, having learnt the lesson of a profligate
grandfather, boasted that all was paid for from yearly income,

out of his determination not to 'saddle posterity with debts for anything which I have myself enjoyed'.

The house closes one side of a square of STABLES AND OFFICES in a way common in Early Georgian planning. They are essentially vernacular, long roughcast C18 ranges with C19 altera-tions. The stables on the S side have vaults springing from lime-stone columns of the kind popularized by *Richard Castle*, here with exaggerated entasis. Filling much of the courtyard is the covered RIDE, attributed to *James Jones* and contemporary with his works for the house, *c.* 1835. Set on axis with the back door and spanning the distance between it and the central archway of the W range, this is an extraordinary building for Ireland. Ten pairs of strong Tuscan columns of cast iron support steel trusses and a slated roof, forming an equestrian stoa, a covered colonnade for exercising the hackneys bred here in the C19, a symbol of the close relationship between the horse and the country house.

Standing over a single-storey range outside the principal stable-yard is the TOWER; part farmyard clock tower, part North African bastion, it was built to *John Madden*'s own design as a coming-of-age present to himself in 1858. It rises over the farm-yard in four diminishing stages – all stacked like building blocks – with walls of squared limestone, strong emphatic quoins, battle-ments, and rounded-headed windows in dressed stone. A small square flag tower with battlements rises in ashlar from the upper storey. An imposing building, placed with a strong sense of the picturesque when viewed with the front of the house from a distance.

The DEMESNE and its DEERPARK represent the finest natural-ized landscape in the region, retaining a great deal of C18 decidu-ous planting, much of it from the era of the first Madden owner. The combination of gentle hills, dense woods and small lakes forms many memorable arcadian vistas, now blended with more exotic C19 perimeter planting. The extensive old kitchen gardens immediately S of the house were replaced in the late C19 by a new red brick walled garden further W. The FORMAL GARDENS and terraces were laid out by *Ninian Niven*, who visited in December 1870.

The CLONES LODGE is a picturesque early C19 three-bay roughcast block, with half-hipped gables, mullioned windows, hoodmoulds, and on the entrance gable, under a lunette, a pretty Regency iron trelliswork porch; set on a rise, it commands the GREEN GATES, an elaborate cast-iron screen of 1868 with piers bearing the Madden falcons. Tucked away in the village, the SMITHBORO LODGE is a simple two-roomed building with a hipped roof and mullioned windows.

HOPE CASTLE *see* CASTLEBLAYNEY

INNISKEEN   MN

An attractive village, well dispersed around a crossroads within an embrace of the River Fane, part of the quiet, easy landscape where Patrick Kavanagh found 'the God of imagination waking in a Mucker fog'. A monastery was founded here in the C6 by St Daig, a protégé of St Ciarian of Clonmacnoise, described as a 'great artificer' who made many bells and shrines. The monastery, supposedly blessed by Columcille (Columba) and first referred to in 636, was burnt in 789 and plundered in 948. Although the death of the last recorded monk, MacSolly, is referred to in 1085, the monastery was burnt again in 1166. In 1178 John de Courcy brought final devastation to the area. A motte to the S of the village, supporting the foundations of an indeterminable stone structure, speaks of the once strategic importance of the place.

MONASTERY OF ST DAIG. The tradition that a MacMahon archbishop and nine bishops lie buried between the graveyard and the crossroads suggests that much of the monastery lay outside the present enclosure. Only the stump of the round tower, built of uncoursed rubble and some 42½ ft (13 m) high, remains today, the shallow projecting coping course added later to support a bellcote. The doorway, 16 ft (5 m) from ground level, is a plain rectangular opening with straight stone lintels and sill. Two grooves on the upper edge of the sill look as though worn by a ladder.

The adjoining former INNISKEEN PARISH CHURCH (C of I) replaces an older structure, according to an inscription (not seen) founded in 1672 by Ardell MacColl MacMahon and described as in good condition in 1810. Rebuilt in 1854 by *Joseph Welland*, reusing materials from the site. A four-bay hall, solid and pleasing, with lichen-covered gables, supported by diagonal offset buttresses. W front of good-quality squared masonry pierced with a quatrefoil window above the doorway, a neat ashlar bellcote on the apex; plain three-light window to the E. The nave has rubble walls with a slight batter to the base. It is lit on either side by three slender ashlar-dressed lancets; at the W end a short wall buttress, and a narrow lancet with a pretty quatrefoil above it to light the gallery. Reroofed in 2006.

Close to the NW corner of the church, a low-walled enclosure with a free-standing arch over the W wall incorporates the remains of the mid-C18 MORTUARY CHAPEL of the Plunketts of Rocksavage. Not found was the inscription recording the foundation of a chapel here in 1672 by Ardell MacColl MacMahon. A simple WAYSIDE CROSS erected in 1729 by his son, Captain Coll MacMahon, is built into the stone wall at the crossroads.

GLEBE HOUSE. To the N, directly across the bridge, on high ground in sheltered pasture that slopes down to the River Fane. An elegant and attractive L-shaped house, built with a loan from the Board of First Fruits in 1821. In 1622 the vicar of Inniskeen was described as residing 'in a house of his own building on temporall lands' because there was no glebe. In 1787 the Rev. Daniel Beaufort observed a 'good' glebe house. The present building is of two storeys and three bays with a low hipped roof supported on bracketed eaves. Roughcast with strip quoins; nicely fenestrated with ground-floor windows in shallow squared recesses. The doorway is set in a shallow porch under a wide segmental fanlight of webbed design.

The basement is open at the back of the house, where a small kitchen yard is accommodated in the angle of the L.

The present BRIDGE over the Fane is carried on five rubble arches with the two to the N skewed to follow the bend of the road. It was built, according to tradition, with stones from the monastery, and replaced the older crossing point further E. A stone on the parapet is inscribed: 'Built by P: Halpen 1801'.

PATRICK KAVANAGH RESOURCE CENTRE (former ST MARY'S CHURCH). Of c. 1820. An awkward composition, dominated by a big low-lying mass hall with a wide gabled roof. At the W end a two-stage tower with battlements and corner pinnacles was later added. The addition only boosts the clumsy appearance of the whole. Raw pebbledashed walls account for some of the grim appearance. Old-fashioned transverse plan with the altar at the centre of the long E wall, lit by five pointed windows in the W wall. Interior quite remarkable and really rather pleasing. An attractive timber inner porch with engaged Tuscan columns at the corners supports a small organ gallery, while the galleries proper are accommodated in the N and S ends. Between them, the ceiling is an extraordinary timber carapace built as a series of narrow pointed vaults running from one wall to the other, like a row of upturned boats, set on long timber beams, certainly one of the most unusual and imaginative roof structures in the country. – STAINED GLASS. On each side of the former sanctuary, St Daig and Mary Immaculate by *Earley & Co.*, 1944.

In the CHURCHYARD, amongst neatly trimmed graves with stained marble headstones, is a strip of worn limestone pavement with a simple wooden cross marking the humble grave of Patrick Kavanagh (1904–67), born at Mucker nearby, whose poetry and autobiography, *The Green Fool*, powerfully evoke this landscape. To the SE a walled enclosure supporting a freestanding arch, similar to its counterpart in the Protestant church graveyard, accommodates the Catholic relatives of the Plunketts of Rocksavage.

MARY, MOTHER OF MERCY. 1 km W. 1974 by *Carr, Sweeney & O'Farrell*. A daring concrete whorl, gleaming in the Monaghan landscape like a living form. The plan radiates from a threestorey tower behind the altar, and descends to low convex eaves which, Ronchamp-like, delimit the outer boundary of the building. The roof is supported on deep free-flowing beams of laminated timber, with the result that the presence of the tower is only evident from the rear. Here, a wide three-storey, fourbay elevation gives the church greater substance but at the same time disguises the tightness of its interior space: roundheaded loop windows light a small room on each level in a compressed oval plan. The tower extends well above the upper storey and is sliced off at an angle. Grand and ambitious architecture, however not always well served by the materials employed: plastic cladding and perspex have deteriorated,

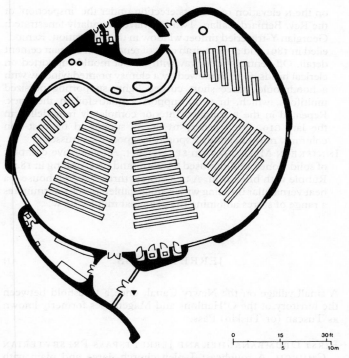

Inniskeen, Mary, Mother of Mercy.
Plan

leaving the building a little tired. – STATIONS OF THE CROSS. Enamels by *Charles Cullen*. – TABERNACLE from the C18 church at Drumcatton.

ROCKSAVAGE. 1.5 km SW. Derelict. Mid-C18 in appearance, relatively plain, with plenty to intrigue and deserving of further study. Essentially a nicely proportioned Georgian front, two storeys and five bays with six-over-six sash windows reduced to three-over-six on the second storey. Roughcast over rubble with a handsome pedimented limestone doorcase; side-lights with diagonal glazing. Despite the uniform appearance, the gables show earlier, narrower gables indicating evolution from an older house. Curious crenellated chimneystack with crow-stepped merlons on the E gable. Tripartite plan with simple low-ceilinged rooms. Square hall with moulded cornice and Neoclassical webbed centrepiece. A half-turn staircase with elaborate late C19 turned newels is reached directly through a segmental archway. Elsewhere mostly mid-C18 joinery. Deep return facing into a quadrangular courtyard, largely C19 in detail. Residence of the Kenny family in the C19.

ST ANNE, DRUMCATTON. 3 km NW. A small and discreetly located chapel of 1796 retaining the modest, unassuming character of a pre-Emancipation mass-house. A slate inscription on the N elevation records its erection under the 'inspection' of the Rev. Bernard Callan. Two-bay nave irregularly fenestrated; Georgian Y-traceried timber window in the N elevation. Remodelled in 1891 and given a drab coat of render and Roman cement detail. Off-centre W doorway with a label mould supported on clerical heads. Overshadowed by a clumsy pointed window with a hoodmould: three short cusped lights supporting outsized multifoils, which, in turn, support a quatrefoil in the apex. Repeated in the E window. Interior completely remodelled in the late C19. Deep gallery to the W supported on cast-iron columns, now enclosed. Exposed kingpost roof trusses.

INNISKEEN MILLS. 0.5 km SE. Derelict. An extensive complex of solid stone buildings used for corn- and tuck-milling in 1840. Rubble with brick trim. A two-storey, three-bay mill house – a neat vernacular building with a small gabled porch – terminates a range of stores adjoining the principal mill to the W.

JERRETTSPASS

A small village on the Newry Canal, once a threshold between the territory of the O'Hanlons and Magennises formerly known as Tuscan (or Tuskin) Pass.

FIRST DRUMBANAGHER AND JERRETTSPASS PRESBYTERIAN CHURCH. A roughcast T-plan church, large and plain with four bays. The transition to its present state is recorded in three plaques between the bays: built in 1751 and renovated in 1897 and 1959. The pleasing Georgian simplicity of the architecture was lost when its big sashes were replaced by leaded windows by *Clokey*, Belfast.

CARRICKROVADDY BRIDGE. Of *c.* 1808 by *John Brownrigg*. A picturesque humpback bridge on the Newry Canal. Generous elliptical arch with neat sandstone voussoirs, broad gabled parapet in rubble, originally roughcast, descending into a gentle curve stopped by cylindrical piers. *John Chebsey* was the builder.

ST MARY, KILBODAGH (C of I) 1.5 km N. 1859 by *W. J. Barre*. A picturesque Victorian church conspicuously set with its VICARAGE against a steep ridge overlooking flat grasslands. In squared, rock-faced silver granite with sandstone dressings. A straightforward four-bay nave, heavily buttressed, with an offset N porch, deep chancel and a tower with broach spire set into the E angle with the chancel. Cusped lights, mostly with clear quarry glazing, and a rose window in the W gable. – STAINED GLASS. E window, the Ascension, *c.* 1903, by *Heaton, Butler & Bayne*, who also executed Charity at the W end of the nave N wall; at the E end, the Good Shepherd, 1895, is signed *Alexander Gibbs & Co.*, London. Across the road, the VICARAGE is contemporary, picturesque in the most sparing way. Two-storey, in an understated Tudor idiom with gablets, bay

windows and narrow sashes divided by mullions. Roughcast,
with red and yellow brick to the rear.

KILBODAGH HOUSE. 1.8 km N. A substantial Victorian villa in
roughcast with granite quoins. Originally a smaller C18 house
on an L-plan, enlarged *c.* 1840 when a long two-storey block
was placed across the front. Five bays on the first floor with
twelve-pane sashes; two large tripartite windows on the ground
floor with stuccoed entablatures and plate glass. The entrance
is deeply recessed to form an open stuccoed porch with a heavy
parapet on giant scrolled brackets, in the robust William IV
style seen in the furniture of *William Henry Playfair* (*see* below),
who may well have been consulted here. Inside, as a result of
the new front, the stair lies deep within the plan, which otherwise retains a straightforward tripartite arrangement; two sizeable Victorian reception rooms gained by the enlargement.

Attractive rubble OUTBUILDINGS enclose a small yard
directly behind, refurbished in 2008 by the *Boyd Partnership*.

DRUMBANAGHER. 3.5 km N. *William Henry Playfair*'s mansion,   *p. 43*
a large Italianate house designed in 1829 for Maxwell Close in
an old demesne purchased from the Moore family in 1818, was
demolished in 1951. The *porte cochère* remains, a monolithic
square *quadrifrons* crisply decorated with heraldic wreaths. For
it and the house, Scottish Old Red Sandstone was brought from
Garscube near Glasgow. In the house Playfair elaborated his
design for Belmont in Edinburgh begun the year before, in
1828, placing the main two-storey block between taller towered
wings, the windows in triplets separated by piers with a character mildly evocative of the Prussian architect Karl Friedrich
Schinkel. There was a strong Neo-Grec accent in both details
and furnishings. The *porte cochère* now leads into scrub and the
extensive ivied ruins of the KITCHEN COURT. A short distance
away the STABLE quadrangle is a reworking, perhaps by
Playfair, of an older building. It is greatly embellished with
stucco ornament, especially prominent on the former STEW-
ARD'S HOUSE, a two-storey block with five bays and a low
hipped roof, set to one side of the archway. Straight entablatures on consoles over the windows and a cornice and balustraded parapet resting just above the first-floor windows all give
it a pleasing Victorian seaside air. Over the archway an elaborate
leaded cupola is not raised as it should be, but instead sits
strangely low behind the balustraded parapet, proof perhaps of
its origins before remodelling. A curiosity of the place is the
numerous dispersed granite columns, here and there grandiosely propping a cart house or used within the quadrangle and
further away on the demesne school; it all suggests a surfeit of
materials, perhaps from the original house of the Moores. One
surviving GATE LODGE is a sumptuous little single-storey stuccoed box, with bold quoins, decorated parapets, varied windows
– two of them Romanesque – and a square porch clearly
intended as a prelude to Playfair's *porte cochère*.

DRUMBANAGHER OLD SCHOOL. 3 km N. Just inside the wall,
on the SE corner of the demesne. An oddly attractive building

with a toy-like quality, established here before 1836 and consisting of a central two-storey roughcast block with a hipped
roof and end stacks; three bays on the front, the ground floor
recessed behind an open screen of four Tuscan columns in
silver granite. The overall arrangement of the plan is rather like
the contemporary example at Taniokey (Poyntzpass), with the
former classrooms standing on either side of the main block
as single-bay wings – here with hipped roofs and tripartite
windows.

THE DEERPARK. 3 km N. On the crest of a hill overlooking
Drumbanagher demesne. A solid gable-ended Late Georgian
block, originally roughcast over squared blue snecked limestone with granite dressings. Three bays on the front, with the
central bay slightly recessed over two storeys. Twelve-pane
sashes and a plain tripartite doorway with narrow side-lights.
A small enclosed YARD behind with attractive buildings in
snecked rubble and red brick; outside the yard is a small BARN,
partly open-fronted, on primitive granite piers. Of particular
interest is the HORSE MILL, retaining the heavy timber horse
wheel and cast-iron machinery, inside a large circular enclosure of rubble, rising into large piers once supporting a large
large conical roof, now replaced with a segmental corrugated roof
on Belfast trusses.

ST LUKE, MULLAGHGLASS (C of I). 2 km SW. 1833 by *William
Farrell*. This substantial church departs from Farrell's familiar
single-cell designs to offer all the indulgent attractiveness of
Regency Gothic. A broad five-bay hall and chancel with an
elaborate projecting entrance front, each corner emphasized
with pinnacled diagonal buttresses. Brownish granite rubble
with copious granite dressings. The three-bay main front has
a particularly spiky appearance, with the buttresses nicely set
in concert with those of the nave and sharply pointed lancets
placed in an ascending pattern; the wider central bay is gabled
between very slender angle buttresses. The windows are a
special feature here, nicely varied and most with clear quarry
glass: tightly grouped lancets with hoods in the nave, richly
patterned oculi with hoods over the side entrances, and a large
Y-traceried E window.

TYRONE'S DITCHES PRESBYTERIAN CHURCH. 4.5 km NW.
There is little of prominence in the surrounding pastoral landscape, even less to evoke the 2nd Earl of Tyrone's late C16
earthen defences that give this place its name, just this little
Georgian church in a grassy hollow. Now cement-rendered
with raised quoins, it retains large round-headed sashes with
Gothick glazing. A plain Victorianized interior.

JONESBOROUGH   AH

A small market town, established when Roth Jones was granted
patents to hold markets and fairs here in 1705. Also known as
Four Mile House in the C18.

CHURCH OF THE SACRED HEART. An ugly building, reminiscent of the unpleasant 1960s churches of *W. H. Byrne & Son*. A broad and angular pebbledashed hall with triangular-headed windows, off-centre side chapel and a lumbering timber porch on the SE corner. An obelisk-shaped copper-clad spirelet breaks the roof ridge. It replaced a T-plan chapel, described as unfinished in 1837.

The building is flanked to the W by the SCHOOLHOUSE, a standard late C19 design in rubble and red brick with a central gable, and to the E by the PAROCHIAL HOUSE of 1896, a solid two-storey, three-bay block over-enriched with stucco.

JONESBORO HOUSE. An Early Georgian house with handsome proportions built by the Jones family at the top of the main street. A gable-ended block of two storeys and five bays with single-storey two-bay wings. Roughcast with narrow Early Georgian windows. The fanlit doorcase is a handsome pattern-book design with an open pediment on engaged Tuscan columns.

RECTORY. A long two-storey gable-ended house. On the ground floor, end bays with tripartite windows and between them a long conservatory. On the first floor, narrow sashes with plate glass.

PARISH CHURCH (former), Flurry Bridge (C of I). 0.75 km NE. 1863 by *W. H. Lynn*. An attractive small church built in silver Mourne granite on the foundations of a predecessor. Designed in the manner of the small gabled churches of *Joseph Welland*, with a three-bay buttressed nave, bellcote, polygonal chancel, S porch, and a rather wide lean-to projection to the N with twin doors to vestry and fuel store. The windows are plain lancets, paired under a vesica on the W gable. Built for £900 under the patronage of Lord Clermont, whose grave lies near the door. The contractor was *Arthur Matthews* of Dundalk.

KILNASAGGART STONE. 2 km S. An important inscribed stone, inside a small rectilinear enclosure. This isolated site once adjoined one of the great roads of ancient Ireland, the *Slighe Miodhheachra* connecting Tara with Emain Macha, and its name, meaning 'church of the priest', suggests the presence of a religious foundation, though the stone's distinctly phallic shape hints at more pagan origins. It is a shaft of greywacke, standing 8 ft (2.5 m) tall, with three faces and an inclined surface at the top. Each surface is inscribed, predominantly with small wheeled crosses; on the S face, below a large incised cross and partly obliterated, are the words IN LOC / SO TANI / MMAIRNI / TERNOCH / MAC CERAN / BIC ER CUL / PETER AP / STEL, translated by the C19 antiquarian George Petrie to read 'This place, Ternoc, son of Ciaran the Little, bequeathed it under the protection of the apostle Peter'. Ternoc has been associated with a personality recorded in the *Annals of the Four Masters*, who died in 716. If true, the connection makes it the earliest datable grave marker in Ireland. A series of scores, too erratic for ogham, are explained by its use as a hone stone. Other smaller stones disposed at the base – two incised with crosses and one with a square socket – are probably associated with early Christian burials uncovered during excavations in 1968.

MOYRY CASTLE. 2.5 km SW. Now in ruins. A very rare instance of a tower house in South Ulster, and more exceptional because its designer is known. However, the building is a modest architectural event that belies its significance. A small square keep of three storeys with rounded corners set within a bawn on a rocky outcrop. Erected in June 1601 by Lord Mountjoy to secure the Moyry Pass – the 'Gap of the North', deemed to be 'one of the most difficult passages of Ireland' – during his Ulster campaign against Hugh O'Neill. Just one year earlier, O'Neill had held fast here among formidable defences described as 'long traverses with huge and high flankers of great stones mingled with turf and staked in both sides with pallisadoes' which he had formed 'from mountain to mountain, from wood to wood, and from bog to bog'. Twice had government forces been repelled from the pass. When Mountjoy found it undefended he acted quickly, erecting the castle and bawn in less than a month, and placed it immediately under the command of Captain Anthony Smith.

Described in its time as 'a pretty castle' that served as 'a good relief to passengers', it is commanding while not very large, and though well-constructed has few architectural distinctions. Rarely are designers of tower houses named, much less for such a rudimentary one as this, but contemporary sources give the design of Moyry to *Levan De Rose*, a Dutch engineer in Mountjoy's train. The hasty, utilitarian approach to its design still shows in the plainness of its walls and the absence of stairs. The ruined tower is square in plan with a circumference of 120 ft (37 m), distinguished by its rounded corners which are pierced with musket loops barely perceptible externally in the closely packed boulder walls. The loops are repeated in the centres on three sides, in the upper levels flanking the windows, and more randomly on the wall walk. The doorway, a large off-centre rectangular opening in the N wall, is defended from above by a crude machicolation projecting from the wall walk. Inside, the upper level is dominated by a large fireplace, its flue carried in a shallow outshot in the windowless N face, projecting from corbels at first-floor level. To the SE is a substantial fragment of the bawn wall.

KEADY   AH

A small milling town that grew up from the linen boom of the mid C18, its name taken from the Irish *Ceide*, 'flat-topped hill'. The River Callan winds its way through a deep glen beside the main street and industries for the finishing processes of the strong linen known as 'stout Armaghs' were established along it, promoted by the main landowner from the Plantation, Trinity

College Dublin, whose provost received the first patent for a market in the town in 1759.

In the C19 Keady suffered in competition with the larger centres at Armagh, Lurgan and Tandragee, but was successfully revived by William Kirk, who acquired an interest in the town in the 1830s. Kirk, described as a man 'of iron energy, of inflexible purpose, and unbending integrity', greatly expanded linen production to an extent still evident in the large industrial complex surviving on the NE side of the town. Consequently the town's appearance is mainly C19; and having been depressed for much of the C20 its streets show a pattern of steady decline. Two of the best Victorian buildings were destroyed in the late C20: the convent off St Patrick's Street, a familiar institutional Gothic design, was lost through zealous expediency; *Fitzgibbon Louch*'s exotic Venetian Gothic Town Hall-cum-Market House of 1870 fell to a terrorist bomb in 1970, and its replacement by a dull small library in brown brick makes its loss even more acute.

ST MATTHEW (C of I). Church Street. A three-bay hall of 1776 to one of *Thomas Cooley*'s 'standard' designs for Primate Robinson. Strangely built without a tower, a deficiency remedied only in 1822 when an extra bay was added to the nave. The tower rises in three diminishing stages, before pinnacles and low battlements. A two-bay transept to the N was added at the same time, both additions probably by *John Bowden*, the works all distinguished by long quarry-glazed lancets. The nave retains *Cooley*'s wide arched windows with timber Y-tracery; the E window has later Geometric tracery in sandstone. Vestry added by *H. C. Parkinson* in 1896. Inside, flat plaster ceilings, simple moulded cornices, and a rare floor of conglomerate stone flags. Some pretty Neoclassical plasterwork survives in the earlier portion. Repewed in 1875 with a new gallery frontal, rather heavy for the delicate C18 clustered colonnettes. – Early C20 sanctuary MURALS inscribed with biblical text by *James Maxwell*, Armagh. – STAINED GLASS. E window: highly transparent figurative panels. Nave: an attractive mid-C20 insert by *Clokey* of Belfast and two bright windows of the 1990s by *David Esler, Leadlines Studio*. – MONUMENTS. Dr Samuel Magee †1833; a very fine tablet on brackets with inverted torches and draped urn. – John Robert Irwin †1872; a marble scroll with a mourning figure resting on a draped column, by *H. Sibthorpe & Son*, Dublin. – The Rev. Canon M. A. Hogg †1931, by *McClements*, Armagh.

ST PATRICK. St Patrick Street. A large T-plan church and tower with lancets. Built in 1857 by the *Rev. Patrick Kelly* P.P. in thin courses of squared blue limestone with sandstone trim. The forestanding tower is a routine design in three stages with battlements and pinnacles. Remodelled *c.* 1989, when the transepts were lengthened using materials from the convent chapel, with vast pointed windows. In the gables these strange aberrant designs are filled with a weak assemblage incorporating the old Geometric tracery. Inside, the complicated open timber roof of arched and braced trusses, the wall MOSAICS and the gallery are the principal remains of a once rich Gothic Revival interior. – STAINED GLASS. Quite varied, with some C19 work by *Clokey*, Belfast.

SECOND KEADY PRESBYTERIAN CHURCH. Davis Street. 1808 and 1857. A large hall, rather plain, of five bays with long round-headed windows and stuccoed quoins. An assured Doric doorcase, large and perfectly detailed, perhaps part of 1857 alterations and additions by *W. J. Barre*. Renovated with new seating in 1932 by *Hobart & Heron*.

In the churchyard the KIRK MAUSOLEUM is a spartan pedimented ashlar box in Dungannon stone. Distinctive cast-iron GATE SCREEN with ogee-topped piers decorated with honeysuckle motifs.

KIRK MEMORIAL. Market Street. 1871 by *Fitzgibbon Louch*. An elaborate Gothic monument to William Kirk, a major figure in Keady's linen industry, philanthropist, landlord, and M.P. for Newry. Vigorous, if lumpish, in Dungannon freestone. From an offset granite base it rises in low stages decorated with short registers carved with Gothic motifs; on each corner buttresses rise from low flying arches into pinnacles to surround the solid central spire. Polished granite plaques set in a cusped recess on each face express the dedicatee's worthiness. The contractor was *John Collen*.

OTHER BUILDINGS. There are few distinguished buildings in the town. In Kinelowen Street, the main street, the NORTHERN BANK of 1904 by *H. C. Robinson* is a large Italianate banking house of two storeys with a dormered attic, in red brick with fine sandstone trim and a handsome Tuscan doorcase. The contractor was *W. Dowling*. Only two other buildings are worth a mention, both on the opposite side of the street: the BANK OF IRELAND, a fussy late C20 design, low fronted with an offset gable and a balustraded parapet, and the late C19 MASONIC HALL, a small four-bay hall with stuccoed quoins, segmental-headed windows and a large mullioned gable window.

KEADY VIADUCT. Crossing the Glen Road NE of the town. A weighty structure, novel for its early use of mass concrete, it was erected for the short-lived Castleblayney, Keady & Armagh Railway, which opened in 1909. Designed by *Sir Benjamin Baker*, with four dramatic and two subsidiary arches in engineering brick rising from tapered concrete piers.

WILLOWBANK. Armagh Road. A seemly Georgian house of two storeys and three bays in roughcast with windows of equal height, elegant doorcase, and a hipped roof with wide eaves on paired brackets. Built *c.* 1820 by the Rev. Joseph Jenkins. The doorcase has an elaborate leaded fanlight supported on engaged Ionic columns necked with rather attenuated, stiff acanthus leaves. Inside, a standard tripartite plan with wide moulded cornices and in the hall a large ceiling rose detailed with lotus leaves.

MANSE. Crossmore Road. 1859. A neat two-storey, three-bay block with a hipped roof. Pebbledashed, with a plain fanlit doorcase.

RECTORY. 1 km N. A familiar Regency design built onto an older rectory of 1779. The new front is bigger than its predecessor, obscuring it entirely with a two-storey, three-bay, gable-ended block with a low-pitched roof on wide bracketed eaves and a square central porch with a handsome timber doorcase set in the side. The fenestration is nicely proportioned, with the taller ground-floor windows recessed under wide relieving arches. Attractive enclosed stableyard to the rear. Now surrounded by a depressing treeless waste.

DUNLARG. 2 km NE. Diminutive Georgian vernacular at its cutest. A quirky early C19 house with modest boxy proportions, to an L-plan; harled, two storeys, with hipped roofs, Georgian glazing. The main front has three bays with a narrow two-storey canted projection excessively fenestrated for its size, given windows in each face on the first floor contrasting with the absence of first-floor windows in the adjoining bays. The sides of the building are expressed as two storeys, with two bays over one.

THE TEMPLE, FIRST KEADY PRESBYTERIAN CHURCH. 3 km N. Set in open countryside, a tidy clutch of buildings – church, lecture hall and school. The first building was established here in 1702 and twice rebuilt in the C18 before the present church of 1834–9. A plain four-bay hall with timber Y-tracery, cement-rendered with raised quoins. Half-hipped entrance gable with twin doors and a lancet between. Good C19 interior with gallery. Internal alterations in 1890 by *J. H. Fullerton*. – STAINED GLASS. Two windows of 1974 and 1975 by *CWS Design*.

The LECTURE HALL of 1896 is a neat three-bay block on a high podium, also by *Fullerton*. Two bays to the front, with decorative bargeboards and tall pointed finial.

MOUNTAIN LODGE, DARKLEY. 4 km SE. Ruined. A neat Late Georgian box. Two storeys over a basement with rendered rubble walls and finely dressed quoins in Armagh limestone. The front has three bays with Tudor hoods of Roman cement and a wide elliptical-headed doorway.

KILCOGY

A rural crossroads in south Cavan.

OUR LADY OF LOURDES, MULLAHORAN. 1.5 km NW. A large stuccoed church set deep in the countryside. Built *c.* 1910, in the understated Romanesque style favoured by *T. F. McNamara*. The plan is cruciform, consisting of a buttressed five-bay nave, transepts, polygonal chancel, a kneelered W gable and set-back buttresses, and a three-stage tower offset on the S side with a steep pyramid roof. Windows are round-headed lancets, in pairs, or arranged with three graded lights in each of the gables. Decoration is spare, limited to moulded strings, hoodmoulds and engaged shafts on the doorway and on the corners in the upper stage of the tower. Inside, the transepts open through a generous two-bay arcade on a single polished granite shaft with a limestone base and foliated capitals; similar colonnettes on corbels support the chancel arch. Exposed hammerbeam roof, elaborated with ornamental kingposts rather like halved wagon wheels. – STAINED GLASS. Chancel: three central and two side-lights, all figurative and attractively coloured, by *Mayer*. N transept: twin lights with the Annunciation, signed *Earley* of Dublin.

DRUMLOMAN FORMER PARISH CHURCH (C of I). 3.5 km S. Derelict. A small Early Georgian church on an impressive windswept site with a view across the SW Cavan lakelands and into Meath and Westmeath. A smooth-rendered single cell with just three bays. Above the doorway on the unadorned W gable, a barely legible plaque records that 'This church was built at the expence of William Gore of Woodford, Esq. in the year 1739'. The blind N wall reveals a pronounced batter that confirms its early origin, supported by the hillocky graveyard and its wayward, tilting monuments. The pointed windows have timber Y-tracery in limestone frames under elegantly thin hoodmoulds, with a similar design enlarged on the E gable with three cusped lights – all presumably part of the repairs made by the Ecclesiastical Commissioners in the 1830s; even with these it was still deemed so simple a structure as 'may defy the church's bitterest enemies to point out any ornament of which they can complain'. Only its sad dereliction at the time of writing warrants any protest concerning such a delightful building.

ST MARY, CORICK. 4 km SE. 1825. A wayside T-plan church with lancets, built under the patronage of the landlord, Gerald Dease of Turbotstown. Smooth-rendered with blocked limestone dressings. The interior is plain, suffused with a dim green light from the coloured glass. Refurbished in 2006 with grotesque sanctuary furnishings of bog yew. – STAINED GLASS. Y-traceried E window by *J. Clarke & Sons*. – MONUMENTS. The Rev. Christopher O'Reilly †1867; a stone plaque with crossed chalice and crucifix. – The Rev. Robert O'Reilly †1875; a plain marble tablet, by *H. G. Barnes*.

A rural parish SW of Belturbet.

CHRIST CHURCH (C of I). Looking like the usual hall-and-tower type, but in fact much older than its standard First Fruits tower suggests. The building began as a low roughcast nave with transepts, C18 or perhaps earlier, recast in 1815 when a three-stage tower was added, to one of *John Bowden*'s most familiar designs, built of rubble and dressed limestone with crowning battlements and spiky pinnacles. The erection of the tower on the S transept gable distorted the appearance of the original T-plan, giving the impression that the tower fronted a conventional nave with a single transept. Internally the plan remained unchanged, with the communion table placed on the long E wall formed by the transepts. Only in 1865 were the internal arrangements aligned with the exterior, when *Welland & Gillespie* sited the sanctuary directly opposite the tower and presumably also refenestrated the whole with hooded lancets. The low pitch of the old roofs remains evident, despite their renewal with exposed kingposts. – STAINED GLASS. Bright figurative E window, signed *Alex. Gibbs*, 10 Bloomsbury St., London. – ARMS. Set into the old nave wall, a flamboyantly carved, and much overpainted, C17 coat of arms of the Cliffords. – MONUMENTS. The Rev. George de la Poer Beresford †1826; a plain marble panel. – Captain Perrott Thornton †1848; a white sarcophagus-shaped tablet with an ascending dove, signed *Killaloe Works*, Dublin. – Mary Clifford †1922; a plain tablet, by *Harrison*. – Captain Robert Clifford †1858; a white sarcophagus-shaped tablet. – Lady Catherine Saunderson †1860. Out of a black marble background a ghostly hand in white marble emerges bearing a scroll; signed *Manderson*, Dublin. – Another similar, to the Rev. Francis Saunderson †1873, signed *Coates*, Dublin.

In the graveyard, the FINLAY MAUSOLEUM is a rugged little Gothic box in rock-faced ashlar with a pyramidal stone roof and cross-loops flanking a Tudor-arched doorway. Across the road, the embanked circular GRAVEYARD is a further indication of distant ecclesiastical origins.

ST DALLAN. 0.7 km NW. 1975. An insipid brown brick hall with tiled roofs, replacing a charming thatched barn church of 1785, which still stands to one side, now utterly disfigured as a parish hall. – STAINED GLASS. Three late C19 figurative windows by *Mayer & Co.* of Munich, brought here from the convent in Belturbet.

CARN LODGE. 1 km N. By the roadside, a model early C19 gentleman's cottage fronting an orderly farmyard. A roughcast gable-ended block, a storey and a half, with lower wings set well back on each side. Bracketed eaves, overhanging the gable-ends with decorative bargeboards. Three-bay front with a bulky square porch stuccoed with strip quoins rising to massive moulded capitals, the moulding continued round as a cornice.

CARN COTTAGE. 1 km NE. Derelict. A somewhat haphazard *cottage orné*, picturesquely set into a hillside overlooking the small kidney-shaped water of Carn Lough. A long two-storey front with unadorned roughcast walls, formed in three ascending blocks, each advancing forward, with the entrance projected under a catslide roof against the square terminal block. The ordered irregularity, the large quarry-paned casements, and the wide oversailing eaves on the taller end block are Regency qualities reminiscent of Nash. Through the C19, the residence of the Clifford family.

KILDALLON GLEBE HOUSE, BOCADE. 1.5 km SE. 1821. A pleasing Late Georgian house sitting well in its small wooded demesne. Built to an L-plan in roughcast, and rising to two storeys over a basement (entirely concealed on the main front), with a bracketed eaves course before shallow hipped roofs. The wide entrance front has three bays, nicely varied with a two-storey canted bay brought forward on one side with Wyatt windows; a deeply set doorway in the centre is a handsome design with panelled pilasters, consoles and an open pediment over a delicate petal fanlight in lead. The STABLES form two parallel ranges behind; the longer N range is a lovely building, symmetrically designed, with a gently advanced carriage arch in the centre flanked by two round-headed doorways, each with a webbed fanlight.

KILDALLON SCHOOLHOUSE. 1.5 km SE. Opposite the gates to the glebe, a long, two-storey, gable-ended block of seven bays in rubble with windows formed under four-centred brick arches. A plaque high in the centre of the façade commemorates the renewal of the school in 1861 in memory of Lady Catherine Saunderson, it having 'fallen into decay'.

MACKAN, also known as MACKAN WOOD. 3 km SW. The lingering two-storey stable block of a vanished house. Built of squared limestone, with a broad, almost gauche front of eight bays, the centre advanced with twin carriage arches and a pediment. In 1837 the house was the residence of Mr Galbraith.

A parish focused on a small rural settlement on the road to Clones; a quaint shop, a schoolhouse of 1852, and two churches set between two hills alongside a fast-flowing stream.

KILLEEVAN ABBEY AND CEMETERY. A circular enclosure with a small ruined church and one of the most important collections of folk art in the region, represented by its gravestones. Traditionally the site of a medieval abbey, but unlikely to have been of great importance, with only the rubble gable of a simple single-cell church (42½ ft by 19½ ft, 13 m by 6 m) standing and some partial remains of the N and S walls protruding from the ground. A small lancet, off-centre and close to the apex, has a simple moulded surround and dripstone that looks C13 or C14. The surrounding C18 gravestones are visually stunning, adorned with every manner of competing heraldic device and *memento mori*, in naïve relief carving; the numerous skulls and crossbones should leave children in no doubt that this was once a pirates' burial ground.

CAMPBELL MAUSOLEUM. Opposite the abbey site. A curious, isolated stone structure commanding impressive views of the surrounding landscape. A square rubble box with a low pyramidal roof, built in the late C18 by the Rev. Thomas Campbell, who was distinguished elsewhere as a writer, diarist, and a member of Dr Johnson's set, as his final resting place. He died in 1795 in London, and so the monument was never used.

St Luke, Shanco. The attractive ruins of an unusual C18 T-plan church, built in 1790 by the Rev. Thomas Campbell. Only the three-stage tower and fragments of the w wall, close to the entrance gates, remain. Date plaque in the lower stage. The body of the church, now indiscernible, seems to have been a standard hall with a large transept-like projection on one side. The tower is roughcast over rubble with tooled ashlar dressings to the strings, quoins, attractive primitive doorcase, and blind oculus above. The diminished belfry stage in ashlar, having lost its pinnacles, is now crumbling.

Killeevan Parish Church (C of I). 1857. A picturesque rural spire with weathercock rising above the approaches to the village does not prepare one for one of *Joseph Welland*'s more sombre parish churches. Built under the patronage of the Archbishop, Lord John George Beresford, with *T. H. Carroll* of Dublin as builder. A big nave, s aisle and chancel and an offset tower on the N front set beside a small lean-to projection; all executed in dark squared limestone with crisp cutstone dressings. Quarry-glazed windows with simple plate tracery on the nave N wall, arranged with paired lancets under a quatrefoil; simpler, without the quatrefoil, on the s aisle. Graded three-light E window. Doorway in the tower set between stepped angle buttresses with a simple arched surround. Above is a short belfry stage with twin louvred lancets, a hollowed cornice enriched with well-spaced foliate nailheads and clover leaves, and a pyramidal base supporting the stout octagonal spire. Inside, the porch rises dramatically into the tower with a short balcony across one side, level with a large plaque commemorating the erection of the building, which only the bellringers could read. The interior is a more cheerful space, filled with light under an exposed timber roof – a series of alternating scissor and braced kingpost trusses. The three-bay arcade, with smooth Caen stone arches resting on round piers, is the handsomest feature. The chancel arch also in Caen stone. – STAINED GLASS. E window: three attractive figural lancets signed *W. F. Clokey*, Belfast, 1919.

St Lavinius. 0.5 km NE. Large four-bay hall of 1818, extended by *W. A. Scott* in 1910 with a chancel, sacristy, and a three-stage tower that looks more suited to a Greek island than to this pastoral scene. Cement-rendered hall with blocked quoins, corbelled eaves and lancets; the gables have interesting elongated kneelers, added by Scott when he raised the roof of the church. The chancel is short, with a graded three-light E window set in a shallow recess; on either side the unusual buttressing in the form of flat projections terminating beneath the kneelers is typical of Scott. The tower is of real interest: a distinctive and original moulded form in concrete with angle buttresses. The lancets in the second stage are set under two

varied hoodmoulds with an attractive metal clock on two
adjoining faces. Open belfry with deep chamfered arches. The
interior is plain and spacious. A good timber roof with barrel-
vaulting and exposed kingpost trusses and an attractive gallery
with panelling and box seating. – STAINED GLASS. E window:
the Crucifixion by *A. E. Child*, 1911.

RECTORY. Derelict. Once an attractive Regency house of seven
bays with the three central bays elegantly projected in a shallow
bow. T-plan formed by a large return. Roughcast with
Georgian windows, nicely diminished to smaller sashes on the
first floor. The more recent removal of the two end bays on
one side, and the shift of the entrance from the bow to the
angle of the return, make it now something of an asymmetrical
oddity. Attractive entrance GATES with stone piers and fancy
ironwork, nicely balanced with the church entrance.

KILLYGORMAN (formerly BESSBROOK). 1.5 km NE. A handsome Late Georgian house of two storeys and three bays with
squared masonry, red brick trim and rusticated quoins. Hipped
roof with paired eaves brackets. The tripartite doorcase is
refined, with a webbed elliptical fanlight and wide side-lights.
Attractive inner porch with side niches. The two principal
rooms interconnect behind the longer four-bay side elevation,
with the staircase placed centrally on the opposite side.

MILLVIEW. 2 km NE. A modest Early Victorian mill house
opposite large vernacular mill buildings, a roughcast two-
storey and three-bay gable-ended block; transformed into an
Edwardian house with the addition of a gabled projection of
three storeys to one side and a single-storey porch in the angle.
Refenestrated at the same time with bipartite windows, plate
glass, and the enlargement of the openings on the first floor.

BALLYNURE. 1.8 km W. Derelict. A compact Late Georgian
villa. Two storeys over a basement, roughcast with a low
hipped roof on paired eaves brackets. Unusually stumpy
chimney stacks. The entrance is recessed in the long side
elevation, moved here in the late C19 when the house was
extended. An unusual semicircular bay window with a sort of
projecting fanlight replaced the original entrance on the three-
bay front.

KILLYCOONAGH. 1.5 km NW. Solid and well-proportioned Late
Georgian house. Two-storey, three-bay block, roughcast with
a big hipped roof on eaves brackets, drawn together in a large
central stack. Handsome timber doorcase with engaged fluted
Doric columns and a finely detailed entablature supporting a
sunburst fanlight. Standard tripartite plan, two rooms deep
with a spacious open-well staircase located centrally beyond
the entrance hall; nicely elaborated with fluted tread-ends and
lighted by a big Georgian Gothick window.

ANALORE MILLS. 1.6 km W. Extensive milling complex sited
picturesquely beside a bridge on the River Finn. Now largely
disused. Corn milling on this site can be traced to the C17,
when a new mill was referred to in 1659. The buildings were
described as only partially standing in 1690, and what survived

was pulled down in 1718 and rebuilt; a new mill for wheat was built in 1758, and in 1829 the miller George Moore claimed to have built a village here, with mills, kilns and houses. Most of what may be seen today belongs to this period. Two adjoining ranges dominate; one is a very large and long three-storey block in limestone rubble with brick trim, the other a higher roughcast block forming a store and residence, set back slightly at one end. Beside this is a detached block of two storeys and three bays, presumably a miller's residence; heavily remodelled with picture windows, but the timber Doric doorcase is rather good and confirms an early C19 date.

KILLESHANDRA

This most Irish-sounding of place-names, Killeshandra, from *Cill na Sean Ratha*, 'church of the old fort', indicates the origins of a settlement here with an early church, set within a ring fort by one of the many lakes seeping through the drumlins to form Lough Oughter. Killeshandra developed first as a Plantation town, having been among the lands in the region granted separately in 1610 to Sir Alexander Hamilton and his son Sir Claude Hamilton as Scottish undertakers for the Plantation of Ulster. A 'strong castle' was built at Keelagh amid the outer lakes of Lough Oughter, and to the E a new settlement and a weekly market were developed near the existing church at Killeshandra, evidently planted with moderate success, as thirty-four 'English-like' houses were recorded here in 1618. By 1621, following the deaths first of Claude, then of Alexander, the property passed to Sir Claude's son Francis, still a minor, held in trust for him by his mother Jane and her second husband, Sir Arthur Forbes. Though considered well defended, the village was burnt by Hamilton in 1642 to prevent it falling into rebel hands. Its recovery was initiated later by Sir Francis's grandson, also Sir Francis, hailed on his tomb in the parish church as 'an example of integrity in evil times, shining as a steady light, the strenuous opponent of heretics and schismatics'. His lasting contribution to the town was to recast the medieval church as a fine specimen of Restoration architecture.

In 1787, when the Rev. Daniel Beaufort passed through, Killeshandra was still little more than a large village with a few neat houses, though more were being built. Eventually it became dependent on an established linen market, centred on a gabled market house in the Main Street, demolished in the C20. The economic benefits of trade were fully evident in 1837, when the town provided 'a cheerful and thriving appearance'.

KILLESHANDRA OLD CHURCH (C of I). Church Street. A singular ruin in a lakeside rath at the N end of the town, roofless except for two barrel-vaulted spaces in the S transept.

Ostensibly a Restoration church, its well-preserved structure the best of this period in Ulster. However, papal registers indicate that a church had been established here by 1436, and evidence for older alterations to the fabric suggests that the core of the sizeable T-plan church standing here today is probably the original medieval building, remodelled to its present appearance in 1688 by Sir Francis Hamilton, whose flamboyant coat of arms appears on the entrance gable of the S transept. Comprising a long nave, 66 ft by 26 ft (20 m by 8 m), and a S transept 29½ ft (9 m) square, it is built of coarse rubble with quoins, formerly roughcast, with traces still remaining across the broad entrance gable of the transept. A Y-traceried window stands out on the E gable, contrasting greatly with the Renaissance style of the others, so that it could be earlier, though similar to the early C17 example at St Mary's, Belturbet and so perhaps another instance of Gothic Survival. The S front is a near-symmetrical, elegantly defined two-bay gable, with round-headed windows set close to the corners, each with a hood and Renaissance-style tracery, a circle over two round-headed arches – a pattern formerly also to be found in the chancel of the Church of Ireland Cathedral at Armagh, according to Blaymire's 1739 view. On the l. side, the window incorporates the door as part of the original design, set in a finely wrought moulded architrave with a scrolled keystone, the clearest example of Jacobean style found in South Ulster; the Hamilton arms in a sculpted limestone frame are set high in the central space between the windows, with the outline of an older opening evident in the masonry below. There is nothing primitive in the details here. The gable itself is equally well-finished, with a thin sandstone coping, nicely scrolled at the eaves, and at the apex flattened as a plinth for a small gadrooned urn. The transept is held between substantial stepped piers with short flying buttresses, a striking and unusual feature investing the front with great character; each pier rises to a moulded cornice with the main eaves before a stepped red brick pyramid, truncated as if intended to support a finial. The buttresses and the offset windows on the S gable are accounted for by two brick barrel-vaults, set in parallel behind the gable and clearly inserted into existing fabric in the C17, so as to cause the old S entrance to be closed.

Today, the entrance opens directly into one of these high vaults; skilfully designed stone stairs lead down to the original floor level, and up in a short flight to a now vanished gallery. The steps are finely carved with scrolled tread-ends, but the best of the design is the open canopy under the rising gallery steps. This has square Tuscan piers to support a low segmental arch formed on two sides with carved spandrels; on one of the piers the initials F.H. are carved, presumably as a reference to the patron. The adjoining vault opens in the centre of the dividing wall. The room here was probably a vestry, with traces of low benches around the walls; it retains much of its stucco, with a plain moulded circle in the centre of the ceiling. A large arched recess high in the end wall is unexplained; an empty limestone frame below the window at the side presumably once held a square plaque. Each of the vaulted spaces has twin-light windows with rounded heads, set high in the walls with deep reveals.

The roofless nave has two windows set close together on the N wall, a slightly simplified version of those on the main front, with a large sloping buttress between them. Traces of older fenestration are apparent near the gables, clearest in the external masonry and evident even around the E window, where the tracery has also been filled in.

Two family mausolea stand inside the gables. In the w end, the plainer HAMILTON MAUSOLEUM is sunken, filling the space with a low, C19 cement-rendered front with battlemented stone copings that belie its more established origins. In the E end, the steep gable of the MARTIN MAUSOLEUM fronts a small Gothic Revival gem, tightly crafted in rock-faced limestone with a stone roof and a trefoiled doorway; the greater architectural sophistication and the richly carved armorial plaque over the door seem to suggest a greater importance for this family compared with the church's patrons opposite.

The graveyard has high walls to the street, opening with splendour through tall classical GATEPIERS of ashlar with a high plinth and a deep frieze, cornice and blocking course before lidless, swagged urn-finials. The date 1688 is carved in the frieze between the piers, and on either side below is a small relief panel, one containing the Hamilton crest, an oak tree sawn through by a frame-saw, the other their shield displaying three cinquefoils.

KILLESHANDRA PARISH CHURCH (C of I). 1838 by *William Farrell & Son*. In the Main Street, a large, buttressed nave of five bays, all the architectural emphasis given to the front, expressed in a spiky Gothic idiom. A big w gable with diagonal buttresses, blind lancets, and a belfry held between pinnacles is set behind a lower two-storey entrance gable projecting deeply between narrow side porches, with polygonal minarets on the corners. The materials are a satisfying contrast of roughcast with local sandstone abundantly used in the buttresses and dressings. Tall lancets to the nave with quarry glazing, elaborated on the façade with thick-set hoodmoulds and bulbous stops. Inside, the spacious rectangular hall retains its corniced flat plaster ceiling, and the windows are tied together under a continuous hoodmould. A narrow chancel arch and short chancel with a simple Perp E window. Unusually, in the original design the doorways on either side of the chancel arch opened to spiral stairs that led up to oriel-like pulpits, long since vanished.

FURNISHINGS. The mid-Victorian PULPIT and READING DESK are ghostly works in Caen stone, the pulpit an especially distinctive circular design; both are the work of an accomplished carver, sharing fine enrichments that include ballflower, quatrefoils and diaper-work. Late Victorian octagonal

FONT, richly carved with short, polished shafts. – STAINED
GLASS. E window: parables of the Prodigal Son and the Lost
Sheep, by *Alexander Gibbs & Co.*, *c.* 1882. – MONUMENTS. Sir
Francis Hamilton †1713. An enormous and sumptuous Early
Georgian monument extolling the manifold virtues of its
subject in a bold architectural composition in grey and white
marble, of the *Kidwell* school, though usually attributed to
David Sheehan, possibly inspired by Kidwell's Godfrey monument in Canterbury Cathedral. It is set over a bracketed base,
where the lengthy inscription is framed by a pair of engaged
Corinthian columns with a plain entablature, surmounted by
a square armorial plaque with a swan-neck pediment, which
in turn is flanked by flamboyant cartouches on plinths decorated with crossed quivers. – William Hales †1831; a richly
layered tablet in grey-and-white marble, with a draped urn
resting on a Greek Revival sarcophagus.

ARTHUR MARTIN MEMORIAL HALL. Main Street. 1898. An
esoteric, gable-fronted hall with a jaunty profile, built of limestone with an ashlar porch; the main gable has rusticated
quoins and a moulded cornice, and is gently advanced in the
centre with shapely copings and ball finials.

PORTALIFF GLEBE. Off the Main Street, close to the church. A
bulky three-storey block, almost palatial in its proportions,
giving it an unexpected presence in its modest grounds. Easily
attributable to *William Farrell*, the front has five bays, symmetrically imprecise but distributed to a careful rhythm that
gives greater spacing to the central bay. The walls are roughcast
with dressed quoins and a platband drawn between the lower
storeys. A heavy bracketed doorcase is flanked by narrow
side-lights. Shallow hipped roofs with massive stacks, set
transversely behind the main ridge.

To the side, a long two-storey range of STABLES AND COACH
HOUSES, in rubble and red brick, is set perpendicular to the
house.

ST BRIDGET. 0.5 km S, at Drumcrow. 1862 by *William Hague*.
Undeservedly sidelined outside the town centre, a large,
sombre church in an earnest Victorian Gothic idiom, built
of rough-hewn local limestone with smooth dressings.
An aisled nave with lower, buttressed transepts, and a deep,
gabled chancel with a big traceried window, flanked by
gabled side chapels; essentially arranged back-to-front, with a
square unfinished tower offset on the NE corner. Inside, an
open timber roof and a three-bay nave arcade with pointed
arches on shafts of Kilkenny marble. – STAINED GLASS. E
window by *John Casey*, Dublin, 1858, repaired by *James
Donnelly*, 1935.

CASTLE HAMILTON. The gate lodge and entrance are within the
town, at the end of Castle Lane, but Castle Hamilton itself (or
what passes for it today) is 0.75 km E. Nothing remains of the
substantial C17 castle founded here by the original Hamilton
grantees, Sir Alexander and his son Sir Claude, other than its
description: 'one bawne of lyme and stone 60 foote square

Killeshandra, St Bridget.
Engraving after W. G. Smith, 1862

[5.6 m²] and 12 foote [3.5 m] in height; and within the same
is built a fayre and sufficient castle or capitall mansion house
of lyme and stone, four storyes in height, with flankers and
turrets'. There was a confusing succession of houses through
the C18 and C19, and today a two-storey house of c. 1930 stands
near the site of the house built for R. H. Southwell, who purchased the estate before the end of the C18. Southwell's house

was a three-storey astylar block with a central bow to the garden front, possibly from a design by *Andrew McLeish*, who appears to have had some connection here in 1822. Burned *c.* 1911. Its replacement is a sedate two-storey roughcast block with an asymmetrical front of four bays, advanced on one side, with a further bay deeply recessed on the opposite side. Steep slate roofs with sprocketed eaves and tall red brick stacks. In the mid C18 Castle Hamilton was the property of Southwell's grandfather, Arthur Cecil Hamilton, and the house, described routinely as handsome and convenient, drew attention for its 'stately spacious hall', grandly claimed in 1739 as the largest of its kind in the kingdom, measuring 40 ft by 36 ft (12 m by 11 m), its height equal to its breadth, and 'properly adorned with Cornish [cornice] pilasters and niches'.

Now, only the YARD BUILDINGS attest to the succession of structures here from the C17. These are fronted by a large quadrangle in rubble and red brick, screened at one end by a battlemented wall with a pedimented archway in ashlar in the centre and a pedestrian doorway to the side. Inscribed on the piers are the dates 1610 and 1789, but there is nothing in the architectural character to ascribe to the earlier period other than a carved armorial plaque embedded later in the wall of the single-storey s range.

Through the C18 Castle Hamilton attracted attention for the quality of its DEMESNE, especially a formal vista, 200 ft (60 m) wide and planted with elms, aligned with the w front of the house and terminating at the town. On the s side there were parterres flanked by wildernesses, kitchen gardens and fruiteries. Four terraces led down to the lake and a banqueting house, while to the E was the deerpark. The demesne extended through the lakes, where on a well-wooded peninsula an octagonal gazebo took in views of the waterbound castle of Clough Oughter. There is still much to be discovered here by the more intrepid visitor.

NEIGHBOURHOOD

CLOUGH OUGHTER CASTLE. 4.5 km NE. A prominent bastion on a rocky isle in Lough Oughter, the substantial remains of a large C13 circular tower, built by Walter de Lacy in one of the most northerly reaches of the Norman hegemony to the E. Built of limestone rubble, 35 ft (10.5 m) in diameter, standing to a height of 60 ft (18.35 m), but badly damaged to the s. Narrow C13 loops at ground level, where there is evidence for a cross-wall dividing the space in two, probably of later medieval origin. Two floors above, with the sockets for first-floor beams visible internally along with three doorways and two windows; larger C17 windows in the upper floor below a battlemented parapet. The castle and its artificial island eventually became one of the primary medieval strongholds of the O'Reillys in the region, until taken into royal possession under the Plantation and granted to Captain Hugh Culme. It was recaptured by the O'Reillys during the 1641 rebellion, when they held Bishop William Bedell captive and where he perished. Fired on by Cromwell's forces in a siege in 1653, it has been ruined ever since.

To the SE, on Camp Hill overlooking the tower, no trace now of the site of the L-plan offices for the castle, built in the early C17.

KILLYKEEN COTTAGE. 3.2 km SE. Now part of Killykeen Forest Park. Picturesquely sited near the water's edge on a peninsula in Lough Oughter, a single-storey early C19 *cottage orné* built by Grace, Countess of Farnham. Originally thatched and now with a tiled hipped roof on generously sprocketed eaves. An oblong plan with two long low fronts, all nicely articulated with rustic columns and walls of decorative pebblework. To the S, the five-bay entrance front has an open three-bay loggia in the centre formed by tree trunk columns with doorways in each of the corners behind. To the N, facing the lake, the reverse, with corners set back, creating a sheltered arbour at either end behind a pair of similar timber columns. Between these are two well-spaced bays with arched windows; around them, as on the main front, the pebblework suggests an elaborate trellis but here the date 1819 is written in quartz. A similarly charming rustic temple immediately to the W has disappeared; the arresting beauty of the setting however still remains.

TRINITY ISLAND. 5 km SE. A remote church ruin on an island in Lough Oughter, reached by a causeway. Close to the water's edge, in a circular enclosure, low rubble walls with a pronounced batter represent the remnants of an undifferentiated nave and chancel 52½ ft by 16½ ft (16 m by 5 m) and S transept 20 ft by 16½ ft (6 m by 5 m); steep W gable topped by a neat twin arched bellcote. A Premonstratensian priory was founded here after 1237, when the island was granted by Cathal O'Reilly to the abbot of Trinity Island, Lough Key in Roscommon. In the gable a pointed window with splayed jambs cleanly formed in dressed masonry is perhaps, with the belfry, part of improvements of *c.* 1427, when indulgences were granted towards restoration. Scattered fragments of window tracery found in the nave are also C15. The main doorway in the W gable is now a ragged, formless opening; it is from here that the Romanesque doorway now set in Kilmore Cathedral is sometimes said to have originated, though the accepted date for its sculpture is C12. An additional doorway (now blocked) can be traced in the nave S wall, tight against the W wall of the transept, suggesting that the transept was a later addition, possibly a part of a recorded restoration in the C17.

PORTLONGFIELD. 4 km SW. An early C19 school, adapted for use as a chapel of ease in 1923. A two-storey roughcast block with a low hipped roof, built by the 5th Lord Farnham and based on designs for schools published 1830 in *A Statement of the Management of the Farnham Estates* and similar to examples

at Kiffagh (Kilnaleck) and Derrylane (Arva), with a long five-
bay front and lean-to entrance bays, recessed on either side.
Mullioned casements with quarry glazing.

HOLY ROSARY CONVENT. 1.5 km NW. Derelict. A modest,
nicely proportioned Late Georgian HOUSE formerly known as
Drumully, built for the Lough family on an exposed hillside,
is now set among the desolate ruins of a vast institution. A
roughcast block, two storeys tall with a three-bay front, mullioned windows with label mouldings, and a hipped slate roof
with wide Tuscan eaves. Extending on one side from behind
the house is a ponderous three-storey SCHOOL WING of 1934
by *Vincent Kelly*, continuing with blunt force until returned, to
advance with a narrow three-bay front. An overwhelming, hard
and factory-like block in cement render, relieved only where
the windows of the two lower storeys are framed together
inside tall recessed arches. Kelly's design for a new CHAPEL in
a bleak Modernist style was abandoned for a more conservative
classical building with terraced gardens of 1947 by *Simon
Aloysius Leonard* of *W. H. Byrne & Son*. Built to balance the
school, it is equally vast, expressed as a two-storey hall with
flat-roofed aisles and a polygonal chancel. The interior was
furnished with mosaics by *Oppenheimer*. Closed in 1985 and
abandoned, leaving a sense of some cataclysmic fallout. The
Italianate terraces and extensive gardens have all gone the way
of the building, including a small circular summerhouse with
Gothic iron windows.

CROAGHAN PRESBYTERIAN CHURCH. 1.5 km NW. Beside
Croaghan Bridge, for a congregation established here by 1670.
The present church is a lowly roughcast hall of four bays with
a simple gabled front, where a ball finial bears the date 1742
on its triangular base; a small C19 plaque below has the weathered inscription 'Glory to God'. A small oculus is set over the
door; the oculus is repeated on the opposing rear gable, set
over two lancets. Remodelled in 1901, when the windows were
given tall Neo-Georgian sashes, incorporating a classic semicircular webbed fanlight in a square-headed design.

CROAGHAN. 1.6 km NW. A mid-Georgian farmhouse, of two
storeys with a five-bay front, gable-ended and nicely proportioned, with the central bay expressed as a plain Venetian
window. Much altered.

AUBAWN. 2.5 km NW. A medium-size Late Georgian villa,
associated in the C19 with the ecclesiastical Beresford family.
A two-storey block with a basement, attics, and lower service
wings to the side, originally roughcast, with a three-bay front,
gabled in the centre with a square ashlar porch. More attractive
on the garden front, where a deep three-bay bow breaks
forward in the centre under a conical roof. Large tripartite
windows flank the bow on the ground floor; originally they,
like all the windows, had moulded entablatures. A characteristic oversailing eaves cornice on paired brackets has since been
replaced by ugly boxed eaves; at the same time the house was

given a new roof with dormers and meanly scaled central
stacks just a portion of the original size. Interiors entirely
rebuilt from a ruinous state in 2005. The setting is impressive,
on a hilltop, inside a ha-ha, to overlook a small well-wooded
demesne with a lake.

KILLINKERE   CN   6090

A rural parish SW of Bailieborough, focused on a small river
crossing, chapel and school.

KILLINKERE PARISH CHURCH (C of I). A small and squarish
    hall-and-tower type of 1817; three-bay rubble hall with plain
    Y-tracery in carved surrounds, dumpy three-stage tower with
    ashlar battlements. N transept of 1866 by *Welland & Gillespie*
    with an elaborated three-light traceried window; interior
    reordered at the same time with exposed kingposts. The con-
    tractor was *James Scanlon*.
ST ULTAN. A spreading T-plan on a rocky outcrop. An unpreten-
    tious church in roughcast with blocked quoins and big lancets,
    built by the Rev. John Fitzsimons in 1829, the year of
    Emancipation. Very plain inside, nave of three bays with
    exposed kingpost trusses. Refurbished 1961, reordered 1995.
    – MONUMENT. The Rev. Bernard McCabe †1902; a decorated
    tablet over a chalice and Host.
RECTORY. 1816. In a small, well-planted demesne. A tall two-
    storey-over-basement block of modest proportions, with half-
    hipped gables and central stacks. Three-bay front of rubble
    with tripartite sashes and a boxy porch. Much restored in 2003
    for community use.
KILLINKERE BRIDGE. A narrow four-arch bridge with cut-
    waters and massive coping stones. Built in two phases. The
    first, probably late medieval, is suggested by the coarsely built
    E face. A visible seam in the soffits of the arches and the
    squared masonry and ashlar voussoirs of the W face confirm a
    C19 widening. – No trace now of the inscribed wayside cross
    recorded beside the bridge in 1974, just a C21 suburban-style
    bungalow.
GALLON OLD CHURCH. 1 km W. Down a narrow boreen, in a
    circular enclosure are these fragmentary remains of a parish
    church mentioned in papal documents in 1406. The footings
    define a rectangular enclosure 53 ft by 19 ft (16.1 m by 5.7 m),
    and the deep, disfigured stump of the W wall still manages to
    preserve the outline of a rectangular window and evidence for
    a transverse vault like those of Lurgan and Killan.
    A primitive CARVED HEAD with inscriptions embedded in
    the gable wall of a house in the adjoining farmstead probably
    originated with the church.

A village founded on a steep hillside in the C18 by John Maxwell of Fellows Hall, who held most of the surrounding land from Trinity College Dublin.

St Mark (C of I). Dominating the w end of the village, an expressive buttressed hall and tower of 1830 by *William Farrell*, in squared limestone with cutstone trim; completed in 1832 at a cost of £1,603 with £5 contributed by the architect. Enlarged in 1874 with a chancel and vestry by *Frederick A. Butler*. The nave has three bays between stepped buttresses, the windows Tudor arches under emphatic hoods, originally with elaborate quarry glazing that survives in the w bays. The battlemented tower has three stages with tall spiky pinnacles rising from quickly diminishing diagonal buttresses; on two sides, a clock face of 1853 is set high in the louvred arches of the belfry. The chancel is a more vigorous design, well finished in perfectly squared, quarry-faced limestone; the contractor was *Richard Cherry* of Loughgall. It projects deeply in two bays with setback buttresses at the angles; the windows, set high on a sloping string, are lightly formed under hoods with cusped Y-tracery; the e window an impressive Dec design with five lights.

Inside, the standard hall with raking w gallery, plain but for the richness of the chancel opening through a deeply moulded arch with tall marble shafts. The nave ceiling has delicate cast-iron trusses, similar to the kind usually found in *Farrell*'s smaller hall churches. A dizzying pavement of encaustic TILES extends down the aisle, greatly elaborated in the sanctuary, where the initials of the patron of the works, Henry Bruce Armstrong, are displayed. Here the walls are lined with blind Gothic arcading in Bath stone. – Low, thick-set REREDOS in the centre, of three gables with shafts of 'dark rouge royal marble' inset with panels of Derbyshire alabaster. The materials, along with the PULPIT and READING DESK, also of Bath stone, were brought here from the Church of Ireland Cathedral in Armagh and reworked by *Butler*. – STAINED GLASS. Rather good late C19 and early C20 figurative works. The big traceried e window of 1874 with scenes from the life of Christ is by *Ward & Hughes*, London, who also designed the Good Samaritan of 1867 in the nave n wall; in the chancel s wall the two attractive windows with pale glass are by *Percy Bacon*, London, c. 1916 and c. 1929. In the e bays of the nave, two colourful medievalizing works of 1865, Jacob blessing his Sons (s) and the Raising of Jairus's Daughter (n), are by *William Wailes* of Newcastle upon Tyne. The Expulsion of Hagar and Ishmael in the s wall is also by *Wailes*. – MONUMENTS. Three ornamental designs stand out. Thomas Knox Armstrong †1840; an attractive Neoclassical tablet with inverted torches. – Lieutenant-Colonel John Cross †1850; a simple tablet with a funerary urn flanked by military officers. – St John Blacker-Douglas †1900;

an ornate Gothic tablet with a crocketed ogee gable by *W. Costigan & Co.*, Belfast.

METHODIST CHURCH. 1903 by *William Fawcett Gilgriest*. A small stuccoed church, built to a T-plan with a gabled porch in the angle between the two main gables. Utterly restrained, with six unadorned lancets, set in pairs, piercing the nave. Steep gables with kneelers, thin moulded copings with varied windows set on a continuous moulded string: a large hooded window with errant Y-tracery in the w gable and three graded lights under a cusped hoodmould in the s gable.

KILLYLEA ORANGE HALL. 1879. A plain gable-end block with overhanging eaves. Two storeys and three bays, the central bay advanced and gabled with braced timber bargeboards. Small rectangular windows, now spoiled with plate glass.

ST MARK'S HALL. Built *c.* 1860 as a schoolhouse, and since 1938 a parish hall. A long, low building in limestone rubble with bracketed eaves. The main front is asymmetrical: single-storey, three bays, with a gabled porch and to one side a two-storey gabled projection. Plain fenestration with twin round-headed lights in the porch. The adjoining street façade has three blind bays in blocked stucco surrounds, with the name in a marble plaque over the central bay.

KILLYLEA RECTORY. N, off the Armagh Road. Of *c.* 1860. An unostentatious roughcast block, two storeys on a half-basement with a low hipped roof on eaves corbels. The main front has three bays, with the entrance in the centre at the head of a narrow flight of steps with attractive railings; the timber doorcase has slender pilasters and a segmental fanlight. The windows, set in pairs on the side elevation, have segmental heads with horizontal glazing bars characteristic of several houses in this area.

DARTON HOUSE. W, on the Armagh Road. A tall gabled-ended block, three storeys and three bays in limestone rubble, built *c.* 1850 beside former coaching stables. Entrance in a long, flat-roofed block built in the late C20 across part of the front.

DARTAN HALL. 0.5 km SW. 1856 by *John Boyd*. Replacing a smaller house existing near this site before 1809. A solid-looking, mildly Italianate, free-standing cubic block, two storeys on a raised basement with a low hipped roof, slightly projected on a bracketed eaves cornice, with tall, rather gaunt stacks. It has rubble walls, sandstone quoins and strings with red brick trim, and plate glass in the windows. Three prominent fronts, each of five bays, the three central bays slightly advanced with tightly grouped round-arched windows so that it shares a family resemblance with Fellows Hall. On the entrance front this central projection is stuccoed with bold tapering keystones to the arches. The entrance, reached by a straight flight of steps, is formed with solid sandstone piers and plain moulded capitals, a simple fanlit door in the centre flanked by tall windows with stilted arches. The interior was rebuilt after a fire in the early C20. In 1837 the residence of Maxwell Cross.

The house stands above a sunken FARMYARD, an older complex with low ranges of vernacular buildings, one with a stone inscribed 'W + C 1809'.

The GATE LODGE of 1870 is a small rugged building in rock-faced masonry to an L-plan with round-headed windows and decorated bargeboards.

ELM PARK. 1.5 km NNE. Tradition and a C19 plaque on the N elevation of this large Late Georgian house place its origin in 1626, though most of what is visible today can only be associated with rebuilding in 1803 and later C19 additions. Its first builder was the Rev. Robert Maxwell, in 1625 Prebendary of Tynan and after 1643 Bishop of Kilmore. There is a tradition that the house was abandoned during the Civil War, perhaps destroyed, and given up entirely when he returned to Ireland after the Restoration and built a now vanished house at nearby Marrasit, which he named College Hall. The Killylea property passed to his nephew Henry Maxwell, and must have been either fixed up or rebuilt. In 1703 we are given a brief glimpse of a 'very good stone house' with 'handsome rooms'; today only the dormered two-storey service range that extends W from the N front, chaotically sloping downhill to the farmyard entrance, hints at anything older than the C19. Significantly, at the junction with the later block, high in the wall, a weathered C17 plaque bears the name of Robert Maxwell and an incomplete date in the 1620s that perhaps confirms the C19 plaque nearby. By the mid C18 the property had passed to Maxwell Close, and what is dominant today is an impressive three-storey block of 1803, built by Samuel Close. Architecturally plain, it has rendered walls of limestone rubble and exposed cutstone dressings, with just three bays on the main front to the E and much deeper sides – deepest on the N front, with eight bays where the two bays at each end are expressed as shallow bows; the four-bay S elevation was later extended with an additional three bays. The entrance front is tall, somewhat vacant, with the central bay slightly advanced, big Georgian sashes, a thin moulded cornice and blocking course before a high pitched roof. The simple carved doorcase is squashed between narrow eight-pane sashes and consequently too weak, that weakness emphasized in thin reeded consoles at either end of a fluted frieze supporting a crisp cornice.

In 1831 Maxwell Close left Elm Park for the house Playfair designed for him at Drumbanagher and the property passed to cousins, the Blacker-Douglas family. For St John Blacker-Douglas in the 1860s *James Rawson Carroll* extended the S elevation to the W to accommodate a large dining room with three closely grouped windows, its wall stepped back slightly with a fine Victorian curved conservatory placed across it, since removed. Carroll had proposed a more elaborate scheme, which involved recasing the house in stucco with rustication, raised panels, entablatures to the windows and a balustraded parapet; a new entrance porch would be echoed by another on the S front. Perhaps in sacrificing these elements a two-storey S porch was built on a larger scale (though narrowed in execution from four to three bays), with large casement windows and Tuscan pilasters, all lazily duplicated on the second storey. The interiors were also reworked by *Carroll*, save for delicate blind arches at the head of the main stairs, the tympana filled with delicate Neoclassical plasterwork worthy of Thomas Cooley – a fan surrounded by swags and bows.

In the first half of the C20 Elm Park was a prep school, and since then it has been a turkey farm, the large decaying Victorian rooms a surreal backdrop to noisy avian inhabitants.

The FARMYARD to the W has closely arrayed vernacular ranges, mostly roughcast. An impressive arched gateway of ashlar to the N bears the date 1884. The long E range that adjoins it was partially refronted to address the house in the late C19, probably by *Carroll*, with three gables in rock-faced masonry, slightly projected on corbels, with decorative bargeboards and a diamond window.

The MAIN ENTRANCE, early C19, has low clustered piers with sharply tapered caps, and a small, much altered, three-bay lodge to one side. The STATION LODGE of 1867 is a solid small block in rock-faced masonry with a three-bay front and mullioned windows, the central bay advanced and gabled. Nice diamond window in the end gable and fish-scale slating to the roofs. The larger NORTH LODGE, derelict at the time of writing, is a later roughcast L-plan block with brick dressings, mullioned timber windows, and ornate bargeboards and finials to the gables. The entrance in the angle is covered by an ornate Gothic veranda.

PURPLE STAR ORANGE HALL. 2.5 km SSE. A charming small building. A single-storey, gabled-ended hall in limestone rubble with brick end stacks. The front has three bays, the entrance in an advanced and gabled projection to one side. Although dated 1898, the carved doorcase looks Georgian, with a blocked architrave and triple keystone; above it nice bargeboards with pierced ornament.

WOOD PARK. 3 km SSE. Ruined. An interesting small castellated block that evolved *c.* 1830 from a house of the Johnston family, present here in 1777. Two storeys over a basement, roughcast, with a shallow central bow on one front that must recall the original house. What remains today is largely the main garden front and fragments of the three-bay single-storey arcade set between buttressed polygonal angle turrets. The arcade has Tudor arches on tall clustered columns, with battlements and pinnacles on the parapet. A Victorian photograph shows this elevation with simple Y-tracery in the windows in similar shallow Tudor arches. Comparison of the arcade with that of Tynan Abbey has attracted an attribution to *Nash*. In the 1830s, the residence of Acheson St George.

FELLOWS HALL. 2 km SSW. A modestly Italianate house, highly idiosyncratic, with a complicated story to tell. Starting in the late C17, the present building embodies four different phases, retaining elements of each earlier phase behind its Victorian façade. The main front has two contrasting storeys on a semi-basement with a spreading hipped roof, oversailing on fussy bracketed eaves, and with tall end stacks. The ground floor is of limestone ashlar, somewhat coarsely finished with wide joints. Here there are five bays and large sashes in moulded architraves of stucco with a plain outer frame and a thin, simplified entablature. In contrast the first floor is of squared masonry, with seven arched bays expressed in flat stuccoed architraves with big keystones resting on a continuous string; and the central three windows are grouped together over the entrance. As below, the windows have horizontal glazing bars and plate glass. The door is set within a flat stuccoed portico pasted on to the wall with Ionic pilasters and an entablature; the pilasters are stretched over the door and side-lights with a certain awkwardness. The pre-existing entrance, still expressed internally as a Venetian window, seems to have been given this stuccoed order to adapt it to the enlarged scale of the Victorian fenestration. At the back, the basement is exposed to reveal a more solid-looking, three-storey block, shorter and plainer than the front, with just three bays, though the disparity between storeys remains, as Regency tripartite windows on the two lower storeys give way to triple arched windows.

The house owes its name to its association with Trinity College Dublin, granted these Crown lands in 1610; Robert Maxwell, a fellow of the College and Bishop of Kilmore, leased them later in the century. Bishop Maxwell's son James, returning to Armagh after the Restoration, built a house here which he named in deference to the owners of the land, just as his father had when he built College Hall nearby. The house was in existence by 1664, the date tendered by two heraldic plaques on the house, and in the same year it appears in the Hearth Money Rolls. It was destroyed by fire in 1752 but some fabric was retained, and the great thickness of the s wall is especially evident in the plan. In a small room later built against this gable in the C19, one of the C17 plaques, set high in the wall, records the erection of the house by James Maxwell and his wife Elizabeth. The tall end-stacks may also be a legacy of this house.

Ten years after the fire, the house was rebuilt as a two-storey block to a single-pile plan. According to one of two further plaques on the largely blind N front, it was rebuilt for Robert and Grace Maxwell 'under the inspection' of their son, John. The resulting C18 plan remains largely intact on the w front, with two small Georgian rooms flanking a handsome dog-leg stair that is pushed off-centre by a closet; the thick newels, sweeping handrails and tightly spaced balusters – three to a tread – are all characteristically Early to mid-Georgian. The joinery, too, has the familiar raised and fielded panels, though combined with much plainer architraves.

John Maxwell retained the core of the Georgian house when he brought the building up to date in 1802, in effect making the old ground floor a basement and reversing the house, placing a new, wider entrance front across the E and raising the entire building by an additional storey. The windows of the W front were widened, with the tripartite sashes that characterize the era. Inside, a tripartite plan was adopted, with larger reception rooms on either side of a deep entrance hall that reaches back to the old stairs. Here and in the adjoining rooms simple moulded cornices and modest foliated roses confirm a light Neoclassical touch that continues into the chimneypieces: in the drawing room a fine Ionic piece in white marble, with fluted pilasters and frieze and putti in low relief in the central panel; in the library, a very refined work in black marble with fluting and an urn in the central panel.

The main front was recast in the late C19 after the property passed to the Armstrong family. The roof was also raised and elaborated at this time; the outline of the old roofs is still evident on the chimneystacks in the cavernous roof space. The date and authorship of these works is unknown; they share something of the character of *John Boyd*'s design of 1856 at nearby Dartan Hall, but they may be by *Frederick A. Butler*, who in 1874 was employed by the Armstrongs at the parish church in Killylea.

Beside the house, to the S, is an impressive FARMYARD fronted by a long two-storey range with gabled end blocks; on the N gable a bellcote and in the S gable a brick dovecote.

At the main entrance the pleasing Regency Revival LODGE of 2007 is by *Brian Esmond*. A tall cubic block of two storeys with a shallow canted porch, casement windows, and a squat pyramid roof with a tall central stack. The walls are rendered, with chamfers to the corners; decoration limited here and on the porch to panels raised in low relief.

MOUNT IRWIN. 4 km SSW. Named for the Irwin family, who were established here in the C18. A modest house of three bays, with a plain two-storey, two-bay wing to one side. The main block is grim Victorian in its appearance, cement-rendered with plate glass and a wide stuccoed porch squashed between bay windows on the ground floor; on the first floor, tripartite sashes under plain gables, steeply pitched, with narrow twin sashes in the attic. The porch has corner pilasters, cornice and blocking course with the entrance between narrow sashes. Round the back the building reveals itself to be an earlier gable-ended house to a T-plan, with flush sash frames suggesting an Early Georgian date; it would certainly reward closer study. Here also nice attic dormers with small sixteen-pane sashes.

Behind the house, an attractive INNER YARD, one side enclosed by a long two-storey roughcast range, also Georgian, with stables and coach houses.

The LODGE is a modest Gothic gem; a single-storey, three-bay block in cement render, the façade gently canted with pointed windows and a central door. The roof is hipped with the shaped rafter toes exposed.

A small rural parish in hilly countryside, focused on a small crossroads village 3 km N of Richhill. Anciently known as Kilmore-Aedhain, from the tradition that a church dedicated to Aidan was founded here by St Mochtee; other sources associate it with *Cill Mhór Ó Nialláin*, 'the great church of O'Niallain'.

ST AIDAN (C of I). The church can list its rectors from 1287; a parish church was in evidence on this site in 1609; and a 'fayre church now built' is mentioned in 1622. The present building is a sizeable hall and tower, the tower a survivor, perhaps even late medieval, and the hall a rebuilding of 1814. Richard Johnston, a nephew of the architect Francis Johnston, was appointed rector here in 1871 and erected the chancel in 1876 as a tribute to his wife, Hester. The three-stage tower betrays its age only in its heavy, thick-set appearance and the slits piercing the NW corner to light the internal spiral stair. The walls are roughcast with zipper-like quoins finishing in battlements with corner pinnacles. A copper-clad octagonal spire erected in 1825 has since been removed. The nave has three bays with hoods to the windows and Y-tracery with small clear panes; the doorway, with a moulded Tudor arch and hood, is set to one side on the S wall. In contrast to the roughcast walls, the chancel is built of squared rock-faced limestone, with angle buttresses and Dec tracery. A late C20 lean-to vestry replaced a small C19 building in the angle between the tower and the nave.
　　Inside, a deep lobby separates the tower and nave. The nave is largely of Johnston's time, with exposed kingposts and a sandstone chancel arch on black polished shafts with foliate capitals. Some nice elements surviving from the early C19 are the clustered colonnettes ending in pendant stops to frame the windows and the polygonal timber columns supporting the gallery. At the E end of the nave are a number of INSCRIBED SLABS, the earliest with raised lettering dated 1633. – STAINED GLASS. E: the Acts of Mercy, a luminous window signed by *H. Hughes* of London, 1876. Nave N: depictions of Christ by *Campbell Bros*, Belfast, *c.* 1906. – MONUMENTS. Mostly plain. Richard Johnston †1907; a brass plaque, marked *A. & N. Aux. G. S. L., London.* – James Hobson †1919; a quirky aedicule in Caen stone with a depiction of the church.
　　The GRAVEYARD has an impressive collection of C18 and C19 grave markers. One of these facing the tower, to Michael Hampton †1825 and Mary Hampton †1817, records puzzlingly that her son 'CRs [Christopher] Primate Hampton' 'laid the first cornerstone of this church and put all species of coin underneath'.

SCHOOLS (former). A C19 building in a Tudor Revival style hanging on the edge of the churchyard. Two-storey gable-ended block with the wide end bay on the front advanced and gabled; a small porch adjoins the S gable. Rubble with dressed quoins, and red brick trim to wide casement windows. The twin entrances form Tudor arches in carved limestone.

OLD RECTORY. Across the road from the church, a boxy two-storey early C20 block with a steep hipped roof. Cement-rendered with narrow plate-glass sashes set in pairs and a short glazed timber porch between bay windows – these nicely expressed with rounded corners.

GREENFIELD HOUSE. Close to the church, a Late Victorian two-storey house to an L-plan, front of three bays with a small central porch, hipped roof and central stacks; longer four-bay side elevation. The walls are roughcast with blocked stucco quoins, label mouldings and a staccato eaves course of moulded yellow brick, repeated on the chimneystacks.

KILMORE HOUSE. A substantial three-storey-over-basement block near the church, built as a glebe house in 1793. A standard Late Georgian design of cubic proportions, cement-rendered, with simple fronts, varied only by the distribution and proportions of the sash windows. The original block still dominates despite being spoiled by additions made after 1871. These included a new entrance to one side in a single-storey projection across the entrance front, dressed up with shaped gables and big mullioned windows of plate glass. The garden front was given large gabled projections at either end, one disproportionately big, both with bay windows and wide mul-lioned windows. These works were for the Rev. Richard John-ston, who acquired the glebe as the Johnston family seat.

VINECASH PRESBYTERIAN CHURCH. 3.5 km NE. 1879. Trim stuccoed hall of three bays with twin lancets.

Close by, a good C19 vernacular HOUSE, two-storey, gable-ended, in blackstone with red brick trim and irregularly spaced small-paned sashes.

ST PATRICK, STONEBRIDGE. 1.5 km SSE. A small C19 stuccoed Gothic hall and chancel. Three bays with plain timber Y-tracery in blocked surrounds and twin-cusped lights in the steep, kneelered gable of the entrance. Here the doorway is deeply recessed in a small gabled porch with a small adjoining lean-to. Alterations in 1908 by *John V. Brennan*, who returned in 1920 to build an unremarkable PRIEST'S HOUSE. Beside the church is a large dry-walled GROTTO; before this, a carved limestone altar, discarded from the church, which commemor-ates Eliza Richardson, who paid for the grotto and the chancel in 1851.

STONEBRIDGE FURNITURE FACTORY. 1.5 km SSE. Post-war Modernism. A long and low two-storey building with a sym-metrical front and a preponderance of big, closely spaced iron windows. The centre is slightly advanced with a raised parapet, gently curved wall, and a battery of vertical windows over the entrance. The walls are roughcast, rising to a parapet that hides the roof; on the broad side elevation the parapet is stepped with a low gable.

Opposite is a NISSEN HUT fronted by a shaped three-bay gable with low curved walls embracing a vehicular forecourt.

Belonging to the same period, it is a small and perfectly formed building well worth a closer look.

BALLYLEANY ORANGE HALL AND HOUSE. On Legacorry Road, 2.5 km SSE. 1923. A small roughcast hall of three bays with lugged stucco and pebble surrounds to the windows. Elongated, with a lower two-bay porch to one side. Beside the hall a pleasing Late Georgian FARMHOUSE. Solid gable-ended, roughcast block of two storeys and five bays with Georgian sashes. Two lower barns adjoining one end.

ANNAHUGH HOUSE. 1.5 km NNW. The epitome of *an teach fada*, the Irish 'long house'. A pleasing vernacular Georgian farmhouse of two storeys with ten bays to the front. The windows have small twelve-pane sashes, mostly with exposed frames, and more irregularly disposed on the ground floor, where a charming fanlit doorcase with attenuated side-lights is placed off-centre. To the rear, a group of equally wholesome whitewashed outbuildings, one rebuilt in 1865, another in 1945.

3000   KILMORE   CN
                   2.5 km SW of Cavan town

A highly picturesque enclave shrouded by venerable oaks and sycamores that give an exalted air and a sense of enchantment to this rural ecclesiastical site, which has been seat of the bishops of Kilmore since the mid C15. The name Kilmore – *Cill Mhór*, 'the great church' – reflects an earlier prominence that the *Annals of the Four Masters* have traced to a late C9 foundation. Of that church there are no physical remains other than perhaps the late Romanesque doorway inserted in the C19 Cathedral which dominates the site today. The only prominent feature associated with early settlement here is an imposing MOTTE AND BAILEY, E of the Cathedral, in the episcopal demesne; erected by Walter de Lacy in 1211 in an effort to extend Norman control into the NW and reduced by Cathal O'Reilly in 1224, it is now clothed in trees as a remnant of the C18 designed landscape of the Old Palace which lies in ruins above it, alongside the C17 Cathedral surviving today as a parish hall.

The reforming bishop William Bedell is Kilmore's most celebrated incumbent. Once chaplain in Venice to Sir Henry Wotton, author of the important architectural text *The Elements of Architecture* (1624), Bedell came to Ireland in 1626 as Provost of Trinity College Dublin and was consecrated Bishop of Kilmore and Ardagh in 1629, remaining until his death twelve years later. He found Kilmore 'under so many disorders' and that 'the King's priests were as bad as the Pope's'; his effort to progress Irish Reformation through the encouragement of the Irish language led to the first Irish translation of the Old Testament. So respected were his actions that during the 1641 rebellion the Irish claimed he was the 'last Englishman they would put out of the county'.

He died a prisoner at Clough Oughter Castle, and was buried here at Kilmore. His grave is marked by a heraldic table monument, elevated over a large vault under the shade of a giant sycamore, reputedly the largest in Ireland, the remnant of a grove that he planted in the early C17.

OLD CATHEDRAL. Until the ancient diocese of Breifne was transferred here from Slanore, and renamed in 1454, Kilmore was little more than a parish church. The incumbents of the early C18 lavished great expense on the palace and garden, but the church was never deemed worthy of enlargement or embellishment, so that what survives today, crowning the hilltop above its successor, is an easily overlooked long rectangular structure in limestone rubble. The building sits across the N side of a rectangular graveyard, well below the present ground level, so that it is undoubtedly a well-established foundation. Probably no later than the C16 or C17, the structure was described in 1646 as having a roof of wood and sods; some time between 1727 and 1739 Bishop Hort 'sashed it, flagged it, pewed and painted it'. In 1810 it was merely 'very small and ancient'. Simply one long hall of three bays, built of limestone rubble with a narrow two-storey block associated with the Old Palace rising over the W end, formerly with three bays and now reduced to one, the outline of the other bays still legible in the masonry. Traces of masonry foundations near the S wall, and corresponding repairs evident near the W end, may indicate the former presence of a transept. Two large rectangular windows to the nave and a smaller one set under the eaves to light the gallery, all with timber Gothic mullions, replacing similar quarry-glazed casements evident in the early C20. John Binns observed in 1837 that the church 'has suffered deplorably from the attempts of some rustic Vitruvian to modernise its exterior'. By 1860 the Romanesque doorway noted here in 1739 had been excised, leaving a deeply splayed doorway as a scar beneath the gallery (it was reset in the new Cathedral, q.v.).

Inside, a cambered plaster vault and a gallery at the W end, where only the clumsy-looking wooden pillars suggest anything of antiquity. Tall rectangular E window with triple lancets in two rows. In the two-storey W end, the two ground-floor rooms are barrel-vaulted in the medieval manner (*see* below).

OLD PALACE. Of the palace what survives is the W ground-floor façade with blocked-up windows and a two-storey portion attached to the W end of the old Cathedral like a tower and still roofed, which could well be C16 or C17 in origin; it has two parallel rooms on the ground floor with barrel-vaults. Having become rather dilapidated, the Palace was rebuilt in the early C18. Bishop Whetnell began the work before 1713. His successor, Bishop Thomas Goodwin, continued it, and by 1720 claimed to have lavished almost £3,000 on the project, resulting in a suite of seven ground-floor rooms – still partly evident in outline – in a range measuring 100 ft by 40 ft

(30.5 m by 12 m), with two floors above. Even so it was still incomplete ten years later, when Goodwin's successor, Bishop Josiah Hort, resumed improvements. In 1739, despite being 'stuccoed', the exterior had evidently been deprived of homogeneity by the sequence of works: it was said to fail 'in that regularity which shines in modern pieces of architecture – which are begun and executed by one plan'. However, the cumulative efforts paid off, and it was eventually adjudged to be among the best houses in Ulster; when the preacher John Wesley visited the Bishop of Kilmore in 1787, he found that 'his house is finely situated, has two fronts and is fit for a nobleman'. It was still intact in 1837, when John Binns described it as 'a capacious building in the Elizabethan style of Architecture'; but by then it had already been superseded by William Farrell's assured Neoclassical block.

The atmosphere of an old LANDSCAPE lingers, and many vestiges of older features still persist at Kilmore; there are even suggestions of where Bishop Goodwin levelled and drained the bog and made a canal 1,500 ft (c. 460 m) long, widening into a 300-ft (90-m) basin in the centre, all aligned with his front door!

ST FEIDHLIMIDH'S CATHEDRAL (C of I). Built at the height of the so-called Second Reformation and dedicated to the memory of Bishop William Bedell, a conscious effort to connect current Evangelical zeal with the enduring reputation of a popular predecessor. A dignified cruciform church by *William Slater*, tightly massed into a squat crossing tower with a crowning slate pyramid, rather monolithic-looking in its emergence from a grassy tree-girt hilltop. This is in part because of the contracted nature of the plan, making less go a long way to achieve a worthy cathedral-like scale, but never quite escaping the impression up close that it is not much more than an oversized parish church. Slater exhibited his designs at the Royal Academy in 1858, and in the harsh polemical environment of the period the *Civil Engineer and Architect's Journal* pronounced the exterior to be deficient 'in point of originality', but allowed that as 'it is carefully put together, we should term it "coldly correct" '. The foundation stone was laid the same year and the contractor employed, locally chosen, was *William Hague Sen.* The completed Cathedral was consecrated in July 1860. The overall compactness and scale certainly enhance the wholesomeness of the building, an otherwise tempered expression of C14 Dec that is most prominent in the clear, thin delineations of the Geometric tracery.

The plan is conventional, with a tall three-bay nave, steeply roofed with lean-to aisles, short transepts, and a two-bay chancel, with a gabled s porch added in 1869, all with thick-set angle buttresses. The square tower is similarly buttressed with a polygonal stair-turret on the SE angle; its overall effect is successful, plainly finished with clean parapets and three closely grouped cusped lancets to the belfry. The walls are built of squared coursed local limestone rubble with smooth

Dungannon sandstone for tracery and other dressings. The main front has a slender appearance, composed around tall twin lancets with simple cusped tracery and an oculus above inset with trefoils; twin doors are set in a generous pointed arch, finely moulded with engaged shafts in the reveals and a diapered tympanum with the episcopal arms and a wheeled motif framing a six-pointed star. Twin lights in the transepts and three lights in the chancel, with a big five-light window in the E gable.

Inside, a tall arcaded nave, narrow and reticent, with a dark timber roof and little architectural elaboration beyond the arcades, composed of simple compound piers and pointed arches, with triangular clerestory windows aligned above. The crossing arch meets the aisles clumsily, made more so by the application of a hoodmould. – FURNISHINGS. Elaborate inlaid REREDOS in Caen stone, and THRONE, a canopied oaken design, both designed by *Slater* and carved by *Forsyth*, London. – Polygonal FONT, on shafts of Connemara marble, and panelled oak PULPIT on a stone base are both by *Purdy & Outhwaite*, Dublin. – STAINED GLASS. E window: parables of the Ten Virgins, Good Samaritan, and Prodigal Son by *William Wailes*, 1869. W window: a large parable composition of 1874 attributed to *Ward & Hughes*, London. Chancel N: W, memorial to Lord and Lady Farnham by *Catherine O'Brien*, *An Túr Gloine*, 1944; E, the Ascension, 1970, attributed to *Clokey*, Belfast. Chancel S: Christ and the Children, signed *Mayer & Co.*, c. 1905; W, Christ flanked by SS Columba and Brigid, by *Clokey*, Belfast, 1972. S transept: the Reaper and Sower, by *Ward & Hughes*, London, 1860. S aisle: a medieval-izing design by *John Richard Clayton* of *Clayton & Bell*, 1860; the Raising of Lazarus, a more conventional design by *Clayton & Bell*, 1867. Single lancets in N and S aisles: the Good Shepherd, 1957, and Christ Blessing the Children, 1961, by *Catherine O'Brien*, *An Túr Gloine*. N aisle: Angel and Women at the Tomb, and the Risen Christ appearing to Mary Magdalene, greenish figurative glass by *James Powell & Sons*, 1888; Christ's charge to Peter, 1886, and Christ disputing with the Doctors, 1900, both by *Mayer & Co.*; and another of 1884 largely patterned with John the Evangelist and St James. – MONUMENTS. In the chancel: the Rev. William Magenis †1825; a draped urn on a Greek Revival sarcophagus, by *Thomas Kirk*. – Mary Beresford †1845 in Rome; an elaborate Gothic aedicule with Connemara shafts and bosses and rich cresting, inset with a circular relief portrait. – George de la Poer Beresford †1906; a plain tablet, by *C. W. Harrison & Sons*. – S transept: Colonel Thomas Nesbitt †1820; an elaborate Neoclassical sarcophagus with torches, surmounted by a funerary urn. – Mary Moore †1833; a plain white pedimented tablet. – Cosby Nesbitt of Lismore †1837; an elaborate white marble pylon with a draped sarcophagus, signed *T. Kirk*. – John Nesbitt †1853; a plain white tablet, signed *White*, Vauxhall Bridge, London.

Kilmore, St Feidhlimidh's Cathedral (C of I), interior.
Engraving by J. R. Jobbins, 1861

20   ROMANESQUE DOORWAY. Now seemingly incongruously set in the chancel N wall, employed as the vestry door. The finest example of Romanesque sculpture in South Ulster, a richly carved doorway largely ignored in studies of the corpus of Romanesque art in Ireland, perhaps because of its loss of context. It has usually been considered to have had a peripatetic existence before its insertion here in 1860: long claimed as the W doorway of the Premonstratensian Priory of Holy

Kilmore, St Feidhlimidh's Cathedral (C of I), Romanesque doorway.
Drawing by K. Mulligan, 2012

Trinity, a few kilometres to the w on Lough Oughter (Killeshandra), it was reputedly moved first to the old episcopal site at
Slanore and then brought to adorn the old Cathedral of
Kilmore, where it was set in the nave wall. There remains the
possibility that it never really left Kilmore, as its suggested late
c12 date is at least a century older than the Premonstratensian
foundation. It is a four-order arch bearing a pronounced
beaded hoodmould; the engaged shafts of the three outer
orders are separated by a beaded fillet, and have enriched bases
and capitals. The capitals especially are ornamented with stylized heads that are rare in Ulster, being more familiar at midlands sites like Clonmacnoise in Offaly or Killeshin in Laois;
the most distinctly human and bearded head is on the w side,
and well preserved. Above the capitals is a beaded abacus. The
outer orders have typical dog-toothed voussoirs or chevron
patterning, both enriched with beading, while the inner arch
is ornamented with continuous strapwork. Three primitive
human heads punctuate the arch of the second order. The
square jambs of the inner order are decorated with diverse
diaper patterns, animal and foliated motifs, of which some
appear in slightly jumbled form – the result of a careless mason
during reassembly – and some too crisp to have weathered the
centuries so well and so must represent repairs.

St Feidhlimidh's Well. Cut into the hillside slope s of the
c19 Cathedral, a simple arched stone canopy of c18 appearance, leading with steps down to a circular well-head.

SEE HOUSE (former). Built *c.* 1835–7 for Bishop George de la Poer Beresford to a design by *William Farrell*. A towering block; when completed it was described as 'too lofty, and in other respects . . . not well proportioned'. Essentially an enlarged version of Farrell's astylar design for Rathkenny (Tullyvin), here with three storeys on a basement, in smooth render with limestone dressings. The tall three-bay front with diminishing proportions is held between the architect's characteristic broad strip pilasters, their projection carried through to the crowning limestone eaves cornice and blocking course. The pilasters are repeated on the central bay, defining a breakfront with a low pediment, its tympanum emblazoned with Beresford's episcopal arms and motto, *Nil nisi cruce* (Nothing but the cross). The ground floor has another of *Farrell*'s favoured devices – big tripartite windows in cutstone frames with substantial mullions and heavy brackets resting on a plinth, separated by a platband from the floors above. A large box-like porch in limestone stands over the area, adorned with thin pilasters and lit by big sashes at the sides. Side elevation of four bays, the central two advanced and with bracketed entablatures across the ground-floor windows. Disconcerting lopsided garden front of five bays; a gentle bow is exquisitely projected from the central three bays, but its elegance is spoiled by the varied width of the end bays, one of which is wider, accommodating a large tripartite window set in a shallow segmental recess.

Inside, a square entrance hall with a plain circular ceiling supported on pendentives leads directly to the inner hall, which introduces an interior on a palatial scale that is at times unbecoming for its plainness, and almost certainly for its comfort. Here vast rooms, simply decorated with Early Victorian cornices and foliated centrepieces, are arranged around the deep, cavernous stair hall, with its bifurcating stair set to one side pushed out on the E elevation and lit by an enormous round-headed tripartite window.

Outside, this window overlooks a very handsome, well-built STABLEYARD and its cupola'd clock tower. On one side, over the kitchens, a small timber-panelled CHAPEL was formed *c.* 1910 with a broad Tudor-arched window overlooking the yard, formerly filled with stained glass of the Last Supper by *Heaton, Butler & Bayne*.

The gently sloping parkland benefits from the great maturity of the Old Palace demesne dotted with magnificent oaks, though the approach was criticized when completed for being 'tortured into short curves, for which the character of the ground is not fitted'. Set beside the main approach to the Cathedral, the entrance is marked by a kneelered Gothic ARCHWAY attributable to *William Slater*, with a small steeply roofed L-plan LODGE alongside; this is a quaint Gothic design also in squared limestone with cusped lancets and a slender bay window in the road gable.

RICEHILL. 0.5 km N. A classic Georgian gentleman's farmhouse in a small demesne. A gable-ended, roughcast block with a nicely ordered, single-storey five-bay front with big twelve-pane sashes and a central fanlit doorway with narrow side-lights. A basement is exposed behind and a lower, single-bay wing stands on one side. The house and its approach are framed by a handsome gateway, with tall square piers, curved sweeps and wrought-iron gates.

TONYMORE CASTLE. 1.2 km SE. Ruins of a stocky tower representing a rare late C16 stronghold in South Ulster. Three storeys, rubble-built, with quoins and well-preserved loops in chamfered surrounds. Its tall battered base and the spiral stair embedded in the SE corner are normal features, leaving nothing architectural to distinguish the building from its medieval fore-bears. W wall now entirely destroyed; entrance and part of a pointed door surviving in the centre of the E wall opposite. The battlements have fallen, though defensive concerns can still be discerned in the loops, one placed directly over the arched doorway, protected also by the murder hole concealed in the thickness of the wall.

ST PATRICK, DRUMCOR. 1.5 km W. A three-bay lancet hall of 1838, altered in 1930 with the addition of a low canted baptis-tery and side porches to the W gable; roughcast. Inside, a simple hall with a timbered W gallery. Flat ceiling that opens to a short barrel-vault at E and W ends, to accommodate an oculus inserted in each of the gables, presumably after the building was remodelled in 1990 by *Philip Cullivan*. – STAINED GLASS. Early C20 by *William Earley*, Dublin.

DANESFORT. 1.5 km NW. In elevated countryside, replacing the Deanery House present here in 1739, a forbidding Victorian house (perhaps by *William Slater*?) raised proudly over an exposed basement. A sizeable two-storey block to an L-plan, built of squared limestone with cutstone dressings. Steep hipped roofs on eaves corbels and tall brick stacks. Irregularly fenestrated front – six symmetrical bays over a discordant five – with plate glass. A large off-centre porch with a gabled front is reached by a walled flight of steps.

KILNALECK   CN   4090

A street village, supported in the C19 by frequent cattle fairs. On the street just three buildings stand out for attention: the broad stuccoed front of the ULSTER BANK, its two storeys raised over the streetscape with a plain astylar classicism, relying for its sophistication on the moulded keystone over the doorway, the bracketed entablature over the first-floor window, and a crowning cornice with nascent pediment; BOYLANS, a two-storey, five-bay house of 1870 in rubble and red brick; and next to it, the smaller premises of JIM LYNCH, which preserves a more authentic traditional shopfront, nicely symmetrical with a big bracketed signboard. Further s on the same side is a handsome rubble-and-red-brick house dated 1911, derelict at the time of writing.

ST PATRICK. 1882. A modest five-bay hall with an offset porch, built in 1882 after the parish church at Crosserlough burned in 1880. Roughcast with limestone dressings. A competent Gothic Revival exercise, if somewhat back-to-front: the kneelered E gable has twin lancets under a quatrefoil with a bellcote over and three graded lights. Flat-roofed porch and side chapel – the latter a long, low extension of the original porch, added in 1973 by *Philip Cullivan*. The interior is plain, with timber-panelled ceiling and exposed kingposts, elaborated with arched braces. Altar on the long N wall, moved there in 1973, and since elaborated with a marble reredos.

Across the road, the PAROCHIAL HOUSE is a sturdy-looking early C20 block of two storeys and five bays, crowned by a big hipped roof with massive end stacks of red brick. Large windows with cross-shaped casements, with lintels joined by a continuous string on the ground floor.

KILDRUMFERTON PARISH CHURCH (C of I). 1.5 km NE. 1812. A perfect rural ensemble of a church and stone-walled graveyard, answered across the road by the small rectoral demesne. The church is a small three-bay hall with simple Y-tracery and a stout, two-stage tower forestanding on the W gable with battlements and short spiky pinnacles. Built of rubble with dressed limestone reveals, hoodmoulds and pronounced quoins. Featureless inside, with a straightforward compartmented ceiling.

RECTORY. 1810. At the end of a picturesque beech avenue. The familiar three-bay roughcast block, two storeys on a raised basement with a hipped roof, central stacks, and a low service return. A polygonal porch with a spreading flight of steps to the side is a late C20 alteration, as are the ugly plastic windows, replacing all but the elegant round-headed sash lighting the stairs in the centre of the rear façade. The WALLED GARDEN behind the house is impressive for the preservation (by neglect?) of formal box hedges, left to grow to untypical proportions; these, with massive boulders of puddingstone, speak of former horticultural glory.

ST MARY, CROSSERLOUGH. 2.5 km NE. 1888 by *William Hague*. Near the foundations of an old church rebuilt in 1830 to a T-plan and destroyed by fire in 1880, set in a circular graveyard raised above a small lake, which gives the place its name, from the Irish *Crois Air Loch*, 'the cross on the lough'. A Gothic church, large and unexpected in this rural situation. Built of regularly coursed, rock-faced limestone with abundant smoothly dressed trim. Straightforward basilican plan with a tall gabled nave, lean-to aisles, a dumpy unfinished tower offset by the S aisle, and a gabled vestry projecting on the NE corner of an undifferentiated chancel; a polygonal stair is tucked in behind the tower, and short lean-to confessionals project between the buttresses from the centre of the aisles. Windows are simple lancets with hoods, cusped in the clerestory. Kneelered gables and stoutly buttressed walls all contribute to a rugged and solid effect. In the w gable, twin pointed doors united under an embracing hoodmould lead into a short lobby. The nave is generously proportioned, unexpectedly tall and deep, with a six-bay arcade of moulded arches on polished granite columns with tall limestone bases and stiff-leaf capitals. An elaborate arch-braced roof with exposed brackets, tie-beams and queenposts; kingposts to the aisles, unusually with braces and posts set transversely on the tie-beams. String-courses and continuous hoodmoulds give a lively articulation to the smooth plaster walls. – STAINED GLASS. Traceried E window, three-light w window and quatrefoil in the s aisle, all bright figurative glass, by *Mayer & Co.*, Munich. – MONUMENTS. The Rev. John Boylan †1899; a white marble Gothic tablet by *E. Sharp*, Dublin. – The Rev. Francis Lynch †1901; the same but unsigned.

KIFFAGH SCHOOLS. 5 km NE. A substantial early C19 rural school to a standard plan published by the 5th Lord Farnham in 1830, perhaps with input from the diocesan architect *William Farrell*. A two-storey block, in roughcast with stuccoed quoins and a hipped slate roof similar to Derrylane and Portlongfield. Five bays wide with rectangular quarry-glazed windows; entrances set back on either side in narrow lean-to projections.

FOXFIELD HOUSE. 1.5 km SW. In a small demesne. A two-storey, three-bay block with gabled ends, plainly rendered, with plate glass and yellow brick stacks. Built *c.* 1920, but retaining part of an earlier, thick-walled house on one side as a low single-storey wing. Other vestiges of an older demesne are the venerable trees and a large walled garden.

ST PATRICK, AUGHALOORA. 4 km W. Neat T-plan church in roughcast with large pointed openings, built in 1844, according to the inscribed datestone now set into the boundary wall. Substantially rebuilt in 1958, with a free-standing belfry.

KILL CHURCH RUINS. 1.5 km NW. An early church site with the densely ivied ruins of a late medieval church, set hard against the edge of an embanked semicircular graveyard. There are C15 references to a church here associated with SS Patrick, Brigid and Carthage, though the ruins seen today belong to a century later. Barely discernible is the outline of a large rectangular structure, 60 ft long and 33 ft wide (18 m by 10 m), built of rubble, with a doorway formed of rough vous-soirs near the SW corner and the outline of two windows in the adjoining wall. The E gable has a narrow lancet retaining two crudely carved stones from its cusped arch.

Dispersed around the GRAVEYARD is an exceptional collection of inscribed stones, the earliest of 1688, but most bearing Early Georgian dates.

KILL DEMESNE. 2 km NW. A solitary ruin in a long forgotten demesne. A small C18 circular gazebo, two storeys tall, set on high ground between Corglass and Kill loughs. The walls are of rubble, originally roughcast, with small square windows on both levels and an entrance formed between two short spur walls projected from the rear façade. Inside, evidence of a fireplace at first-floor level.

St Joseph, Drumkilly. 3.5 km NNW. A plain lancet hall of four bays in cement render, built in 1847, altered in 1861, and heavily remodelled in 1968, probably by *Philip Cullivan*, with a harsh bell-cast roof, low flat-roofed porches and a tall offset belfry. The belfry, linked to the church by a thin ledge extended across the front to roof the porch, is formed in concrete with an unsettling open middle stage; it replaces one in limestone of 1876, which survives to the SW – a neat ashlar structure with a tall tapering base, bold string-courses and a pyramid roof, between equally tall sentinel yews. Inside, a big rectangular hall with a flat plaster ceiling divided into decorative panels. – STAINED GLASS. Unremarkable abstract work by *Earley*, Dublin. – MONUMENTS. Beside the entrance: the Rev. Patrick O'Reilly †1825, by *H. Ryan*, Dublin. – Outside, on the S wall: the Rev. Patrick Galligan †1877, by *C.W. Harrison*, Dublin.

KINGSCOURT   CN

A Georgian market town remarkable for its extraordinarily long and wide Main Street. Its history is elusive. Its name – in Irish *Dún-an-Rí*, 'fort of the king' or 'king's court' – derives from its earlier prominence as the centre of a frontier kingdom; a scatter of pronounced hill-forts in the environs of the town attest to a concentration of regional power here in the past. The modern town was founded in the late C18 by Mervyn Pratt of Cabra and was formally planned along the expansive Main Street, running in a straight line N–S and rising gently at the centre, where as in most Cavan towns it opens into a square market place. The unwarranted demolition of the market house in the mid C20 deprived the town of its pivotal building: architecturally one of its best and most imposing, this had a broad two-storey front with an understated Gothic arcade extending on either side of a yawning pedimented central archway bridging the side street that cut through the market place. Today the Georgian character of the town survives largely in the building profiles – steep roofs and stocky stone chimneystacks – and in a diminishing number of stone doorcases, varying from primitive Gibbsian designs to rarer, more refined examples with fanlights. GARTLAN'S PUBLIC HOUSE at the N end of the street, with its pleasantly proportioned façade, thatched roof, traditional shopfront, stone doorcase and offset carriage arch, best preserves a sense of the Georgian ambience, while the CENTRAL STORES provide a more formal contrast, symmetrically arranged with a five-bay front, big stacks, large twelve-pane sashes and a central Gibbsian doorcase with a leaded fanlight.

St Ernan (C of I). A large Late Georgian church, set well back in a large open graveyard at the s end of the Main Street. Hall-and-tower type, built of rubble with sparse stone dressings. Three-bay nave and half-bay chancel, all with Y-tracery and quarry glazing. The three-bay w front incorporates the ashlar lower stages of the tall square tower as its central bay, flanked by the stairs and vestry, each with a lancet and a small quatre-foil above. The keystone over the entrance is carved with a primitive clerical head and the date 1780. The two upper stages of the tower break through the nave roof; the tall belfry is finished in battlements with short ball-topped pinnacles. Inside, a wonderful serpentine gallery in Carpenter's Gothic on thin clustered shafts with strange fluted capitals, arcaded frieze and quatrefoil-decorated panels; otherwise Victorianized with heavy pine kingposts and oak furnishings. – STAINED GLASS. Sombre three-light E window, 1892, with the Transfigu-ration by *Clayton & Bell*, dedicated to Mervyn Pratt. The remainder removed from St Jude, Kilmainham, Dublin, installed here in 1985; the largest, signed *A. L. Moore* of London, 1904, consisting of four panels, now incongruously broken up between two windows in the nave. – MONUMENTS. Two plain marble tablets by *C. W. Harrison & Sons* of Dublin: Lieutenant Samuel Adams †1916 at Jutland, and Sergeant R. Wolfe †1917 at Ypres.

Church of the Immaculate Conception. Hall Street. 1869 by *William Hague*. Set on a high plateau above the town with impressive views over open countryside, across to Armagh and the distant bulk of Slieve Gullion. A large and heavy Gothic church replacing the old pre-Emancipation chapel whose E front, a tall battlemented gable of rubble with a bell-cote flanked by square pinnacled towers, has been retained as a striking gateway. The new church, given a more imposing position further w, is built of squared local limestone with paler dressings of Carrickmacross limestone, much of it in boldly pronounced Gothic detail: billet eaves, kneelers, finials and Geometric plate tracery. The plan is cruciform, consisting of a three-bay nave with buttressed lean-to aisles, transepts, a polygonal chancel deeply projecting between gabled side chapels, and a square tower offset to the SE, unusually filling the angle between the transept and chancel. The contractor was *Hugh Kelly* of Granard. The tower has a pronounced batter with angle buttresses, rising in just two stages. It was left unfin-ished with a ridiculous pyramid roof; in 1914 *W. H. Byrne & Son* proposed completing it with a broach spire, but the ambi-tion was unfulfilled until 2011. Steeply gabled w front with offset buttresses and flanking aisles, the centre impressively filled by a big plate-traceried rose window framed in a moulded arch with engaged sandstone shafts; here and in the entrance below, a good deal of stonework remains uncarved, the crockets of the entrance gable left as stark projecting blocks, finials, stops and capitals likewise left as plain, hard-edged blocks – an economy employed with such consistency as to seem almost stylistic.

The interior is narrow, with a high timber-panelled pine roof. Ample sculptural details; an arcaded nave on round granite piers with thick, blocky capitals, uncarved and cushion-like. Clerestory of paired lancets and roundels, alternating with polished shafts that support the arched trusses of the roof. Chancel lit by three Geometric windows united under a continuous hood. Three-bay choir gallery on slender shafts of Middleton marble. – Lady Chapel ALTAR by *W. H. Byrne & Son*, 1910, completed in 1937 with a carved relief of the Annunciation in Caen stone. – STAINED GLASS. An important C20 collection. Chancel: the Annunciation, the Crucifixion and the Ascension, richly coloured figurative work by *Evie Hone*, 1947. Lady Chapel: the Miracle of the Sun, also by *Hone*. Aisles: *Harry Clarke Studios*, a little staid for such a distinguished name. w window: the Creation, weakly coloured and cartoon-like, by *Eoin Butler*, 2000. – MONUMENT. The Rev. Peter O'Reilly †1878; a large marble slab bordered with encaustic tiles, in the floor of the N aisle.

ST JOSEPH'S PRIMARY SCHOOL. Nobber Road. 1953. A long unrelieved twenty-bay range in local red brick with big square-headed windows, terminated at one end by a square tower in Flemish bond brickwork with a sparse pattern of projecting headers; a register of square piercings in the parapet; parabolic archway on the ground floor, and above this a relief sculpture of St Joseph and the Christ Child feeding chickens by *Garry Trimble*, who was perhaps also the architect.

ST ERNAN'S HALL. 1889 by *J. F. Fuller*. On a triangular site facing down the Main Street. A small gabled hall and porch in red brick, of four bays with mullioned windows in gently rusticated brick surrounds. Decorative bargeboards, moulded eaves brackets and terracotta ridge cresting.

ST MARY'S HALL. Hall Street. 1888. A big two-storey, gable-ended block, cumbersomely set into the sloping streetscape. Built of rubble with moulded terracotta eaves and red brick window trim. Broad, with six bays across the first floor and big Victorian sashes with segmental heads and plate glass to light the hall; gabled entrance porch projecting near the centre, a steep flight of steps forming wings on either side.

BANK OF IRELAND (former HIBERNIAN BANK). Main Street. 1920–2 by *W. H. Byrne & Son*. A two-storey, gable-ended building inserted into the streetscape with a stuccoed front in a cheerful Neoclassical style with bracketed eaves. Five-bay first floor with plate glass; three bays below, with a pedimented fanlit doorcase flanked by wide segmental-arched windows decorously stuccoed with perfect Adamesque urns and swags in the tympana. Good, but much too frivolous and lighthearted for the building's purpose.

LARKFIELD GLEBE. 0.75 km E. *c.* 1831. A substantial house consisting of two gable-ended blocks placed back-to-back, raised on a basement, with two storeys and attics, built of rubble with red brick dressings and decorative bargeboards. The main front has three bays, with the entrance in a narrow gabled projection recessed on one side.

CABRA DEMESNE, now DÚN AN RÍ FOREST PARK. 1 km N. The old demesne established in the late C17 by Colonel Thomas Cooch around the remains of a castle of the Flemings, in the deep, wild valley of the River Cabra. In 1699 it passed by marriage to the Pratts, who continued to exploit the natural qualities of the landscape so admired by Mrs Delany: visiting in 1732, she speaks of Mervyn Pratt as a virtuoso who 'discovers *whim* in all his improvements'. The old Fleming castle had been enlarged and made habitable, enhanced with gardens, ponds and two terraced walks. Stone was extensively quarried from outcrops within the demesne and used for a number of important Georgian buildings here, including a flax mill that had long exploited the thundering waters of the river. The village of Cabra built to support it has long vanished, surviving only until Kingscourt was founded in the later Georgian period. Today, all the demesne buildings with the exception of bridges are neglected ruins, though architecturally they remain of the first importance, including the disfigured remains of a small Palladian villa and remote stables.

The decline here appears to have begun in the early C19 after the Pratts transferred their attention to the neighbouring demesne of Cormey, where they established the present Cabra Castle (*see* below). Mrs Delany's greatest pleasure was reserved for 'a rivulet that tumbles down from rocks in a little glen, full of shrub-wood and trees . . . [where] a fine spring joins the river, of the sweetest water in the world'. Long known as the 'Wishing Well', this natural feature remains the central attraction of the demesne in its present incarnation.

THE COTTAGE. Now a flat-roofed shelter and machine shed; only the series of elegant brick round-headed windows reaching to the ground on the N front suggests that this unassuming rubble building represents the remains of the small sophisticated villa almost certainly designed by *Sir Edward Lovett Pearce* for his cousin, Mervyn Pratt, the 'little commodious lodge' in a hollow referred to by Mrs Delany 'where Mr Prat lived whilst his house [*see* Fleming's Castle] was repairing'. The principal surviving space, now windowless and open as a shelter, is large and finely proportioned, with its four tall bays facing N down a verdant slope toward the river, directly aligned with a former carriage drive carried across the deep ravine. Its walls are stripped of plaster and irregular; only closed arches on one side of a chimney-breast and irregular recesses in each corner hint at a once sophisticated interior.

Kingscourt, Cabra, elevation.
Drawing by K. Mulligan, 2012

Relationship to the architect alone has never stood as a basis for the attribution of a building to Pearce. But like Lord Burlington to England, Pearce was the Palladian envoy to Ireland, and in this instance Cabra's original appearance and its likely association with Pearce seem confirmed by a portrait of Pratt by James Latham in which the E front of the building is shown with a broad pedimented façade, close to Lord Burlington's brand of Palladianism, the pediment filled with a big Diocletian window and adorned with urns. Examined closely, this image and what remains of the building together suggest a design simplified from Burlington's wings for Tottenham Park, which in turn were derived from Palladio's design for the Villa Valmarana at Vigardolo.

Only part of the E façade survives, with its three central bays now a closed arcade gently recessed behind the taller end bay to the N, with the ghost of an earlier arch on one side an indication of alterations or unfulfilled ideas. Its completion on a more substantial and regular plan can now only be confirmed by the Ordnance Survey, suggesting that the L-plan block seen today must amount to less than half the original building. That was evidently enlarged to the W with a further three arched bays, now disfigured and closed as a store.

Through an arched passageway behind, a large complex of rubble buildings, mostly two-storey, appear to be the remains of the FLAX MILL.

FLEMING'S CASTLE. Now a decayed ruin. These towering, ivy-thatched walls are those of the main house which Mrs Delany found 'on the side of a high hill with some old tall trees about it and gardens that were small but neat'. The old Fleming castle which appeared on the Down Survey in 1656 had by the time of Mrs Delany's visit been recently 'modernised, and made very pretty' for Mervyn Pratt; now just a little of all that she had found remains here still. Beyond thick, wayward laurels, the fragmentary walls stand above a murky rectangular pond. They are those of two staggered towers, four storeys tall, joined to the N by the slightly more complete remains of a two-storey gable-ended block. Most of the W portions of the building are lost; what stands is largely of rubble and brick with dressed quoins and traces of roughcast. The S tower appears to be the older, perhaps early C17, with the remains of mullioned windows visible at a low level on the S wall, while one of the quoins on the SE corner is carved in raised relief with the initials FF, an association perhaps with its Fleming builders. An extraordinary feature is the use of a chamfered brick course, now heavily eroded, to form a plinth, its appearance here representing an important early use of the material. The internal walls are lined with brick on the lower levels, probably done as part of Early Georgian works, and in the N wall a small plastered niche survives with its internal reeded impost moulding still intact. The adjoining tower seems contemporary with these works, remodelled with an open-well staircase; light still penetrates the ivy-meshed walls to reveal a succession of pointed windows that lit the cantilevered stone stairs in their ascent around the walls – a rare example of Gothic Survival in the region.

CROMWELL'S BRIDGE. High over a ravine, a wide rubble arch and narrower subsidiary one, together taking the old approach to the Cottage spectacularly across the River Cabra. Now leading disappointingly to a dead end.

To the SE the STABLES, a sad ruin known as the Barracks, which in their former state, like the Cottage they once served, may justly be considered a building worthy of *Pearce*. Long Early Georgian lofted range in rubble with sandstone dressings. One main front, to the E, with ten bays; the fenestration is limited to a row of high lunettes resting on a continuous and pronounced string-course, rather similar to *Richard Castle*'s designs for stables at Leinster House of the 1740s. Two doorways, incorporating two of the lunettes, flank the centre and are now stripped of their surrounds. The lunettes have been filled with masonry, perhaps as a result of the building's supposed use as a military barracks. Immensely worthy of restoration and surely deserving of some loving care. Opposite, the KENNELS are a small rubble range with four bays and low barrel-vaulted rooms.

Conveniently set on a steep wooded hillside overlooking the ornamental lake, the ICE HOUSE is the conventional domed brick egg, reached by a short barrel-vaulted passage.

SARAH BRIDGE. 1801. A single-arched carriage bridge with low parapets, built of rubble with channelled ashlar voussoirs.

GATE LODGE. Close to Kingscourt, opposite a handsome ashlar gate sweep. A Late Georgian single-storey lodge. Symmetrical three-bay roughcast front with a low hipped roof, central stack, and decorative timber eaves, narrow paired sashes, and a central stone doorcase with plain pilasters and entablature.

CABRA CASTLE. 2.5 km NE. To the E of the old Cabra demesne, on the opposite side of the road. A large and earnestly picturesque castle with a haphazard plan and a convulsion of bold battlemented projections. The setting in open parkland is flat and rather tame, closed to vistas but well planted with several magnificent oaks. The early history is sketchy, but like many Late Georgian castles it appears to have evolved from an older structure. Originally known as Cormey Castle, it was remodelled by Henry Foster *c.* 1808 as trustee of his cousin Augustus Foster, and sold in 1813 to Colonel Joseph Pratt of Cabra. He transferred his seat from Fleming's Castle the short distance across the road, and enlarged the castle here with greater seriousness and swagger, all unified under roughcast with stone dressings and simple indented crenellations. It was largely complete to its present plan by 1837. Now a hotel, with late C20 enlargements recessed to the s.

The old house emerges on the corner, and only just, as a hefty block of four storeys with three bays; its bulk might imply the massing of a tower house thinly disguised with crenellations, but the fenestration offers Georgian proportions instead with an orderly arrangement of pointed windows – originally sashed with Gothick tracery – before changing on the upper floor into small square openings. Enlarged on the s side with a massive forestanding entrance tower with machicolated corner turrets and a massive splayed doorway of striking simplicity, and to the N with the big canted bay that was common to Late Georgian castles. Beyond this, a longer range is altogether more consciously Tudor in style, with big mullioned windows and label mouldings, interrupted by a tall square flagstaff tower before projecting forward to terminate in a circular bastion on the angle. This uncrenellated tower is the beginning of a wide symmetrical entrance to the stableyard, with a central turreted gateway which reverts to the simpler, toy-like castle style and is thus perhaps a discrete element of Foster's work brought into play by the later enlargements.

Inside, the older house is present in small rooms with modest Georgian proportions and Neoclassical swagged ceiling roses. The earliest manifestation of Gothicization survives on the ground floor, with broad ogee arches and remains of shutter panelling in a thin Regency Gothic style. Behind the entrance, the towering stair hall is a dominant feature of the later works, with an imperial staircase rising to the first floor and overlooked by a gallery surrounding the second floor, all brightly lit by large mullioned windows with clear leaded glass. Ceilings richly patterned with saltires in low relief. The first floor is treated as a *piano nobile*, the large rectangular drawing room projecting over the entrance with a thin cornice and a Regency Gothic chimneypiece in white marble.

STABLEYARD. Set hard against the kitchen yards and much too close for comfort or effect. A yard within a yard, consisting of a big outer quadrangle with well-built limestone ranges enclosing an imposing U-plan block, completed after 1837. The main front is two storeys tall with a mixture of rubble and red brick between pedimented wings of ashlar with big relieving arches, and a severe three-bay frontispiece, also of ashlar, with a bellcote and a gauche Gibbsian doorcase weakly projecting with V-channelled blocks.

GATE LODGE. 1857. Behind a grandiose Gothic sweep with spired piers of open cast-iron. A Tudor-style block in squared limestone with a long return forming a T-plan. Modest three-bay front with central kneelered gable, mullioned windows, and square drip mouldings. A toy castellated tower extends from the return, elaborately screening a small yard.

OUR LADY OF MOUNT CARMEL, MUFF. 3.5 km w. 1858. A three-bay lancet hall and chancel with kneelered E and W gables, roughcast with sandstone dressings. W front with a pointed doorway under a big lancet, both set in a narrow projection with offsets and flanked by small round windows. Inside, a bright hall with exposed kingposts. – STAINED GLASS. E window: the Crucifixion, by *Harry Clarke Studios*.

ST JOSEPH, CORLEA. 6 km NW. Of *c.* 1836. A scenic vernacular church set in uplands. Cruciform, essentially consisting of the traditional T-plan with a sacristy projecting from the E arm. Roughcast, with stuccoed strip quoins and tall Gothick sashes. Inside, low-ceilinged with timber panelling and quarry-tiled floors. Altar in the centre of the long E wall and galleries in each arm. The polished shafts and moulded arches framing the high altar and flanking doorways correspond to the marble FURNISHINGS of 1916 by *W. H. Byrne & Son*.

LARAGH

9 km NNW of Carrickmacross

Mostly deserted and ruined. Just two simple rows of labourers' houses, one inhabited, the other derelict, are left to recall the existence of one of the largest linen industries in the region, established here by the early C19. The linen mills were founded by Messrs F. and A. Davidson, who operated two separate buildings for spinning and weaving. The power was supplied by a water wheel and in 1825 ten power looms were installed, the first of their kind in Ulster. By 1835 there were thirty frames under the supervision of young women for spinning, and about six hundred looms operated by men. The mills closed in 1880 and have left virtually no traces.

ST PETER (C of I). Derelict. A forlorn roadside fairytale in tin: a novel miniature church built for the McKean family, high on a rocky outcrop (appropriately for its dedication to Peter), in a densely wooded gorge. Two-bay hall with an offset tower and vestry, all sheeted in corrugated iron, with good Dec windows in wood. The tower is ornate, in three diminishing stages with a tin needle spire and a cockerel weathervane. The entrance, reached up steps edged with moss-covered rocks, is a Tudor-arched doorway in the lower stage. Above it are paired lancets with louvres and hoodmoulds, followed by a heavy moulded timber cornice; the boxy middle stage has emphatic quatrefoils; then a short hipped roof covered in tin moulded to a fish-scale pattern, and a short polygonal lantern which supports the spire. Once-attractive interior, entirely wood-panelled, with scissor trusses and stained glass. A granite plaque on the E wall dates it to 1890. Wonderful polygonal GATEPIERS in cement with Gothic panels and grotesque stone cappings assembled in a confection like a Mr Whippy.

LARAGH HOUSE. A simple but pleasing Late Georgian house built for Mr Davidson, owner of the mills. Two-storey three-bay roughcast block with windows set in raised stone reveals. Hipped roof with central stacks and an interesting eaves detail of paired console brackets, widely spaced in a deep frieze. Burnt out in the late C20 and restored with a new two-storey brick return to connect the house to the L-plan yard behind.

ST MARY, LISDOONAN. 2.5 km SE. A primitively carved stone plaque at the rear of the building gives the date of erection,

Laragh, St Mary, Lisdoonan, inscribed plaque.
Drawing by K. Mulligan, 2012

1812. A modest four-bay hall in roughcast, remodelled later in the C19 and given big pointed windows in blocked stucco surrounds under hoodmoulds. Central gabled porch. Interior completely gutted after 1974 and now pitiful. Walls lined with concrete blocks under a clutter of puny prefabricated roof trusses. Sanctuary retained on the long E wall. Windows in the gables indicate the presence of former galleries. – STATIONS OF THE CROSS in wood, carved by *J. Haugh*.

LATTON
MN 6010
6 km SSW of Ballybay

ST MARY. 1823. A long six-bay hall, cement-rendered with blocked quoins, large pointed windows and single-storey porches in the end bays. Small sacristy on the rearward E wall with an unusual masonry bellcote, built later, towering above it, in two stages with a tapered base of dark squared limestone with sandstone quoins, the same ashlar forming the gabled upper stage. Internally plain with a flat timber-panelled ceiling. A polygonal sanctuary with good carved altar rails is placed traditionally on the long E wall, between two small windows, with the seating arranged around it. Handsome rusticated GATEPIERS and excellent iron GATES with curlicued spears. The inscription *Deo soli laus honor et gloria* (To God alone praise, honour and glory) is carried across the piers in a frieze panel.

ST MARY'S PAROCHIAL HALL. 1886. A neat single-storey block, the front of three bays with a central gablet and a porch to the side, two storeys to the rear. Rubble with red brick trim.

PAROCHIAL HOUSE. The standard two-storey late C19 block with a three-bay front, box-like porch, and a single-storey return. Roughcast with plain plaster quoins, plinth and an eaves band. High hipped roof with central stacks. Lovely iron gateway with curved side sections.

LISNADILL
AH 8040
4.25 km S of Armagh

ST JOHN (C of I). 1772 by *Thomas Cooley*. Probably the best-preserved of Cooley's 'standard designs' for Primate Robinson. Hall-and-tower type with a forestanding three-stage tower in rubble with cutstone dressings, almost exactly as in Cooley's 'Design No. 9' – flat angle buttresses, simple battlements, and corner pinnacles. As with all of Cooley's identifiable designs, the date of erection is inscribed boldly on the tower. The nave is a boxy, roughcast three-bay block with wide pointed windows and timber Y-tracery; all delightfully enlivened with old glass.

Roof hipped over the E end, where there is no E window. Inside, a plain old-fashioned space with flat plaster ceilings and box pews.

RECTORY. A charming small Late Georgian house. Two storeys on a raised basement with three bays, the centre bay advanced and gabled; a steep flight of steps to a handsome rusticated doorcase with Gothick fanlight. Improvements by *J. H. Fullerton* in 1885.

ST PATRICK, BALLYMACNAB. 1.75 km S. A late C19 church in the heavy rusticated Gothic style of *J. J. McDonnell*. A solid buttressed hall of five bays in squared blue limestone trimmed with Armagh limestone; paired lancets; polygonal chancel. The gabled front is busy with clasping buttresses, bellcote, ashlar string-courses and a gabled doorway flanked by lancets; above, two twin lights with bar tracery under a rose window. The airy interior disappoints. Unexceptional timber-panelled mansard-shaped ceiling. High in the nave N wall a curious RELIEF of the Crucifixion looks C18. Colourful figurative STAINED GLASS in the sanctuary. Additions of 1910–11 by *John V. Brennan*.

LOUGH EGISH

In picturesque countryside 10 km SE of Ballybay. A mélange of monolithic industrial structures associated with the modern creamery, beside a crossroads overlooking the lake of the same name. Distances are taken from the crossroads.

TEMPLEMOYLE. 1 km NE. On an isolated peninsula on the N shore of Lough Egish, a ruined single-cell church. Simple rectangular rubble-built structure (59 ft by 36 ft, 18 m by 11 m) with a small rectangular W window and evidence of a larger pointed E window. Doorway in the centre of the S wall. Possibly no earlier than the C18, when a Franciscan friary was recorded here.

CHURCH OF THE SACRED HEART, TULLYNAMALRA. 1 km SW. An unspoilt early T-plan chapel, present by 1837 and enlarged in 1886. A long symmetrical E front, trim with a central gabled projection and two bays on each side. Cement-rendered with a stone bellcote on the W gable at the back; simple Y-traceried windows in blocked surrounds, set under an oculus in the end gables. E window of three graded lights closely grouped. On the front, a doorway for each of the sexes in the end bays. Plain stone crosses on all four gables. Lovely graded slate roofs on the rear slopes. Internally, the space is traditionally planned with the altar placed on the long E wall in a shallow projection and raking galleries extending through each of the arms of the cross on four Tuscan columns of cast iron. Panelled timber roof of 1886 with arch-braced trusses.

CROSSDUFF PARISH CHURCH (C of I). 3 km SW. 1829. A short two-bay hall and squat W tower, built as a chapel of ease for

Aughnamullen. Rubble with crisp limestone dressings and pretty Y-tracery. The tower is in three stages with battlements and pinnacles rising from polygonal corner piers on the upper stage. The roof pitch of the hall was raised later in the C19.

ST MARY, CARRICKATEE. 4 km NW. Rebuilt 1890–3. There are enough similarities between this cement-rendered T-plan building and the church at Tullynamalra to invoke a sense of *déjà vu*, if not the suggestion of a shared builder. The same symmetrical E front with a shallow gabled projection and a stone bellcote on the W gable at the back. Here the fenestration is simpler, with lancets widely spaced under a continuous hoodmould and three graded lights to the E gable. The doorways are flat pointed arches in the end bays leading into small timber-panelled porches. Galleries, though here given more elaborate timber fronts, are also supported on Tuscan cast-iron columns in each of the arms under the same arch-braced roof.

LOUGH FEA* MN 8000

Meandering walls S of Carrickmacross conceal this large Elizabethan Revival house in a demesne that remains remarkably complete in the modern world. Far above the sheltered 'lake of the rushes' that gives the place its name, the house, built between

Lough Fea, hall, interior
Lithograph by E. Walker, *c.* 1850

* Permission to view the interior was denied.

1825 and 1848, spreads picturesque, low-lying pinnacled wings in every direction. Impressions of a collegiate complex are out of place in this rural setting, yet they are not unwarranted; the fast-changing silhouettes of the different ranges include a chapel and cloister, a great hall, and a clock tower.

The estate lies on the edge of the w moiety of Farney, a barony which was the Shirley family's share of the Essex inheritance after that was divided between two daughters in the C17. Perhaps to affirm the Elizabethan origins of the property, Evelyn John Shirley in 1825 initiated plans for a new house that somewhat dourly evokes the era of his ancestor, Walter Devereux, Earl of Essex, and the Queen who had granted the barony in 1576. The Shirleys' inheritance made them the largest landowners in Monaghan. Though their Irish estate was greater than the property they held in England, they remained absentees and continued to reside at Ettington Park in Warwickshire, where they had been lords of the manor since Domesday. Before building their new house here the family divided their temporary residence in Ireland between Shirley House, an C18 building in Carrickmacross shared with their agent (demolished), and a commodious house surviving beside the walled garden in the present demesne, known in 1835 as 'The Cottage'. The *Ordnance Survey Memoirs* in 1835 provide a curious description of this house, of 'neat appearance on the outside' but so vast internally as to exceed 'what it might be supposed to afford . . . [with] no less than 27 bedrooms'.

The design was begun in 1825 by the Birmingham-based architect *Thomas Rickman*, author of *An Attempt to Discriminate the Styles of [Gothic] Architecture in England*. In 1824 Rickman, with his junior partner *Henry Hutchinson*, had on paper at least remodelled the Shirley seat at Ettington Park in a Neoclassical style. In September of that year Hutchinson travelled to Ireland to inspect the proposed site, and designs were still being prepared exactly a year later. Two phases of building, subtly evident in the architecture, confirm the participation of separate architectural forces. The core building represents Rickman's (and presumably Hutchinson's) work, a mixture of Elizabethan and Jacobean ideas, largely reticent in its details, with none of the brio expected of an expert in Gothic styles. Hutchinson died in 1831; Rickman had retired by 1838 and his involvement ended soon after. The recent discovery of papers relating to the building makes it clear that it was completed substantially between 1838 and 1850 by *William Walker* and *George Sudden*. Though relatively obscure in Irish architectural history, they deserve recognition as the real designers of the elements that completed Lough Fea, principally the Baronial Hall and Chapel, which are distinguished from the earlier phase by a richer, more varied treatment of the architecture. George Sudden first appears in the accounts in 1832 as a clerk of works on the Shirley estate, principally in connection with works to Shirley House.

The different ranges of Lough Fea rise, without too much chaos on the skyline, in a well-dispersed plan punctuated by three square towers, tightly grouped octagonal chimneystacks, and spear-topped pinnacles. From a distance the appearance is orderly and harmonious and the impression of scale effective; at close quarters the plan seems to contract, revealing a tighter grouping of the ranges, with individual elements such as the Chapel retaining a sense of independence from the core building – an arrangement possibly determined more by a protracted building programme than by an overall scheme.

The principal front faces W, its close, crouching ranges formidably set to the fore, poised somewhat defensively, around a broad entrance court. Here the Chapel and Baronial Hall form a cold embrace on either side of the entrance axis that passes over a dry moat topped by a palisade with arched openings, more picturesque than protective. A wide single-storey porch marking the entrance is offset to the N as if to confirm the fundamental asymmetry of the elevation; it is an ornamental piece with canted sides bearing the flourishing Shirley arms on a gablet above twin Tudor arches. It contrasts with *Rickman*'s plain frontage to which it is attached, and highlights the more indulgent approach to decoration in the later additions. Changes in the masonry of the front also indicate two phases of building activity. Rickman's work is limited to the central portion, a long two-storey range framed by square three-storey towers formerly adorned with neat pagoda roofs. Built of a soft grey limestone tinged with yellow, the block accommodated an earlier chapel and presumably originally the principal reception rooms, with its plan centred on the entrance hall with the main staircase at the back, placed behind an arched screen; to the E it projects in a large square three-storey tower dominating the garden front.

Work at Lough Fea either proceeded slowly or had been halted, since the house was still described as 'erecting' as late as 1835. But by 1838 the porch had been added and the new Chapel was under construction. What distinguishes the new work of *Walker* and *Sudden*, as much as their more wilful architectural detail, is their use of a different pinkish freestone that was found on the estate. The new Chapel is set transversely, bisecting the N range, with an E window facing into the court. A short cloister extends to the W, ending in a neat diminutive structure – a curiosity of country houses – the Justice Room. The Baronial Hall dominates the S side of the court. An orangery, a small but highly ornamental skeletal link, joins it to the house. At the end of January 1841 Walker sent plans for the hall, outlining its location relative to the Chapel so that foundations could be laid. The position of the orangery was indicated as something to be built at a later stage. It is with these ranges that the architectural detail becomes more lively. Buttresses begin to shoulder out of the wall plane, and windows push up into the string-courses, causing gablets with spiky finials to appear with the battlements on the parapets.

In April the architects were concerned with windows, and Evelyn John Shirley indicated that those in the Hall were to be executed in the 'old style', with stone transoms and mullions and no timber elements. Work progressed quickly and by September

Walker was anxious to see the Hall. In anticipation of covering the building he forwarded a drawing for the roof, a design with hammerbeam trusses that he based on a church roof by Edward Blore (as yet unidentified), 'executed at 41 feet [12.5 m] span . . . though opposed to the wishes of the church commissioners'. Walker had postponed sending the drawing until he had received confirmation of its effectiveness: 'I find it has not sunk in the least and has now been finished nine years . . . I am not the least afraid of this plan being used at Lough Fea.' In effect the roof was executed more elaborately, with greater integral support, as may be seen in Edmund Walker's contemporary engraving. The orangery was constructed in 1842, connecting the Hall and the Drawing Room and positioned to give access to the terrace on the E front.

Three years later Walker altered the elevation of the E front, adding, under a single hoodmould, a row of seven new Tudorarched openings overlooking the terrace garden. Despite this enlivening alteration the front remains austere, extending along two sides of a formal terraced garden. The boxy three-storey stair-tower is plainly expressed with a pair of high chimneystacks on the end walls. A lower block with projecting oriels on two storeys adjoins it to the N. A short single-storey range extends E along the N side and terminates in the clock tower – a two-storey block with an orderly three-storey polygonal corner projection. Behind this the ground falls away and the powerful massing of the building is more dramatically revealed; though it faces into the service yards, it was this side that Evelyn John Shirley chose to illustrate in his magisterial *History of the County of Monaghan*.

The sobriety of the architectural detail in *Rickman*'s part of the building is not assisted by the horizontal emphasis. This is even more marked in the broad expanses of ashlar, formed in a patchwork that is at times distracting, arranged in stages weakly defined by the thinnest of string-courses. In the upper stage the stringcourse is reluctantly widened to form a cornice supporting deep parapets, a particularly determined horizontal detail that is interrupted only by the square towers and the occasional chimneystacks that cling to the surface. On each principal elevation windows are arranged proportionately, mostly two- or three-light mullions that pierce the wall surface under stern hoodmoulds. Only once, with an attractive oriel window on the first floor, does the pattern deviate. The abiding restraint in Rickman's building – somewhere between quiet sophistication and parsimony – contrasts sharply with his contemporary designs for St John's College in Cambridge which bristle with Perp ornament. Less sparing are the embellishments on the building pertaining to the Shirleys' aristocratic origins, conveyed in many heraldic devices such as the Ferrers horseshoe and the insignia of Walter Devereux, or crucial dates in the story of the family's rich inheritance.

The BARONIAL HALL. A. W. N. Pugin stressed the idea of a baronial hall as the *sine qua non* of the Victorian country house and was adamant as to its attributes: 'a bay window, high open roof, two good fireplaces, a great sideboard, screen, minstrel gallery – all or none'. All of these are represented at Lough Fea. Contrary to the impression given by Edmund Walker's view, the Hall is not vast, 75 ft by 35 ft (23 m by 10.5 m), but it is striking and evocative. To John Ynyr Burges, visiting in 1870, it was 'very fine in effect, full and noble as any one of the ancient kind in England or abroad. It is in such perfect keeping, nothing belonging to it poor or trifling.' It forms a long two-storey room with big mullioned windows flooding the space with light from the SW. Along the N wall, a gallery only accessible from the Hall overlooks it and heightens the sense of grandeur. The lower walls are lined with linenfold panelling, executed in plaster and painted to imitate wood. Two architectural chimneypieces on the N wall are executed in sandstone with sloping mantels, polygonal corner buttresses and tall pinnacles; on one is carved the motto of the C17 Bishop John Hacket, 'Serve God and be Cheerful'. As one would expect for a family with a long and noble ancestry, heraldic motifs dominate in the decoration: the Shirley family pedigree is painstakingly represented in the great bay window of 1843, tracing their descent from the C11 lords of Ettington. The Victorian tradition of entertaining under rules of paternalistic obligation was realized here when the Hall was used to host a biennial dinner for tenants of the estate. The buildings had only recently been completed in the winter of 1848, but Evelyn John Shirley, keen to use the new hall and unwilling to put off the event, hosted an inaugural ball at which a gathering of two hundred people were played to by a band in the gallery.

The CHAPEL is a plain gable-ended structure with diagonal buttresses, reached from the E where the doorway displays the motto *Omne bonum – Dei donum* (Every good thing is from God) and the date 1840. The interior contains many sculptural furnishings in wood, including an extraordinary pulpit, its lectern borne by a near-life-size angel – a sort of Gothic caryatid – and a sumptuous altarpiece with scenes from the Passion of Christ, apparently C15 Flemish, brought to Lough Fea in 1835 and formerly set in panelling in the Library. The floor is composed of alternate squares of bog oak and common oak. – STAINED GLASS. In the E window 'Gloria in excelsis Deo'; in the W, armorial bearings.

The DINING ROOM has a ceiling ornamented with the initials of Evelyn John Shirley together with the horseshoe that proclaimed his descent from Lord Ferrers. The LIBRARY, where Evelyn Philip Shirley, son of the builder of the house, kept his famed Irish collection, has a ceiling apparently derived from the 'Brown Room' at Wiston, a Shirley house in Sussex. In 1866 *George Thomson* completed bookcases to his own design, which is presumably when some of the Flemish carvings were moved to the Chapel. In 1880 five strong cases were sent from London by the *Soho Marble & Stone Galleries* containing 'a finely carved Italian chimneypiece' with a heraldic frieze for the Library. The SMALL DRAWING ROOM, possibly the South Room referred to in 1859 (and described as the ante-room by Burges), has clustered scagliola columns of *verde antico*, probably from the Lambeth works of *William Croggan*, who had supplied the Shirleys' house in Warwickshire. Florid C19 wallpaper. The chimneypiece is of alabaster mined on the estate; it is Elizabethan in style, with strapwork decoration in the frieze and repeated in the overmantel, which frames a group of oval portraits.

The DEMESNE is exceptional as much for its survival as a single entity as for its beautifully wooded parkland, most impressive when viewed towards the s from the raised terrace garden created in the 1830s on the E of the house. In 1835 the demesne was said to be in its infancy; many of the plantations and walks were new, having been laid out by the agent, *Alexander Mitchell*, whose name is commemorated in a straight avenue to the w of the house. However it does harbour the layers of history that characterize so many Irish demesnes. Near the s boundary, E of the lake, a great MOTTE with a surrounding fosse suggests a presence here from the C12. This naturally enhanced the sense of romance that guided a Picturesque approach to the landscape here in the beginning; that sense of the Picturesque is heightened in a deep glen in the woods NE of the house which exploits natural rock outcrops and caves, and a fanciful association with the mythical Irish giant Fionn MacComhaill (Finn McCool) whose rocky 'chair' lies there – possibly the 'wishing stone' visited by John Ynyr Burges. A more formal addition is the great terraced ALLÉE, centred on the formal terrace garden, and cut through the Home Wood leading SE to frame a giant CELTIC CROSS in limestone erected after 1856 by Evelyn Philip Shirley to commemorate his father. A fine Tudor-style FOUNTAIN and WROUGHT-IRON GATES also break the vista. An enclosed deer-park lies immediately to the s.

To the SE, on the N side of the derelict walled garden, The GARDEN HOUSE represents 'the Cottage', described by the *Ordnance Survey Memoirs* in 1835 as a 'place of antiquity . . . of neat appearance on the outside' but so vast internally as to exceed 'what it might be supposed to afford . . . [with] no less than 27 bedrooms'. In its outward appearance today this is the classic Irish mid-Georgian house. A gable-ended block of five bays with a round-headed fanlit door to the centre; twelve-pane sashes, and, on the s gable, two Tudor-style windows with mullions and hoodmoulds, inserted *c.* 1840.

The HOME FARM to the NE is a neat cluster of largely vernacular buildings. Grotesque water-worn masonry appears here to decorative effect; it is found throughout the demesne, capping walls and gatepiers, and is presumably local. An ORNAMENTAL DAIRY with a small battlemented turret perched above the yards is a finer feature of the farm. There are also a substantial number of mid-C19 LODGES – Tudor in style, varied in scale, but consistent in quality and probably by *Walker* and *Sudden*. HOME LODGE, the most picturesque, is an elaborate two-up-two-down building in pink ashlar with quarry-glazed mullioned windows and stairs contained in a striking octagonal tower. BRACKEN LODGE, built for the land agent, is the largest, though hidden away at the back of the estate; two storeys to an H-plan, a double-gabled front, and single-storey porch to the side. SFORZA LODGE commemorates a Shirley's marriage with Italian nobility; single-storey, T-plan, with a projecting gable which displays the ducal crest of the Sforzas. LAKE AVENUE LODGE, the smallest and neatest, lies half-in and half-out of the railed entrance screen; gable-ended with off-centre porch and rear projection. Tidy out-buildings to the rear.

Outside the demesne wall to the s, the former LOSSET SCHOOL is a charming building in the estate's Tudor Revival livery. A long one-and-a-half-storey block of six bays in cottage style with end gables carrying familiar spear-topped finials. Gables echoed by small projecting porches; between these a veranda runs across the front with a pair of dormer windows above. An expanded and sophisticated version of the school at Corvalley.

DERRYLAVAN MILLS. 1.5 km NW. Mid-C19 industrial complex for the Shirley estate. A self-contained picturesque group in a modest Tudor style. The MILL HOUSE is an irregular two-storey gabled block of rubble with ashlar dressings, similar to Bracken Lodge, but T-plan, with plainer three-storey stores attached to the s. The disused CORN MILL lies nearby to the E; a long two-storey range in an attractive russet stone with a twin gabled projection to the N.

DERRYLAVAN HOUSE, SE of the Mills, is contemporary and closely similar. A perfect model farm, built for a tenant or agent of the Shirley estate. Three-bay two-storey gable-ended block with the central bay advanced and gabled, in rubble with ashlar trim. Attractive paired sashes in mullioned frames with hood-moulds. Bulky, off-centre return facing into a generous yard with opposing ranges whose neat end gables flank the house in the Palladian spirit.

LOUGH GOWNA   CN   3090

A small town formerly called Scrabby, picturesquely set within lakelands – 1,200 acres of water that stretch into the neighbouring counties of Leitrim and Longford.

LOUGH GOWNA PARISH CHURCH (C of I). A modest early C19 church, probably by *William Farrell*, in roughcast with rather stiff Gothic details in dressed limestone. Basically a three-bay hall with an offset buttressed porch to the side, tall quarry-glazed lancets and a squarish bellcote on the w gable.

LOUGH GOWNA PARISH CHURCH. 1903 by *Hague & McNamara*. Refurbished in 2009. An understated church; a six-bay buttressed hall and polygonal chancel with plain lancets. Pebbledashed with limestone dressings. The kneelered w gable has a simple Gothic elegance, with a traceried rose window held between clasping buttresses ending in tall, spiky pinnacles. Inside, the roof is a combination of plain hammerbeams and ornamental kingposts. – STAINED GLASS. Rather anodyne figurative work by *Stained Glass Creations*, Kilkenny, 2009.

The nearby PRESBYTERY is a solid-looking two-storey block in roughcast with stuccoed quoins and tall bay windows on the main front.

DRUMHAWNAGH PORTAL TOMB. 3.75 km E. Upstaged by a late C20 house, stranded on the lawn in the front garden. A tight jumble of megaliths form a portal tomb with a polygonal chamber, entered from the NW and covered by a roof slab almost 2 sq. m (21½ sq. ft) in size.

MIDDLETOWN PORTAL TOMB. 4.5 km E. A wayside tomb, like Drumhawnagh. A massive sloping capstone teetering on two orthostats covers a chamber 6.5 ft (2 m) long; the entrance, framed in the usual way by two portal stones, is on the SE side. Unnecessarily set in a semicircular walled enclosure with mean battlemented copings, built in 2010 – presumably to prevent its escape?

ST JOSEPH, LOUGHDUFF. 4.5 km E. 1908 by *T. F. McNamara*. Refurbished in 1979 and 2010. A large stuccoed church, cruciform in plan, with a polygonal chancel and a kneelered W gable between clasping buttresses, given a fussy array of round-headed lancets with hoodmoulds. Four-bay nave with the windows cramped between offset buttresses; two-bay transepts with catslide roofs forming porches on the W sides. Inside, a complicated hammerbeam roof with twin-arched bracing. – FURNISHINGS. Plain marble altar with recessed panels, moved from the Convent of Mercy at Granard in Co. Longford in 2010.

LOUGHGALL   AH

A substantial street village, picturesquely developed by the Cope family over the C18 and C19. The property had been granted to the 7th Lord Saye and Sele by James I in 1610; Sir Anthony Cope acquired it the following year. While Lord Saye and Sele's promise to build a new town named after Sir Robert Cecil did not materialize, Cope conformed to the principles of the Plantation and erected a bawn at Drumilly, described in 1619 as 'a building of lime and stone, one hundred and eighty feet square [17 sq. m], fourteen feet [4.3 m] high, with flankers and in three of these were good lodgings, three stories high'. Cope settled the property on his sons, whose descendants eventually formed two adjoining demesnes surrounding the 36-acre lake that gives the place its name.

The street is lined mostly with trim Georgian houses with a pleasing variety of fanlit doorcases, all nicely preserved as a model village. An exception is the former DISPENSARY at the N end, a large stuccoed Victorian building of five bays with plate-glass windows and bracketed doorcase. The ordinary building beside it is notable only as the place where the Orange Order in Ireland was founded in 1795. A fuller architectural potential might have been realized had two buildings designed for Robert Cope by *Sir Edward Lovett Pearce*, a market house and an 'office house', ever been built. Still, staying here as a guest of Cope's in 1722, Jonathan Swift found Loughgall a perfect oasis: 'the People, the Churches and the plantations make me think I am in England. I mean only the scene of a few miles about me, for I have passed through miserable Regions to get to it.'

OLD CHURCH RUINS. In the graveyard in the centre of the village. Only the large rubble W gable of a church apparently established here in the C13. A low doorway, crudely arched, with a small ogee lancet of a common late medieval kind. In 1622 the building was described as well repaired but in 1641 it was ruined; it was largely rebuilt in 1734, when a square bellcote was added; deemed dangerous in 1798, the nave was demolished and the materials sold.

ST LUKE (C of I). In 1788 the ruinous state of the old church together with its 'bad situation' resulted in the decision to rebuild on the present site, work undertaken by a committee that included the architect *George Ensor*. As built in 1795 it formed a straightforward rectangular three-bay hall and tower, the battlemented tower not forestanding but rising from the central entrance bay between the vestry and gallery stair. Here the building is faced in dressed stone, the architecture given ample expression with lesenes, strings and hoodmoulds. Enlarged in 1864 by *W. J. Barre*, who added transepts with a buttressed E gable rising between them to the E, all in squared limestone. The transepts are raised on deep battered plinths, with steep gables and sinuous Y-tracery. The builder was *Richard Cherry*, a local contractor. The interior is plain, the nave ceiling with flat recessed panels, and a W gallery on clustered colonnettes; additional galleries added in 1822 were later removed. The transepts, opening through plain arches, are roofed with exceptionally light scissor trusses. The sanctuary was reordered in 1930 by *R. F. C. Orpen*. – STAINED GLASS. Three-light E window, a bright florid work, gifted in 1866 by Mrs Cope of Drumilly. – MONUMENTS. The Rev. Silver Oliver †1844; an elaborate tablet with sarcophagus and inverted torches. – The Rev. Savage Hall †1851; a similar design with an urn.

RECTORY. 1933 by the Diocesan Architect, *Henry C. Dorman*. Built to replace the large C18 rectory destroyed by fire in 1926. A two-storey block with large picture windows, dormered attics and broad end gables. The contractors were *Thomas Hyde & Sons* of Portadown. Large stone and brick outbuildings of the earlier house remain, with handsome Neoclassical gatepiers at the entrance.

COURTHOUSE AND MARKET HOUSE. At the high end of the Main Street of 1746. The familiar combination, the former above the latter. Much more rustic than the restrained Palladian design proposed by *Sir Edward Lovett Pearce*: a plain Georgian block of rubble with a hipped roof and four-bay front with a simple arcade on the ground floor formed with large rough-hewn voussoirs; tall corresponding sashes above with flush frames, divided with nine small panels over six.

ENSOR MASONIC HALL. Main Street. 1902. A small Gothic hall and porch with lancets, brick stacks over the gables, and a short, flèche-like ventilator in the centre of the ridge. The doorway is a Tudor arch in moulded red brick.

LOUGHGALL DISTRICT ORANGE HALL. Main Street. A large stuccoed hall of one storey and three bays, with a bulky gabled porch with decorative bargeboards and a large fanlit door. The big round-headed sashes have hoodmoulds, plate glass and marginal glazing bars. The date 1907 is given in a plaque above the door. Attached on one side of the hall is a pretty two-bay, two-storey house.

ERASMUS SMITH SCHOOL (former). Beside the church. A compact two-storey, roughcast block with half-hipped roof and a squat central stack. Three bays with large Georgian sashes, unusually divided on the ground floor with eight small panes over twelve. The datestone over the door is inscribed: 'This School House erected by the / Trustees for the Charities of the late / Erasmus Smith & endowed with two / Acres of land for ever by Robert / Camden Cope Esqr. was built / AD 1811'.

COPE SCHOOLS. Main Street. 1861 by *W. J. Barre*. The TEACHER'S HOUSE is a small gable-ended block in red-and-yellow brick with fish-scale slating and ridge cresting on the roof. Busy three-bay front with a small gabled central porch and gables over the first-floor windows, all with frilly bargeboards. Behind, the SCHOOLHOUSE extends in a more modest red brick range with a broad canted bay window on one side under a steep polygonal roof.

LOUGHGALL HOUSE. Main Street. A substantial, somewhat unexpected early C19 house associated with the steward of the Cope estate. A two-storey, three-bay block in roughcast with a hipped roof on wide bracketed eaves and four short stacks. Hoodmoulds give the Georgian sashes a modest Tudor expression; the windows are wider on the ground floor, where the sashes are set in pairs under rectangular panels with geometric glazing. Between them is a handsome doorcase with engaged Ionic columns, plain entablature, narrow geometric side-lights and an elliptical leaded fanlight to a petal design. To the rear, the house rises tall over an exposed basement, with a handsome timber-glazed room on the first floor projecting from the return to hang perilously over a raised open veranda.

In the adjoining street wall, a curious low BASTION of rubble with battlemented parapet breaks forward onto the pavement with a shallow bow. Of uncertain date, it formerly stood on the edge of a large enclosed garden or orchard.

ROSE COTTAGE. Off the Main Street. A pretty late C19 house in rubble with red brick trim. A single-storey gable-ended block with projecting end stacks; three bays with small twelve-pane sashes and an advanced and gabled porch.

THE MANOR HOUSE, now a Department of Agriculture research station. Off the Main Street. The entrance, expressed as a rumbustious architectural fantasia of striking immediacy, and the spectacular, steeply rising avenue of limes, reduce this modest if rambling two-storey Tudor Revival house to an anti-climax. Begun in 1874 for the Cope family to the designs of *Frederick A. Butler*. The main front to the W is irregular with plain graduated gables, all rendered with stone dressings. The larger N gable is deeply advanced with a short link to a low gabled porch faced in pale sandstone with a large archway, its hoodmould terminated in big medieval-looking heads. Cross-mullioned windows, some with triangular heads and hood-moulds, and all with sashes rather than casements. A more regular gabled façade on the terraced E front with four bays, and a lower kitchen range set back with a further four gabled bays given triangular-headed windows on the first floor and an additional end bay, broad and advanced, with a plain gable. Inside, the plan has been greatly altered to provide offices, with some remaining Victorian decoration.

The STABLEYARD adjoins the kitchen yard to the N, a small quadrangle, mostly two-storey in rubble with generous lime-stone dressing, plate-glass windows, and on the N range a large gabled projection with a timber cupola and clock; the iron weathervane on its steep leaded roof bears the remains of a date in the 1870s.

The sheer whimsy of the main ENTRANCE would seem pompous but for the diminutive scale: rarely has so much architecture been packed into so little space, in a bristling Jacobethan design with twin lodges facing each other behind a four-piered gate screen between balustraded sweeps; the equally fanciful wrought-iron GATES by *R. Marshall*, Caledon, are stamped and dated 1842. The piers are built in crisp blocks of vermiculated and diamond-faced rustication, with strap-work decoration in the frieze and finial-topped by the Cope fleur-de-lis and issuing dragon's head. The LODGES are set back on either side of the avenue, with crazy-paved walls of polygonal rubble, much like *opus incertum*, with ample carved dressings. Built to an L-shaped plan with an elaborate open porch supported on Elizabethan tapered piers with squashed Ionic capitals. The gables have small oriel windows with honeycomb iron casements, then the Cope quarterings and motto – *Aequo adeste animo* (Be ready with constancy) – in Keene's cement, and finally shaped gables with a flurry of spikes, most finished in bulbous Eastern-looking finials. It is perhaps just as well that any intended architectural promise was never fulfilled in the house.

In the DEMESNE a great deal of ornamental planting remains, mostly Victorian, with the yew walk near the house and the great lime avenue representing elements of an older demesne, presumably associated with the landscape of Cope's C17 house.

The ICE HOUSE is the usual brick egg concealed in an ornamental mound, entered through a rustic arch. Set against a small hill near the lake, the HERMITAGE, built within Drummilly demesne and now part of this property, is a domed garden building in grotesque masonry, of a common C18 type, with two wide arched openings and a sloping buttress between; an entrance on one side leads through a long indented passageway to a brick-vaulted hexagon.

ST PATRICK, EAGRALOUGHER. 1 km NW. A curious rough diamond of a church, large and vaguely Romanesque with an offset tower and apsidal chancel, built in 1912 to replace a chapel of 1787. All highly textured in a manner that is reminiscent of *W. A. Scott*, with nubby roughcast walls, porridge-like in texture, amply trimmed with rock-faced limestone. The hall is bulky with four bays, covered by a heavy slated roof projecting on flat mutules and fronted with a big gable and three graded lights; sympathetic porch of 1992. The gable is partially stepped at the base with flat buttresses set back from the corners, made taller and broader at the front so as to read like antae. The tower is an unusual design, square in plan and rising from a stepped plinth in three stages to the belfry, where the corners are set back as chamfers and capped by a pyramid roof projecting like that of the nave; on the ground floor three slit windows united under a deep semicircle form an attractive motif, repeated on each face. Inside, an exposed hammerbeam roof.

LAUREL HILL. 1.5 km N. Set on a drumlin sheltered by trees. A charming Late Georgian house in roughcast with blocked quoins, hipped roof and short centre stacks. Two storeys and three bays, the central bay set back to accommodate a railed balcony on the first floor. The windows are Georgian sashes, unusually with hoodmoulds; the fanlit doorcase is elliptically arched with fluted Ionic columns – all features shared with Loughgall House. Inside, vigorous foliate plasterwork.

FREE PRESBYTERIAN CHURCH, BALLYMAGERNEY. 2 km N. Discreet little C19 gabled hall, roughcast with three bays.

CASTLE RAW. 2 km NE. Ruinous. Chiefly the tottering rubble gable wall of a three-storey castle built in 1611 in 'freestone and hard stone' by Sir Anthony Cope and largely destroyed after 1641. The rest remains in outline as a basement, its plan following a Greek cross that is comparable only with a later house at Ightermurragh in Co. Cork, built in 1641. Inspiration probably came from Cope's homeland in Northamptonshire, where there are the late C16 cruciform houses of Lyveden and Gayton. The interior of Castle Raw adopted a simple layout of two rectangular rooms 30 ft by 20 ft (9 m by 6 m) extending side by side the full depth in the middle, with a square room occupying each of the other two arms. The overseer was named in official sources as *William Pearson*, given a force of some fifteen workmen, nine carpenters, and a large team of horses and oxen to draw materials. Stone and

Loughgall, Castle Raw.
Isometric drawing by E. M. Jope, 1960

timber were all sourced within eight miles (13 km), except for the freestone quoins and windows which were 'prepared' somewhere beyond Armagh.

LURGAN

AH   0050

INTRODUCTION

Anciently this place bore the unwieldy title of Lurganvallivackan, which translates from the Irish into the equally cumbersome 'townland of the MacCanns on the shin-like ridge'. Nothing else is known of the earliest settlements here. The modern town was

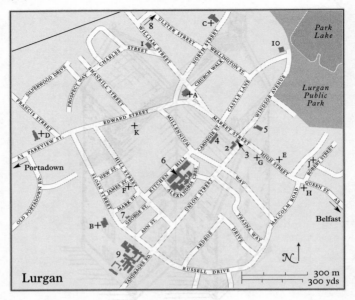

Lurgan

A	Christ Church (C of I)
B	St John (C of I)
C	St Peter
D	St Paul
E	First Lurgan Presbyterian Church
F	Hill Street Presbyterian Church
G	High Street Methodist Church
H	Queen Street Methodist Church
J	Quaker Meeting House
K	Mount Zion Convent Chapel

1	Courthouse (former)
2	Town Hall
3	Mechanics' Institute
4	Carnegie Library
5	Masonic Hall
6	Lurgan College and High School
7	Hill Street Presbyterian School
8	Lurgan Minor Model School
9	Lurgan Hospital (former Workhouse)
10	Brownlow House

founded following the Plantation, developing in the C18 as an estate town before passing into the C19 as a thriving linen market, eventually becoming an increasingly industrialized centre for linen production in the region.

In 1610 John Brownlow of Nottingham and his son William were granted between them the manors of Dowcoran and Ballynemony, in all about 2,500 acres extending to the s shore of Lough Neagh. They were resident in the region by 1611, when Sir George Carew noted that they were inhabiting an 'Irish House'; their plans to erect two bawns were reflected by their retinue, which included six carpenters, one mason, and six workmen. By 1619 the settlement established on this broad ridge was sufficient to be described by Pynnar as 'a fair town, consisting of 42 houses ... inhabited with English families, and the streets all paved clean through also two water mills, and a wind mill, all for corn'. The younger Brownlow built his house and bawn on the edge of the ridge to the NE of the settlement, completed by 1622. Some of the fabric of the old house survives, incorporated in *William Henry Playfair*'s Elizabethan Revival mansion and yards of 1833.

William Brownlow's commitment to the Plantation project was recognized with a knighthood, and in 1629, having succeeded his father, those lands were combined with his own and raised into the manor of Brownlowsderry. The town, then shortened to Ballylurgan, was officially recognized by patent at the same time, which in the hard language of conquest consolidated the Plantation ideals by preventing settlement in any part of the town centre to 'any one being mere Irish or who shall not be of English or British race'. Landlord and settlers paid the price when the new town was amongst the first to be attacked in 1641, torched by rebels led by Sir Conn Magennis. Brownlow and his family were taken prisoner and the townspeople were forced to flee; released in 1642, the family returned to rebuild the fabric and quickly set about laying the foundations of its future prosperity. The town had been laid out along the broad High Street with a succession of long linear plots in the manner of a medieval borough, limited on the S side by the watercourse of the River Pound and more generously to the N by Brownlow's demesne. A triangular market place was set on the highest point at the W end, where a market house and windmill stood; at the beginning of the C18, the parish church was moved to this site, afforded a pre-eminence which it retains today, enhanced by rebuilding works of the mid C19.

The beginnings of commerce in the district came early, when the planters cleared the surrounding derries or oak woods for tanning, improving the boggy hinterland in the process. The more challenging clay fenlands closer to Lough Neagh were unaffected, and these largely retain a distinctive, uncultivated quality today. It was in the improved hinterland that Quaker families from the North of England settled, to play a crucial role in organizing the nascent linen industry. Their presence is evident from 1653, when the first Quaker Meeting House in Ireland was established in the developing town. Ultimately by fixing its success on finer linens such as cambric and later damasks, Lurgan was quickly established as the hub of the region's linen economy, proclaimed in 1682 as the 'greatest linen manufacture in Ireland'. As a centre for the distribution of linen, its markets eventually exceeded those of Armagh. In 1703 it could claim to be 'one of the most thriving and flourishing and a most considerable market town in the province of Ulster'; Sir William Brownlow's grandson, Arthur, described it that year as 'a large village consisting of a great many stone houses well shingled and finished and abounding with a great number of British inhabitants who are industrious and trading people and have considerably advanced and improved several manufactures and especially the linen manufacture there'.

The landlord may have downplayed his role, but through shrewd investment and wise management, assisted by an Act of 1697 for the promotion of the industry, the single resident influence of the Brownlows had certainly given the town advantages over neighbouring centres such as Portadown and Armagh. In 1708 Thomas Molyneux affirmed it as the greatest centre in the region and attributed this solely to the methods of the landlord, 'who on his first establishing the trade here, bought up everything that was brought to the market of cloath and lost at first considerably; but at length the thing fixing itself, he is now by the same methods a considerable gainer'. In 1776 the agriculturalist Arthur Young was shown around the market by William Brownlow. He observed how the cambrics 'all made in a circumference of not many miles' were sold in the first half of the morning with the remainder sold between eleven and twelve o'clock, and recorded that 3,000 pieces a week were sold here, amounting to trade worth £5,250, and per annum £273,000.

Linen production grew steadily from a cottage industry to a heavily industrialized process in the C19 and in 1876 as many as thirty-three manufactories were listed in the town and its environs. The corresponding expansion of the town is evident in the long brick and stuccoed terraces that rose up in around the factories, which were concentrated in streets close to the railway – William Street, Victoria Street, North Road and Brownlow Terrace. While the arrival of the Ulster Railway in 1841 was an important factor in the industrial growth of the town, Portadown as an important junction profited more.

Today the wide, undulating thoroughfare combining Queen Street, High Street and Market Street displays all the solidity of a C19 provincial town in its mostly stuccoed façades. Together these streets continue to provide a central axis to the greatly expanded town of the C21, now extending to the s into a concentrated street network blending with Craigavon's eastern sprawl but still limited to the N, where the reduced former demesne with its lake dominates as a large public park.

CHURCHES ETC.

CHRIST CHURCH, SHANKILL PARISH CHURCH (C of I). 1861 by *Welland & Gillespie*. Dominating the triangular market place in a railed enclosure, a big blackstone church with a soaring helm spire. In 1718 the parish vestry met to consider plans for a new church on Lurgan green to replace the old church of Shankill. It was completed in 1725, followed by the tower in 1736, and finished with an octagonal wooden spire twenty years later and described in 1837 as a 'handsome Grecian edifice'. The present building is an unashamed Gothic rebuild, E.E. in style, consisting of an aisled nave with an undifferentiated chancel, transepts, and a forestanding w tower with flanking porches. Built in uncoursed blackstone rising from a battered plinth and trimmed with biscuit-coloured sandstone from Dungannon. Windows are predominantly lancets with quarry glazing, set in groups – paired in the aisles, with three lights under an oculus in the transepts, and three graded lights for the E window. The cost was £6,000 and the builder was *Thomas H. Carroll*. The tower, completed later in 1869 by *Robert McConnell*, has diminishing clasping buttresses and a polygonal sandstone spire with a series of recessed discs on each face. Rubble masonry on the tower and porches could suggest their survival from the older church, though thoroughly remodelled, with porches entirely in sandstone ashlar on the W front. The interior is plain and capacious, with a broad nave under open trusses with clerestory lighting and galleried aisles. Renovated in 1911 by *James A. Hanna*; chancel enlarged in 1930 by *Richard F. C. Orpen*. – FONT. 1684. A handsome Renaissance pedestal supporting a polygonal bowl with a beaded rim moulding. – STAINED GLASS. In the chancel S wall, Baron Lurgan memorial window: Faith, Hope and Charity, 1853. N transept: figurative with sombre colours, by *Heaton, Butler & Bayne*, c. 1917.

BROWNLOW MAUSOLEUM. At the N end of Shankill Street. On the site of the old parish church and central amongst a clutter of imposing headstones, a cement-rendered box, built by Elizabeth Brownlow for her husband William †1737. The walls are unadorned, with a prominent cornice and blocking course before a conical roof, topped by a funerary urn. Refurbished in 1959 by the 4th Baron Lurgan.

ST JOHN (C of I). Sloan Street. A simple Victorian Gothic hall of five bays with paired lancets and an advanced and gabled entrance in the centre with a lower projection at one end and a subsidiary gabled entrance between. Roughcast over polychrome brick, exposed to the rear. Timber Y-tracery in the E gable.

ST PETER, SHANKILL PARISH CHURCH. North Street. A large and assured church in a familiar French Gothic style with an imposing offset tower and spire flanking the gabled front. Built in rock-faced blackstone copiously trimmed with pale grey limestone, giving a uniformity to the architecture that fails to betray a complicated evolution. The earliest church was established here on a site presented by Charles Brownlow in 1829. Dedicated in 1833, it was described as being in the 'later English style' decorated with 'minarets' and Gothic windows. That building was greatly enlarged in 1867 by *John Murray* with a chancel and transepts, which survived when the nave was rebuilt with aisles in 1893 by *J. J. McDonnell*. The plan is a straightforward one of aisled nave with deep transepts and chancel flanked by side chapels, all in highly textured masonry, the distinctions between the phases only obvious in the fenestration, where the Geometric tracery of Murray's works contrasts with McDonnell's plain lancets. McDonnell's proposals for a spire in 1897 appear to indicate that a central tower had preceded the present four-stage structure erected in 1901. The spire, added in 1925 by *Ashlin & Coleman*, was raised on a polygonal drum between tall pinnacles. The w front appears to have been remodelled in the same period: a narrow gable with twin windows under a rose, all of unembellished bar tracery; below, the doorway projects in a gable with a deeply recessed arch on polished shafts of pink marble and a sculptural tympanum of 1927 depicting St Peter receiving the keys of the kingdom, signed *JFDM*.

Until refurbishment in 2011 the interior had largely escaped meddling hands, still attractively furnished in a full-blown Gothic Revival display, down to medievalizing brass light-fittings. Though the high altar and mosaics have been retained, the sanctuary now intrudes into the nave on an incongruous polished pavement, while pews and floor tiles have been needlessly replaced by garish replicas. As it was, it was largely the achievement of extensive works by *Ashlin & Coleman* in 1927; these may have involved remodelling the nave arcade, replacing tame Gothic piers with polished shafts of grey granite rising into large, spreading foliate capitals to support amply moulded arches. Above, a lofty open wagon roof with the main trusses rising from corbels between cinquefoil clerestory lights. – HIGH ALTAR. A bold architectural composition with crocketed gables, pinnacles and spires flanked by statuary niches. – MOSAICS. Sanctuary and side chapels richly clad in the manner of *Oppenheimer*. – STAINED GLASS. Extensive, mostly of late C19 date, in sombre colours that contribute to the atmospheric gloom. – MONUMENT. High in the s transept, a heavy Gothic gable supported on corbels with pious angels.

The PAROCHIAL HOUSE is a three-storey five-bay block of 1834 enlarged on one side with a cumbersome gabled block, plainly decorated with stucco bands with a battlemented bay window and porch. The PARISH HALL opposite is a small Gothic design of 1897 with six bays in blackstone rubble and sandstone trim. Gabled entrance porch flanked by lean-tos.

ST PAUL. Francis and Parkview Streets. 1963 by *Thomas J. Ryan*. A large and stylish church, somewhat unexpected for the period, built originally as a chapel of ease. A towering nave of four bays to an oblong plan, canted at each end and skirted by low aisles which extend into polygonal vestibules that project diagonally on the w front. Built of concrete, mostly roughcast, with low-pitched copper roofs and a tall, slender spirelet over the ridge on the w end. Lit from the clerestory, where bronze lattice windows in large rectangular frames are set high in recessed panels clad with ceramic tiles. Unusually, over the w door is a flamboyant coat of arms and motto of St Paul in monochrome tiles, the gift of the architect. Inside, the high nave is bright and impressive, with walls partly lined in timber and a roof with massive beams formed rib-like in star shapes to support the flat concrete ceiling. The aisles are more human in scale, opening through slender mosaic-clad pilotis and atmospherically lit; here small rectangular panels in STAINED GLASS display the Stations of the Cross in intense deep-coloured vignettes.

FIRST LURGAN PRESBYTERIAN CHURCH. High Street.
Unevenly hemmed in by three-storey blocks. A large Victorian
hall, five bays deep, with a stuccoed façade and a prostyle
Roman Doric portico between rounded corners that offer a
cautious lean towards the Baroque. On the ground floor channelled rustication and round-headed windows, traceried with
paired lights under an oculus; niches at the corners, all dressed
up with keystones, lugged architraves and bracketed sills. The
portico betrays an unsure hand: the pediment is too steep, and
the intercolumniation increases in the centre to accommodate
the entrance; the awkward proportions continue with the pediment carried on brackets over the entrance. Inside, after a
vestibule with flanking stairs, a handsome galleried interior
with dark timber furnishings. The galleries are cantilevered
over fluted Ionic columns. Remodelled and reseated 1889,
possibly by *Young & Mackenzie*, who designed a new lecture
hall to the rear in 1878 (since replaced). – MONUMENT. John
Dobbin †1831; a lengthy eulogy on white marble attractively
framed with polished slate, by *W. Fitzpatrick*, Belfast.

HILL STREET PRESBYTERIAN CHURCH. Hill Street. 1861 by
James McNea. A five-bay hall and offset tower with highly
faceted surfaces of rock-hewn blackstone trimmed with sandstone. The tower has two stages with angle buttresses, deep
parapets and hefty pinnacles. The polygonal copper spire was
added after 1888.

The MCCLURE HALLS, built *c.* 2000, are in a pretentious
box-like appendage to the rear. Cement-rendered walls with
slate cladding projected slightly in a large panel on the side
over a low strip window, disintegrating at the time of writing.

HIGH STREET METHODIST CHURCH. High Street. A modest
stuccoed façade of 1888, blended into the streetscape and
fronting a church of 1826. Two storeys and three bays with
quoins, vermiculated with channelled rustication on the
ground floor, and a cornice and blocking course concealing the
roof. Plain round-headed windows on the first floor, given
hoods with foliate bosses. Major repairs in 1910 by *Henry
Hobart*.

QUEEN STREET METHODIST CHURCH. Queen Street. An odd-
looking building set back-to-front with a three-bay lancet hall,
transepts and a large gabled front to the street. Here a small
pointed-arched doorway linked with side-lights under a continuous hood suffers from an overbearing large traceried
window.

The detached HALL to the rear is a modest brick building,
repaired in 1913 by *Henry Hobart*.

QUAKER BUILDINGS. High Street and Johnston's Row. A large
complex with housing, shops, and both old and new Meeting
Houses. To the High Street, a Late Victorian range two storeys
tall and twelve bays long with attics and a mixture of gables
and dormers on the roof-line, built in squared blackstone
trimmed with yellow brick. The brick used again exclusively
to form the w elevation in the late C20 after the adjoining

buildings were removed to open a new street (Johnston's Row). Behind, reached by a passage to the E, stands the former MEETING HOUSE of 1880 by *F. W. Lockwood*, a substantial two-storey Italianate block. A building was founded on this site in 1696, erected by Ezokiall Bullock for a congregation first established in Lurgan in 1653. The main, E, front, richly stuccoed with classical details, faces a small court, its unpainted cement render effecting a dourness unworthy of its architectural detail. Four bays wide with a central pedimented breakfront. On the ground floor a portico is set *in antis* with stylized Doric columns and responds and a central pediment over which the first-floor Venetian window is playfully forced upwards. This and the adjoining S front are bound tightly together with numerous moulded string-courses, either run through as continuous sills or halted as imposts on which the upper window architraves rest. The ground-floor windows have segmental heads, those above taller with rounded heads, all with plate glass and marginal glazing bars.

The back of the chapel is exposed in Johnston's Row, with a projecting porch labelled 'Quaker Buildings'. Further N on the same side is the new MEETING HOUSE of 1996 by *Alwyn Sinton*, a more modest affair. A simple single-storey five-bay block in red brick with slender paired buttresses and a yawning arched entrance in a central gabled projection.

On the W side of Johnston's Row, back towards the High Street and easily missed, trapped in a garage car park and sadly decayed, is a modest architectural gem. Said locally to have been a gate lodge to the Brownlow demesne, but not evident as such on the Ordnance Surveys. A diminutive two-storey, two-bay block, cement-rendered over brick, with an ogee-gabled front. The entrance is to one side, a small ogee arch between irregular piers, suggestive of an early date.

MOUNT ZION HOUSE (former MERCY CONVENT). Edward Street. Founded in 1866. A large stuccoed block, two storeys tall, with a big hipped roof and a seven-bay frontage with a meagre Tuscan portico; extended in 1876 to the E to accommodate a boys' school, in a two-storey L-plan range in red brick with stone dressings. The CHAPEL to the W, built *c.* 1900 by the Rev. James McKenna P.P., gives the entire building added prominence. Gabled and stuccoed with blind arches in an early Renaissance style with a thick-set Italianate tower to one side. Inside, a lofty top-lit space with an apsidal end. Decoration by *Ashlin & Coleman*, with rich mosaics on the sanctuary walls.

Adjoining the chapel to the E, ST MARY'S PRIMARY SCHOOL, perhaps early C20, has a plain seven-bay front, extended *c.* 1960 with a three-storey flat-roofed block to the side.

PUBLIC BUILDINGS ETC.

TOWN HALL. Union Street. 1868 by *Young & Mackenzie*. On a side street, upstaged by the adjoining Mechanics' Institute and given little of the architectural prominence deserved by a public building. Impressive largely for its scale, with a ponderous front nine bays wide, the surface only relieved on the end bays by strip pilasters which die into a prominent brick eaves course, above which the roof projects on brackets. Built over a raised basement with a tall ground floor in blackstone rubble and brick trim with tall round-headed sashes. Above this the walls are of brown brick, with smaller windows paired on a shared sill. The contractor was *John Archer*.

COURTHOUSE (former), now a public house. Charles Street. 1872 by *Thomas Turner* in partnership with the County Surveyor, *Henry Davison*. It has more the air of a railway station than a judicial venue. Two-storey, gable-ended block of four bays in polychrome brick, fronted by a low flat-roofed projection, extending on one side where a two-bay pedimented gable steps forward. A deep semicircular bow addresses the forked street corner with a pediment expressed in the gable above; over the apex here, and on the opposite gable, the tall chimneystacks are distinctive, bridged with arches in a Vanbrughian manner. The windows have segmental heads with large, irregularly proportioned sashes and plate glass. The entrance, inset in the centre of the main front, has twin arches on squat sandstone columns with richly carved foliate capitals. Remodelled as a public house in 1996 by *Michael Doyle*.

MILLAR MEMORIAL. William Street and Charles Street. 1859 by *John Robinson*. An elegant thin small Gothic monument in sandstone, set on a stepped base enclosed by railings. Formed as an octagonal arcade around a central column with shafts of polished granite, steep gables and a needle spire. The square pedestal has angle buttresses and an enriched nailhead cornice. On each face arched panels of white marble record the worthiness of the Rev. Thomas Millar †1858, a victim of the Trent Valley railway disaster near Nuneaton in England.

WAR MEMORIAL. Market Street. 1928 by *R. Lynn*. Raised on a podium in a small landscaped green, a domed Tuscan pavilion in granite crowned by a bronze Victory by *L. S. Merrifield*. Inside, the ceiling springs from a central polygonal pier lined with bronze panels cast with the names of the war dead.

MECHANICS' INSTITUTE. Of 1857, a winning competition entry by *William Raffles Brown*. Prominent on the corner of Union and Market streets, a stuccoed Italianate block of cubic proportions with a campanile perched above the street corner. The main front in Market Street is richly decorated, in contrast to the simplified treatment on Union Street. Two storeys tall with narrow advanced end bays, ground floor rusticated with vermiculated window and door surrounds, and tall round-headed windows on the first floor, set out singly or in groups below an enriched modillion cornice. The tower rises in two stages above the blocking course: on the lower stage a triple arcade, and above a recessed oculus between pilasters, crowned by a low pyramid roof on eaves brackets.

CARNEGIE LIBRARY. Carnegie Street. 1906 by *Henry Hobart*. A quixotic design in red brick with red sandstone dressings. The three-bay front is asymmetrical with large windows and has a fanciful outline consisting of a central pyramid-roofed tower flanked by wide gabled side bays, varied in height and fenestration, all decorated with ball finials, scrolled copings and a queasy mixture of classical and Gothic elements. The entrance has short, portly Ionic columns under a cusped arch with a lumpish ogee hood. Extended in 1992, with the main gable weakly mimicked at one end of a long, dull range in poorly matched brick.

MASONIC HALL. Windsor Avenue. 1900 by *G. W. Ferguson*. Red brick with terracotta and sandstone dressings. A sizeable two-storey hall of five bays with a shaped gable of two bays on the front. A bulky stair-tower projects diagonally from one side with chamfered corners, a steep chisel roof and a narrow porch to the side. The tower fenestration is treated playfully, with tall, narrow windows reducing to correspond with the ascent of the stairs inside while the string-course, employed as a continuous sill on the adjoining façades, slices off the upper panes. Elsewhere the quirky glazing divisions are characteristic of the time, mostly with sashes divided into six panes over two.

LURGAN COLLEGE AND HIGH SCHOOL (former TECHNICAL SCHOOLS). Kitchen Hill. 1957–61 by *G. P. & R. H. Bell*, extended in 1966. In a familiar 1950s institutional style in red brick with flat roofs, oversailing eaves, and expansive glazing.

HILL STREET PRESBYTERIAN SCHOOLS. George Street. 1888 by *Young & Mackenzie*. A small single-storey school with a frontage of four bays, with the entrance in a small porch to one side. Built in English-garden-wall-bond red brick with gabled end bays, pilasters, and a high string-course of saw-toothed brickwork. Windows both segmental- and round-headed.

WATT ENDOWED SCHOOL. College Walk. Tucked away off the Lough Road. A school and master's house of 1873 by *Young & Mackenzie*. Collegiate Gothic with a long and varied front in red brick with thin bands of black brick and red sandstone trimmings. Mostly single-storey, with dormered attics. A central square entrance tower, steeply roofed with a slate-clad pyramid and a small lantern set diagonally on the summit. Large mullioned windows in recessed arches with tympana of herringbone brickwork. At either end are projecting blocks. The simpler has bow windows under a gable. The other, with a kneelered gable, fronts a buttressed hall, with twin windows united under a hood with a slender buttress between; the design is separated by stonework into two stages, with heraldic glass in the lower stage and attenuated Perp tracery in the upper stage. This design is Arts and Crafts in spirit and presumably one of the several early C20 additions to the original building, all difficult to isolate: 1922 by *R. Lynn*; 1927 by *James A. Hanna*; 1955 by *Bell & Malcolmson*.

MINOR MODEL SCHOOLS. Brownlow Terrace. 1861 by *J. H. Owen*. A large Italianate school, departing notably from the familiar Gothic and Tudor Revival idioms favoured by Owen as at Monaghan. Though established as a Minor Model School, the building equals that of any of the District Schools. Built with a mixed palette of materials, predominantly of red-and-yellow brick with sandstone dressings, set on an impressive rusticated basement with battered walls of rock-faced blackstone. The builders were *Patrick Kerr* and *George Carolin*. The building follows a U-plan with a long ten-bay range set deep between the wings. The bays are generous, set in recessed panels of red brick framed by machicolated yellow brickwork with tall round-headed windows. Prominent eaves corbels and hipped roofs. The square entrance tower is a stately campanile projecting diagonally from the w wing, four storeys tall with a short arcaded belfry, boldly corniced with brackets under a squat pyramid roof. Framing the lower stages are broad clasping pilasters of yellow brick supporting a rusticated arch with a framed oculus above; both details have large expressive heads for keystones, the upper ones hirsute and sage-like. The successful arrangement of the plan and the impact of the tower have been upset by additions of 1931 by *James St John Phillips* and again of 1938 by *G. A. Henry*, which created a low link between the wings with new entrances and added a bulky block to the w crudely aping the character of the original.

LURGAN HOSPITAL. Sloan Street. The former Union Work-house of 1841 by *George Wilkinson*, extended by him in 1850, refronted in 1929 by *Ferguson & McIlveen*. Some of Wilkin-son's familiar ranges survive, largely concealed behind the front, a lumbering three-storey range, partly of red brick with rendered wings and bulky terminal blocks with hipped roofs. Never a very attractive building, now greatly disfigured by messy flat-roofed extensions and mixed fenestration.

COMMERCIAL BUILDINGS

ULSTER BANK. Market Street. 1911 by *Vincent Craig*. Something of an oddity, a five-bay, three-storey block in buttery Mountcharles sandstone on low courses of dull Aberdeen granite. More embellished on the advanced ends bays, which have gawky round gables, diagonal pilasters set buttress-like on the corners, and elaborate window surrounds. A wide mul-lioned window in a shallow bow dominates in the centre of the first floor.

BANK OF IRELAND. Market Street. 1922 by *Tulloch & Fitzsimons*. Three storeys and five bays, with a fussy stuccoed front over a nicely ordered ground floor in ashlar with engaged Tuscan columns. Plate-glass windows in classical surrounds with boldly expressed lugs, aprons and keystones on the upper floor before a weighty cornice and open balustraded parapet.

NORTHERN BANK. Corner of Market Street and Union Street. 1901 by *G. W. Ferguson*. A compact corner building of two storeys, with bold architectural details adopting reliable

Italianate forms typical of the turn-of-the-century Classical Revival. Red brick over channelled sandstone rustication with the first floor treated as a *piano nobile*, fenestrated in aedicules with alternating bracketed pediments. The entrance, on the canted street corner, is an imposing lugged doorcase in black polished marble under an open pediment. On Union Street the heavy modillion cornice is continued on the plainer three-storey annexe.

LURGAN CREDIT UNION. Church Place. Built in 1765 for the Rev. A. Fforde, though its present appearance suggests a substantial Early Victorian town house. Three storeys tall with gabled ends and a plainly stuccoed four-bay front with plate glass. Channelled rustication on the ground floor and a wide, fanlit doorcase with Ionic columns set in an elliptical arch. Renovations in 1996 by *John Kelly*.

YARN FACTORY. Victoria Street. Of *c.* 1890. An industrial brick leviathan, probably by *Young & Mackenzie*, who enlarged the building in 1911. Originally built as a power-loom factory for the firm of Johnston & Allen with a capacity of 500 looms, producing yarn for local weavers. Three storeys tall in red brick banded with thin courses of black brick, with wide segmental-headed windows and strip pilasters on the upper floors, rising to an emphatic cornice and blocking course. On one side, a handsome pedimented gateway with a segmental arch and a carved head on the keystone. On Woodville Street, an off-centre square tower barely disrupts the monotony of the long twenty-two-bay façade. Across the street, the terrace of brick HOUSES, distinguished by crowstepped gables on the central and end houses, is of 1888 by *Young & Mackenzie*. The same architects may also have been responsible for the nearby Late Victorian church, now occupied by INGLEWOOD PRESS. Red brick with a gabled front and a short offset tower with battlements. A deep plan of seven bays, part buttressed, with central, slightly projecting gables.

Two commercial buildings deserve notice on the main artery. On the N side of Market Street, w of the Bank of Ireland, is a tall three-storey building with gabled ends and attics which rises over the adjoining streetscape. It has a narrow two-bay front with impressive polychrome brickwork above an arcaded shopfront in faience draped with thick swags, with a Shakespearean head on the central keystone. Further E, on the High Street, HOUSTONS is a sort of Arts and Crafts-styled fairytale castle in red brick and sandstone, three storeys tall and five bays wide, with a large central gable flanked by dainty dormers with hipped roofs; the squat, paunchy columns on the first floor, supporting the central bays, are of a kind favoured by *Henry Hobart*, who is known to have designed premises on the street.

OTHER BUILDINGS

Some of the best housing was found at the SE end of the High Street. The GOSPEL HALL preserves the sorry remains of two imposing stuccoed houses by *Thomas Jackson*, built here in 1837 for the Cuppage family and named Bengal Place. Formerly of three storeys over a basement with tall windows, deep parapets and steep roofs; now only the ground floors and handsome tetrastyle Ionic porticoes, with fluted columns and Greek-key patterning in the frieze, are preserved. Bomb-damaged in 1974, the upper floors were subsequently demolished and the ground floor absurdly given a flat roof to accommodate the Gospel Hall, to which the porticoes continue to offer some measure of dignified access. The two adjoining houses are the finest surviving Late Georgian town houses in the centre, with handsome proportions, tall chimneystacks, original sashes, and handsome railed steps leading to fanlit timber doorways.

BROWNLOW HOUSE, also known as LURGAN CASTLE. Windsor Avenue. Now an events venue owned by the Orange Order. A large Tudor Revival house of 1833 by *William Henry Playfair*. Robert Graham, like Playfair a Scot (whose relation Lord Lynedoch had been a patron of William Henry and of his father James Playfair), visited the incomplete building in September 1836, when work was well advanced, and described it as Playfair's 'first Elizabethan house', which 'does him great credit'. Graham acknowledged that the plan was 'a little hampered by the remains of an old house and a court of offices, which are in some places new-faced and re-adapted to the general plan'. Two years later he was shown around by a Mr Gowan, the master of works; then the building detritus had been tidied up, the masonry had been completed, and progress was rapidly being made with the carpentry work. Though he considered it 'altogether a most comfortable house', he remained convinced that Playfair's Drumbanagher (Jerrettspass) was the better house, the architect not having been 'tied up to any restriction by having part of the old house retained'.

The old house was that initially built by Sir William Brownlow not long before 1622, when Lord Charlemont observed a three-storey building of 'stone and brick layed with lime', enclosed in a bawn 159 ft (*c.* 48 m) long with walls 14 ft (4.3 m) high, defended by one 'fair flanker square to the southeast', and another proposed to be built opposite. A survey of the estate in 1751 shows an irregular, predominantly triangular complex. In 1813 it was described as a very antique castle, enclosed by walls, evidently with many additions. Sir William had bequeathed his property to his grandson, Arthur Chamberlain, a scholar of the Irish language and patron of Irish scribes, who for a time was keeper of the Book of Armagh. His successors perhaps had a similar antiquarian bent, remaining in the old castle throughout the C18, content to make small improvements rather than rebuild, even as their financial and political standing was raised. William Brownlow succeeded in 1747 and was M.P. for Armagh from 1753 until his death in 1794; unlike many of his peers he preferred to invest his time and patronage in Dublin, where he built the most richly decorated house on Merrion Square, at No. 12.

William Brownlow's second son, Charles Brownlow, later 1st Lord Lurgan, succeeded his brother William in 1815, but only gave thought to building almost twenty years later. His choice of architect stemmed from a connection through his education in Edinburgh: there he had studied and lodged with the mathematician Professor John Playfair, and the Professor had in his care his nephew, the young *William Henry Playfair*. Brownlow appears to have temporized with the architect, considering designs without commitment, at an early stage giving consideration to what Playfair termed a 'Roman Villa', heroic in scale with a truly imperial Corinthian portico. Perhaps he had already made up his mind for a Tudor design, and was reluctant to ask that of an architect so readily associated with the creation of Edinburgh as 'the Athens of the North'. But Playfair confidently left behind Attic purity.

What Playfair created is a large house, of Scottish Old Red Sandstone from the Stevenson Quarry near Ardrossan, extended into existing lower ranges to the NW, which he remodelled along with a trapezoidal courtyard to the S. Any difficulty apparent to Graham in adapting older structures is hidden behind Playfair's success in giving all parts a unified character. To the SE, the main front is composed of two angled three-storey ranges facing an open court, with subsidiary two-storey elements breaking forward on the S side, in part concealing the sunken courtyard behind. The elevations are a lively and competent display of Tudor kneelered gables, bay windows with strapwork crowns, and broad mullioned windows under hoods. Impressive raggedness is given to the silhouette by steep roofs and a battery of pillar chimneystacks, individually carved with characteristic Tudor motifs; rising among these is an exotic ogee-domed tower set diagonally behind, its surfaces bristling with bold panel decoration. A short avenue leads to the entrance in the r. range, where the doorway occupies a narrow, deeply projecting three-storey gable. The NE front is less grand, with three gabled bays – each with two-storey canted bay windows – and one spaced further away and projecting forward; beside it a large Tudor-arched opening carries the cipher of Charles Brownlow and his second wife, Jane McNeill, and the date 1833. Round the corner the arrangement to the NW is more picturesque, formed as a sparsely fenestrated open court, with the two-storey family apartments extending NW in a long wing, all a little introverted and forbidding but still rather grand in effect. The tower is prominent at the centre of the plan, but its diagonal stance is a calculated reinforcer of wilful disarray. To the SW, the family wing displays a livelier façade, with a small polygonal turret at the angle between it and the main block. Here a low range extends away to the SE. This range, forming the SE side of the stable courtyard, with its line of small eaves gables and big cross-mullioned windows subtly graduated in scale, gives a sense of real Tudor design, suggesting that it may be what Robert Graham took to be 'a wing of the old house' containing the children's apartments.

Inside, steep mural stairs rise to a small square waiting room, which leads directly into a large, brightly lit octagonal Saloon – the centre of the plan and the main circulation space. In a highly original arrangement, the primary axis passes through on a true N–S axis, creating a diagonal enfilade between the Drawing Room and the diametrically opposed bow-ended Dining Room. This is not a Tudor feature: it owes more to

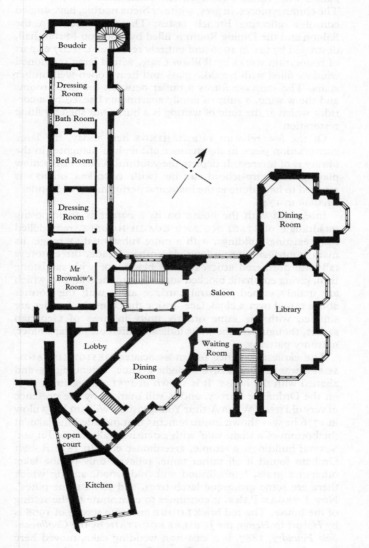

Lurgan Castle.
Plan by K. Mulligan, 2012

Playfair's reaction to the site, and his response to the Picturesque. The walls of the Saloon, decorated by *Hay & Co.* of
Edinburgh, have large panels painted to imitate marble with a
jewelled strapwork frieze, and oddly contrasting *trompe-l'œil*
overdoors in Louis Quatorze style, with classical portraits in
elaborate gilded frames supported by cherubs. The ceiling
here, as in all the main rooms, is flat, with heavily moulded
panels with varied strapwork embellishments and pendants.
The chimneypieces, in grey, white or Siena marble, have angled
consoles reflecting French tastes. The space between the
Saloon and the Dining Room is filled by a big top-lit stair hall,
destroyed by fire in 1996 and entirely recreated *c.* 2007 as part
of restoration works by *William Craig*, with a large mullioned
window filled with heraldic glass and heavy open-well timber
stairs. The staircase forms a buffer between the main rooms
and the W wing, a suite of family apartments backed by a corridor which at the time of writing is a burnt-out shell awaiting
restoration.

Of the few relevant FURNISHINGS here today, the large
conversation piece in the manner of Stephen Slaughter in the
library is of interest. It depicts the youthful William Brownlow
playing the harpsichord, as he (with countless others) is
reputed to have done at the inaugural performance of Handel's
Messiah in 1742.

Integrated with the house on its S corner is an imposing
quadrangle of STABLING AND COACH HOUSES, remodelled
from existing buildings, with a more substantial SE range, its
main front facing SE: a long eleven-bay façade, three storeys
tall with dormered attics, built of blackstone with sandstone
trim, giving emphatic blocked surrounds to the windows which
are mainly sashed. Central carriage arch, with the dormer
above raised over a clock face. Inside the court the façades are
simpler, with the same orderly unity in rows of Georgian
sashes, though here the walls indicate different, perhaps older,
masonry patterns.

The earliest evidence for an associated DESIGNED LAND-
SCAPE was an impressive straight avenue, extending SE and
aligned with the house. It is shown in 1751 and again in 1836
on the Ordnance Survey, and is still marked by the presence
of very old trees. When Arthur Young visited William Brownlow
in 1776 he was shown improvements that included the lake 'at
the bottom of a slight vale' with extensive walks around it and
'several buildings, a temple, greenhouse etc.' In 1836 Robert
Graham found it all rather tame, relieved only by the lake;
otherwise grass, 'embellished with old wood, among which
there are some grotesque larch trees, and some stone pines'.
Now LURGAN PARK, it continues to contribute to the setting
of the house. The red brick LODGE and gate screen of 1908 is
by *Hobart & Heron*; the JUBILEE FOUNTAIN by the *Coalbrookdale Foundry*, 1887, is a cast-iron wedding cake, moved here
from the town centre.

NEIGHBOURHOOD

DERRY LODGE. Lough Road. A low mid-C19 Neoclassical villa sometimes attributed to *Thomas Jackson*. A single-storey astylar design with wall surfaces subtly modelled in stucco: coupled pilasters reinforcing the corners are reduced virtually as shadows to an elegant simplicity under a deep frieze and wide bracketed eaves. Essentially an L-plan block consisting of two long adjoining façades, S and E, with the entrance set well back in a discrete two-bay block at the W of the main S front. Each of the fronts has five bays with large sash windows stretching to the ground, all with unevenly proportioned glazing and plate glass of a kind often found in Jackson's houses. On the S front a wide central breakfront with a shallow bay window; the bay window is repeated in the end bays of the E front and to the W where the entrance block steps back. Inside, off a central top-lit corridor, the elegant sophistication of the exterior gives way to large, bright rooms with ebullient Victorian cornices and roses.

THE DEMESNE. Off Kilmore Road. 1911 by *Young & Mackenzie*. Set in extensive gardens on the edge of Lurgan Golf Course, once part of the demesne of Brownlow House. An attractive Arts and Crafts-inspired house built for Thomas B. Johnston in red brick with red sandstone dressings. Two storeys with attics and substantial diagonal stacks. Broad asymmetrical front of three bays with gabled ends and a large central gable, truncated on one side by a chimneystack where the façade recedes in the end bay. The windows are a mixture of timber and stone mullioned frames with leaded casements. The entrance projects in a wide canted porch with false battlements, mullioned side bays and a Tudor-arched doorway. The side elevations are varied with twin gables and bay windows.

A GARAGE extends from the rear, novel for its time with wide, glazed folding doors. The STABLE in the nearby paddock is a diminutive red brick structure with a central gabled archway and hipped roof.

SOLITUDE. Off Kilmore Road. Now swamped by suburban housing, depriving its name of meaning. A modest two-storey farmhouse with a return, perhaps Georgian, remodelled *c.* 1906 when taller, canted wings were added by *Hobart & Heron* for Frederick W. Bell. This resulted in a long Edwardian façade in terracotta-colour cement render with plate-glass windows: on the first floor these are sashes with segmental heads set in pairs; below, the fenestration is increased with taller windows and irregularly divided upper sashes with coloured glass panels.

ST MICHAEL'S GRAMMAR SCHOOL. Cornakinnegar Road. The former Industrial School for Boys, developed exponentially in the C20 into a sprawling complex of large institutional buildings. The main interest is a discrete two-storey Early Victorian house with a long stuccoed front. The ground floor has channelled rustication with vermiculated quoins and bay windows flanking a tetrastyle Ionic portico; the upper floor has five bays with a cornice and blocking course. Built to an L-plan with a longer six-bay façade to the side, since extended. Additions by *Ashlin & Coleman* are recorded in 1906. The most notable C20 building is a small five-bay CHAPEL, built in pre-cast concrete to imitate rock-faced masonry and competently styled with Romanesque details.

PROVIDENCE HOUSE (former Industrial School for Girls). Across the road. 1890. A large two-storey block in an institutional Gothic style reminiscent of *J. J. McDonnell*. Cement render over red brick with roughcast on the upper floor. The main front has seven bays with a shallow entrance projection at one end and a large projecting gable on the opposite side.

KINNEGOE HOUSE. 3.5 km NW. A two-storey Late Georgian roadside farmhouse with gabled ends. The main front is five bays wide, the rhythm slowed in the centre to reflect a tripartite plan. Though now roughcast with stucco embellishments, it retains twelve-pane Georgian sashes and a timber doorcase with an elliptical webbed fanlight and plain side-lights. Interiors of a mid-Georgian kind with raised and fielded panel joinery, chunky cornices, and in the main room a large centrepiece to the ceiling with scrolled leaves transformed into basket-bearing figures of Plenty.

Small YARD to one side enclosed by vernacular buildings.

8090   MAGHERNACLOY CASTLE   MN
6 km SSE of Carrickmacross

Standing abruptly on a hilltop, watchful over a wide area, this is a rare survivor in a region largely bereft of castles. Essentially a fortified house of two storeys with a basement, like an Irish tower house but lower, with a somewhat Scottish oblong plan and, unusually, a near central stair-tower. Its defensive posture is evident, while not always wholehearted. Maghernacloy was the stronghold of 'Hadsor's fee farm' – half the parish of Magheracloone, granted by the 3rd Earl of Essex in 1618 to 'reconcile the feelings' of John Hadsor of Capoge in Co. Louth whose daughter he had seduced. Presumably built by Hadsor shortly afterwards, the castle was captured in 1643 by Henry Tichborne and confiscated. Later part of the Brownlow estate, it was tenanted throughout the C18. In 1785 Richard Clinton begged in his will that his wife and children should 'live amicably at the castle of Mahernacligh'.

Built of rounded rubble stones, roughcast, with complete battlements, machicoulis, gun loops, and a noticeable taper to the walls, the form of the castle is simple, but for the expressive treatment of the chimneystacks which are carried outside the wall on corbels above ground-floor level. In its arrangement the building is similar to the Z-plan houses of the C17, Scottish in origin, defined by flankers placed on opposing corners. A flanker duly projects at the SE. Its counterpart to the N, given over entirely to a stone stair, occupies a more central position on what was the original entrance front. It stands as a solid structure, largely without windows, with narrow loops tight against the main wall to the E to defend adjoining windows on each storey. Other security devices are found. The original door was at basement level, facing W, in the angle between the stair-tower and the main block, protected by a machicoulis high on the parapet. The treatment of the chimneystacks as machicolations allowed a wall walk behind the high parapets, and an opening in the battlements along the W side of the flanker is well placed to protect the S front, though this may not be of C17 origin. A close parallel with Maghernacloy, geographically and architecturally, was provided by the recent rediscovery of the castle of Newry, built for Sir Nicholas Bagenal, where much the same plan is confirmed by documents of 1568. There the entrance was also in the angle between the stair-tower and the main block, signified by the location of the machicoulis, confirming the arrangement at Maghernacloy.

All defensive concerns were abandoned in the early C18 when the plan was reversed, and the new façade adopted the more benign appearance of a castellated Georgian farmhouse with a new S entrance – a plain round-headed doorway of tooled limestone ashlar. The fenestration was essentially regularized. Probably at the same time, the original stair was demoted, and replaced by a timber dog-leg staircase in the entrance hall; this

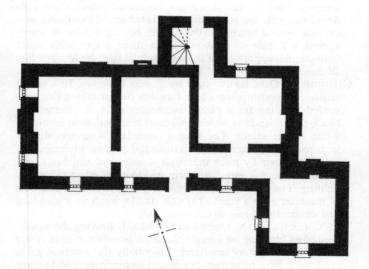

Maghernacloy Castle.
Plan by K. Mulligan, 2012

has since been removed. The w wall was pierced by four large windows, which retain their Georgian sashes on the ground floor; those on the upper floor have since been closed. The remaining windows were renewed to a similar pattern in 2005.

The interior was also extensively remodelled in the C18, although the division of rooms with timber stud-work is a distinctly C17 practice. There are three principal rooms, with the entrance hall at the centre. A masonry wall separates the room to the E, to form a corridor to the S leading to the flanker. Surviving entirely is the original spiral stone stair with generous rough-hewn blocks of limestone that winds irregularly between the storeys from basement to attic. It is reached at each level through archaic arched doorways, essentially medieval in style. In 2005 the castle was heroically made habitable again, having fallen into ruin in the C20.

9060

MAGHERY   AH

A small settlement on the S shore of Lough Neagh.

ST MARY. Forsaken but happily retained. A dinky hall and tower closing an impressive vista on the S approach to the village. Built in 1840 by the Rev. John Keating, and recorded on a plaque similar to the one on Keating's later church at Collegelands (Charlemont). Rubble with dressed quoins and strings. Three-bay nave, the walls boldly rendered with wide recessed lines to imitate shallow rusticated ashlar. Plain rendered chancel, the roof with sprocketed eaves extending to a catslide over a vestry on the S side. Stocky square W tower against a kneelered gable rising in three stages with squat battlements; apparently it is later, built in 1927 by *Michael Fay & Sons*.

CHURCH OF OUR LADY. 1977 by *Patrick Haughey*. In a sea of tarmac. The visitor would be forgiven for mistaking this flat-roofed building for a public swimming pool. A strange low block that abandons all ecclesiastical convention in favour of a C20 leisure idiom. The plan is essentially a square, shaped with rounded corners. Any merit in the original intention has been let down by poor materials – industrial red brick and metal cladding – with high strip windows to effect clerestory lighting. The contractors were *Bradley & McElhatton*. The best of the interior is a reset STAINED GLASS window, a standard C19 design by *Mayer & Co*.

THE CHIMNEYS. On Derrywarragh Island. Braving the south-westerlies blowing on Lough Neagh, a tottering rubble tower isolated on a grassy headland. Essentially the external gable stack of a long forgotten C17 house, sometimes said to have been an O'Connor or an O'Neill stronghold, though the land had been granted to Sir Toby Caulfeild in 1607. The walls are coarsely built with fieldstone and a good deal of red sandstone, gradually diminished in stages and once finished with ornamental brickwork, shaped not unlike the chimneys of Charlemont Fort, but now reduced to just a few suggestive stumps. The stack gathers three flues and so suggests this was once a three-storey structure. Now chiefly remarkable for its tenacious survival and the light it sheds on chimney construction.

ST ANDREW, MILLTOWN PARISH CHURCH (C of I). I km SE. A small rural parish church with a striking battlemented tower. The building began as one of *William Farrell*'s single-cell designs similar to Clare, with nave and chancel and the entrance in a large recessed arch in the W gable. Built in 1839 and twice enlarged, first in the mid C19 with the addition of a transept and vestry on the S side. The slender tower was probably added at the same time, and its upper stage was added or rebuilt in the early C20. The lower stages are of rubble, changing to roughcast with stucco trim at belfry stage before finishing with steep Irish battlements, machicolated in the centre. As first built the roughcast nave had just two bays with plain lancets and three graded lights to the E. The additions, probably by *Joseph Welland*, are in blackstone rubble with larger quarry-glazed lancets in dressed stone frames. Inside, the two main phases are evident, with Farrell's iron trusses giving way to heavy intersecting kingposts. – STAINED GLASS. E window c. 1920, attributed to *Joshua Clarke & Sons*, Dublin. The remainder are C20, the best signed *W. F. Clokey*, the remainder cartoon-like designs by *Caldermac* and *Campbell Glass Studio*.

BALLYNARRY METHODIST CHURCH. 3 km SSE. 1874. A small, effortless church design of just two bays. Cement-rendered with raised quoins, a porch, steep gables and triangular-headed windows.

DERRYLEE METHODIST CHURCH. 2 km SW. In a railed enclosure at a road junction. Small roughcast hall of three bays with round-headed windows and a tiny porch, present here in 1837.

CLONMORE CHURCH. 5 km SW. A trim C19 lancet hall with an offset gabled porch. Roughcast with heavy stucco trim. Interior plain with timber panelled ceiling, W gallery, *Minton*-tiled floors and coloured glass by *Clokey*, Belfast.

MARKETHILL

A small market town developed by the Achesons on the edge of Gosford Castle demesne (q.v.). Henry Acheson was granted land in the district in 1610 and with his brother, Sir Archibald, who succeeded him in 1628, laid the foundations for the town. In 1664 Markethill was an established hamlet of five houses, growing within thirty years to a more substantial settlement with more than fifty houses aligned on the street that labours steeply to the top of the hill that gives the place its name. Markethill continued to develop in the c18 and c19 but today it remains essentially a small Georgian town, with many good town houses. Most are on the Main Street, substantial in size with five bays, either rendered or in blackstone, with a variety of fanlit doorcases; regrettably the best are derelict at the time of writing.

CHAPEL OF EASE (C of I). Main Street. 1859. It looks more Georgian. A modest T-plan church with a plain, pedimented frontispiece with a bellcote placed between rather two-dimen-sional-looking porches. Built as a gift by the rector, Lord John de la Poer Beresford, around the time when he succeeded his brother as Marquess of Waterford. Along the street, nice railed walls with ashlar piers and ball finials.

FIRST PRESBYTERIAN CHURCH. Fairgreen Road. 1899. A large Gothic church in squared rock-faced limestone with vivid red brick trim. The straightforward plan consists of a five-bay hall with lancets, polygonal chancel and unfinished offset tower. The main gable has three graded lights framed between stepped buttresses. Inside rather plain, with an expansive tim-ber-panelled ceiling and exposed hammerbeam trusses. – MONUMENT. In the porch, a large aedicular First World War memorial signed *W. Lendrum*, Clones.

METHODIST CHURCH. Keady Street. A charming hall church of Late Georgian appearance, in coursed blackstone with three large round-headed windows with multiple glazing bars; entrance in the plainly pedimented w gable; twin windows to the E. Interior remodelled in 1860 by *W. J. Barre*.

SECOND PRESBYTERIAN CHURCH. Water Lane, off Newry Street. 1956. A small four-bay hall and porch, replacing a church of 1769. Roughcast with blocked quoins. The round-headed windows have stained glass in bronze frames.

COURTHOUSE (former). Main Street. 1842 by *Thomas Duff*. A large two-storey cruciform block with bulky proportions in coursed blackstone and Armagh limestone. Three-bay front with the central bay deeply advanced and pedimented. Behind the pediment an octagonal domed cupola sits at the centre of the roof. The first floor is treated as a *piano nobile* with large Georgian sashes in plain reveals and tripartite frames in the centre and side elevations. The sills form a continuous plat-band above the squat ground floor. There the end bays are blind with small recessed panels; more elaborate bracketed entablatures to the windows in the sides of the projecting bay denote the original doorways. Closed in 1952, and renovated in 1999 by *Consarc*, who transformed the old entrances into windows and formed a new entrance to the front out of a long window opening; it carries an awkward entablature on brackets illiterately interpreted from the details of Duff's original entrances. Also part of these works is a flat-roofed annexe to one side, faced in stone with a cedar-clad oriel providing a weak Modernist statement.

ALEXANDER'S (former MARKET HOUSE). Keady Street. An imposing three-storey block in the style of *Thomas Duff* and showing the same broad proportions evident in the Courthouse, with three bays and a wide advanced and pedimented central bay. Dark rubble walls with Armagh limestone dressings. Gable-ended, the gables given pediments in the same manner as the front, with a blind oculus. The entrance is a wide elliptical archway, now with a poorly detailed glazed door. More gruesome alterations include enlarged rectangular openings with plastic windows and cement-render aprons; the projecting slate-roofed canopies of the ground-floor shopfronts equally detract.

NORTHERN BANK. Main Street. A tall, unremarkable block of two storeys and three bays with gabled ends, the massing unchanged since its depiction in a sketch of the street by Cornelius Varley in 1808. Rendered, with segmental-headed windows, replacement red brick stacks, and a late C20 flat-roofed porch lying asymmetrically across the front.

PEMBROKE HOUSE. Main Street. An attractive end-of-terrace Late Georgian house in blackstone rubble. Two storeys with an attic and a partially slate-clad gable. The entrance front has three bays with large Georgian sashes in flush frames and a handsome doorcase with engaged Ionic columns and webbed fanlight.

The architecture bleeds into two more modest houses to the N which are symmetrically arranged with smaller sashes and a shared central carriage arch.

See also GOSFORD CASTLE, p. 344.

NEIGHBOURHOOD

MULLAGHBRACK HOUSE. 3 km N. A handsome former rectory, built in 1829 for the Rev. Samuel Blacker. A large three-storey-over-basement block with a low hipped roof oversailing on bracketed eaves. The main front has three bays, the central bay slightly advanced and given all the architectural emphasis, with ashlar quoins, wide tripartite windows in blocked reveals, and a handsome doorcase in crisp Armagh limestone with four leaded geometric side-lights. The doorcase projects from a wide recessed elliptical arch of the kind associated with *Thomas Duff*, with an entablature and blocking course supported on pilasters with plain consoles.

ST JAMES, MULLAGHBRACK. 2.5 km NW. A T-plan church, originally with quarry glazing and stepped gables, replaced after 1870 with plain lancets and straight gables with decorative bargeboards. Discreet repairs by *W. H. Byrne & Son* in 1923, including a shallow sanctuary with three graded lights. The nicest feature is the unusual Art Nouveau gutter hoppers in the angles of the building. Since then ugly concrete porches have been added to the gables. Inside, a large space with W gallery and an elaborate timber-panelled roof with exposed kingposts. – The ALTAR is a fine solid work in brown marble.

ST JOHN, MULLAGHBRACK (C of I). 3 km NNW. On a site where there has been a church since at least 1608. The present tower of 1814, probably by *John Bowden*, was added to an older nave, itself a late C18 rebuilding of a structure found out of repair in 1657. Trebled in size in 1830, when the nave and tower were flanked by large three-bay aisles with hipped roofs, hooded lancets and timber Y-tracery; at the w end, mullioned Tudor windows with hoods over pointed doorways. The tower rises in three stages from a splayed plinth of Armagh marble; emphatic moulded string-courses define the short middle stage; stepped battlements between corner pinnacles on the upper stage.

Inside, the nave is opened up with tall clustered colonnettes rising close to the ceiling with elided capitals supporting rather flat and plain Tudor arches. A raking gallery runs through nave and aisles at the w end. Altogether an attractive space with box pews, most notable for its collection of monuments. – STAINED GLASS. Four-light E window: the Ascension, 1936. Tower: a simple early C21 work by *Calderwood Glass*. – MONUMENTS. The best are in the sanctuary: on the S wall a large and naïve Jacobean work of 1638 with a plain pediment bearing aloft ball finials and the Hamilton arms between scrolled supports. – Opposite, Sir Arthur Acheson †1749; an elaborate stele inset with a fine bust by *Jan van Nost the Younger*. – Adam Bell †1775; a small lugged tablet, signed *C. W. Harrison & Sons*, Dublin. – The Rev. John Jones †1790; a Neoclassical urn with swags and classical figures in low relief, by *John Bacon the Elder*, 1794. – Lieutenant George Lambert V.C. †1860, by *Edwin Smith*, Sheffield. – Margaret Wann †1877; a plain marble tablet. – N aisle: James Walkinshaw Bell †1841; a large white marble tablet topped by a weeping willow and urn. – Martha Lina Boyd †1842; a Neoclassical funerary urn in an aedicular frame, signed *J. Johnston*, Belfast. – S aisle: the 2nd Earl of Gosford †1849 is commemorated by the Acheson Memorial, by *David McCullough* of Armagh, 1867, an exceptionally fine arcaded Romanesque monument worthy of the builder of Gosford Castle. – The Rev. John Henry Potts †1835; marble stele surmounted by an urn. – Jane McAnally †1887; a plain tablet, signed *J. McCullough*, Armagh. – Elizabeth Margary Blacker †1836; a plain tablet. – The Rev. John Gibson †1867; an ornate Neoclassical tablet by *J. McCullough*, Armagh.

DRUMFERGUS. 3 km NNW. A handsome two-storey Victorian farmhouse. Gable-ended with three bays, plate glass in the windows, and a wide doorway with a depressed arch filled with a spoked fanlight, side-lights and engaged columns.

REDROCK PRESBYTERIAN CHURCH. 4 km W. 1861. Bulky lancet hall. Roughcast with four bays and three graded lights in the entrance gable. Renovated in 1932 by *Hobart & Heron*.

MEIGH

A small crossroads town lying in the shadow of Slieve Gullion.

St Luke (C of I). Forkhill Road. Derelict. 1831 by *William Farrell*. A variation of the design for the churches of Clontibret and Munterconnaught (Virginia). A small three-bay hall with Farrell's familiar pinnacled belfry and deep battlemented porch. The walls are roughcast with dressings of Mourne granite, nicely displayed in the solid pinnacle-topped buttresses framing the entrance gable and porch. The windows are plain lancets with hoodmoulds, made impossibly slender on either side of the porch. Inside, the roof is supported on exposed cast-iron trusses.

Close by (s), the former RECTORY is a small Late Victorian house, picturesquely designed with an asymmetrical front. The asymmetry is set by the windows, varied in size and irregularly disposed, and a two-storey gabled end bay with the ground-floor bay window projected under a lean-to roof. The walls are roughcast with timber-mullioned windows in blocked surrounds with hoodmoulds. A timber Gothic porch is offset between the gable and the tall staircase window.

St Joseph. Camlough Road. A large cruciform church of 1852 in squared limestone with dressed trim. A compact and understated Gothic design with tall gables and short transepts. The entrance is a modest arched opening under a narrow Perp window with lithesome timber tracery. Long low vestry, extending from the s transept, part of additions and alterations of 1905 by *Ashlin & Coleman*. Inside, plain with a segmental vault divided into square compartments.

Heath Hall. 3 km NE. Ruinous. This was a plain two-storey Georgian house with a seven-bay front in which the three central bays were canted. The property was sold by Thomas Seaver in 1853 when he emigrated to Australia. His son, Jonathan Seaver, a civil engineer and adventurer, restored the property to the family before 1896 and employed his architect cousin *Henry Seaver* of Belfast to design a tall entrance tower in place of the old canted front to celebrate the return of his ageing father, who died in 1900. Stranded amidst slatted sheds, the ruined tower is square in plan, in three stages with a corner bartizan and machicolated battlements. The walls and details are cement-rendered, with the windows of the upper stages set in recessed panels; the granite doorcase with its wide elliptical fanlight comes from the old entrance.

Ballymacdermot Megalithic Tomb. 4 km NE. A court tomb of the Neolithic period, sited on a raised plateau projecting from the s slope of Ballymacdermot mountain. Originally a large wedge-shaped cairn formed with a circular entrance court to the N, the orthostats now standing exposed like teeth from a great skeletal jaw. The entrance leads to three small spaces, roughly oval in shape, arranged in sequence with a smaller antechamber leading directly to two larger burial chambers. The chambers originally had corbelled stone roofs, and the lower course of granite slabs partly survives to the W.

CHURCH OF THE SACRED HEART, CLOGHOGUE. 4.5 km NE. Designed in 1911 by *Ashlin & Coleman*. Dedicated on Easter Day 1916. A prominent basilican church, the tower with its signal copper-clad dome visible from afar, offering a touch of Eastern exotica to the Forkhill roundabout. The design is more overtly Lombardic than Hiberno-Romanesque, vigorously textured in rock-faced Mourne granite with nave, aisle and offset tower. The entrance gable is studiously recessed with a large multiple-foiled rose window above a row of blind arcading; the eaves here and on the N aisle have an expressive corbel table. The tower dominates, with angle buttresses framing the tall lower stage where a statue of Christ is set in a discordant Gothic canopy above three graded lights. The belfry stage is arcaded on stocky columns with scalloped capitals and finished with a flourish in the ogee dome, its surface bristling with fish-scales and ridge crockets.

Inside, the nave arcade has five round-headed arches in Caen stone on clustered piers of Portland stone with scalloped capitals. In the spandrels paired shafts rise up between the triple clerestory windows to support ribs crossing a panelled barrel-vault. The aisles terminate in side chapels that open off the chancel through twin arches on paired shafts of grey polished granite. The chancel and chapels are covered in gold mosaic in an opulent Byzantine manner, perhaps by *Oppenheimer*. – Elaborate HIGH ALTAR adorned with angels gracefully in prayer. – STAINED GLASS. Coloured figurative glass in the manner of *Mayer & Co.*, with dark tones.

The PAROCHIAL HOUSE to the N is also by *Ashlin & Coleman*, a gabled block in rock-faced granite, plainly detailed with plate-glass windows.

ST MICHAEL, KILLEAN. 3.5 km E. A large church in local granite, unusually sophisticated for its isolated location. The plan is cruciform – an aisleless lancet hall with unusual gabled transepts set in parallel and almost independent of the side walls. The entrance gable has stepped clasping buttresses with pinnacles, bellcote and a small porch, gabled on three sides, all in ashlar. The windows here and in E gable have very slender timber tracery, Perp in style. Inside, a six-bay nave opens to the transepts through two pointed arches on limestone shafts with bell capitals. Four-centred chancel arch with hoodmould. Open timber roof, principally of arched and braced trusses, with kingposts changing to hammerbeams over the E end.

CLONTYGORA MEGALITHIC TOMB. 5 km SE. The impressive remains of a large Neolithic court tomb. Imposing megaliths form a deep U-shaped forecourt with traces of three burial chambers behind, the first with a massive capstone. Finds of flint arrowheads and a polished axe and evidence of cremated burial are more meagre traces of this early farming society.

HAWTHORN HILL. 1.75 km SW, in Slieve Gullion Forest Park, Annahaia. A handsome two-storey Regency box on a basement, built in 1815 for Hunter W. Chambre. Roughcast with an irregular two-bay front; the offset entrance bay is slightly advanced, with a large round-headed doorway inset with engaged Tuscan columns and above this a tripartite window. In the adjoining bay the ground-floor window is set within an elliptical relieving arch – an arrangement repeated on the symmetrical side and rear elevations.

To the N a decent quadrangular STABLEYARD with quarry-glazed casements adjoins the walled garden, managed as part of the Forest Park. The GATE LODGE, opposite a simple gate sweep, is a delightful small building in snecked granite, of three bays with rich geometric-patterned iron windows and a high pyramid roof rising to a central stack.

KILLEVY CASTLE, later BELL'S CASTLE. 1 km W. A delightful toy castle rising above a castellated terrace against the wooded slopes of Slieve Gullion. In both architecture and picturesque effect the design recalls Charles Augustus Busby's dramatic Gwrych Castle near Abergele in Wales. The building began as a small late C18 villa with two storeys over a basement, a three-bay front, and a central bowed projection to the rear. This was remodelled in 1836 by *George Papworth*, who did little more than dress it up for Powell Foxall. Even if the design was constrained by the existing house and failed to extend across the rear façade (probably because of Foxall's finances), a lot has been achieved in a small compass: by the addition of an entrance tower, corner turrets, string-courses, battlements, attenuated slits, flat label mouldings and mullioned windows, what was effectively a decent farmhouse has been impressively transformed. This began with the addition of towers to the corners – a slightly enlarged square tower with Irish battlements on the SW corner, and opposite, on the NW corner, a stout and tall circular turret that rises well above the roof-line. With a small conservatory to the S (since removed), these were the only conscious efforts to suppress the underlying symmetry. On the main front Papworth placed similar square turrets at either end, varied in fenestration only slightly, with a canted entrance tower in the centre. On the ground floor, between the towers, the wall was brought forward and opened up with wide Tudor arches in which the existing windows were deeply recessed; overhead, the walls are battlemented to form terraces outside the first-floor windows. The tall narrow doorway is flanked by stepped buttresses, the door an ornate Gothic design bristling with studs and set under a Tudor arch and a machicolated bay window with three round lancets. The Foxall arms are displayed in Roman cement on the upper stage. Here the battlements are cleverly extended rearward, projecting slightly to align with, and disguise, the stacks of the C18 house – a successful trick were it not openly exposed on the rear elevation, where its neat bowed projection and hipped roof remain unembellished between the two varied towers. There is little dressed stonework in the design, and Papworth's additions are distinguished from the rubble of the C18 work by rough ashlar blocks – of limestone rather than the local granite – with wide uneven joints. On the side elevations, presumably as an economy, he concealed the old wall by replicating the newer pattern in stucco, using a composition render, as he had done at Headford (Co. Galway) in 1829.

The plan is straightforward, originally a tripartite arrangement with the hall leading directly into the bowed drawing room with rooms on either side. In 1852 the rooms were named as 'a parlour, with a wine cellar and store-room, adjoining a drawing room, with library and conservatory attached; also a study and office'. The plan has since been altered to provide just two principal rooms. The library extends from front to rear on the S side. The dog-leg stairs lie directly off the hall in the NE corner, with the room behind to the W opened up to the drawing room.

The TERRACE forming an arc at the front is an impressive battlemented structure with miniature bartizans raised on high buttressed walls overlooking the ornamental CANAL. To the S, in a small enclosed farmyard, the STABLES, a neat roughcast block of late C18 appearance with an advanced and gabled central bay. In 1881 the property was acquired by Joseph Bell and thereafter known as Bell's Castle.

KILLEVY OLD CHURCHES. 2 km NNW. The remains of an important early Irish nunnery sheltered in a tree-lined enclosure at the foot of the E slopes of Slieve Gullion. The name Killevy, from the Irish *Cill Sléibhe Cuilinn*, 'the church of Slieve Gullion', indicates an early foundation. There is confusion surrounding its founding abbess, known variously as St Darerca, St Monnena, and locally as Blinne; she died in 518. The early house was plundered at least twice by the Vikings, last in 923, but fully recovered to serve as a convent under Augustinian rule until suppressed in 1542, when its last abbess is recorded as Alicia O'Hanlon.

What survives, though ruined, remains impressive: it consists of one very long gabled range – approximately 112 ft (34 m) in extent – which is in fact the remains of two independent churches. The western church is smaller and earlier, mostly of C12 construction, though its architectural significance lies in an earlier, pre-Romanesque trabeated W doorway, neatly constructed of large squared blocks with a cyclopean granite lintel suggesting an origin in the C10 or C11. In the E gable a small Romanesque light pierces the wall, featureless but for an external concave rebate. The later, eastern, church shares the E gable of the older building, but no communication exists between the two. The walls are constructed of rubble, battered at the base, with a later date indicated by the use of dressed quoins and copings on its own E gable. Here a pointed window indicates the C15: now much decayed and without mullions, its carved jambs remain and each impost block has a crowned head in a late medieval style. Offset on the S wall is a simple lintelled doorway.

Outside the SW corner of the older church the low footings of a rectilinear building are evident, and in the same area the base of the round tower, known to have collapsed in 1768, was uncovered during repairs in 1907.

MIDDLETOWN AH 7030

A small crossroads town midway between Armagh and Monaghan, developed under the benefaction of Dr Sterne, Bishop of Clogher, who bequeathed the existing village and surrounding lands to a charitable trust in 1772. From 1829 the Trustees began to erect public buildings that included a fever hospital, dispensary and market house. In 1837 there were 187 houses in Middletown, all 'large and well-built'. At the W end of the Main Street, an attractive two-storey house demonstrates the town's original architectural character: it is a brave end-of-terrace survivor (and only just), with three bays, Georgian sashes, and a handsome recessed fanlit doorway with engaged Tuscan columns.

ST JOHN, MIDDLETOWN PARISH CHURCH (C of I). In a field at the end of Church Street. 1793. A charming small hall-and-tower type, unusually with the battlemented tower only slightly advanced on the W gable, breaking through it in three short stages. Roughcast with sparse stone dressings, three bays and timber Y-tracery. Original entrance in the tower with Georgian Gothick fanlight, replaced in the C19 with a plain pointed doorway to the N. Inside, a neat space with exposed kingposts; the gallery of 1833 was refronted by *J. F. Fuller* as part of refurbishment with new fittings in 1893. The contractor was *Mr Dunwoody*. – STAINED GLASS. E window: 'Blessed are the pure in heart' by *Jones & Willis*, 1905. – MONUMENTS. Numerous marble tablets, the best of these Hugh Harris †1840; a large white marble tablet with an angel supported by mourning cherubs, by *T. Lawrence*, Dublin. – Alexander Cross †1842; a weeping figure crouched beside an urn. – Hugh Harris †1904; a plain scroll, by *C. W. Harrison & Sons*, Dublin.

MIDDLETOWN PRESBYTERIAN CHURCH. Church Street. 1829, for a congregation formed in 1826. A plain hall of three bays with a wide gabled front. Partially roughcast with walls of coursed limestone, red brick dressings and round-headed windows. Equally plain interior with box pews.

ST LOUIS CONVENT. Off Church Street. A large Late Victorian complex with austere institutional buildings in red Coalisland brick. The main building incorporates an existing house, formerly known as Fee Farm House, which was acquired by the St Louis Sisters of Monaghan in the 1870s. The roughcast and whitewashed farm buildings survive to form an attractive small court behind the convent. The proportions of the old house are perhaps still represented in the three-bay gable-ended block, which was entirely encased in red brick, relieved only by stone string-courses – the finely moulded eaves course was probably reused – and windows set in pairs with plain sashes. The plan is a standard tripartite one, the rooms plainly finished with some surviving Late Georgian joinery; in the inner hall the inner doorway with an arched petalled fanlight marks the old entrance. Also added to the house were a battlemented porch, dormers and slender brick stacks; the building was extended asymmetrically with a gabled two-bay projection to the E and, adjoining it, a lower recessed section connecting with the CHAPEL of c. 1900. This is the best element, a five-bay hall with lancets under hoods and a polygonal chancel which is presented on the main convent frontage, the reverse of the more familiar arrangement where the entrance gable is displayed here; to the S, the chapel's gabled entrance front has a bellcote and plain Geometric tracery. The interior is an atmospheric space with a panelled wagon roof, the walls and ceiling richly stencilled with *Pugin*-inspired decoration. – ALTAR FURNITURE by *Pearse & Son*. – STAINED GLASS. Colourful figurative windows by *Mayer & Co.*, Munich.

To the N, the former INDUSTRIAL SCHOOLS of 1876 are in the same idiom yet plainer, with two large two-storey gabled blocks joined by a recessed entrance link with twin Gothic arches. Refectory of 1930 by *Hugh Lamont*.

MARKET HOUSE. The Diamond. 1829. A handsome if chaste building with a two-storey, four-bay front of limestone ashlar, the two central bays recessed. The ground floor has wide segmental arches, originally open in the centre, with doorways set in the outer bays. Built to accommodate a courthouse in the upper storey. According to a plaque it was 'Erected by the trustees of Bishop Sterne's Charities'. No trace of the clock and cupola recorded in 1837. The building is flanked by handsome GATEWAYS with stout piers and wrought-iron gates.

MONUMENT. Opposite the Market House. A small sandstone obelisk, now truncated, erected to David Smith M.D., Superintendent of the Fever Hospital, who succumbed in 1847 to an occupational hazard 'at the commencement of the fatal epidemic of this season' – cholera.

ELIZABETHAN HOUSE (former FEVER HOSPITAL). Main Street. A neat two-storey C19 building labouring under a misnomer. In roughcast with dressed stone trim, the windows in blocked surrounds with voussoir arches and mostly retaining attractive Georgian sashes. The Fever Hospital was built by Bishop Sterne's Trustees in 1834 with four wards to accommodate sixteen patients; the building was later converted to an elementary school, and is now in part a residence. The irregular plan comprises a T-plan residential block with two bays to the front and a long four-bay ward range set at right angles. The latter became the classroom block; its interior remains untouched. A handsome pedimented GATEWAY in ashlar stands before a small yard formed in the angle to the NE.

DISTILLERY (former). Main Street. 1831. A large three-storey vernacular building with rubble walls and red brick dressings lying to the s at the w end of the street, derelict and overgrown at the time of writing. It was established by Matthew Johnston, produced 80,000 gallons of whiskey annually, and promoted grain markets in the town. Lower annexes in advanced ruin.

WESTPORT HOUSE. Main Street. A Late Victorian two-storey house in red brick with rusticated quoins; three-bay front with bay windows on the ground floor. Built by Matthew Burke J.P., whose initials ornament an attractive pedestrian gate.

NEIGHBOURHOOD

ST JOHN, ASHFORT. 1 km SE of the Armagh Road. Hidden in the generous folds of grassy drumlins, a large pre-Emancipation barn church of 1826 with a tower of 1857 projecting from the centre of the long N wall. The hall has four well-spaced bays in rubble with red brick surrounds to wide round-headed windows. The tower has three stages in pale squared limestone, with cutstone dressings and a battlemented upper stage. The odd relationship between the hall and tower, once unified with render, has been exacerbated by a harsh refurbishment in 1994 by *Dennis O'Neill* which leaves the incongruous stonework exposed with raised pointing bulging across the surface like veins. Interior completely reordered and refitted with ugly, ill-proportioned timber windows. To these works a plaque on the tower now proclaims an unwitting aesthetic truth: 'How terrible is this place'; the remainder, 'This is no other but the house of God and the gate of heaven', the date 1826; a further inscription dated 1843 was to the memory of the Rev. Bernard J. Loughran, whose name has long been erased from the stone.

PORTNELLIGAN. 2.25 km SE. A vernacular Georgian farmhouse on a hilltop beside Doogary Lough. A long two-storey roughcast range with gabled ends and four large and unwieldy late C19 brick stacks. The front has seven bays, irregularly spaced, though the windows are nicely proportioned, with later horizontal glazing bars and plate glass. The doorway is off-centre under a matchstick-like porch with fluted cast-iron columns supporting a thin flat shelf; the entrance was apparently moved here in the C19. The former doorway at the other end is marked by a damaged plaque with an erased cross and part of an C18 date and the inscription 'Haec Domus Construct . . . Cross', possibly a reference to Richard Cross, who acquired the land here in 1731. Inside, just one room deep, accessed from a corridor across the front; good mid-Georgian joinery with raised and fielded panels. Between 1775 and 1842 this was the seat of Alexander Cross. His son-in-law Thomas J. Tenison must have been in mind to rebuild, having obtained designs from his kinsman *F. Cross*, who in 1848 exhibited at the Royal Academy designs for a villa here at Portnelligan.

Behind the house are various modest vernacular FARM
BUILDINGS, one bearing the date 1857 and on the gable a
fragment of a medieval hoodmould with a primitive terminal
head. Close to the house, beside traces of former terraced
gardens, is an unusual GARDEN MONUMENT; in effect a miniature medieval village cross, it is essentially an assemblage of
architectural fragments composed of a church pinnacle with
an elaborate foliated top rising from a stone crisply inscribed
with the date 1774; the base plinth is faced with a heraldic
plaque.

The Middletown LODGE is a neat symmetrical single-storey
brick building of three bays with paired sashes and a steep
hipped roof with central diagonal stacks.

CREEVEKEERAN CASTLE. 3.5 km SE. A gaunt and perilous
castle ruin encircled by a late C19 beech plantation. Originally
a keep of at least three storeys, now reduced to one shapeless
wall with traces of first-floor barrel-vaulting, mural passages
and musket loops.

BONDIVILLE. 2 km NNW. A chaste two-storey Late Georgian
house in squared limestone with a low hipped roof. The front
has three bays, the entrance now obscured by a boxy early C20
porch. Internally quite plain, to a tripartite plan, the stairs
opening off the hall through an arched doorway with an elaborate webbed fanlight. Modest Neoclassical cornices and roses
in the main rooms. Eponymously named after Edward Bond
acquired the property from John Hamilton in 1708; in the early
C19 the residence of H. C. Bond.

MILFORD   AH
2 km SW of Armagh

A red brick mill town founded by the weaving firm of Messrs
Robert McCrum & Co. (after 1886 McCrum, Watson & Mercer).
In 1808 William McCrum established a linen mill here on the
River Callan, which was greatly expanded throughout the C19 by
his son, Robert Garmany McCrum. In 1850 the mills began
weaving damasks, of which they became one of the most substantial producers. Nothing of the once extensive manufacturing
process remains today; the last of the mills were demolished in
1996 and only the orderly two-storey terraces of back-to-back
houses, occasionally varied with yellow-brick trimming, remind
one of its industrial importance. The only buildings of any real
prominence now are at the centre of the main street, Hill Street:
two semi-detached early C19 houses, then the OLD SCHOOL-
HOUSE, in a cottage style with steeply gabled end bays and a
veranda between, and CALLAN HOUSE opposite, of 1913 by
James St John Phillips, built as an assembly hall; a substantial
two-storey, five-bay block in red-and-yellow brick, with a gabled
centre bay and a rather flat Ionic sandstone doorcase.

MANOR HOUSE (MILFORD HOUSE). Immediately s of the village, off Ballyards Road. An early C19 house, enlarged and remodelled into a sprawling Italianate mansion in 1880 by *Young & Mackenzie*, who as a novelty for the time employed mass concrete on a large scale. Two storeys with extensive stucco enrichments and plate-glass windows. The main front is asymmetrical with six bays, the end bay advanced, and formerly with an elaborate cast-iron *porte cochère* at the entrance; tall sashes on the ground floor set in channelled rustication between clasping pilasters, and a deep entablature between the storeys with a dentil cornice. Segmental-headed windows with moulded hoods and keystones on the first floor, below a bracketed eaves cornice and solid blocking course, concealing the low hipped roof. Round the s side a more extensive, equally varied garden front punctuated by three projecting elements: three bays under a pediment to the w, then a single-storey bowed projection in the centre, and finally a bulky two-storey canted bay, set back by one bay from the E end. Also in 1880 *William Fraser Haldene* laid out formal Victorian gardens here with parterres and a fountain; a large polygonal conservatory was built among the parterres, linked to the house by a lower range. In institutional use 1936–87, acquired by Armagh District Council in 1996 and sold in 2002; derelict at the time of writing.

ROSEBROOK HOUSE. 1.5 km NW. A small venerable house, with a modest villa-like front. Traditionally dated to 1733, built as a manse for the Rev. John Maxwell, and despite the early C19 appearance of the front there is no reason to doubt the underlying antiquity of the L-plan block. Single-storey three-bay front in smooth render with a trim low-gabled porch, the surfaces nicely delineated with shallow recession and restrained Neoclassical mouldings below the gable. The side bays have tall tripartite sashes with gentle cambers to the heads and a plain hoodmould that droops down on either side of the window. Keener interest is roused by the diagonal stacks which follow the C17 manner, and round the sides and back where the walls are roughcast with narrow early sashes in flush frames.

SUMMER HILL HOUSE. 2.5 km NW. A long single-storey Regency house of five bays with a central gabled porch on solid-looking Tuscan columns in timber. Roughcast with rusticated stone quoins and square-headed windows, tightly set in shallow recesses with big sashes and marginal glazing. In the porch an imposing segmental-headed doorcase with engaged Tuscan columns and pilasters, side-lights, and a big leaded fanlight.

MILLTOWN CN 3010

A quiet street village 4.5 km SSW of Belturbet.

ST PATRICK. 1868 by *William Hague*. A gaunt church, all angles, with a tall belfry on the narrow gable-fronted nave, tapering upwards with kneelers and offsets and flanked by lean-to aisles. The severity of the composition is greatly eased by the big rose window with cusped petals. At the w end the chancel steps down, and is narrow enough to allow circular windows with plate tracery on either side. The materials are rubble and dressed limestone, blended with Hague's favoured yellow brick, here matched with pale sandstone around the windows. The contractor was *Hugh Kelly* of Granard. Inside, a lighter touch with nave and aisles separated by tall arcades, supported on lithesome shafts with tame foliated capitals. A panelled wagon roof, interrupted by unbraced arched trusses carried on tiny polished shafts in the spandrels of the arcade. Chancel disappointingly plain. Repairs made in 1935 by *James Donnelly*. – STAINED GLASS. Three-light e window: the Crucifixion, by *Harry Clarke Studios*, 1938, with all the piercing blues that distinguish the artist's work.

KILLICAR LODGE. 2.5 km NW. A modestly proportioned Late Georgian gable-ended house, of two storeys and three bays, with generous twelve-pane sashes and a plain round-headed doorway. Lower two-storey wing set back on one side with a later single-storey wing opposite. In 1865 the residence of Arthur Nesbitt.

ST COLUMBA, DRUMLANE PARISH CHURCH (C of I). 3 km NW. A modest hall-and-tower design of 1819 by *John Bowden*, for which he received payment in 1820. A forestanding tower in three stages with a tall battlemented belfry; nave of three bays with pretty cusped twin windows in timber with bold hoodmoulds. Roughcast and dressed limestone. Enlarged *c.* 1863 by *Welland & Gillespie* with a bulky, steep-roofed s transept and small gabled vestry, built of squared limestone, so that by contrast they appear overweening. Here the windows have reticulated tracery. The contractor was *William Hague Sen.* Inside plain, with a w gallery and a Victorian roof of kingposts with strange cusping to the rafters. – STAINED GLASS. e window, central lancet: Mary washing the feet of Christ, by *William Wailes*, *c.* 1880, brought in 1964 from Monivea, Co. Galway. – MONUMENTS. John Moutray Jones †1835; a gabled tablet with acroteria and a snake eating its tail. – The Rev. George Moffatt †1874; a simple white marble pylon, by *Coates*, Dublin.

ASHGROVE HOUSE. 3 km E. A handsome Georgian villa. Now rather exposed, its site bereft of the fine planting that had grown up around the building and gifted it its name. Apparently the site of an early C17 bawn built by the Bakers. The present house, a well-proportioned block of two storeys on a deep plinth with a hipped roof and stout stacks, perfectly characterizes provincial Georgian classicism of the 1760s. Roughcast and quoinless, the main front has three well-spaced bays, nicely diminished on the first floor and with all the emphasis given to the central bay in a typical mid-C18 way: an unadorned Venetian window over a similar fanlit doorcase in a boldly blocked surround. Windows all now cruelly disfigured by plastic frames. The Venetian motif reappears as blind windows, set high in the side elevations.

The former STABLE BLOCK extends on one side, screened from the front as a blind arcade with rounded buttresses.

MONAGHAN

6030

INTRODUCTION

Monaghan is a large market town set among lakes and folding hills in the northernmost spur of the county. In such a setting, it naturally takes its name from the Irish *Muineachan*, 'a cluster of hills'. Tradition that a monastery was founded here by St Moclodius in the C6 is supported by the Four Masters, who record its plunder in 830 and 931; it is understood to have survived into the C12, but nothing is known of it after this and no physical traces remain.

From the later Middle Ages the region around Monaghan lay under the control of the MacMahons, supporters of the O'Neills in Tyrone and much given to faction fighting. By the C15 a crannog, still discernible in Convent Lake, was the centre of their petty kingdom of West Oriel, and close by the lake shore a Franciscan friary was founded by Phelim MacMahon in 1462. In the aftermath of the Battle of Bellahoe, Lord Deputy Grey advanced to Monaghan in 1540 and laid waste to 'the abbey' and beheaded 'the abbot'. With nominal loyalty from the MacMahons, the county was eventually shired in 1585 and Monaghan was chosen as the county town; strategically it lay midway between Newry and Enniskillen, and presumably it was by then already an established settlement of some kind.

The MacMahons were capricious in their loyalties and treacherous to each other; officially they were regarded as 'the proudest and most barbarous sept among the Irish and do ever soonest repine, and kick and spurn the English Government'. A succession feud amongst them in 1589 led the Lord Deputy, Sir William Fitzwilliam, to break up the three ruling MacMahon factions decisively. Marching on the town in 1590 he sought out Hugh Roe MacMahon, brother of the recently deceased loyal subject Sir Ross MacMahon, put him on trial, and had him hanged. Afterwards Fitzwilliam proceeded to partition the county to

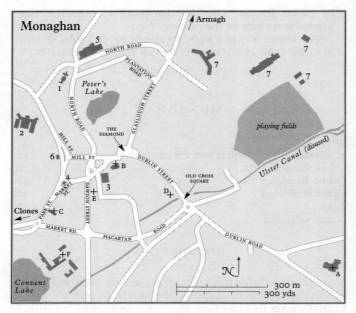

Monaghan

↑ Armagh

NORTH ROAD

PLANTATION ROAD

GLASLOUGH STREET

Peter's Lake

NORTH ROAD

HILL ST.

THE DIAMOND

MILL ST.

DUBLIN STREET

OLD CROSS SQUARE

playing fields

Ulster Canal *(disused)*

Clones ←

PARK ST.

MARKET ST.

DAWSON STREET

MARKET RD.

MACARTAN ROAD

DUBLIN ROAD

ROAD

Convent Lake

300 m
300 yds

A   St Macartan's Cathedral
B   St Patrick's Church (C of I)
C   St Joseph's Church
D   First Monaghan Presbyterian
     Church
E   Methodist church
F   St Louis Convent

1   Model School (former)
2   County Hospital
3   Courthouse
4   Market House
5   Railway station (former)
6   Aviemore
7   County Asylum
     (St Davnet's Hospital)
     (former)

weaken the clan's power. These actions were to be central to the
onset of the Nine Years War, during which the town was attacked
several times by the Irish, so that this 'new reformed place' was
soon 'wasted to the utter ruin'. Passing into rebellious MacMahon hands who held it fast for seven years, it suffered further
attack, to become 'a place of no strength but the walls of an old
church and some little trenching that the soldiers had made'.
When the town was reclaimed by government forces in 1602 and
a garrison re-established it was placed in a small fort on the hill,
with Captain Edward Blayney as the first governor. Although the
county was not part of the systematic Plantation of Ulster, the
town was subsequently planted under the private enterprise of
Blayney, the only sizeable town in the county that developed
under these circumstances. In 1604 Blayney was confirmed seneschal and in 1606 he obtained from James I a lease of the castle
and town, gaining rights to markets in 1611. The town was incorporated in 1613.

Monaghan, map.
Drawn by R. Bartlett, *c.* 1602

The development of a settlement between two small lakes, and the irregular, somewhat haphazard street pattern, both suggest a natural development within the topography that belies the establishment of a garrison and castle defences along formal lines at the beginning of the C17. Two separate impressions of the town survive from this period – maps of the town, including one by Richard Bartlett, and a description by Sir John Davies. In the maps fancy and fact are hard to reconcile. Barthelet's view of

c. 1602 shows the crannog settlement of the MacMahons overlaid
by an established settlement close to the friary ruins, dominated
by a star trace typical of C17 fortifications, with a smaller earthen
fort in the background. But in 1606 when Sir John Davies visited
the town, which he believed 'doth not deserve the name of a good
village', it consisted simply of 'divers scattered cabins, or cottages', and while observing the 'little fort' he fails to mention the
more elaborate star fort; he finds the foundation of a new castle
in the village, 'which being raised ten or twelve feet [3 m–3.5 m]
from the ground, and so left neglected for the space of almost
two years, is now ready to fall into ruins again'. Blayney eventually completed the castle at his own expense, 'making of it more
convenient for himself for his own tyme'.

A more elaborate early C17 map of the town published in Shirley's *History of the County of Monaghan* (1879) indicates a well-
developed street pattern within walls, and shows the castle set in
a square bawn with two diagonally disposed square bastions and
formally laid out gardens and fishponds extending to the lake.
The castle is shown as a large square block with square towers
projecting on each corner, as was common in C15 castles. The last
remains were taken down in the mid C19 and no trace survives;
the approximate location is usually identified with the site of the
Westenra Arms Hotel. The present Diamond can be associated
with the old market place, and much of the area now occupied by
the town-centre car park to the NW seems to correspond to the
former castle garden meadows, although archaeological trials in
the vicinity have so far failed to yield supporting evidence.

The castle was short-lived, as the town witnessed great upheav-
als during the rebellion of 1641. It was Edward Blayney's son
Henry, 2nd Lord Blayney, who escaped from Blayney Castle and
brought to Dublin news of the rebellion on 23 October 1641. The
events were particularly devastating for the family: his brother
Richard was hanged in the castle garden by the insurgents, and
he himself was killed at Benburb, Co. Tyrone, in 1646. Ultimately
the castle at Monaghan and Castle Blayney (*see* Castleblayney)
were ruined and never rebuilt. In 1680 the 5th Lord Blayney sold
this portion of his Monaghan estate; but just as had happened
with Castle Blayney, it was temporarily restored to the family by
marriage when the 7th Lord, Cadwallader, married the only
daughter and heiress of Sir Alexander Cairnes to whom the estate
had passed. However, when Lord Blayney died in 1732 his widow
remarried the Rt Hon. Lieutenant Colonel John Murray M.P.,
to whose daughters the Monaghan estate descended and whose
husbands, including the Earl of Clermont, steered the town
through the C18. The second daughter married Robert Cuninghame, created Baron Rossmore in 1796. Eventually the entire
inheritance passed to the youngest daughter, who married Henry
Westenra in 1764, and their son, Warner William, brought the
honours and fortunes together on the death of his uncle, succeeding as 2nd Lord Rossmore in 1801.

The late C18 coincided with a period of considerable growth,
but there was no sense of formality in the town's development,
the haphazard pattern of descent being somehow reflected in the

layout. In 1788 the Rev. Daniel Beaufort found 'a good large town, very neat, but streets narrow', while in 1801 Monaghan appeared to Sir Charles Coote as 'whimsically built, branching triangularly from the centre'. In fact the underlying pattern is essentially a great arc of streets, developed by the C18 and extending NE from Park Street through Market Street and the long Church Square to the larger Diamond and on to Dublin Street leading SE. C18 development was spread out all along the line of the arc and concentrated between the Market Square and the Diamond, where the streets were more confined. Until the C19 the only intersecting roads were from the N, with Hill Street leading to the Market Square and Glaslough Street to the Diamond. The latter was long established as a market place, with the Old Cross set in the centre.

The parish had been served by a C17 church at Rackwallace, but in 1725 a parish church was built between the old Gaol (site of the present Courthouse) and the Diamond. Daniel Beaufort considered it to be of 'Casselian stile'; others offered less kind but intriguing descriptions of 'an ugly narrow tower' over the w end, peculiar in shape as 'an irregular pentagon'. In the early C19 the church was re-roofed and it was proposed to replace the 'old shaken and unsightly' steeple; in 1825, however, Lady Rossmore committed funds for a new church, and in 1831 the vestry agreed to rebuild on the site. By then a new public space, now Church Square, was being created through street widening and realignment to improve the flow in the town centre. A sketch of 1816 by Alexander Fleming shows his proposal for 'the round house' that still survives in part at the E end of Mill Street, addressing the square. In 1825 the North Road was created and united with the newly formed Dawson Street to form the primary N–S axis bisecting the arc.

The first three decades of the C19 shaped much of the modern town, which acquired a series of new public buildings. In 1824 it was noted that the 'streets of Monaghan have been much widened, the thatched cabins taken down, and good limestone houses, well slated, and two or three storeys high, occupy their places'. A new Courthouse was built on the site of the old Gaol in 1827. That had been replaced by a new COUNTY GAOL designed by *John Behan* on the standard radial plan and built on a new site NW of the town between 1814 and 1821, overseen in its final year by *John Bowden*. Part of this was demolished at the end of the C19 when the surviving building became the new County Infirmary, then that too was demolished to make way for the County Hospital in 1937. The small Catholic chapel built on Park Street in 1824, its stepped gable with spiky pinnacles contributing a striking Gothick curiosity to the streetscape, is a more regrettable loss.

In 1839 a further boost was given when the Ulster Canal reached the town, and by the middle of the century when the Great Northern Railway had arrived Monaghan was a thriving market town. The decision to make it the episcopal seat culminated in the building of *J. J. McCarthy*'s 'Dream of Beauty' far to the SE.

ST MACARTAN'S CATHEDRAL AND PRECINCT

High Victorian Gothic reaches high drama on this tremendous windswept site more than a kilometre SE of the town centre. St Macartan's is the full flowering of the Gothic Revival, conceived in a vigorous French-influenced Dec style with an offset tower and spire 245 ft (74.6 m) tall, dramatic as the situation itself and ensuring dominance within the rural landscape. That such an urban-scale building should lie so removed from the centre seems at first explained less by ambition than convenience. In 1850 Charles McNally, Bishop of Clogher, established Monaghan as the new episcopal seat. His predecessors in this expansive diocese, effectively stretching coast to coast from Donegal to Louth, were peripatetic, though chiefly resident in the E portion. In 1858 it was decided to build a cathedral on an 8-acre site above the old chapel at Lathlorcan (now the Lathlorcan Mortuary Chapel: *see* p. 466). There could be no greater contrast than that between the unabashed triumphalism of the Cathedral on the hilltop and the modest vernacular of the lowly sequestered hall which served the Catholics of the town since the C18. The architect was *J. J. McCarthy*, assisted by *John Farrell* as clerk of works. There is evidence that the Cathedral had a more personal significance for McCarthy himself: in 1865 he said that it was the fulfilment of his architectural and patriotic ambitions, as represented many years before in a promise he had made to the nationalist Sir Charles Gavan Duffy, a native of the town.

The foundation stone was laid in June 1861, and by August the following year the foundations, according to contemporary sources formed by a series of massive load-bearing arches, had been completed. The plan is compact and clearly articulated along Puginian lines to provide a straightforward cruciform arrangement of nave with clerestory and well-lit aisles, short transepts, and an apsed chancel flanked by chapels. A polygonal baptistery projects from the N aisle. To the E of the N transept a short cloister passage runs outside the N side chapels to join the solid gabled block of ashlar known as the Chapter House. The nave is two and a half bays shorter than originally intended, but the effect is no less imposing. The deep polygonal apse gives the E end a true French flavour, forming in essence a chevet, though flanked by straight-ended chapels expressed externally with tall gabled projections. The material is a hard limestone that varies from brown to buff; it was quarried from the bottom of the hill, given freely by the 4th Lord Rossmore and carted by willing men of the district.

Typically, the building work progressed haltingly. In October 1873 working drawings for the roof and details of the tower were submitted but in 1875 the roof remained unfinished. As in many of McCarthy's churches the spire, planned from the outset, was commenced many years later, and completed by *William Hague* only after McCarthy's death in 1882. There were only minor alterations from the published design, principally in the canopies over the broaches, changed from steep chisel-shaped roofs to

p. 48

polygonal turrets. The work was however beset by problems when the contractors, the *McElhatton Bros*, were accused of 'violating the specification' in their pointing of the stonework as well as 'carrying up the spire in an irregular manner and of unequal sides instead of having the four faces alike'. They eventually reformed, and completed the spire in 1884. The building was finally dedicated in 1892.

The general impression is one of ordered strength, most evident in the uncompromising symmetry of the wide showy w front. Solid polygonal turrets faced with stepped buttresses frame the nave gable and lean-to aisles, rising well above them with

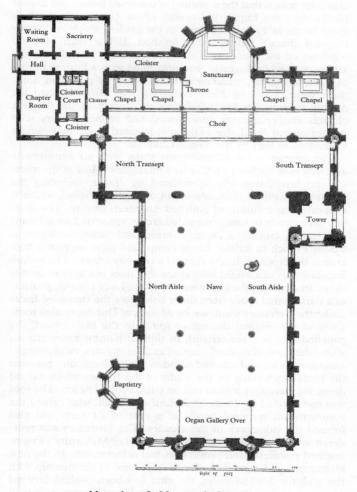

Monaghan, St Macartan's Cathedral.
Plan, 1868

highly ornamented pinnacles – more like minarets, providing a little flavour of Eastern exoticism. Elsewhere stepped buttresses define the architecture, angled at corners or again rising into pinnacles on the transepts and there graduated so as to relate to lower elements and indulge the skyline. The walls are of squared masonry, smoothly dressed at ground level and changing subtly to a more rugged rock-faced finish higher up, providing a greater contrast with the ashlar quoins and carved tracery. The provision of windows is fulsome and the tracery, Dec in style, is articulate, though on the w front and side elevations details are largely under-embellished, framed by plain shafts with polygonal bases and capitals. The emphasis on scale to achieve the principal character means that the economy of uncarved bosses and impost blocks does not impair the overall effect. Greater emphasis is given to the large rose windows in the gables, which are deeply recessed though still sparsely finished. Below each of these windows on the transepts is an arcade, initially intended by the architect as a blind arcade, and now filled with a host of statues in Carrara marble, standing out like a row of porcelain dolls; these were carved by *Pietro Lazzerini*, who also furnished the marble tympana in low relief over the entrances. In the side chapels and apse more complicated and refined tracery with greater cusped detail, that of the apse inspired in part by Beauvais Cathedral, in part by the Sainte-Chapelle.

The interior is on an ambitious scale, with an atmospheric austerity now far from McCarthy's intentions. Most of the interior and furnishings were completed by *Hague*, including the organ loft, with an elaborate organ of 1891 by *Telford*, which is supported on columns of polished Aberdeen granite. The four-bay nave arcade of simple moulded arches supported on columns with varied crocketed capitals carved with acanthus leaves is wholly French in feeling. Large compound piers support a high arch at the crossing. In the chancel a two-bay arcade. The overall impression is of a bright lofty space that does not appear unduly short. In contrast, the baptistery, now the Lady Chapel, projects as a dark canted space from the N aisle; here the stencilled frieze under the clerestory windows, by *Mannix* of Dublin, retains some sense of the original decorative spirit. In the main vessel, the panelled roof is a masterwork in timber: hammerbeam trusses above the nave, elaborately carved and set in pairs, yield over the sanctuary to an undecorated wooden vault. Continuity between the roofs is provided by the shafts of the trusses which extend down the clerestory wall to rest on paired corbel heads. The roof was constructed by *Purdy & Millard* of Belfast, who carved the hammerbeam terminal angels at a cost of £1 each and also formed the stonework of the arcades. The sanctuary was reordered in 1982 and is a regrettable betrayal of McCarthy's Pugin-inspired manifesto and proud personal achievement. In the new arrangement, designed by *Gerald MacCann* in partnership with the sculptor *Michael Biggs*, the altar has been pushed forward onto a spreading tiered pavement of polished Travertine which has even been extended up the rear walls to achieve a glorious mismatch of striking coldness. Swept away were all the elements of the C19 furnishings, deemed 'ecclesiastical bric-a-brac', including additions made by *W. A. Scott* between 1913 and 1916.

FURNISHINGS. The old PULPIT, FONT, ALTAR and CATHEDRA were all discarded in favour of brooding organic masses of granite carved by *Michael Biggs*; wilfully opposed to the character of the setting, these furnishings appear somewhat misshapen and are now more dated than the items they replaced. – A small cylindrical CONFESSIONAL, a curious hermetic pod in Travertine ashlar also by *Biggs*, is the most interesting feature of the arrangement, though without any true sense of place it stands in one of the s chapels, an object more of curiosity and symbolism than of function. – TAPESTRIES, lining the E wall, give dizzying blasts of colour in contrast to the hard polished surfaces; the religious scenes, depicted in a collage style, are by *Francis Biggs* and *Terry Dunne*. – SCULPTURE. In the Lady Chapel (formerly the baptistery) the *Pietà* of 1989 is a rigid bronze by *Nell Murphy*. The contemporary sanctuary Crucifix is a becoming primitive tubular depiction in cast bronze on oak by *Richard E. King*. – STAINED GLASS. Most of the windows, including those of the apse, are by *Mayer & Co.* and date from 1884–92; the depiction of the Virgin and St Anne in the s aisle is noteworthy because the dedication is to the architect William Hague and his wife Anne Frances. Other windows are by *Earley & Powell* and *Cox & Buckley*.

On the NE corner, the CHAPTER HOUSE is a neat, well-finished block in ashlar, two storeys with asymmetrical fronts and elaborate windows, as though surplus from the clerestory and nave. From the Cathedral chancel the building is reached by a narrow 'cloister' passage extending behind the N chapels. The plan is arranged around a small offset 'Cloister Court'; the cloister passage resumes to the W and S around two sides of the Court to lead to the chapter room. The GATE LODGE, by *Hague*, is a complementary small Gothic building with rich embellishment, neatly sited inside the grandiose gate screen which was installed in 1948 as a prelude to the dramatic terraced approach.

E of the Cathedral lies the CATHEDRAL HOUSE of 1903, probably by Hague's partner *Thomas F. McNamara*. A two-storey block in squared rock-faced ashlar with dressed window surrounds and moulded string-courses. The centre bay is set between canted bays, with the entrance recessed under a pointed segmental arch supported on polished granite colonnettes. Above it is a fussy oriel window with heavily moulded detail and a steep miniature pediment, filled with early C20 stained glass by *Michael Healy* depicting SS Brigid, Patrick, Macartan and Dympna. Robust, compact and well finished.

OTHER CHURCHES ETC.

ST PATRICK (C of I). 1836 by *William Farrell*. A hall and tower prominently sited on Church Square, built to replace the Early Georgian church with its 'oddly shaped' tower. Broad six-bay nave with aisles and a three-stage tower and spire linked by porches to the W front; short chancel projection with side porches. All in finely wrought ashlar. The builder was *John Clarke*. The nave is a solid rectangle with a battery of pinnacled buttresses framing tall lancets. In the details, whether the languid window hoods or the carved diaper frieze, the scale is uncouth, with a certain hardness in the finish reflecting a problem found in many of Farrell's buildings, where the detail satisfies until it leaves the paper. The tower is the best feature of the design, its slender form well-gauged with stepped angle buttresses tapering to receive the octagonal needle spire, which is given added lightness with ribbed arrises and pierced on alternate faces with diminishing lucarnes.

62   Internally a lighter touch is evident, with a wide nave under a delicately ribbed vault carried on clustered columns defining the aisles and supporting the galleries. On either side of the chancel arch, facing the nave, are episcopal and baronial seats, little Gothic fancies in mahogany with delicate open fretwork and pinnacles; one bears a mitre, the other the Rossmore coronet. Some alterations were proposed by *Joseph Welland* in 1854. – The PULPIT and READING DESK, in Caen stone and Irish marbles, were added in 1865 by *James E. Rogers*, carved by *Charles W. Harrison*, much too tough for such a refined interior. – The ORGAN of 1860 is by *William Telford*, an ornamental Gothic case with pinnacles bearing aloft the Rossmore arms. The attractive E window, a three-light Perp exercise in sandstone, was installed in 1862 to receive a richly patterned and coloured testimonial STAINED GLASS window to the 3rd Lord Rossmore, by *F. S. Barff*.

The primary interest of the interior is in the extraordinary array of C19 MONUMENTS. These include three in the chancel to members of the Rossmore family. 'The Parting Glance' for Lady Rossmore †1807, a poignant portrayal of personal anguish in marble by *Thomas Kirk*, exhibited at the Royal Hibernian Academy in 1843. – Lieutenant the Hon. Charles Westenra, missing in action 1824, in India; also by *Kirk* and exhibited at the Royal Hibernian Academy in 1841, it depicts a touching vignette of a cavalryman's funeral with a caparisoned riderless horse. – 'The Vacant Chair', to another Lady Rossmore †1840, is a more meditative image by *Lewis* of Cheltenham. – In the S gallery is one of the most elaborate, a sarcophagus festooned with military trophies, designed by *A. K. Young* for Captain John Lucas †1845 and carved by *Joseph Robinson Kirk*. – In the N gallery, the monument to Henry Lloyd †1879 at Isandula, by *Purdy & Millard* of Belfast, is remarkable for its contrasting supporters: a stiff and hirsute sword-bearing officer and formidable Zulu warriors with assegais and shields.

LATHLORCAN MORTUARY CHAPEL. Derelict. Discreetly sited in a depression below the Cathedral. An important pre-Emancipation chapel, built *c.* 1780–90. From 1850 it served as the procathedral until the dedication of St Macartan's in 1892, when it was downgraded to a mortuary chapel. A trim gable-fronted

Gothic hall in roughcast, with large pointed windows and Georgian sashes with Y-tracery. Given a facelift in the late C19 with a buttressed stone front – perhaps in two stages, as implied by the combination of squared masonry and rock-faced ashlar. Here two windows are set far apart on the corners, perhaps originally intended to receive a door between them, with a quatrefoil above. Plain interior: plastered walls and a flat panelled timber ceiling with exposed beams on corbels. The pews have been stripped out, though (superstitiously perhaps) the altar was placed between the windows inside the long E wall. Door on the W side, offset between the windows.

LATHLORCAN HOUSE. Next to the chapel, built as the Parochial House on land granted by the 2nd Lord Rossmore in the early C19. Later used as the bishop's palace before the present residence (Cathedral House) was built. A very pleasant Late Georgian farmhouse in the vernacular tradition. Two storeys and three bays, roughcast, with sash windows and a hipped roof. Attractive doorcase, proportioned like a Wyatt window, with long side-lights and an oblong geometrical fanlight. Originally with a big glazed porch and balcony, removed in the C20, leaving the partially glazed window on the first floor as something of an oddity. Very handsome entrance with octagonal stone piers and railed side walls.

ST JOSEPH. 1898 by *William Hague*. The dominant building on Park Street. A quirky and rugged Gothic church in rock-faced ashlar, built to replace the old town chapel of 1824. In 1897 Bishop Owens leased ground adjoining the old chapel from Lord Rossmore for a church and presbytery. The foundation stone was laid the following year and the church was dedicated by Cardinal Logue in 1900. The builder was *Patrick Nolan*. The new building is a four-bay buttressed hall with a big gabled front and a three-stage gabled tower, offset and recessed on the S side. The front has heavy stepped angle buttresses elaborated on the gable with pinnacles and miniature turrets, framing a big four-panel Perp window with cusped transoms and mullions; the blind lower panels disappear behind the entrance. Set in a heavy stepped gable, this forms a noteworthy composition, with a trefoil-headed doorway in a tall recessed pointed arch flanked by a single niche and three small cusped lights. The tower is an interesting composition in its own right, nicely decorated with twin cusped lights and an unusual round window with cruciform tracery. The ground floor is an open porch, leading under the organ loft into the tall and gloomy nave with a high panelled ceiling and exposed hammerbeam trusses. At the E end the chancel arch is formed as a trefoil with low cusps, supported on Hague's favourite device of short colonnettes in polished marble. Wide and rather plain E window, formed of five graduated lights. – Marble ALTAR and elaborate REREDOS by *E. Sharp* of Dublin. – STAINED GLASS. E window: brightly coloured glass by *Mayer & Co.* S nave: a darker three-light memorial window to Patrick Nolan, the builder of the church, and his wife, by *J. Clarke & Sons*. –

MONUMENT. The Rev. Hugh O'Neill †1910; plain marble shield in the nave, by *E. Stuart* of Monaghan.

Set against the corner of the tower, the PRESBYTERY is a handsome contemporary block of two storeys, in the same rock-faced masonry with dressed trim. The plate-glass windows are arranged in pairs, larger on the ground floor, with the frames nicely rounded in the upper corners, and given a surrounding moulding formed as a flat ogee arch under segmental hoods that look rather like eyebrows.

On the opposite side, the datestone of the old chapel was incorporated in the base of ST MACARTAN'S HALL, a plain gabled structure faced in stucco, built in 1907 by *Thomas F. McNamara* with a reading room and billiard room.

FIRST MONAGHAN PRESBYTERIAN CHURCH. Dublin Street. 1827, rebuilt 1900–2 by *W. J. M. Roome & R. S. Boag* of Belfast. A formidable Gothic church in rock-faced limestone with dressed stone trim. Big three-bay buttressed hall with sharp three-light lancets and a solemn gabled front with plate tracery. Three-stage, stepped, offset tower with a pyramidal cap where the architects intended a tall broach spire, balanced by a pinnacled buttress and a shorter subsidiary tower. The deeply recessed and gabled doorway is raised well above ground level, with an impressive flight of steps arching over the entrance to the hall below. The bulky mass, presenting a façade much too cumbersome for the short hall, is explained by the concealment of the early C19 church within the structure. The decision to rebuild stemmed from a need to provide a meeting hall for the congregation. In 1896 a new site and stone from the later C19 Gaol were acquired, and three churches in Co. Down – Ballywillan, Ballywalter and Bangor – were inspected by a delegation. When the plans were abandoned in 1899 it was decided instead to raise a new church over the existing building, which would become the new hall. Of the three churches visited, the resulting façade is closest to Ballywalter. The contractors were *Bright Bros* of Portadown.

The old church projects to the rear – a gabled, rendered block with limestone trim retaining timber Y-traceried sashes and a very nice Gothic door. It was a typical Gothic hall with a big gabled front of three bays, with square three-light windows on two levels, built by the *Rev. John Bleckley*; according to a contemporary, he employed masons and carpenters and with 'himself as architect, superintended the building until it was finished'. In fact the design is closely similar to the church of Sligo town. Inside the porch at ground level the beefy Tudor doorcase survives and at first-floor level the hoods of the old windows can be seen with the 1827 datestone; below this is an earlier stone with the date 1745 and the initials D. H., taken to be those of Dacre Hamilton.

Inside, the new church is a big airy space with timber-panelled ceiling, exposed hammerbeam trusses, and a raking gallery at the back. – STAINED GLASS. On the N side, 'I have fought the good fight' is a very finely coloured early C20 memorial window filling three lights. – MONUMENTS. Mostly simple classical tablets in statuary marble, the best to the Rev. John Bleckley †1873; an ornate Gothic gable in white marble with polished marble shafts, by *J. Robinson & Son*, Belfast.

METHODIST CHURCH. Dawson Street. Of *c.* 1861. A simple Gothic hall of four bays. Wide gabled front in squared limestone with a good Dec window of cusped tracery and an ashlar bellcote above, now vacant; small side porches with Tudor-arched doorways. The building replaced an earlier Primitive Wesleyan church of 1824, according to a datestone embedded in the boundary wall.

The former MANSE adjoining to the N is a tall cement-rendered block of three bays with a central gabled projection. The ASSEMBLY ROOMS to the S are *c.* 1900 in appearance, a long rendered block of two storeys and six bays with string-courses and a central gabled projection. The principal spaces are on the first floor with large casement windows; Tudor hoodmoulds to the smaller openings in the low ground floor. Entrances and stairs are accommodated in lower recessed blocks against the end gables.

ST LOUIS CONVENT. S of Market Road. In 1859, at the invitation of Bishop McNally of Clogher, three nuns made their way from France to establish here the first convent of the Sisters of St Louis in the country. After establishing a female school on Mill Street, the sisters moved to the large C18 brewery complex beside Spark's Lake (now Convent Lake) which they redeveloped in the late C19 and early C20 into a complex of large institutional buildings. The principal building overlooks the lake and was erected in 1885. A rather intense three-storey seven-bay structure in institutional Gothic built in long blocks of rusticated brown masonry with an ashlar trim. The central bay is advanced and gabled with a single-storey porch, ornately finished with a pointed doorway and a traceried fanlight. Heavy stone canopies break the eaves of the middle bay on each side, while the windows are nicely varied on each level, those on the ground floor linked by a string-course which rises over them as hoods. Contract drawings signed by the local contractors *Patrick Nolan* and *Joseph Woods* are preserved in the convent heritage centre; they correspond closely to the style of *William Hague*, who at this time was busying himself with the completion of the spire of St Macartan's. The same architecture bleeds into the adjoining rendered ranges which incorporate the original two-storey brewery buildings; these front the plainer ancillary buildings extending in different directions behind, which may be the additions carried out in 1901–3 by *Thomas F. McNamara*.

Running parallel behind the convent is the CHAPEL, a long low building in rock-faced brownstone, dedicated in 1863 and reworked and extended with side chapels by *Thomas J. Cullen* between 1933 and 1939. Internally, the stencilled decoration, carved reredos and hammerbeam chancel roof were notable losses in the 1930s; the space is now quite plain, with a simple roof of exposed arched braces, though the old chancel arch has been retained halfway along the nave. – SANCTUARY and ALTAR in *opus sectile*. – The PIETÀ in the N chapel is an accomplished work in statuary marble by *Edmund Sharp*. – Noteworthy also are the finely worked ceramic STATIONS OF THE CROSS set in frames of Siena marble. – STAINED GLASS. Three-light E window with the Crucifixion, brightly coloured and exceptionally vivid, signed by *Earley*, Dublin, 1937.

To the N, near the Clones Road, is the FEMALE NATIONAL SCHOOL of 1876. A severe two-storey, seven-bay T-plan block with plate-glass windows, cement-rendered, with a high hipped roof and absurdly small chimneystacks in polychromatic brickwork; the central bays are advanced and gabled with tripartite windows. In the first three decades of the C20 there was extensive new building, much of it carried out by *J. J. McDonnell*. The former INDUSTRIAL SCHOOL of 1906 is an austere three-storey block of ten bays in red brick relieved by strings of black industrial brick. The end bays are advanced and gabled, breaking up the long façades; in one of these is an attractive Tudor doorcase in sandstone with carved spandrels and stiff-leaf foliate bosses.

Other structures include the former NOVITIATE BUILDING of 1922 by *McDonnell, Lamont & McDonnell*, a largely unexciting T-plan block of three storeys with sash windows and sparse Gothic detail. Built of concrete blocks successfully cast to imitate rock-faced ashlar. The same material and technique were employed in the large gable-fronted CONCERT HALL to the SE, designed in 1930 by *Hugh Lamont*, of which the Art Deco-style entrance – three deeply recessed doors grouped under a deep moulded architrave – is the most appealing feature.

PUBLIC BUILDINGS ETC.

73 COURTHOUSE. Church Square. 1827 by *Joseph Welland*. A heavily massed classical box built on the site of the old Gaol. *William Deane Butler* had produced designs in 1826 which were not accepted. This is Welland's most conspicuous debt to his master John Bowden, and one of the few classical buildings attributable to him. The builder was *Thomas Stewart*. The broad five-bay façade, in a crisp biscuit-coloured stone, is extended by carriage arches on either side. Welland, a predominantly ecclesiastical architect, was perhaps a little ill-at-ease in the Greek idiom. The engaged Doric portico rising through two storeys with a pediment is just a little too thick-set, lacking the Doric frieze, all hard and angular but for the fluted columns of the portico. The ground floor has channelled rustication that extends into the carriage arches. Two string-courses separate the floors. Above, the windows, which are the most distinctive element of the design, have lugged architraves in an Egyptian fashion tapering inwards, almost imperceptibly, from the sills.

The pediment bears the royal arms, excellently carved, in Portland stone. To the rear the building extends to a less homogeneous assemblage of ranges finished in rubble with ashlar trim. Though haphazard in appearance, the arrangement was standard, comparing closely to *William Farrell*'s designs for the courthouses in Cavan and Carrick-on-Shannon. In each of those the side elevations are dominated by large round-headed windows lighting the court chambers. Altered in 1930 by *John P. McArdle* and damaged by fire in the 1980s, the interiors are entirely modern and unprepossessing.

In front of the Courthouse is a SCULPTURE by *Ciaran O'Cearnaigh* erected in 2004 to commemorate the victims of a bomb in 1974: a tall cylinder half in pink sandstone and half in polished metal, with the names of the victims inset in the stonework on strips of bronze.

MARKET HOUSE. Market Street. 1792 by *Samuel Hayes*. Set to one side on a tight, sloping peripheral site, a highly pleasing Neoclassical building by an accomplished amateur for his friend, Robert Cuninghame. Originally set on a low stepped podium, it is essentially a quadrangular single-storey structure, in large blocks of rough-hewn stone with dressed limestone trim – unfortunately scarred by nasty cement pointing – and panels of Portland stone with drapery festoons and paterae above each bay, a hallmark of Neoclassicism from Adam to Gandon. On the long façades the three central bays are arcaded in an advanced and pedimented section. The outer bays have blind windows with bold rectangular frames and a large patera above. The gable-ends are more finely treated, each a pedimented front with a large central arched doorway flanked by niches. The lower half of the wall is nicely rusticated with V-channelled masonry, which extends to the quoins and voussoirs in the upper half. In the pediment at the E end is a small oval plaque framed in a bay wreath, inscribed 'Dedicated to the convenience of the inhabitants of Monaghan by the Rt. Hon. Lieutenant Gen. Robert Cunninghame. M.D.CC.XC.II. S. H. of Avondale Del.' The reference is apt, since some of the same architectural character can be found on the house Hayes designed for himself at Avondale in Co. Wicklow. In the pediment at the W end the date is carved in the frieze, and the pediment contains a very finely carved coat of arms, showing those of Cuninghame impaled with those of Murray, framed by delicate sprays of bay. At once simple and sophisticated, this is a gracious building that deserves greater prominence. In the year of its erection the Earl of Clermont was granted rights to hold a weekly market in the town.

DAWSON MEMORIAL. 1857 by *W. J. Barre*. A ghostly obelisk in silver granite ashlar erected in 1857 by Lord Cremorne to commemorate his brother, Lieutenant-Colonel Thomas Vesey Dawson of the Coldstream Guards, who fell at the Battle of Inkerman in 1854. A more modest reworking of Barre's unsuccessful design submitted the previous year for a memorial to

Lord Londonderry on Scrabo Hill in Co. Down. Set on a stepped base, the plinth boldly projects on each face, formed in the manner of Egyptian sarcophagi with simple channelled rustication, deep rabbeted panels and shallow angular pediments with cat's-ear acroteria carved with anthemia. Two sides of the obelisk carry the inscriptions ALMA and INKERMAN.

ROSSMORE MONUMENT. The Diamond. Curiously exotic in the middle of the square. A High Victorian richly embellished fountain, erected to commemorate the 4th Baron Rossmore, 'Rosie', who was killed at the age of twenty-two while steeplechasing at Windsor in 1874. His death was witnessed by Queen Victoria, who called off the next day's racing as a mark of respect. Octagonal, with three diminishing stages, each domed but for the last which ends in a spirelet. Constructed of

Monaghan, Rossmore Monument.
Engraving, 1877

dissolving red sandstone, it stands on eight grey polished granite columns with foliate capitals supporting a gabled arcade of pointed arches with the letters R-O-S-S-M-O-R-E spelled out above. A stout polished pink column rises from the central fountain to support a stone vault. The arcaded arrangement is repeated in miniature on the upper stages, strengthened in the middle stage with square two-stage piers instead of columns. Between the boldly crocketed gables is a series of heavily eroded heraldic motifs and a dedication. A more slender variant of Timothy Hevey's Martin Memorial in Shrigley, Co. Down, this was possibly conceived by *E. J. Tarver*, who at the same time designed a mausoleum at Rossmore Park to receive the young Lord's remains (*see* p. 483).

MONAGHAN COUNTY MUSEUM, Hill Street. *See* p. 478.

MONAGHAN TOWN LIBRARY, North Road. *See* p. 478.

GARDA STATION. Plantation Road. 1875 by *E. T. Owen*. Tall gabled block of three storeys to an L-plan. Roughcast with brick trim. A standard design, though much simpler than Owen's designs for Caherciveen and Dungannon.

Beside is the DIVISIONAL HEADQUARTERS, built in 1986 by the *Office of Public Works*, a grim block in grey brick.

BARRACKS. Emyvale Road. Built for a 'troop of horse' *c.* 1800. Two parallel ranges, each a long, modestly classical two-storey block in limestone rubble with dressed stone trim. The doorcases are striking, with big blocked surrounds which seem more mid-C18 in character. The central bays of the principal range were advanced with a pediment until *c.* 1914, when the building was adapted to accommodate Belgian refugees. The centre was then opened up with a wide Tudor-arched carriageway and completely reworked as an asymmetrical battlemented gateway. The buildings were incorporated into BELGIAN SQUARE, a local authority housing development of dormered cottages of 1922 by *Patrick McCarthy*, sympathetically built in limestone and brick along two sides of the old parade ground.

WORKHOUSE (former). Emyvale Road. Only the administration block survives of *George Wilkinson*'s typical plan, to house 900 inmates, 1841–2. The usual U-plan block of two storeys and five bays in squared limestone with dressed trim; dormer windows on the first floor with decorated bargeboards. Now subdivided into separate housing units. On the site of the former accommodation ranges is BELGIUM PARK, part of the redevelopment of the old workhouse between 1922 and 1936, with some of the houses designed by *Frank Gibney*. Neat terraces of quite standard one- and two-storey houses, some in rendered concrete and others built of random rubble.

COUNTY HOSPITAL. High Street. 1937 by *J. F. McGahon* of Dundalk with *W. H. Byrne & Son* as consulting architects. Built on the site of the late C19 County Infirmary, which incorporated the remains of the County Gaol of 1821. An uninspiring building with the familiar early C20 plan of monotonous three-storey angled ranges fronted by a lower two-storey block of three bays, the central bay recessed with a concrete tetrasyle portico.

MONAGHAN REGIONAL MODEL SCHOOL. Swan Park. 1860 by
James H. Owen. An asymmetrical and somewhat haphazard
composition, nominally Gothic, in limestone rubble with
dressed quoins and window surrounds. Essentially a long single-storey buttressed range with square casements and big roof
spans, interrupted by two big gabled projections, both with
small gabled porches to one side. The central gabled block is
wide, with a large three-light window; the end block housing
the domestic quarters is narrower, of three storeys, with a small
boxy addition to the side of 1925.

RAILWAY STATION (former). Of *c.* 1862 by *Sir John MacNeill* for
the Ulster Railway (Portadown–Clones line), subsequently the
Great Northern Railway. In red-and-yellow brick, a short boxy
single-storey arcaded block, flanked by long low ranges poised
like waiting railway carriages. The central block is massive and
rather sepulchral with a five-bay arcade, the central three open,
glazed in the end bays with the same motif simplified across
the wings. Emphatic eaves cornice on paired brackets with a
heavy blocking course and squat pediments projecting in low
relief on each façade. More modest than the later stations of
Armagh and Portadown, though closely similar to them, and
the only survivor. The line was abandoned in 1960.

OTHER BUILDINGS

109 BANK OF IRELAND (former HIBERNIAN BANK). 1874 by *O'Neill
& Byrne.* Successfully fitted on a triangular site at the meeting
of Dawson Street and Church Square, a decorative and highly
textured two-storey building, its wedge-shaped plan giving two
fronts, quite anomalous in this regular streetscape. Eclectic
Gothic in the spirit of Ruskin, though here the decoration is
more consciously Hiberno-Romanesque. The contractor was
P. Brodigan. Two pleasing and varied façades built of squared
rock-faced blocks meet at a rounded corner, skewed slightly
towards Dawson Street. Here the main portal, framed with
heavy polished granite columns, projects boldly and partially
supports an ornate balcony. Its highly carved frieze extends
beyond the door, supported on long notched corbels. The
longer Dawson Street façade is more irregular and incorporates the bank manager's house. The principal architectural
character of the building is expressed in the windows, predominantly segmental-headed, deeply set, framed by engaged colonnettes with foliate capitals, on the ground floor elaborated
as Romanesque arches to light the banking hall. On each level
they are linked by the impost mouldings, enhancing the strong
horizontal emphasis given by the bold projection of the sills.

AVIEMORE. Hill Street. A big Georgian town house built for Sir
James Hamilton and altered at different times in the C19. Commanding the long vista down Mill Street, this is probably the
best sited building in the town. It is a three-storey block of
three bays over a raised basement with big plate-glass sashes

dressed up with elaborate Roman cement trim. On the ground floor vermiculated quoins, banded rustication, elaborate lugged surrounds with segmental heads; plainer on the upper floors, but finished on the parapet with a double frieze of rosettes set above a rinceau band. The wide fanlit doorcase is Regency, with fluted Doric columns and a Greek-key frieze, now with a plate-glass fanlight and side-lights and an elaborate stucco frame. The side elevations reveal the façade as a sham, exposed where the parapet fails to extend to the massive stacks. The explanation for this curiosity lies in the C18 roof structure – three parallel pitched roofs running from front to rear. Something of the original appearance of the façade is suggested in the half-gabled rear elevation, which retains the Georgian glazing.

Internally the standard tripartite plan, two rooms deep, with a combination of Late Georgian and Regency joinery. The hall communicates directly with a chunky dog-leg staircase, Early Georgian in feeling with tightly grouped balusters, ramping swan-neck handrails and richly carved tread-ends, given heightened interest by the way in which the terminal volutes alternate with pheasant-like heads.

Remarkably good buildings to the rear, retaining exceptional Regency joinery worthy of the house. In the stables the stalls are divided by clustered columns and decorated with other Gothic details.

FARMEEHULL. On the Ballybay Road. 1875. A gaunt house with an unusually high hipped roof almost extending beyond the small stacks. Two storeys and three bays in squared limestone with brick trim, casement windows on the first floor, and sashes set in small canted bays on the ground floor, flanking a big fanlit doorcase. Built for Matthew Rushe and the home of his son, Denis Carolan Rushe, the historian of Monaghan.

TRANQUILLA. On the Clones Road. A trim house with a hipped roof and brick stacks, built in squared limestone with dressed quoins, string-course, and plate-glass windows with red brick trim. Plain doorcase with side-lights and a fanlight etched with the date 1875. Once quite rural, it now sits comfortably amongst bungalows in a developed suburban setting.

MANSE (former). 1883. A large boxy stuccoed Victorian house set above the Clones Road. Two storeys and three bays in smooth render with string-courses, big plate-glass windows, and a hipped roof with dormers. The narrow single-storey porch has paired round-headed windows echoing the central windows of the first floor. The two-bay side elevations have bay windows at ground level. Typical Late Victorian interiors with two large rooms to the front plainly decorated with moulded cornices.

COOLSHANNAGH. Emyvale Road. A Late Victorian curate's house. Two storeys with an asymmetrical and somewhat confused front with varied fenestration, including long paired sashes and an offset half-hipped gable. All in red brick with a variation of yellow and black brick and dressed limestone trim.

Simple Tudor-arched doorway set in a short single-storey projection.

COOLSHANNAGH HOUSE. Emyvale Road. A lugubrious Late Victorian house built for the medical master of the Asylum (*see* St Davnet's Hospital). Two-storey, three-bay block with a steep hipped roof, roughcast with plaster rusticated quoins, plate-glass windows and a central canted bay on the first floor set over the porch. The porch has a plain Tudor-arched doorway, heavily moulded cornice, and frilly wrought-iron parapet.

KILNACLOY. Off the High Street. A large Late Victorian house, asymmetrical, with an irregular T-plan. Two storeys over a raised basement with hipped roofs and red brick stacks. Roughcast with dressed quoins. The fenestration is varied, with plate-glass windows and timber bay windows on the ground floor of the S and E fronts, which project over the area. The main entrance is placed in a narrow two-storey block in the SE angle, reached by a flight of steps spanning the area. The rear entrance is prettier, covered with an open porch, cottage-style, in rustic timber. The area and garden terraces are bounded by Elizabethan Revival BALUSTRADES by *William Burn*, brought from the destroyed Dartrey Castle (*see* p. 310).

HILDEN. Off the High Street. An attractive Late Victorian house of two storeys and three bays in red brick with a hipped roof. Bay windows on the ground floor flanking a neat little glazed timber porch.

TIRKEERAN. A tall Late Georgian house on Poundhill. Two-storey gable-ended block of three bays with big Georgian sashes of equal height on both storeys. Roughcast with dressed quoins and a decorative eaves course with small moulded consoles. Extended with an additional storey in the C20. In 1824 it was known, appropriately, as Town View, and was the residence of Samuel McDowell, surgeon.

TOUR

Monaghan is remarkable for the quantity of stone-built houses that line its curving streets and for the constant presence of the countryside, visible from the ends of the roads and from the upper floors of houses. Most visitors will leave their cars in one of two large car parks: to the N behind the Diamond, approached from Glaslough Street, or to the S between Church Square, the Courthouse and the modern Shopping Centre, approached from the New Road (Macartan Road). It is easy to find the centre from either park.

Three irregular open spaces make up the core of the town. To the SW is Market Square, triangular, with the C18 Market House (*see* p. 471) set on a sloping site. Church Square is a little to the E, defined by the front and spire of *William Farrell*'s St Patrick's Church and the solid presence of *Joseph Welland*'s Courthouse, facing the robust Victorian Bank of Ireland (*see* pp. 465, 470 and 474). Further E again is the Diamond, an attractive formal urban space now pleasantly paved and improved by restricted traffic routes. The architecture is essentially Victorian, dominated by the reassuringly solid red brick façade of the WESTENRA ARMS by *William Hague*, who had canvassed the Rossmore agent for the commission in 1872. It has a heavy corbelled cornice and pedimented attic windows; on the ground floor elaborate tripartite windows set in pedimented limestone frames flank a bulky porch on square pillars, originally supporting a first-floor conservatory. The same architect seems to have shoehorned what was the TOWN HALL into the narrow site to the E. With much the same feeling as the hotel, it is a tall pedimented building in red brick and limestone, sharing its quoins. The pediment carries the Rossmore arms in red sandstone. The name of the hotel is the family name of the Barons Rossmore, Victorian proprietors of the town, who erected the Rossmore Monument, a fountain at the centre of the Diamond (*see* p. 472). W of the hotel two houses were adapted by *Beckett & Harrington* in 1922 for the Munster and Leinster Bank, now the AIB, dressed up with understated classical detail in pale sandstone; the same architecture was applied to the lower house to the N, set well back and extending into the small alleyway at the side of the hotel.

While most of the major buildings are at the very centre, two short walks may be suggested that amplify the picture of the town. Each begins at *W. J. Barre*'s Dawson Memorial obelisk in CHURCH SQUARE and starts by walking past the side of the Bank of Ireland (for obelisk and bank *see* pp. 471 and 474) up North Street to the first crossroads at Mill Street.

For the first walk, turn l. into MILL STREET, which leads uphill to the W and focuses on the white-painted façade of Aviemore. On the N side at first a row of rubble-built C18 houses, then a tall stuccoed town house with canted bays. In the centre of the S side the POST OFFICE of 1907 is by *Robert Cochrane* and *G. W. Crowe*. Red brick front with dressings of Castlewellan granite and Ardbraccan limestone; originally single-storey with wide segmental windows framed by rusticated pilasters; raised by one floor *c.* 1950 with the addition of a flat-roofed box in paler brick.

At the end is HILL STREET, where a thin wedge of garden divides the street into two levels. Turning r. from here, tucked away at the N end of Hill Street, the former SAVINGS BANK of 1855 is visible, a disarming small building by *William Deane Butler*. A storey-and-a-half block of three bays, gable-ended, with a porch at either end. Built in squared limestone with much dressed stone detail, less successful now that the render has been stripped off. On the façade rusticated corner pilasters with bracketed capitals frame round-headed casement windows with bold architraves and keystones, forming a neat arcade; the mesh of circular patterned glazing bars adds a lighter touch. Turn back, past the front of a house with a battlemented porch and then the extraordinary façade of Aviemore (*see* p. 474).

Beyond, on the same side, are two interesting Georgian houses, both two-storey, gable-ended blocks, nicely fenestrated, with good internal joinery, and thatched roofs up to recent times. From here the road leads downhill past a pair of semi-detached town houses of c. 1860, now joined and in use as the MONAGHAN COUNTY MUSEUM. A solid symmetrical block in squared limestone, three storeys high on a basement; each former house has three bays with plate-glass windows and a central doorway approached up steps with bold ironwork; the pair are tied together by a substantial cornice, blocking course and balustraded parapet.

At the bottom of the street continue past the Market House on the l., into PARK STREET, with a succession of painted vernacular houses leading on the l. to St Joseph's Church (see p. 467). Across the junction with Market Road, lining the E side of the N entrance to the St Louis Convent grounds, is LAKE VIEW (with no direct views to the lake!), an attractive terrace of five two-storey early C19 houses, possibly built as workers' houses for the former brewery. Rubble, each with two bays and, for four of the houses, windows only on the l. side with a neat fanlit door to the r. Most doors and windows are now crude C20 replacements. Turn l. into MARKET ROAD, now a modern link road, out of scale with the character of the old town, though its construction has undoubtedly saved the centre. At the first junction, round the massive white Dunnes Stores, is DAWSON STREET on the l., where a sense of the history of the place returns, to some extent, with some smaller buildings and a Gothic Methodist church on the r. (see p. 469). Dawson Street leads back into Church Square.

For the second walk cross Mill Street and continue on NORTH ROAD away from the centre, passing a mess of undistinguished modern buildings. MONAGHAN TOWN LIBRARY, a Modernist white two-storey block on a concrete grid of 1969, renovated and extended in 2005, is on the l., then the gabled and turreted front of the JOHNSTON AND MADDEN MEMORIAL ORANGE HALL of 1882, attributed to *William Batt*. A jaunty L-shaped gabled hall with offset octagonal tower; red brick, mixed with black brick to form a patterned string-course, with half-timbered gable and porch. Next comes the projecting cream sandstone cash office of the former PROVINCIAL BANK, c. 1900, with a pyramidal slate roof and glazed square cupola. It was added on to and obscures the two-storey banking hall behind, attached to a handsome Late Georgian house by the local builder *John Clarke*, who built St Patrick's Church. Five bays and two storeys in squared limestone with red brick trim to the windows. The elegant front door is framed by Ionic columns with a webbed elliptical fanlight. Single-storey wing to the N. Well-to-do architecture; in contrast to most of the houses that open directly off the streets, it faces onto the trees and open ground that surround Peter's Lake, one of the many pieces of water that characterize this part of Ulster, which here comes into the town. Its presence is welcome.

The walk continues by skirting the l. shore of the lake, but further up North Road on the l. is the Model School and further on again the former railway station (*see* p. 474). At the N end, on the r., SWAN PARK, three-bay blocks built after 1835, some nicely fenestrated with canted bays and all with good doorcases.

From the lake the visitor can appreciate the extent of modern building within the town centre, which here presents as a continuous wall of for the most part clean and clear architecture. Follow the path round the lake to where a pair of twisted stainless-steel ribbons marks the entry to the N car park. Directly opposite the gates is GLASLOUGH STREET, one of the historic streets of the town, lined by tall vernacular houses. Here too the MASONIC HALL, mid-C19, a gable-ended block of two storeys over a raised basement, cement-rendered with red and polychromatic brick trimming; Tudor-arched doorway reached by a fanciful perron with good ironwork. Glaslough Street leads on the r. into the Diamond, with the Rossmore Monument as its focal point. In the Diamond turn l. along DUBLIN STREET which, curving to the SE, opens a view to the tower and spire of St Macartan's Cathedral, far away on its hillside out of the town. There are some good houses built over shops with wide elliptical arches, and at the end of the street the Presbyterian church (*see* p. 468). Here, in the past, the street opened into a low rectangular shambles, now replaced by a roundabout and approach roadways. The Old Town Cross, largely a reconstruction, is on the l. The best way back to the centre is to return along Dublin Street, past the present TOWN HALL, the former ROYAL BANK, extensively altered by *Bradbury & Evans* in 1930; a decent building with an astylar stuccoed front of two storeys and seven bays, the three central bays advanced and pedimented as a stylized engaged portico. Attractive stone doorcase in a minimal Art Deco style.

NEIGHBOURHOOD

ST DAVNET'S HOSPITAL. On Mall Road, 0.75 km NE. 1863–7 by *John McCurdy*. A large institutional complex on the edge of the town. A competition for the District Lunatic Asylum – the largest in Ireland – was announced in 1863, the specifications advocating a combination of the block and corridor systems as found in the Cheshire and Derby county asylums. McCurdy's winning design is a lesson in the architecture of economy, a sprawling complex that lacks a primary focus, with ranges diverting off here and there at right angles so that the general appearance is incoherent. Despite the impression, the plan is symmetrical. The principal section is a long unrelieved block of two storeys and ten bays with a hipped roof, flanked by similar recessed blocks, all with big segmental windows and metal casements and distinguished only by central canted bays. Uniting these ranges is a glazed lean-to canopy which extends across the entire front to give access to detached infirmaries at either end. Behind these, with only the most tenuous link to the main block, are the 'retired wings' intended for more disruptive patients. It remains a good building; its aesthetic qualities lie in the minutiae, primarily in the quality of the stonework – squared rock-faced limestone with bold red brick trim. The contractors were *Wardop & Sons*. Internally there were 1,000 yds (915 m) of corridor, and when it opened in 1867 the hospital was the largest in the country. Unassuming additions were carried out in 1883–6 by *William Hague*, the contractor *W. Connolly & Son*. Further buildings were added by *Thomas F. McNamara* in 1904 and by *W. H. Byrne & Son* in 1909.

Near the entrance, the former CHIEF MEDICAL SUPERINTENDENT'S house, also by *McCurdy*, is a large, mildly picturesque building in the same materials. Essentially an L-plan block with wide eaves on paired brackets and a hipped roof. The front is recessed in stages with a showy Italianate campanile to the side to heighten the asymmetry. Plate-glass windows, mainly segmental-headed, some in a tripartite arrangement. The interior has good Late Victorian plasterwork.

Two CHAPELS, Catholic and Protestant, sit harmoniously cheek-by-jowl a short distance from the main block, added in 1897 and 1900 respectively. In painted render with salient elements in moulded red brick trim, they offer a lively contrast in such serious surroundings. Both probably by *Hague & McNamara*, who are known to have designed the Protestant chapel. The CATHOLIC CHAPEL is the larger, with a classical bearing, a long gabled hall of eight bays with deep semicircular apse and big round-headed sashes with marginal glazing bars. The two end bays are gabled, projecting on the S side for a vestry. The gables are framed by twin buttresses, essentially piers topped with ball finials that give a decidedly Baroque feeling, enhanced on the front by a dinky brick porch with a squashed pediment and Tuscan pilasters. Plain interior, with exposed arched trusses and good timber altar rails formed as a Tuscan arcade. The PROTESTANT CHAPEL is a more compact five-bay hall, in a robust Romanesque style. Straightforward plan with a vestry, polygonal apse, and long round-headed windows set between thin buttresses of brick and rock-faced limestone. The W front is strengthened by thicker angle buttresses that read as primitive antae. A deep-set rose window with simple petal tracery floats prominently above the gabled porch. Inside, timber-panelled ceiling; chancel arch on short Romanesque columns. Repaired in 1910 by *W. A. Scott*.

MENTAL HOSPITAL. 1938–43 by *C. T. MacLynn* of Belfast. On higher ground nearer the town, a successful Art Deco design less forbidding than McCurdy's buildings. Large red brick and sandstone ranges, essentially T-plan. Central entrance block of two storeys with advanced end bays and tall rectangular windows with typical 1930s glazing. Between the end bays the ground floor is of pale ashlar. The central bay is advanced slightly and rises through three storeys as a square tower with a stylized aedicular surround to the first-floor window. The doorcase, flanked by two shallow canted bays, is in limestone with simple mouldings and lugs; fish-scale-patterned leaded fanlight. A short link to the rear connects with a long ward range of twenty-six bays with single-storey canted wings at either end – plain but for the studied recession of the end bays, the unusual division of the windows, and the projection of the central bays under a deep parapet.

The NURSES' HOME to the s is in the same cast of red brick laid in English-garden-wall bond with raised quoins and sandstone trim. A large astylar block of two storeys and nine bays with a hipped roof. The central bay advances with a small balcony carried on brackets over the entrance.

STANLEY TERRACE and WESTENRA TERRACE. On the Armagh Road, 0.8 km NNE. Two large Late Victorian terraces of three-storey blocks in red and yellow brick make for a strange isolated urban incident removed from the centre. Clearly a concerted effort to extend the town, but how did they come to be here? Westenra Terrace, the southernmost block, is more attractive, made up of four tall two-bay houses with neat railed front gardens and round-headed doorways with spoked fanlights. An additional bay on one of the end houses accommodates a carriage arch leading to a pleasant range of roughcast mews buildings and long garden plots. Stanley Terrace is more severe, a long and ponderous façade like a row of inflated industrial cottages; the only architectural incident is the advancement of the four central houses. All the windows in both terraces replaced by nasty plastic glazing units.

ST MACARTAN'S SEMINARY. 2 km N. 1840–8 by *Thomas Duff*. A brooding no-nonsense building on a rural hilltop. Cold, stripped-down classicism that marks a sort of halfway house between domestic and public architecture. In 1864, soon after its completion, the *Freeman's Journal* regarded the building as a 'noble structure . . . well calculated to excite the warmest admiration'. The work was superintended by the Rev. Thomas Bogue, a friend of Duff's, who claimed that 'accident had given him some practical knowledge of building as he had been concerned in the erection of different chapels'.

Duff's design was clearly influenced by the architecture of the Maynooth Seminary, with a similar central block of three storeys and five bays, the three central bays advanced and pedimented; here, however, the president's house is gable-ended, executed in crisp squared limestone with dressed trim, so that it has more of the appearance of a provincial mid-C18 farmhouse. The institutional character is conveyed by the straight two-storey side wings of five bays, slightly recessed behind the main block and extending to narrow three-storey end blocks with hipped roofs distinguished only by a large segmental-headed tripartite window at first-floor level. The ranges are all brought together by a continuous sill course and string-course forming a deep band between the lower storeys.

102

The end blocks return rearward to give the plan its U-shape; one contains the chapel and hall, the other kitchens and refectory. These ranges were extended by *J. J. McDonnell* in 1908 in a sympathetic and plain institutional manner with squared masonry and brick trim; the main event is the dramatic five-storey toilet block to the rear with a giant chisel-shaped roof that breaks the skyline. Internally the planning is straightforward, with a long spine corridor to the rear spanning between the end ranges.

The CHAPEL is the most formal space, designed as a large double-height room with eight Corinthian columns supporting a panelled dome over the altar. The original decoration was by *G. B. Steer & Co.* The interior was simplified by *T. J. Cullen* in 1939. – STATIONS OF THE CROSS in opal glass by *Richard E. King.* – STAINED GLASS. E window by *M. & A. O'Connor & Co.*, London.

The commanding position is enhanced by terraced lawns to the front, which with the main avenue were laid out in the last decade of the C19 by *William Sheppard* of Dundrum. Coach houses were added in the same period by *William Hague.*

The CONVENT was added in 1946 for the Sisters of St Louis, a neat classical block with a hipped roof in squared limestone with red brick trim. Two storeys and five bays with a stocky Doric doorcase. Built with stone from the Hamilton mansion, Cornacassa, an important Georgian house 2 km away demolished in 1934. The complex has spread on the E side with independent classroom ranges. The earliest of these, flat-roofed blocks of 1966 by *S. & G. MacCann*, represent institutional Modernism, in one and two storeys with nothing architectural other than concrete and close vertical fenestration. Later additions of 1984 by *C. J. Falconer* have the same functional inelegance: two-storey blocks with hipped roofs, clad in machined limestone.

WILLVILLE. 1.4 km SE. On the hill above Lathlorcan. An attractive small Georgian farmhouse, built *c.* 1764 when William McKenna bought the surrounding farm. Gable-ended, with a nicely proportioned front of two storeys and five bays with a round-headed window and door in the centre, which if given side-lights would look a little less isolated. Roughcast with strip quoins. Simple interior with corner fireplaces and raised and fielded panel joinery. The birthplace in 1771 of General Don Juan McKenna, Liberator of Chile.

ROSSMORE PARK. 3 km SSW. The story of Rossmore is the too-familiar tale of a historic Irish demesne – the estate succumbing to fragmentation, architectural vandalism, coniferous monoculture and golfing greens. As always the fundamental natural features remain, and it was the rolling topography that gave the place its name in the C18, Cortolvin Hills; the original gable-ended house was described in 1801 as 'a paltry cabin, unfurnished and mean'. It was retained as a service wing when *William Vitruvius Morrison*, towards the end of a partnership with his father *Richard*, greatly enlarged the house in a

p. 41

Jacobean cast for the 3rd Lord Rossmore in the 1820s. It was then further remodelled and enlarged, first in 1854 by *William Deane Butler*, and again just four years later by *W. H. Lynn*, the castellated result bringing together in a short time the impression of three centuries of architectural development in a spreading assemblage of disconcerting battlemented and gabled blocks with an array of disproportionate towers. The castle was abandoned in the 1940s, stripped and lay ruinous until ignominiously blown up by the local authority in 1974, leaving only its footprint and a small battlemented block.

The principal LODGES remain. The Tudor-style BALLY-LECK LODGE is a neat gable-ended block of one and a half storeys, with quarry glazing and a deep projecting porch bearing the lion rampant of the Rossmore crest. It stands across the road from an imposing gateway, possibly of earlier date. The tall classical piers have V-channelled rustication and florid iron gates and are flanked by pedestrian gates formed as chaste aedicules. The COOTEHILL LODGE is an odd red brick box with yellow brick trim, raised ashlar quoins and an unusually high pyramid roof, hidden behind an elaborate cast-iron gate screen.

Lost deep in the demesne woods is the MAUSOLEUM of 1876 by *E. J. Tarver*. Approached by a gloomy yew-lined avenue, it is a sad and quirky little Gothic building combining a squat gable-fronted hall with a domed cylindrical tower that clings perilously to rocks above a rushing stream. It was built to receive the remains of the young 4th Baron, killed in 1874 in a riding accident at Windsor (also commemorated in the memorial fountain in the Diamond, p. 472), and commissioned by his brother Derry, who believed the building 'so beautifully situated that it may well be said to make one in love with Death'. The low-slung roof is the dominant feature; clad with clay shingles and ridge tiles with unusual square perforations, it sweeps down to low side walls, raised on a deep offset plinth and impressed with a row of rectangular panels. The walls, of limestone ashlar, still have a knife-edge sharpness best appreciated in carved details such as the doorway, which is deeply set within chamfered pointed arches with slender engaged shafts and an unusual wide outer frame with stocky square shafts. A bulky timber bell-canopy projecting over the door is a rudimentary construction on brackets. At the rear the roof is hipped, colliding awkwardly with the tower that emerges as a dalek-like projection; the most pleasing part of the design is the way the tower's neat cylindrical body is roofed with a plump dome, formed of precision ashlar like an orb and bearing aloft a large stone cross. A shallow gable, projected on corbels above the ravine, is filled with a large three-light window with simple Y-tracery. Long vandalized and ruinous, now with ongoing restoration (2012) the interior is again impressive, a brick-lined space, laid out like a church with nave, aisles, and a raised apsidal sanctuary in the tower. Two-bay arcade with pointed arches of moulded brick on short

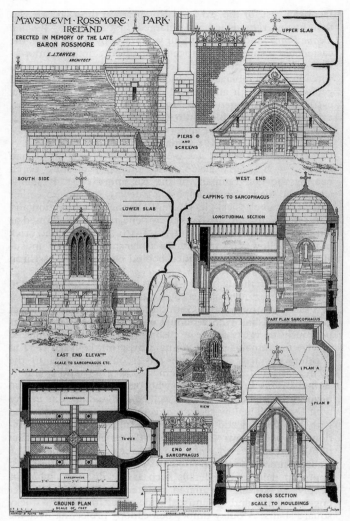

Monaghan, Rossmore Mausoleum.
Drawings by Maurice B. Adams, 1876

limestone columns with bell capitals and high bases. Elaborate
ironwork between the bays to screen the coffins. Overhead is
a simple timber-sheeted ceiling on a cornice formed in brick
as a billet moulding. The floor is richly patterned with mosaic
tiles centred on the Rossmore arms. The armorial stained-glass
window by *Heaton, Butler & Bayne* has been smashed to
pieces.

MOUNT NORRIS AH 9030

In November 1600 Lord Mountjoy occupied a bivallate ring fort here in his strategy to confine Hugh O'Neill N of the Blackwater. The site, elevated over low ground that was once an extensive morass, was described by Fynes Moryson as 'a hill like a promontory, all invironed with bogges, a river, and great store of wood'. The fort, named after Sir John Norris, Mountjoy's respected former general who had skirmished with Tyrone in the district five years before, was enlarged in 1601 and was described a decade later by Sir George Carew as 'a good fort well rampiered, with bulwarks, and a palisade and a fair deep ditch'. It was probably planned by *Levan De Rose*. The ring fort was modified from its circular form into an octagon, enclosing a cluster of houses, shown in Richard Bartlett's survey *c.* 1602 as little more than primitive thatched cabins, though they came to include some of cage-work. Nothing remains of the C17 defences except suggestive outlines, and today Mount Norris is a village with some well-preserved Late Georgian housing. The best of this is two whitewashed farmhouses, both with weather-slated gables, on the outskirts. The smaller of the two, on the Mowhan Road, is a three-bay, single-storey Regency cottage with Georgian sashes and a segmental fanlit doorway; the larger house, at No. 111 Bessbrook Road, has two storeys with Wyatt windows and a pleasing clutter of outbuildings behind.

MOUNT NORRIS PRESBYTERIAN CHURCH. Elevated off the Main Street, dull architecture unworthy of its prominent position. The origins of the church in 1791 are utterly unrecognizable in this roughcast T-plan structure.

ST PATRICK, LOUGHGILLY PARISH CHURCH (C of I). 2 km NE. 1811, rebuilt in 1828 and enlarged in 1863. A Board of First Fruits hall and tower of rubble with granite dressings, enlarged with chancel, vestry and transepts in rock-faced granite by *Welland & Gillespie*. The contractor was *Arthur Henry*. The nave was refenestrated in the same period with simple plate tracery. Inside, plain to the point of austerity. – Of primary interest is a C17 polygonal FONT which attests to the antiquity of the site. Formed from a single piece of tapering limestone with an inscription carved in relief above recessed panels, it was erected in the old parish church by the Rev. George Synge in 1637.

Beside the churchyard, the former WIDOWS' ALMSHOUSES, a vernacular two-storey gable-ended block in roughcast with quarry glazing. Built in 1811 for the Rev. Thomas Vesey Dawson to accommodate four 'respectable' aged women in a two-up, two-down scheme, the upper rooms entered from the gables by external stairs. Each of the houses is elegantly numbered on a granite keystone above the door.

LOUGHGILLY HOUSE. 2 km NE. Derelict. The N wing of a substantial glebe house. Originally a solid three-storey block built in 1782, enlarged by the Rev. Thomas Vesey Dawson *c.* 1806, when two-storey wings were added to the N and S and linked by a corridor across the front of the house. The addition cost £1,819, twice the cost of the original house. The architect was *Francis Johnston*, who a decade earlier had designed Townley Hall in Co. Louth for Dawson's brother-in-law. What survives has two storeys over a basement, walls of roughcast over rubble and red brick with granite dressings on the w front. Crudely adapted as a smaller house in the C20; the s front now exposes expanses of red brick that hint at its former place in a larger house. Johnston's work is evident only on the narrow w façade; here the recession of the single ground-floor window in a wide elliptical arch is an elegant Regency device favoured by the architect. The tall window above this is more unusual, with a carved pediment on tapered corbels rising above the eaves course. The plainer E front had Wyatt windows.

KINGSMILLS PRESBYTERIAN CHURCH. 4 km SSE. A plain pebbledashed hall with half-hipped gables. A date on the porch suggests an origin in 1788; another says rebuilt in 1837 by the Rev. A. Henry. Five bays with round-headed windows, all now horribly fenestrated in plastic.

TULLYHERRON CHURCH. 1 km S. A small C19 stuccoed church with a bellcote and hooded lancets in blocked surrounds. Cruciform, with clumpy buttressing to the three-bay nave. Inside, accomplished carpentry work in the gallery frontal; otherwise plain. – STAINED GLASS. Routine work by *Clokey*, Belfast.

GLENANNE HOUSE. 1.5 km SW. An unpretentious two-storey Victorian block in roughcast, with a low hipped roof on wide oversailing eaves. Built *c.* 1860 in front of a compact gable-ended Georgian house, still prominent round the back. Three-bay front with tripartite windows, plate glass and a large central stuccoed porch. Just one room deep, with bay windows in the end walls. In the early C19 the residence of William Atkinson, who established the nearby COTTON MILLS, later acquired and expanded by George Gray & Sons, and now decaying.

TULLYALLEN PRESBYTERIAN CHURCH. 1.5 km NW. A church was established here in 1742 by the Rev. John Mulligan. Rebuilt in 1780, its origins now unrecognizable in the rather dull six-bay hall. Roughcast with a tiled roof.

In the churchyard, the tiny three-bay COTTAGE is a rare survivor more worthy of notice.

MOUNT NUGENT   CN

A small village picturesquely situated beside Lough Sheelin. Associated with the Nugent family of Farren Connell, who were first established in the district in the C15, based at Racraveen, where a substantial motte and bailey survives. In 1762 Robert Nugent was granted a patent to hold fairs and markets at Mount Nugent.

ST BRIDE (C of I). A hall-and-tower church built, according to a plaque over the entrance, in 1804 on ground gifted by Oliver Nugent of Bobsgrove (now Farren Connell). A small rectangular church of rubble with just two bays and a short chancel. Pretty three-stage tower with battlements and finials, set between a small lean-to vestry and stairs, added later and much lower than the main gable. Inside, attractively plain with plastered ceilings and a galleried W end. – MONUMENTS. William Evans †1898 and Georgina Evans †1904; a plain marble scroll by *C. W. Harrison*. – Oliver St George Nugent †1929; an allegory of Psalm 75 incised in plaster, by *Percy Oswald Reeves*, 1933, signed with the monogram of the artist.

ST BRIGID. An early C19 pebbledashed church with big lancets in stone frames. The familiar vernacular barn, with a cruciform plan, altered in 1887 when the chancel was given a highly finished kneelered gable in squared rock-faced limestone with a traceried window. Plainer entrance front with a big hooded oculus; altered in the late C20 with short lean-to projections at the side, resulting in a strange sprocketed gable and a shallow entrance projection in rusticated limestone between three narrow lancets. Inside, plain with plaster ceilings and nice internal timber porches. – STAINED GLASS. Traceried E window with bright figurative glass signed *Cox, Sons, Buckley & Co.*, London and New York, 1887. – MONUMENTS. Patrick Ahern †1884; a white marble scroll with shamrocks. – Philip Sheridan †1889; a Gothic tablet with polished shafts over a stoup. – The Rev. Michael Fannan †1907; a Romanesque tablet in white marble, signed *Edmund Sharp*, Great Brunswick Street, Dublin.

KILNACROTT. 2.5 km NE. A middle-size house, in a Tudor Revival style with pinnacled gables and an extraordinary *porte cochère*, evoking all the attenuated Regency elegance found in the work of the Reptons, and a picturesqueness that brings to mind Sir Jeffry Wyatville's Endsleigh in Devon. In 1609 the

Mount Nugent, Kilnacrott.
Lithograph by Hodges and Smith, *c.* 1850

castle and lands of 'Killnecroitt' were granted to the Countess
of Delvin and her son, Sir Richard Nugent, but by 1661
Abraham Clements was resident here, having been granted the
property under the Act of Settlement three years before. Before
the end of the C18 it belonged to the Mortons of nearby Drum-
rora (demolished). Pierce Morton resided here in the early C19,
having inherited after the suicide of his brother Charles in
1832. They were descended from the physician Dr Charles
Morton, Librarian of the British Museum in the late C18,
whose two successive marriages to ladies of the Pratt family
are commemorated in the carved arms above the entrance.
There is now no trace of the castle or its site.

The house, known in 1837 as Kilnacrott Cottage, was remodelled soon after, perhaps following Pierce Morton's marriage to
Louisa Somerville in 1839. The extent of the works was much
greater than what is to be seen today. A lower, distinct range to
the W was demolished before the end of the C19. Substantial in
its own right, it was overall more Nash-like, with projecting
gabled end blocks, wide bracketed eaves, and Regency canopied hoods over the ground-floor windows. Its loss explains
something of the present disjointed appearance, as nothing
balances the yard enclosure to the E, with its long curtain wall
and steep angular archway. In 1853 the property was purchased
from the Landed Estate Court by *William Hague Sen.*, who
local tradition records had been the contractor for the house
some years before. Hague leased out the house and is said to
have pulled down the wing, probably in 1880, when the rateable
valuation was reduced by half. The younger William Hague
inherited but appears not to have lived here either, and his son
sold it in 1903. It passed in 1931 to the Norbertine Order, who
built Holy Trinity Abbey nearby from 1948.

What remains is essentially a near-symmetrical two-storey
block in smooth plaster with limestone dressings, four bays
wide with kneelered gables as shallow projections to the end
bays, made asymmetrical first by an oriel window on the E
gable and more completely by the lanky *porte cochère* on the
opposite side, looking even more unwieldy after the loss of the
W range. Independently, the *porte cochère* is an architectural
peach, a joyful creation executed entirely in pale cut limestone,
and undecorated but for a panelled Gothic frieze interrupted
in the centre by the coat of arms breaking the parapet, under-
scored by the Morton motto, *Sub nexu nunquam servili* (Never
bound by slavery). It has three bays with tall four-centred
arches, framed between polygonal turrets flaring into wide
crowning battlements. Similar elements are reduced in the
centre to become engaged shafts set against the piers, but
reduced almost to splinters; these reappear with the same
proportions as soaring finials on the gables, enhancing the
sense of elegant fragility and giving the building one of its most
striking features. The windows are rectangular, generously
proportioned, and mullioned with plate glass and label mouldings; the two central windows on the first floor break the

eaves line in an unusual fashion, forcing the eaves moulding upwards, resulting in a rather squarish, abruptly terminated appearance.

The interiors have a spare Regency Gothic charm, oblivious to the coming ebullience of the Victorian age. The square entrance hall has plaster rib-vaulting with pendants; a more elaborate quadripartite vault in the stair hall is geometrically patterned with plaster ribs, frugally decorated with foliate bosses. Otherwise the ceilings of the main rooms are flat, compartmented with plaster ribs, each compartment in the drawing room displaying a wreathed coat of arms and motto.

HOLY TRINITY ABBEY. 1948 by *Downes & Meehan*. A large, rather bland, institutional block on the edge of the Kilnacrott demesne. Three storeys tall, in pebbledash on a rusticated limestone plinth with gabled ends and cleated copper roofs. The real architectural force of the abbey was, alas, not realized, as funds never materialized to complete the large cruciform church. Instead, the big round-headed arches of the cloistered return peter out in raw concrete arcades, all weathered and ancient-looking.

KILDORAGH CHURCH (C of I). 3.75 km NE. 1862 by *Welland & Gillespie*. A rather special small Gothic church, shamefully forlorn at the time of writing. Built of limestone rubble with cutstone dressings, to a perfectly simple Tractarian plan consisting of a three-bay nave and chancel with a gabled vestry set in the SE angle between them. The entrance is in a small buttressed tower, forestanding to the SW, its square plan broached in the upper stage before a steep octagonal spirelet. The nave windows have sharply pointed lancets, grouped together with quarry glazing; Geometric tracery in the chancel. The contractor was *Patrick Sharp*. Inside, an exposed timber roof with scissor trusses. – MONUMENT. The Rev. Andrew Hogg †1871; a Gothic tablet of marble and sandstone with a boldly crocketed gable.

KILDORAGH GLEBE HOUSE. 3.75 km NE. 1818. The familiar two-storey-over-basement block, solid and dependable, with a hipped roof and a big central stack. Roughcast with chunky dressed limestone reveals. The main front has three bays with twelve-pane Georgian sashes on the ground floor and smaller sixteen-pane sashes above. The entrance was remodelled *c*. 1930 in a rather handsome arrangement when a closed porch with a round-headed window replaced the former distyle portico, whose columns and pilaster responds were set up to form two open porches on either side of the porch proper, though the greater success of the design is let down a little by the absence of capitals. The garden front is more irregular, with tripartite windows on one side, indicating the position of the drawing room in the plan. Inside, a compact arrangement of three rooms around a central hall with apsidal stairs set to one side on the front, the curve not expressed externally.

FARREN CONNELL (formerly BOBSGROVE). 4 km SSW. Its twin name evocative of romance and enchantment, this is an old demesne insulated by big trees with a house and yards buried deep at its heart. The house is a two-storey, five-bay gable-ended block with wide overhanging eaves, the roofs extended out over the gables to include the prominent projection of the chimneystacks. The entrance front has big Victorian sashes with plate glass and an off-centre square porch. Behind, a large and irregular three-storey return, partly raised on a basement. Farren Connell was long known after the C18 as Bobsgrove, having been named for Robert Nugent, whose family, a cadet branch of the earls of Westmeath, were already well established here before the end of the C17. The old house, of indeterminable date and never very substantial, was recast in the early C20 by General Sir Oliver Nugent and his wife Catherine Percy Lees, but more modestly than they originally intended; a drawing preserved in the house signed by *Thomas Manly Deane* in 1907 shows a substantial Tudor Revival house with big gables, bay windows and a castellated porch. This was superseded by a scheme by *Sir Thomas Drew*, whose plans, dated 1909, proposed a new entrance block to the E. This too was not realized, and it seems that the Nugents settled instead for refurbishment of the old house. Drew's plans show the outline of the present house, suggesting the survival today of a much older structure beneath; this is apparent not least in the thickness of the w gable, the massive chimneystacks, the modest room proportions, and the presence of corner fireplaces in the return. It seems probable that *Drew* was responsible for the more limited scheme to remodel the old house, essentially confined to refitting the interiors and creating a heavy iron-balustraded open-well stair in the newly formed entrance hall, communicating between two large reception rooms placed one above the other on one side of the plan. The drawing room, on the ground floor, is a bright rectangular space with a moulded cornice; the carved timber chimneypiece is a handsome design of *c.* 1760 with a Rococo frieze, presumably from the old house.

The YARDS, close by to the w, are fronted by an attractive C18 L-plan range, two storeys tall, in roughcast with round-headed windows on the first floor. The w front was remodelled in the early C20 with half-dormers.

WOODLAWN. 2 km NW. A handsomely proportioned Late Georgian house set in a small demesne beside Lough Sheelin. A three-bay roughcast block, two storeys on a basement, with twelve-pane sashes, hipped roof and central stacks. The original entrance, behind a later flat-roofed porch, is a narrow, round-arched doorway in a moulded limestone frame with a leaded petal fanlight. Set back discreetly on either side are low vernacular wings with lunettes, the short ends of more substantial L-plan ranges. These enclose a large sunken yard, where they become two-storey buildings formally framing the house. This stands to its full height at the head of the yard, set squarely with the segmental archway in the enclosing curtain wall at the opposite end. Wholesome vernacular architecture enriched on understated Palladian principles.

MOUNTAIN LODGE CN 5000

A rural crossroads 11 km NW of Bailieborough.

ST PATRICK, CARRICKALLEN. 2 km NW. 1844. A small barn church with lancets, enlarged in 1859 to a T-plan with a deep three-bay projection to the rear. Roughcast with stuccoed strip quoins. Wide doorcase in the W gable in a simple blocked surround with a slender, similarly treated lancet above. Inside, the original placing of the altar in the centre of the long E wall survives; otherwise nothing of architectural interest now. Meanly furnished, with the sanctuary wall hideously stone-clad like a badly conceived fireplace in an olde worlde public house. – FONT. A handsome limestone design with crested decoration on the rim. – MONUMENTS. The Rev. Anthony Smith †1862; a white marble tablet, signed *Moss*, Drogheda. – Another similar, unsigned, to the Rev. Peter McCann †1878.

ST BRIGID, TUNNYDUFF. 4 km SE. A large and very ordinary T-plan church, painted brilliant white. Roughcast with plain lancets. Broad W gable with a narrow tower-like projection in which an embedded stone plaque records the builder, the Rev. Patrick Brady P.P., and the date, 1845. Not recorded here is the name of the stonemason, *Mr Murray* from nearby Knocknalossett. The bulky flat-roofed porches and the tower are additions by *Patrick Gaffney* of 1952. Tower offset on the W gable with a linking screen wall; tall and cardboard-like, its three diminishing stages and copper pyramid roof are the most appealing elements of the building. Inside plain, with a raking W gallery. Sanctuary enclosed with marble altar rails; three-light E window in a shallow semicircular recess, flanked by big lancets, all with early C20 stained glass. – STATIONS OF THE CROSS. Noteworthy mid-C20 panels with scenes painted in a cartoon-like manner against a gilded background.

ST MICHAEL, CLIFFERNA. 5 km SW. A T-plan church of 1821 replacing a long, low thatched chapel of 1796 on a different site. Roughcast with four-bay front and low-set pointed windows. Renovated in 1973, and again, more extensively, in 2005–6, including a new sacristy and stone-clad porches on the end bays. A crudely carved stone embedded in the front wall came from the church of 1796, the barely legible inscription recording its erection by the Rev. Edward McCormack.

MULLAGH CN 6080

A small market village on the road between Kells and Bailieborough, with a single wide street lined with good two- and three-storey houses.

ST KILIAN. On the Virginia Road. Dedicated to a local saint martyred in Würzburg in the C7. Located outside the village, a hall-and-tower church of 1857 in a restrained Gothic idiom, that looks as though it might have been cribbed from a Board of First Fruits plan and enlarged. The architect was the parish priest, the *Rev. John Conaty*; the builder *Mr McGennis* of Tullyvin. Rubble walls with ashlar trim. A large four-bay nave, said to accommodate a congregation of 2,000. Clasping buttresses with pinnacles to the W, diagonal to the E. Simple lancet windows with hoodmoulds and stained glass. Three-stage W tower with S doorway, parapets with central gables and corner pinnacles. Unusually tall lancet on the W elevation, flanking lancets on the adjoining gable. Single-storey porch of ashlar between the bays on the SW corner, possibly added later. Chancel added in 1862, somewhat more expressive and assured, with ogee-headed triple lancet window. Formerly richly decorated with a fine Gothic reredos and side altars, the interior has been 'improved' to provide a sterile environment of brightly coloured glass, royal blue carpets and a collection of bizarre sculpted tree-trunks as sanctuary fittings. – Original BELL by *Murphy* of Thomas Street, Dublin. – Limestone STATUE of St Kilian by *H. Flanagan* O.P., *c.* 1989.

The PAROCHIAL HOUSE opposite the church facing the village is the standard mid-C19 rendered two-storey, three-bay house with hipped roof, rear return and contiguous outhouses.

74 MULLAGH PARISH CHURCH (C of I). 1 km NW. 1819. A charming diminutive hall-and-tower church in a small tree-filled enclosure, perfectly scaled and suited to its picturesque setting beside Mullagh Lake. Typical, ornamental rather than academic, early C19 First Fruits Gothic, presumably the work of *John Bowden*. Three-bay nave of rubble with ashlar trim. Central gabled vestry to the S and battlemented W tower in three diminishing stages. Attractive windows with hoodmoulds and timber Y-tracery (a rare survival), unusually embellished with flat cusps applied to the outer frame.

To the W a ruined single-cell structure with limestone rubble walls, referred to locally as TEAMPALL CEALLAIGH ('Kilian's church'). Possibly no earlier than the C18, this large building is entered in the NW corner. Square-headed E window opening and remains of an off-centre window on the S wall. Small fireplace on the W wall with stack expressed externally.

KILLEETER NATIONAL SCHOOL. 2 km NNW. Derelict. An attractive rural school of 1834 on the side of Killeeter Hill. Plain two-storey, three-bay rendered block with eight-over-eight Georgian sash windows, hipped roof and flanking side porches.

LAKEVIEW. 2 km SW. A curious but attractive limewashed house, built in the mid C19 for the Mortimer family and perfectly suited to its beautiful setting by Mullagh Lake. Originally a small three-bay block with rambling returns, to which a deep and somewhat ungainly central projection was added in an Arts and Crafts manner with an open pediment naïvely supported on scrolled brackets. The first floor was carried out on corbels and given big metal windows. The proportions and arrangement of the windows on the original block, forming tripartite compositions with plate glass, are not always happy, though they are part of the building's distinctiveness and appeal. Adjoining the house are very fine gardens, restored and enhanced 1997 by *Daphne Levinge Shackleton*.

MULLAGHBAWN

AH . 9010

A village in south Armagh in the valley of the River Forkhill.

ST MARY. 1857 by *Richard Hynes* of Newry. A neat cruciform chapel with lancets. Roughcast with stuccoed quoins, window surrounds and hoodmoulds. The gables have large pointed windows; the s window is housed in a short gabled projection. Inside, the kingpost trusses are sparing and functional. – STAINED GLASS. Colourful three-light E window by *Clokey*, Belfast. In the s transept a simple symbolic design by *McManus Design*, 1982. – MONUMENT. The Rev. Hugh Mulligan †1878; a grey marble tablet.

SILVERBRIDGE HOUSE. 3 km SW. An attractive Early Victorian house in a small picturesque demesne. L-plan with two adjoining fronts in roughcast with mullioned timber casements and flat label mouldings. The main front has two storeys and three bays, the end bays gabled with decorative bargeboards and bay windows on the ground floor formed of Armagh limestone. The entrance front is to the side, of three bays, the centre bay advanced and gabled with an attractive Ionic doorcase and fanlight below a small oriel window. The service wing is a gaunt three-storey block at right angles to the entrance front, with three bays and a hipped roof rising above the main house. The later addition of the upper floor with plate-glass windows accounts for its incongruous appearance. Adjoining one- and two-storey vernacular ranges form a very handsome farmyard to one side.

BALLYKEEL DOLMEN. 3 km N. The best example of a portal tomb in the region. Three triangular uprights supporting a flat sloping triangular capstone enclose a burial chamber at the s end of a wedge-shaped cairn or barrow, defined now by the surviving kerbstones. The low stone between the paired ortho- stats to the s marks the entrance. Excavations in 1963 uncov- ered large quantities of Stone Age pottery which confirmed the Neolithic origin of the monument, *c.* 3500 B.C. A stone-lined cist was also found in the N end of the cairn.

OUR LADY, QUEEN OF PEACE, AUGHANDUFF. 3.5 km NW. 1957 by *Simon Aloysius Leonard* of *W. H. Byrne & Son*. A large five-bay hall with pebbledashed walls, stucco quoins, and wide boxed eaves supported on iron brackets. The windows are plain round-headed lancets with rusticated surrounds. To one side a slender free-standing tower adds elegance to the structure; square in plan and tall, with unrelenting quoins, it gently tapers until capped abruptly by a low pyramid roof. Inside, plain and lofty; the ceiling is pitched and, like the E wall, is divided into recessed panels pierced with a cross pattern.

A large ring fort beside the town indicates early origins of settlement here and gives the town the Irish name *Liosdarrach*, 'fort of the oaks'. This area was anciently held by the MacMahons until acquired by Gilbert Nicholson in the C17, eventually passing in the early C18 to Sanderson Stevenson, who sold his lands to Andrew Ker in 1730. Ker's son Robert built a house here in 1740 and developed the town when he gained the rights to hold fairs and markets in 1751. It was still a small town at the end of the C18, with one wide street that despite its great scale would never achieve much consequence. Under the shadow of NEWBLISS HOUSE, rebuilt in 1814 (demolished in the 1940s), there was considerable growth in the early C19. In 1821 there were forty houses, which more than doubled to ninety-five in 1837. Many of the houses found on the main street today are large three-storey blocks, built as if in expectation of a greater expansion that never materialized.

NEWBLISS PARISH CHURCH (C of I). Cootehill Road. Of *c.* 1838 by *William Farrell*. Built as a chapel of ease under the patronage of Dr Andrew Ker. An exciting small church, dramatically sited against a hillside on the edge of the town with a whimsical tower bristling with needle-like pinnacles. Irregular cruciform plan formed by a wide gabled projection to the N and a smaller S arm, occupied by the vestry. Rubble, with carved details; angle buttresses and belfry of ashlar. The windows are quarry-glazed, those of the nave lancets with hoodmoulds, contrasting with a large E window with three graded round-headed lights, unusually separated simply by slim, plain chamfered mullions and with a transom. A blind miniature group overhead, intended as a roof vent and repeated on the N gable. The tower is in three diminishing stages, arranged like Russian dolls, with striking outer pinnacles on the upper stages, rising to a tall octagonal spirelet. The lower stage is differentiated with gables and angled buttresses, like those on the nave. These are finished abruptly with small gabled caps that look as if they might once have been extended into pinnacles. The tower was intended as an eye-catcher for vistas from Newbliss House to the W (*see* above). A watercolour sketch by William Greenlees dated February 1839 shows the tower scaffolded in anticipation of its pinnacles and demonstrates the mutual relationship between the church and the patron's demesne.

As so often is the case, any expectation of similar architectural drama inside is disappointed; the interior is truly spartan, but with a good sense of space. Lofty ceilings follow a shallow pitch rather mundanely broken up by plaster ribs with foliate bosses, all simple unfussy stuff. The Murray-Ker seat is elevated on the N side, taking up the larger arm of the cross and perched over the family burial vault. – MONUMENTS. Andre Allen Murray-Ker †1892; a decent Gothic tabernacle. – Mary Anne Murray-Ker †1900; a plain white marble scroll, by *Purdy & Millard*, Belfast.

PRESBYTERIAN CHURCH. Monaghan Road. A dispute with the landlord brought about the setting up of this church on the edge of the town, completed in 1842. Trim four-bay hall, gable-fronted, with a minister's house forming a T-plan to the E. Roughcast with blocked ashlar quoins, chamfered window reveals and carved hoodmoulds. Simple Y-tracery with quarry glazing, greatly enhanced by the survival of crown glass. Low Tudor-arched entrance set in the gable between windows with a deep chamfered reveal and a compound roll-moulded surround. Plain interior with compartmented timber-panelled ceiling. – STAINED GLASS. A pair of highly decorative panels flanking the pulpit, the Holy Bible and 'Ardens sed Virens' (Burning but flourishing), by *Ward & Partner*, Belfast, c. 1901. – MONUMENTS. Edward B. McCaldin †1942, and the Rev. W. Keers †1943, both signed *Harrison Ltd*, Dublin.

COURTHOUSE. Main Street. Of c. 1820. Unassuming two-storey L-plan block. Originally symmetrical, of three bays with the central bay recessed, later extended by a further bay on one side to accommodate a now closed carriage arch. Rubble, roughcast. Sash windows on the first floor; big tripartite casements in shallow relieving arches on the ground floor, giving an air of sophistication.

MARKET HOUSE. At the centre of the Main Street. The familiar Late Georgian type, a tall block of two storeys and five bays, made clumsy by fussy narrow projecting end bays and a shallow hipped roof with stumpy brick chimneys. Also an unhappy mixture of materials: rubble, red brick, sandstone and limestone. The odd contrast is especially prominent on the first floor and in the end bays, which are too complex and too weak to support the more robust centre, where the three arched bays on the ground floor are in clean limestone ashlar. The side arches now closed in brick and fenestrated; the central carriageway leads through to the rear and its more agreeable rubble-and-brick elevation.

MASONIC HALL. Main Street. 1927 by *William R. Potts*. A trim structure of small proportions. Three-bay hall, pebbledashed with stucco details, red tiled roof and a small flat-roofed porch extending across the front. Masonic symbols and date on the gable.

PARISH HALL. Corner of the Main Street and Clones Road. Simple roughcast hall of four bays with plain lancets in ashlar surrounds and sloping pier buttresses between the bays. Formerly a Presbyterian church, built in the C18 under the patronage of the Ker family. A visitation in 1778 deplored the bad repair of the meeting house, the prevalence of drunkenness, oaths and clandestine marriages, and the numbers who attended horse-racing. Rebuilt in 1816. A pleasant little building not improved by C20 additions.

MAIL COACH INN (former). Of c. 1820. A welcoming Regency building with a tall well-proportioned front on the Main Street facing the approach from Clones. A solid three-storey block with three bays on the principal front and two on the sides. Roughcast with blocked limestone quoins, low hipped roof, and solid red brick stacks, emphatically detailed in cutstone. Handsome recessed doorcase with pulvinated pilasters and scrolled brackets, side-lights and a plain radial fanlight. The fenestration pattern is interesting, with windows set in recessed arches on the ground floor and Wyatt windows on the first floor, diminishing to smaller uniform sashes across the upper storey. Contemporary two-storey range of outbuildings to the rear in rubble and brick with a pedimented projection.

NEIGHBOURHOOD

GLYNCH HOUSE. 1 km N. Of c. 1815. A drawing by *Richard Morrison*'s draughtsman Owen Fahy indicates that an ambitious scheme for a castellated mansion was originally proposed here for a Mr Joseph Rogers. A symmetrical version of the castle style employed by Morrison at Castle Freke (Co. Cork) and Moydrum Castle (Co. Westmeath), the design was rather stiff and unpromising. Only the symmetrical clarity was retained in the present house, a crisp Regency villa of two storeys over a half-basement, plainly rendered with Georgian windows, a low hipped roof, and oversailing bracketed eaves. There are two principal fronts: a three-bay entrance front with windows set in relieving arches with segmental heads on the ground floor, and a longer, plainer elevation to one side with four bays. The porch is a sophisticated composition set up on a podium which reads as a simplified version of Morrison's portico for Mount Henry (Co. Laois), with slender Doric columns on square bases, set *in antis*, and a shallow pediment. Apart from this there are few of the characteristics of Morrison's work, so that if he was involved here, as Fahy's drawing might suggest, Glynch is a restrained and much less idiosyncratic example of his smaller villas.

Internally the house has none of Morrison's distinguishing traits, nor of his finesse. The plan lacks the overall coherence one would expect: two large rooms on either side of a deep hall are isolated at the front. The rooms are plain, with little decoration; only the six doves fluttering in isolation, in very low relief, around the ceiling rose in the drawing room relate to Morrison's decorative repertoire. Beyond the hall, the staircase and adjoining rooms are subsidiary spaces, tucked away at the back of the house and unremarkable. The house is closely similar to Aghafin near Clones, and the two may well share the same local architect. In 1837 the residence of J. Thompson and afterwards of William Dawson Mayne.

RAILWAY STATION (former). 0.5 km NE. 1860 by *William G. Murray* for the Dundalk & Enniskillen Railway. The same understated Gothic employed by Murray at Ballybay. Two-storey and single-storey gabled blocks linked by a short arcaded range, raised on a high plinth with substantial steps leading to the entrance in the link building under Tudor arches. The contractor was *John Nolan* of Dublin. Undergoing reconstruction at the time of writing.

ST MARY, LATNAMARD. 5 km NE. A lively church of 1812 dominated by its ornamental tower and spire added in 1867. A big roughcast rectangular hall with stucco quoins, large pointed windows in blocked surrounds with hoodmoulds, and pronounced eaves corbels. The tower is square in plan, its height accentuated in five diminishing stages, defined by simple string-courses, and finished with a very fine broach spire in cutstone with dummy lucarnes and turret-like pinnacles on the corners. The entrance is on the S side through an ordinary pointed doorway, facing a neat polygonal baptistery projecting on the N side of the tower. The interior is airy, with an open-truss roof on corbels with arched braces and iron ties. The canted timber gallery with a balustrade pierced by quatrefoils, the marble ALTAR RAILS, and the HIGH ALTAR with its crocketed spires are all remarkable survivors. – The STATIONS OF THE CROSS are particularly noteworthy, presenting relief images in sturdy Gothic frames. – STAINED GLASS. Three-light E window, extending awkwardly into the attic space, with richly coloured glass in the manner of Harry Clarke Studios.

DRUMKEEN PRESBYTERIAN CHURCH. 5 km E. A pleasing rural hall of five bays with a lower, two-storey minister's house set back on one side. Built in 1803; a plaque over the doorway records works to the fabric in 1828 and 1889. Roughcast with plain stucco detail. Pointed windows with basic Y-tracery. Unusually, the entrance is placed to one side on the main elevation, with a pointed doorway set in a deep moulded surround. The most interesting aspect of the interior is the raking floor; further to ensure the attention of the congregation, the seats along the side walls are all angled towards the pulpit. Interior refurnished in 1889 with a gallery to the rear. – Good Victorian entrance with cast-iron PILLARS and wrought-iron GATES.

DRUMBREAN COTTAGE. 5 km E. A perfect Late Georgian house, modest in scale, with simple proportions – proof that all that is good in Georgian architecture can be seen in the simplest designs. A rectangular roughcast block of two storeys and three bays with a hipped roof and unusually slender brick stacks. Plain Georgian sashes, carefully diminished on the first floor, and an exquisite timber doorcase with fanlight and sidelights. The quality of the joinery is carried through to the interior, evident in fine shutter detailing.

LISDARRAGH RECTORY. 0.5 km SE. An attractive Early Victorian Tudor Gothic cottage, rather like a simplified version of Annaghmakerrig nearby. Three-bay gable-ended block with a central two-storey gabled projection. Rubble with red brick and sandstone trim, paired sashes, a high-pitched roof with oversailing eaves, and central chimneys with diagonal stacks. The breakfront has a heavily moulded coping with a carved finial and elongated kneelers like those at Annaghmakerrig, but here ornamented with primitive heads of a monastic cast. The entrance is through a discreet doorway in the side gable. A lower two-storey return adjoins to form an L-plan. Nice frilly bargeboards on the end gables, detailed with a form of inverted Vitruvian scroll.

AGHABOG PARISH CHURCH (C of I). 2.5 km SE. 1875 by *G. C. Henderson*. Built to replace an C18 church – a 'plain rectangular building without a spire' – of which no trace survives. A gable-fronted single cell with a bellcote, polygonal apse, and diagonally opposed porch and vestry, all modestly scaled like Welland's smaller rural churches, though here the result with solid E.E. detail in rubble and limestone trim is more ponderous; the carved details, however, are excellent. High-pitched roofs resting on carved corbels over the nave and on a continuous cornice around the apse. Plain lancets with chamfered reveals, on the W gable set as a pair under an oculus in a recessed arch with a quatrefoil overhead. Henderson had been engaged on improvements at Annaghmakerrig at this time, working with *Albert E. Murray*. The builder was *John Maguire* of Newtownbutler. Burial place of Sir Tyrone Guthrie and his ancestors.

DRUMSWORDS OLD CHURCH (C of I). 4.5 km SW. A roofless single-cell church in a quiet rural graveyard. Simple rectangular structure with strong rubble walls. Round-headed openings, two in the S and N walls; carved stone frames and evidence of a central mullion and basic Y-tracery suggest a C17 origin for the building. The E window is barely discernible beneath the ivy; a blocked doorway is visible in the W gable. Later door in the N wall; a heavily eroded MONUMENT with an elaborate coat of arms is fixed to the inside of this wall.

LISALEA. 0.5 km NW. A plain mid-C19 house of two storeys over a basement to a standard L-plan. Three-bay front, plainly rendered with blocked quoins, plate-glass windows, and a low hipped roof with projecting eaves on paired brackets. The porch is a narrow boxy projection with stuccoed strip quoins, cornice and blocking course.

NEWTOWNHAMILTON   AH

A small town with tight meandering streets in the uplands of the Fews Mountains. Alexander Hamilton sought a patent to hold a fair at Tullyvallen in 1746, and by 1795 it was stated that a considerable town had grown up around the well-supplied weekly linen market. Sixty houses were recorded here in 1837. Today the best are to be found in a late C19 red brick terrace with a central carriage arch at the s end of the Main Street.

ST JOHN (C of I). Shamble Lane, beside the market place. 1867 by *Welland & Gillespie*. The church opened in 1869; the contractor was *Walter Doolin*. A forbidding, highly textured church in dark limestone with sandstone trim and the hard angular plate tracery often favoured by the architects. This is a complicated and playful design consisting of a three-bay buttressed nave, offset tower and polygonal chancel. The tower lies flush with the gable, its tall belfry stage finishing with heavy pinnacles. Asymmetry is reinforced by a squat vestry lying opposite under a steep chisel roof. On the side elevation, the pitch of the nave roof changes dramatically over the bays to indicate aisles, while the E bays are enlarged with gables to form transepts. Inside, neither is represented in the plan, and the space is a rather ordinary single cell, unusually brick-lined, but with an interesting roof: along the walls a series of pocket vaults with timber ribs, springing from corbels to support a pointed tunnel-vault; spanning the vault, a series of heavy tie-beams propped by diagonal struts extending from the corbels, in an expression of structural rationalism worthy of Viollet-le-Duc. – STAINED GLASS. In the chancel three largely decorative mid-C20 windows with figurative panels by *Clokey & Co.*, Belfast.

ST MICHAEL. Dundalk Road. A compact lancet hall, rendered, with Armagh limestone dressings. Three bays, the central bay shortened over small confessional outshots. Pleasing gabled front with ashlar angle buttresses and windows arranged under hoods. Built by the Rev. Michael Caraher, as recorded in a replacement plaque over the door that gives the date as 1834; other sources suggest it opened a decade later. Inside, a hollow space with a timber-panelled ceiling. Gallery installed in 1857; further works by *Richard Hynes* in 1877. Completely refitted in the late C20, destroying the C19 interior; the sole survivor is the FONT, an elegant Gothic design in statuary marble supported on a cluster of grey columns. – STAINED GLASS by *Clokey*, Belfast.

SECOND NEWTOWNHAMILTON PRESBYTERIAN CHURCH. Castleblayney Street. 1821. A large three-bay stuccoed hall, square in plan, with pointed windows, a steep hipped roof, and a deep projecting gabled front. On the front, flat pilaster strips unite over the central bay in an arch to frame an oculus. Alterations of 1907 by *Samuel Wilson Reside*.

NEWTOWNHAMILTON OLD CHURCH, TULLYVALLEN (C of I). 2.5 km s. Ruinous. A bereft hall and tower, built to one of *Thomas Cooley*'s 'standard' designs for the parish newly formed here in 1773, and abandoned in 1869. A plain hall of three bays with rubble walls and gaping pointed windows. The tower is similar to that of Salters Grange, with subtle lesene strips punctuated by blind loops and three stages, elongated in the middle stage with an intermediary cornice; unusually large openings to the crenellated upper stage. As at Lisnadill the date – here 1775 – is carved in c18 script on the string-course.

FIRST NEWTOWNHAMILTON PRESBYTERIAN CHURCH, CLARKE'S BRIDGE. 3.5 km SW. A neat T-plan church with half-hipped gables, roughcast walls and stuccoed quoins. The main block has five bays with pointed windows. – STAINED GLASS. Coloured glass in Art Nouveau patterns. Good mid-C20 stained glass in the E windows.

ALTNAMACKAN PRESBYTERIAN CHURCH. 3.5 km SW. Abandoned. A four-bay roughcast hall, built in 1837 by the Rev. Daniel Brown. Moulded Gothic doorway in the entrance gable, flanked by lancets, all with hoodmoulds.

TULLYVALLEN SECESSION MEETING HOUSE. 3 km W. 1851. A four-bay hall, roughcast with stuccoed quoins, half-hipped gables and pointed windows. A pleasant building but for the ugly plastic windows.

HOLY TRINITY, ARMAGHBREAGUE (C of I). 4.5 km NW. 1831 by *William Farrell*. Remotely situated amidst the conifer belts of the Fews Mountains. A fine example of Farrell's smaller Board of First Fruits designs. A three-bay gabled hall and porch with rubble walls and limestone dressings. S windows quarry-glazed, timber Y-tracery to the N. The entrance gable has angle buttresses and a decorative ashlar bellcote topped by a spiky pinnacle. Inside, a plain space with an open-truss roof. – Pleasing vernacular ENTRANCE with quadrant walls, slender stone piers, and hooped iron gates.

The former GLEBE HOUSE lies across the road; a plain c19 house, two storeys, gable-ended, with three bays, a porch and Georgian glazing. Improvements by *J. H. Fullerton* in 1885.

ARMAGHBREAGUE PRESBYTERIAN CHURCH. 5.5 km NW. Built in 1847 and renovated in 1890. Large five-bay hall with hipped gables. Grimly modernized with cement render, tiled roof and plastic windows.

ORAM   MN

A rural crossroads 4 km NE of Castleblayney.

ST JOHN. Of *c.* 1830. A plain T-plan chapel set in a gentle declivity. Smooth rendered walls and simple pointed windows with coloured glass. The carefully graded slate roof is now something of a rarity. Attractive interior with exposed kingpost truss roof of roughly hewn timber. Timber gallery at the W. The sanctuary is defined by two pairs of bold pilasters with deep fluting applied to the E wall; these frame the altar and two flanking pointed windows. Communion rails of cast iron in a Gothic design.

GARMANY'S GROVE PRESBYTERIAN CHURCH, FORMIL. 1 km NE. C19 gabled hall of five bays, roughcast. Big round-headed windows now fitted with obscured lavatory glazing. A number of good late C19 architectural gravestones in the surrounding cemetery.

FAIRVIEW REFORMED CHURCH, MULLYASH MOUNTAIN. 2 km NE. Two adjoining cement-rendered gabled halls with round-headed windows. Irredeemably dull.

MCKELVEY'S GROVE PRESBYTERIAN CHURCH. 4 km NNW. The most interesting and remote of a group of Presbyterian churches hidden in this rural corner of Monaghan. Stocky three-bay hall with triple-gabled porch; the central gable is larger and accommodates the doorway, which is flanked by small timber lancets with Y-tracery. An inscription high in the S gable records the date 1847 and presumably the first minister, the Rev. Matthew McAuley. Abutting the N gable, the two-storey, four-bay former MINISTER'S HOUSE.

SCHOOLHOUSE. On the opposite side of the road. Extremely pretty small-scale single-storey block of four bays with square windows, all quarry-glazed. Flanking porches with attractive pointed windows in the end walls. Two-storey schoolmaster's house behind. Altogether a happy vernacular survival.

PORTADOWN AH 0050

Portadown – from the Irish *Port an Dúnáin*, 'port of the little fort' – appears to owe its earliest prominence to a stronghold of the MacCanns, elevated near the ford formed where the River Bann broadens into a shallow pool. The modern town developed around the manor of Ballywarren, originally bestowed on William Powell at the Plantation but sold soon after to the Obins family. Prudence and John Obins obtained a patent for markets and fairs in 1631, built for themselves 'a large mansion in the Elizabethan style', and erected fourteen houses for English settlers around a large market place pinched in the centre and on axis with the river crossing.

Having suffered greatly in 1641, when 'so many protestants' were drowned in the river by the rebellious hands of Captain Toole McCann, the town recovered only gradually over the succeeding decades with little more than the original number of houses shown on Francis Nevill's 1703 map of the district. Thomas Molyneux in 1708 found Portadown a pretty village but was forced to cross the river by wherry because a 'large and handsome' new bridge was not yet finished. This, like its predecessors, was a timber bridge; it proved too restrictive to navigation in the seasonal floods, and it was eventually replaced by a seven-arched masonry bridge in 1761–4. By then Portadown was

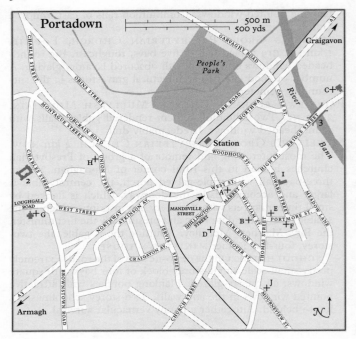

Portadown

A	St Mark (C of I)
B	St Patrick
C	First Portadown Presbyterian Church
D	Armagh Road Presbyterian Church
E	Methodist church
F	Quaker Meeting House
G	St Columba (C of I)
H	Epworth Methodist Church
J	Presentation Convent (former)
I	Town Hall
2	Sir Robert Hall Memorial School
3	Bann Bridge

emerging as a nexus in the development of transport in South Ulster. Its potential arose from the ready agricultural markets of the rich pastoral hinterlands and from linen – the Ulster staple – which was given encouragement when a market for it was established in the town in 1762. Strategically sited on the first river crossing s of Lough Neagh, with the opening of the Newry Canal in 1742 the navigation routes already established between the Bann and Lough Neagh were greatly extended. Agricultural produce was transported to Newry in return for coal, and general merchandise – slate, timber and iron. A century later the arrival of the Ulster Railway secured the town's fortune as the most important junction of the road, canal and railway networks between Armagh, Newry and Belfast; with the onset of the industrial revolution it was poised for rapid growth.

In 1814 Michael Eyre Obins sold his interest in Portadown to Millicent Sparrow, whose marriage in 1822 to Viscount

Mandeville, later 6th Duke of Manchester, brought the town under the patronage of that family. The old Obins residence has disappeared, now only vaguely recalled in the name of Castle Street, and by 1837 the demesne had been carved up, with the exception of the wooded core that survives today as the People's Park, off the Garvaghy Road. In 1842 the town was admired as 'airy clean and pleasant', a description not entirely evocative of the major industrial centre that earned the sobriquet 'the hub of the North'. When W. M. Thackeray called the following year he found 'the little brick town of Portadown, with its comfortable, unpretending houses, its square and marketplace, its pretty craft along the river, a steamer building on the dock close to the mills and warehouses that look in a full state of prosperity . . .' The variety of industries established here ranged from conventional ones like weaving, distilling and ironfounding to brick and soap manufacturing; of all these it was linen that brought greatest wealth – though in this Portadown always played second fiddle to Lurgan – and at its apogee at the end of the C19 there were seven large factories mainly specializing in cambric manufacture.

Eventually the railways won out over the canal, and Portadown was expanded as a junction to Armagh and the NW. The peripheral industrial developments of the late C20 associated with the Craigavon City vision ensure that its label as a northern hub is still a relevant one today. Now, at the beginning of the C21, it is the road networks that dominate, strangling the periphery and congesting the town centre.

The market place remains the focus of the modern town; the wide thoroughfare extending as Market Street and High Street flares at either end into large triangular spaces, an unusual urban form that resulted from a convergence of the old approach roads. The town centre is dominated by C19 buildings, mainly Victorian in character, focused on the parish church, which provides a central authority at the E end of Market Street.

ST MARK (C of I). A substantial Gothic church in blackstone with sandstone dressings. The commanding square tower is the last in a series of additions to the standard hall-and-tower church established here on the market place in the early C19. The parish, originally dedicated to St Michael, was formed out of Drumcree in 1824, and a new parish church was built two years later on a site granted for the purpose by Viscount Mandeville. Keeping pace with the expanding town, the building was enlarged with transepts about a decade later, and in 1861 three-bay aisles were added by the Ecclesiastical Commissioners – all highly textured additions in rock-faced blackstone with simple Y-tracery. *J. F. Fuller* carried out further additions, completed in 1885 at a cost of £5,000, raising the nave, adding a new polygonal chancel, and greatly enlarging the transepts; plainer E.E. fenestration denotes his work. As a result of the additions only the aisles preserve some sense of the scale of the old hall church. The contractors were the local firm of *Collen Bros.* In 1919 *Henry Hobart* was appointed architect for an extension and spire, but this seems to have come to nothing, and by 1922 the vestry were inviting plans for a church extension and a 75-ft (23-m) high war memorial tower with a large w window. Designs for a 100-ft (30.5-m) tower by *Henry Seaver* were approved subject to costs. These proved too high, and having discussed the scheme with *Blackwood & Jury* the vestry deferred their decision. It was not until 1927 that they resumed discussions with Seaver and finally accepted his design, deciding that the tower should be in the centre, not at the side as proposed. To receive the tower the nave was extended by an additional bay over the site of the old tower and the new structure was raised in four stages. The tower is perhaps a little too broad and too dominating in its scale, where a narrower tower would have added greater elegance with equal presence. It certainly is more compatible than its predecessor, with matching masonry and plain E.E. details married perfectly to Fuller's work. Polygonal buttresses on the corners add to the solidity, rising to short pinnacles around elaborated battlements with smaller spiky pinnacles to the centres.

Even on the brightest of days, cement-rendered walls lend a pervading grey gloom to the interior. In a rare display of architectural ornament, compound piers with bell capitals support the arcades, whose moulded arches are pointed; quadripartite vaults spring from wall-shafts between the arches. The clerestory has multifoil windows deeply set in triangular-arched recesses, helping to suffuse an atmospheric light. The nave opens through high arches into the generous transepts. – In the chancel the Gothic REREDOS with shafts of red Cork marble and inset panels of Connemara marble was installed in the early C20. – STAINED GLASS. Plentiful, brightly coloured, and of varied quality. Three-light E window: the Ascension by *Mayer & Co.*, 1891; N transept: the Transfiguration, signed *Tiroler Glasmalerei*, Innsbruck, *c.* 1894. C20 examples in the aisles include the Baptism of Christ, one of six windows in the church from the studios of *Shrigley & Hunt*, 1971, and King David and Michael the Archangel by *Calderwood*, *c.* 2001, the best of the later examples. – MONUMENTS. Alexander Bredon †1866; a draped sarcophagus, by *Coates*, Dublin.

On the island before the church, two monuments flank the gateway. To the r., and earliest, is the SAUNDERSON MONUMENT by *W. Goscombe John*, 1908. A formidable bronze statue of Edward James Saunderson, M.P. for Armagh 1885–1906, cast by *A. B. Burton* of Thames Ditton. The later WAR MEMORIAL by *Henry Fehr* is an allegory, also in bronze, with an imposing winged Victory and a wounded soldier.

ST PATRICK. On William Street, with none of the prominence of its Protestant counterpart. Outwardly a straightforward cruciform Gothic church with a forestanding battlemented tower. A plaque on the s nave wall gives the date 1835; consecrated in 1837, when it was described as 'a neat stone building corniced with freestone and having 4 minarets in front and 2 in

the rear'. Its appearance was transformed when it was enlarged
c. 1860, including the addition of the transepts and tower. The
four-bay nave is roughcast, though faced in stone on the w
gable between clasping buttresses. Pointed openings throughout with thick hoods, and simple timber lights with supermullions. Gabled masonry porches to the transepts. The tower has
three stages, built in squared blackstone with sandstone dressings. Plate tracery on the w face and twin lights in the upper
stages. Clasping offset buttresses give the structure a certain
vigour, upset by the crowning battlements and corner pinnacles, all rather oddly executed in a jarring pale limestone and
therefore possibly renewed work. Inside, the roof has well-
spaced trusses with semicircular arched braces. Deep raking
gallery with attractive carved Gothic frontal. The chancel is
decorated with rich mosaic work in the late C19 manner of
Oppenheimer. – Fine Gothic ALTAR in marble adorned with
crocketed spire and pinnacles. – STAINED GLASS. E window: a
tableau of saints in two tiers, brightly coloured.

FIRST PORTADOWN PRESBYTERIAN CHURCH, Bridge Street.
1858 by *W. J. Barre*. A distinguished stuccoed church in an
Imperial Roman style. A distyle Corinthian portico is set *in
antis* in the central bay, flanked by single bays framed by the
pilaster responds of the portico and corresponding pilasters on
the corners. The absence of parapets over the side bays is a
noticeable omission. The wall surface is channelled, with plain
round-headed windows, given thick surrounds and keystones
in the three lights under the portico. *Mr Davidson* of Lurgan
was the builder. Inside, a gallery was added in 1875. The nature
of further alterations and improvements by *Young & Mackenzie*
in 1882 is not known, but transepts were added later, in
1891. The building replaced a T-plan church of 1822, set back
from the street to the rear of the site, later converted as a
schoolhouse.

ARMAGH ROAD PRESBYTERIAN CHURCH. 1868 by *Boyd &
Batt*. A small gable-fronted Gothic hall in Church Street (the
road to Armagh) sited to close the vista down Hanover Street.
The foundation stone was laid by the 7th Duke of Manchester;
the contractor was *John Collen*. A buttressed hall of four bays
in blackstone rubble, with a three-bay façade where the
masonry is squared with Dungannon sandstone dressings. The
central bay steps forward slightly with angle buttresses; above
rises a slender pinnacle on an angular base. A squat pointed
doorway is set between the buttresses, with a reticulated tracery
window above. Quatrefoils in the side bays over lumpish
Y-traceried windows with hoods that appear to have once been
open as side doors. This alteration and the concrete super-
mullioned windows of the nave are possibly additions by
T. Houston recorded in 1903.

METHODIST CHURCH. Thomas Street. 1858 by *John Boyd*. An
imposing stucco-fronted classical church with a tetrastyle
Corinthian portico across the central three of its five windowless bays; pilastered responds and corners, which – unlike the

columns – are fluted. Blind recessed panels between the orders on the upper stage, with a nice Vitruvian scroll between the stages. On the sides the stucco is returned for just one bay, the remaining four bays of coursed blackstone rubble with brown-brick trim; here the windows are set in pairs, tall and round-headed in the upper gallery level and smaller with segmental heads below.

The former MANSE is a detached stucco block to the N; two storeys, with quoins, projecting cornice, and distinctive tripartite windows on the ground floor; originally of three bays, but extended by a further two with a matching Tuscan porch. The SCHOOLHOUSE adjoining the E end on Portmore Street is a lower continuation of the church, in the same materials, with a deep gabled projection in the centre. The builders were *Browne & Ross* of Belfast.

QUAKER MEETING HOUSE. On Portmore Street, facing the S end of Edward Street. 1905 by *Joseph Chandler Marsh*. A quaint Arts and Crafts hall with a polygonal projection set back on one side; all in red brick sparsely trimmed with pale sandstone. The gabled front has a small glazed timber porch flanked by single bays with a Venetian window above; here and in the paired windows of the hall the arch is supported on slender barleysugar timber shafts.

ST COLUMBA (C of I). Loughgall Road. 1970 by *Gordon McKnight*. An unconventional church on a cruciform plan in brownish brick, consisting of a square nave with pyramidal slate roof, glazed, before a short copper-clad spirelet; lean-to chancel and transepts with a disjointed bowed stem, with side porches and a copper roof rising gracefully to a point topped by a sailboat as a symbol of the patron.

EPWORTH METHODIST CHURCH. Union Street. Dull late C19 hall in coursed rubble blackstone with paired round-headed windows to the nave. Not improved by unsightly additions.

METHODIST CHURCH AND MANSE (former). Thomas Street. Sold in 1861 after the new church was built further down the street, and converted to commercial use; derelict at the time of writing. A large boxy hall on a high podium, with three bays to the front in squared blackstone with sandstone dressings. The central bay is advanced with a gabled parapet bearing an oval plaque inscribed 1832, and corner pinnacles. Big round-headed windows on the first floor with Gothick sashes; segmental below. The former manse stands to one side, a narrow detached block rather like a doll's house in red brick with sandstone quoins; three storeys tall and two bays wide with a hipped roof, Georgian sashes and a fanlit doorcase to one side.

SALVATION ARMY HALL, Edward Street. *See* p. 509.

PRESENTATION CONVENT (former). Thomas Street. Familiar institutional Gothic, reminiscent of *J. J. McDonnell*. A long, sparsely ornamented red brick block of 1902 with bands of black brick and stone dressings on the gabled projections in the centre and end bays. Plate-glass windows with cambered heads. The chapel (N wing) was added by *McDonnell, Lamont & McDonnell* in 1924. Now in residential use.

The contiguous CONVENT PRIMARY SCHOOLS consist of a group of red brick buildings in a plainer, less appealing institutional idiom. Built in 1900, extended first by *Hugh Lamont* in 1934 and again by *McLean & Forte* in 1951.

TOWN HALL. Edward Street. 1890 by *Thomas & Robert Roe*. A heavy, twin-gabled municipal block, nominally Flemish, with a curious mix of classical detail. Red brick with red sandstone dressings and modest terracotta ornaments. Just one main front, five bays wide, with the entrance squashed into a narrow bay between the gables: a round-headed arch set between twin brick pilasters with rich scrolled brackets supporting a balcony for the window above. The ground floor has big round-headed windows with keystones breaking through the hoods; more classically minded lugged surrounds to the windows above; all with heavy mullioned frames. The gables rise over an emphatic brick cornice, decorated with applied pilasters topped with ball finials and, on the apexes, snarling terracotta dragons bearing heraldic shields associated with the crest of the town patron, the Duke of Manchester.

CARNEGIE LIBRARY. Edward Street. 1904 by *J. W. Walby*. An irregular two-storey block in red brick. An Ionic order in stucco pasted across the four-bay ground floor, with channelled brickwork; a single-storey entrance bay is set to one side with zany engaged columns with swelling, bottle-like proportions and Scamozzian capitals. Three bays on the first floor with a canted oriel in the centre and pedimented stucco surrounds in the side bays, all projecting with gables above the wide bracketed eaves.

LIBRARY. Market Street. 2000 by *Maurice Cushnie*. An unforgivable gable-ended lump, three storeys tall and part-rendered with rusticated quoins and a wasteful central pedimented projection in sandstone; all meanly fenestrated.

MILLENNIUM COURT ARTS CENTRE. William Street. The former Municipal Central Markets of 1929, by *Ferguson & McIlveen*, remodelled internally in 2000 by *Harry Porter Architects*. A long single-storey arcaded front in red brick with high segmental arches and steep central gable. To the S, a short discreet stretch of adjoining shops, enhancing the streetscape but marred by cheap signage.

SIR ROBERT HART MEMORIAL SCHOOL. Charles Street. 1932 by *James St John Phillips*, completed by *Henry Hobson*. In an industrial Art Deco style, a large, formal design in red brick trimmed with sandstone. Bulky central block with half-hipped gables and five-bay front with defining flat buttresses separating tall paired iron casements under a continuous Greek-key frieze. Flat-roofed wings front extensive classroom blocks to the rear. Named for the accomplished Inspector General of Chinese Customs, who was born on this site in 1835.

ST COLUMBA'S PUBLIC ELEMENTARY BOYS' SCHOOL. Carleton Street. Derelict. A large cement-rendered two-storey L-plan block of 1933 by *Hugh Lamont*, copiously fenestrated with tall multiple-pane metal casements. Behind, an open-fronted shed with short columns from the Portadown foundry.

FERGUS HALL. Church Street. Formerly the Church National Schools, established here in the early C19 and known then as the Duke's School. Rebuilt in 1889 as a large stuccoed block, two storeys tall, with a hipped roof and single central stack. Odd in appearance: the front is six bays wide with a central gable set between bold pilasters, channelled on the upper level and panelled below; pilasters repeated on the corners. Tall, narrow windows in blocked stucco surrounds, set in pairs in the end bays and with triangular heads on the first floor. Additions by *Hobart & Heron* in 1916.

BANK OF IRELAND. High Street. 1868 by *Sandham Symes*. The familiar banking palazzo, tall, with three storeys and five bays. Built of Mourne granite, ornately carved on the ground floor with vermiculated arches to the central bays and classical heads in the keystones of the end bays, where the doorways are set in concave surrounds edged with rope mouldings; alternating aedicules on the first floor, and a console-bracketed cornice with an open parapet above. The contractors were *A. & N. Hammond* of Drogheda.

FIRST TRUST BANK (former PROVINCIAL BANK). Market Street. 1931 by *Blackwood & Jury*, in a Georgian Revival style. A broad seven-bay front in red brick with rusticated pilasters and a decent modillion brick cornice, gabled over the advanced central bays. Ground floor plainly stuccoed with asymmetrical fenestration and an offset doorway where a Doric entablature is irreverently carried on scrolled brackets.

ULSTER BANK. High Street. 1932 by *Blackwood & Jury*. A large three-storey block in Armagh limestone with walls of channelled ashlar and copious ornamentation. Four bays with the twin central bays projecting, rising to an emphatic shelf-like modillion cornice before a deep blocking course with corner urns and flamboyant arms in the centre. The fanlit entrance stands to one side, balanced by a carriage arch opposite.

BANN BRIDGE. 1834 by *Arthur Williamson*. In 1761–4 the architect *Christopher Myers* replaced a succession of timber bridges here with a rather routine affair of seven arches. The C19 design makes the crossing with greater elegance in three wide elliptical arches, gently humpbacked in the centre, and small semicircular subsidiary arches at either end. The original structure is now evident only on the N side: granite ashlar, with round bollard-like cutwaters with broad, gently inclined lesenes extending above these to die beneath the bold roll moulding at the base of the parapet. The bridge was completed in 1838 at an estimated cost of £9,000. Widened twice on the s side, first in 1922 and again in 2005, when its concrete face was garishly clad in machined granite.

COLLEN BROS. Hanover Street. A frivolous Late Victorian building. Twin-gabled, of two storeys with rubble walls on the ground floor and decorative red-and-yellow brickwork above. Segmental-headed windows with plate glass, irregularly spaced on the ground floor, are set in elaborate moulded brick surrounds under a continuous nailhead string. The string is repeated on the wide rectangular windows above and along the gable parapets.

The nearby SHED has an impressive Belfast-truss roof, nicely articulating the widely cambered street-front gable.

TAVANAGH FACTORY. Church Street. A sprawling industrial complex beside the railway line. At the centre is a large C19 block in brown brick, of two storeys on a basement with a small pyramid-roofed tower to one side. Greatly enlarged by various single-storey Edwardian ranges in industrial red brick with red sandstone dressings; at the entrance a twenty-one-bay range of 1907 with deep parapets, the bays set in shallow recesses between emphatic arched end bays.

OTHER BUILDINGS. On the High Street, the NORTHERN BANK, in a 1980s bunker style, is a three-storey, five-bay block primarily of orange brick, with long capsule-like protrusions in opaque glass on the upper floors; it replaces a building of 1922 by *Henry Seaver*. Opposite is the PROGRESSIVE BUILDING SOCIETY, 1993 by *Gerry Hamill*, a conventional gable-ended form in red brick, made modern with irregular fenestration. Beyond the island car park at the N end, into Castle Street, HALDENE FISHER is a substantial mid-Victorian warehouse built by *Thomas Averill Shillington*; nicely proportioned front in brown brick with plate-glass windows and yellow-brick eaves courses; exceptional long N range, partly of coursed rubble.

At the corner of Mandeville and West streets, MCCON-VILLE BROS, built as a large Victorian hotel, formerly the Mandeville Arms, three storeys tall with a bracketed cornice and tall segmental-headed windows with plate-glass windows on the upper floors; the date 1865 inset in an elaborate stuc-coed projection rather like a chimneystack, rising above the eaves on the W front. Further down the street, creating a dead end on Shillington Street, a massive red-and-yellow brick arch with flanking doorways fills the lively stepped brick gable of the FORMER BUTTER, EGG AND FOWL MARKET; it faces the contrasting neat Modernist essay of TAYLOR'S on the corner with Market Street (2008 by *Harry Porter Architecture*), a two-storey, look-at-me building with walls of opaque glass and floating concrete panels. Nearby on the one-sided West Street, KNOX'S FOOD COURT occupies a late C19 former Temper-ance hall with a big gabled front in red brick trimmed with decorative yellow brick; triangular-headed windows and a plain rose window under a pointed hood; ground floor obscured by ugly C20 shopfronts.

The CONSTABULARY BARRACKS on Edward Street is a functional red brick block of 1885 by *Edward Kavanagh*; two storeys with a three-storey gable to one side and a canted bay window on the ground floor. Next to it the SALVATION ARMY HALL of 1939 has a plain Art Deco façade of machined red brick in English-garden-wall bond with a central stepped gable, topped with limestone blocks rising over the slightly advanced side bays. Its reserve contrasts with the loud poly-chrome brick façade of the former METHODIST INSTITUTE, a broad late C19 block with a notable doorcase of engaged columns, now incomplete, with handsome carved door panels.

On Thomas Street, the MASONIC HALL of 1897 by *J. J. Phillips & Son* is a ponderous red brick block with gables and a large square tower set back on one end. Round the corner on Carleton Street, the ORANGE HALL is a tall Victorian building, three storeys high with five bays, altered and enlarged in 1908 by *James W. Walby* with a lively brick-and-stucco frontage. Beside it is the big gable-fronted ST MARK'S PAROCHIAL HALL of 1954 by *Hobart & Heron*, who had prepared designs for the building as early as 1936. In red brick with a large stone tripartite window above a low ground floor faced in ashlar. Wide Art Deco-style entrance with narrow side-lights canted inward under a thin concrete ledge. The contractors were *R. J. Heathwood & Sons*.

At the end of an imposing terrace on Church Street, CARLETON HOUSE is a large and brooding Edwardian block built as a maternity hospital. In red brick with red sandstone dressings and plate glass, it is predominantly three storeys tall with a balustraded parapet; the front is asymmetrical, with on the corner a narrow diagonal tower four storeys tall with a copper ogee dome. Shallow pilaster strips define the entrance bay with a singular Corinthian doorcase and a deflated segmental pediment over short bulging columns, part fluted with medievalizing capitals.

NEIGHBOURHOOD

EDENDERRY MEMORIAL METHODIST CHURCH. Carrickblacker Road. 1953 by *Robert Frater*. A large red brick hall of five bays with tall twin lights and a wide gabled front with a low protruding porch; above this, five round-headed lights are closely grouped under orientalizing ogee hoods. To one side, the Late Victorian church is a modest four-bay hall (since enlarged) in yellow-and-red brick with a large mullioned sandstone window in the gable.

DRUMCREE PARISH CHURCH (C of I). Drumcree Road, off Garvaghy Road. A large and unforgiving Tractarian church, visible from afar on its exposed hilltop above Portadown. Drumcree was the site of an old church, whose rectors can be traced back to 1414; in 1837 Samuel Lewis described it as 'a large ancient building', but only traces of the nave walls s of the tower are evident today. In 1854 *Joseph Welland* retained the solid three-stage tower of snecked blackstone and granite in an otherwise complete rebuilding, reshaping it with an ashlar broach spire, and reorienting it as an offset at the w end of a large aisled nave and chancel. The result is a convincing uniformity between old and new, with only the coarse granite trim on the tower distinguished from Welland's smooth sandstone. The executant architect was *William Turney Fullerton* with *Hugh Henry & Son* as contractors. The aisles are lit by paired lancets with quarry glazing; smaller triple lights in the clerestory, and three graded lights in the lower chancel. Inside, a cavernous space, drably cement-rendered, with an elaborate open timber roof of scissor trusses alternating with arch-braced hammer-beams. Four-bay sandstone arcades with pointed arches on round piers. – FONT. A heavy sandstone bowl, perhaps C17, carved below the thick rim with lunettes and a rope moulding; now incongruously set inside a plain C19 Gothic font. – MONUMENTS. Miles and Margaret Atkinson, a handsome classical monument of 1811 with a draped Adamesque urn and heraldic shield. – Meredyth Workman †1795; an early C19 white marble tablet. – A plain slab records the benevolence of Mary Johnston towards the poor of the parish, 1809.

The GRAVEYARD is extensive, with some early markers; the best is Early Georgian, c. 1734, with florid scrolled supports, embedded in the wall beside the entrance gates.

The PARISH HALL of 1902 by *James W. Walby* is a buttressed hall in coursed blackstone with four bays and a forestanding gabled porch with low side bays; now much enlarged to the rear.

Across the road the SEXTON'S HOUSE is a stuccoed gabled block possibly also by *Walby*, built to replace the old steep-roofed C19 cottage in the graveyard.

THE ROCKERY. Off Drumcree Road. A small mid-C19 villa, a single-storey, gable-ended block with a loft storey in roughcast. Bay windows with plate glass are probably a later addition, linked across the entrance by a continuous shallow lean-to roof; the doorway has a wide, squat elliptical arch with a webbed fanlight over geometric side-lights. The place owes its name to the ornaments in the small enclosed garden at the front, where a well and playful arches are constructed of large grotesque flints.

ST JOHN THE BAPTIST. Garvaghy Road. 1977. On the outer fringe of Portadown's N sprawl. A large square church with a skewed porch and a slender offset bell-tower. Walls of textured concrete with strip clerestory lighting under a heavy pyramid roof of natural slate with a glazed apex. Inside, an uninspiring diagonal plan with an axial coffered ceiling on pilotis.

ROBB'S FERRY COTTAGE. Off Derrycarne Road. An important vernacular cottage set in a cobbled yard, separated by level fields from the Bann and the former ferry crossing served by the occupants. A long and low lofted range with Georgian sashes and a deep, lean-to porch. Mud-walled and now with corrugated tin over its thatched roof. Inside, a classic lobby-entry plan with two principal rooms and an impressive oak purlin roof. The rural setting has been spoiled somewhat by brash C21 suburban-style housing.

MAHON METHODIST CHURCH. Mahon Road. 1828. A trim two-bay hall. A plaque over the door records the building as a gift from Henry Ripley to the Primitive Wesley Methodist Society.

MAHON PUBLIC ELEMENTARY SCHOOL. Mahon Road. 1847.
A single-storey eight-bay block combining classrooms and residence under one roof. Roughcast with wide eaves and a gabled
porch in the centre, with the date inscribed in a Gothic panel
over the Tudor-arched doorway.

MAHON HOUSE. Off Mahon Road. Derelict. A two-storey Late
Georgian house to an L-plan. Roughcast over red brick with
raised stucco quoins and a hipped roof with central stacks.
Longer side elevation of six bays. In the late C18 the residence
of Meredyth Workman, an improving farmer with whom the
agriculturist Arthur Young stayed in 1776. Most of the grounds
now encroached on by housing, but some good planting
remains in the embrace of the River Annagh.

s of the house ST PATRICK'S WELL is a domed red brick
vault of early C19 appearance.

A street village set tight against the border with Co. Down,
halfway between Newry and Portadown. The townland name of
Federnagh aptly describes the surrounding area as the 'in-
between place'. It owes its present name to Lieutenant Charles
Poyntz, who in 1598 held this 'encumbered pass' through marsh-
lands on the Glan Bog between Armagh and Down against the
advances of Hugh O'Neill, Earl of Tyrone; for this he was made
a small grant of the surrounding lands and built himself a bawn
on a site N of the present town, establishing a small settlement
there which he named Acton from his origins in Iron Acton,
Gloucestershire. It still survives, little changed from its description in 1837 as one street with a group of 'indifferently built'
houses; the late C17 parish church built by Sir Toby Poyntz is
gone, but its graveyard remains evident SW of the village. By 1641
the name Poyntzpass first emerges with a site S of Acton, though
represented by little more than a causeway and timber bridge
over the River Staroagh. Sir Toby Poyntz established a monthly
fair here in 1685, at the expense of the earlier settlement at Acton.
The modern town however was largely developed in the late
C18 by his descendant, Alexander Thomas Stewart (who inherited the Poyntz property through his mother), including the two
churches that stand at either end of the principal street. In the
C19 ownership passed to the Close family of Drumbanagher
(Jerrettspass).

ACTON PARISH CHURCH (C of I). Main Street. Initially a hall-
and-tower type of c. 1790, replacing Sir Toby Poyntz's C17
church at Acton. A standard plan with a three-bay nave and a
forestanding tower of two stages with attenuated belfry before
a deep battlemented parapet with ornate pinnacles; all in
roughcast, with dressed granite quoins to the nave and the

lower stages of the tower. Windows mostly quarry-glazed. The church was first 'enlarged and improved' in 1829, but in 1835 it was considered 'altogether much out of repair'. In 1861 *Welland & Gillespie* added a N aisle in rock-faced masonry, extending to four bays before ending in a gabled porch. Later additions of 1891 by an unknown hand are the chancel with a large Y-traceried E window in red sandstone, and an open lean-to porch on the tower. Inside, the nave has exposed oak tie-beams, each carved with a foliate boss repeated from the Arts and Crafts porch, presumably part of the later C19 works. The aisle opens through two arched bays springing from a short limestone pier. Refurnished as part of late C19 works. – STAINED GLASS. Five-light E window: scenes from the Life of Christ attributed to *Shrigley & Hunt*, Lancaster, 1891. N aisle: Christ Blessing the Children, also attributed to *Shrigley & Hunt*. Nave: the Baptism of Christ, a staid composition by *Leadlines & David Esler Studio*, 1999. – MONUMENT. A plain scroll to the Bennet family, by *C. W. Harrison & Sons*, 1912.

On the N face of the tower the SUNDIAL of 1819 by the local schoolmaster *Thomas McCreash* is a worthy curiosity, the simplest of three examples in the locality.

ST JOSEPH. A prim little roughcast hall. Built on land granted in 1792 by Alexander Stewart to the Rev. John Maguire. Four bays with the end bays stepping forward slightly, originally to accommodate twin porches at either end, of which only the E one survives. The position of the porches indicates an old-fashioned plan with the altar on the long N wall between galleries, later moved to its present location at the W end. Simple, unaffected interior with open roof trusses. In the wall beside the entrance is the earliest surviving example of a SUNDIAL by *Thomas McCreash*, made in 1817 for the Rev. Henry Campbell.

POYNTZPASS PRESBYTERIAN CHURCH. 1836. An unremarkable roughcast hall with four bays and a large gabled porch.

OLD NATIONAL SCHOOLS. Derelict. Off Railway Street, now lost in the corner of a suburban garden. A small idiosyncratic mid-C19 building which local tradition has ascribed to *William Henry Playfair*, perhaps because of the patronage of the Close family. It is certainly a distinguished building, symmetrical in plan, with two large classrooms, three bays deep, set in parallel. The main front has twin porches with half-hipped gables and frilly bargeboards joined by a narrow recessed two-bay link. The architecture is striking chiefly because of the squat kneelered gable rising over the central link to support a jaunty little bellcote in ashlar with sweeping copings. Cement-rendered with chunky bevelled ashlar casings to the windows. The only obvious connection with Playfair is the large Victorian sashes with a prominent central glazing bar and plate glass, similar to those used at Drumbanagher, where the proportions favour the lower sash. A plaque below the bellcote reveals nothing other than the function of the building.

ACTON GLEBE HOUSE. 1 km N. Originally a modest gable-
ended house of 1799 with two storeys and attics, small Georgian rooms, and a long service range running off to the rear.
Enlarged in the mid C19 when a new hall, staircase and large
drawing room were accommodated in a square two-storey
block placed over two bays of the old five-bay E front. The
result was a new irregular four-bay entrance front to the S, all
in roughcast with stucco quoins. Here the old house remains
distinct with its three storeys and Georgian sashes; a gable
stack rising over the parapet was added to unite the two buildings. The adjoining two-storey section steps forward slightly,
with a fanlit doorway on one side and a rectangular timber bay
window to the drawing room, beautifully detailed with narrow
cross-glazed sashes.

ACTON. 1.5 km N. Set in sweeping elevated parkland, a perfect
small Neoclassical villa displaying a sophisticated elegance,
perhaps the work of *Thomas Cooley*. Built in 1775 for Alexander
Stewart. It replaced Sir Toby Poyntz's 'brick and lime house'
and its bawn. Here is grandeur on a small scale, with a stocky,
compact block of two storeys and attics over a basement. The
walls are roughcast, with the first-floor windows carried on a
continuous stone sill course, and above these a carved eaves
cornice and blocking course before the hipped roof. The main
front has three bays with tall twelve-pane sashes set in shallow
recessed arches on either side of the generous fanlit door, a
handsome Neoclassical design with engaged Composite
columns, lion masks and swags in the entablature, and a large
webbed fanlight and leaded geometric side-lights. The garden
front to the E has five bays, the central three advanced in a
shallow elliptical bow, widely expressed with what seems an
almost independent conical roof. The elevation was altered in
the late C19 when the N bay beside the bow was pulled forward;
other smaller additions distort the effect even more.

Inside, the oval dining room is the focus of the double-pile
plan, and if *Cooley* was indeed involved here the elliptical form
anticipates his design for Caledon. It is reached directly from
a barrel-vaulted entrance hall. Cooley employed a barrel-vault
in this period for the entrance hall at Ardbraccan, though here
it is plainly treated, nicely converted to a groin-vault at the end
of a hall where a short passage to the side leads on to the
staircase; that rises in a half-circle, its curve tangential to the
dining room. In general the decoration of the rooms is sparing.
Fine six-panel mahogany doors enrich the hall, but economy
seems all too obvious here, with just four flat pilasters – the
kind favoured by Cooley and used for example in the Primate's
Chapel in Armagh – placed at either end of the vault to correspond with a decorated soffit band. Elsewhere decoration is
limited to delicate foliated cornices, in designs similar to some
of those found in a sketchbook from Caledon that is attributed
to Cooley. Both drawing room and dining room have good

contemporary marble chimneypieces, each finely decorated
with Neoclassical urns, the dining room example especially
nice as it follows the pronounced curve of the end wall.

DRUMINARGAL. 3 km N. A gable-ended house of two storeys
and five bays, with a distinctive fanlit doorway and side-lights
set in a rather flat elliptical arch, originally all very nicely
leaded. Built c. 1830 and remodelled c. 1900 with leaded casement windows and an oversailing pitched roof. The birthplace
of Charles Davis Lucas, first ever recipient of the Victoria
Cross, awarded to him in 1857 for valour during the Crimean
War.

TANIOKEY SCHOOL. 3.5 km SW. Nestled in a fork in the road,
this interesting building is as curious as its name. Built as a
rural school in 1840 under the patronage of Colonel Close
of Drumbanagher (Jerrettspass) and not dissimilar to the
former demesne school there. A formal grouping of neat
stuccoed buildings consisting of the former schoolmaster's
house – a boxy two-storey block with a big hipped roof and
tall end stacks – flanked by the male and female classrooms in
lower pedimented ranges, five bays deep, with big casement
windows.

CREMORE PRESBYTERIAN CHURCH. 3.5 km SW. A long, low
hall established here by the Rev. John Caldwell in 1802.
Cement-rendered with round-headed windows. The s end lies
outside the body of the church, expressed as two storeys on
the gable, suggesting that the plan originally incorporated the
minister's residence.

CHURCH OF THE IMMACULATE CONCEPTION, LISSUMMON.
6 km SSW. 1933 by *W. H. Byrne & Son*, replacing an older
church here dedicated to St Patrick. An arresting diminutive-
looking church in an Italian Romanesque idiom, successfully
expressed in the unusual combination of brown machined
brick and reconstituted stone. The front has a kneelered gable
with the classic Romanesque reference of a tall recessed arch
inset with an oculus over the doorway and above this an
emphatic corbel table and a bellcote. Despite the dinkiness of
the front, the plan is in fact a very deep hall lit on both sides
by six tall round-headed lancets, three on either side of an
oculus, above a low gabled confessional outshot that echoes
the main gables. Three graded lights in the E gable. The ornate
slate SUNDIAL on the adjoining wall is by *Thomas McCreash*,
made in 1828 for the Rev. Bernard Loughran.

REDHILLS   CN   4010

A quaint village in the north Cavan uplands, named for the iron-
rich soils of the district. Planned round a green outside the high
walls of the old picturesque and densely wooded demesne of the
Whyte family, who settled here in the C17.

REDHILLS HOUSE. Standing inside the demesne walls, near the village, the rubble remains of a near square fortified house of indeterminate date but generally accepted as the C17 house of the Whytes, which has been ruined since it burned c. 1820. The walls are much repaired and rebuilt, revealing no architectural characteristics other than evidence for external roughcast, so applied as to suggest blocked quoins and window surrounds. The succeeding house, a substantial Regency block, enlarged by *James E. Rogers* for the Rev. Arthur Whyte-Venables in 1867, was burnt in 1922 and modestly rebuilt in 1934 and c. 1990. All that now remains of the C19 house is a heraldic roundel, elaborately carved with the Venables crest of a wyvern devouring a child, set in a blank wall beside the present house. The antiquity of the adjoining demesne is still attested by a broad yew avenue and traces of rectangular fishponds in a broad flat expanse NE of the fortified house ruins.

To the S, the demesne is marked by a fine Georgian ENTRANCE, with square stone piers topped by big sculpted pinecones. Inside was a small Italianate gate lodge, richly stuccoed with a canted frontispiece, all under a low hipped roof with ornate eaves brackets. Now crudely rebuilt, this once worthy Late Victorian design was probably also by *James E. Rogers* when involved here in 1867.

STONE PARK ORANGE HALL. 1 km SE. Set well back from the roadside, a Late Victorian two-storey gable-ended block, in smooth render with rusticated sandstone quoins and a continuous sill course on the first floor. Originally of three bays, it was enlarged in the C20 with an extra bay, given the same distinctive iron frames with a crosshairs pattern and marginal glazing.

KILLOUGHTER PARISH CHURCH (C of I). 2 km SE. A hall-and-tower church of c. 1813, in the usual elementary Gothic style, with a lower, Late Victorian chancel, probably designed by *James E. Rogers*. Rubble walls with limestone dressings throughout. Three-bay nave with lancets under Tudor-style hoodmoulds. The tower has three stages with a richly patterned oculus in the middle stage and crowstepped battlements and pinnacles on the tall belfry. The entrance in the tower N wall is a pointed arch with a hoodmould stopped by carved male heads. Inside, a dark timber roof with exposed kingposts. The nave windows are delicately framed by slender colonnettes with moulded hoods. – STAINED GLASS. Memorial E window, with rich Geometric tracery: 'The Sower' by *Catherine O'Brien, An Túr Gloine*, 1954. Nave S: 'I have fought the good fight', bright, richly patterned window, signed *Watson*, Youghal, c. 1919. – MONUMENTS. John Boyle White †1827 and James Whyte †1830; by *Thomas Kirk*, 1831. Against a slate pylon, a bas-relief in white marble with a mourning female figure, seated under a weeping willow beside two draped urns. Erected by their mother; on the monument their father Francis Whyte is cited as the 'sole representative of those two most ancient families Whyte of Tuddington and White of De Albaville' (accounting for the difference in spelling).

The former RECTORY lies in a small, well-wooded demesne behind the church. A two-storey roughcast block of 1822 with a low hipped roof. Four-bay front, with two bays projecting forward on one side where the ground-floor windows are recessed in shallow segmental arches in the usual way; the entrance, with an open porch, is set in the angle between.

ST BRIGID. 2 km SSE. Built in 1839, remodelled in 1948. A four-bay lancet hall and chancel in roughcast with stuccoed quoins. Unusual cruciform E window. – STAINED GLASS. All by *A. W. Lyons*, Dublin.

RICHHILL   AH *9040*

The manor of Legacorry, from the Irish *Log an Choire*, 'the hollow of the cauldron', was granted to Francis Sacheverell in the Plantation of 1610. It passed by marriage to the Richardson family, who established their seat here, renaming it after 1683 when a patent for markets and fairs was granted to Edward Richardson. Today Richhill is a busy market town, developed in the C18 and C19 around two principal streets converging on a square and the Richardsons' C17 mansion.

RICHHILL CASTLE. Behind the church, crowning the steep *p. 18* ascent of the Main Street. One of the most interesting houses in Ulster, and the only true C17 house in this region still inhabited. To Lieutenant Bennett of the Ordnance Survey, writing in 1835, it was 'a very old and substantial building but of no particular beauty'. Agreement for a late C17 date has recently been refined to *c.* 1664 by dendrochronological analysis of the oak timbers in the surviving butt-purlin roof. The house probably owes its origins, as it does its name, to Major Edward Richardson M.P., who married Anne Sacheverell in 1654. In 1664 no payment of hearth tax is recorded here, and Richardson was then resident in Loughgall; in 1668 he disposed of some 1,300 acres in Armagh obtained under the Restoration land settlement, and it seems not unrealistic to link that sale with the financing of a new house here.

Plan and elevation are equally of interest. Apart from the Georgian doorcase and Victorian fenestration, the house retains a C17 look. Two storeys with attics and partly cellared, to a U-plan, it has a symmetrical front of five bays set between square pavilion wings, three storeys tall, strongly advanced and crowned with Dutch gables; all roughcast over rubble, with later stucco dressings most prominent on the gables. The attic dormers on the inner faces of the wings and over the intermediate bays on the main front have the same gables, reduced in scale. The butt-purlin roof is an innovation derived from English houses, that allowed slate to replace thatch as a covering. Towering over the roof-line, the big decorated brick chimneys, now roughcast, complete the evocation. They are panelled

Richhill Castle, staircase.
Drawing by L. Mulligan, 2012

with blind arcades that follow early C17 types as existed at
Brazeel House, Dublin; here attenuated arches with prominent
imposts are arranged in a single tier in groups of three.

Despite its name, there is nothing in the character of Richhill
Castle to suggest defence other than the posture of the two
wings, flankers set in an echelon position overlapping the
corners of the main, s, front: an arrangement considered by
Maurice Craig to be a 'slightly more economical and less
secure version of the four-flanker type' as at Mountjoy in

Tyrone (1605). In this instance the wings are well-fenestrated, with a window at each level, on the main and inner faces, though these are perhaps later modifications. The plan is elaborated by a stair projection to the N, which is in some ways anachronistic when considered beside C17 houses of the same type at Gort and Athleague (both in Roscommon), but is a feature that persisted among the conventions of C18 planning. The pedimented doorcase – a typically robust Georgian type with engaged Tuscan columns and Doric frieze – probably replaced a timber doorcase. The windows (now with Victorian plate glass) were probably also sashed in the same period; however it is not too difficult to imagine cross-mullions, and on the stair return rectangular mullions remain, renewed, but retaining a medieval look with their deep internal oak linings.

The interior is plain, mostly with C18 and C19 joinery. The house is now subdivided as three residences, but the original plan remains discernible, just one room deep, divided into two rooms on the ground floor as a legacy of medieval planning – hall and kitchen – with the stairs closed off behind and smaller rooms in the wings at either end. A more conventional tripartite plan was later created, the C17 stairs now opened up to provide the main focus at the back of the central hall. The open-well staircase is the best feature, a heavy oaken work with satisfying turned balusters and a thick bevelled handrail. In the E wing, a wonderful lugged bolection doorcase survives with an equally impressive six-panel door, unusually carved with timber discs on the rails and stiles.

Richhill's flamboyant GATE SCREEN of 1745 by the *Thornberry Bros* of Falmouth in Cornwall was moved to Hillsborough Castle, Co. Down, in 1936.

ST MATTHEW. Main Street, overlooking the Square. A hall-and-tower type, more engaging than usual, this emerged from a market house built in 1753 by William Richardson. The precise date of the conversion is not known, except that it probably involved two phases, the first complete by 1837, when it was in use as a chapel of ease. In the first instance, a nave would have been created within the market house simply by replacing its low round-arched bays with three pointed windows with Y-tracery. The walls seem to have been raised at this time too, though the prominent eaves corbels seem true to the C18 building, betraying a subtle camber in the wall surface. In 1862 *Welland & Gillespie* added a N transept, chancel and vestry; in contrast to the plain roughcast hall these are vigorous buttressed structures in rock-faced masonry with elaborate sandstone tracery. The well-proportioned tower is later still, added by *W. Sampson Jervois* in 1912. It is a striking if simple design in roughcast and cement with lancets, rising to a crisp cornice before simple battlements, distinctively raised higher over one corner.

Inside, the low thick walls of the market house and its openings remain evident as blind recesses. A high flat plaster ceiling in the nave gives way to exposed timber in the Victorian additions. In the gallery, an exceptionally fine Regency ORGAN by *Telford* with a carved Gothic frontal, brought here from Gosford Castle as the gift of the 4th Earl of Gosford in memory of Louisa Bacon †1881. – STAINED GLASS. Three-light E window: Christ the Good Shepherd, 1862, attributed to *Alexander Gibbs & Co*. Otherwise mostly Late Victorian. N transept: Faith, Hope and Charity, signed by *James Cameron*, Wigmore St., London, probably also the designer of the window in the nave N wall of *c.* 1880. Nave S: SS Paul and John, attributed to *Mayer & Co.*, *c.* 1890. – MONUMENTS. James Best †1898; a plain scroll, by *Purdy & Millard*, Belfast. – Francis James Best †1907; a white marble relief with an angel, by *W. Costigan & Co.*, Belfast.

COLTHURST HALL. Main Street, beside the church. A pleasing early C19 building of two storeys and three bays in roughcast with paired sashes nicely set in shallow segmental arches.

PRESBYTERIAN CHURCH (former). Off Irish Street. A big Gothic hall, established here by 1835 and renovated in 1889 by *John Boyd*. Five closely spaced bays with tall triangular-headed windows and stucco hoodmoulds.

METHODIST CHURCH. Tandragee Street. A nicely proportioned Victorian church. Stuccoed, with four well-spaced lancets to the nave under a continuous hoodmould. In the buttressed entrance gable a gabled porch set between lancets under a plain rose window.

FRIENDS MEETING HOUSE. 1793. Tucked away behind the houses on Irish Street, a Georgian vernacular building, deeply pleasing in its simplicity. A large roughcast hall with two adjoining lean-to projections to the E and big gables, the N gable expressed as three storeys with two widely spaced bays. Mostly Georgian sashes, all varied in proportion, with two larger Victorian windows to the meeting room. Inside no less abstemious but still attractive; most notable for the collection of good C17 FURNITURE it contains, including a primitive oak bench brought here from the now demolished Ballyhagan Meeting House near Kilmore in Armagh.

ORANGE HALL. Off the Main Street. A deep early C20 hall with a well-ordered little pedimented frontispiece to the street, flanked by carriage arches. Roughcast, with a tall fanlit door in a blocked stucco surround flanked by small round-headed windows.

MASONIC HALL. Irish Street. A boxy C19 hall under a hipped roof. Plain, with stuccoed walls and round-headed windows set high up.

TEMPERANCE HALL. Tandragee Street. 1875. A small roughcast building, suitably circumspect, with nothing more than an entrance and an inscribed plaque on its gabled front.

RECTORY. Hamiltonsbawn Road. A compact stuccoed house, the date 1874 carved in a quatrefoil on the main front. Two storeys with pointed gables, a small glazed porch, and steeply roofed bay window on the side. Typical Victorian details of chamfered window reveals, continuous meandering strings, and incised ornament in blind arches, combined with more unusual raised zigzag brickwork in the gables.

T. H. HARDY ELEMENTARY SCHOOL. The New Line. 1927 by *James St John Phillips*. Well suited to its surroundings. A very long, low front in brick and cement. Sixteen bays in all, the two end bays advanced and set under gables between rusticated piers.

NEIGHBOURHOOD

LISKYBOROUGH MANSE. 1 km W. A small house of Regency proportions. Two storeys and three bays with a hipped roof and central stacks. Victorian stucco detail with rusticated strip quoins on the ground floor, blocked above; windows in moulded stucco frames with straight entablatures and twelve-pane sashes on the ground floor and nine-pane sashes on a continuous sill course above. Segmental-headed doorcase with engaged Ionic columns, fanlight and side-lights, all in a fussy stucco surround.

FRUIT FIELD. 1.3 km E. A sturdy Late Georgian farmhouse built to an L-plan; two storeys in roughcast with big twelve-pane sashes. Front of three bays with a central porch and hipped roof; longer gable-ended side of four bays.

COURSE LODGE. 1.3 km S. A modest two-storey Regency villa in roughcast with stucco trim. Three-bay entrance front with two neat bows flanking a central fanlit door. The twelve-pane sash windows are made to look disproportionate in blocked stucco surrounds. Long side elevation extended by a service wing.

FIR GROVE. 1.5 km SE. 1872. A two-storey Late Victorian block with a steep hipped roof and central stacks. Three-bay front with plate-glass windows and a central fanlit doorcase.

KILNAHARVEY. 2 km SE. An attractive Georgian gentleman's house, a late C18 version of an early C18 type. Two storeys with attics, gable-ended. Five bays to the front with twelve-pane sashes, all evenly spaced. Now coated in early C20 pebbledash with quoins, string-course and architraves in plaster. Wide central doorcase with side-lights, reeded pilasters and an elliptical webbed fanlight.

ROCKCORRY MN 6010

A picturesque estate village developed on the old road from Cootehill to Monaghan. Established in the C17 as Newtowncorry by Walter Corry, who also built a castle here, now long-vanished. In the C18 the family estate on the edge of the village was called Fairfield. It was inherited in 1785 by Thomas Charles Steuart

Corry, who seems to have employed the architect *Benjamin Hallam* in the first decade of the C19 to create a model village around a market house and Presbyterian church. The principal street was neatly lined with two-storey houses, and industry was provided by a corn mill, powered by the small river that skirts the village. After the death of Corry's first wife in 1821 things began to slide: he married a servant, had a large family and became heavily indebted. The town and castle fell into a dilapidated state. Corry eventually sold much of his estate to Lord Dartrey, who absorbed it into the adjoining demesne of Dawson's Grove at Dartrey, while Corry retired to Glenburn Cottage, a house he had built beside the village. Things picked up later in the C19 under the patronage of Lord Dartrey. Almshouses were erected in 1847, a model agricultural school the following year, and eventually a new church at the S end of the village.

84 ST JAMES (C of I). 1854–61 by *W. J. Barre*. A compact Victorian church picturesquely sited beside the village green. Barre exhibited his design at the Royal Hibernian Academy in 1861. Nave and chancel with diagonally opposed vestry and porch and a neat tower offset beside the porch, all tightly grouped with stepped buttresses in a dark pitch-faced masonry, squared and uncoursed with wide mortar joints, and crisp cutstone trim. Good plate tracery to the nave, with two lancets under a quatrefoil; simple quarry-glazed lancets elsewhere. Graded three-light window with hoodmoulds on the W gable and a more elaborate five-light design for the E window. The tower provides the finishing touch. Small and square, in three stages with stepped diagonal buttresses, it is drawn into an octagon by deeply chamfered corners over the second stage, stepped and pitched in smooth ashlar to support a short belfry and continued to form the spire. A simple Tudor-arched doorway on the W face with a hoodmould and unusual carved stops. The principal entrance is through a much more expressive pointed doorway, deeply recessed in the gabled porch adjoining the tower to the E with a fat outer roll moulding. Simple but impressive interior with a high roof of exposed trusses with arched braces. The chancel, behind a plain arch, has scissor trusses. – MONUMENTS. Lieutenant-Colonel Thomas Vesey Dawson, †1854 at Inkerman (commemorated on the Dawson Memorial obelisk in Monaghan).

PRESBYTERIAN CHURCH. 1830. A plain Gothic hall of five bays; rubble with rusticated quoins and plain dressed stone window surrounds with small keystones. The doorway, the oculus above it, and the two windows on either side all stand out in bold relief on the rendered front gable. Old photographs show plinths on the apex and at eaves level.

The MANSE is a solid gable-ended house set in an attractive garden beside the church. Two storeys and three bays in dark rubble with blocked ashlar quoins and red brick reveals. Sash windows with marginal glazing on the ground floor.

METHODIST CHURCH (former). 1807. A trim little roughcast hall of three bays, arranged asymmetrically with a simple round-headed doorway and two Georgian sashes.

MARKET AND SESSIONS HOUSE. A neatly proportioned cubic block built in 1805, possibly by *Benjamin Hallam*. Roughcast with rusticated quoins. Two storeys and three bays; tall recessed arches on each façade, their imposts linked by a continuous platband. Pedimented breakfront on the main façade. Altered with new fenestration in the C20.

WIDOWS' ALMSHOUSES. A long, low range overlooking the village green. Two storeys and twelve bays with advanced and pedimented end bays. Identical plaques in both pediments state: 'These houses were built by Jos. Griffiths for destitute widows A.D. 1847'. Solidly built in squared masonry with rusticated quoins and red brick trim. There are four houses, each of three bays with a central round-headed doorway with a spoked fanlight.

MILL. A derelict gable-ended rubble block of two storeys with tapered brick stack to the rear. Other vestiges include TEA POT ROW, a charming row of six rubble and brick cottages, built for mill workers, sloping with the street down to a small C18 BRIDGE with fine rounded arches in shale.

ST MARY, CORRAVACAN. 1.5 km NE. 1866 by *William Hague*. A small slate-roofed building was erected here *c.* 1815 as a chapel of ease for Edergole, 3 km W. The new church, now serving the parish of Ematris, replaced it just fifty years later. It is a stocky single cell with a bellcote over the E gable and two identically designed but differently scaled projections – a porch and a sacristy – on the S wall. The principal elevations are built in coursed squared limestone with sandstone trim. The windows are nicely varied between simple lancets and plate tracery: best is the E window, which stands out in sandstone against the dark limestone with three well-spaced lights, each under a circular window – the larger central one an elaborate quatrefoil. The N elevation, cement-rendered, has paired lancets. Entrance in the W gable below a heavy canopy, a dull, flat piece carried by stumpy colonnettes with foliate capitals on moulded corbels. Plain shouldered doorway with a pointed tympanum carved in low relief. An attractive, well-lit interior with figurative stained glass. Timber-panelled ceiling with exposed kingpost trusses.

SALTERS GRANGE AH 8040

A rural parish 3.5 km N of Armagh, once one of the granges of the Abbey of SS Peter and Paul, known by the extended appellation of Grangeballymarramacquoid until granted at the Plantation to the London Company of Salters.

ST AIDAN (C of I). A steepled church by *Thomas Cooley*, standing today as the focus of a small hilltop settlement. Built by
Archbishop Robinson, whose arms, with those of Dean Hugh
Hamilton, are displayed over the door; above these, the date
1773 is written in lead on the string-course. The church follows
Cooley's more elaborate 'Design No. 10', with a tall three-stage
tower and polygonal spire flanked by battlemented vestries. In
1843 transepts were added to the sizeable roughcast hall, with
a small ashlar porch set in the angle of the N transept as a
private entrance for the Molyneux family of Castle Dillon,
patrons of the church, whose arms emblazon the gable. Presumably also refenestrated at the same time, with heavy timber
tracery and clear quarry glazing; all too lumpish to be from
Cooley's hand; better in the orderly Perp E window. The tower,
flanked by battlemented vestries with blind windows, rises in
three stages with lean limestone dressings and short pinnacles
before the ashlar polygonal spire. The junction of the tower
and spire seems a little too abrupt, even if the base is decorated
with nice Gothic panelling, and it is now greatly exacerbated
by the stripped rubble walls of the tower and vestries, which
yearn for roughcast.

Inside, the nave retains Cooley's simple space with a flat
plaster ceiling surrounded by a cornice of deep Gothic pendants. Raking W gallery on impossibly slender shafts. In 1854
the interior was given 'many gratifying ameliorations' for the
Molyneux family. – The FONT is by *Philip Charles Hardwick*, a
rich polygonal design in Caen stone on a cluster of marble
shafts. Possibly also by Hardwick are the more sedate PULPIT
and READING DESK, in the same combination of stones. –
STAINED GLASS. The E window is an exceptionally fine, vivid
figurative work of 1910 by *Beatrice Elvery*: eight panels, the four
Evangelists and parables below. – MONUMENTS. Excellent
array of sculpted white marble memorials to worthies of the
Molyneux family. Sir Capel Molyneux †1797; an urn-topped
tablet. – Sir Capel Molyneux †1832; a plain tablet supporting
a draperied heraldic scroll and a portrait bust, signed *T. Kirk*.
– General Sir Thomas Molyneux, Bt †1841; an urn draped
under a regimental flag. – Sir George King Adlercron Molyneux
†1848; a portrait bust in a Soanean arch, by *J. McCullough*,
1863. – The Rev. Graham Murphy †1903; a Gothic aedicule,
by *M. Walker*, Armagh. – Turner Macan †1813; an oval tablet
in a classical frame with slender Tuscan columns, a disproportionate cornice, and shallow Neoclassical urn.

In the CHURCHYARD a good collection of Neoclassical
monuments, the best of these a small box tomb to the Perry
family with diminutive fluted Doric columns recessed in the
corners. The ENTRANCE has big C18 gatepiers flanked by twin
three-bay lodges.

HOCKLEY LODGE. 3.5 km E. A single-storey, stuccoed Regency
villa built for Henry Caulfeild, the younger son of the 1st Earl
of Charlemont, in a prosaic Neoclassical style attributable to
William Murray. Raised over a high basement with a long five-

bay entrance front, facing W, extended to the N by a large
two-bay service block recessed on one side. The three central
bays are advanced, and an enclosed Tuscan portico projects at
the head of a steep pyramid of steps. On the longer garden
front facing S the five central bays are recessed with a delicate
iron veranda between pedimented pavilions. Twelve-pane
sashes set in pairs in the end bays on both fronts; tall casements
to the veranda. Inside, three large rooms are placed in enfilade
on the long S front with a passage behind. The rooms have high
coved ceilings, all plainly treated. The library, once much
admired for its contents, retains bookcases embellished in a
William IV style with lotus-leaf capitals. The dining room has
a late C18 gessoed chimneypiece, the drawing room a heavy
Doric chimneypiece in grey marble.

Behind the house, the sunken COACH HOUSE is a long two-
storey range in rubble and red brick with wide segmental
arches on the ground floor; over the larger central bay a plaque
with the initials of Henry Caulfeild and the date 1838. The
outer yards include an impressive array of low lean-to buildings
of ashlar with red brick arcading. Rising in the centre of a long
single-storey range is the ornamental DAIRY, an octagonal
building of brownstone and red brick with a shallow roof,
central lantern and decorative mullioned casements set high in
the wall. The GATE LODGE is a charming L-plan block, roughcast over red brick with a hipped roof and a quarry-glazed bay
window.

DRUMMANMORE. 1.5 km SE. Overlooking Drumman More
Lough, a handsome vernacular farmhouse, single-storey with
lofts and a formal, asymmetrical front of six bays with an off-
centre doorway and narrow side-lights. Roughcast with a roof
of reed thatch. Above the door an exposed keystone is inscribed
with the initials R. McC. and the date 1785. The windows have
flush sash frames with plate glass and horizontal glazing bars.
The house is characteristically set beside an intimate group of
yard buildings, the largest of these a two-storey rubble block
attached to one end of the house.

CASTLE DILLON. 2.5 km SE. 1844 by *William Murray*. In institutional use for much of the C20 and derelict at the time of
writing. An austere mansion of pink Armagh limestone ashlar,
built for Sir George Molyneux, 6th Bt. The last in a succession
of houses on this site overlooking the picturesque triangular
lake. There are no remains of the castle of the Dillon family,
who resided here until the mid C17, when the property passed
to the highly cultured Molyneux family. The French-born
Thomas Molyneux, an administrator in the Elizabethan court,
came to Dublin in 1576 and became Chancellor of the Court
of Exchequer in Ireland in 1590. Advanced by opportunity and
landed wealth, his descendants were physicians, engineers,
astronomers, politicians and controversialists at the centre of
intellectual life in the capital, most notably perhaps with the
foundation of the Dublin Philosophical Society by William
Molyneux in 1683. In 1664 Captain Samuel Molyneux, a

surveyor and master gunner known as 'Honest Sam', bought
the Castle Dillon estate. His grandson Samuel, an informed
commentator on Irish gardening, spent two years improving
the estate in the first decade of the C18 before leaving Ireland
to become Secretary to the Prince of Wales; in that sphere he
developed his interests and tastes in architecture and gardening
to some repute, but without necessarily applying these at
home. The little that is known of the estate in the C18 owes a
great deal to the work of Sir Capel Molyneux, who politicized
the landscape, following in the great Whig tradition, erecting
at least two conspicuous obelisks commemorating the patriotic
ideals of the late C18, of which only one remains.

The C18 house, dismissed in 1804 by Sir Charles Coote as
'very old-fashioned', had probably evolved over a long period;
it was remembered by the adopted daughter of the 4th Baronet
as 'a low straggling house, the centre, a sort of pavilion containing the reception rooms, and of one storey only. The wings
were of two. Odd staircases and steps within obviated the differences of level.' In a late C18 painting it appears as a long,
low, gable-ended block with a pedimented frontispiece recessed
between substantial five-bay wings.

Today the C19 Castle Dillon is an overstated two-storey
block, nine bays long and five bays deep with single-storey
three-bay wings at either end. The main front faces N with a
Doric porch similar to *Murray*'s design for the Archbishop's
Palace in Armagh, with paired fluted columns projecting diagonally from the corners. The basement is exposed on the
garden front, which otherwise shares with the N front two
storeys of equal height and big Georgian sashes before a
cornice and blocking course, partly concealing a low hipped
roof with ridiculously stubby central stacks. In such broad
expanses of crisp masonry one could be forgiven for confusing
Neoclassical sophistication with puritanical severity. The contractors were the Scottish builders *John & Charles McGibbon*.

Inside, austerity is succeeded by monotony. The double-pile
plan is dominated by a cavernous entrance hall and spinal
corridor behind with staircases grandly disposed at either end.
Numerous generously proportioned well-lit rooms are all decorated with repetitious Early Victorian cornices. The most
appealing space is the small top-lit lobby in the W wing, its oval
lantern handsomely decorated with an anthemion chain in the
encircling frieze.

The E wing encloses a sunken kitchen YARD, opening
through an archway bearing the date 1844. Facing the kitchen
yard are the imposing but ruinous STABLES, designed before
1782 by *Thomas Cooley*. A long free-standing block with two
storeys and thirteen bays to the front, faced in limestone ashlar
with a shallow string-course, cornice and blocking course. The
three central bays are slightly advanced under a pediment,
formerly crowned by a domed cupola. The ground floor is
expressed as an arcade, open in the centre, and elsewhere
forming shallow windowed recesses with imposts and large

keystones. Behind, the ground falls away steeply to reveal an astonishing towering façade on a vaulted understorey.

On the N side of the demesne the formidable PARK ENTRANCE is a singular Piranesian evocation, perhaps also by *Cooley*. Here twin pedimented lodges in massive V-channelled rustication are separated by blank screen walls from stout gatepiers under massive capstones, once taller than the lodges but now pitifully reduced by a third. The former monumental elegance of the gateway once so captivated visitors as to be considered 'the most costly park gates of hewn stone in the three kingdoms'.

Further N, prominent on Cannon Hill, just outside the demesne walls, stands the VOLUNTEER OBELISK, a finger of pale grey limestone. The survivor of at least two obelisks erected in the C18 by the patriotic Sir Capel Molyneux, this one, of 1782, celebrated the legislative independence of the Irish Parliament. A plaque on one face is inscribed: 'This obelisk was erected by the Rt Hon. Sir Capel Molyneux of Castle Dillon, Bart. in the year 1782, to commemorate the glorious revolution which took place in favour of the constitution of the Kingdom, under the auspices of the volunteers of Ireland.' Probably to a design by *Thomas Cooley*, it is an elegant, well-proportioned obelisk in rubble with dressed quoins on a pedestal of squared limestone.

THE GRANGE. 0.5 km w. 1781. An attractive roughcast house of two storeys and three bays with a low hipped roof. The fenestration varies between large sixteen-pane sashes on the ground floor and smaller nine-pane sashes on the floor above. Central doorcase in a simple moulded surround with a straight classical entablature. Tripartite plan with a central hall passage and a generous open-well stair behind.

ST COLUMCILLE, KNOCKACONEY. 2 km NW. 1957 by *McLean & Forte*. A substantial church in finely wrought sandstone ashlar, mildly Egyptian in inspiration, with trapezoidal openings and strange, rather flat, undeveloped ornament. The plan consists of nave, chancel and S transept, with an offset square tower linked by a flat-roofed porch to the W front. Here the kneelered gable is decorated with unpleasant blunt sawtoothed detail, repeated in a shallow recess between triangular windows from which a narrow gable projects with a big trapezoidal window. The nave has six bays with trabeated windows set high in shallow trapezoidal panels. Inside, a broad nave lined with pilasters, and flat coffered ceiling. The decoration is even stranger here, with panels and windows ornamented with Celtic interlace. – STAINED GLASS. W window: St Columcille (Columba), a radiant work inset in patterned glass. In the transept, the Baptism of Christ, a small brilliant work by *D. I. Braniff*.

BOND'S MILL. 2 km NNW. Pleasing early C19 vernacular buildings consisting of two conjoined gable-ended blocks at a crossing of the River Callan. The main building has two storeys with a long six-bay front and twelve-pane sashes in flush frames, taller on the first floor. It was built in two phases, evident in the seam dividing the stonework on the front wall between rubble on one side and older squared limestone on the other. The distinction is most apparent in the red brick trim, where deeper red brick is used more extensively in the later section. The plain doorway is offset in the original building, apparently reduced within a wider brick arch when the building was enlarged. Inside, the proportions are small, with low ceilings. In the hallway is some modest plaster decoration with scallop shells in the corners of the ceiling and a rope-edged centrepiece covered in shamrocks with long intertwining stems.

4010

SCOTSHOUSE MN

A small village on the w shoulder of Monaghan which developed on the periphery of Hilton Park demesne.

ST ANDREW, CURRIN PARISH CHURCH (C of I). A large hall-and-tower church of 1812, roughcast with stone trim. Four-bay nave, with simple quarry-glazed Y-tracery inserted in 1859. Small vestry in rubble added about the same time. Chancel of 1905, in squared pitch-faced limestone, reusing the older E window. The tower, tall and stark, is in three diminishing stages with battlements and pinnacles. Internally a simple and attractive single cell with a small gallery over the w end. Re-roofed by *Welland & Gillespie* in 1866 with a very good hammerbeam-truss roof. The contractor was *Henry Sharpe*. – STAINED GLASS. E window: Christ with SS Patrick and Michael in muted colours, by *Percy Bacon*, London, 1918. – MONUMENTS. Colonel John Madden †1844; a white marble tablet with Corinthian pilasters, by *Sharp & Emery*. – Ernest W. King, †1912 on the *Titanic*.

CHURCH OF THE IMMACULATE CONCEPTION. 1924 by *R. M. Butler*. A severe Celtic Revival chapel in rock-faced limestone. Though inspired by the earlier work of W. A. Scott, Butler is an original and interesting designer. The plan, a long nave and aisles of five bays, is straightforward, but the outward expression offers a more severe and vigorous development of the basilican plan, an indication of Butler's ability to innovate within tradition. The front is asymmetrical, subtly in the minor differences between the antae that support the gable, and more wilfully with an offset bellcote rising from the corner of the nave. As in Butler's church at Newport, Co. Mayo, the aisles are long rectangular ranges with paired Romanesque windows; the flat roofs perhaps reflect the influence of modern architectural forms rather more than an interest in the possibilities of new materials. Throughout the building carefully selected masonry is well finished to achieve contrast and effect. Blue rock-faced limestone dominates, with a greyer variety concentrated at the corners and in the buttresses. The same pale stone is smoothly finished, giving hard chiselled definition to the windows, especially in the formation of their distinctive shape, which, following the pattern of Irish Romanesque models, widens subtly at the base so that they read like keyholes. The same treatment can be seen in the square-headed windows and doors of the sacristy on the SE corner, giving it the defensive appearance of a bunker. The salient gabled doorway on the W gable, with its flanking blind arches, is an austere version of the C12 arrangement at St Cronan's, Roscrea, and exploits the crisp qualities of the carved limestone to enhance the shadows of the recessed door and to anticipate the dim Byzantine atmosphere of the interior.

Internally an eloquently simple and coherent space. The nave is barrel-vaulted with flat transverse ribs carried on long corbelled brackets, and lined by arcades of clean round arches carried on squat tapered piers with scalloped capitals. The piers are square in the last bay, which is reduced in size to enhance the impression of scale. – STAINED GLASS. E window: the Virgin with her parents, SS Joachim and Anne, a brooding blue three-light window by *Harry Clarke*.

RECTORY. A busy Late Victorian brick house. Two storeys and three bays with a central gabled projection, three-bay sides and a ground-floor bay window on one elevation. Wide eaves with paired brackets halted on the projection to form an open pediment, hipped roof, and massive brick stacks. Red brick in Flemish bond with string-courses and arches over the openings of yellow brick. The bricks are combined in a stretcher bond to form a patterned frieze below the eaves. The door, in the projection, is set in a shallow recess with the outer cambered head in yellow brick descending to carved foliate capitals. Above the doorway two narrow round-headed windows rest on the same sill.

ST MARY, TURE. 3 km NE. Hall and tower built in 1843. Gabled hall of four bays with lancets under emphatic hoodmoulds with unusual mallet-like stops. Roughcast with ashlar trim. Neat two-bay sacristy added later on the E. The rubble tower, in three diminishing stages with short pinnacles and miniature battlements, stands over the W gable. The W face is orderly, with pointed openings at each level; one original sash with Y-tracery survives in the middle stage. The S face is less so, though the off-centre position of the main doorway, shared by the inscribed dedication plaque and blank clock face above, give it a certain naïve quality.

ST ALPHONSUS, THE CONNONS. 4.5 km NW. 1844. A bulky four-bay lancet hall. Roughcast with rusticated quoins, and a masonry belfry on the rear gable. Orderly front gable with a pointed doorway and two lancets, all with Gothick glazing and hoodmoulds with mallet-like stops similar to those at St Mary, Ture. Dull interior with exposed kingpost trusses; porch, confessionals and organ gallery combined in a single wooden structure.

St Mary, Drummully (C of I). 5 km NW. 1844. A big road-side church set in a small area of land extending into Ferman-agh, where most of the parish is. The old church lies in ruins across the border. A symmetrically planned church, not the usual *Joseph Welland* type, but similar to his design for Swan-linbar, the other of his two earliest churches in the region: three-bay hall with bellcote, tall gabled porch, and chancel flanked by single-storey vestries, all in squared limestone with crisp cutstone trim. Quarry-glazed lancets, paired on the main elevations and arranged as three graded lights in the chancel. The elevations are divided into three registers by playful string-courses that run continuously around the building, through window sills, around buttresses, rising intermittingly to form hoodmoulds. The porch, a lofty space, leads one to expect a greater volume beyond. Inside, the doorway from the porch is set in a giant pointed recess, where the real interest is a pair of Gothic fireplaces set into the splays. The nave is airy and bright with exposed kingpost trusses, nicely detailed with cusping on the rafters and struts.

SCOTSTOWN   MN

St Mary, Urbleshanny. 0.75 km NE. A remarkable C19 lime-stone church evoking Monaghan's most intriguing and unfor-tunate C18 house, Gola, an important Palladian house that stood nearby until its destruction by fire in 1923, leaving just one of its wings. When and how the elements from that house came to be used here is not recorded. Initially a large and unremarkable four-bay hall set N–S in squared limestone, with big round-headed windows and large square towers marking an entrance at either end. The towers were originally identical, with wide Gothick fanlit doorways, the upper stage a sham with two adjoining walls hiding a lean-to roof, masked further to the front by stepped battlements supporting a cross between two pinnacles. The N tower was then remodelled, and given an upper belfry stage in materials that have an important prove-nance: the distinctive Venetian openings on opposing faces show it to be a well-conceived reuse of the attic tower from Gola. The belfry stage is a handsome box in crisp ashlar with rusticated quoins, a deep and well-defined entablature, and squat pyramid roof. String-courses and architraves from Gola give the tower greater elaboration in its present reincarna-tion; a larger round-arched opening on the N face set in a bold Gibbs surround is derived from the sophisticated tripartite doorcase of the house, while the simple oval hiding on the S face once filled an open eaves pediment there. Inside, the old layout is preserved under a dark kingpost roof with the altar placed on the long E wall and galleries on three sides. – MONUMENT. The Rt Rev. James Murphy, Bishop of

Clogher †1824; black-and-white marble displaying episcopal paraphernalia.

At the rear, a large two-storey PRIEST'S HOUSE projects from the E wall; a three-bay roughcast block, this is a rare instance in Monaghan of an arrangement that stems from the residential tower of the medieval parish church.

GOLA HOUSE. 2 km SW. Only a disfigured wing survives of the intriguing Palladian house built here, it is said, for Joseph Wright in 1703. The original two-storey house was a gable-ended block with a handsomely proportioned front of five bays with a broken pediment to the centre, floating over the eaves. The design was apparently elaborated later by the addition of single-storey wings with Venetian windows, and the same motif was more prominently displayed in a most remarkable lantern-topped attic tower that straddled the roof, a structure which only finds comparison in Ireland at Woodlands in Co. Dublin, a house usually accepted to be by Sir Edward Lovett Pearce. (Something of the same idea was later expressed in the C19 tower built at Ancketill's Grove, Emyvale.) The Palladian motifs at Gola, continued in the rusticated tripartite doorcase, all shared in Pearce's kind of classical sensibility, even if overall the design as conveyed in old drawings and photographs seems a little provincial. Some sense of the quality of the stonework survives, however, in the fragments integrated with the disembodied tower which was rebuilt at the nearby church of St Mary, Urbleshanny (*see* above). Today the once impressive wide, straight avenue, still very evident along its NW–SE alignment (which continues to the SE in the public road), but defined now by just a few limes and yews, terminates at the remodelled N wing. This is a two-storey block just one bay wide, with a gabled front in squared limestone with rusticated quoins. The door is off-centre, set in a corner of the original

Scotstown, Gola House.
Engraving, 1879

Venetian window, its form with a triple keystone still evident though flush with the surrounding masonry.

ST JOSEPH, KNOCKTALLON. 6 km NW. A large and unexpected early C20 church deep in the countryside on the lower slopes of Slieve Beagh. An ambitious Gothic design in rock-faced limestone. Cruciform, with unfinished tower and vestry flanking the S transept and a small stair-turret projecting at the W end. Plain lancets in the five-bay nave, Geometric bar tracery in the W gable and transepts, and a more eccentric bipartite E window. Inside, the nave opens to the transepts and side chapels through a pair of pointed arches on a round sandstone pier. Elaborate roof combining hammerbeam and kingpost construction.

7000   SHERCOCK   CN

A small street village set on a height between two small lakes and at the tail of the more expansive waters of Lough Sillan. No trace here today of the 'handsome house' of the same name, overlooking the lake, that Mrs Delany saw in 1732. Some good C19 housing, and a church at either end of the street.

KILLAN PARISH CHURCH (C of I). Hall-and-tower type in a walled graveyard, elevated above the S approach. A simple three-bay roughcast hall with a shallow apsidal chancel built c. 1780, to which a forestanding tower was added c. 1830, in three diminishing stages, with bold quoins, battlements and sharply tapering pinnacles. Timber Gothic sashes, and small traceried E window in Portland stone. Mid-C19 lean-to vestry on the N. Inside, a simple unadorned hall. – MONUMENTS. Joseph John Fitzpatrick †1842; a plain plaque bearing a relief carving, 'Young man I say unto thee arise'. – The Very Rev. Samuel Adams, Dean of Cashel †1856; a white marble plaque with inverted torches and a snake eating its tail.

ST PATRICK. On a low site on the edge of Muddy Lough. A bulky gable-fronted hall of 1838 with a slender square tower offset on the NE angle. Roughcast with stone trim; simple Y-tracery, and ogee-headed doorways in the gable and tower on the W front. The chancel and sacristy were added in 1908 by J. J. McDonnell, and in 1912 he raised the nave walls, adding a new roof and leaded lights. The tower was also raised and given a tall belfry, yet even with its steep copper-clad pyramid roof it remains disproportionately weak. Inside, a deep coved plaster ceiling on an enriched string-course, and square coffers in the centre similarly enriched. Reordered in 1988 by Gerald Fay and Gerald Stapleton, with artist contributions by Ray Carroll: the altar is awkwardly placed in the aisle, with seating arranged transversely; the furniture and its effect now tired and dated. – ALTAR. By Earley & Co., 1908. – STAINED GLASS.

Bright and colourful three-light E window with Jesus, Mary and Joseph, and St Patrick in an upper roundel, probably by *Earley*, *c.* 1938.

WESLEYAN CHAPEL. 1838. Derelict. On a narrow side road leading off the Bailieborough Road, a modest three-bay rough-cast hall, gable-fronted with a Gibbsian doorcase in low relief.

MARKET HOUSE. 1825. A substantial two-storey block with a hipped roof, stepping forward at the N end of the Main Street to expose a big recessed arch on the gable with rustication and a hooded plaque displaying the date of erection. Main front of seven bays. The windows on the upper floor have bold rusticated surrounds; the ground floor is now disfigured by shopfronts, the voussoirs of the arcade peeping out behind the fascia boards.

NATIONAL IRISH BANK (former NORTHERN BANK). Origin-ally a long two-storey roughcast house, remodelled *c.* 1920 by *G. W. Ferguson* as a bank with stuccoed dressings and plate glass. Handsomely understated.

GLASLECK PRESBYTERIAN CHURCH. 3 km SSW. 1836. Dere-lict. A boxy Gothic hall, small and attractively plain, with four large pointed openings still with Gothick timber sashes; a plaque between the windows is inscribed 'A.C. MDCCCXXXVI'. Roughcast with dressed quoins and reveals and a hipped roof. A porch is recessed on one side and a two-storey, two-bay former minister's house projects in a modest gable-ended return.

ST JOSEPH, KILLCROSSBEG. 3 km SW. Wedged into a tight triangular site at a small rural crossroads. A roughcast early C19 Gothic church with later C19 stuccoed decorations. It makes the most of the limited site with nave, transepts, various porches, and two diminishing projections to the E.

KILLAN OLD CHURCH. 5 km SW. Prominent at a rural cross-roads, raised on a grassy mound within a large circular enclo-sure. The thick rubble gables of a ruined rectangular church 72 ft by 26 ft (22 m by 8 m) with a closed, vaulted chamber incorporated at the E end, a mausoleum of the Cosby family; the vault is set transversely to the nave, with evidence for a gallery accommodated above it. Single window in the W gable, repaired with a triangular arch.

LOUGH SILLAN HOUSE (formerly Carrickcreery Glebe House). 2 km NW. 1819. In a small demesne overlooking Lough Sillan. A Regency house, built to a haphazard plan resulting in an assemblage of two-storey-over-basement blocks with hipped roofs and bowed projections on either side. Remodelled *c.* 2001 to achieve a more coherent design. Originally rough-cast, now cement-rendered. The entrance front remains largely unchanged with two storeys and two bays, the entrance bay recessed slightly with engaged columns and a thin cornice. The main front is now to the side, where the two-bay bowed projec-tion has been centred in the enlarged façade. Here the area has been pulled away to present a more imposing three-storey edifice; on this new ground level a leadwork Regency-style canopy projects over a glazed veranda on one side of the bow. The staircase projects in a narrower bow behind, facing into an enclosed kitchen yard.

Attractive stables and vernacular outbuildings, of rubble and red brick, arranged in two groups behind the house.

5030   SMITHBOROUGH   MN

A small village between Monaghan and Clones, formed when Henry Smith established a market here in 1717. In 1837 it had a Presbyterian church, school and police station, and these continue to provide the main focus of the present street village. The POLICE STATION was replaced in 1927 by an attractive Neo-Georgian design for the Gardí.

PRESBYTERIAN CHURCH. A large gable-fronted hall, *c.* 1830, with a hooded oculus and long round-headed windows flanking a small gabled porch. All pebbledashed with exposed sandstone trim. The hall is lit from the S by five large round-headed windows with exaggerated blocked surrounds. Bright interior, utterly spartan, with coloured glass. – MONUMENTS. Frederick Welsh †1918, signed *W. Lendrum*. – The Rev. Arthur Rose †1926, by *J. Edgar Winter*, Belfast.

A sizeable SCHOOL BLOCK projects to the side with two oversized square-headed windows; also pebbledashed with sandstone trim.

THORNHILL. 1.5 km NE. A neatly formed Late Georgian villa. There is an undated design for the house by *William Farrell* for John George, but instead of Farrell's very plain three-storey block with a Tuscan portico what is seen here today is a simplified version of Richard Morrison's distinctive midlands villas of Bellair and Cangort in Co. Offaly. It is uncertain whether Farrell had a hand in this rather unsophisticated and solid two-storey block (no basement) with a hipped roof and wide oversailing eaves on paired brackets. It has two show fronts, built in finely worked squared limestone with expressive brick dressings. Like the Offaly villas, it has a compact three-bay front and a longer side elevation with a central bow. The bow, too small to accommodate three bays, looks unresolved, with just two windows that seem too far apart. Morrison's influence is apparent in the entrance formed as a deep concavity, unadorned but for a prominent rusticated keystone in the outer masonry arch; the handsome fanlit doorway is quite lost within it, though there is a delicacy in the way the doors continue the line of the curve. The plan is a simplified version of Cangort, with the stairs disposed to the side off an axial hallway. The rooms while attractively scaled are disappointing, lacking Morrison's elegant finish.

BALLINTOPPIN HOUSE. 1.5 km S. A small Late Georgian villa. Roughcast, with a broad single-storey front of three bays. The roof is hipped, with central brick stacks; round-headed windows with Georgian sashes and bold reveals. The wide doorcase has side-lights and an elliptical fanlight with an unusual blocked surround like those around the windows of Smithborough Presbyterian Church, exaggerated with elongated projections.

ST MARY, MAGHERARNEY. 1 km SW. A large lancet hall with an assured gabled front, built in squared limestone with ample cutstone trim. The old thatched chapel on the site was destroyed during the notorious storm – the 'night of the big wind' – on 6 January 1839, and rebuilt in the same year; further alterations were made in 1859, and that date seems right for the present architecture. The old hall was enlarged and given long lancets under hoodmoulds and a belfry, projecting from the W gable in hammer-dressed stone with simple buttressing and a small gabled porch at its base. Parallel with the S wall is a small sacristy, its plain Gothick windows presumably reflecting the original fenestration. Inside, the space is broad, with a flat panelled ceiling set out as a grid. The sanctuary is set behind an elaborate Gothic arcade on clustered shafts with stiff-leaf capitals, nicely articulated with a wide three-centred arch in the middle, flanked by smaller subsidiary arches, all hand-somely detailed with moulded arches decorated with ball-flowers. The motif is repeated on the E wall, with more robust decoration.

LOCK HOUSE. 1.3 km SW. A small lock-keeper's house, surviving as an isolated curiosity beside the abandoned lock, which now lies exposed on dry land like a beached whale. Built for the Ulster Canal Company c. 1835, possibly by *Henry, Mullins & McMahon*, who were awarded the original contract to build the canal in 1830, though ultimately they were superseded by *William Dargan* and *William Cubitt*. Built, like the nearby lock house at Glear, as a long single-storey block with a deep canted bay, wide oversailing eaves, and a central stack; extremely well finished in large square blocks of masonry. The summit canal linking Lough Neagh and Lough Erne, with twenty-six locks over 74 km, was doomed to failure by the decision to econo-mize by making the locks narrower, thus ruling out most of the craft employed on the other Ulster navigations. It was abandoned in 1931.

LOUGHOONEY. 2 km SW. A small, sophisticated Neoclassical villa with an attractive single-storey front. Built c. 1800, on a hill overlooking Lough Ooney, the site of an important crannog mentioned in the *Annals of Ulster* and the *Annals of the Four Masters* and the centre of the petty kingdom of Fernmag. The house is L-plan with a long low front, hipped roof with squat stacks, and wide oversailing eaves on carved stone brackets, set in pairs. The walls are neatly coursed in small squared blocks. The front is cheerfully composed with four elegant windows: big sashes tightly set in crisp recessed arches with blind tympana. The two central windows are grouped together with the doorway which is similarly expressed and overlaid with tall and slender engaged Tuscan columns that push a simple entablature right up into the eaves; worked in finely droved limestone, it remains an elegant composition despite this awkward collision. To one side, the front wall is set back slightly beyond the end bay with a two-storey kitchen and service wing extending out to the rear. In 1837 the residence of Mrs Murray. Handsome entrance GATES with cast-iron piers, pierced with a Greek-key pattern.

STRADONE   CN

5000

Small estate village, set in the wooded vale of the River Stradone, developed with a market by the Burrowes family of Stradone House. In 1835 the Ordnance Survey noted among the sixty-seven houses five grocery shops, five spirit retailers and ten lodging houses, 'a dispensary and a small detachment of police'. Now there are just a few vernacular houses mixed with light industry, with a dilapidated Regency-style police barracks of 1926 still prominent at the heart of the main street. To the s is the well-planted demesne of STRADONE HOUSE; the large Neoclassical house for Colonel Burrowes for which *J. B. Keane* exhibited plans at the Royal Hibernian Academy in 1828 has long vanished, but the farm buildings and a small classical gate lodge remain.

LARAH PARISH CHURCH (C of I). 1832 by *William Farrell*. The familiar chapel-of-ease design, consisting of a small Gothic hall of three bays with a short chancel. Pinnacled front gable in limestone ashlar with bellcote and battlemented porch. The standard design is varied on the side, where flat rubble buttresses project between the bays. Lancet windows with light geometric tracery and quarry glazing. Inside, repewed later in the C19 but retaining the usual ceiling of exposed cast-iron trusses. – STAINED GLASS. E window: Christ the Good Shepherd between the Angels of Life and Death, by *Heaton, Butler & Bayne,* memorial to Robert Burrowes †1893. – MONUMENTS. A good variety of C19 tablets. Major George Burrowes †1834; a Neoclassical tablet with a draped urn. – Alexander and Bell Burrowes and family, a Greek Revival pedimented tablet in sandstone, crisply carved with scrolls, anthemions and egg-and-dart cymatium, by *J. Kirk*, 1855. – James Edward Burrowes †1860; a Perp Caen stone tablet. – Susan Burrowes †1862 and family; a hooded Gothic tablet. – Robert Burrowes †1881; a brass plaque, by *Jones & Willis*, London.

ST BRIGID, LARAH. 1981–4 by *Gaffney and Cullivan*. An ostentatious building from the era of *Battlestar Galactica*, unsuited to its quiet rural situation. A lozenge-shaped plan with walls of squared hammer-dressed sandstone; strip windows under thick slate-hung eaves and a big hipped slate roof. A monolithic porch dominates the front with its bizarre wedge-shaped roof, mirrored by a similar protrusion at the E end. Here a small toilet block with a steep pyramid roof and central stack has infinitely greater appeal. Inside, a broad hall with an expansive timber-clad ceiling. Altogether a regrettable replacement for the handsome Late Georgian barn church sited here, which had been restored in 1937 by *W. H. Byrne & Son*. – ALTAR FURNISHINGS. Hammered copper by *David J. King*.

LARAH PARISH SCHOOL (former). 1837. A handsomely plain gable-ended block in smooth render with decorative barge-boards. Symmetrical five-bay front with big windows and a central round-arched door with a spoked timber fanlight.

LAVEY PARISH CHURCH (C of I). 1.5 km SW. 1817. A Board of First Fruits hall-and-tower type of the smallest proportions, built in limestone rubble with carved dressings. Three-bay nave with pointed windows in chamfered reveals with hoods, cheaply refenestrated apart from the cusped timber Y-tracery on the E gable. This gable is unusually given exaggerated buttresses, built as stout sloping piers against the corners. The tower has three stages with battlements and short spiky pinnacles. All that is known of an older church on this site is old burials and a sheila-na-gig found here in 1842, now in the National Museum in Dublin.

ST DYMPNA, LOWER LAVEY, KILLYCONNAN. 2.5 km SW. 1979 by *Gaffney & Cullivan*. A harsh angular building, essentially a lean-to structure in mass concrete with a radial plan. The sweeping slate roof is brought low to a thick beam projecting over extensive glazed walls, canted at either end and with triangular buttresses interspersed between. An angular slate-clad projection on the roof with square windows, rather like a military look-out. Pretentious and strange; inside, vacant and dull.

ST DYMPNA, UPPER LAVEY. 5 km W. 1859 by *John Ryan*, greatly remodelled in 1960 by *Philip Shaffrey*. A bulky lancet hall of four bays with a polygonal apse and a low tower offset by a short link to the W gable. Roughcast with stucco quoins and a curious arcade fringe on the eaves and gables. The tower is decidedly odd, solid-looking with angle buttresses, a circular stair-turret on the NW corner, attenuated lancets, and a neat pyramidal roof with louvred dormers. Interior now a bleak, empty hall; the canopied Crucifix above the altar and the ceiling, gridded with square coffers, seem inspired by *W. H. Byrne & Son*'s 1958 design for St Columcille's Church at Kells, Co. Meath.

SWANLINBAR

A straggling street village on the River Claddagh, which owes its location in the remote mountainous region of north Cavan to the rich iron deposits found nearby on Cuilcagh. Although the old name of *An Muileann Iarainn*, 'iron mill', probably refers to a long-established industry, the present town largely grew up around an iron foundry established in the C17, of which the ruins were still present W of the town in 1837, in the telling townland name of Furnaceland. The origin of the new name, at first 'Swandlingbar', was explained by Jonathan Swift in 1728 as an acronym extracted from the surnames of the foundry's promoters – *Swi*ft (his uncle Godwin Swift), *Sand*ers, Dar*ling* and *Bar*ry. By 1760 the smelting works were closed, having consumed all of the surrounding timber. By then the iron-rich geology had begun to provide a greater source of wealth for the town: sulphuric waters rich in iron, sulphur and magnesium, which from 1740 onwards were exploited for medical conditions well beyond the usual gouty complaints. The *Poste-Chaise Companion* in 1786 advertised the excellence of Swanlinbar water for the treatment of 'scurvey [*sic*], nerves, low spirits and bad appetite'. And though it is difficult now to consider Swanlinbar in any way comparable to a North Yorkshire spa resort, its reputation from April to September each year was indeed once as great as Harrogate's, its attractions largely concentrated E of the town at Uragh Spa, where a 'handsome' pump room was situated in 'tastefully planted grounds'. In 1786 a fire devastated the town, burning twenty-two houses; in 1787 the Rev. Daniel Beaufort noted a 'tolerable sized village' with 'a wonderful paucity of decent houses for a place of such concourse'; in 1802 'the ravages of the fire' were still evident, and yet Sir Charles Coote could observe that 'a great deal of harmony and sociability prevails in this retired watering place'. More retiring still today, as its prominence as a great resort faded entirely with the C19.

ST AUGUSTINE (C of I). 1844 by *Joseph Welland*, built as a chapel of ease for Kinawley parish (which extends into Fermanagh). A solid ashlar hall and tower. Buttressed three-bay nave and chancel with a vestry and porch projecting in the re-entrant angles between the nave and chancel. The windows are quarry-glazed lancets set in orderly pairs with hoodmoulds. The square tower dated 1849 is a revision of the original design for a W porch, and in its execution repeats the design built at Drummully (Scotshouse); it has three stages with clasping buttresses on the lower stage and battlements on the tall upper belfry, made distinctive by the absence of pinnacles. Inside, a broad nave under an open timber roof of braced kingposts. Tall and narrow chancel arch framing a tall E window of three graded lancets. – STAINED GLASS. E window: patterned around panels of the Parable of the Prodigal Son set under the Crown of Life, attributed to *Alexander Gibbs & Co.*, London, *c.* 1898. Nave N, twin lancets: l., the Ascension by *Mayer & Co.*, Munich, *c.* 1920; r., the Resurrection, signed *Alexander Gibbs & Co.*, London, *c.* 1900. – MONUMENTS. The Rev. William Grattan †1844; in white marble, a draped urn set over a sarcophagus with eagle feet and inverted torches on either side.

– James Johnston †1846; a white tablet on which rest a helmet and sword, by *Coates*, Dublin. – Captain John Johnston †1864; a white marble tablet surmounted by a draped sarcophagus. – Albert Hutton †1887; an enriched Gothic tablet. – Martha and Andrew Veitch †1925; both signed *Lendrum*, brought here in 1997 from the Methodist church.

RECTORY. Adjoining the churchyard, a plain rendered two-storey block with three bays, a small porch, plate-glass windows and a steep hipped roof.

ST MARY. 1975 by *Hubert Duffy*. On an attractive riparian site, a nondescript pebbledashed church to a radial plan with a long low front, partly stepped back with an open concrete canopy on short pillars, and a tall belfry to one side comprising four slender concrete shafts arranged in a square. Replacing a church of 1828 renovated in 1927 and 1959 and bombed in 1974.

METHODIST CHURCH (former). A plain end-of-terrace hall of *c.* 1840 in smooth render. Three-bay front with Gothick sashes.

DROMOD SPA. 1 km SE, just off the roadway. The most accessible of the surviving sulphur spas in the hinterland of Swanlinbar. A small, near-inconsequential, whitewashed stone canopy over a circular well-head.

TIRCAHAN LODGE. 2.5 km SSE. Elevated in a well-treed park, a plain stuccoed gentleman's house with plate-glass windows, of Late Victorian appearance but remodelled out of an older building. Two storeys and three bays with a prominent square projection in the centre, bay windows on the narrow side elevations, and a large return. Long two-storey coach house to one side.

ST PATRICK, GLANGEVLIN. 12 km W. A remote roadside church encompassed by the Cuilcagh and Slievenakilla mountains. A greatly remodelled lancet hall of six bays in roughcast with smooth quoins, built in 1856 by the Rev. Hugh Magauran. Altered in 1978, when a broad gabled porch was placed incongruously on the main front, and the nave roof was given an exaggerated sprocket, clad with tiles. Interior unprepossessing except for a timber barrel-vault punctuated by circular king-post trusses, presumably part of improvements of 1916 by *J. J. McDonnell*. – PAROCHIAL HOUSE also by *McDonnell*, 1920.

TANDRAGEE AH

Tandragee owes its name to the Irish *Tamlacht Gliad*, 'burial ground of strife', or *Tóin re Gaoith*, 'backside to the wind'. History may resonate in the former, but the latter best reflects the topography. C19 visitors could share a favourable impression of an attractive small town, memorable in appearance, with handsome, well-built houses gracing the steep Main Street. Sir Charles Coote wrote in 1801 that 'the neat appearance of the town, its gradual elevation from a valley through which a beautiful stream winds between lofty and undulating banks . . . affords a pleasing prepossession to the traveller; nor are his expectations balked in viewing the town and its vicinity; every place corresponds with this engaging picture.'

Tandragee was the centre of the medieval petty kingdom of Orior ruled by the O'Hanlons, whose power surged in the C15 through alliance and competition with the neighbouring O'Neills. Their estates were forfeited in the early C17 and Tandragee was granted by James I to the servitor Sir Oliver St John under the terms of the Plantation of Ulster. By 1622 he had paled around the elevated O'Hanlon stronghold, creating a 'pleasant park' with a handsome church, and in its shadow developed a village of twenty-seven houses 'well built of the English fashion, making a fair large street'. The distinctive broad arc of the Main Street, climbing steeply uphill before widening formally at the entrance to the demesne of the castle, is a product of St John's C17 planning and is clearly shown on a 1703 map of the district by Francis Nevill.

Situated as the town is on the River Cusher, milling was a long-established industry. In the early C19 the flour and meal mills run by John Creery at the s end of the town could grind 2,000 tons of wheat and 1,000 tons of oats annually. Milling reaching its zenith in the late C19, with both industry and markets well served by the not-too-distant Newry Canal and the Dublin & Belfast Junction Railway. However, Tandragee's reputation was made with the production of fine linens, in which it was rivalled only by Lurgan and Armagh; damask production was introduced in 1805, and the town became the main producer in the region. Accompanying the growing industrial activity, Tandragee was improved and renewed by the St John descendants – first by the Sparrows in the C18 and then by successive dukes of Manchester, who gradually from 1819 raised the formidable silhouette of a new castle on the site of the old one.

The C20 has been harsh to the architectural accomplishments of the town. The castle is a burnt-out shell, while the loss of many of the dignified terraces on the Main Street is most keenly felt in the replacements, poorly mimicking the older houses with inferior material. The linen mills are silent, and only the great red brick hulks of White's Mills continue the industrial traditions into the C21.

St Mark (C of I). A big parish church raised above the Mall in a corner of the castle demesne. In 1622 Sir Oliver St John built on this site a 'fair church of brick, covered with tiles, with seats and needful ornaments'. Burnt in 1641 and rebuilt by Henry St John; replaced by the present church in 1812, enlarged in 1818 to the designs of *John Bowden*, whose familiar three-stage tower is evident here. Further enlarged by *Joseph Welland* in 1846 with a chancel, vestry and transepts, including the Duke of Manchester's private entrance on the s transept. A consequence of these additions is an irregular huddle of buildings around the chancel. All in dark limestone rubble, with regular courses in the additions; the distinctions between the two phases all too obvious now with the loss of the render, which also left the hoodmoulds on the nave awkwardly exposed. Plain Y-tracery to the nave, elaborated with cusping on Welland's additions, and best in the large E window.

The interior is disappointing, having been reroofed and repewed c. 1963. The gallery was removed at the same time, and internal works of c. 1884 by J. F. Fuller entirely erased. Still, the nave remains a lofty space with the transepts and chancel opening through tall moulded arches with colonnettes. Simple rib-vaulting with a central gilded boss survives in the chancel ceiling. – A remarkable addition to the interior is the CARVED WOODWORK brought here in 1956 from the chapel of Tandragee Castle. The oak REREDOS is an ebullient C18 classical composition with a central segmental pediment, Ionic pilasters, chubby winged cherub heads above the capitals and square funerary urns along the cornice. The PANELLING in the chancel and in the adjoining small WAR MEMORIAL CHAPEL (remodelled from the Manchester porch) has vigorous foliated motifs that are decidedly French in feeling. The most intricate carved work is to be seen in the musical instruments on the PLAQUES now adorning an otherwise utilitarian organ horribly suspended over the W end. – The PULPIT of 1908 is an elaborate work in Caen stone with polished marbles and free-standing figures of the apostles set in niches. – STAINED GLASS. Mostly early C20 and highly figurative; many of the windows are memorials to the Manchesters, the best of them the E window, signed Alfred O. Hemming, 1906. Chancel S: attributed to Abbott & Co., Lancaster, c. 1918. N transept: two windows, by Heaton, Butler & Bayne, c. 1908. S transept: two windows attributed to O'Connor & Taylor, London, c. 1892. Nave S: the Good Samaritan, attributed to Shrigley & Hunt, Lancaster, c. 1927. – MONUMENTS. William Loftie †1833, agent to the Tandragee estate for thirty-five years, signed Thomas Kirk. Under a palm tree, a draped sarcophagus decorated with a snake eating its tail, set over an elaborate tablet. – In the S transept, tender Late Victorian alabaster relief of Lady Mary and Lady Alice Montagu, signed a.c.

ST JAMES, BALLYMORE PARISH CHURCH. Cornmarket Street. 1852 by J. R. McAuley. A hall and slender tower in dark coursed limestone rubble with Dungannon sandstone dressings. A confident design; the unusually attenuated proportions of the tall tower are explained by the church's placing to the rear of a narrow plot in a gap in the street terrace, the effect destroyed when the adjacent houses were demolished. The forestanding tower diminishes in three tall stages before a pinnacled parapet with one pinnacle much larger than the rest. The entrance is in the W face, deeply recessed, with moulded arches, colonnettes, and a hoodmould with carved stops. Steeply roofed, buttressed nave of four bays with twin lancets; five graded lights in the chancel. The interior is spacious, under an exposed timber roof of arched trusses alternating with scissor trusses; otherwise plain.

METHODIST CHURCH. 1835. Set back discreetly on the Main Street. A galleried three-bay hall with a familiar Wesleyan Gothic frontispiece in squared limestone with granite dressings, probably by *Isaac Farrell*. A plaque on the façade gives the date. Three bays wide with pointed windows, enlarged over the door in the wider, gabled centre bay. The bays are separated by rather stiff buttresses with offsets rising into tall pyramidal pinnacles. The parapets are battlemented over the end bays.

PRESBYTERIAN CHURCH. Markethill Road. 1828 (the original datestone lies discarded against the churchyard wall). A sizeable three-bay roughcast hall with stuccoed quoins. Large round-headed windows and an oculus in the entrance gable, all with coloured glazing. Built at a cost of £700 and inaugurated in 1829 by the Rev. Dr Henry Cooke. Works in 1899 presumably included the addition of decorative bargeboards; further works in 1977 added the large gabled porch with an incongruous Tuscan portico.

The MANSE of 1894 is a familiar two-storey rendered block of modest proportions. Three bays to the front with bay windows on the ground floor.

TANDRAGEE MASONIC HALL. Church Street. 1894. An embellished Gothic hall, to a T-plan. Roughcast with stucco quoins. Three-bay gabled front with Tudor arches to the openings, all linked under a continuous rope moulding with Masonic symbols in carved panels above. An attractive small building, now diminished by the loss of its tall diagonal stacks, and an ungainly C20 hall that collides with the N side.

TANDRAGEE CASTLE. Off the Square, on a densely wooded rise with a haunting silhouette visible from a distance. A large and rugged Victorian castle of dark grey limestone in a tightly massed group, built in two distinct phases clearly evident on the main front, overlooking a terraced lawn to the S.

The powerful O'Hanlon chiefs in Armagh possessed a tower here, perhaps similar to Tonymore, which was forfeited by them in the early C17, and afterwards rebuilt. Having been given improved defences, the old castle at Tandragee was attacked and destroyed when the O'Hanlons avenged their losses in 1641. It was eventually replaced in a newly enclosed demesne embellished with formal gardens around a large ornamental canal. Precisely when is unclear. A seven-bay, two-storey block with a central doorcase in a Gibbsian surround is shown in Daniel Kelly's 1751 survey of the demesne, suggesting that any late C17 rebuilding of the house had been brought up to date or rebuilt in the Georgian manner, possibly by Sir Francis St John, and before the estate passed *c.* 1756 to Sir John Bernard, who married Mary St John in 1737.

In 1789 Tandragee was inherited by Robert Bernard Sparrow. The present castle was begun in 1830 for Lord Mandeville, son of the 5th Duke of Manchester and himself the future 6th Duke, who in 1822 had married the heiress Millicent Sparrow.

It was largely completed in 1837. The old house, with its early C19 painted interiors by *Gaspare Gabrielli*, was entirely swept away, and replaced by a building rather like a modest C16 Tudor hunting lodge. The architect was *Isaac Farrell* of Dublin, and his design has some distinctive original qualities. The W portion of the main front is a wilfully asymmetrical three-storey block raised over a basement, with tall polygonal stacks, a large offset gable, and irregularly disposed mullioned windows with Georgian sashes piercing the unadorned wall surface. The walls, of squared limestone quarried locally from Tullyhue, give a feeling of austerity, dictated perhaps more by economy than style, the family finances having been acutely embarrassed by Lord Mandeville's father. The same sparing approach lends an arresting quality to the square bartizan corbelled out diagonally from the SW corner, rising in two tiers of hard-edged ashlar with gaping three-bay mullioned windows and a flattish ogee roof. A single-storey glazed porch projected from the recessed E bay, but this has largely been demolished.

To this building was added a formidable boulder-faced keep, heavily machicolated, with crowstepped gables and narrow chamfered windows, supported by a lower battlemented tower that adjoins the entrance porch. The date of this work is not known. In style it suggests *W. H. Lynn*, and perhaps even *William Burn*, who carried out works at Kimbolton (Huntingdonshire) in 1864 for the 7th Duke. Burn's influence is suggested by Scottish baronial features such as the steep crowstepped gables. There is no sign here, however, of the circular turrets and bartizans preferred by those architects. In fact the small corbelled-out bartizans at the corners, projecting diagonally perhaps to compliment Farrell's distinctive turret, only find a close parallel at this time in Ireland in G. Fowler Jones's work at Castle Oliver (Co. Limerick) of about 1850; even the elaborate, staged projection of the gable stack, inset with heraldic devices, is similar. The only architect whose name is associated with work here is *John Millar*, who some time before his emigration to Australia in 1854 designed additions to Tandragee in a Renaissance style; though little of his architectural activity is known, he may well have been responsible for the executed design. There are mid-C19 designs for the decoration of a ceiling in the castle by the London interior decorator *Leonard W. Collmann*. The work may be linked to the 6th Duke's second marriage in 1850, and completed by his son William Drogo, the 7th Duke, after his succession in 1855. On the main front the cipher – GM – under a ducal coronet belongs to the 6th Duke, while the more complicated cipher of the 7th Duke is displayed under an inferior coronet between the base corbels of the gable stack. Above this are the flamboyant Manchester arms above another related set.

Behind the main block *Farrell* formed an enclosed STABLE-YARD, all in the same squared masonry, though it does appear to follow closely the footprint of its C18 predecessor. With a handsome succession of wide segmental arches along the w range, the yard is entered through two very different gateways – on the W a wide, rather austere battlemented gateway, and on the N a more muscular design with polygonal turrets, crowned by an ogee-topped turret with the crisp ashlar work displayed in Farrell's bartizan. To the S, a lower two-storey range with ogee-headed lights on the first floor houses Farrell's CHAPEL, now stripped of its rich wooden interior to adorn the neighbouring parish church.

The family withdrew from Tandragee in 1925; sold in 1955, it has since 1956 been the unlikely headquarters of the Tayto potato-crisp factory. Largely burnt out in the late C20, the castle stands derelict and partly roofed but otherwise substantially preserved with the stableyard in use as the company offices.

The DEMESNE has three main entrances, only two with LODGES, both of the 1850s; the best of these now serves a golf course on the S approach to the town. Behind an arched and battlemented screen wall, a gable-ended block with a projecting pyramid-roofed tower on the front rising in two stages and supported on one side by a partly open timber porch, all in boulder-faced limestone with narrow paired sashes and decorative fretwork on the tower. A plaque on the face of the tower displays the cipher of the 6th Duke and the date 1852. To the E, on the Clare Road, a more discreet gable-ended lodge is partly hidden behind a formidable crenellated gateway and screen walls.

TANDRAGEE LIBRARY. Market Street. 1970 by *McCormack & Co.* of Lurgan. An earnest modern building that breaks entirely with the conventions of the historic streetscape. For the most part a long, low range in glass and steel, vaguely Miesian in character, extending back from the street frontage. A heavy angular timber-clad box on impossibly thin pilotis projects over the entrance; the purpose of this element, other than to display a giant clock face, is not declared.

CARGANS MEMORIAL ORANGE HALL. Scarva Road. 1923. A small, classically inspired stuccoed Art Deco-style hall. Gable-fronted with three bays between square piers at the corners topped with spheres. The wider central bay, where the door is set in a shallow recessed arch, is advanced with kneelers; at the apex of the gable, a plinth with a rather tame-looking lion couchant.

The large red brick building to the S is the PROTESTANT HALL, opened in January 1913 by the Duke of Manchester. A two-storey gabled block with large mullioned windows, moulded brick hoods, and sashes with multiple panes over plate glass. The date 1912 is carved above the doorway.

WHITE'S MILLS. Scarva Road. A tall roadside Georgian monolith, now standing as an adjunct to a stuccoed Victorian house, is the earliest element in the massive milling complex that dominates both sides of the street at the S extremity of the town. Four storeys high and three bays wide with a hipped roof and roughcast walls, nicely punctuated front and rear with small twelve-pane sashes, it shows that a flour and corn mill was here before the 1830s, when John Creery operated a thriving business. Today the mill, producing porridge oats, occupies two utilitarian late C19 brick blocks further down on both sides of the road, rising and falling along it, mostly four storeys tall and in parts windowless, as if to emphasize the unrelenting severity of the life inside such Victorian industrial behemoths.

SINTON'S FLAX-SPINNING MILLS. Off Glebe Hill Road. Derelict and stranded in a housing development. After 1868 Thomas Sinton of Laurelvale converted the existing watermills to steam power. Behind a towering polygonal brick stack, the main factory block is three storeys high and fourteen bays long, in limestone rubble with yellow-brick trim. It is flanked by similar lower ranges, some with red brick, that once extended to form a large quadrangle. The NE angle is now entirely demolished. Surviving in the NW angle is a two-storey stuccoed Victorian house with bay windows.

ORANGE HILL. Off Gilford Street, on a hilltop on the edge of the town overlooking the River Cusher and its extensive milling enterprises. A tall Late Georgian gable-ended block of two storeys over a basement with attics and a single-storey wing to one side. Cement-rendered, with weather-slating on the S gable. Enlarged to an L-plan c. 1890 when a substantial gable-ended block was placed at right angles to the front, crossing the wing which was retained at single-storey level. Old and new were reroofed with attic gables and yellow-brick dentils to the eaves. A flat-roofed porch over the old entrance extends into the angle, creating a long hallway linking the C19 addition. Interesting provincial plasterwork in the inner hall, with primitive lion masks on a reeded cornice around an oval foliated centrepiece. In 1837 the residence of the miller John Creery.

BALLYMORE RECTORY. Off Glebe Hill Road, on a sheltered, elevated site facing N towards the town. A substantial two-storey Late Victorian block in red brick with yellow brick dressings, built in 1860 for the Rev. Arthur Malony. Three-bay front with a low hipped roof and irregularly disposed stacks; large sashes with plate glass and horizontal glazing bars. Set back to one side is a large two-storey service wing of two bays with multi-pane sashes.

A collection of CARVED STONES in the garden, near the front of the house, including an elaborate foliate finial, are understood to have come from St Patrick's Church of Ireland Cathedral in Armagh.

NEIGHBOURHOOD

PROSPECT HOUSE. 2.5 km NNE. A handsome two-storey block with half-hipped gables and central stacks. Rendered, with three bays to the front, large sixteen-pane sashes, and a segmental doorway with side-lights and a webbed fanlight. Bay windows with large casements in the gables. All early C19 in appearance, but a plaque embedded in the front wall is dated 1724 with the initials SWE, said to represent a member of the Emerson family.

MANDEVILLE HALL. 3 km NNE. A modest Early Georgian house, attractively sheltered in trees on an elevated site with open views to the NE over Co. Down. A two-storey gable-ended block with attics and a shallow C19 bow to the E gable. Three bays to the front with the central bay projecting into the attic and gabled. Later tripartite timber doorcase in an unappealing C20 stuccoed surround. The LODGE, now overgrown, retains a pointed doorway with a pleasing Gothick fanlight.

DERRYALLEN. 1 km SW, off the Markethill Road. A modest Late Georgian block. Originally the mill house to a long vanished corn mill, it has two storeys and three bays with a hipped roof, oversailing eaves on paired brackets, central stacks and big twelve-pane sashes. Rendered, with rusticated granite quoins. Attractive timber doorcase in a segmental arch, with slender pilasters, side-lights and a petalled fanlight. The house is two bays deep, with a lower return to the rear which looks contemporary but was added c. 1910; it has a two-storey canted bay on the garden front. Inside, the central hall and stairs are flanked by large reception rooms with Victorian cornices. Over the stairs the ceiling rises into a tapering polygonal void, dated to the early C20, perhaps intended to end in a lantern to improve the lighting of the stairs after the return was built.

MULLAVILLY PARISH CHURCH, LAURELVALE (C of I). 2.5 km NW. An exceedingly plain hall-and-tower church that long pre-dates the large milling settlement that grew up around it in the C19. Sources say either 1736 or 1755; the primitive Gibbsian doorcase at the base of the tower supports the earlier date, even if the lintel and keystone are concrete repairs. The tower is a tall, plain structure with pinnacles. To the three-bay nave transepts and a chancel were added by *John Bowden*, whose plans were approved by the vestry in December 1818, resulting in a rather elongated body. Roughcast, sparingly trimmed with sandstone. There is no clear distinction between Bowden's additions and those of *J. F. Fuller*, who in 1897 rebuilt the chancel and formed a small vestry to the S. The windows are more obvious later additions, round-headed openings inset with simple Y-tracery, including the five-light E window, and so all presumably part of Fuller's campaign. Inside, the tower leads into a short passage, through an archway lined with C18 raised-and-fielded panelling. The nave was Victorianized, probably as part of *Fuller*'s works, and is far too ponderous, with heavy wood furnishings and a roof of laminated arched trusses. – The only C18 survivor is a limestone FONT, primitive but elegantly inscribed 1751, now tucked away in a corner under the gallery. – STAINED GLASS. Bright figurative glass, mostly C20. E window late C19. N tran-sept: the Ascension, by *Heaton, Butler & Bayne*. S transept: 'She hath done what she could', by *George Wragge*, Manchester, c. 1913. Nave: 'The Good Shepherd' and 'The Light of the

World' by *Campbell Bros*, *c.* 1920; also two late C20 windows, one by *Solaglas Studios*, Lisburn, the other in the distinctive garish colouring of *Calderwood Stained Glass*. – MONUMENTS. In the N transept, two imposing marble plaques topped with urns: Thomas Kelly †1779 and Elizabeth Kelly †1807.

The CLOCK, by *Mangin* of Cork, was gifted to Louth Parish Church in 1846 by the Rev. Elias Thackeray, and installed here in 1949.

ESSEX RIDGE, Laurelvale. 2.5 km NW. 1944 by *T. F. O. Rippingham*. An interesting terrace of semi-detached red brick weavers' houses, built for Sinton's Mills. Two storeys and two bays each, with prefabricated monopitch concrete roofs, sloping to the rear and oversailing the façades on multitudinous beams. Large rectangular windows and tapered concrete canopies around the doors.

ST MARY, LAURELVALE. 3 km NW. A roughcast two-bay hall, completely remodelled in 2007, leaving little now to commend it. The kneelered gables are echoed on the small W porch and the pointed windows have blocked stucco surrounds with fancy aprons to the sills.

TARTARAGHAN AH 9050

A rural parish in north Armagh with a small settlement close to the parish church.

ST PAUL, TARTARAGHAN PARISH CHURCH (C of I). The familiar hall-and-tower type, picturesquely sited in a hilltop graveyard, reached by a short procession of beech trees. Built in 1816 by *John Bowden* with the patronage of James Verner of Church Hill nearby (demolished) and a grant of £1,300 from the Board of First Fruits; extended rather late in the C19 with a chancel and vestry. Forestanding three-stage tower with a tall battlemented belfry stage without pinnacles. Three-bay nave of coursed rubble with thick mortar joints, a perfect foil to the cusped Y-tracery and other dressings in sandstone. In contrast the buttressed chancel and flanking projections are in squared blackstone, though trimmed with the same sandstone. Inside the tower a circular vestibule supports a cantilevered stone staircase. Heavy, overbearing kingposts in the nave. – STAINED GLASS. E window: the Angel and the Women at the Tomb, a pale figurative work by *A. L. Moore*, London, *c.* 1906. In the vestibule, St Paul by *Abbott & Co.*, Lancaster, 1959. – MONUMENTS. Annie Edith Broadwood †1897; a florid Gothic tablet. – Joseph Atkinson †1903; a broken pediment on Connemara marble shafts, by *Sharp & Emery*. – Joseph Atkinson †1916; a simple tablet, by *C. W. Harrison*. – First World War memorial by *R. McClements*: an elaborate white marble tablet with downcast officers in alabaster. – Red-tiled LYCHGATE *c.* 1955.

112

LAUREL COTTAGE. Beside the approach to the church, formerly the sexton's house. A Late Georgian cottage, charming in its simplicity. A low single-storey block in roughcast with a steep hipped roof. Four-bay front with twelve-pane sashes, the door placed off-centre. – Behind, adjoining vernacular BARNS of one and two storeys.

Nearby is the SCHOOLMASTER'S HOUSE. 1903 by *James William Walby*. A curious, diminutively scaled house. Three bays with a hipped roof and large casement windows.

THE HEAD O' THE ROAD. Clontylew Road, opposite the church. A quaint vernacular spirit grocery, precious for its survival. A long, gable-ended roughcast house, two storeys and five bays. Irregularly fenestrated with C19 nine-pane sashes.

BELMONT. On the corner of Clontylew and Belmont roads, an unexpected roadside house. A smart two-storey block, Late Georgian in appearance, with a broad front of five bays and a hipped roof. Broader side elevation with irregular fenestration. Roughcast with stuccoed quoins, string-course and architraves. The windows have twelve-pane sashes in thick exposed frames; also a narrow rectangular leaded fanlight in a pretty geometric design. Contemporary farmyard across the road with a long roughcast BARN of two storeys.

CLONTYLEW HOUSE. 0.75 km S. A large Neoclassical-style house, built *c.* 1970 to replace the old house of the Obré family. Brown brick with rusticated quoins, frieze, and an emphatic modillion cornice all in stucco. The front has six bays, the central two advanced under a pediment. The portico, raised on a podium reached by steps, is too broad, but has convincing columns – the capitals an attenuated Tower-of-the-Winds type – and pilaster responds. Round the back the central bay on the first floor is recessed to form an open balcony between the pedimented end bays. It is the kind of design usually decried as pastiche, a charge certainly warranted in the use of cheap materials, but overall well-suited to the small established demesne.

Across the road is the WALLED GARDEN entered by a Gothic arch; a weathered sandstone plaque in the wall gives the distances between 'Clantilew' and a list of places, usefully set out in miles, furlongs and perches.

TARTARAGHAN MASONIC HALL. 0.5 km E. 1893. A captivating little three-bay hall with brick detailing. Built of a brownish red brick, alternating with a paler brick around the openings. The gabled front has a gingerbread look about it with round-headed windows flanking the door and an *œil-de-bœuf* window above. The gable is emphasized like a corbel table, the corbels a continuous zigzag of projecting bricks, and all the windows have billet hoods. The best detail of all is the line of Masonic instruments hanging from the narrow metal tie-plates between the bays.

ST JOHN, EGLISH. 1.5 km W. A small idiosyncratic single-cell church of three bays. Roughcast with stucco decoration and timber Y-tracery. A stucco plaque high in the gable says built in 1826 and rebuilt in 1914. Unusual gables, stepped at the base like double kneelers, with the oversailing eaves of the nave sticking out on each side, giving the front a distinctly odd look. Inside, an airy space with rudimentary stick-like scissor trusses strengthened with a system of iron tie-bars.

TARTARAGHAN PRESBYTERIAN CHURCH, BALLYNARRY. 1.5 km N. 1824. A modest four-bay hall with kneelered gables, flanked by lower wings: a small porch and a two-bay session room of 1950. Roughcast, with a neat symmetrical front and wide Tudor-arched windows in stucco frames with stained glass. Nice duchess slates on the rear roof slope and twin conical topped ventilators on the ridge.

COCKHILL WINDMILL. 2 km S. A prominent battlemented tower rising over a hilltop orchard. Built for Edward Hoope of Crow Hill before 1723 and once part of a group that included a horse mill, malt kiln and millers' houses. A 40-ft (12-m) bulging drum of roughcast over rubble, finished with sloping brick battlements added after the machinery was stripped out in the early C20. The peripatetic minister John Wesley preached in its shadow in 1778.

TASSAGH AH 8030

A rural crossroads on the River Callan, 3 km NE of Keady.

TASSAGH PRESBYTERIAN CHURCH. In a very pretty setting, reached across the rushing River Callan. Built in 1777 to a T-plan with later two-storey additions. Roughcast with round-headed windows and etched glass. Interior completely refitted in 2008.

DUNDRUM. A once-handsome Georgian house, gable-ended with two storeys and five bays. Typical artful rhythm to the spacing of the windows; doorcase of an Early Georgian type, a rusticated Venetian window form with round-headed doorway and glazed side-lights, all blocked out in a Gibbsian manner. Repairs were carried out by *J. H. M. Wilson* in 1909 and since then the C18 interior has been destroyed. Now unsympathetically re-roofed, re-rendered and fenestrated with modern materials.

TASSAGH HOUSE. A gable-ended block of two storeys and three bays. Roughcast with blocked quoins, Georgian sashes, and a segmental-headed doorcase with a webbed fanlight. Occupied by Mr F. Stringer in 1837.

MILL VIEW. 1 km N. A two-storey Late Georgian house with a double-pile plan consisting of two gable-ended blocks placed back-to-back and a lower two-storey block with a half-hipped roof to one side. The main front has three bays, cement-rendered, with plate-glass windows and a lovely timber door-case with very ornate leaded fanlight and side-lights.

St Mary, Granemore. 1.75 km SSE. 1909 by *J. F. McGahon*.
A small, dignified stuccoed church. Economical Romanesque. The entrance front has a squat gable with prominent
kneelers over clasping buttresses, and an equally squat gabled
doorway flanked by round-headed windows with three similar
graded lights above. An ashlar bellcote rises from a corbel
table. The sides are two-dimensional in feeling, subtly modelled with flat pilaster strips into five bays, with round-headed
windows in the centre three. The interior is quite smart, with
an open-truss roof of kingposts with arched braces. The sanctuary has been handsomely remodelled with heavy Travertine
FURNISHINGS carved with a mesh of graduated Y-tracery. –
STAINED GLASS. Good figurative glass by *F. Foster*, 1968. E
window earlier and more striking, a richly coloured vesica set
in timber tracery.

107   TASSAGH VIADUCT. 2.5 km NW. 1903–11 by *Sir Benjamin Baker*
for the Castleblayney, Keady & Armagh Railway. A heroic
structure spanning the River Callan, magnified by its restricted
channel. Eleven arches on slender splayed piers of mass concrete. Unlike its smaller counterpart at Keady, the spandrels
and parapet here are highly textured, built with squared rock-
faced masonry in the C19 tradition.

The viaduct dwarfs a large three-storey MILL, an impressive
vernacular structure of thirteen bays, well-preserved in quiet
abandonment.

ROWAN COTTAGE. 3 km NW. A small gable-ended house, built
before 1837 to a T-plan, with a low pitched roof on scrolled
eaves brackets. Single-storey front with big Georgian sashes
and a wide open porch, the entrance arched on square piers
with moulded panels, large limestone capitals and plain angular
base blocks. The doorcase is a refined work in timber with
reeded pilasters and wide elliptical spoked fanlight. Attractive
tall casement windows to the side with upper square panels
glazed in a pretty petalled design.

ROUGHAN HOUSE. 3.5 km NW. An attractive Victorian house
overlooking the River Callan. Two-storey, three-bay block with
a steep pitched roof. Once roughcast, now stripped with rubble
walls, with Georgian glazing and a wide arched timber doorcase with side-lights.

2010   TEMPLEPORT   CN

A highly picturesque rural parish S of Bawnboy, notable for a
large concentration of megalithic monuments at Kilnavart.

ST MAEDOC, MOGUE'S ISLAND. Accessible by boat from
Corboy on the W shore. An island cemetery with the partial
ruins of a rectangular church, supposedly the site of a
monastery founded in the C6 through its association with St

Mogue, also known as Maedoc or Aidan, whose birthplace this was. The present remains look later, corresponding perhaps to the church that was known here in 1496 and shown still roofed in a baronial map of 1609. Today only the substantial, overgrown foundations of a rectangular rubble cell remain, measuring 40 ft by 17½ ft (12 m by 5 m), with much of the W wall standing; a large rectangular window opening high in the wall is the only significant architectural element.

St Peter, Templeport Parish Church (C of I). A spired church picturesquely sited near the E shore of Templeport Lough. A church by the name of Aghavanne was recorded on this site in 1609. Apart from a small number of vaulted tombs, anything earlier was lost in two phases of C19 building. Of the first, the 'very neat edifice' of 1815, only the roughcast battlemented tower with its ashlar needle spire and a gabled vestry in the centre of the N wall survive. In 1860 the three-bay nave was remodelled with twin lancets, and a lower single-bay chancel with a three-light E window was added by *Welland & Gillespie*, who also formed a new roof and reordered the interior.

Inside, arch-braced trusses in the nave and scissor trusses in the chancel. – FONT. Flared from a slender stem, an octagonal bowl of sandstone, crisply inscribed on the rim: 'This font was given by Majr Willm Blachford of Lisnover to the parish church of Templeport in the year of our Lord God 1721, IA Fecit', a work of delightful simplicity. – STAINED GLASS. E window: Angel and Women at the Tomb, by *Heaton, Butler & Bayne*, London, 1929; notable for its portrait of the dedicatee, Mary Elizabeth Johnstone. N nave, twin-light window: the Ascension and the Risen Christ, also signed *Heaton, Butler & Bayne*, 1923. – MONUMENTS. John Blachford †1727; erected by his son, Major William Blachford. A sumptuous Corinthian aedicule in marbleized sandstone with a broad scrolled pediment, just a little too broad and too heavy for the columns, framing an inscribed plaque and adorned with urns, scroll brackets and festoons; the pediment supports a large circular frame with the Blachford heraldry against an impressive military panoply. – George Finlay †1855; a crested Neoclassical tablet, by *Manderson*. – Frederick Betty †1863; a crested tablet with a white marble scroll. – George Henry L'Estrange †1870; a plain Gothic tablet, by *P. J. Neill & Co.*, Dublin. – Emma Anne Betty †1874; a plain tablet under a draped urn, by *C. W. Harrison*, Dublin. – The Rev. Joseph Rawlins †1907; a marble scroll, by *Louis Harrison*, Dublin.

Templeport House. 1 km NNE. Set above attractive countryside, a small Regency block, two storeys tall and quite rectory-like, with a three-bay roughcast façade crowned by a hipped roof and central stacks. Twelve-pane sashes, made just a little narrower on the first floor, and an elegant trabeated doorcase with tall side-lights and a shallow segmental fanlight of webbed design.

CORVILLE. 1.25 km NE. A handsome Late Georgian farmhouse
of the middle size: two-storey roughcast block with smooth
quoins, a shallow hipped roof and central stacks. Three bays
across the front with a broad, shallow porch in the centre,
nicely articulated with chamfered corners and finished with a
prominent cornice. Twelve-panel door under a spoked fanlight,
flanked by narrow eight-pane sashes.

BAWNBOY ROAD STATION (former). 0.5 km SE. A single-storey
polychrome station of 1885 built for the Cavan & Leitrim
Railway, serving Belturbet and Dromod; possibly by *W. H.
Mills*.

CHURCH OF THE IMMACULATE CONCEPTION, KILNAVART.
2 km SE. 1866–8 by *William Hague*. A conspicuous church,
erected on a rural hilltop as a memorial to the Rev. Tom
Maguire of Ballinamore, who is buried alongside. Straightforward Dec Gothic, consisting of a tall nave with undifferentiated chancel, low aisles, short transepts, and an offset,
unfinished, square tower. Built of squared rock-faced limestone with smooth dressings and tracery of Bath stone. Steep
gables with offset buttresses and a big plate-traceried window
on the E front. The manner in which the aisles are returned to
flank the W front is unusual: they are given hipped rather than
lean-to roofs. The best of the design is here, with small lancets
nicely emphasized in miniature arcades with polished shafts.
The contractor was *Hugh Kelly* of Granard and the cost £3,500.
Repaired in 1920 by *Patrick J. Brady*; the whole composition
made ugly by a concrete roof with sprocketed eaves formed
in 1997.

   Inside, an airy nave lit by a clerestory of deeply set quatrefoils under a polygonal plaster vault with timber ribs. Arcade
of four bays with stilted arches, with the three arches of the W
bays set on dumpy piers of red Cork marble. – ALTARS by
Sibthorpe & Son. – MONUMENTS. Some moved here from an
older church. Catherine Murray †1837; a limestone plaque
with winged cherubim, in a moulded frame with a bracketed
apron. – Mrs Catherine McNally †1842, by *Wade*, Dublin.
– The Rev. Patrick Dean Smith P.P. †1876; a white tablet
with acroterion by *Pearse & Sons*, Dublin. – The Rev. Dean
Magauran P.P. †1895; a white marble Gothic aedicule by
T. H. Dennany, Glasnevin.

   Across the road, the PRESBYTERY is a trim two-storey block
in roughcast with stuccoed quoins, of three bays with a hipped
roof and central brick stacks. Small boxy porch and sash
windows with twelve upper panes above plate glass.

KILNAVERT WEDGE TOMB. 2 km SE. The exposed gallery of a
ruined wedge tomb set in a ring of sycamore trees. The most
impressive of a group of prehistoric tombs, stone circles and
standing stones in the area.

BALLYMAGAURAN TOWER HOUSE. 3 km S. The fragments of
an early C17 castle on the N shore of Ballymagauran Lake. Built
of rubble in at least two phases; the remains indicate a rectangular plan of two storeys. Today, a small rectangular window

and a fireplace are found at opposite ends of the long s wall, while a grotesque head lurks behind the ivy on the NW quoins.

CORBOY GLEBE. 0.75 km SW. A handsome mid-Georgian house, beautifully sited, facing on to the waters of Templeport Lough. Broad seven-bay front of two storeys with a central pedimented breakfront. Carefully proportioned with nine-over-six sashes on the ground floor and six-over-three above; narrower windows flanking the central bays, blind lunette in the pediment, and Gibbs surround to the fanlit door. The interior has a tripartite plan, preserving a cantilevered stair in the central hall; good C18 lugged architraves and raised and fielded panels to doors and shutters.

KILDOAGH OLD CHURCH. 1 km NW. Now disused and under-appreciated, this remains the purest of a small number of surviving Georgian vernacular churches; as inscribed in a Latin plaque displayed on the front, it was built for the Rev. Patrick Maguire in 1796. Originally a long thatched barn type in roughcast with five bays, it was slated in 1860, given an extra bay, and refenestrated on the main front. The façade only then became symmetrical, with separate entrances for men and women flanked by pointed windows with hoods. The window openings correspond on the back, all retaining their Georgian sashes with small panes and a flourish of Y-tracery. Inside, a space of charming simplicity where the altar rests against the long s wall between the gendered galleries. All the PEWS and earthenware floor TILES survive.

OWENDOON. 2.5 km NW. A distinctive Victorian house, mildly Italianate in style, with spare Gothic and Moorish elements, built c. 1850 for George Henry L'Estrange, who died in 1870 (and whose memorial is a Gothic tablet in St Peter's, Templeport). By an unknown but accomplished architect familiar with the new attitude toward Gothic design being promoted by Ruskin, this is a long two-storey building with plate-glass windows and an oversailing hipped roof on brick eaves with notched timber brackets. Luxuriously finished, with highly textured façades in rock-faced limestone with smooth dressings. The main front has nine bays, some set in pairs, the last three advanced, accommodating a somewhat oversized gabled porch in the angle between. The ground-floor windows adjoining the porch to the r. are tall, with transoms intruding across the centre of the upper sash – an arrangement repeated across the ground floor on the rear façade. Round the side, the staircase window is an elaborate tripartite design high in the wall, with slender shafts supporting notched mullions and transoms above; this same Moorish serration is repeated on a bay window offset to the side. The interior follows a well-considered plan, the porch opening into a hall where the stair is set to one side, the dining room and drawing room placed side by side across the back of the house, and two smaller rooms to the front. A corridor dividing the plan leads to the service areas and a back staircase. Simple moulded cornices throughout.

THREE MILE HOUSE

A small village located some 5 km SW of Monaghan town centre.

ST MARY. A C19 church destroyed by fire in 1924 and rebuilt by *R. M. Butler*. A tight budget or else most unambitious patronage was responsible for retaining the appearance of the traditional gable-fronted vernacular building with a stone bellcote. A narrow five-bay roughcast hall with a flat-roofed aisle to the N and a shallow chancel. A gable-fronted baptistery projects transept-like from the centre of the S wall and a low flat-roofed porch spans the W gable. Only the windows with their modest Romanesque outlines – paired lights and a small circular window integrated in an arched surround on the N and S walls, and small tapered lights on the porch and W aisle wall – suggest Butler's involvement.

Inside, the feeling is much more C20, with the aisle separated by a six-bay arcade of round-headed arches with concave mouldings that merge with the concrete pillars – a stylized treatment showing how far Butler could embrace new materials and methods. The dark-stained roof trusses are more old-fashioned, with their arched braces pierced by quatrefoils. The seating, designed with squared ends that are nicely finished as fielded panels, is noteworthy, also the small raking gallery, carried on four cast-iron columns, with a distinctive and attractive open timberwork front. – STAINED GLASS. Three-light E window and baptistery window in the style of *Harry Clarke Studios*.

DRUMSNATT PARISH CHURCH (C of I). 2 km NW. Substantial early Board of First Fruits hall-and-tower church set in attractive countryside. Rectangular cement-rendered hall of four bays with pointed windows filled with coloured glass. Good masonry E window with three cusped lights. Standard three-stage rubble tower with simple string-courses, battlements and spiky pinnacles. Repaired in 1834. Vestry with a hipped roof added in 1866. The entrance is in the tower, leading into a narrow space plainly finished with a high timber-panelled ceiling. The E window is filled with brightly coloured figurative glass.

In the churchyard, the grave of Oscar Wilde's half-sisters Emily and Mary, who were tragically killed by fire at nearby Drumaconnor House in 1871.

DRUMSNATT GRAVEYARD. 2 km NW. A mounded circular enclosure peacefully sited above Drumsnatt Lake. Now only a very good and interesting collection of C18 and C19 headstones can be seen, on a site considered to be the place where St Molua founded a monastery at the end of the C6.

GLEBE HOUSE. 2 km NW. Of *c.* 1800. Facing the graveyard, a modest roughcast block of cubic proportions. L-plan with two storeys over a raised basement and a familiar three-bay front with windows set in recessed arches with segmental heads on the ground floor, greatly diminished to small six-pane sashes on the first floor. The arrangement is repeated on the two-bay side elevation. Gabled Victorian porch with ornate bargeboards.

ST MICHAEL, CORCAGHAN. 4.5 km SE. 1842. Boxy five-bay lancet hall, built on the site of an earlier chapel of 1806, recorded by an inscription on the sacristy. Roughcast with blocked stone quoins and a pleasant gabled front with three lancets arranged around a pointed doorway. Stone window surrounds and hoodmoulds with decorated polygonal stops. Ashlar bellcote on a rubble base on the gable. Interior disappointing, now a big open carpeted space spanned by jumbo kingpost trusses and filled with uninteresting furniture. – STAINED GLASS. In the simple three-light E window, the Crucifixion in bright figurative glass.

The adjoining PAROCHIAL HOUSE is a vernacular gable-ended house of two storeys and three bays with a small flat-roofed porch.

THE WREN'S NEST, STRANOODAN (C of I). 5.5 km SE. 1860. A small Victorian country church, built as a chapel of ease under the patronage of the 4th Lord Rossmore, almost certainly by *Welland & Gillespie*. Two-bay lancet hall with chancel, vestry and an unusual offset tower, all with angle buttresses. Uncoursed limestone rubble with corbelled eaves course. Tower in two stages with a tall gabled belfry, pierced by tall lancets and an almond window, raised on haunches over a squat lower stage. Reprieved from dereliction at the time of writing and reroofed as a residence with timber from the nearby Lough Bawn estate.

TULLYCORBET   MN   7020

A rural parish N of Ballybay.

ST MARY, CORVOY. A low-lying cement-rendered church with a modest tower highly finished with battlements and spire. Founded at the end of the C18; rebuilt a century later. A long four-bay hall with a polygonal apse, gabled porch and a three-stage W tower. Narrow round-headed windows. The tower is by far the most interesting element, with its elongated belfry stage finished in sandstone ashlar with a French Romanesque flavour complete with gargoyles, miniature cylindrical towers with conical caps, and a copper-clad crocketed spire. Internally a plain and cheerful space with arched timber roof trusses and exposed rafters. Moulded chancel arch on short marble shafts of the kind popularized by William Hague. The apse is an attractive space with windows set in a blind arcade to good effect. – STAINED GLASS. Four brightly coloured windows in the apse, including the Virgin, Christ and St Joseph, by *Mayer & Co.*, Munich.

ST PATRICK (C of I). 1.5 km N. A roofless hall and tower on a wooded mound, probably by *William Farrell*. In 1824 the vestry agreed to replace an older church established on this site before 1415. Built in 1831, the church was a plain two-bay hall with angle buttresses on the W gable and a forestanding square tower. Squared limestone and sandstone trim with ashlar for the tower. The vestry minutes name *John Clarke* as contractor. Contrasting with the dowdiness of the traditional Board of First Fruits type, the three-stage tower forms an articulate piece of architecture with the kind of emphatic detail employed by Farrell on his churches. The short middle stage finishes with a deeply moulded cornice that dramatically changes into a widely scooped plinth supporting the diminished belfry, a rectangular box with corner pilasters, louvred lancets and deeply moulded cornice, finished with a short octagonal spire that gains from the elevated site. The doorway is in the W face, a simple pointed arch under a hoodmould; an empty clock face occupies the stage above.

GLEBE HOUSE. 1.5 km NNW. A substantial two-storey, five-bay block with gabled ends and heavy square stacks. Built in 1773 and according to Samuel Lewis in a very dilapidated state in 1837. Entrance now obscured by an ungainly porch with absurd Ionic columns. Attractive stable range directly behind.

CLOVERHILL. 4.5 km SW. A boxy mid-C19 block of two storeys and three bays with a flat-roofed porch, regular sashes and hipped roof. Roughcast with raised stucco quoins. Adjoining yard buildings form an L-plan.

LISNAVEANE. 5 km SW. Attractive late C18 house of two storeys and three bays. A modest roughcast block with good proportions, the windows smaller on the first floor. Central bay advanced and gabled; a further gabled bay forming an addition to one side. Sweeping hipped roof with sprocketed eaves.

CAHANS PRESBYTERIAN CHURCH. 5 km W. Disused. A plaque high on the S wall recalls the trepidation of the minister John Rogers at the erection of the building in 1779, with a plea to 'God's providence' for protection. This is an important Presbyterian foundation, established as the first Seceder church in Monaghan. The Scottish Seceder missionary Thomas Clark was ordained at Cahans in 1751, and later Irish ministers were trained here. The present building, replacing an earlier undescribed C18 foundation, is substantially the 1779 structure, altered *c.* 1840 when the walls were raised marginally, entirely refenestrated, and extended at the W end to provide a new entrance front with two-storey accommodation in a narrow space behind. The church today is a generous four-bay hall of rubble with sandstone trim; large pointed windows with timber Y-tracery and attractive quarry glazing. The broad façade has a central door with a lancet and plaque set above it – 'Christ is all and in us all M. McAuley 1840' – and big pointed windows on either side. The doorcase is Perp in style with a Tudor arch, carved spandrels and square label stops. Internally the space is plain, except for two wonderful ogee-headed doorways opening from the lobby to the body of the church. What makes this building particularly special is the survival of all the panelled BOX PEWS, along with the carved PULPIT and JURY BOX.

TULLYVIN

The road between Cootehill and Cavan thunders through this small village, even smaller now than the settlement recorded here in 1835 of twenty stone- and mud-built cabins established around a yearly livestock fair.

TULLYVIN HOUSE. A substantial roughcast house, built c. 1820 for Maxwell Boyle, with a well-proportioned three-bay front to the E, two storeys tall with twelve-pane sashes, and a wide hipped roof with paired brackets to the eaves. A large three-bay porch, raised on a podium with steps, projects from the centre, built in dressed limestone and nicely articulated with Tuscan pilasters framing tall sashes, with an entrance in each side. Round the sides of the house the basement is exposed, with a longer four-bay façade to the S, and just two bays to the N.

Across the road, facing an elaborate cast-iron GATE SCREEN, the LODGE is a stuccoed three-bay block, single-storey with bracketed eaves and a hipped roof. The wide windows retain their Tudor hoodmoulds, but their mullions and elaborate geometric glazing have been destroyed. Fortunately the petal fanlight remains, set inside a tall pilastered door surround.

GARDA STATION. 1931. A quaint single-storey building in a plain revived Georgian style. A five-bay roughcast block with a central pedimented entrance bay, twelve-pane sashes, cogged brick eaves, and a large hipped roof with tall stacks. A police presence of similar prominence was recorded here in 1835.

ST PATRICK, CORICK. 1.5 km NE. 1863 By *William Hague*. An understated Gothic Revival church. Modest five-bay nave with chancel and an entrance tower with a buttressed belfry offset on the plain W gable. Built of limestone rubble with sandstone and yellow brick dressings; lancets in unusual blocked surrounds. Unremarkable interior with exposed kingposts and a pointed chancel arch.

CORNABRAHER. 1 km E. A large two-storey Regency house to an L-plan, in smooth render with a low hipped roof. The main front has three bays with tripartite windows on the ground floor, nine-pane sashes above, and a central pedimented porch. Pleasing vernacular buildings of rubble and red brick with hipped slate roofs enclose a small yard behind.

KILLDRUMSHERDAN PARISH CHURCH (C of I). 2.5 km SE. 1857 by *Joseph Welland*. A small Victorian church established on a new site to replace a Late Georgian church, described in 1835 as 'a small oblong building with elliptical windows'. A highly finished structure, with walls of quarry-faced limestone and smooth dressings; a three-bay gabled hall with a lower chancel, both with angle buttresses, a gabled s porch, lean-to vestry to the N, and a bellcote over the W gable; the bell chain disappears into a small lean-to projection beneath the gable windows. Twin lancets to the nave with quarry glazing, three graded lights in the chancel. Inside, a scissor-truss roof with exposed rafters and purlins. – STAINED GLASS. E window by *Solaglas Caldermac*, Lisburn, 1993. – MONUMENTS. Sarah Adams, †1929, by *C. W. Harrison & Sons*. – Stored under the W window, Allen Johnston †1763 and Johannes Johnston †1770; a marble armorial plaque in a boldly carved egg-and-dart frame, perhaps brought from the old church; the arms are those of the family of the architect Francis Johnston.

ST BRIGID, KILL. 3 km SE. A prominent stone-built tower of 1846, in three stages with pinnacles and a steep pyramid roof, now set against a large nondescript T-plan church of 1977. According to various stone plaques around the church, the tower was built by the Rev. Eugene McQuaid for a church that itself replaced another of 1826, built by the Rev. Felix McCabe. – STAINED GLASS. Three early C20 windows, attractive relics from the old church. St Brigid by *William Earley*, late C20.

DRUMELTON. 3.5 km SE. A large Late Victorian gabled house in roughcast with red brick dressings. Broad, two-storey entrance front, well-fenestrated, with steep three-bay gables deeply projecting before the corners at either end. The entrance, under a bracketed timber canopy, is to one side, in a single-storey, five-bay lean-to set between the deep projection of the gables; subsidiary two-bay gable in the centre of the first floor above. In each of the three gables, a brick roundel filled by a limestone plaque depicting the arms and crest of William Adams, for whom the house was built, and those of his wife, Sarah Chatterton, whom he married in 1870.

KILMOUNT PRESBYTERIAN CHURCH. 6 km SE. A solid-looking lancet church built for a congregation established here in 1861. Four-bay gabled hall in smooth render with stone dressings. Altered and extended in 1924 by *Patrick J. Brady*. – STAINED GLASS. The Good Shepherd, by *McManus Design*, late C20.

CHURCH OF THE IMMACULATE CONCEPTION, DRUNG. 5 km SW. 1948 by *Simon Aloysius Leonard* of *W. H. Byrne & Son*. Big, bulky rectangular church with a disproportionately slender offset square tower. A five-bay stuccoed hall with an apsidal chancel and a broad gabled front, nicely expressed as an open pediment with a deep concave cornice supported from the corners by narrow, gently projecting end bays with thin rectangular windows in recessed frames. Here the walls have channelled rustication with the effect of strip pilasters. The rustication is continued across the lower façade and around a large concave recess in the centre, where the main entrance is set beneath a large round-headed window and flanked by side entrances with massive keystones like those employed on the windows throughout. Sacristy and mortuary chapel in low flat-roofed projections on either side. The big proportions result in a rather spare interior; interesting ceiling on a deep cornice, raised in the centre into a shallow barrel-vault carried on a coving enriched with swags.

DRUNG PARISH CHURCH (C of I). 5.5 km SW. Hall-and-tower type, built in 1834 to a familiar design by *William Farrell*. Roughcast with limestone dressings. The nave is buttressed with three well-spaced bays, lancets with pretty iron tracery, gabled chancel and a forestanding three-stage tower with battlements and pinnacles. Inside, an exposed roof with Farrell's favoured cast-iron trusses. The chancel is simply vaulted with close vertical ribs. At the W end, the seat of the Lucas-Clements family of Rathkenny is in the tower, opening impressively to the nave through a deep archway with a canted timber frontal decorated with Gothic panels. – MONUMENTS. Robert Clements †1722; a tall marble plaque in a carved frame bearing urns and an armorial cartouche. – Edward Shuckburgh Clements †1836; a plain tablet. – Margaret Whitney Upton †1836; a marble plaque with draperies borne aloft by cupids, carved in Rome by *William Theed*, 1840. – Thomas Edward Lucas Clements †1852; a draped Greek Revival tablet with a portrait bust set within a snake eating its tail, signed *J. R. Kirk*. – The Rev. Ralph Hope †1908; a scrolled tablet signed *Lendrum*, Clones.

DRUNG OLD CHURCH. 6.5 km SW. In a hillside cemetery, the overgrown ruins of a small rectangular church (65½ ft by 26 ft, 20 m by 8 m), apparently of 1635, which survived in the early C19 as a low house with a shingled roof.

CORRAVAHAN HOUSE. 8 km SW. A tall and commanding three-storey-over-basement block, built *c.* 1825 as a rectory; attributable to *William Farrell*. Rubble walls with red brick trim, mostly smooth-rendered, with a low hipped roof. To the N, symmetrical three-bay entrance front and a small cubic porch; the proportions diminish on the upper floors. Round the side, the ground floor is more irregular, given two tripartite bays, one projecting in ashlar as a bay window rather like a porch, with tall sashes. On the S front a shallow bow, offset on one side, rises through the house, breaking forward with a kind of gentle reluctance. The staircase is at the centre of the plan, extended into a shallow two-storey projection on the W front. Lower service wing to the W, enclosing one side of the kitchen and stableyard.

MILLVALE. 0.75 km W. A cubic Early Victorian former mill house. Two storeys over a basement with three bays to the front, a tall pilastered doorcase, and a steep hipped roof oversailing on wide bracketed eaves. Rubble with dressed quoins and red brick trim to the windows. Twelve-pane sashes, with larger proportions to the ground-floor windows. Scenically set in grounds that describe an imposing hemicycle around the main front.

RATHKENNY. 2.25 km w. An old demesne straddling the River
Annalee, established by the Clements family who came here
in the mid C17. A visitor in 1739 admired how the river was
'beautified by an elegant house, improvements and large plantations on the southern shore, and on its northern bank by
extensive gardens and terraces'. While the terraced gardens
survive, we know nothing more of the character of the old
house; today on the s bank of the river, on part of its site or
near it, stands the sizeable four-square Regency house built in
1829 for Theophilus Lucas-Clements to designs by *William
Farrell*. An attractive astylar block, it is essentially a smaller
version of Farrell's later design for the See House at Kilmore
in Cavan, with much the same bold emphasis in its three-bay
entrance front held between giant strip pilasters, here of two
storeys, with an advanced, pedimented centre. The house, formerly rendered, is now stripped back to its rubble walls revealing sandstone dressings; finely wrought limestone is reserved
for the pediment, emphatic cornice, plain frieze, the blocking
course that conceals a low hipped roof, and for all the ground-
floor windows. Here the tall twelve-pane sashes have plain
surrounds under a pronounced bracketed entablature, with the
same design elaborated over the doorcase and side-lights.
Round the side, the four-bay elevation seems somewhat over-
articulated, with the two central bays projecting; facing the
river, the articulation changes once again with pilasters framing
each of three bays, those at either end set back from the
corners.

Inside, a square entrance hall leads into a long stair hall
extending beyond the centre to the E, where the staircase is lit,
as at the See House, by an ample round-headed window on
the half-landing. The plan is developed around the stair hall,
the main sequence of generously proportioned rooms comprising a library, drawing room and dining room. The use of
shallow recesses gives an elegance to each of the rooms, and
architectural restraint continues throughout the internal decoration, with plain cornices modestly overlaid by Greek Revival
details in the ceiling roses. A good selection of marble chimneypieces: in the library, white with brackets and Greek decorations; in the drawing room, a clean Doric design also in white
marble; the dining-room example was brought here in the late
C20 from Ashfield, the demolished Clements house near
Cootehill, and is an impressive piece in dove-grey marble with
tall, graceful brackets.

Across the broad, slow-moving waters are the TERRACED
GARDENS, reached by an impossibly thin concrete bridge. The
gardens are set out in terraces over a natural declivity, and are
traditionally said to have been centred on the old house on the
opposite bank; they are open entirely to the river where the
low quay wall is framed on either side by tall urn-topped piers
that serve also as terminals to the enclosing side walls. Aligned
with the axial path, framed by yew trees, is the Georgian TEA
HOUSE. Set between low quadrant walls in the centre of the

upper wall, it is a large rectangular Gothic structure faced in red brick with rusticated quoins and a battlemented parapet; three-bay front with tall lancets and a large central panelled doorway.

ST PATRICK, THE BUNNOE CHAPEL, LISBODUFF. 6 km NW. 1838 by the *Rev. Peter O'Reilly* P.P., replacing a clay-built cabin of 1780. A four-bay roughcast hall and porch with big lancets in blocked limestone surrounds. Repaired in 1952 by *P. Gaffney*.

PAROCHIAL HOUSE. 1921 by *Patrick J. Brady*.

LISLIN HOUSE. 7 km NW. In the valley of the River Annalee, the ruins of an Early Georgian farmhouse. A roughcast gable-ended block with central brick stacks, formerly thatched, with a slated gabled stair return. Two storeys with a five-bay front, Georgian sashes, and a round-headed fanlit door. Enlarged to the rear in the early C20.

TYHOLLAND   MN   7030

A small rural parish NE of Monaghan town.

ST SILLIAN, TEMPLETATE, TYHOLLAND PARISH CHURCH (C of I). A hilltop hall and tower. The site is associated with a Patrician foundation given over to the charge of St Cillin. In 1787 a small roughcast hall of three bays with a neat apsidal chancel was built under the patronage of Alexander Montgomery of Bessmount. A tower was added in 1827, of standard design – three stages in limestone rubble and dressed quoins, with crenellations and spiky corner pinnacles. The nave windows, placed only in the S wall, are large pointed openings now filled with crude Y-tracery frames.

Inside, the interior remains C18 in feeling, an intimate cubic space with a deep coved ceiling and thickly moulded cornice, from which the seating and gallery, added by *J. F. Johnston* in 1844, in no way detract. The gallery has fluted Tuscan columns supporting a balustrade with cusped openings. Repairs to the interior were carried out by *J. H. Fullerton* in 1891. – STAINED GLASS. In the E window, a single pointed opening, richly coloured geometric glass of 1887. – MONUMENTS. A surprisingly good collection. The Rev. Edward Stanley †1812; a simple plaque, by *Reeves & Son*, Bath. – Eliza Montgomery †1827; a handsome pedimented slab, also by *Reeves & Son*. – The Rev. Charles Henry Crookshank †1836; a sarcophagus slab topped by an urn, by *Thomas Kirk*. – Mark Anthony Montgomery †1844; a white pedimented slab against grey marble, by *Knowles*, Manchester. – Major Edward Richardson †1938; a more elaborate plaque with coloured marble Gothic shafts, by *Harrison*, Dublin. – The finest, to Alexander Nixon Montgomery †1837, is unsigned. The design is typical, with a large plaque in white marble supporting a squat obelisk in grey marble; against this, a plain classical sarcophagus with in relief a snake eating its tail; the whole topped by an urn below an armorial shield and crest. – Inside the porch, a plain slab to John Williams †1723, ancestor of the physician Sir William Whitla.

Below the church, the GLEBE HOUSE is a pleasing rough-cast block of two storeys over basement with a hipped roof. Though c18 in origin, the present appearance agrees entirely with it having been improved in 1820. The front is of five bays with Georgian sashes, diminished in scale on the first floor. The doorcase, added in the late c20, is a simple arrangement with underscaled Ionic columns.

Close by, on the main road at Tuckmilltate, is a quaint Gothic former SCHOOL of 1821. Of T-plan with a two-storey gabled central block with crenellations and large pointed windows, flanked by single-storey two-bay wings with hipped roofs – unharmoniously raised on one side – with wide Tudor-arched windows. The front is in squared limestone with dressed quoins and window surrounds. A large limestone plaque above the door explains that the school was built with a legacy from the Rev. Dr John Maxwell of Falkland.

ST PATRICK, LEITRIM. 0.75 km E. A large understated mass-house, erected in 1827 according to the plaque on the exterior. A roughcast hall of four bays with large pointed arches and thick-set Y-tracery, to which *W. A. Scott* made alterations in 1921. He added an expressive bellcote tower to the W front, devised with three stages in hammered limestone with offset buttresses set against one another. A tall arched window recess occupies the middle stage, with a pointed doorway below. He also added tall lancets with blocked reveals on either side of the belfry, and at the E end three graded lancets, widely spaced, within a rash of hammer-dressed limestone. Inside, the spacious hall is remarkable only for the elaborate roof structure, expressed as a mansard; in effect like a railway station, it is a dizzying mesh of exposed trusses, combining kingpost and queenpost construction, set out on heavy timber corbels. The E window is filled with figurative STAINED GLASS, garishly coloured.

Outside, against the S wall, is a large Celtic Revival MONU-MENT to James Blayney Rice, Fenian leader †1908, by *O'Neill & Co.*, Belfast. A fussy architectural piece in dark limestone, full of symbolism with the usual Nationalist icons – pikes, a harp, Irish wolfhound, and ivy-garlanded round tower – forming a theatrical display in high relief.

CASTLE SHANE. 4 km SSE. A fragile and overgrown external wall in dense woodland is all that survives of the stuccoed castle built for the Lucas family in 1836 on the site of a c16 Mac-Mahon stronghold and burnt in 1920. The castle was an uncompromising three-storey block with canted end bays and sparse Elizabethan details – emphatic string-courses, mullioned windows and gabled parapets. At the heart of the plan was a four-storey machicolated tower, claimed to have been copied from the now vanished castle of the O'Neills at Ardgonnell, a few kilometres to the N in Armagh. The GATE LODGE is an attractive picturesque building which Samuel Lewis uncharacteristically described as handsome and 'in the later English style of architecture', a reference to its Tudor Gothic style. It is an asymmetrical two-storey L-plan block, with a neat open porch and twin gables with richly carved bargeboards. Now greatly disfigured by enlarged window openings. Good stone PIERS and iron RAILINGS.

BESSMOUNT. 1.5 km SW. A large and vigorously modelled house in Ruskinian Gothic, a truly splendid example of High Victorian display. Originally a Late Georgian house built by Alexander Nixon Montgomery *c.* 1807. This was the familiar two-storey, five-bay block distinguished by a Wyatt window at first-floor level and a boxy entrance porch, all heavily massed, with a hipped roof on bracketed eaves. Sold in 1840 to John Hatchell; the Georgian box must have seemed dull to his daughter and her new husband, William Henderson, and in 1868 they recast it into a High Victorian fancy. The architect remains unknown, though *John McCurdy*, who was at the same time completing his work for the District Lunatic Asyum in Monaghan, might be considered, as might *W. J. Barre*; he died in 1867, but his design for Danesfort (Belfast) of 1864 has some of the same qualities, especially its massing around a prominent entrance tower. With the addition of an extra storey, a proud steeply roofed entrance tower and a panoply of architectural devices and decoration, the remodelling is a very clever success.

All symmetry has been cast aside in a series of projections except at the rear, where the old house betrays itself in the simpler underlying elevation. Largely retaining the roughcast finish, the surface is broken up with bands of red-and-yellow brick which collide with the blocked quoins, solely in yellow brick. The addition of steep gabled projections, square eaves turrets, and a fairytale oriel turret on the principal corner establishes the asymmetry. This is reinforced by the variety of big mullioned-and-transomed windows, formed in limestone and filled with deep-set plate glass. The windows are varied, with plain chamfered reveals or with pointed and trefoil heads,

Tyholland, Bessmount, carved capital.
Drawing by K. Mulligan, 2012

and set singly or in groups under decorative brick arches. It is in this stylistic arrangement that *McCurdy*'s involvement is most strongly suggested, the trefoil-headed windows in particular bearing close comparison with Knocktopher Abbey (Kilkenny) which he had just completed. The primary architectural incident is similarly a square entrance tower ascending above the roof into the water tower (the tanks have been removed), here worked up to a polychromatic frenzy in red-and-yellow brick, expanding outwards and textured with diaper-work, arcading, string-courses and eaves cornice. It tapers off in a steep pyramid roof with sprocketed eaves clad in fish-scale slating and topped by a vertiginous railed platform. Preceding the tower is a short gabled porch of sandstone ashlar with a cusped archway, framed by a heavy billet moulding. Under the gable the crests and mottos of Hatchell and Henderson are displayed, while in the spandrels are portraits of the patrons themselves, Mrs Henderson rendered with an Elizabethan ruff and hair-do. Of real interest are the capitals, extending across the piers between the simple corner shafts, in effect transformed into highly elaborate imposts with virtuoso carvings of playful, microcosmic flora and fauna in a Ruskinian manner worthy of Deane & Woodward, and more especially the carving of the O'Shea brothers. Nicely contrasting land and water: on one side gluttonous herons, symmetrically posed, wade in bullrushes between a trout and a menacing pike, watched by nervous frogs and unsettled water hens; on the other side, squirrels start as a misplaced monkey boldly emerges from oak leaves, while a spreadeagled bat and an owl are hidden in the underbrush.

97   The garden elevation to the side is equally imposing: a tall off-centre gabled projection dominates the composition here, and a certain lightness is achieved by exposing the basement, extended outwards in an open arcade. The arcade supports a simple Gothic conservatory which runs through the gabled projection and emerges with a deeply bowed projection at its base. On the opposite side, a large single-storey 'music hall' adjoins the house with a short gabled link; a charming gabled block, chapel-like, with graded Gothic windows under decorative bargeboards. The elevation on this side has three plain and closely grouped sashes set below short cusped windows which form a sort of clerestory, with elaborate timbered dormers. A trefoil window high in the main gable records its erection in 1869 by William Henderson.

Inside, the plan of the old house was not significantly altered: the staircase retains its old position to the rear at the centre, though plumped out with a stocky timber newel, handrail and pierced balustrade. The principal rooms remain disposed on each side, the dining room enlarged into the gabled towers and the drawing room given a bay window. Ceilings with typical Late Victorian cornices. A number of good Neoclassical chimneypieces survive from the old house, lined with spectacular *Minton* tiles.

LISCARNEY. 1.75 km SW. A plain two-storey Late Georgian house with a hipped roof projected on eaves brackets. The front has four bays, three of them advanced to form in effect an L-plan, with the entrance accommodated in the narrow angle. Limestone rubble walls with brick trim, deprived of render and now all unhappily exposed, with plastic sash windows.

COOLMAIN HOUSE. 2.3 km SW. An Early Georgian house on a modest scale, gable-ended with basement and attics; the broad gables indicate a deep plan, with the attic windows widely spaced and close to the eaves. Nicely ordered single-storey front, now cement-rendered with blocked quoins: seven bays with the centre three slightly advanced, perhaps formerly with a pediment but now with the main roof simply extending over the wall-head at eaves level. Refenestrated with nasty plastic casements. It does however retain a handsome early doorcase in sandstone, with panelled architraves and moulded brackets supporting a cornice in an arrangement identical to that at No. 40 Abbey Street, Armagh. Before 1761 the seat of Colonel George Graham; in 1837 of John Goudy. Historic maps indicate that the house was originally aligned with a straight avenue to the E, now partly overlaid by the public road.

TYNAN AH 7040

An attractive nucleated estate village that grew up around the parish church on a hilltop overlooking Tynan Abbey demesne. Its name comes from the Irish *Tuíneán*, 'place of the water-course', which implies an early milling tradition on the River Tynan to the E. The origins are obscure, but two high crosses, and part of at least one other, indicate that this was an early Christian site, dedicated to St Uinnic or Vindic. By 1837 it possessed all the characteristics of a small estate village, with a courthouse, police barracks, schoolhouse, dispensary and Post Office. At Dartan Ree facing the church on the N side of the village, two prim white houses with long two-storey fronts still preserve that character, the plainer of the two, distinguished by handsome tripartite windows, formerly the dispensary.

VILLAGE CROSS. A large sandstone cross prominently sited on the roadside outside the churchyard. It is 15 ft (4.5 m) tall, assembled in three unrelated sections, with the arms and pierced nimbus of the upper portion greatly restored. Decoration is limited, with semicircular cusps to the arcs, five rimmed bosses in high relief on the main faces, and a lozenge motif carved on one side. A single panel decorates each face of the lower shaft, all badly weathered and barely legible; the fall of Adam and Eve is recognizable on the E face, iconographically close to the crosses of Arboe and Donaghmore (Tyrone).

St Vindic (C of I). A large and attractive church, built *c.* 1780 and thrice enlarged in the C19. This is essentially the standard hall-and-tower type, in limestone with cutstone dressings, given transepts in 1822. The tower is similar to Lisnadill, with shallow, undeveloped angle buttresses, rising in three stages to battlements and spiky pinnacles. There is no evidence of the spire mentioned by the Rev. Daniel Beaufort in 1787. The windows have simple Y-tracery, gently looped above the lights, probably added in the 1860s when the Ecclesiastical Commissioners built a vestry on the S transept and refitted the interior. In 1867 a small gabled porch was added to the N transept, as a private entrance for Sir James Stronge and his servants. A low plaque on the vestry wall marks the family crypt, carved with interlace designs inspired by one of the high crosses in Tynan Abbey demesne.

Inside, the roof is exposed with unusually complicated trusses, combining all the elements of kingposts and queenposts with arched braces; plain kingposts in the transepts. The late C18 gallery survives on elegant clustered columns with tall plinths. The sanctuary was reordered in 1893, the carved communion rails and oak prayer desk brought here from the Church of Ireland Cathedral in Armagh. Further repairs by *W. Sampson Jervois* in 1916. – STAINED GLASS. Decorative three-light E window, *c.* 1862; colourful late C19 glass in both transepts. – MONUMENTS. A large collection, mostly in the transepts; the best are pedimented tablets. The Rev. William Mauleverer †1840, with a draped urn and inverted torches. – James Mauleverer †1847, similar but less elaborate. – Colonel Sir James Matthew Stronge †1885, by *J. McCullough*, Armagh. – Sir John Calvert Stronge †1899, by *W. Costigan & Co.*, Belfast.

St Joseph. Chapel Hill Road. 1813. A neat pre-Emancipation barn church nicely sheltered against a hillside overlooking Tynan. Cement-rendered with buttresses. Irregular fenestration: three bays grouped in the centre of the N wall, five evenly spaced bays on the S, all pointed, one with Gothick glazing. The plain gabled front was elaborated in the mid C19 with kneelers and a cutstone bellcote; to one side in the gable a small sandstone plaque is inscribed 'Rev. John Hugh P.P. Tynan AD 1813'. Inside equally plain, with late C20 furnishings and some figurative STAINED GLASS. – The entrance to the CHURCHYARD has handsome octagonal piers with cusped lancets recessed in panels.

Tynan Parish Hall (former ERASMUS SMITH SCHOOL). Derryhaw Road. 1860 by *W. J. Barre*, extended 2006. Built under the patronage of Sir James Stronge and the Archbishop of Armagh. A stuccoed Italianate building, to a T-plan formed by the projection of the two-storey teacher's residence at the rear. The main front has five bays with raised quoins and a pitched roof projected on thin moulded eaves brackets. The central bay is advanced and gabled as a porch, with a large round-headed window, simple timber tracery, and plate glass; otherwise segmental-headed windows in blocked surrounds.

In the s gable a large Venetian window is placed in a similar surround. Extended in the same idiom in 2006 with two bays added in a lower block to the N gable.

TYNAN RECTORY. Off Derryhaw Road. 0.5 km SE. An attractive Georgian house, two storeys on a basement with half-hipped gables and a lower two-bay block to one side. Nicely proportioned three-bay front in limestone rubble, with a central carved Gibbsian doorcase with blocked architrave, large triple keystone and cornice, and flanked by narrow side-lights. Described by the Rev. Daniel Beaufort in 1787 as 'a good looking glebe house well situated', it enjoys pleasant views towards the village and the tower of the hilltop parish church.

The LODGE is a neat single-storey block under a pyramid roof with a single tripartite window (like those of Dartan Ree in the village) and a recessed porch to one side.

TYNAN ABBEY DEMESNE. 1 km SW. The destruction of Tynan Abbey by fire in 1981, when the 8th and 9th baronets were murdered together in the library, is a painful episode in late C20 history. The burnt-out shell stood gaping over the surviving formal terraces until 1998 when it was demolished, leaving just two standing elements – the sandstone entrance porch and part of the terrace arcade – as poignant reminders of the picturesque Gothic Revival castle that evolved in the C19. There was never an abbey here: the name derives solely from the romantic motivations that inspired Sir James Stronge c. 1810 to remodel and extend the existing C18 house, then known as Fairview. The property had passed to the Stronges after Dr John Stronge, Rector of Tynan, married Elizabeth Manson in 1714. A two-storey house certainly existed here at that time, built by Captain Manson and briefly described by Thomas Ashe in 1703 as 'a very prittie house well timbered and regularly built'; it was evidently a modest building, with a

Tynan Abbey.
Engraving, 1854

'handsome parlour' and a 'common hall' with 'good chambers and garrets above staires'. It was rebuilt in the mid C18.

The 2nd Baronet, Sir James Matthew Stronge, began to remodel the house about the time of his marriage to Isabella Calvert in 1810. A stocky square entrance tower was symmetrically flanked by lower battlemented ranges with pointed windows, buttresses and crocketed pinnacles. The canted gable terminated in a spectacular flourish with a full-length traceried window. The building extended back with a long façade overlooking formal terraces and the lake; here the design was more consciously Tudor, with a tall gable projecting in the centre flanked by low arcades, on one side fronting a conservatory that terminated in a spiky polygonal tower. Unexecuted proposals in this period, since destroyed in the building, were signed by *A. C. Pugin*, an assistant in the office of *John Nash*, who was almost certainly the designer here. The works coincided with Nash's involvement at Caledon, and elements of the design are consistent with his work at Luscombe in Devon and Kilwaughter in Antrim, though the absence of his characteristic turrets is noteworthy. On the garden front, laid out with a series of steep Tudor gables, the open loggia with four-centred arches was a feature beloved by Nash. Stronge's mother-in-law revealed the aesthetic chaos that ensues from such ambitious remodelling; visiting during the reconstruction in 1816 she exclaimed, 'I don't think I shall ever like the house': with the exception of some bedrooms, she had found 'all the other rooms . . . are unfinished even without windows . . . the staircase without banisters and all about unfinished . . . unplastered and full of rubbish and workmen . . . every part of the house is open and unprotected.'

By 1836 one visitor (James Graham) could find 'a very nice moderately sized gothic house [with] a very nice dining room and drawing room, with library and music room running back from the latter'. Later the castle was made more consciously Victorian, first when *W. J. Barre* was involved in work *c.* 1866 that included removing the orangery and raising this portion with gables to correspond to the opposite side. In 1877 *W. H. Lynn* proposed alterations to the entrance front including the surviving Tudor porch, composed as a shallow battlemented projection with a deep, heavily moulded archway with carved spandrels. Earlier in the same year John Ynyr Burges noted a 'handsome new staircase and a boudoir' which may have been part of Barre's or Lynn's additions.

The DEMESNE of Tynan Abbey is a highly picturesque landscape with broad and varied vistas filled with many venerable trees, most impressively oaks. The STABLEYARD is an attractive C18 quadrangle formed of low, lofted rubble ranges, broken on the N and S sides by larger central blocks with hipped roofs. Each front is differently expressed, on the S front raised high over vaults to form an impressive cubic house with an attractive three-bay front, finishing in a shallow hipped roof and central chimneystack.

If *Nash* was involved here, then it is reasonable to assume the two main entrances are to his design. The CASTLE GATE is a forbidding battlemented structure to an L-plan with high walls of squared limestone, battered at the base and terminating in towers with Irish battlements; the stout keeper's house at one end is a two-storey polygonal tower, answered opposite by a slender square turret. The gateway is a pointed opening set in a square machicolated recess. The LEMNAGORE LODGE is a charming picturesque Tudor Revival essay in limestone rubble and red brick formed of two adjoining blocks, one lower and slightly recessed. The main part, of three bays, has a deeply projecting gable with a half-timbered upper storey oversailing an open red brick porch below. The steep roofs have diagonal slating with ornamental clay pots to the main stacks.

DEMESNE CROSSES. Dispersed in the demesne are three sandstone ringed high crosses, one from the village and two others brought here before 1837 by Sir James Stronge from Glenarb in the nearby parish of Artaloo in Co. Tyrone. All the crosses have been partially restored. While they are slightly more sophisticated than the fragments at Eglish, dating is problematical; none can be considered later than the C12.

TERRACE CROSS, apparently brought from the village in the early C19, now stands in a gloomy arbour of yew trees at the end of the formal terraces of Tynan Abbey. A tall, decorated ringed cross restored on a stepped base, standing to a height of 11 ft (3.4 m). The ring is pierced with rebated arcs. The front is relatively plain, with an inscribed margin and flat undecorated paterae in the panels of the shaft. The opposite face is outlined with more prominent linear mouldings, extended to form panels in each terminal that are filled with paterae decorated with interlace in low relief; the longer shaft panel has a lozenge at the base; all the designs are linked together by a narrow raised stem to a plainer central patera. The sides of the shaft have smaller labyrinthine paterae isolated at the top and bottom of the narrow panels.

WELL CROSS. Brought from Glenarb. Raised on a stone   16
arch over a well in a small railed enclosure close to the avenue and the Lemnagore gate. Approximately 8 ft 6 in. (2.5 m) high, it appears plain but is heavily weathered, with faint decoration, and a restored base and lower shaft. It has an unpierced ring, though the segments between are recessed with semicircular cusps to the arcs of the ring; the ring face is decorated with interlace and on the sides of the arms and shaft there are square decorated panels. A weak outline of the Crucifixion is suggested on the W face, while the E face is embellished with a common pattern of flat central boss and narrow raised stems.

ISLAND CROSS. Also from Glenarb. Standing in a circle of yews on a narrow point in the lake facing the site of Tynan Abbey. This is the smallest – 7 ft 6 in. (2.3 m) high – and plainest of the group, assembled in three parts, with most of its lower portion restored. The ring is pierced and decorated with Celtic interlace; the cross has linear margins, and a carved patera in the centre of each side decorated with a La Tène pattern of linked spirals.

TYNAN RAILWAY STATION (former). 1 km N. A small rural station of rare sophistication and charm, now abandoned. Built c. 1859 for the Ulster Railway serving the Armagh–Monaghan–Clones line, and designed by an architect known only as *Mr Clayton*. Like the Glaslough station which he also designed, this is an earnest Gothic Revival conceit. The *Civil Engineer and Architect's Journal* in 1859 unfairly dismissed it as 'absolutely ugly', while accepting the Glaslough design as 'a happier conception'. Built in squared rock-faced sandstone, presenting two gabled end bays to the platform, one with a bay window, and a lean-to timber canopy between. The entrance front is more varied, consisting of nicely layered gabled blocks, graduated asymmetrically. The largest of these, the passenger hall, dominates in the centre and has an unusual four-light mullioned window with small star-like upper panels. An entrance tower to one side is the most ambitious element: square in plan, it converts abruptly to an octagon as the base for a vanished or unfinished broach spire. Inside, the main hall is an airy space with exposed trusses, its present state adding to an overall impression of Gothic gloom.

The station stands between characteristic late C19 two-storey WORKERS' HOUSES, the best of these in a semi-detached block of rendered red brick with camber-headed windows. Beyond them, the ENGINE SHED is a more forceful building, formed as a long gabled block joined to a wide, equally long lean-to, resulting in an irregular front in squared masonry, propped by three massive stepped buttresses with large triangular doorways between.

TYNAN MILL. Coolkill Road. 1.25 km NNE. An impressive four-storey gable-ended block in squared limestone with red brick trim. Eight bays to each of the main fronts. The unusual extension of two internal dividing walls so as to project through the roof is explained by the rotating conical cowl of the oast house rising from the ridge between them. The tall gable towers over the road, with a plaque bearing the date 1844 and a Diocletian window above.

LISCLOONEY PRESBYTERIAN CHURCH. 1 km SE. A large roughcast hall proclaiming the foundation date 1714 on its gabled front. Nothing in its plain appearance suggests this date; it has five pointed bays with moulded surrounds and a taller and narrower central bay. The interior has late C19 furnishings and stained glass.

VIRGINIA CN

A small estate town located on the road between Kells and Cavan on the N shore of Lough Ramor. Under the Ulster Plantation,

Virginia, view of the lake.
Engraving, c18

1,000 acres in the vicinity were granted with a patent to Captain
John Ridgeway, who in 1611 occupied a castle here and had by
then established a small settlement and a watercourse for a mill.
The patent was later reassigned to Captain Hugh Culme, the
servitor who was also granted Clough Oughter Castle near Killeshandra. Culme was allowed 250 acres for the purpose of building a town, which he named Virginia in honour of the late Queen.
By 1619 there were eight timber houses already in evidence – all
lived in by English tenants, one of whom was a minister who kept
a 'good school' – along with 'a large bawn in a strong situation'
in which a two-storey house was under construction, 'the roof
ready to be set on'. In 1622 Culme's interest was purchased by
Lucas Plunkett, 1st Earl of Fingall; he failed to develop the town
satisfactorily under the terms of the commission, and it was
captured by Colonel Philip O'Reilly and devastated in 1642.

After the Restoration, the 3rd Earl was confirmed in his possession of the property in 1662. By 1746 the Virginia estate had
been acquired by Sir Thomas Taylour, 2nd Bt, whose ancestor
and namesake had been an associate of Sir William Petty in the
Down Survey. Two years before Taylour acquired it, Virginia was
dismissed as a 'poor despicable place not affording a tolerable
inn'.

Leaving no trace of its precise original location or c17 buildings, the town was greatly revived and rebuilt in the early c19
under the patronage of the marquesses of Headfort, Taylour's
descendants, who built a hunting lodge here. Two phases of
development are evident. In the early part of the century, coinciding with the period when *Alexander McLeish* was working on the
grounds at Virginia Lodge, it began to acquire the character of a
well-planned estate town, gaining a new parish church at the w
end of the Main Street, at the intersection of the roads to Cavan

and Ballyjamesduff, which was overlooked by a new market house (now the Courthouse). The Main Street was lined with good, pleasing two-storey houses, some distinguished in a modest cottage style with mullioned windows with small panes. Later in the century a series of attractive estate cottages were built about the town. Virginia's principal industries were a distillery and a flax mill, both served by the stream – presumably Ridgeway's early C17 watercourse – that winds its way into Lough Ramor behind the Main Street.

LURGAN (VIRGINIA) PARISH CHURCH (C of I). A hall and tower picturesquely framed by a long avenue of limes and beeches at the W end of the Main Street. The intimate alignment of the tower with the entrance to Virginia Lodge reflects the proprietorial interest of the Taylours and their foundation of the church. An earlier structure of unknown origin was destroyed in 1818 after a storm threw down the spire on to the nave. It was rebuilt to a design by the Cavan architect *Arthur McClean*. In 1821 *Alexander McLeish* gave 'directions for enclosing plantations at the church'. On Christmas night 1832 disaster returned, when the new church was burnt; a source in 1837 states that the building was 'entirely consumed', and the charred timber lintels surviving in the tower tell of this event.

The present building is modest in scale for its big site – a triangular island formed from the old fair green and bounded by yews. Three-bay nave with battlemented gables, pinnacled diagonal buttresses and a battlemented W tower in stages with an octagonal needle spire. Built of limestone rubble, formerly rendered, with ashlar trim; the exceptionally poor quality of the carved limestone is revealed by the blistering of the surfaces of the window surrounds. The pinnacles were unusually embellished with cast-iron crockets and finials; there are a few tenacious survivors. Quarry-glazed timber windows, Perp in style, with tracery carved to imitate stone and forming three lights. A chancel projection to the E neatly accommodates the vestry and Sunday School in the basement below, reached directly from outside and by a discreet stair tucked into the SE corner of the nave.

The interior is arranged as a plain hall with a shallow-vaulted ceiling, now even plainer since the removal of stucco ribs and bosses which survive in the chancel only. – REREDOS erected by Lady Headfort in 1890 as a memorial to her son by her first marriage, John Alfred Wilson Patten: Christ in Majesty with saints, an elaborate composition of *opus sectile* and mosaic designed by *Frank Mann* of *James Powell & Sons*. – STAINED GLASS. E window with Christ as the Good Shepherd, a memorial to Lady Madeline Crichton †1876, daughter of the 3rd Marquess of Headfort, by *Clayton & Bell*. – BELL. By *John Rudhall* of Gloucestershire, 1832.

Outside the S door, a handsome diminutive pair of carved Celtic crosses in red granite commemorates the 3rd Marquess and Marchioness of Headfort.

CHURCH OF MARY IMMACULATE. Bailieborough Road. 1988. Built to replace an earlier church on the Main Street. A visually harsh modern structure with a gabled weather-slated spire and bright pebbledashed walls, set within a large car park. The interior reflects the later C20 interest in radial planning. In the car park, a BRONZE BELL by *M. O'Byrne*, 1913, set up as a souvenir of the old church.

COURTHOUSE (former MARKET HOUSE). A two-storey, three-bay building in roughcast with dressed limestone trimming. The purpose for which it was built in 1830 is easily recognizable in the two big arches on the ground floor, in blocked stone surrounds. These were closed and fenestrated in 1930 when the building was converted to a courthouse. The diminutive windows on the first floor originally had mullioned casements of a type shared by several early C19 estate houses in the town, possibly as the work of *Alexander McLeish*; those were replaced by twelve-pane sashes in 2008, perhaps in the erroneous belief that the existing windows were themselves replacements. The courtroom, with simple panelled pine fittings, is reached by a narrow entrance between the arches. Office area to the rear with cells to one side. Upper floor reached from the side elevation to the w by external stairs with attractive cast-iron balusters.

RAMOR THEATRE. Main Street. Built as a Catholic church in 1845. Neatly shoehorned into the streetscape like a stage set, a modest buttressed Gothic frontispiece to a plain rendered five-bay hall. Gabled with battlements, the façade is built of limestone ashlar with three lancets set under a continuous hoodmould; two buttresses flank the larger central window, and diagonal buttresses at the corners rise to sharp pinnacles. On either side of the gable are low doorways with crowstepped battlemented and four-centred arches. A small former vestry lies behind the E doorway; access to the hall is made discreetly through the w doorway via an open side passage which leads on to a small enclosed graveyard extending down to the banks of the river. Effectively arranged back-to-front: the altar was located on the N side, behind the street façade. Closed in 1989, and the interior stripped.

A simple three-bay, two-storey former PAROCHIAL HOUSE with hipped roof adjoins the vestry.

OTHER BUILDINGS. Beside the Theatre the NATIONAL IRISH BANK is a late C19 three-bay, two-storey stuccoed Italianate block. A tidy composition with flanking archways incorporating attractive intersecting arches to the E. Façade enriched by a bracketed eaves cornice, raised quoins, and string-courses. Elaborate surrounds with segmental pediments to the first-floor windows, which have marginal glazing; on the ground floor, plainer round-headed windows with keystones flanking a projecting porch. Interior remodelled, but typical Late Victorian plasterwork survives on the first floor. To the w a pair of handsome early C19 houses, raised over basements with railed gardens, form the end of a short terrace extending along the bend of the street down to the bridge. The largest of these, COIS ABHAINN, remains most intact, with a four-bay façade, Georgian sash windows and leaded teardrop fanlight. Masonry BRIDGE on four segmental arches over the river, 1894. Adjoining the parapet of the bridge to the NE is the gable of a former MILL, a long three-storey range with rubble walls, terminated by a tall five-storey block to the N; converted in the late C20 to residential use.

The centre of the town is dominated by two three-storey buildings on the Main Street. On the N side, the former LAKEVIEW HOTEL, a much altered rendered block. Facing it is a more handsome counterpart, distinguished by its exposed red brick façade, which retains its fenestration and paired timber shopfronts with finely crafted Corinthian capitals – degraded by modern signage. There are several mid-C19 former estate cottages around the town: the best-preserved are found on the Cavan and Ballyjamesduff Roads, arranged in semi-detached pairs with squared limestone walls, dormered attics and stout central brick stacks. The pretty open porches add a delicate touch, with ornamental bargeboards deceitfully supported on rustic timbers of cast iron. The former VIRGINIA NATIONAL SCHOOL on the Cavan Road, of 1909, is a plain rendered L-plan building with paired gables and ungainly modern porches. OAKFIELD, off the Kells Road, is a neat cement-rendered block built c. 1940 by the town doctor.

NEIGHBOURHOOD

VIRGINIA LODGE. 1 km W. A long and handsome sporting box, enjoying wonderful views over the wooded islands of Lough Ramor. Initially built before 1800 for the Taylour family of Kells, earls of Bective and after 1800 marquesses of Headfort; Sir Charles Coote commented that here the Marquess of Headfort 'delights to spend the autumnal months'. Three principal periods of development are evident. On the main, E, front the three-bay gable-ended block in the centre is the original house, a plain building just one room deep. The symmetrical plan remains evident in the small rooms on either side of the present entrance hall, which now serve as lobbies to later accommodation. The small and elegant staircase at the centre of the plan must also belong to the original house. The building was first extended c. 1820, with a further range to the W, resulting in a double-pile plan divided by a narrow spinal corridor. The architect may have been *Alexander McLeish*, who between 1821 and 1824 was employed by Lord Headfort on the gardens at Headfort near Kells and in laying out the demesne here. The house was remodelled in a simple Tudor idiom with rubble walls, brick trim and octagonal chimneystacks, and arranged with its principal entrance to the W, contained in a single-storey porch with multiple gables, altogether more ornamental than the restrained E front. The timber doorcase survives in

the modern ballroom at the rear of the building, but the elliptical fanlight has lost its original glazing; outside, a Tudor gable
survives above the parapet, largely concealed by later additions.
The house continued to be extended in the C19, principally
when it was remodelled *c.* 1860 to serve as a dower house, with
the addition of two wings dominating the E front, which were
given richly carved bargeboards.

The grander accommodation provided in these wings was
then reached through the original little rooms, given bay
windows. The dining room to the S has a coved ceiling with an
enriched Victorian cornice bearing grapes and a heavy centrepiece. Here, an exceptionally fine Ionic Georgian chimneypiece of Siena and Carrara marble with an elegant frieze
decorated with a human mask between swags; its origin and
when it was installed here are not recorded. The former
drawing room again has a coved ceiling, this time with understated Adamesque plasterwork, a style still evidently fashionable to the owners of Headfort. The oversized Renaissance-style
marble chimneypiece is a more flamboyant Victorian design,
mostly in white marble, similar to examples at Uppercourt, Co.
Kilkenny.

Substantial COURTYARD to the W. A carved plaque over the
central carriage arch is inscribed 'Bective 1834'. The W range
with gabled breakfront and red brick trim was built in 1874 to
designs of *J. F. Fuller.*

TOWN LODGE. In February 1823 *Alexander McLeish* laid
out a new approach from Virginia Church, and by March a
new lodge was under construction; presumably it is this single-
storey, two-bay lodge with roughcast walls, decorated bargeboards and quarry-glazed windows, discreetly placed behind
the entrance with its gable overlooking the avenue. The
BALLYJAMESDUFF LODGES are of the same period and
presumably also by *McLeish.* They form an attractive pair of
single-storey houses, placed back-to-back in an H-plan. Roughcast rendered walls, brick porches and ornate bargeboards.
OLDCASTLE LODGE, *c.* 1880, probably by *Fuller,* contrasts
with the simple cottage style of the other lodges: a fussy two-
up-two-down building of squared limestone with ashlar trim,
crammed with detail, including a decorated open timber porch
and ground-floor oriel window in the gable. Cruciform-plan
GATEPIERS with gabled fronts and trefoils.

ST PATRICK, LURGAN PARISH CHURCH, COPPANAGH. 2.5 km
NW. A large roadside chapel to a cruciform plan, with a shallow
chancel and a handsome kneelered gable to the front with
narrow proportions, a pointed doorway and a hooded quatrefoil. Built in 1831 by the Rev. John O'Reilly, remembered in a
plaque above the entrance; enlarged *c.* 1920 when the walls
were raised. Roughcast with blocked quoins and the simplest
Y-tracery. Inside, pleasantly simple with panelled timber ceilings and a big two-tiered timber porch. – STAINED GLASS.
In the three-light E window, figurative glass with rich blues
and purples, the gift of Cardinal O'Connell of Boston. –

MONUMENTS. The Rev. John Brady †1831; a tall limestone slab with a rope-edged oval and winged cherubs. – The Rev. John O'Reilly †1844; a plain tablet. – The Rev. James Fitzsimmons †1898; a white marble tablet, by *Farrell & Son*, Glasnevin. – The Rev. Hugh J. Brady †1916; a decorated tablet.

LURGAN OLD CHURCH. 4 km NW. In a circular enclosure in open countryside, the ruins of a long rectangular church, 52½ ft by 26¼ ft (16 m by 8 m). A section of an impressive voussoired vault built against the W gable is possibly of a different phase, but as at Gallon (Killinkere) and Killan (Shercock) it is set tranversely, perhaps to support a gallery. Apparently quarried in 1818 to supply the new parish church in Virginia. Nice collection of primitive C18 grave markers with naïve scripts.

RAFFONY. 3 km NE. The much restored ruin of a small single-cell church, internally 44 ft by 19 ft (13.5 m by 5.7 m). Evidence for a segregated space at the W end, perhaps originally vaulted, as at Gallon (Killinkere) and Lurgan (Virginia).

Nearby are a well, rath, souterrain and wedge tomb – all evidence for ancient settlement here.

RAHARDRUM. 1 km SE. Long plain two-storey house of four bays, nicely sited beside the lake. Present in the early C19. Roughcast with hipped roof and red brick stacks. Boxy off-centre porch. Fenestration altered in the early C20 with metal casements.

ST MATTHEW, MAGHERA. 5 km SE. A bulky Gothic hall, built by the Rev. John O'Reilly in 1858 to the designs of *John Ryan*. Positioned with its E end to the fore and skew to the road, with an assertive W front looking out over the Cavan countryside and the Loughcrew Hills to the SW. Seven-bay hall with roughcast walls and simple lancets, formed as a group of three at the E end. Single-storey porches flank the gabled W front, where a two-stage tower advances. Repaired by *Michael Grace* in 1926. The spire was removed later, but its absence barely diminishes the building's presence in the landscape. Interior bright and airy, with a basic hammerbeam roof. – STAINED GLASS including the four Evangelists and the local saints Columcille (Columba) and Oliver Plunkett.

MUNTERCONNAUGHT PARISH CHURCH, KNOCKATEMPLE (C of I). 3 km S. One of *William Farrell*'s ubiquitous small single-cell designs, picturesquely set at the rear of a graveyard with views to the N over Lough Ramor. In 1837 'a very neat building', newly erected. It has a three-bay nave of limestone rubble with quarry glazing. Gabled W front of ashlar with bellcote and square corner buttresses, elegantly converted to octagons to support pinnacles and repeated on the single-storey battlemented porch. Short chancel with plain E window with stained glass in Art Nouveau style. Vestry added later to the N. The interior retains box pews and cast-iron roof trusses.

ST BARTHOLOMEW, KNOCKATEMPLE. 3 km S. A large, plain hall on an exposed site overlooking Lough Ramor. Described in 1837 as a 'good stone building'. Rebuilt in 1858. Five-bay nave with roughcast rendered walls and gabled fronts with identical battlemented Gothic doorcases of limestone ashlar. The E gable more elaborate, with the entrance to the sacristy flanked by windows below a triple lancet. Interior completely remodelled *c.* 1960; the altar canopy and use of cork tiles recall the work of *W. H. Byrne & Son*. Bell-frame to the w supported on piers of rusticated ashlar.

GLOSSARY

Particular types of an architectural element are often defined under the name of the element itself, e.g. for 'dog-leg stair' see STAIR. Literal meanings, where specially relevant, are indicated by the abbreviation *lit.* Of the terms here defined, not all are necessarily used in this volume. The abbreviations E.E., DEC, and PERP, referring to stylistic subdivisions in English Gothic architecture, have little relevance to Irish medieval patterns. They are retained here principally because they provide a convenient shorthand with which to indicate the character of much C 19 Gothic Revival architecture in Ireland which, particularly in the first half of the century, was often based on English models.

ABACUS (*lit.* tablet): flat slab forming the top of a capital, *see* Orders (fig. 16).

ABUTMENT: the meeting of an arch or vault with its solid lateral support, or the support itself.

ACANTHUS: formalized leaf ornament with thick veins and frilled edge, e.g. on a Corinthian capital.

ACHIEVEMENT OF ARMS: in heraldry, a complete display of armorial bearings.

ACROTERION (*lit.* peak): pointed ornament projecting above the apex or ends of a pediment.

AEDICULE (*lit.* little building): term used in classical architecture to describe the unit formed by a pair of columns or pilasters, an entablature, and usually a pediment, placed against a wall to frame an opening.

AGGREGATE: small stones added to a binding material, e.g. in harling or concrete.

AISLE (*lit.* wing): passage alongside the nave, choir or transept of a church, or the main body of some other building, separated from it by columns or piers.

AMBO: raised platform or pulpit in early Christian churches.

AMBULATORY (*lit.* walkway): aisle at the E end of a chancel, usually surrounding an apse and therefore semicircular or polygonal in plan.

ANNULET (*lit.* ring): shaft-ring (q.v.).

ANSE DE PANIER (*lit.* basket handle): basket arch (*see* Arch).

ANTAE: (1) flat pilasters placed at the ends of the short projecting walls of a portico or colonnade, which is then called *In Antis*. *See* Orders (fig. 16). The bases and capitals of antae differ from, and are more simple than, the columns of the order that they accompany. (2) the side walls of a building projecting at the gables, typical of many early Christian churches in Ireland.

ANTEFIXAE: ornaments projecting at regular intervals above a classical cornice. *See* Orders (fig. 16).

ANTHEMION (*lit.* honeysuckle): classical ornament like a honeysuckle flower (*see* fig. 1).

Fig. 1 Anthemion and Palmette Frieze

APSE: semicircular (i.e. apsidal) extension of an apartment. A term first used of the magistrate's end of a Roman basilica, and thence especially of the vaulted semicircular or polygonal end of a chancel or a chapel.

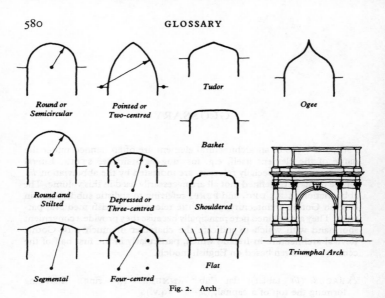

Round or Semicircular

Pointed or Two-centred

Tudor

Ogee

Basket

Round and Stilted

Depressed or Three-centred

Shouldered

Segmental

Four-centred

Flat

Triumphal Arch

Fig. 2. Arch

ARABESQUE: type of painted or carved surface decoration, often with a vertical emphasis and consisting of intertwined foliage scrolls sometimes incorporating ornamental objects or figures.

ARCADE: a series of arches supported by piers or columns. *Blind Arcade*: the same applied to the surface of a wall. *Wall Arcade*: in medieval churches, a blind arcade forming a dado below windows.

ARCH: for the various forms *see* fig. 2. The term *Basket Arch* refers to a basket handle and is sometimes applied to a three-centred or depressed arch as well as the type with a flat middle. *Transverse Arch*: across the main axis of an interior space. A term used especially for the arches between the compartments of tunnel- or groin-vaulting. *Diaphragm Arch*: transverse arch with solid spandrels spanning an otherwise wooden-roofed interior. *Chancel Arch*: across the w end of a chancel. *Relieving Arch*: incorporated in a wall, to carry some of its weight, some way above an opening. *Strainer Arch*: inserted across an opening to resist any inward pressure of the side

members. *Triumphal Arch*: Imperial Roman monument whose elevation supplied a motif for many later classical compositions. *See also* Rerearch.

ARCHITRAVE: (1) formalized lintel, the lowest member of the classical entablature (*see* Orders, fig. 16); (2) moulded frame of a door or window. Also *Lugged* (Irish) or *Shouldered Architrave*, whose top is prolonged into lugs (*lit.* ears).

ARCHIVOLT: under surface of an arch or the moulded band applied to this curve. Also called Soffit.

ARRIS (*lit.* stop): sharp edge at the meeting of two surfaces.

ASHLAR: masonry of large blocks wrought to even faces and square edges.

ASTYLAR: term used to describe an elevation that has no columns or other distinguishing stylistic features.

ATLANTES: male counterparts of caryatids, often in a more demonstrative attitude of support. In sculpture, a single figure of the god Atlas may be seen supporting a globe.

ATTACHED: description of a shaft

or column that is partly merged into a wall or pier.

ATTIC: (1) small top storey often within a sloping roof; (2) in classical architecture, the top storey of a façade if it appears above the principal entablature of the façade.

AUMBRY: recess or cupboard to hold sacred vessels for the Mass.

BAILEY: open space or court of a stone-built castle; *see also* Motte-and-Bailey.

BALDACCHINO: free-standing canopy over an altar or tomb, usually supported on columns. Also called Ciborium.

BALLFLOWER: globular flower of three petals enclosing a small ball. A decoration used in the first quarter of the C 14.

BALUSTER (*lit.* pomegranate): hence a pillar or pedestal of bellied form. *Balusters*: vertical supports of this or any other form, for a handrail or coping, the whole being called a *Balustrade*. *Blind Balustrade*: the same with a wall behind.

BARBICAN: outwork defending the entrance to a castle.

BARGEBOARDS: projecting inclined boards, often decoratively pierced and carved, fixed beneath the eaves of a gable to cover and protect the rafters. Common in C 15 and C 16 architecture and revived by Picturesque designers in the C 19.

BARROW: burial mound.

BARTIZAN (*lit.* battlement): turret, square or round, corbelled out from a wall or tower of a castle, church, or house. Frequently at a corner, hence *Corner Bartizan*.

BASE: moulded foot of a column or other order. For its use in classical architecture *see* Orders (fig. 16). *Elided Bases*: bases of a compound pier whose lower parts are run together, ignoring the arrangement of the shafts above. Capitals may be treated in the same way.

BASEMENT: lowest, subordinate storey of a building, and hence the lowest part of an elevation, below the main floor.

BASILICA (*lit.* royal building): a Roman public hall; hence an aisled building with a clerestory.

BASTION: one of a series of projections from the main wall of a fortress or city, placed at intervals in such a manner as to enable the garrison to cover the intervening stretches of the wall. Post-medieval and developed for use with artillery (first at Rhodes), bastions are usually polygonal or semicircular in plan.

BATTER: inward inclination of a wall.

BATTLEMENT: fortified parapet, indented or crenellated so that archers could shoot through the indentations (crenels or embrasures) between the projecting solid portions (merlons). After the invention of gunpowder had made them obsolete, battlements continued in use as decoration until at least the C 17. *Irish Battlements*: a system where the up-and-down rhythm of merlons and embrasures is interrupted at the corners, which are built up in a series of high steps, typical of late medieval architecture in Ireland.

BAWN (*lit.* ox fold): defensive walled enclosure attached to, or near, a tower house or Plantation castle.

BAYS: divisions of an elevation or interior space as defined by any regular vertical features (arches, columns, windows, etc.).

BAY WINDOW: window of one or more storeys projecting from the face of a building at ground level, and either rectangular or polygonal in plan. A *Canted Bay Window* has a straight front and angled sides. A *Bow Window* is curved. An *Oriel Window* projects on corbels or brackets from an upper floor and does not start from the ground.

BEAKHEAD: Norman ornamental motif consisting of a row of bird or beast heads with beaks biting usually into a roll moulding.

BELFRY (*lit.* tower): (1) bell-turret set on a roof or gable (*see also* Bellcote); (2) room or stage in a tower where bells are hung; (3) bell-tower in a general sense.

BELL-CAST: *see* Roof.

BELLCOTE: belfry as (1) above, with the character of a small house for the bell(s).

BILLET (*lit.* log or block) FRIEZE: Norman ornament consisting of small blocks placed at regular intervals (*see* fig. 3).

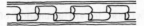

Fig. 3.   Billet Frieze

BLIND: *see* Arcade, Balustrade.

BLOCKING COURSE: plain course of stones, or equivalent, on top of a cornice and crowning the wall.

BOLECTION MOULDING: convex moulding covering the joint between two different planes and overlapping the higher as well as the lower one, especially on panelling and fireplace surrounds of the late C 17 and early C 18.

BOND: in brickwork, the pattern of long sides (stretchers) and short ends (headers) produced on the face of a wall by laying bricks in a particular way (*see* fig. 4).

BOSS: knob or projection usually placed to cover the intersection of ribs in a vault.

BOW WINDOW: *see* Bay window.

BOX PEW: pew enclosed by a high wooden back and ends, the latter having doors.

BRACE: *see* Roof (fig. 22).

BRACKET: small supporting piece of stone, etc., to carry a projecting horizontal member.

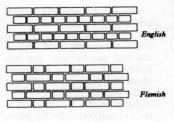

English

Flemish

Fig. 4.   Bond

BUCRANIUM: ox skull, used decoratively in classical friezes.

BULLAUNS: boulders having an artificial basin-like hollow. Now frequently regarded with superstition, they are found at early monastic sites and killeens and were probably used for pounding and grinding grain.

BULLSEYE WINDOW: small circular window, e.g. in the tympanum of a pediment. Also called *Œil de Bœuf*.

BUTTRESS: vertical member projecting from a wall to stabilize it or to resist the lateral thrust of an arch, roof, or vault. For different types used at the corners of a building, especially a tower, *see* fig. 5. A *Flying Buttress* transmits the thrust to a heavy abutment by means of an arch or half-arch.

CABLE MOULDING or ROPE MOULDING: originally a Norman moulding, imitating the twisted strands of a rope.

CAMBER: slight rise or upward curve in place of a horizontal line or plane.

CAMPANILE: freestanding bell-tower.

CANDLE-SNUFFER ROOF: conical roof of a turret.

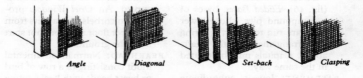

Angle   Diagonal   Set-back   Clasping

Fig. 5.   Buttresses at a corner

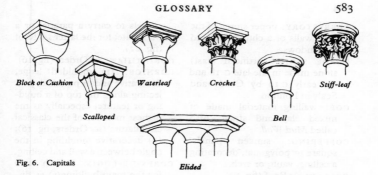

Block or Cushion   *Waterleaf*   *Crocket*   *Stiff-leaf*

Scalloped   *Bell*

Fig. 6.   Capitals   *Elided*

CANES: *see* Quarries.

CANOPY: projection or hood over an altar, pulpit, niche, statue, etc.

CANTED: tilted, generally on a vertical axis to produce an obtuse angle on plan, e.g. of a canted bay window.

CAPITAL: head or top part of a column; for classical types *see* Orders (fig. 16); for medieval types *see* fig. 6. *Elided Capitals*: capitals of a compound pier whose upper parts are run together, ignoring the arrangement of the shafts below.

CARRIAGE ARCH: *see* Pend.

CARTOUCHE: tablet with ornate frame, usually of elliptical shape and bearing a coat of arms or inscription.

CARYATIDS (*lit.* daughters of the village of Caryae): female figures supporting an entablature, counterparts of Atlantes.

CASEMATE: in military architecture, a vaulted chamber, with embrasures for defence, built in the thickness of the walls of a castle or fortress or projecting from them.

CASEMENT: (1) window hinged at the side; (2) in Gothic architecture, a concave moulding framing a window.

CASTELLATED: battlemented (*q.v.*).

CAVETTO: concave moulding of quarter-round section.

CELLURACH: *see* Killeen.

CELURE or CEILURE: panelled and adorned part of a wagon roof above the rood or the altar.

CENTERING: wooden support for the building of an arch or vault, removed after completion.

CHAMFER (*lit.* corner-break): surface formed by cutting off a square edge, usually at an angle of forty-five degrees.

CHANCEL (*lit.* enclosure): that part of the E end of a church in which the altar is placed, usually applied to the whole continuation of the nave E of the crossing.

CHANTRY CHAPEL: chapel attached to, or inside, a church, endowed for the celebration of masses for the soul of the founder or some other individual.

CHEVRON: zigzag Norman ornament.

CHOIR: (1) the part of a church where services are sung; in monastic churches this can occupy the crossing and/or the easternmost bays of the nave, but in cathedral churches it is usually in the E arm; (2) the E arm of a cruciform church (a usage of long standing though liturgically anomalous).

CIBORIUM: canopied shrine for the reserved sacrament. *See also* Baldacchino.

CINQUEFOIL: *see* Foil.

CLAPPER BRIDGE: bridge made of large slabs of stone, some built up to make rough piers and other longer ones laid on top to make the roadway.

CLASSIC: term for the moment of highest achievement of a style.

CLASSICAL: term for Greek and Roman architecture and any subsequent styles inspired by it.

CLERESTORY: upper storey of the nave walls of a church, pierced by windows.

COADE STONE: artificial (cast) stone made in the late C 18 and the early C 19 by Coade and Sealy in London.

COB: walling material made of mixed clay and straw. Also called *Mud Wall.*

COFFERING: sunken panels, square or polygonal, decorating a ceiling, vault, or arch.

COLLAR: *see* Roof (fig. 22).

COLONNADE: range of columns supporting an entablature.

COLONNETTE: small column or shaft in medieval architecture.

COLUMN: in classical architecture, an upright structural member of round section with a shaft, a capital, and usually a base. *See* Orders (fig. 16).

COLUMNA ROSTRATA: column decorated with carved prows of ships to celebrate a naval victory.

COMPOSITE: *see* Orders.

CONSOLE: ornamental bracket of compound curved outline (*see* fig. 7). Its height is usually greater than its projection, as in (*a*).

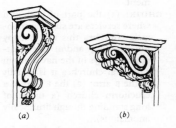

(*a*)   (*b*)

Fig. 7.   Console

COPING (*lit.* capping): course of stones, or equivalent, on top of a wall.

CORBEL: block of stone projecting from a wall, supporting some feature on its horizontal top surface. *Corbel Course:* continuous projecting course of stones fulfilling the same function. *Corbel Table:* series of corbels to carry a parapet or a wall-plate; for the latter *see* Roof (fig. 22).

CORINTHIAN: *see* Orders (fig. 16).

CORNICE: (1) moulded ledge, decorative and/or practical, projecting along the top of a building or feature, especially as the highest member of the classical entablature (*see* Orders, fig. 16); (2) decorative moulding in the angle between a wall and ceiling.

CORPS-DE-LOGIS: French term for the main building(s) as distinct from the wings or pavilions.

COURSE: continuous layer of stones etc. in a wall.

COVE: concave soffit like a hollow moulding but on a larger scale. A *Coved Ceiling* has a pronounced cove joining the walls to a flat surface in the middle.

CREDENCE: in a church or chapel, a side table, often a niche or recessed cavity, for the sacramental elements before consecration.

CRENELLATION: *see* Battlement.

CREST, CRESTING: ornamental finish along the top of a screen, etc.

CROCKETS (*lit.* hooks), CROCKETING: in Gothic architecture, leafy knobs on the edges of any sloping feature. *Crocket Capital: see* Capital (fig. 6).

CROSSING: in a church, central space opening into the nave, chancel, and transepts. *Crossing Tower:* central tower supported by the piers at its corners.

CROWSTEPS: squared stones set like steps to form a skew; *see* Gable (fig. 9).

CRUCK (*lit.* crooked): piece of naturally curved timber combining the structural roles of an upright post and a sloping rafter, e.g. in the building of a cottage, where each pair of crucks is joined at the ridge.

CRYPT: underground room usually below the E end of a church.

CUPOLA (*lit.* dome): small polygonal or circular domed turret crowning a roof.

CURTAIN WALL: (1) connecting

wall between the towers of a castle; (2) in modern building, thin wall attached to the main structure, usually outside it.

CURVILINEAR: *see* Tracery (fig. 25).

CUSP: projecting point formed by the foils within the divisions of Gothic tracery, also used to decorate the soffits of the Gothic arches of tomb recesses, sedilia, etc.

CYCLOPEAN MASONRY: built with large irregular polygonal stones, but smooth and finely jointed.

DADO: lower part of a wall or its decorative treatment; *see also* Pedestal (fig. 17).

DAGGER: *see* Tracery (fig. 25).

DAIS: raised platform at one end of a room.

DEC (DECORATED): historical division of English Gothic architecture covering the period from *c.* 1290 to *c.* 1350.

DEMI-COLUMNS: engaged columns, only half of whose circumference projects from the wall.

DIAPER (*lit.* figured cloth): repetitive surface decoration.

DIOCLETIAN WINDOW: *see* Thermae Window.

DISTYLE: having two columns.

DOGTOOTH: typical E.E. decoration applied to a moulding. It consists of a series of squares, their centres raised like pyramids and their edges indented (*see* fig. 8).

Fig. 8. Dogtooth

DONJON: *see* Keep.

DORIC: *see* Orders (fig. 16).

DORMER WINDOW: window standing up vertically from the slope of a roof and lighting a room within it. *Dormer Head*: gable above this window, often formed as a pediment.

DORTER: dormitory; sleeping quarters of a monastery.

DOUBLE-PILE: *see* Pile.

DRESSINGS: features made of smoothly worked stones, e.g. quoins or string courses, projecting from the wall which may be of different material, colour, or texture. Also called *Trim*.

DRIPSTONE: moulded stone projecting from a wall to protect the lower parts from water; *see also* Hoodmould.

DRUM: (1) circular or polygonal vertical wall of a dome or cupola; (2) one of the stones forming the shaft of a column.

DRY-STONE: stone construction without mortar.

E.E. (EARLY ENGLISH): historical division of English Gothic architecture covering the period 1200–1250.

EAVES: overhanging edge of a roof; hence *Eaves Cornice* in this position.

ECHINUS (*lit.* sea-urchin): lower part of a Greek Doric capital; *see* Orders (fig. 16).

EDGE-ROLL: moulding of semicircular or more than semicircular section at the edge of an opening.

ELEVATION: (1) any side of a building; (2) in a drawing, the same or any part of it, accurately represented in two dimensions.

ELIDED: term used to describe (1) a compound architectural feature, e.g. an entablature, in which some parts have been omitted; (2) a number of similar parts which have been combined to form a single larger one (*see* Capital, fig. 6).

EMBATTLED: furnished with battlements.

EMBRASURE (*lit.* splay): small splayed opening in the wall or battlement of a fortified building.

ENCAUSTIC TILES: glazed and decorated earthenware tiles used for paving.

ENGAGED COLUMN: one that is partly merged into a wall or pier.

ENTABLATURE: in classical architecture, collective name for the three horizontal members (architrave, frieze, and cornice) above a column; *see* Orders (fig. 16).

ENTASIS: very slight convex deviation from a straight line; used on classical columns and sometimes on spires to prevent an optical illusion of concavity.

ENTRESOL: mezzanine storey within or above the ground storey.

ESCUTCHEON: shield for armorial bearings.

EXEDRA: apsidal end of an apartment; *see* Apse.

FERETORY: (1) place behind the high altar where the chief shrine of a church is kept; (2) wooden or metal container for relics.

FESTOON: ornament, usually in high or low relief, in the form of a garland of flowers and/or fruit, hung up at both ends; *see also* Swag.

FIELDED PANELLING: panelling, or wainscot, characteristic of the late Stuart and early Georgian periods (1690–1770), in which each panel is bordered by a sloping chamfered edge, creating a flat panel or 'field' in the centre.

FILLET: narrow flat band running down a shaft or along a roll moulding.

FINIAL: topmost feature, e.g. above a gable, spire, or cupola.

FLAMBOYANT: properly the latest phase of French Gothic architecture, where the window tracery takes on undulating lines, based on the use of flowing curves.

FLÈCHE (*lit.* arrow): slender spire on the centre of a roof.

FLEUR-DE-LYS: in heraldry, a formalized lily as in the royal arms of France.

FLEURON: decorative carved flower or leaf.

FLOWING: *see* Tracery (Curvilinear; fig. 25).

FLUTING: series of concave grooves, their common edges sharp (arris) or blunt (fillet).

FOIL (*lit.* leaf): lobe formed by the cusping of a circular or other shape in tracery. *Trefoil* (three), *Quatrefoil* (four), *Cinquefoil* (five), and *Multifoil* express the number of lobes in a shape; *see* Tracery (fig. 25).

FOLIATED: decorated, especially carved, with leaves.

FOSSE: ditch.

FRATER: refectory or dining hall of a monastery.

FREESTONE: stone that is cut, or can be cut, in all directions, usually fine-grained sandstone or limestone.

FRESCO: painting executed on wet plaster.

FRIEZE: horizontal band of ornament, especially the middle member of the classical entablature; *see* Orders (fig. 16). *Pulvinated Frieze (lit.* cushioned): frieze of convex profile.

FRONTAL: covering for the front of an altar.

GABLE: (1) peaked wall or other vertical surface, often triangular, at the end of a double-pitch roof; (2) the same, very often with a chimney at the apex, but also in a wider sense: end wall, of whatever shape. See fig. 9. *Gablet*: small gable. *See also* Roof.

GADROONING: ribbed ornament, e.g. on the lid or base of an urn, flowing into a lobed edge.

GALILEE: chapel or vestibule usually at the W end of a church enclosing the porch; *see also* Narthex.

GALLERY: balcony or passage, but with certain special meanings, e.g. (1) upper storey above the aisle of a church, looking through arches to the nave; also called tribune and often erroneously triforium; (2) balcony or mezzanine, often with seats, overlooking the main interior space of a building; (3) external walkway projecting from a wall.

GARDEROBE (*lit.* wardrobe): medieval privy.

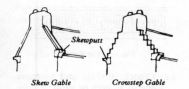

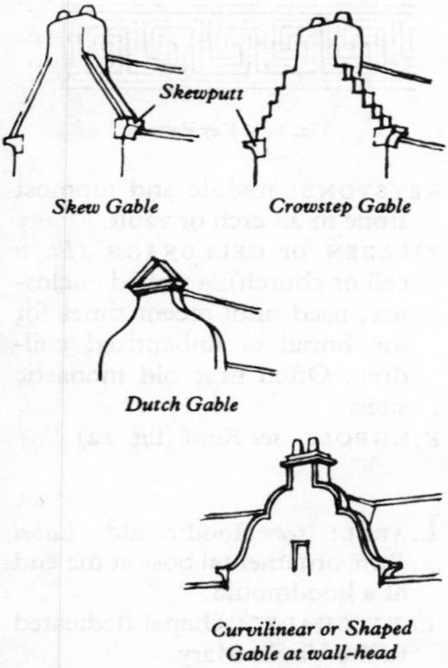

Skew Gable   *Crowstep Gable*

Dutch Gable

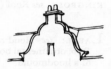

Curvilinear or Shaped Gable at wall-head

Fig. 9. Gables

GARGOYLE: water spout projecting from the parapet of a wall or tower, often carved into human or animal shape.

GAZEBO (jocular Latin, 'I shall gaze'): lookout tower or raised summer house overlooking a garden.

GEOMETRIC: historical division of English Gothic architecture covering the period *c.* 1250–90. *See also* Tracery (fig. 25). For another meaning, *see* Stair.

GIB DOOR: doorway flush with the wall surface and without any visible frame, so that the opening appears to merge with the wall of the room. It often has the skirting board and chair-rail carried across the surface of the door.

GIBBS SURROUND: C 18 treatment of door or window surround, seen particularly in the work of James Gibbs (1682–1754) *see* fig. 10).

GLACIS: in military architecture, a bank, extending in a long slow slope from a fort, on which attackers are exposed to fire.

GLEBE-HOUSE: a house built on and counting as part of the portion of land going with an

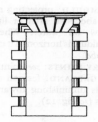

Fig. 10. Gibbs Surround

established clergyman's benefice.

GNOMON: vane or indicator casting a shadow on to a sundial.

GRC: glass-fibre reinforced concrete.

GROIN: sharp edge at the meeting of two cells of a cross-vault; *see* Vault (fig. 26a).

GROTESQUE (*lit.* grotto-esque): classical wall decoration of spindly, whimsical character adopted from Roman examples, particularly by Raphael, and further developed in the C 18.

GUILLOCHE: running classical ornament formed by a series of circles with linked and interlaced borders (see fig. 11).

Fig. 11. Guilloche

GUN LOOP: opening for a firearm.
GUTTAE: *see* Orders (fig. 16).

HAGIOSCOPE: *see* Squint.
HALF-TIMBERING: timber framing with the spaces filled in by plaster, stones or brickwork.
HAMMERBEAM: *see* Roof.
HARLING: *see* Rendering.
HEADER: *see* Bond.
HERM (*lit.* the god Hermes): male head or bust on a pedestal.
HERRINGBONE WORK: masonry or brickwork in zigzag courses.
HEXASTYLE: term used to describe a portico with six columns.

HOODMOULD: projecting moulding above an arch or lintel to
throw off water. When the
moulding is horizontal it is called
a *Label*.

HUNGRY JOINTS: *see* Pointing.

HUSK GARLAND: festoon of nut-
shells diminishing towards the
ends (*see* fig. 12).

Fig. 12.   Husk Garland

IMPOST (*lit.* imposition): horizontal moulding at the spring of
an arch.

IN ANTIS: *see* Antae, Orders (fig.
16), and Portico.

INDENT: (1) shape chiselled out
of a stone to match and receive
a brass; (2) in restoration, a
section of new stone inserted as
a patch into older work.

INGLENOOK (*lit.* fire-corner):
recess for a hearth with provision
for seating.

INTERCOLUMNIATION: interval
between columns.

IONIC: *see* Orders (fig. 16).

JAMB (*lit.* leg): one of the straight
sides of an archway, door, or
window.

KEEL MOULDING: *see* fig. 13.

Fig. 13.   Keel Moulding

KEEP: principal tower of a castle.
Also called Donjon.

KEY PATTERN: *see* fig. 14.

Fig. 14.   Key Pattern

KEYSTONE: middle and topmost
stone in an arch or vault.

KILLEEN or CELLURACH (*lit.* a
cell or church): a walled enclosure, used until recent times for
the burial of unbaptized children. Often near old monastic
sites.

KINGPOST: *see* Roof (fig. 22).

LABEL: *see* Hoodmould. *Label
Stop*: ornamental boss at the end
of a hoodmould.

LADY CHAPEL: chapel dedicated
to the Virgin Mary.

LANCET WINDOW: slender pointed-arched window, often in
groups of two, five, or seven.

LANTERN: a small circular or polygonal turret with windows all
round crowning a roof (*see*
Cupola) or a dome.

LAVATORIUM: in a monastery, a
washing place adjacent to the
refectory.

LEAN-TO: term commonly applied not only to a single-pitch
roof but to the building it covers.

LESENE (*lit.* a mean thing): pilaster without base or capital.
Also called pilaster strip.

LIERNE: *see* Vault (fig. 26b).

LIGHT: compartment of a
window.

LINENFOLD: Tudor panelling
ornamented with a conventional
representation of a piece of linen
laid in vertical folds. The piece
is repeated in each panel.

LINTEL: horizontal beam or stone
bridging an opening.

LOGGIA: sheltered space behind a
colonnade.

LOUVRE: (1) opening, often with
lantern over, in the roof of a
building to let the smoke from a
central hearth escape; (2) one
of a series of overlapping boards
placed in a window to allow ven-
tilation but keep the rain out.

LOZENGE: diamond shape.

LUCARNE (*lit.* dormer): small window in a roof or spire, often capped by a gable or finial.

LUGGED: *see* Architrave.

LUNETTE (*lit.* half or crescent moon): (1) semicircular window; (2) semicircular or crescent-shaped surface.

LYCHGATE (*lit.* corpse-gate): wooden gate structure with a roof and open sides placed at the entrance to a churchyard to provide space for the reception of a coffin.

LYNCHET: long terraced strip of soil accumulating on the downward side of prehistoric and medieval fields due to soil creep from continuous ploughing along the contours.

MACHICOLATION: in medieval military architecture, a series of openings at the top of a wall head, made by building the parapet on projecting brackets, with the spaces between left open to allow missiles or boiling liquids to be dropped on the heads of assailants.

MAJOLICA: ornamented glazed earthenware.

MANSARD: *see* Roof (fig. 21).

MARGINS: dressed stones at the edges of an opening.

MAUSOLEUM: monumental tomb, so named after that of Mausolus, king of Caria, at Halicarnassus.

MERLON: *see* Battlement.

METOPES: spaces between the triglyphs in a Doric frieze; *see* Orders (fig. 16).

MEZZANINE: (1) low storey between two higher ones; (2) low upper storey within the height of a high one, not extending over its whole area.

MISERERE: *see* Misericord.

MISERICORD (*lit.* mercy): shelf placed on the underside of a hinged choir stall seat which, when turned up, provided the occupant with support during long periods of standing. Also called Miserere.

MODILLIONS: small consoles at regular intervals along the underside of some types of classical cornice. Typically a Corinthian or Composite element.

MOTTE: steep earthen mound forming the main features of C 11 and C 12 castles.

MOTTE-AND-BAILEY: post-Roman and Norman defence system consisting of an earthen mound (motte) topped with a wooden tower within a bailey, with enclosure ditch and palisade, and with the rare addition of an internal bank.

MOUCHETTE: motif in curvilinear tracery, a curved version of the dagger form, specially popular in the early C 14; *see* Tracery.

MOULDING: ornament of continuous section; *see* the various types.

MUD WALL: *see* Cob.

MULLION: vertical member between the lights in a window opening.

MUNTIN: post forming part of a screen.

MURDER HOLE: small rectangular trap in the ceiling of an entrance passage in a castle or tower house.

NAILHEAD MOULDING: E.E. ornamental motif, consisting of small pyramids regularly repeated (*see* fig. 15).

Fig. 15. Nailhead Moulding

NARTHEX: enclosed vestibule or covered porch at the main entrance to a church; *see also* Galilee.

NEWEL: central post in a circular or winding staircase; also the principal post when a flight of stairs meets a landing.

NICHE (*lit.* shell): vertical recess in a wall, sometimes for a statue, and often round-headed.

NIGHT STAIR: stair by which monks entered the transepts of their church from their dormitory to attend services at night.

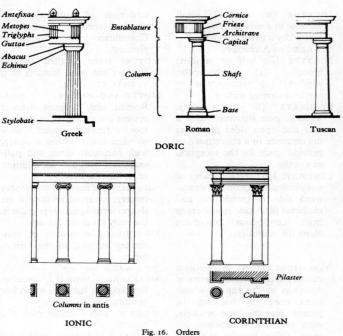

Fig. 16. Orders

NOOK-SHAFT: shaft set in an angle formed by other members.

NORMAN: *see* Romanesque.

NOSING: projection of the tread of a step. A *Bottle Nosing* is half-round in section.

OBELISK: lofty pillar of square section tapering at the top and ending pyramidally.

OCULUS: circular or oval window or other opening, used to create a conscious architectural effect.

ŒIL DE BŒUF: *see* Bullseye Window.

OGEE: double curve, bending first one way and then the other. *Ogee* or *Ogival Arch: see* Arch (fig. 2).

ORDER: (1) upright structural member formally related to others, e.g. in classical architecture a column, pilaster, or anta; (2) one of a series of recessed arches and jambs forming a splayed opening. *Giant* or *Colossal Order:* classical order whose height is that of two

or more storeys of a building.

ORDERS: in classical architecture, the differently formalized versions of the basic post-and-lintel structure, each having its own rules of design and proportion. For examples of the main types *see* fig. 16. Others include the primitive Tuscan, which has a plain frieze and simple torus-moulded base, and the Composite, whose capital combines Ionic volutes with Corinthian foliage. *Superimposed Orders:* term for the use of Orders on successive levels, usually in the upward sequence of Doric, Ionic, Corinthian.

ORIEL: *see* Bay window.

OVERHANG: projection of the upper storey(s) of a building.

OVERSAILING COURSES: series of stone or brick courses, each one projecting beyond the one below it; *see also* Corbel Course.

PALLADIAN: architecture following the example and principles of Andrea Palladio, 1508–80.

PALMETTE: classical ornament like a symmetrical palm shoot; for illustration *see* Anthemion, fig. 1.

PANTILE: roof tile of curved S-shaped section.

PARAPET: wall for protection at any sudden drop, e.g. on a bridge or at the wall-head of a castle; in the latter case it protects the *Parapet Walk* or wall walk.

PARCLOSE: *see* Screen.

PARGETING (*lit.* plastering): usually of moulded plaster panels in half-timbering.

PATERA (*lit.* plate): round or oval ornament in shallow relief, especially in classical architecture.

PATTE D'OIE (*lit.* goose foot): a common element in French baroque garden design, much copied in c 17 and c 18 Europe, where three radiating avenues focus on a single point.

PEBBLEDASHING: *see* Rendering.

PEDESTAL: in classical architecture, a stand sometimes used to support the base of an order (*see* fig. 17).

Fig. 17. Pedestal

PEDIMENT: in classical architecture, a formalized gable derived from that of a temple, also used over doors, windows, etc. For the generally accepted meanings of *Broken Pediment* and *Open Pediment see* fig. 18.

PEND: covered archway passing through a terraced building to give vehicular access to gardens or yards behind. Also called a *Carriage Arch*.

PENDANT: hanging-down feature of a vault or ceiling, usually ending in a boss.

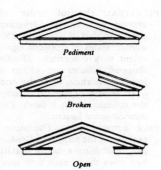

Pediment

Broken

Open

Fig. 18. Pediments

PENDENTIVE: spandrel between adjacent arches supporting a drum or dome, formed as part of a hemisphere (*see* fig. 19).

Fig. 19. Pendentive

PERISTYLE: in classical architecture, a range of columns all round a building, e.g. a temple, or an interior space, e.g. a courtyard.

PERP (PERPENDICULAR): historical division of English Gothic architecture covering the period from *c.* 1335–50 to *c.* 1530.

PERRON: *see* Stair.

PIANO NOBILE: principal floor, usually with a ground floor or basement underneath and a lesser storey overhead.

PIAZZA: open space surrounded by buildings; in the c 17 and c 18 sometimes employed to mean a long colonnade or loggia.

PIER: strong, solid support, frequently square in section. *Compound Pier*: of composite section, e.g. formed of a bundle of shafts.

PIETRA DURA: ornamental or scenic inlay by means of thin slabs of stone.

PILASTER: classical order of oblong section, its elevation similar to that of a column. *Pilastrade*: series of pilasters, equivalent to a colonnade. *Pilaster Respond*: pilaster set within a loggia or portico, or at the end of an arcade, to balance visually the column which it faces. *Pilaster Strip*: see Lesene.

PILE: a row of rooms. The important use of the term is in *Double-pile*, describing a house that is two rows thick, each row consisting of three or more rooms.

PILLAR PISCINA: free-standing piscina on a pillar.

PILOTIS: French term used in modern architecture for pillars or stilts that carry a building to first-floor level, leaving the ground floor open.

PINNACLE: tapering finial, e.g. on a buttress or the corner of a tower, sometimes decorated with crockets.

PISCINA: basin for washing the communion or mass vessels, provided with a drain; generally set in or against the wall to the s of an altar.

PLATBAND: deep, flat stringcourse, frequently employed between a rusticated lower storey and ashlar work above.

PLINTH: projecting base beneath a wall or column, generally chamfered or moulded at the top.

POCKED TOOLING: hammerdressed stonework with a pocked appearance characteristic of Irish masonry from the C 14 to the C 16.

POINTING: exposed mortar joints of masonry or brickwork. The finished form is of various types, e.g. *Flush Pointing, Recessed Pointing. Bag-rubbed Pointing* is flush at the edges and gently recessed in the middle of the joint. *Hungry Joints* are either without any pointing at all, or deeply recessed to show the outline of each stone. *Ribbon Pointing* is a nasty practice in the modern vernacular, the joints being formed with a trowel so that they stand out.

POPPYHEAD: carved ornament of leaves and flowers as a finial for the end of a bench or stall.

PORCH: covered projecting entrance to a building.

PORTAL FRAME: a basic form of pre-cast concrete construction where walls and roof are supported on a series of angled concrete beams which, meeting at the ridge of the roof, form 'portals'.

PORTCULLIS: gate constructed to rise and fall in vertical grooves at the entry to a castle.

PORTE COCHÈRE (*lit.* gate for coaches): porch large enough to admit wheeled vehicles.

PORTICO: roofed space, open on one side at least, and enclosed by a row of columns which also support the roof (and frequently a pediment). A portico may be free-standing: more usually it forms part of a building, often in the form of a projecting temple front. When the front of the portico is on the same level as the front of the building it is described as a *portico in antis*.

POSTERN: small gateway at the back of a building.

PREDELLA: (1) step or platform on which an altar stands; hence (2) in an altarpiece the horizontal strip below the main representation, often used for a number of subsidiary representations in a row.

PRESBYTERY: the part of the church lying E of the choir. It is the part where the altar is placed.

PRINCIPAL: see Roof (fig. 22).

PRIORY: monastic house whose head is a prior or prioress, not an abbot or abbess.

PROSTYLE: with a row of columns in front.

PULPITUM: stone screen in a major church provided to shut off the choir from the nave and also as a backing for the return choir stalls.

PULVINATED: see Frieze.

PURLIN: see Roof (fig. 22).

PUTHOLE or PUTLOCK HOLE: putlocks are the short horizontal timbers on which during construction the boards of scaffolding rest. Putholes or putlock holes are the holes in the wall for putlocks, and often are not filled in after construction is complete.

PUTTO: small naked boy (plural: putti).

QUADRANGLE: inner courtyard in a large building.

QUARRIES (*lit.* squares): (I) in stained glass, square or diamond-shaped panes of glass supported by lead strips which are called *Canes*; (2) square floor-slabs or tiles.

QUATREFOIL: *see* Foil.

QUEENPOSTS: *see* Roof (fig. 22).

QUIRK: sharp groove to one side of a convex moulding, e.g. beside a roll moulding, which is then said to be quirked.

QUOINS: dressed stones at the angles of a building, usually alternately long and short.

RADIATING CHAPELS: chapels projecting radially from an ambulatory or an apse.

RAFTER: *see* Roof (fig. 22).

RAGGLE: groove cut in masonry, especially to receive the edge of glass or roof-covering.

RAKE: slope or pitch.

RAMPART: stone wall or wall of earth surrounding a castle, fortress, or fortified city. *Rampart Walk*: path along the inner face of a rampart.

RANDOM: *see* Rubble.

RATH: circular or near-circular enclosure consisting of one or more earthen (or occasionally stone) banks with ditches outside, classified as univallate, bivallate, or trivallate. Most date from early Christian times and housed single farms or served as cattle enclosures for the farms. Also called *Ring Forts*.

REBATE: rectangular section cut out of a masonry edge.

REEDING: series of convex mouldings; the reverse of fluting.

REFECTORY: dining hall (or frater) of a monastery or similar establishment.

RENDERING: the process of covering outside walls with a uniform surface or skin to protect the wall from the weather. *Stucco*, originally a fine lime plaster finished to a smooth surface, is the finest rendered external finish, characteristic of many late C 18 and C 19 classical buildings. It is usually painted. *Cement Rendering* is a cheaper and more recent substitute for stucco, usually with a grainy texture and often left unpainted. Shoddy but all too common in Ireland. In more simple buildings the wall surface may be roughly *Lime-plastered* (and then whitewashed), or covered with plaster mixed with a coarse aggregate such as gravel. This latter is known as *Rough-cast* or, in Scotland and the North of Ireland, as *Harling*. A variant, fashionable in the early C 20, is *Pebble-dashing*: here the stones of the aggregate are kept separate from the plaster and are thrown at the wet plastered wall to create a decorative effect.

RERE-ARCH: archway in medieval architecture formed across the wider inner opening of a window reveal.

REREDOS: painted and/or sculptured screen behind and above an altar.

RESPOND: half-pier bonded into a wall and carrying one end of an arch. *See also* Pilaster Respond.

RETABLE: altarpiece; a picture or piece of carving standing behind and attached to an altar.

RETROCHOIR: in a major church, an aisle between the high altar and an E chapel, like a square ambulatory.

REVEAL: the inward plane of a jamb, between the edge of an external wall and the frame of a door or window that is set in it.

RIB-VAULT: *see* Vault.

Fig. 20. Rinceau

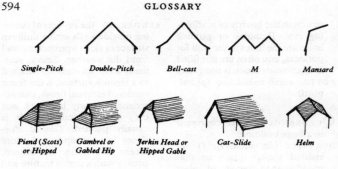

Single-Pitch Double-Pitch Bell-cast M Mansard

Piend (Scots) or Hipped Gambrel or Gabled Hip Jerkin Head or Hipped Gable Cat-Slide Helm

Fig. 21.   Roof Forms

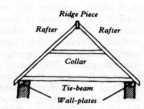

Ridge Piece

Rafter   Rafter

Collar

Tie-beam

Wall-plates

Common Roof Components

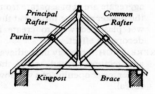

Principal Rafter   Common Rafter

Purlin

Kingpost   Brace

Roof with Kingpost Truss

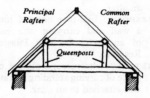

Principal Rafter   Common Rafter

Queenposts

Roof with Queenpost Truss

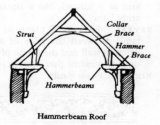

Strut   Collar Brace

Hammer Brace

Hammerbeams

Hammerbeam Roof

Fig. 22.   Roof Construction

RINCEAU (*lit.* little branch) or antique foliage: classical ornament, usually on a frieze, of leafy scrolls branching alternately to left and right (*see* fig. 20).

RING FORT: *see* Rath.

RISER: vertical face of a step.

ROCK-FACED: term used to describe masonry which is cleft to produce a natural, rugged appearance.

ROCOCO (*lit.* rocky): the light-hearted last phase of the baroque style, current in most continental countries between *c.* 1720 and *c.* 1760, and showing itself in Ireland mainly in light classical elements and scrolled decoration, especially in plasterwork.

ROLL MOULDING: moulding of semicircular or more than semicircular section.

ROMANESQUE: that style in architecture which was current in the C 11 and C 12 and preceded the Gothic style (in England often called Norman). (Some scholars extend the use of the term Romanesque back to the C 10.)

ROOD: cross or crucifix, usually over the entry into the chancel. The *Rood Screen* beneath it may have a *Rood Loft* along the top, reached by a *Rood Stair*.

ROOF: for external forms *see* fig. 21; for construction and components *see* fig. 22. *Wagon Roof*: lined with timber on the inside, giving the appearance of a curved or polygonal vault. *Belfast roof truss*: segmental roof truss designed to cover a wide span and built as a lattice beam, using (according to the origin of its name) short cuts of timber left over from the shipbuilding industry in Belfast.

ROPE MOULDING: *see* Cable Moulding.

ROSE WINDOW: circular window with patterned tracery about the centre.

ROTUNDA: building circular in plan.

ROUGH-CAST: *see* Rendering.

RUBBLE: masonry whose stones are wholly or partly in a rough state. *Coursed Rubble*: of coursed stones with rough faces. *Random Rubble*: of uncoursed stones in a random pattern. *Snecked Rubble* has courses frequently broken by smaller square stones (snecks).

RUSTICATION: treatment of joints and/or faces of masonry to give an effect of strength. In the most usual kind the joints are recessed by V-section chamfering or square-section channelling. *Banded Rustication* has only the horizontal joints emphasized in this way. The faces may be flat but there are many other forms, e.g. *Diamond-faced*, like a shallow pyramid, *Vermiculated*, with a stylized texture like worms or worm-holes, or *Glacial*, like icicles or stalactites. *Rusticated Columns* may have their joints and drums treated in any of these ways.

SACRAMENT HOUSE: safe cupboard for the reserved sacrament.

SACRISTY: room in a church for sacred vessels and vestments.

SANCTUARY: area around the main altar of a church (*see* Presbytery).

SARCOPHAGUS (*lit.* flesh-consuming): coffin of stone or other durable material.

SCAGLIOLA: composition imitating marble.

SCALE-AND-PLATT (*lit.* stair and landing): *see* Stair (fig. 24).

SCARCEMENT: extra thickness of the lower part of a wall, e.g. to carry a floor.

SCARP: artificial cutting away of the ground to form a steep slope.

SCISSOR TRUSS: roof truss framed at the bottom by crossed intersecting beams like open scissors. Frequently used in C19 churches in conjunction and alternating with kingpost trusses. Where the scissors occur with each rafter and are not formed into separate trusses the structure would be called a scissor-beam roof.

SCREEN: in a church, usually at the entry to the chancel; *see* Rood Screen and Pulpitum. *Parclose Screen*: separating a chapel from the rest of the church.

SCREENS or SCREENS PASSAGE: screened-off entrance passage between the hall and the kitchen in a medieval house, adjoining the kitchen, buttery, etc.

SEDILIA: seats for the priests (usually three) on the S side of the chancel of a church.

SET-OFF: *see* Weathering.

SHAFT: upright member of round section, especially the main part of a classical column. *Shaft-ring*: motif of the C12 and C13 consisting of a ring like a belt round a circular pier or a circular shaft attached to a pier.

SHEILA-NA-GIG: female fertility figure, usually with legs wide open.

SHOULDERED: *see* Arch (fig. 2), Architrave.

SILL: horizontal projection at the bottom of a window.

SLATE-HANGING: covering of overlapping slates on a wall, which is then said to be *slate-hung*.

SLOP STONE: drainage stone designed to carry kitchen waste through the thickness of a wall. A domestic gargoyle.

SNECKED: *see* Rubble.

SOFFIT (*lit.* ceiling): underside of an arch, lintel, etc. *See also* Archivolt.

SOLAR (*lit.* sun-room): upper living room or withdrawing room of a medieval house, accessible from the high table end of the hall.

SOUNDING-BOARD: horizontal board or canopy over a pulpit; also called Tester.

SOUTERRAIN: underground stone-lined passage and chamber.

SPANDRELS: surfaces left over between an arch and its containing rectangle, or between adjacent arches.

SPIRE: tall pyramidal or conical feature built on a tower or turret. *Broach Spire*: starting from a square base, then carried into an octagonal section by means of triangular faces. *Needle Spire*: thin spire rising from the centre of a tower roof, well inside the parapet. *Helm Spire: see* Roof (fig. 21).

SPIRELET: *see* Flèche.

SPLAY: chamfer, usually of a reveal.

SPRING: level at which an arch or vault rises from its supports. *Springers*: the first stones of an arch or vaulting-rib above the spring.

SQUINCH: arch thrown across an angle between two walls to support a superstructure, e.g. a dome (*see* fig. 23).

Fig. 23. Squinch

SQUINT: hole cut in a wall or through a pier to allow a view of the main altar of a church from places whence it could not otherwise be seen. Also called Hagioscope.

STAIR: *see* fig. 24. The term *Perron* (*lit*. of stone) applies to the external stair leading to a doorway, usually of branched or double-curved plan as shown. *Spiral* or *Newel Stair*: ascending round a central supporting newel, usually in a circular shaft. *Flying Stair*: cantilevered from the wall of a stairwell, without newels. *Geometric Stair*: flying stair whose inner edge describes a curve. *Well Stair*: term applied to any stair contained in an open well, but generally to one that climbs up three sides of a well, with corner landings.

STALL: seat for clergy, choir, etc., distinctively treated in its own right or as one of a row.

STANCHION: upright structural member, of iron or steel or reinforced concrete.

STEEPLE: a tower together with a spire or other tall feature on top of it.

STOUP: vessel for the reception of holy water, usually placed near a door.

STRAINER: *see* Arch.

STRAPWORK: C 16 and C 17 decoration used also in the C 19 Jacobean revival, resembling interlaced bands of cut leather.

STRETCHER: *see* Bond.

STRING-COURSE: intermediate stone course or moulding projecting from the surface of a wall.

STUCCO (*lit*. plaster): (1) smooth external rendering of a wall etc.; (2) archaic term for plasterwork.

STUDS: intermediate vertical

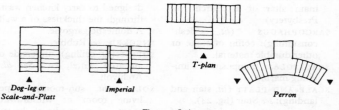

Dog-leg or Scale-and-Platt   Imperial   T-plan   Perron

Fig. 24. Stair

members of a timber-framed wall or partition.

STYLOBATE: solid base structure on which a colonnade stands.

SWAG (*lit.* bundle): like a festoon, but also a cloth bundle in relief, hung up at both ends.

TABERNACLE (*lit.* tent): (1) canopied structure, especially on a small scale, to contain the reserved sacrament or a relic; (2) architectural frame, e.g. of a monument on a wall or free-standing, with flanking orders. Also called an Aedicule.

TABLE TOMB: raised memorial tomb in the shape of a table or altar, often with recumbent effigies on the table top.

TAS-DE-CHARGE: stone(s) forming the springers of more than one vaulting-rib.

TERMINAL FIGURE or TERM: upper part of a human figure growing out of a pier, pilaster, etc. which tapers towards the bottom.

TERQUETRA: *see* Triquetra.

TERRACOTTA: moulded and fired clay ornament or cladding, usually unglazed.

TESTER (*lit.* head): bracketed canopy, especially over a pulpit, where it is also called a sounding-board.

TETRASTYLE: term used to describe a portico with four columns.

THERMAE WINDOW (*lit.* of a Roman bath): segmental or semicircular window divided by two mullions. Also called a *Diocletian Window* from its use at the baths of Diocletian in Rome.

THOLSEL: exchange or market-house.

TIE-BEAM: *see* Roof (fig. 22).

TIERCERON: *see* Vault (fig. 26b).

TILE-HANGING: *see* Slate-hanging.

TIMBER FRAMING: method of construction where walls are built of timber framework with the spaces filled in by plaster or brickwork. Sometimes the timber is covered over with plaster or boarding laid horizontally.

TOMB-CHEST: chest-shaped stone coffin, the most usual medieval form of funerary monument.

TOURELLE: turret corbelled out from the wall.

TOWER HOUSE (Scots and Irish): compact fortified house with the main hall raised above the ground and at least one more storey above it. A C15 type continuing well into the C17 in its modified forms.

TRACERY: pattern of arches and geometrical figures supporting the glass in the upper part of a Gothic window, or applied decoratively to wall surfaces or vaults. *Plate Tracery* is the most primitive form of tracery, being formed of openings cut through stone slabs or plates. In *Bar Tracery* the openings are separated not by flat areas of stonework but by relatively slender divisions or bars which are constructed of voussoirs like arches. Later developments of bar tracery are classified according to the character of the decorative patterns used. For generalized

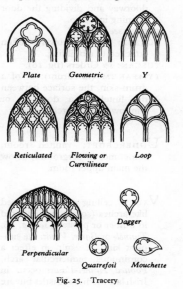

Plate   *Geometric*   *Y*

Reticulated   *Flowing or Curvilinear*   *Loop*

Perpendicular   *Dagger*   *Quatrefoil*   *Mouchette*

Fig. 25.   Tracery

illustrations of the main types *see* fig. 25.

TRANSEPTS (*lit.* cross-enclosures): transverse portions of a cross-shaped church.

TRANSOM: horizontal member between the lights in a window opening.

TREFOIL: *see* Foil.

TRIBUNE: *see* Gallery (1).

TRIFORIUM (*lit.* three openings): middle storey of a church treated as an arcaded wall passage or blind arcade, its height corresponding to that of the aisle roof.

TRIGLYPHS (*lit.* three-grooved tablets): stylized beam-ends in the Doric frieze, with metopes between; *see* Orders (fig. 16).

TRIM: *see* Dressings.

TRIQUETRA: a symbolic figure in the form of a three-cornered knot of interlaced arcs, common in Celtic art. Hence also *Terquetra*, a knot formed of four similar corners.

TRIUMPHAL ARCH: *see* Arch.

TROPHY: sculptured group of arms or armour as a memorial of victory.

TRUMEAU: stone mullion supporting the tympanum of a wide doorway and dividing the door opening into two.

TRUSS: *see* Roof.

TURRET: small tower, often attached to a building.

TUSCAN: *see* Orders (fig. 16).

TYMPANUM (*lit.* drum): as of a drum-skin, the surface between the lintel of a doorway or window and the arch above it.

UNDERCROFT: vaulted room, sometimes underground, below the main upper room.

VAULT: ceiling of stone formed like arches (sometimes imitated in timber or plaster); *see* fig. 26. *Tunnel-* or *Barrel-Vault*: the simplest kind of vault, in effect a continuous semicircular arch. *Pointed Tunnel-Vaults* occur in Irish late medieval castles but are

Tunnel or Barrel   *Pointed Tunnel*

Pointed Tunnels with Surface Ribs

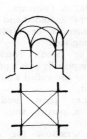

Groin   *Quadripartite*

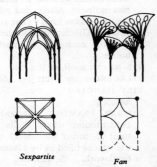

Sexpartite   *Fan*

Fig. 26. (a) Vaults

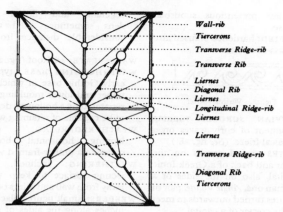

Fig. 26 (b). Ribs of a late Gothic Vault

Wall-rib
Tiercerons
Transverse Ridge-rib
Transverse Rib
Liernes
Diagonal Rib
Liernes
Longitudinal Ridge-rib
Liernes
Liernes
Tranverse Ridge-rib
Diagonal Rib
Tiercerons

otherwise rare. *Groin-Vaults* (usually called *Cross-Vaults* in classical architecture) have four curving triangular surfaces produced by the intersection of two tunnel-vaults at right angles. The curved lines at the intersections are called groins. In *Quadripartite Rib-Vaults* the four sections are divided by their arches or ribs springing from the corners of the bay. *Sexpartite Rib-Vaults* are most often used over paired bays. The main types of rib are shown in fig. 26b: *transverse ribs, wall ribs, diagonal ribs, and ridge ribs. Tiercerons* are extra, decorative ribs springing from the corners of a bay. *Liernes* are decorative ribs in the crown of a vault which are not linked to any of the springing points. In *stellar vault* the liernes are arranged in a star formation as in fig. 26b. *Fan-vaults* are peculiar to English Perpendicular architecture and differ from rib-vaults in consisting not of ribs and infilling but of halved concave cones with decorative blind tracery carved on their surfaces.

VAULTING-SHAFT: shaft leading up to the springer of a vault.

VENETIAN WINDOW: *see* fig. 27.

VERANDA(H): shelter or gallery against a building, its roof supported by thin vertical members.

Fig. 27. Venetian Window

VERMICULATION: *see* Rustication.

VESICA (*lit.* bladder): usually of a window, with curved sides and pointed at top and bottom.

VESTIBULE: anteroom or entrance hall.

VILLA: originally (1) Roman country-house-cum-farmhouse, developed into (2) the similar C 16 Venetian type with office wings, made grander by Palladio's varied application of a central portico. This became an important type in C 18 Britain, often with the special meaning of (3) a country house which is not a principal residence. Gwilt (1842) defined the villa as 'a country house for the residence of opulent persons'. But devaluation had already begun, and the term implied, as now, (4) a more or less pretentious suburban house.

VITRIFIED: hardened or fused into a glass-like state.

Fig. 28.   Vitruvian Scroll

VITRUVIAN SCROLL: running ornament of curly waves on a classical frieze. (*See* fig. 28.)

VOLUTES: spiral scrolls on the front and back of a Greek Ionic capital, also on the sides of a Roman one. *Angle Volute*: pair of volutes turned outwards to meet at the corner of a capital.

VOUSSOIRS: wedge-shaped stones forming an arch.

WAGON ROOF: *see* Roof.

WAINSCOT: timber lining on an internal wall.

WALLED GARDEN: C 17 type whose formal layout is still seen in the C 18 and C 19 combined vegetable and flower gardens sometimes sited at a considerable distance from a house.

WALL-PLATE: *see* Roof (fig. 22).

WATERHOLDING BASE: type of early Gothic base in which the upper and lower mouldings are separated by a hollow so deep as to be capable of retaining water.

WEATHERBOARDING: overlapping horizontal boards, covering a timber-framed wall.

WEATHERING: inclined, projecting surface to keep water away from wall and joints below.

WEEPERS: small figures placed in niches along the sides of some medieval tombs; also called mourners.

WHEEL WINDOW: circular window with tracery of radiating shafts like the spokes of a wheel; *see also* Rose Window.

WYATT WINDOW: early C 19 term for the type of large tripartite sash window made popular by the Wyatts.

INDEX OF ARTISTS, ARCHITECTS,
PATRONS, RESIDENTS AND VISITORS

The names of architects and artists working in the area covered by this volume are given in *italic*. Entries for partnerships and group practices are listed after entries for a single surname. Minor differences in title are disregarded.

Also indexed here are the names of families and individuals (not of bodies or commercial firms) recorded in this volume as having commissioned architectural work or owned or lived in properties in the area. The index includes monuments to members of such families and other individuals where they are of particular interest. Significant visitors to the area are also included.

INDEX OF PLACES

Principal references are in **bold** type; demolished buildings are shown in *italic*.

The counties are abbreviated as AH = Armagh, CN = Cavan, MN = Monaghan.